Lecture Notes in Computer Science   8516

Commenced Publication in 1973
Founding and Former Series Editors:
Gerhard Goos, Juris Hartmanis, and Jan van Leeuwen

T0185396

Constantine Stephanidis   Margherita Antona (Eds.)

Universal Access in Human-Computer Interaction

Design for All and Accessibility Practice

8th International Conference, UAHCI 2014
Held as Part of HCI International 2014
Heraklion, Crete, Greece, June 22-27, 2014
Proceedings, Part IV

 Springer

Volume Editors

Constantine Stephanidis
Foundation for Research and Technology - Hellas (FORTH)
Institute of Computer Science
N. Plastira 100, Vassilika Vouton, 70013 Heraklion, Crete, Greece
and University of Crete, Department of Computer Science
Heraklion, Crete, Greece
E-mail: cs@ics.forth.gr

Margherita Antona
Foundation for Research and Technology - Hellas (FORTH)
Institute of Computer Science
N. Plastira 100, Vassilika Vouton, 70013 Heraklion, Crete, Greece
E-mail: antona@ics.forth.gr

ISSN 0302-9743   e-ISSN 1611-3349
ISBN 978-3-319-07508-2   e-ISBN 978-3-319-07509-9
DOI 10.1007/978-3-319-07509-9
Springer Cham Heidelberg New York Dordrecht London

Library of Congress Control Number: 2014939292

LNCS Sublibrary: SL 3 – Information Systems and Application, incl. Internet/Web and HCI

Typesetting: Camera-ready by author, data conversion by Scientific Publishing Services, Chennai, India

Printed on acid-free paper

Springer is part of Springer Science+Business Media (www.springer.com)

Foreword

The 16th International Conference on Human–Computer Interaction, HCI International 2014, was held in Heraklion, Crete, Greece, during June 22–27, 2014, incorporating 14 conferences/thematic areas:

Thematic areas:

- Human–Computer Interaction
- Human Interface and the Management of Information

Affiliated conferences:

- 11th International Conference on Engineering Psychology and Cognitive Ergonomics
- 8th International Conference on Universal Access in Human–Computer Interaction
- 6th International Conference on Virtual, Augmented and Mixed Reality
- 6th International Conference on Cross-Cultural Design
- 6th International Conference on Social Computing and Social Media
- 8th International Conference on Augmented Cognition
- 5th International Conference on Digital Human Modeling and Applications in Health, Safety, Ergonomics and Risk Management
- Third International Conference on Design, User Experience and Usability
- Second International Conference on Distributed, Ambient and Pervasive Interactions
- Second International Conference on Human Aspects of Information Security, Privacy and Trust
- First International Conference on HCI in Business
- First International Conference on Learning and Collaboration Technologies

A total of 4,766 individuals from academia, research institutes, industry, and governmental agencies from 78 countries submitted contributions, and 1,476 papers and 225 posters were included in the proceedings. These papers address the latest research and development efforts and highlight the human aspects of design and use of computing systems. The papers thoroughly cover the entire field of human–computer interaction, addressing major advances in knowledge and effective use of computers in a variety of application areas.

This volume, edited by Constantine Stephanidis and Margherita Anton, contains papers focusing on the thematic area of Universal Access in Human-Computer Interaction, addressing the following major topics:

- Web accessibility
- Design for all in the built environment

- Global access infrastructures
- User experience in Universal Access

The remaining volumes of the HCI International 2014 proceedings are:

- Volume 1, LNCS 8510, Human–Computer Interaction: HCI Theories, Methods and Tools (Part I), edited by Masaaki Kurosu
- Volume 2, LNCS 8511, Human–Computer Interaction: Advanced Interaction Modalities and Techniques (Part II), edited by Masaaki Kurosu
- Volume 3, LNCS 8512, Human–Computer Interaction: Applications and Services (Part III), edited by Masaaki Kurosu
- Volume 4, LNCS 8513, Universal Access in Human–Computer Interaction: Design and Development Methods for Universal Access (Part I), edited by Constantine Stephanidis and Margherita Antona
- Volume 5, LNCS 8514, Universal Access in Human–Computer Interaction: Universal Access to Information and Knowledge (Part II), edited by Constantine Stephanidis and Margherita Antona
- Volume 6, LNCS 8515, Universal Access in Human–Computer Interaction: Aging and Assistive Environments (Part III), edited by Constantine Stephanidis and Margherita Antona
- Volume 8, LNCS 8517, Design, User Experience, and Usability: Theories, Methods and Tools for Designing the User Experience (Part I), edited by Aaron Marcus
- Volume 9, LNCS 8518, Design, User Experience, and Usability: User Experience Design for Diverse Interaction Platforms and Environments (Part II), edited by Aaron Marcus
- Volume 10, LNCS 8519, Design, User Experience, and Usability: User Experience Design for Everyday Life Applications and Services (Part III), edited by Aaron Marcus
- Volume 11, LNCS 8520, Design, User Experience, and Usability: User Experience Design Practice (Part IV), edited by Aaron Marcus
- Volume 12, LNCS 8521, Human Interface and the Management of Information: Information and Knowledge Design and Evaluation (Part I), edited by Sakae Yamamoto
- Volume 13, LNCS 8522, Human Interface and the Management of Information: Information and Knowledge in Applications and Services (Part II), edited by Sakae Yamamoto
- Volume 14, LNCS 8523, Learning and Collaboration Technologies: Designing and Developing Novel Learning Experiences (Part I), edited by Panayiotis Zaphiris and Andri Ioannou
- Volume 15, LNCS 8524, Learning and Collaboration Technologies: Technology-rich Environments for Learning and Collaboration (Part II), edited by Panayiotis Zaphiris and Andri Ioannou
- Volume 16, LNCS 8525, Virtual, Augmented and Mixed Reality: Designing and Developing Virtual and Augmented Environments (Part I), edited by Randall Shumaker and Stephanie Lackey

- Volume 17, LNCS 8526, Virtual, Augmented and Mixed Reality: Applications of Virtual and Augmented Reality (Part II), edited by Randall Shumaker and Stephanie Lackey
- Volume 18, LNCS 8527, HCI in Business, edited by Fiona Fui-Hoon Nah
- Volume 19, LNCS 8528, Cross-Cultural Design, edited by P.L. Patrick Rau
- Volume 20, LNCS 8529, Digital Human Modeling and Applications in Health, Safety, Ergonomics and Risk Management, edited by Vincent G. Duffy
- Volume 21, LNCS 8530, Distributed, Ambient, and Pervasive Interactions, edited by Norbert Streitz and Panos Markopoulos
- Volume 22, LNCS 8531, Social Computing and Social Media, edited by Gabriele Meiselwitz
- Volume 23, LNAI 8532, Engineering Psychology and Cognitive Ergonomics, edited by Don Harris
- Volume 24, LNCS 8533, Human Aspects of Information Security, Privacy and Trust, edited by Theo Tryfonas and Ioannis Askoxylakis
- Volume 25, LNAI 8534, Foundations of Augmented Cognition, edited by Dylan D. Schmorrow and Cali M. Fidopiastis
- Volume 26, CCIS 434, HCI International 2014 Posters Proceedings (Part I), edited by Constantine Stephanidis
- Volume 27, CCIS 435, HCI International 2014 Posters Proceedings (Part II), edited by Constantine Stephanidis

I would like to thank the Program Chairs and the members of the Program Boards of all affiliated conferences and thematic areas, listed below, for their contribution to the highest scientific quality and the overall success of the HCI International 2014 Conference.

This conference could not have been possible without the continuous support and advice of the founding chair and conference scientific advisor, Prof. Gavriel Salvendy, as well as the dedicated work and outstanding efforts of the communications chair and editor of *HCI International News*, Dr. Abbas Moallem.

I would also like to thank for their contribution towards the smooth organization of the HCI International 2014 Conference the members of the Human–Computer Interaction Laboratory of ICS-FORTH, and in particular George Paparoulis, Maria Pitsoulaki, Maria Bouhli, and George Kapnas.

April 2014   Constantine Stephanidis
                                    General Chair, HCI International 2014

Organization

Human–Computer Interaction

Program Chair: Masaaki Kurosu, Japan

Jose Abdelnour-Nocera, UK
Sebastiano Bagnara, Italy
Simone Barbosa, Brazil
Adriana Betiol, Brazil
Simone Borsci, UK
Henry Duh, Australia
Xiaowen Fang, USA
Vicki Hanson, UK
Wonil Hwang, Korea
Minna Isomursu, Finland
Yong Gu Ji, Korea
Anirudha Joshi, India
Esther Jun, USA
Kyungdoh Kim, Korea

Heidi Krömker, Germany
Chen Ling, USA
Chang S. Nam, USA
Naoko Okuizumi, Japan
Philippe Palanque, France
Ling Rothrock, USA
Naoki Sakakibara, Japan
Dominique Scapin, France
Guangfeng Song, USA
Sanjay Tripathi, India
Chui Yin Wong, Malaysia
Toshiki Yamaoka, Japan
Kazuhiko Yamazaki, Japan
Ryoji Yoshitake, Japan

Human Interface and the Management of Information

Program Chair: Sakae Yamamoto, Japan

Alan Chan, Hong Kong
Denis A. Coelho, Portugal
Linda Elliott, USA
Shin'ichi Fukuzumi, Japan
Michitaka Hirose, Japan
Makoto Itoh, Japan
Yen-Yu Kang, Taiwan
Koji Kimita, Japan
Daiji Kobayashi, Japan

Hiroyuki Miki, Japan
Shogo Nishida, Japan
Robert Proctor, USA
Youngho Rhee, Korea
Ryosuke Saga, Japan
Katsunori Shimohara, Japan
Kim-Phuong Vu, USA
Tomio Watanabe, Japan

Engineering Psychology and Cognitive Ergonomics

Program Chair: Don Harris, UK

Guy Andre Boy, USA
Shan Fu, P.R. China
Hung-Sying Jing, Taiwan
Wen-Chin Li, Taiwan
Mark Neerincx, The Netherlands
Jan Noyes, UK
Paul Salmon, Australia

Axel Schulte, Germany
Siraj Shaikh, UK
Sarah Sharples, UK
Anthony Smoker, UK
Neville Stanton, UK
Alex Stedmon, UK
Andrew Thatcher, South Africa

Universal Access in Human–Computer Interaction

Program Chairs: Constantine Stephanidis, Greece, and Margherita Antona, Greece

Julio Abascal, Spain
Gisela Susanne Bahr, USA
João Barroso, Portugal
Margrit Betke, USA
Anthony Brooks, Denmark
Christian Bühler, Germany
Stefan Carmien, Spain
Hua Dong, P.R. China
Carlos Duarte, Portugal
Pier Luigi Emiliani, Italy
Qin Gao, P.R. China
Andrina Granić, Croatia
Andreas Holzinger, Austria
Josette Jones, USA
Simeon Keates, UK

Georgios Kouroupetroglou, Greece
Patrick Langdon, UK
Barbara Leporini, Italy
Eugene Loos, The Netherlands
Ana Isabel Paraguay, Brazil
Helen Petrie, UK
Michael Pieper, Germany
Enrico Pontelli, USA
Jaime Sanchez, Chile
Alberto Sanna, Italy
Anthony Savidis, Greece
Christian Stary, Austria
Hirotada Ueda, Japan
Gerhard Weber, Germany
Harald Weber, Germany

Virtual, Augmented and Mixed Reality

Program Chairs: Randall Shumaker, USA, and Stephanie Lackey, USA

Roland Blach, Germany
Sheryl Brahnam, USA
Juan Cendan, USA
Jessie Chen, USA
Panagiotis D. Kaklis, UK

Hirokazu Kato, Japan
Denis Laurendeau, Canada
Fotis Liarokapis, UK
Michael Macedonia, USA
Gordon Mair, UK

Jose San Martin, Spain
Tabitha Peck, USA
Christian Sandor, Australia

Christopher Stapleton, USA
Gregory Welch, USA

Cross-Cultural Design

Program Chair: P.L. Patrick Rau, P.R. China

Yee-Yin Choong, USA
Paul Fu, USA
Zhiyong Fu, P.R. China
Pin-Chao Liao, P.R. China
Dyi-Yih Michael Lin, Taiwan
Rungtai Lin, Taiwan
Ta-Ping (Robert) Lu, Taiwan
Liang Ma, P.R. China
Alexander Mädche, Germany

Sheau-Farn Max Liang, Taiwan
Katsuhiko Ogawa, Japan
Tom Plocher, USA
Huatong Sun, USA
Emil Tso, P.R. China
Hsiu-Ping Yueh, Taiwan
Liang (Leon) Zeng, USA
Jia Zhou, P.R. China

Online Communities and Social Media

Program Chair: Gabriele Meiselwitz, USA

Leonelo Almeida, Brazil
Chee Siang Ang, UK
Aneesha Bakharia, Australia
Ania Bobrowicz, UK
James Braman, USA
Farzin Deravi, UK
Carsten Kleiner, Germany
Niki Lambropoulos, Greece
Soo Ling Lim, UK

Anthony Norcio, USA
Portia Pusey, USA
Panote Siriaraya, UK
Stefan Stieglitz, Germany
Giovanni Vincenti, USA
Yuanqiong (Kathy) Wang, USA
June Wei, USA
Brian Wentz, USA

Augmented Cognition

**Program Chairs: Dylan D. Schmorrow, USA,
and Cali M. Fidopiastis, USA**

Ahmed Abdelkhalek, USA
Robert Atkinson, USA
Monique Beaudoin, USA
John Blitch, USA
Alenka Brown, USA

Rosario Cannavò, Italy
Joseph Cohn, USA
Andrew J. Cowell, USA
Martha Crosby, USA
Wai-Tat Fu, USA

Rodolphe Gentili, USA
Frederick Gregory, USA
Michael W. Hail, USA
Monte Hancock, USA
Fei Hu, USA
Ion Juvina, USA
Joe Keebler, USA
Philip Mangos, USA
Rao Mannepalli, USA
David Martinez, USA
Yvonne R. Masakowski, USA
Santosh Mathan, USA
Ranjeev Mittu, USA

Keith Niall, USA
Tatana Olson, USA
Debra Patton, USA
June Pilcher, USA
Robinson Pino, USA
Tiffany Poeppelman, USA
Victoria Romero, USA
Amela Sadagic, USA
Anna Skinner, USA
Ann Speed, USA
Robert Sottilare, USA
Peter Walker, USA

Digital Human Modeling and Applications in Health, Safety, Ergonomics and Risk Management

Program Chair: Vincent G. Duffy, USA

Giuseppe Andreoni, Italy
Daniel Carruth, USA
Elsbeth De Korte, The Netherlands
Afzal A. Godil, USA
Ravindra Goonetilleke, Hong Kong
Noriaki Kuwahara, Japan
Kang Li, USA
Zhizhong Li, P.R. China

Tim Marler, USA
Jianwei Niu, P.R. China
Michelle Robertson, USA
Matthias Rötting, Germany
Mao-Jiun Wang, Taiwan
Xuguang Wang, France
James Yang, USA

Design, User Experience, and Usability

Program Chair: Aaron Marcus, USA

Sisira Adikari, Australia
Claire Ancient, USA
Arne Berger, Germany
Jamie Blustein, Canada
Ana Boa-Ventura, USA
Jan Brejcha, Czech Republic
Lorenzo Cantoni, Switzerland
Marc Fabri, UK
Luciane Maria Fadel, Brazil
Tricia Flanagan, Hong Kong
Jorge Frascara, Mexico

Federico Gobbo, Italy
Emilie Gould, USA
Rüdiger Heimgärtner, Germany
Brigitte Herrmann, Germany
Steffen Hess, Germany
Nouf Khashman, Canada
Fabiola Guillermina Noël, Mexico
Francisco Rebelo, Portugal
Kerem Rızvanoğlu, Turkey
Marcelo Soares, Brazil
Carla Spinillo, Brazil

Distributed, Ambient and Pervasive Interactions

Program Chairs: Norbert Streitz, Germany, and Panos Markopoulos, The Netherlands

Juan Carlos Augusto, UK
Jose Bravo, Spain
Adrian Cheok, UK
Boris de Ruyter, The Netherlands
Anind Dey, USA
Dimitris Grammenos, Greece
Nuno Guimaraes, Portugal
Achilles Kameas, Greece
Javed Vassilis Khan, The Netherlands
Shin'ichi Konomi, Japan
Carsten Magerkurth, Switzerland

Ingrid Mulder, The Netherlands
Anton Nijholt, The Netherlands
Fabio Paternó, Italy
Carsten Röcker, Germany
Teresa Romao, Portugal
Albert Ali Salah, Turkey
Manfred Tscheligi, Austria
Reiner Wichert, Germany
Woontack Woo, Korea
Xenophon Zabulis, Greece

Human Aspects of Information Security, Privacy and Trust

Program Chairs: Theo Tryfonas, UK, and Ioannis Askoxylakis, Greece

Claudio Agostino Ardagna, Italy
Zinaida Benenson, Germany
Daniele Catteddu, Italy
Raoul Chiesa, Italy
Bryan Cline, USA
Sadie Creese, UK
Jorge Cuellar, Germany
Marc Dacier, USA
Dieter Gollmann, Germany
Kirstie Hawkey, Canada
Jaap-Henk Hoepman, The Netherlands
Cagatay Karabat, Turkey
Angelos Keromytis, USA
Ayako Komatsu, Japan
Ronald Leenes, The Netherlands
Javier Lopez, Spain
Steve Marsh, Canada

Gregorio Martinez, Spain
Emilio Mordini, Italy
Yuko Murayama, Japan
Masakatsu Nishigaki, Japan
Aljosa Pasic, Spain
Milan Petković, The Netherlands
Joachim Posegga, Germany
Jean-Jacques Quisquater, Belgium
Damien Sauveron, France
George Spanoudakis, UK
Kerry-Lynn Thomson, South Africa
Julien Touzeau, France
Theo Tryfonas, UK
João Vilela, Portugal
Claire Vishik, UK
Melanie Volkamer, Germany

HCI in Business

Program Chair: Fiona Fui-Hoon Nah, USA

Andreas Auinger, Austria
Michel Avital, Denmark
Traci Carte, USA
Hock Chuan Chan, Singapore
Constantinos Coursaris, USA
Soussan Djamasbi, USA
Brenda Eschenbrenner, USA
Nobuyuki Fukawa, USA
Khaled Hassanein, Canada
Milena Head, Canada
Susanna (Shuk Ying) Ho, Australia
Jack Zhenhui Jiang, Singapore
Jinwoo Kim, Korea
Zoonky Lee, Korea
Honglei Li, UK
Nicholas Lockwood, USA
Eleanor T. Loiacono, USA
Mei Lu, USA

Scott McCoy, USA
Brian Mennecke, USA
Robin Poston, USA
Lingyun Qiu, P.R. China
Rene Riedl, Austria
Matti Rossi, Finland
April Savoy, USA
Shu Schiller, USA
Hong Sheng, USA
Choon Ling Sia, Hong Kong
Chee-Wee Tan, Denmark
Chuan Hoo Tan, Hong Kong
Noam Tractinsky, Israel
Horst Treiblmaier, Austria
Virpi Tuunainen, Finland
Dezhi Wu, USA
I-Chin Wu, Taiwan

Learning and Collaboration Technologies

**Program Chairs: Panayiotis Zaphiris, Cyprus,
and Andri Ioannou, Cyprus**

Ruthi Aladjem, Israel
Abdulaziz Aldaej, UK
John M. Carroll, USA
Maka Eradze, Estonia
Mikhail Fominykh, Norway
Denis Gillet, Switzerland
Mustafa Murat Inceoglu, Turkey
Pernilla Josefsson, Sweden
Marie Joubert, UK
Sauli Kiviranta, Finland
Tomaž Klobučar, Slovenia
Elena Kyza, Cyprus
Maarten de Laat, The Netherlands
David Lamas, Estonia

Edmund Laugasson, Estonia
Ana Loureiro, Portugal
Katherine Maillet, France
Nadia Pantidi, UK
Antigoni Parmaxi, Cyprus
Borzoo Pourabdollahian, Italy
Janet C. Read, UK
Christophe Reffay, France
Nicos Souleles, Cyprus
Ana Luísa Torres, Portugal
Stefan Trausan-Matu, Romania
Aimilia Tzanavari, Cyprus
Johnny Yuen, Hong Kong
Carmen Zahn, Switzerland

External Reviewers

Ilia Adami, Greece
Iosif Klironomos, Greece
Maria Korozi, Greece
Vassilis Kouroumalis, Greece

Asterios Leonidis, Greece
George Margetis, Greece
Stavroula Ntoa, Greece
Nikolaos Partarakis, Greece

HCI International 2015

The 15th International Conference on Human–Computer Interaction, HCI International 2015, will be held jointly with the affiliated conferences in Los Angeles, CA, USA, in the Westin Bonaventure Hotel, August 2–7, 2015. It will cover a broad spectrum of themes related to HCI, including theoretical issues, methods, tools, processes, and case studies in HCI design, as well as novel interaction techniques, interfaces, and applications. The proceedings will be published by Springer. More information will be available on the conference website: http://www.hcii2015.org/

General Chair
Professor Constantine Stephanidis
University of Crete and ICS-FORTH
Heraklion, Crete, Greece
E-mail: cs@ics.forth.gr

Table of Contents – Part IV

Web Accessibility

Design for All in the Built Environment

Global Access Infrastructures

User Experience in Universal Access

Web Accessibility

A Framework to Facilitate the Implementation of Technical Aspects of Web Accessibility

Roberto Cícero de Oliveira[1], André Pimenta Freire[2], Débora Maria Barroso Paiva[1],
Maria Istela Cagnin[1], and Hana Rubinsztejn[1]

[1] School of Computing, Federal University of Mato Grosso do Sul (UFMS)
P.O. Box 549, 79070-900, Campo Grande, MS, Brazil
{rco.ufms,dmbpaiva,istela,hanaksr}@gmail.com
[2] Department of Computer Science, Federal University of Lavras (UFLA)
P.O. Box 3037, 37200-000, Lavras, MG, Brazil
apfreire@gmail.com

Abstract. The expansion of the internet has become apparent in recent years, both by the number of users, and by the number of services available on the network. Considering such an expansion it is essential that the content be accessible to all people, regardless their abilities or different disabilities. Thus, it is necessary that IT professionals dedicate time and effort in planning accessible online solutions. In this paper, we proposed the Homero framework in order to support the development of accessible interface layer of web applications. Developed using the PHP language, the Homero framework automates the generation of web pages in accordance with guidelines defined in Web Content Accessibility Guidelines (WCAG) 2.0. In order to provide evidence of the quality of web applications generated using the framework, an empirical study was conducted. The results showed the effectiveness of Homero to assist the development of accessible web applications, achieving level AAA in automatically detectable WCAG 2.0 success criteria.

Keywords: Web Accessibility, Framework, Empirical Study, Web Interfaces, WCAG.

1 Introduction

The expansion of the internet has become more and more apparent in recent years due to the number of users and the number of services available on the network, such as e-banking, e-learning and e-commerce.

Considering this expansion, it is necessary that professionals in Information Technology (IT) dedicate time and effort in planning intelligent and accessible online solutions, in order to enable all people to have access to information and web services. Based on the definition of accessibility provided by ISO 9241-171 - Ergonomics of Human-System Interaction Guidance on Software Accessibility - web accessibility could be defined as the possibility of a website to be used by people with widest range of abilities, including people with disabilities [1].

C. Stephanidis and M. Antona (Eds.): UAHCI/HCII 2014, Part IV, LNCS 8516, pp. 3–13, 2014.

Additionally, the W3C (World Wide Web Consortium) published the WCAG (Web Content Accessibility Guidelines) [2], currently at version 2.0. The guidelines provide recommendations to help make the content of web pages more accessible to people with disabilities [2].

WCAG 2.0 consists of twelve accessibility guidelines, broken into 61 success criteria. These guidelines are organized around four principles (that content should be Perceivable, Operable, Understandable and Robust). In order to check the conformance to guidelines, developers can perform automatic evaluations of some success criteria, but manual evaluation is necessary to evaluate all criteria, including those that cannot be automatically evaluated. The completeness of automatic evaluation tools ranges between 14% and 38% for WCAG 2.0 success criteria [3].

However, developing accessible web applications is not always a trivial task, due to the knowledge needed to implement interface components in an accessible manner. One way to reduce the effort employed in the development of accessible web applications is using software reuse techniques such as software frameworks, which can contribute especially to the implementation of more technical accessibility requirements.

In this paper, we proposed the Homero framework in order to support the development of accessible interface layer of web applications. This framework automates the generation of web applications in accordance with the guidelines in WCAG 2.0, especially those which are related to more technical aspects, in order to reduce the effort spent by developers and the chance of occurring some common errors.

An empirical study was conducted to evaluate the number of violations of automatically detectable WCAG 2.0 success criteria in web applications generated using the framework. The study measured the number of elements implemented in the given time and the conformance level to WCAG 2.0 success criteria that can be evaluated automatically.

The paper is organized as follows. In Section 2, we discuss related work. In Section 3, the Homero framework is explained. In Section 4, the empirical study planning, execution and results are described. Finally, in Section 5 the conclusions are presented.

2   Related Work

Significant work has been dedicated to developing automated accessibility evaluation tools, such as Total Validator [4], CynthiaSays [5], iMergo [6] and others. Such automated evaluation tools can help developers detect many problems that otherwise would be very tedious to check. However, those tools cannot identify many problems that would require a manual evaluation. Even the problems that could be automatically detected often are identified in a late stage of the development, as developers do not always run such tools on their web pages as frequently as would be necessary.

Other works in the literature have reported on different approaches to help develop more accessible content, including those that enable users and developers to embed Javascript codes into rendered web pages in their client browser and others that propose frameworks and model-based development approaches.

The scripting framework Accessmonkey [7] was developed in order to help end users and developers to incorporate Javascript code into web pages in order to make them more accessible. The framework allows for the inclusion of more general and specific codes in web pages in order to automate task that are commonly performed by users or to work around accessibility issues that are commonly encountered in web pages. However, the proposal of the framework is focused on the automation of page adaption in client-side operations.

Velasco [8] propose a framework to help develop more accessible rich internet applications (RIA) using a service-oriented architecture. The framework provides resources to help developers incorporate broader web-compliance requirements in the development of their projects. The framework allows for the use of resources to detect and adapt content according to web accessibility compliance requirements, especially for RIAs, which frequently have content that is dynamically generated after web pages were rendered.

Another proposal was made by Yan [9] by means of the SourceProbe tool, which embeds comments in HTML code of pages generated by server-side scripts. By means of those indications, when the final HTML code is evaluated using the client browser, it is possible to track where exactly in the server-side code the given part of resulting HTML with accessibility problems was generated.

Moreno et al. [10] proposed a Model-Driven Development (MDD) approach for modeling web accessibility and generating more accessible web applications. They developed the AWA – Accessibility for Web applications, which incorporates the AWA-Metamodel and a process for generating the code of web applications that follow basic principles of accessibility.

Martín et al. [11] proposed an approach based on Aspect-Oriented development to create more accessible web applications. Their approach consists of enriching User Interaction Diagrams with interaction points that incorporate accessibility requirements that can be modeled when the interface is designed. They use a Softgoal Interdependency Graph (SIG) template to include WCAG 1.0 requirements.

Although there are several mechanisms to help develop more accessible content, we could not find empirical studies in the literature that detailed the impact of using such approaches on adhering to the guidelines and on developers' productivity.

3   The Homero Framework

The Homero framework [12] automates the generation of user interfaces of web applications in accordance with a set of WCAG 2.0 guidelines, in order to reduce the effort spent by developers and the chance of occurring some common errors. One of the simplest examples of the framework usage is related to Success Criterion 1.1 in WCAG 2.0, which states: "Provide text alternatives for any non-text content so that it can be changed into other forms people need, such as large print, Braille, speech, symbols or simpler language". In this case, the framework can prevent developers from omitting alternative texts for images.

It should be noted that the Homero framework does not intend to address WCAG 2.0 success criteria that require manual human evaluation. For example, success criteria included in guideline 3.1 of WCAG 2.0 are related to "Making text content readable and understandable". The Homero framework is not able to determine whether content is completely readable and understandable automatically.

Homero is a black-box object-oriented framework [13], producing HTML 5.0 compliant code. It was developed using best practices in PHP development. The user interface layers of web applications generated by Homero are in accordance with success criteria of WCAG 2.0 AAA level that are related to technical aspects that can be checked automatically. Its classes were defined to prevent the overwriting of their methods, and thereby affecting the accessibility validations implemented.

By reusing Homero classes, developers implement the user interface layer of web applications using only PHP language. This enables the creation of clean and readable source code and reduces the cost of having to deal directly with HTML code, which is generated automatically by the framework.

The Homero framework has thirty-nine classes, organized into eleven groups to facilitate understanding. Each group consists of one or more classes, as shown in Fig. 1.

The Media group is responsible for media of user interface (audio and video). The Objects group represents external components (i.e. flash plug-in) which may be incorporated in the interface. The Link group deals with links or anchors of the interface. The Images group treats the images that are part of the application context. The Layout group works with the divisions of the site layout. The application tables are handled by Tables group. The Lists group was created to deal with lists. The Texts group consists of ten classes and works with different types of texts. The Form group is responsible for managing forms. The Header group deals with header of HTML pages. The Page group represents the web page to be developed.

The Homero instantiation must begin by creating an object of Page class. This object has a header attribute, that accepts an object of the Header class, and a set of objects of Element class, which are instances of other classes (such as Media, Object, Link, Image, Table, Superscript, etc), according to the inheritance relationships with the Element class, illustrated in Fig. 1.

During the methods invocation of Homero classes, the developer must provide as parameters all required accessibility data. Otherwise, an accessibility validation warning of the user interface of the web application is presented, as can be seen in the warning shown on the right side of Fig. 2. In this case, the alternative text of the image represented by img object of Image class (line 9, Fig. 2) has not been defined, because the second parameter of the constructor method was defined as null, causing an accessibility error.

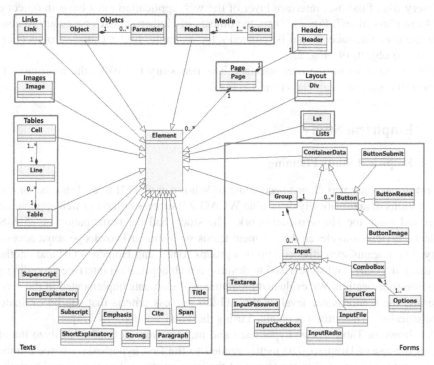

Fig. 1. Homero class diagram

```
1  <?
2  include ("Homero.php");
3  $header = new Header("Homero preview");
4  $header->setMeta('http-equiv="Content-Type"
5       content="text/html; charset=iso-8859-1"');
6
7  $interface = new Page("pt-br");
8  $interface->setHeader($header->generate());
9  $img = new Image("icons/logo.png", null,
10      "Homero", null, null);
11 $interface->setBody($img->generate());
12 $interface->generate();
13 ?>
```

Warning: Image's alternative text was not specified.
in D:\\www\Homero\Image.php on line 9

Fig. 2. Example of the Homero instantiation

For the Homero instantiation, a property of the PHP language is employed. In order to use classes, it is necessary only to include them in the source code with the following PHP native functions: include or include_once. Thus, a file called Homero.php was created with all framework classes, which must be included in all project files.

Initially, it is just necessary to include the Homero.php file in the file where the user interface will be created (line 2, Fig. 2) and to add the folder that contains the files of framework classes in the folder of the web application project.

Every file of the user interface layer of the web application must have an object of the `Page` class (line 7, Fig. 2). Then, the objects of Homero classes necessary to compose the user interface should be created - for example, line 3 (`header` object) and line 9 (`img` object) of   Fig. 2.

Finally, to generate the user interface it is necessary to invoke the `generate()` method of object of `Page` class (line 12, Fig. 2).

4   Empirical Study

4.1   Empirical Study Planning

An empirical study was planned according to Wholin et al. [14] to evaluate the number of violations of automatically detectable WCAG 2.0 success criteria in web applications generated using the Homero framework. The study had the participation of 25 MSc students, divided into eleven development teams with similar knowledge about accessibility. These teams were divided into two groups (one using Homero - GH and another not using it - GnH) and were asked to develop a web application interface according to the same specification. We evaluated the number of elements implemented in the given time and the conformance level of WCAG 2.0 success criteria that can be evaluated automatically.   The latter was obtained using the Total Validator tool [4].

As shown in Table 1, two hypotheses and metrics were defined to analyze the effect of the use of Homero. The metric related to the first hypothesis was the number of elements implemented in the layout of the user interface. For the second hypothesis, the metric was the level of accessibility achieved by the application, considering WCAG 2.0 (A, AA or AAA), using Total Validator tool.

Table 1. Hypotheses and metrics of the empirical study

H_0	There is no difference in the number of elements developed using, or not, Homero
H_{a0}	There is a significant difference in the number of elements developed using, or not, Homero.
Metric	**Number of elements implemented in the layout**
H_1	There is no difference in level of accessibility achieved by using or not Homero.
H_{a1}	There is a significant difference in the level of accessibility achieved by using or not Homero.
Metric	**Level of accessibility in WCAG 2.0**
Legend: H - Null hypothesis, H_a - Alternative hypothesis	

Before conducting the empirical study, a survey was conducted to analyze the level of knowledge, theoretical and practical, of the participants in object-oriented programming, web development using PHP and HTML languages. Moreover, the level of experience of the participants with concepts of web accessibility and WCAG 2.0 guidelines was identified. This survey was conducted through a questionnaire answered by the participants and the level of knowledge of participants is presented in Table 2.

Table 2. Level of Experience of Participants

Level of theoretical knowledge	None	Little	Reasonable	High
Object-oriented programming	0	6	16	3
PHP	3	11	7	4
HTML	1	9	11	4
Web Accessibility	5	14	6	0
WCAG 2.0 guidelines	22	3	0	0

Considering the results in Table 2, a training was offered to groups about object oriented programming, PHP language, Homero framework, tableless development, HTML language and WCAG 2.0.

Participants were organized into teams of 2 or 3 people. To allow comparison between development using Homero and development without the use of Homero, teams were divided into two groups: one group, called GH, used Homero in the development and the other, called GnH, which did not use Homero. The formation of teams and groups was made so that each team in each group had equivalent knowledge in relation to technologies used for developing activities.

The execution plan of the study was composed of a single phase, in which the teams from the two groups had to develop the proposed interface layout. At the beginning of the study we provided the teams with the interface model to be developed, a consent form to use the information and an activities execution form to assess the framework usage. The participants were provided with:

1. A mockup of a semantically accessible application, used as template of the interface;
2. An image of the expected appearance of the interface, with the divisions of the proposed layout;
3. A CSS file containing the style characteristics of the interface, and
4. A folder containing five images used in the interface.

4.2   Execution and Results of the Empirical Study

After the execution of the activities assigned to the participants, some results were analyzed as shown below.

During the evaluation of the hypothesis 1 it was observed that the average number of elements implemented by teams of GnH group was higher (9.6 versus 6.2 of GnH group), as can be seen in Fig. 3.

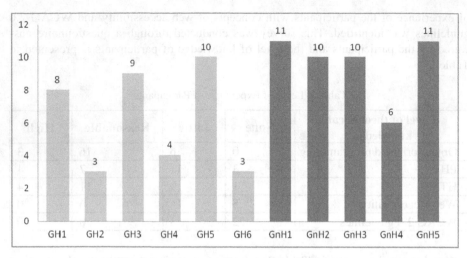

Fig. 3. Number of elements implemented by teams

As observed, half of GH teams could implement few elements. We believe that this discrepancy may be due to lack of knowledge of Homero framework. In the form of activities execution of the GH group, it was observed that this was the main difficulty (50% of the teams indicated this); despite the Homero training had been offered before the empirical study execution.

To evaluate the hypothesis 2, the source files developed by participants were validated using the Total Validator tool. The result of this validation is the number of errors of accessibility automatically evaluated in each user interface (Fig. 4) and the level of WCAG 2.0 reached (Fig. 5). On the y-axis of Fig 5, number 1 corresponds to level A of WCAG 2.0, number 2 corresponds to level AA and number 3 corresponds to the level AAA.

The results showed that teams of GnH group developed interfaces with a larger number of elements. However, all of them presented accessibility errors. In contrast, all interfaces developed by the GH group teams, even with a smaller number of elements implemented, had no violations of automatically detectable WCAG 2.0 success criteria of AAA level.

Therefore, we concluded that the use of Homero framework may help avoid developers running into common accessibility mistakes that can be detected automatically earlier in the development, saving time and effort that can be dedicated to performing manual evaluations and user testing. Additionally, Homero contributes to widening the use of Web accessibility guidelines and to making accessibility a concern throughout the development of web applications.

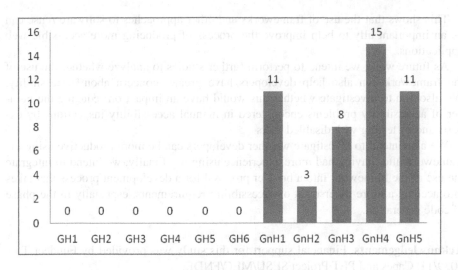

Fig. 4. Number of errors of accessibility by groups

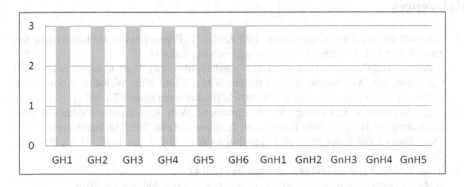

Fig. 5. WCAG 2.0 conformance level achieved by groups

5   Conclusion

This paper presented a study consisting of the development of a framework to help develop more accessible web applications with easier implementation of accessibility requirements from guidelines that can be automatically detected.

Along with the proposal of the framework, an empirical study with 25 participants was conducted to verify the extent to which the framework helped implement technical requirements of accessibility and the productivity of developers using the framework or not.

The initial results from this first study showed that, despite lowering the productivity of developers who used the framework for the first time, the number of technical accessibility errors in the generated web pages is substantially reduced.

This shows that the use of frameworks and other approaches to software reuse can be an important ally to help improve the process of producing more accessible web applications.

As future work, we intend to perform further studies to analyze whether the use of the framework can also help developers have greater concern about accessibility. We also aim to investigate whether this would have an impact on reducing the number of accessibility problems encountered in manual accessibility inspections by experts and by testing with disabled users.

We also intend to investigate whether developers can be more productive using the framework after having had more experience using it. Finally, we intend to integrate the use of the framework into a broader proposal for a development process that takes into account a more diverse set of accessibility requirements, especially in the phase of code generation.

Acknowledgements. Financial support for this study was provided by Fundect T.O. 0039/11, Capes and PET Project SESU/MEC/FNDE.

References

1. International Standards Organization: ISO 9241-171: Ergonomics of Human-System Interaction. Part 171: Guidance on software accessibility (2008)
2. Caldwell, B., Cooper, M., Reid, L.G., Vanderheiden, G.: Web Content Accessibility Guidelines 2.0. Web Accessibility Initiative (WAI), World Wide Web Consortium (W3C) (2008), http://www.w3.org/TR/WCAG20 (accessed October 23, 2013)
3. Vigo, M., Brown, J., Conway, V.: Benchmarking Web Accessibility Evaluation Tools: Measuring the Harm of Sole Reliance on Automated Tests. In: 10th International Cross-Disciplinary Conference on Web Accessibility (W4A 2013), pp. 1–10. ACM, New York (2013)
4. Total Validator – accessibility evaluation tool (2014), http://www.totalvalidator.com/ (last accessed February 4, 2014)
5. Hisoftware. CynthiaSays – accessibility evaluation tool (2014), http://www.cynthiasays.com (last accessed February 4, 2014)
6. Mohamad, Y., Stegemann, D., Koch, J., Velasco, C.A.: Imergo: Supporting Accessibility and Web Standards to Meet the Needs of the Industry via Process-Oriented Software Tools. In: Miesenberger, K., Klaus, J., Zagler, W.L., Burger, D. (eds.) ICCHP 2004. LNCS, vol. 3118, pp. 310–316. Springer, Heidelberg (2004)
7. Bigham, J.P., Ladner, R.E.: Accessmonkey: A Collaborative Scripting Framework for Web Users and Developers. In: 2007 International Cross-Disciplinary Conference on Web Accessibility (W4A 2007), pp. 25–34. ACM, New York (2007)
8. Velasco, C.A., Denev, D., Stegemann, D., Mohamad, Y.: A Web Compliance Engineering Framework to Support the Development of Accessible Rich Internet Applications. In: 2008 International Cross-Disciplinary Conference on Web Accessibility (W4A 2008), pp. 45–49. ACM, New York (2008)
9. Yan, S.: SourceProbe: Web Accessibility Remediation Framework. In: 2010 International Cross Disciplinary Conference on Web Accessibility (W4A 2010), article 26, 2 pages. ACM, New York (2010)

10. Moreno, L., Martínez, P., Ruiz, B.: A MDD Approach for Modeling Web Accessibility. In: 7th Int. Workshop on Web-Oriented Software Technologies, pp. 1–6 (2008)
11. Martín, A., Rossi, G., Cechich, A., Gordillo, S.: Engineering Accessible Web Applications. An Aspect-Oriented Approach. World Wide Web 13(4), 419–440 (2010)
12. Oliveira, R.C.: Homero: A Framework for Developing Accessible User Interface of Web Applications. Master Thesis, College of Computing, Federal University of Mato Grosso do Sul (2013) (in Portuguese)
13. Fayad, M.E., Johnson, R.E.: Domain-specific Application Frameworks: Frameworks experience by industry, 1st edn. John Wiley & Sons (2000)
14. Wohlin, C., Runeson, P., Höst, M., Ohlsson, M.C., Regnell, B., Wesslén, A.: Experimentation in Software Engineering. Springer (2012)

Preserving Privacy – More Than Reading a Message

Susanne Furman and Mary Theofanos

National Institute of Standards and Technology, 100 Bureau Drive,
Gaithersburg, Maryland, 20899, USA
{Susanne.Furman,Mary.Theofanos}@nist.gov

Abstract. Social media has become a mainstream activity where people share all kinds of personal and intimate details about their lives. These social networking sites (SNS) allow users to conveniently authenticate to the third-party website by using their SNS credentials, thus eliminating the need of creating and remembering another username and password but at the same time agreeing to share their personal information with the SNS site. Often this is accomplished by presenting the user with a dialog box informing them that they will be sharing information. We were interested in determining if SNS users authenticating to a third-party website with their SNS credentials, were reading the informational message and if changing the message format would impact the choice to continue or cancel. Format type did not alter the participant's choice to continue. Eye-tracking data suggests that the participants who chose to continue read some of the words in the message.

Keywords: Access to the Web, privacy, eye tracking, authentication.

1   Background

By creating an identity on a website, users gain the ability to engage in a wide range of activities like e-mail, online shopping and banking, or in social networking activities.   Today's Web is very site-centric where the user is expected to maintain a separate copy of their username and corresponding password for each site they join [14]. To create and maintain these separate identities, users must create and remember their usernames and passwords; populate a profile often with the same data across sites; and remember each site's different password rules [9].

Federated identity management offers the user a solution to reduce the burden of multiple identities. It provides a technology that websites can offer to users as a single sign-on (SSO) experience. SSO offers the user an easier experience through a more consistent and less frequent log-on process. The user can authenticate once and access their protected resources across multiple websites [9].

Facebook[1] offers its users a type of SSO that allows users to connect their SNS identity, friends, and personal information to any site that offers this service.

---

[1] Disclaimer: Any mention of commercial products is for information only; such identification is not intended to imply recommendation or endorsement by the National Institute of Standards and Technology, nor is it intended to imply that these entities, materials, or equipment are necessarily the best for the purpose.

C. Stephanidis and M. Antona (Eds.): UAHCI/HCII 2014, Part IV, LNCS 8516, pp. 14–25, 2014.
© Springer International Publishing Switzerland 2014

Through this technology, a user's SNS ID becomes a gateway that provides access to the digital world. The third-party website offering this service benefits through distributing their services with minimal effort to SNS users and the SNS users benefit by eliminating the cumbersome process of registering, and creating and remembering a username and password [8].

Social media has become a mainstream activity where people share all kinds of personal and intimate details about their lives; photos of their children, family and friends; their email address; and even their physical location. Many of these users are unaware that both their personal information as well as that of their friends is passed to these third parties when they authenticate using their SNS credentials.

SNS websites do inform users (through a pop-up dialog window) that authentication to a third-party website using their SNS credentials results in their personal information being shared with the website. The user is typically given the option to agree to or cancel the authentication request.

Privacy advocates are concerned that these SNS authentication services pose new sets of concerns about how data are collected and shared among websites. One major concern is that because users don't completely understand how these services work and have the mistaken impression that their data isn't being collected [8].

Many popular SNS applications transmit users' identifying information to dozens of ad and internet tracking companies. This practice affects millions of SNS application users, even those who implement the strictest privacy settings. Ten of the most popular applications reviewed transmitted not only a user's ID and personal information but also personal information about the user's friends to outside companies [13]. Approximately 850 million times per month, apps have asked SNS users to release their basic information [17].

Most SNS do not make it clear exactly what user information is shared and to whom it is given, so many SNS users make the assumption that their information is safe [12]. Also, SNS privacy settings are often difficult to manage and users often do not change them from their defaults, which are generally set to maximize the visibility and sharing of users' profile information [7].

So, it is not surprising that SNS users are unaware of and don't understand the privacy dangers from data sharing with third-party apps or websites that they connect to using their SNS accounts. Many users believe that online communities are safe and don't understand privacy policies [16]. They do not realize the extent to which they share not only their own information, but that of their friends as well [2]. As a result, they feel their risk of unwilling or inadvertent disclosure of personal information is very low [15].

Motivation is directly tied to attention so the more motivated a person is to perform a particular task, the more effort and attention they will devote [3]. Authentication tasks (i.e., entering a username and password) or privacy and security tasks (e.g., reading a privacy policy) are not considered primary tasks but are viewed as secondary and a requirement for completion of primary tasks.

Another factor impacting attention is that often security messages resemble other non-essential pop-up dialogs. As a result users often fail to realize that they contain important information about how their privacy and security will be affected by taking a certain action. Often users disregard or do not read these dialogs and only click "Agree" or "OK" to close the dialog message [18].

Message format can also impact reading. Information presented in a list format can benefit users who are searching for information that is embedded in other text. List formats facilitate easier information acquisition than paragraph formats, due to their lower print density [19]. The results of a 1995 study demonstrated that older patients were better able to find, understand, and later recall medication instructions that were presented in list format rather than paragraph format [10].

2   Research Goal

Millions of SNS users are utilizing their SNS identities to authenticate to third-party websites. Many are unaware that both their personal information and that of their friend's is passed to these third parties. SNS websites typically inform the user via a dialog message in a pop-up window that by agreeing they will be sharing personal data with the third-party website. However, the user does have the option to agree or cancel the authentication request.

We wanted to investigate if users read the authentication dialog message explaining that their personal information would be shared with a third-party website. Also we wondered if manipulating the format of the dialog message (i.e., sentence-style, list-style, and list with personal data displayed) would impact whether participants would decide to continue with the authentication process. Previous research testing message formats explains the lack of observable effects by claiming that participants did not read or were habituated to the dialog messages. The study supported this explanation with screen capture videos that show the message was displayed for a period of time but clarifies that without an eye tracker they could not be certain users read the message [5]. Specifically we were interested in:

- Will SNS users authenticate to a third-party website using their SNS credentials after being informed that their personal information will be shared with the website?
- Will manipulating the format of the dialog message (i.e., sentence-style, list-style, and list with personal data displayed) influence a participant's choice to continue with the authentication process? Figure 1 shows the three formatted messages.
- What information does the eye-gaze data show about the content participants viewed in the dialog message if any? Does the format of the message make any difference in a participant's authentication choice to continue?

Fig. 1. Format message conditions

3   Methodology

3.1   Participants

A study was conducted at NIST for a period of four weeks to examine these three message conditions. Participants were required to have an SNS account and received $50 for participation in a 30 min session.

Of the 120 participants initially recruited, 117 completed the study. One participant withdrew, and hardware malfunctions prevented two others from completing the study. Participants ranged in age from 17 to over 60 and age groups were fairly equally represented. There were fewer males (35 %) than females (65 %). Most of the participants (92 %) had at least some college experience.

3.2   Instruments and Apparatus

Software code was written to intercept and replace the original SNS authentication message dialog. The code replaced the original dialog message with a similar message in one of three formats identified above. Participants were randomly assigned to one of the three format conditions at the start of their session.

The study used a PC integrated with the Tobii T60XL[1] eye tracker paired with a high-resolution 24" TFT wide screen monitor having a display pixel resolution of 1900 x 1200. The eye tracker looked like a normal computer display, and its high resolution cameras were invisible to the participant. The online version of the Wall Street Journal (WSJ.com website)[1] was shown in Internet Explorer 9. All precision measurements were done at 60 Hz sampling rate, and all participants completed a nine point eye calibration prior to the start of the session. Gaze data was logged by Tobii Studio software.

3.3   Sessions

After signing the consent form, participants logged into their SNS account. The researcher started the intercept software, assigned the participant to one of the three format conditions, and started the eye-tracking device. The intercept software launched the online version of the third-party website. The researcher asked participants to find a news story of interest, and once selected, the researcher provided the following scenario:

> You are sitting at home and are very interested in reading this news story but you don't have time right now. Given the number of times that news sites refresh their content, you are concerned that you may not find the story when you come back. Please save the news story so that you can read it later.

The researcher instructed the participant to do whatever they would do at home. Saving the news story on the site required the participant to set up an account or use their SNS credentials to authenticate to the third-party website.

If the participant chose not to use their SNS credentials to authenticate, the researcher stopped the eye tracker and instructed them to complete an online survey about their SNS use and privacy concerns. If the participant chose to use their SNS credentials to authenticate, the choice was recorded, the eye tracker captured the participant's interaction with the dialog message, and particpants completed the online survey.

After session completion, the researcher logged the participant out of their SNS account, removed the intercept application from their SNS apps, asked if there were any questions, and thanked the participant for their time. Participants were compensated for their time prior to leaving the laboratory.

4   Results

4.1   Authentication Using SNS Credentials

The participants were randomly assigned to one of the format conditions at the start of their session resulting in 40 participants in the sentence-style format, 38 in the list, and 39 in the list with data displayed formats. Fifty-nine (51 %) of the 117 participants chose to use SNS credentials to authenticate to the third-party website.

Of the 40 participants in the sentence-style format, 23 (58 %) authenticated using their SNS credentials; of the 38 participants in the list-style, 17 (45 %) authenticated; and of the 39 in list with data format, 19 (49 %) authenticated. A chi squared test was performed to determine whether the format conditions were equal with respect to authentication choice. Although there were more participants using their SNS credentials to authenticate in the sentence-style format, use/did not use data comparing the three conditions were not significant, χ^2 (2, N= 59) = 1.3382, p > 0.5.

4.2 Eye-Tracking Data

Tobii Studio software captured the gaze data as participants viewed the third-party website. Of particular interest was where participants allocated their visual attention when the SNS SSO dialog box appeared. For that reason, only those participants who chose to use their SNS credentials and those who started to use their SNS credentials but did not continue were included in the eye-tracking analyses.

AOI 1 – Dialog Message Analyses. An area of interest (AOI) is a user-defined area on the stimulus that is used for capturing and analyzing the eye-tracking data (see Figure 2). The message content, title, and action buttons on the SNS authentication dialog message were marked as the initial AOI. Of particular interest was the amount of attention the AOI received. Therefore, the mean and standard deviations were calculated for the following metrics: (1) fixation count: the number of times the participant fixates or pauses over areas of interest - this indicates how many times the participant looks at the area; (2) total fixation duration: measures the sum of the length of time for all fixations or pauses within an AOI measured in seconds; (3) total visit duration: how much time in seconds the participant spent within an area of interest - this indicates the level of the participant's involvement with the area. The overall mean total visit duration was 5.56 s. Participants in the list format condition spent less time viewing the AOI than those in the sentence-style or list with data displayed format conditions. Individuals who chose not to connect had the longest total visit duration. Table 1 shows the total visit duration, fixation counts, and fixation duration means and standard deviations across format conditions.

The mean fixation count for all participants was 21.04 fixations. The mean fixation count showed similar results with the sentence-style format having fewer fixations than the list or the list with data displayed formats. However, the participants who did not choose to connect had the most fixations.

The mean fixation duration for all participants was 4.39 s. The results across format condition show that the participants in the sentence format condition spent less time fixating within the AOI than the list format participants.

Table 1. AOI total fixation, fixation count, and total fixation duration (seconds) mean and standard deviations across format condition

Format Condition	Total Visit Duration(s)		Fixation Count		Fixation Duration(s)	
	Mean	St Dev	Mean	St Dev	Mean	St Dev
Sentence-style	4.85	4.35	16.75	14.11	3.28	2.78
List	4.70	3.74	17.8	11.16	3.59	3.97
List with Data	8.07	6.42	26.67	21.8	6.16	5.1
Did Not Connect	13.01	5.94	31	16.02	6.03	2.6

Multiple AOI Analyses. We separated the dialog box into separate AOIs, including the basic information area (e.g., name, email, gender), the profile picture, and the participant's photos of friends. The sentence-style format did not include any shared photos and is not included in these analyses.

The main content AOI included the personal information that the participants shared from their profile. Participants spent less time fixating within the list format AOI than within the AOIs in the sentence-style, and the "did not connect" format conditions.

The list format had fewer fixations than the sentence-style format, list with data format and didn't connect format groups. They also had a shorter visit duration than the sentence-style format, list with data format, and didn't connect format conditions. Table 2 shows the fixation duration, fixation count, and total visit duration means and standard deviations across format conditions.

Table 2. Multiple AOI total fixation duration, fixation count, and total fixation duration means and standard deviations

Format Condition	Total Visit Duration (s)		Fixation Count		Fixation Duration (s)	
	Mean	St Dev	Mean	St Dev	Mean	St Dev
Personal Information Message Content						
Sentence	1.95	2.53	8.93	10.17	1.63	2.19
List	1.66	1.64	7.25	6.21	1.45	1.37
List with Data	4.13	4.82	17	19.93	3.68	4.44
Did Not Connect	6.85	3.38	18.6	11.59	3.6	1.79
Photos of Friends						
Sentence	*Did not have photos on their message dialogs*					
List	.75	.56	3.83	2.17	.62	.55
List with Data	1.47	1.25	4.86	3.44	1.32	1.25
Profile Photo						
Sentence	.61	.13	3.33	.58	.58	.16
List	.21	.13	1.25	.05	.21	.13
List with Data	.38	.21	2.33	1.53	.38	.21

Large within group standard deviations precluded significant results for any pairwise comparisons, but there appeared to be a trend in the data across formats. A trend analysis attempts to spot a pattern or trend in the data. A Likelihood ratio test was conducted and showed a significant monotonic trend for fixation count and total visit duration for both the dialog box AOI and personal content AOI, $p < 0.05$. This was also the case for the fixation count for the dialog AOI.

A heat map was created to visualize the eye-tracking data (see Figure 2). The heat maps were consistent with the eye-tracking data and showed that the majority of participants did read some of the content of the dialog message that indicated their personal information would be shared with the third-party website.

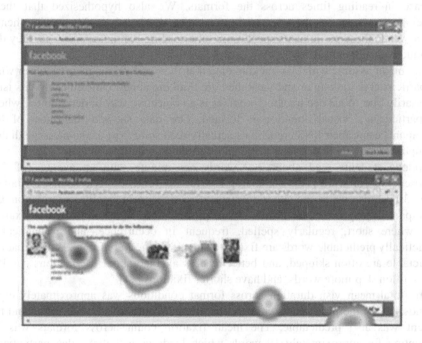

Fig. 2. AOI and heat map example

Survey Responses. Our online SNS use and privacy survey data shows that 57 % of the 117 participants change their SNS privacy settings once a year and approximately 80 % of those individuals set the level at strict or extremely strict where only their friends can see their information.   The majority of participants were very concerned about having their cell phone (91 %), postal address (91 %), email address (78 %), and picture (64 %) shared with a third-party website without their permission. That concern does not appear to transfer to SNS accounts where the respondents are willing to share their name (83 %), gender (80 %), birthday (61 %), picture (72 %), interests (71 %), friends (64 %), current city (65 %), and education (66 %).

5   Discussion

We asked participants to save a news story they selected from a third-party website requiring authentication either by setting up an account or using their SNS credentials. Approximately half of the participants chose to use their SNS credentials to authenticate to the third-party website.

We hypothesized that participants who were presented with the list with data format would spend more time reading the dialog box than the other formats. Unfortunately the standard deviations precluded finding any significant differences for pairwise comparisons. However, we did see a trend showing that there is a significant increase in reading times across the formats. We also hypothesized that these participants upon seeing their personal information displayed would cancel authentication. While these participants spent more time reading the dialog message, they did continue with authentication.

One might assume with eye-tracking data that there is a relationship between what the participant is looking at and what they are thinking about. Unfortunately this isn't necessarily true. What eye tracking provides is an objective way of determining where the participant's visual attention is located. Our data showed that most of the participants using their SNS credentials actually read some part of the message dialog pop-up informing them that their personal information would be shared.

College students read about 300 words per minute with an average of 200 microseconds per word [19]. The dialog box for the sentence-style format contained about 30 words, while the other formats were dependent on the information the participant displayed in their profile. Word processing in text is reflected in fixation time where short, regularly spelled, frequent in occurrence, and semantically/ syntactically predictable words are fixated for a shorter period of time. Words that are predictable are often skipped, and better readers average about 84 fixations per 100 words, often skip more words, and have shorter fixations [11].

The total mean visit duration across format conditions was approximately eight seconds, giving the participants enough time to read approximately 10 words and the content was also predictable. The mean fixation count across formats was 23 accounting for approximately 19 words which leads us to believe that participants read the content in the dialog box.

6   Conclusions

Our eye-tracking data shows that participants read content in the SNS authentication dialog message box but also continued with authentication even though they were informed their personal information was about to be shared. Although this does not indicate they processed any of the words or content, it does seem to suggest that they did not habituate to the dialog box or just select the agree button to close the dialog so that they could continue with their main task.

There was a signficant trend in reading times across formats. But the format style did not impact participants' decision to continue with authentication. Participants chose to share their personal information by selecting to 'allow' the SNS to authenticate to the third-party website.

Participants comments were inconsistent with their actions. Participants admit to sharing many types of personal information on their SNS pages but are more concerned with sharing personal information with others (e.g., ad companies or marketers). They were adamantly opposed to sharing their personal information with a third-party website without their consent. Even though participants gave consent, they didn't seem to realize that their SNS privacy settings did not apply to the sharing of their personal information when they authenticated using their SNS credentials.

Some researchers think that the SNS authentication message is too generic and does not adequately convey this data sharing. They believe that users do not realize they share so much information with these third-party websites and applications [2]. While others believe that the average user is reacting to these interruption dialog messages with responses that range from mild irritation to annoyance, and users quickly learn to visually and cognitively dismiss them [1]. Still others think that over the years, users are trained to click dialogs away to complete the primary task. Because these interception dialogs interrupt the user's primary task, the users do not bother to read them and as a result, do not heed warnings [4].

Our participants may not have fully understood the risks associated with innocent-appearing disclosure of information like their hometown or current city. As we are quite aware, users' attention is scarce, and identity management is seldom a user's primary goal. The participants in our study may have quickly scanned the message and did not fully understood what they were consenting to. Or quite simply, our participants may have continued authentication even though they were informed that their personal information was being shared because they believed the third-party website to be a reputable site that would protect their information.

Having a single sign-on method such as SNS identity eases the burden for users trying to authenticate to a new online service. Often users are willing to trade-off some possible or unknown risks for the convenience of not having to set up another account, and create and remember another username and password [6]. The Federal Trade Commission and others have policy goals of adequately informing users of when their personal information might be shared. Future research should explore other types of alerts and explore whether users understand the potential implications and consequences of their choices.

References

1. Bahr, G.S., Ford, R.A.: How and why pop-ups don't work: Pop-up prompted eye movements, user affect and decision making. Computers in Behavior 27(2), 776–783 (2010)
2. Besmer, A., Lipford, H.R.: Users' (mis)conceptions of social applications. In: Mould, D., Noël, S. (eds.) Graphics Interface, pp. 63–70. ACM, New York (2010), http://hci.uncc.edu/pubs/Misconceptions.pdf (retrieved)

3. Bitgood, S.: The role of attention in designing effective interpretive labels. Journal of Interpretation Research 5(2), 31–45 (2000), http://www.jsu.edu/psychology/docs/5.1-role_of_attention.pdf (retrieved)

4. Bohme, R., Kopsell, S.: Trained to accept?: a field experiment on consent dialogs. In: Proceedings of the 28th International Conference on Human Factors in Computing Systems, pp. 2403–2406. ACM (2010)

5. Egelman, S.: My profile is my password, verify me! The privacy/convenience tradeoff of facebook connect. In: Proceedings of the SIGCHI Conference on Human Factors in Computing Systems, pp. 2369–2378. ACM (2013)

6. Good, N.S., Grossklags, J., Mulligan, D.K., Konstan, J.A.: Noticing notice: a large-scale experiment on the timing of software license agreements. In: Proceedings of the SIGCHI Conference on Human Factors in Computing Systems, pp. 607–616. ACM (April 2007)

7. Gross, R., Acquisiti, A.: Information revelation of the privacy in online social networks. In: Proceedings of the 2005 ACM Workshop on Privacy in Electronic Society, pp. 71–80. ACM, New York (2005), doi:10.1145/1102199.1102214

8. Ko, M.N., Cheek, G.P., Shehab, M.: Social-networks connect services. Computer 43(8), 37–43 (2010), doi:10.1109/MC.2010.239; MacMillan, D.: FB connect: Your 8,000 hidden friends. Bloomburg BusinessWeek: Technology (April 2, 2009) http://www.businessweek.com/technology/content/apr2009/tc2009041_649562.htm (retrieved)

9. Maler, E., Reed, D.: The venn of identity, options and issues in federated identity management. IEEE Security & Privacy 6(2), 16–23 (2008), doi:10.1109/MSP.2008.50

10. Morrow, D., Leirer, V., Altieri, P.: List formats improve medication instructions for older adults. Educational Gerontology: An International Quarterly 21(2), 151–166 (1995), doi:10.1080/0360127950210204

11. Rayner, K., Juhasz, B.J., Pollatsek, A.: Eye Movements During Reading. In: Snowling, M.J., Hulme, C. (eds.) The Science of Reading: A Handbook, pp. 79–97. Blackwell Publishing Ltd., Oxford (2008), doi:10.1002/978047-757642.ch5

12. Roberts, K.K.: Privacy & perceptions: How facebook advertising affects its users. The Elon Journal of Undergraduate Research in Communications 1(1), 24–34 (2010), http://www.elon.edu/docs/e-web/academics/communications/research/03RobertsEJSpring10.pdf

13. Steel, E., Fowler, G.A.: Facebook in privacy breach: Top-ranked applications transmit personal IDs, a journal investigation finds. The Wall Street Journal (October 17, 2010), http://online.wsj.com/article/SB10001424052702304772804575555 8484075236968.html (retrieved)

14. Sun, S.T., Boshmaf, Y., Hawkey, K., Beznosov, K.: A billion keys, but few locks: The crisis of web single sign-on. In: Proceedings of the 2010 Workshop on New Security Paradigms, pp. 61–72. ACM, New York (2010), doi:10.1145/1900546.1900556

15. Tow, W., Newk-Fon, H., Dell, P., Venable, J.: Understanding information disclosure behavior in Australian Facebook users. Journal of Information Technology 25(2), 126–136 (2010), doi:10.1057/jit.2010.18

16. Tuunainen, V.K., Pitkanen, O., Hovi, M.: Users' awareness of privacy on online social networking sites – case Facebook. In: BLED 2009 Proceedings (Paper 42) (2009), http://aisel.aisnet.org/bled2009/42 (retrieved)

17. Wang, N., Xu, H., Grossklags, J.: Third party apps on facebook: Privacy and the illusion of control. In: Proceedings of the 5th ACM Symposium on Computer Human Interaction for Management of Information Technology (Article No. 4), ACM, New York (2011), doi:10.1145/2076444.2076448
18. West, R.: The psychology of security. Communications of the ACM 51(4), 34–40 (2008), doi:10.1145/1330311.1330320
19. Wolgater, M.S., Shaver, E.F.: Evaluation of list vs. paragraph text format on search time for warnings symptoms in a product manual. Advances in Occupational Ergonomics and Safety 4, 434–438 (2001)

An Ergonomic Evaluation of the Adaptation of Polish Online Stores to the Needs of the Elderly

Krzysztof Hankiewicz[1], Marcin Butlewski[2], and Wiesław Grzybowski[2]

[1] Poznan University of Technology, Chair of Management and Computing Systems, Poland
krzysztof.hankiewicz@put.poznan.pl
[2] Poznan University of Technology, Chair of Ergonomics and Quality Management, Poland
{marcin.butlewski,wieslaw.grzybowski}@put.poznan.pl

Abstract. Recently websites have been a key intermediary in the exchange of information. The share of trade conducted based on online services transactions is also dynamically growing. Among people using online services and communicating this way, are now also the elderly. These are often people whose first contact with these technologies occurred during adulthood. Many of elderly people did not use a computer in their work, and their first contact with the Internet has been during their retirement. In conclusion, the currently operating focus in Poland on young online shoppers is faulty. With the increasing proportion of elderly people in Polish society and the dissemination of computer technology among them, the need for senior-friendly online stores will grow. The choice of this form of purchase will be decided by convenience, price, range of goods and delivery terms. However, the ultimate determinants of whether elderly users will enjoy the benefits of online shopping are the ergonomic features of services, particularly criteria such as: security, ease of use, rule transparency and ascetic aesthetics.

Keywords: elderly design, ergonomic evolution, usability, online shops for seniors.

1 Introduction

Internet technologies, though initially inaccessible, have become almost universally good. They ceased to be a domain of the young and modern users and have become an obligatory tool. This change led to broad consequences. Internet resources must give the opportunity to be used by groups with different levels of experience and perception, including the elderly. The similar situation is characteristic to online shops, whose more and more customers are so called the early. In Poland today, according to date from the National Census in 2011, nearly 35% of the population has exceeded the age of 50 years (34.89%) [18]. It is expected that due to the aging process, this percentage of the population will increase, so that even greater number of potential customers will be elderly. The increase in older online shoppers will involve decreasing motor

C. Stephanidis and M. Antona (Eds.): UAHCI/HCII 2014, Part IV, LNCS 8516, pp. 26–36, 2014.

abilities of these people. The above-mentioned factors cause a greater demand for solutions with the appropriate level of ergonomic quality [4], and the solutions of this type will be required in every manifestation of human activity [12].

However, the problems of the elderly connected with the use of online shops constitute a complex methodical problem. This is due the fact that they constitute a combination of weakening physiological function - such as the weakening ability to see close objects - which starts after the completion of 40-45 years of age [16, p 121] and psychological determinants - aversion to the unknown solutions. For that reason, it is impossible to be certain whether older people do not use modern technologies just because they are too modern for their cognitive system, or simply they do not have the need, habit, or what is most essential, have not been "infected" by the computer skills because they were born much longer time ago. The identified problems of the elderly connected with the use of modern technology have been combined with the usability, in order to diagnose the interfering and assisting factors for the elderly people in the use of online shops. The aim of the article is to present the study on the characteristics of online shops as well as their adaptation to the needs of the elderly in Poland.

2   Literature Review

Among the many publications on internet websites for elderly people, there are only a few that describe problems of the elderly with the use of online stores [10]. In addition to the small spread of this form of shopping among the elderly, the reason for this could be methodological problems - behavioral differences in terms of the behavior of older and younger customers are of a cohortative nature [17].

Among the identified problems connected with web technologies of older, the most common ones are problems with finding broken links, viewing graphics, searching for new information and re-visiting previously used pages. [14, p 375]. However, a significant factor which increases the difficulty of their operations and extends the time for their implementation is the disorganized site, with a large number of links, different colors and placement of navigation elements in unexpected places (especially at the bottom of the page) [14, p 396].

The rules concerning ergonomic websites design for elderly people are included in many guides [3]: SPRY, 1999 - Older Adults and the World Wide Web: a Guide for Web Site Creators [9], AgeLight, 2001 - Interface design guidelines for users of all ages [2], NIA / NLM, 2002 - Making your Web site senior friendly - A checklist [15], Coyne & Nielsen, 2002 - Web usability for senior citizens [5], de Sales & de Abrew Cybis, 2003 - Development of a checklist for the evaluation of the web accessibility for the aged users [6], AARP, 2004 - Designing Web Sites for older adults: heuristics [1], Fidgeon, 2006 - Usability for older web users [7]. They were used to build a model of the criteria described in the next part of the publication.

3   Research Method

This method is based on a multi-level set of criteria. It was assumed that performance quality of an evaluated site has a three-level hierarchical structure (Figure 1) comprising a primary criterion, the group criteria and elementary criteria (detailed). Overriding the primary criterion results from meeting the criteria formed by the group of appropriate elementary criteria. This ensures the logical clarity and relational correctness of the model on the levels of the adopted structure. This method has already been applied in other studies of Web pages [8].

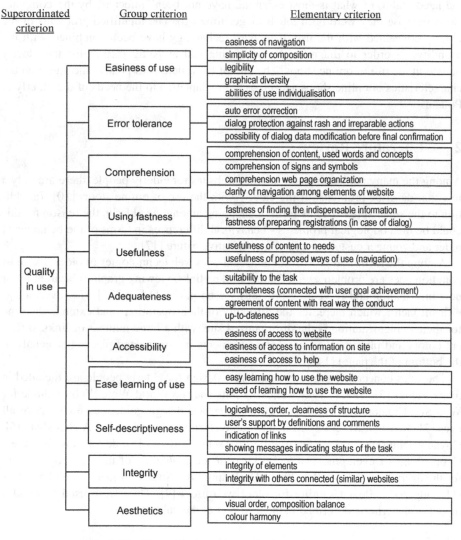

Fig. 1. The hierarchical quality model for use of WWW [8]

The process of the research was directed to identify the features which, according to the users, pose problems when using the web pages by the elderly.

The analysis of preferences, priorities and level of satisfaction with the usefulness of particular criteria was performed using a self-completion questionnaire.

The process of subjective quality assessment consisted of three steps:

1. establishing a set of criteria: Group evaluation criteria resulting from the general adaptation of the utility structure shown in ISO 9241-10 [11],
2. preparation of assessment: transforming a set of criteria into a list of questions about the degree of users satisfaction with the fulfillment of the criterion;
3. making an assessment using a hierarchical model:
   (a) determining preferences of the users, which consists of indicating the significance of a group functional characteristics using an ordinal scale,
   (b) an assessment of the widely understood usefulness by means of a verbal scale.

This course of study was due to the adopted hypothesis that the fulfillment or non-fulfillment of the needs and expectations of the users decide on the satisfaction of the operated website.

The structure of the questionnaire was divided in two parts. The aim of the first part of the questionnaire was to identify the priorities of users in relation to the validity of group characteristics forming a hierarchical model of functional quality. The aim of the second part was to assess the level of users satisfaction with meeting particular elementary criteria.

Satisfaction (dissatisfaction) was evaluated on the basis of responses to closed questions about satisfaction with the degree of meeting the criterion. Verbal scale was used to make an assessment: yes / rather yes / rather no / no. In case of difficulty to indicate the evaluation, a respondent had a choice of 'do not know'.

4   Object of Research – The Evaluated Aspects and Their Users

It was noted that the needs of elderly people concern mainly products of everyday use. That is why, stores got limited to offer only such products. The choice was related to the fact that these types of stores operate locally, ie even nationwide stores have their logistics centers in larger cities. Only in this way can they ensure the delivery at the acceptable time to the customer, freshness of foods with a short shelf life and transport parameters associated with the delivery of frozen products. It turned out that some elderly people, until they are able to go shopping on their own or someone close to them can do it, avoid using e-shops. These concerns arise from the lack of trust to such shops and the lack of ability to look closely at the goods. For this reason, after a preliminary analysis of the available suppliers in a given area, a renowned service was chosen.

Purchasing service was given an assessment. Its main functions were:

- to present the product range,
- the purchase of selected goods while ensuring their delivery to the indicated address in the selected period,
- the purchase of goods based on registered lists of shopping - repeatability of a fixed set of products without the necessity to select them again,
- choice of payment method and its service in the case of payment by bank transfer or credit card prepayment,
- reviewing past purchases and creating shopping lists based on them.

Users of the site can be either regular customers or occasional ones. Forcing them to register by entering e-mail address and password assigned is likely to encourage them to use the service more often, as it significantly reduces the amount of data that is necessary to enter. Creating an account allows to view previously made purchases and even to repurchase the same products.

The research users were elderly people aged over 70 and comparatively younger people aged 20-25. The users were asked to trace the shop's offer and the possibility of purchasing the selected goods.

It was assumed that the study would be preliminary. The research sample was limited to 10 persons, in accordance with the assumptions developed by Steve Krug [13, p 138].

5   Results

Table 1 presents the results of validity assessment of the group criteria in hierarchical model, specified by the studied group of elderly people, and a Table 2 indicates a reference group made up of younger people.

Table 1. Assessment results of the validity of group criteria by older persons

Characteristics of functional quality	Evaluation [%]				
	Very important	Important	Of little importance	Not important	Do not know
Easiness of use	40%	40%	0%	0%	20%
Comprehension	25%	75%	0%	0%	0%
Using fastness	33%	67%	0%	0%	0%
Usefulness	33%	34%	33%	0%	0%
Adequateness	33%	67%	0%	0%	0%
Ease learning of use	0%	67%	0%	0%	33%
Accessibility	50%	50%	0%	0%	0%
Self-descriptiveness	17%	25%	25%	8%	25%
Integrity	0%	100%	0%	0%	0%
Aesthetics	0%	67%	17%	0%	16%

Table 2. Assessment results of the validity of group criteria by younger people

Characteristics of functional quality	Evaluation [%]				
	Very important	Important	Of little importance	Not important	Do not know
Easiness of use	**43%**	26%	23%	8%	0%
Comprehension	42%	**54%**	4%	0%	0%
Using fastness	**57%**	29%	0%	14%	0%
Usefulness	43%	**57%**	0%	0%	0%
Adequateness	**71%**	29%	0%	0%	0%
Ease learning of use	14%	**71%**	15%	0%	0%
Accessibility	36%	**50%**	7%	7%	0%
Self-descriptiveness	18%	**36%**	25%	21%	0%
Integrity	0%	**86%**	14%	0%	0%
Aesthetics	14%	36%	**50%**	0%	0%

The satisfaction of service users with regard to group criteria was specified on the basis of particular assessments of elementary criteria. The results obtained for the elderly and a comparative group of younger individuals respectively was shown in Table 3 and 4.

Table 3. Assessment results relating to satisfaction of service use by older persons

Characteristics of functional quality	Evaluation [%]				
	Yes	Rather yes	Rather no	No	Hard to say
Easiness of use	**33%**	27%	20%	7%	13%
Comprehension	**75%**	25%	0%	0%	0%
Using fastness	33%	**67%**	0%	0%	0%
Usefulness	33%	**67%**	0%	0%	0%
Adequateness	**67%**	33%	0%	0%	0%
Ease learning of use	**67%**	0%	0%	0%	33%
Accessibility	**33%**	**33%**	17%	17%	0%
Self-descriptiveness	0%	25%	8%	0%	**67%**
Integrity	**67%**	33%	0%	0%	0%
Aesthetics	17%	**67%**	0%	0%	17%

The comparison of distribution of positive verbal evaluations ("Yes" and "Rather yes" collectively) is shown in Fig. 2. In order to show precisely the details of the assessment, Fig. 3 contains only "Yes" answers and a Fig. 4 contains "Rather yes" answers.

Table 4. Assessment results relating to satisfaction of service use by younger people

Characteristics of functional quality	Evaluation [%]				
	Yes	Rather yes	Rather no	No	Hard to say
Easiness of use	**46%**	31%	9%	14%	0%
Comprehension	**57%**	32%	11%	0%	0%
Using fastness	**57%**	29%	0%	14%	0%
Usefulness	43%	**57%**	0%	0%	0%
Adequateness	**71%**	14%	14%	0%	0%
Ease learning of use	**57%**	29%	14%	0%	0%
Accessibility	36%	**57%**	7%	0%	0%
Self-descriptiveness	36%	**39%**	11%	11%	4%
Integrity	29%	**71%**	0%	0%	0%
Aesthetics	**64%**	36%	0%	0%	0%

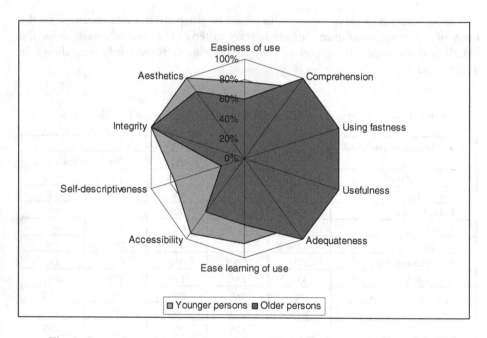

Fig. 2. Comparison of the verbal assessments "Yes" and "Rather yes" collectively

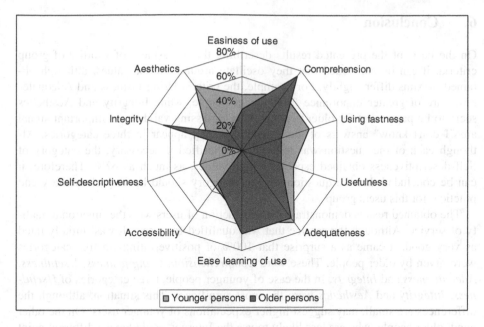

Fig. 3. Comparison of the verbal assessments "Yes"

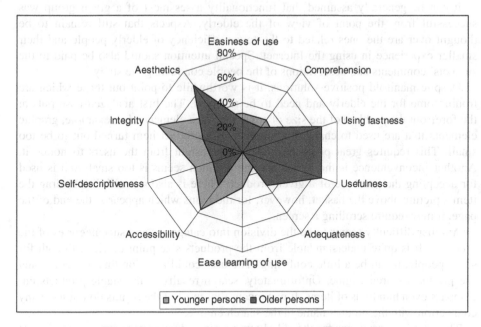

Fig. 4. Comparison of the verbal assessments "Rather yes"

6   Conclusion

On the basis of the presented results describing the assessment of validity of group criteria, it can be concluded that they oscillate around similar values, although obtained maxims differ slightly. For example, the criteria Using fastness and Adequateness are of greater importance for younger people, while Integrity and Aesthetics seem to be paramount for older people. When assessing validity, an important signal are "I don't know" answers of the elderly and they appear in three categories. Although each of the question was individually clarified if necessary, the category of Self-descriptiveness obtained especially high values, as much as 67%. Therefore, it can be concluded that the questions in this category should be very elementary and practical for this users group.

The obtained results demonstrate the satisfaction of users with the functional quality of service. Although the service that was qualified for research was initially rated as very good, it came as a surprise that 100% of positive ratings in five categories were given by older people. These were *Comprehension*, *Using fastness*, *Usefulness*, *Adequateness* and *Integrity*. In the case of younger people, three categories of *Usefulness*, *Integrity* and *Aesthetics* were the most significant. This situation, although the differences are small, may suggest higher expectations of younger users. On the other hand, older people, who are less likely to use the Internet, could have a different point of reference when it comes to previously visited pages, and online shops in particular.

It can be generally assumed that functionality assessment of a given group was successful from the point of view of the elderly. Aspects that still remain to be thought over are the ones related to the lower efficiency of elderly people and their smaller experience in using the Internet. Special attention should also be paid to the subjects' comments and observations of the people conducting the study.

Despite manifold positive solutions, it is worthwhile to point out those which are troublesome for the elderly and need to be resolved. The first analyzed case puts at the forefront the problem of the size of some interface elements. For example, graphic elements that are used to change the number of a product item turned out to be too small. This requires great precision and good eyesight from the users to notice it. Another inconvenience is the basket's symbol which seems is too small and is used for accepting the purchase of a given product. There is also a possibility to drag the item's picture above the basket, however, for the items which appear at the end of the page, it may require scrolling a screen.

Another difficulty seems to be the division into categories and subcategories of the products. It is quite understandable from the products size point of view, though for some people, it can be a little confusing. The user could abandon this procedure and use products search engine. Unfortunately, search results of the staple products encompass even hundreds of items. It may occur that most of the results do not have any connection with the product name in the search engine.

The next inconvenience for the elderly was an introduction of indispensable data of the orderer. While entering the name and address was understandable, inasmuch giving an e-mail address and a password not. It was impossible to skip it and it was not adequately explained. It can be assumed that those who do not use an e-mail will need to quit shopping.

In contrast, payment options in the analyzed case seem to be quite exemplary. For example, card payment terminals carried by a courier delivering purchases give an opportunity of not preparing cash and enables elderly people to make bank transfers.

Finally, it should be noted that the technology of online stores, apart from the natural psychological resistance of older users, did not constitute a significant barrier and after appropriate adjustments the elderly can successfully take advantage of the benefits of trading via the Internet. However, using Internet technologies needs to be performed with caution so that it will not be a way for the alienation of the elderly from the rest of society.

References

1. AARP: Designing Web Sites for Older Adults: Heuristics (2005), http://www.aarp.org/olderwiserwired/oww-resources/designing_web_sites_for_older_adults_heuristics.html
2. Agelight: Interface Design Guidelines for Users of all Ages. Agelight LLC (September 2001), http://www.agelight.com/webdocs/designguide.pdf
3. Arch, A., Abou-Zhara, S.: How Web Accessibility Guidelines Apply to Design for the Ageing Population (2008), http://www.w3.org/WAI/WAI-AGE/Papers/York_ADDW_waiage_paper.doc
4. Butlewski, M.: Extension of working time in Poland as a challenge for ergonomic design. Machines, Technologies, Materials, International Virtual Journal, Publisher Scientific Technical Union of Mechanical Engineering (VII issue November 2013) ISSN 1313-0226
5. Coyne, K.P., Nielsen, J.: Web Usability for Senior Citizens - design guidelines based on usability studies with people age 65 and older, p. 126. Nielsen Norman Group (April 2002)
6. de Sales, M.B., de Abrew Cybis, W.: Desenvolviment de um checklist para a avaliaçã de acessibilidade da web para usuários idosos (Development of a checklist for the evaluation of the web accessibility for the aged users). In: Proceedings of the Latin American Conference on Human-Computer Interaction, Brazil. ACM International Conference Proceeding Series, vol. 46, pp. 125–133 (2003)
7. Fidgeon, T.: Usability for Older Web Users. WebCredible (February 2006), http://www.webcredible.co.uk/user-friendly-resources/web-usability/older-users.shtml
8. Hankiewicz, K., Prussak, W.: Quality in use evaluation of business websites. In: Pacholski, L.M., Trzcieliński, S. (eds.) Ergonomics in Contemporary Enterprise, pp. 84–91. IEA Press, Madison (2007)
9. Holt, B.J.: Komlos-Weimer. M.: Older Adults and the World Wide Web: a Guide for Web Site Creators. SPRY Foundation, p. 36 (1999)

10. Kuo, H.-M., Fu, H.-H., Hsu, C.-H.: Exploring the difficulties of Internet shopping behavior between the elderly and young consumers. Journal of Information and Optimization Sciences 30(3), 447–462 (2009)
11. ISO 9241-10: Ergonomic requirements for office work with visual display terminals (VDTs). Part 10. Dialogue principles (1996)
12. Jasiulewicz-Kaczmarek, M.: The role of ergonomics in implementation of the social aspect of sustainability, illustrated with the example of maintenance. In: Arezes, P., Baptista, J.S., Barroso, M., Carneiro, P., Lamb, P., Costa, N., Melo, R., Miguel, A.S., Perestrelo, G. (eds.) Occupational Safety and Hygiene, pp. 47–52. CRC Press, Taylor & Francis, London (2013)
13. Krug, S.: Don't Make Me Think: A Common Sense Approach to Web Usability. New Riders, Berkeley (2006)
14. Morrell, R.W., Mayhorn, C.B., Bennett, J.: A survey of World Wide Web use in middle-aged and older adults. Human Factors 42(2) (Summer 2000)
15. National Institute on Aging and National Library of Medicine: Making Your Web Site Senior Friendly: A Checklist, NIH & NLM (September 2002), http://www.nlm.nih.gov/pubs/checklist.pdf
16. Starzycka, M., Starzycka-Bigaj, E.: Zmiany w narządzie wzroku związane z wiekiem. In: Marchewka, A., Dąbrowski, Z., Żołądź, J.A. (eds.) Fizjologia Starzenia się: Profilaktyka i Rehabilitacja. Wydawnictwo PWN, Warszawa (2013)
17. Teller, C., Gittenberger, E., Schnedlitz, P.: Cognitive age and grocery-store patronage by elderly shoppers. Journal of Marketing Management 29, 3–4 (2013)
18. The results of the National Census of Population (2011), http://www.stat.gov.pl/bdl/app/strona.html?p_name=indeks

A Showcase for Accessible Online Banking

Sebastian Kelle, Christophe Strobbe, and Gottfried Zimmermann

Responsive User Interface Experience Research Group
Hochschule der Medien, Nobelstr. 10, 70569 Stuttgart, Germany
{kelle,strobbe,zimmermann}@hdm-stuttgart.de

Abstract. Online banking systems pose especially high requirements to web architectures with particular respect to the end-user interface. Although the number of online banking users is steadily increasing, they commonly face "one-size-fits-all" user interfaces rather than personalized user interfaces that are tailored to their individual needs and preferences. In this paper we present a prototypical online banking demonstrator that is based on the Global Public Inclusive Infrastructure (GPII), a new technical framework for the development, identification and delivery of accessibility services, assistive technologies and automatic personalization capabilities; and on the Universal Remote Console (URC) technology, a framework for pluggable user interfaces.

Keywords: Accessibility, Web accessibility, online banking, GPII, URC, URC Light.

1 Introduction

The usage of Internet banking (also known as online banking) has steadily been rising. According to data collected by Eurostat [1], by the end of 2013 42% of EU-27 citizens (rising from 25% in 2007) and 43% of Euro area citizens (rising from 20% in 2005) were using online banking. However, the percentages of current usage vary strongly between the individual member states: from 82% in Denmark and the Netherlands to 4-5% in Romania and Bulgaria.

One of the primary advantages of online banking is the reduction of effort in accessing banking services without having to worry about opening hours, queues or the actual trip to the physical bank of choice. In a survey in the USA in 2004, the two main reasons for using online banking given by respondents were convenience and saving time [2]. This makes banking more accessible to people with reduced mobility, taking into account that not just people with disabilities or the elderly may benefit, but also those bearing the responsibility of childcare or other constraining circumstances. It is therefore desirable to bring forth a way to enable inclusive design of online banking web services with considerably lower effort in comparison to the current state. According to Vanderheiden and Treviranus [3], the implementation effort of assistive technology is quite high due to the degree of specialization involved and the small market. Additionally, as described by Vigo and Brajnik [4], the cost of accessible design rises further because of the necessity of validation by experts.

C. Stephanidis and M. Antona (Eds.): UAHCI/HCII 2014, Part IV, LNCS 8516, pp. 37–45, 2014.
© Springer International Publishing Switzerland 2014

2   Background

In 2004, Michelle Bayes published the results of a survey about the use of online banking services [2]. She found that the most frequent banking activities were — in decreasing order of frequency — checking account balances (weekly), viewing or paying bills (monthly), downloading statements (less than once a month), transferring funds between accounts at the same bank, checking credit card balances, and paying credit card bills. A Spanish study in 2009 found that customers used the following functions in order of frequency: checking account balances, money transfers, paying bills, recharging phone cards, services related to investments, services related to loans, and services related to insurances [5]. Bayles also asked respondents to rate the importance of online banking features. Among the features at the top of this list were quick access to information you are looking for, clearly indicating that a function has been completed, clear feedback on the status of past transactions, and clear and simple terminology. Some other usability-related findings are worth highlighting: "account activity and balances should be immediately accessible after login", terminology should be more meaningful (e.g. respondents found "payee" ambiguous), and feedback on the acceptance or rejection of information should be provided [2].

A comparison of several online banking applications (i.e. those by HSBC, Barclays and Halifax in the UK) showed that there a considerable differences with regard to the complexity in the screens and processes for the frequently used banking functions identified by Bayles [2] and Muñoz Leiva [5]. Some applications display account balances on the home screen (the screen immediately visible after logging in), while others require customers to go through a menu or to select something like "My accounts" from a navigation menu on the home screen. Forms for money transfers can have different types of labels: some banks use simple labels such as "Amount", "Name of recipient", and "Date", while others use questions such as "What's the amount?" and "When do you want to send this payment?" For money transfers, there are two basic approaches: either the customer first selects the account from which the transfer will be made, then selects the function called "Pay a bill", "Make a transfer" or something similar; or the customer first selects the function "Pay a bill" or "Make a transfer" and in one of the next screens selects the account from which the transfer will be made. It is this type of differences in the detail that illustrate the heterogeneity of different online banking solutions, posing a challenge to work towards inclusive design.

Concerning the bigger picture, according to Gourdazi et al. [6], online banking bears several properties that are critical for user acceptance: accessibility, privacy, security, quality and usability. Although our focus is accessibility, the other factors are critical, too, and cannot be sacrificed.

3   The Cloud4all Online Banking Demo Application

The online banking demo application is being developed in the context of Cloud4all [7], an EU-funded project run by a consortium of 27 partner organizations drawn from academia, non-profit and private sector. The goal of the project is to advance the Global Public Inclusive Infrastructure (GPII) [8] to a level that enables accessibility across different platforms and devices. To do so, it is of special interest to create or enhance platforms for automatic personalization so they suit the end-users' needs best. This is especially relevant for platforms that are used by large audiences, such as online-banking web sites. GPII's personalization is meant to work on different platforms and devices, including desktop operating systems, mobile devices, ATMs, browser and web applications. A special requirement for the online banking application is that the personalization should work across three layers: the web application itself, the web browser in which it runs, and the underlying operating system.

At the start of the development process, we decided that one of the main components of our online banking demo should be an extension of a standard content management system capable of simulating authenticated banking transactions (in our case Drupal [9]) with a front end based on Fluid Infusion [10,11], a JavaScript library including modular components that enable multi-modal accessibility enhancements of web content.

In our demonstrational prototype, we focus on personalization features for the following four user scenarios:

- Users who need textual representation of content and highly configurable visual enhancements (e.g. visually impaired users).
- Users who need sign language communication, especially for complex content (i.e. deaf users with sign language as their native language).
- Users who need alternative and possibly simplified interaction approaches, for example by using keyboard only, switch or scanner (e.g. users with motor impairments).
- Users who need an overall simplified representation of content, for example by using pictograms instead of text (e.g. users with cognitive disabilities).

Although this list of addressed user needs seems short, it is important to take into account that the complexity of user preferences increases with a growing number of platforms, applications, and assistive technologies. Also, the need for special arrangements can occur in any combination and degree of strength.

Therefore, instead of using static settings, the goal is to always allow the user to change the adaptation parameters via a "personal control panel" that has been built into the application. The personal control panel is based on the Infusion user interface options toolkit [10, 11]. One of the functionalities we plan to add is that a user is presented with suggested adaptations of the site, while still being able to override them, and the system will learn from this. In general, though, we aim for a system that instantiates a close-to-ideal user interface for a specific user so that the user needs to make only little or no customization.

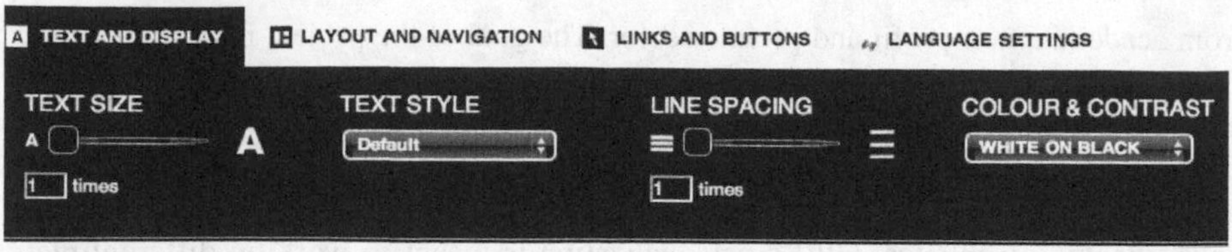

TEXT AND DISPLAY   **LAYOUT AND NAVIGATION**   **LINKS AND BUTTONS**   **LANGUAGE SETTINGS**

TEXT SIZE   TEXT STYLE   LINE SPACING   COLOUR & CONTRAST
A ⚪———   **A**   [Default   ⬍]   ≡ ⚪———   ≡   [WHITE ON BLACK   ⬍]
[1] times   [1] times

Fig. 1. Online banking demo: the floating panel at the top, featuring adaptation control elements for text and display configuration. In this figure the color and contrast scheme has been set to "white on black", affecting also the floating panel.

The functionality for "manual" adjustments is provided in a JavaScript extension called "floating panel", which is visualized as an overlay element that can be folded out as shown in figure 1. It is also illustrated how the floating panel's settings affect the overall presentation of the visual content. For users with low eyesight, the floating panel provides several modes adapting the font size, line spacing, font type as well as amplification of visual contrast.

For users with little or no hearing, the prototype includes a sign language extension (figure 2), which can currently switch between American Sign Language (ASL), German Sign Language (GSG) and International Sign (ILS) (see figure 2). The sign language extension was included because some users can interpret sign languages more easily than textual content. The sign language extension is included by means of videos that can be positioned freely as an overlay box around the application space, featuring either avatar-based sign language representation or videos of human interpreters.

Fig. 2. Online banking demo, featuring the floating panel for sign language settings, in this view showing a video of a human interpreter explaining the user dialog fields

4   Technical Background

Each bank typically runs its own proprietary user interface, despite the general trend of common UI toolkits. This makes accessible design expensive and laborious, with each bank having to implement their separate solution of multimodal presentation channels and respective content media.

To address this problem, we suggest a more standardized approach with an infrastructure for personalized user interfaces on the basis of standardized web technology. The foundations for this approach are the Infusion JavaScript toolkit, the Global Public Inclusive Infrastructure (GPII) and the Universal Remote Console (URC) framework.

4.1   Infusion JavaScript Toolkit

The Infusion JavaScript toolkit [10, 11] is a library that enables the construction of a control panel on web sites, presenting adjustments to the user, and allowing the user to adjust preference settings that enable enhancements for online accessibility. This is achieved using renderer components that add contents to a HTML template at runtime. Several CSS settings can be overridden on web sites, for example font type, font size, and line height. This control panel can be combined with the "URC Light" methodology, as described below. One of the most important aspects to take into account is that the presentational aspects of a web site must not be hard-coded into the layout, but can only contain relative style settings, for example using "em" measurements. The control panel presents one of the key elements of the solution because it is the main starting point to the user. The user needs to be able to intuitively and quickly modify settings and be able to reset them. The complex logic behind this front layer needs to be hidden to the user while still providing the adaptive experience that is needed.

4.2   Global Public Inclusive Infrastructure (GPII)

The Global Public Inclusive Infrastructure (GPII) [8] is a global effort for user interfaces that automatically adapt to the user's needs and preferences.

In this infrastructure (see figure 3), a "matchmaker" will provide suggestions on how to transform a user interface so that it becomes more "personally accessible" for a specific user with their particular needs and preferences. For this purpose, a personal preference set is created and maintained for every user. This preference set is stored on a central cloud-based service called Preference Server, with a "Flow Manager" routing the traffic of preference sets and other payloads between the Preference Server, the matchmaker and the components on the user's client. For example, the font size may be enlarged and/or the contrast theme set to "white on black" for a visually impaired user (see figure 2.). Sign language videos may be added to complex Web forms so that a deaf user can understand what to fill into the fields. A "switch-optimized" Web page may be shown to a user employing a switch and scanning for text input. Or a simplified user interface (with reduced functionality) may be shown to a cognitively impaired user.

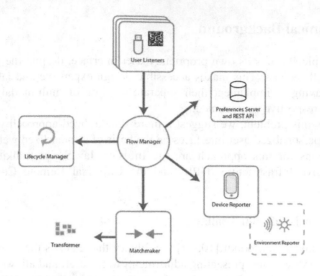

Fig. 3. GPII Architecture, simplified diagram

The GPII architecture also enables adaptation capabilities for accessible interfaces on local system environments. Users will want to use their devices also for services not directly connecting to the internet, which demands for an authentication method used by means of a USB token or QR code. GPII architects have developed a user listener that needs to be installed locally, enabling adaptations that go beyond the web browser. Additionally, a device reporter (a service that detects the type of device while monitoring user behavior) enables accessibility settings that can be re-used across different platforms and mobile devices. Tapping into this additional feature set for the use of the online banking demo will bring the approach further towards a proper "one size fits one" type of holistic personalization.

4.3   Universal Remote Console (URC)

The Universal Remote Console (URC) framework [12] enables pluggable user interfaces for the control of devices and services (target applications). In the URC ecosystem, target applications and their user interfaces are decoupled from each other, and are only linked together at runtime by the user interface socket, a modality-independent user interface model. In this approach, the user interface socket description represents a "contract" between the target developer and the user interface designer. Thus, user interface designers from any party (including third parties such as human factors experts and user groups) can contribute pluggable user interfaces that are specialized for a particular type of user and/or particular personal devices (controllers). At runtime, the controller can pick an appropriate user interface from the set of available pluggable user interfaces, based on some automatic mechanism or on the user's choice (or both).

In the URC ecosystem, a resource server acts as a global marketplace for pluggable user interfaces and their components (collectively called user interface resources). Atomic resources include any media items that could be used as part of a pluggable user interface, such as text labels, icons, fonts, audio clips, videos, captions and audio descriptions. At runtime, when a target application has been discovered, the controller (or a middleware component between the controller and the target) will build a suitable user interface, based on the user interface resources available on the resource server.

While the user interface socket has been designed for the control of devices and simple services in mind, the principle of pluggable user interfaces in combination with reusable user interface resources deployed to a resource server can be applied to more information-heavy applications such as Web applications. By eliminating the user interface socket, a significant overhead for employing the URC technology is eliminated, but the approach still facilitates flexible user interfaces that are built from existing resources on demand at runtime. We call this approach URC Light.

In the URC Light approach, a Web designer should build their Web interface with exchangeability in mind. Every component, down to icons and labels, may get replaced at runtime through alternate resources from the resource server. Therefore, the Web designer should assign unique identifiers to the components of a Web page, so that they can be referenced and replaced or extended at runtime. Basically, every part of the Web page, including the whole Web page itself, can get substituted or extended by supplementary resources when the full context of use is known at runtime.

Currently, we are working on URC Light implementation guidelines which will likely include the following use cases:

Label substitution/augmentation: A label gets replaced or extended by a supplementary label (including multimedia labels such as icons, audio clips, videos).

- *Input component substitution/augmentation:* An input component can get replaced or extended. For example, a drop-down menu is replaced by a set of radio buttons.
- *Output component substitution/augmentation:* An output component gets replaced or extended. For example, an image gets an alternate text added.
- *Subpage component substitution/augmentation:* A part of a page gets replaced or extended. For example, a <div> component may get replaced by a <div> resource with an alternate presentation.
- *Style sheet substitution/augmentation:* The style sheet of a Web page gets replaced or extended.
- *HTML header substitution/augmentation:* The page title gets replaced or extended.
- *HTML document substitution/augmentation:* A whole HTML page gets replaced by an alternate version, or extended by additional information.

In the Cloud4all online banking demo, we currently focus on the application of the label augmentation use case for sign language annotation. In Web forms (e.g. the wire transfer form described in section 2), if the user prefers sign language, we check for every input field whether a supplementary label is available for it in the form of a sign language video. If so, we display a small button with an icon for sign language next to the input field (see figure 2). When the user presses the button, the input field is explained in a sign language video that is played in an overlay window.

5   Discussion and Outlook

Although this technology can potentially be used for any kind of web application or service, online banking has been chosen as a proof-of-concept application and as an acid test for our infrastructure:

On the one hand it has especially high requirements with respect to user acceptance, because of ranging within the focal point between security and accessibility/usability. High security and privacy requirements usually are in opposition with usability and accessibility enhancements. This can be illustrated with the increasing demand for Human-Interaction Proof tools or CAPTCHAs, which are typically inaccessible by design and impossible to solve for visually impaired users [13, 14].

Furthermore, as a tool of daily routine for almost all citizens, it is a matter of public interest that online-banking services should be accessible, due to people with disabilities being often less mobile than others, and therefore likely profiting even more than the average customer.

From an implementation perspective, especially with regard to the level of integrating adaptive accessibility both to the web interface and the operating system environment to the same degree and simultaneously, an important challenge emerges. While the operating system can be modified offline and with local settings, it is an ongoing debate how a web-based (and hence, decentralized by default) adaptation of the web site can possibly be synchronized with local settings. Since the old paradigm of the "personal computer" that relies purely on local memory more and more evaporates, it is from a somewhat opportunistic point of view questionable whether a local instance of an OS-based personalized control panel is still necessary at all. With this perspective, however, we might quickly be excluding parts of society who are not as appreciative towards always-on internet availability as others.

Acknowledgments. This work has been funded by the European Commission, under Grant 289016 (Cloud4all). The opinions herein are those of the authors and not necessarily those of the funding agency.

References

1. Eurostat - E-Banking and E-Commerce,
   http://epp.eurostat.ec.europa.eu/tgm/table.do?tab=table&
   init=1&language=en&pcode=tin00099
2. Bayles, M.: Online Banking: Why People Are Branching Out. Software Usability Research Laboratory (SURL), Wichita State University, Usability News (July 12, 2004),
   http://www.surl.org/online-banking-why-people-are-branching-out/

3. Vanderheiden, G., Treviranus, J.: Creating a Global Public Inclusive Infrastructure. In: Stephanidis, C. (ed.) Universal Access in HCI, Part I, HCII 2011. LNCS, vol. 6765, pp. 517–526. Springer, Heidelberg (2011)
4. Vigo, M., Brajnik, G.: Automatic web accessibility metrics: Where we are and where we can go. Interacting with Computers 23, 137–155 (2011)
5. Muñoz Leiva, F.: Caracterización de los clientes de la Banca Electrónica. Revista de Estudios Empresariales. Segunda Época 1, 4–30 (2009),
   http://revistaselectronicas.ujaen.es/index.php/REE/article/download/356/319
6. Goudarzi, S., Ahmad, M.N., Zakaria, N.H., Soleymani, S.A., Asadi, S., Mohammad-hosseini, N.: Development of an instrument for assessing the Impact of trust on Internet Banking Adoption. Journal of Basic and Applied Scientific Research 3, 1022–1029 (2013)
7. Cloud4all Project Website, http://cloud4all.info/
8. GPII Architecture Overview - wiki.gpii,
   http://wiki.gpii.net/index.php/Architecture_Overview
9. Drupal.org - Open Source CMS, https://drupal.org/
10. Infusion Web Accessibility Framework,
    http://wiki.fluidproject.org/display/fluid/Fluid+Infusion
11. Fluid – Infusion, http://fluidproject.org/products/infusion/
12. myurc.org - home, http://myurc.org/
13. Sauer, G., Holman, J., Lazar, J., Hochheiser, H., Feng, J.: Accessible privacy and security: a universally usable human-interaction proof tool. Universal Access in the Information Society 9, 239–248 (2010)
14. May, M.: Inaccessibility of CAPTCHA: Alternatives to Visual Turing Tests on the Web - W3C Working Group Note (November 23, 2005),
    http://www.w3.org/TR/2005/NOTE-turingtest-20051123/

Using Eye Tracking to Understand the Impact of Cognitive Abilities on Search Tasks

Efi A. Nisiforou, Eleni Michailidou, and Andrew Laghos

Department of Multimedia and Graphic Arts
Cyprus University of Technology, Limassol, Cyprus
{efi.nisiforou,eleni.michailidou,andrew.laghos}@cut.ac.cy

Abstract. Nowadays, there is an increase of studies that examine individuals' cognitive characteristics in correlation to visual perception. The present study investigated the association between cognitive abilities and Web page complexity. Specifically, differences within simple, medium and complex Web pages were observed among the field dependent, independent and mixed cognitive groups via a task completion time with the use of the eye tracking technology. The results showed that task completion time is significantly different in medium and complex pages between the FD and FI users, while, in the simple pages, no statistical differences appeared. Furthermore, it was supported that users' FD-I cognitive construct style can be identified using innovative techniques like eye tracking studies by analyzing users' scan path and heat maps.

Keywords: Field Dependent-Independent, cognitive abilities, visual complexity, ViCRAM algorithm, eye tracking.

1 Introduction

The visual appearance of interactive systems, such as Web pages and e-learning environments, tend to convey more information than one can imagine. Contact points that users make first to perceive such a system affect the rest of the interaction process [1]. Individuals' cognitive characteristics and Web pages visual complexity have been gaining ground in the literature. This study is a pilot investigation towards a project that aims to formulate a framework and suggest guidelines in designing adaptive environments by understanding how users of different cognitive types interact with different tasks [2]. The use of eye tracking technology as a measure of noticing users' cognitive ability during visual processing will be investigated as a methodology in achieving the above objective. Cognitive style data is being incorporated into adaptive systems for the development of personalized user models. The link between eye tracking and cognitive modelling is an extremely intuitive and fruitful area of research. It is important therefore, to understand precisely what the eyes reveal in order to model human behavior by designing suitable and adaptive environments based on the assumption that individuals interact differently. Developing a new objective method of

C. Stephanidis and M. Antona (Eds.): UAHCI/HCII 2014, Part IV, LNCS 8516, pp. 46–57, 2014.

measuring the cognitive behavior of humans, instead of solely relying on questionnaires, is of paramount importance. Finally, by understanding sighted users' visual understanding of Web page complexity in relation with the time of task completion, important information should reveal with refer to the cognitive effort required for interaction with that page.

A previous pilot study examined the potential of eye tracker as a tool in detecting users' cognitive dimensions with respect to the FD-I classification and identified differences between the three cognitive construct styles and tasks time completion [2]. It was mentioned that complexity consists an interesting concept with its applications to be used in for a wide range of uses, from cognitive psychology to computer science [3]. An earlier study conducted by Michailidou [4] found that visually complex pages generate users' disoriented navigation while, visually simple pages produce the opposite perspective with the use of the ViCRAM algorithm. This presented study was designed to investigate whether eye tracking can assess subjects' differences on cognitive dimensions and examine the correlation between these styles and tasks time completion. Specifically, it attempts to identify users' cognitive ability based on their Web behavior and relate individuals' cognitive characteristics such as visual attention patterns in terms of field dependent-independent construct style with Web pages' visual complexity. The use of eye tracking technology as a measure of noticing users' cognitive ability during visual processing gives insight to how this information and cognitive overload affects user ability to interact.

Therefore, the following research question is addressed:

1. How does users' Web behavior in terms of task time completion differ in simple, medium and complex Web pages among FD, FI and FN users?

2   Related Work

Access to and movement around complex hypermedia environments has long been considered an important issue in the Web design and usability field [5]. With the rapid and constant advancement of technology, new ways are continually being introduced to present information that leads to visually complex Web pages. Cognitive overload is a result of the boost of information presented on the Web. The information on most of these Web pages is visually fragmented and organized into groups [6]. In this way, when users reach a Web page, they can scan the page and obtain a comprehension of it in a few seconds. Cognition refers to the ability of the human mind to acquire and manage information [7] and comprises different mental processes such as attention, memory, perception, problem solving and learning [8]. Moreover, it describes the tendencies as the modes in which humans approach, acquire, organize, process, interpret information [9] and how they use these interpretations to guide their actions [10]. Visual perception encompasses complex cognitive processes that are involved in other forms of conceptualization and learning [11].

2.1 Field Dependent-Independent

The field dependent-independent (FDI) construct lies within the most broadly studied of a variety of cognitive style dimensions appearing in the literature and especially in the educational technology field [12]. These dimensions are formed based on the individual's reliance on the context to extract particular meaning and describe users. The key difference between FD and FI learners is visual perceptiveness. FD learners, who are asked to identify a simple geometric figure that is embedded in a complex figure, will take longer time to detect the simple figure than FI learners, or they may not be able to find it at all. On the contrary, FI learners have difficulty in abstracting relevant information from visual instructional materials. In line with the results of previous work [12, 13], it is hypothesized that FI learners will outperform FD learners as well in terms of problem-solving performance.

Much of the research on FD-I dimension has focused on examining the effects of FD-I on learners' computer performance [14]. A study by Ford, Miller, and Moss [15] demonstrated individual cognitive-style differences in Web searching tasks. It is important to note that most studies rely heavily on the prior completion of questionnaires by system users. Since the completion of questionnaires can be time consuming for users, potentially improving the measurement methods of users' cognitive load is meaningful.

2.2 Visual Complexity

Complexity can be defined as "the degree of difficulty in providing a verbal description of an image" [16]. Textures with repetitive and uniform oriented patterns are less complex than disorganized ones. A visual pattern is also described as complex if its parts are difficult to identify and separate from each other [16]. Complexity perception of an image depends on the amount of grouping, the quantity of the parts an observer perceives in the scene, familiarity with the scene and existing knowledge of objects inside the scene. Visual complexity is mainly represented by the perceptual dimensions of quantity of objects, clutter, openness, symmetry, organization, and the variety of colors [16, 17].

Studies try to identify Web page design metrics that predict whether a site is highly rated with regard to complexity [18, 19]. These studies relate Web site design guidelines with complexity explaining that the way a Web site is presented depends on the way the page itself is designed and what elements (metrics) are used; Web page code complexity was not examined. Others [19] propose cognition, content and form as the three primary factors that affect the complexity of a Web site. Tuch et al. [20] mentioned that visual complexity of Websites has several effects on human cognition and emotion.

The above studies [18-20] tried to develop techniques to empirically examine all aspects of Web site design, but without being able to define and investigate visual complexity. ViCRAM [4], which is the algorithm employed in this study, used the afore-mentioned characteristics and findings concentrated on Web page design and the structure that defines visually simple and complex interfaces. The specific algorithm was used since it was based both on users' perception and the underlying structure of the page.

2.3   Eye Tracking

Cognitive and semantic aspects of a stimulus play an important role in visual and scene perception [17]. Eye movements are driven by properties of the visual world and processes in a person's mind [17]. Eye tracking and usability evaluation studies try to investigate and understand user behavior [17, 21] with an increasing interest to Web page behavior. A general conclusion is that user interaction depends on the visual factors (nearby visual features) and scene semantics (general knowledge about the scene layout). The idea that user' features such as cognitive abilities and personality are affecting the effectiveness of information visualization techniques is continuously growing. An eye tracking study conducted by Toker et al. [22] investigated the relationship between such characteristics and fine-grained user attention patterns. Their findings revealed that user's cognitive abilities such as verbal working memory and perceptual speed have a significant impact on gaze behavior in terms of visualization type and task difficulty.

3   Methodology

A comparative evaluation of two methodologies was conducted: users' cognitive abilities identification based on the Field Dependent-Independent classification using Hidden Figures Test (HFT) and Web page visual complexity using an automatic algorithm (ViCRAM). It was hypothesized that field independent learners' will need less time in identifying a task in a Webpage, whereas, field dependent learners' will take more time in completing a task and therefore a more disoriented behavior will be occurred. In addition, participants' visual attention was measured and analyzed based on the scan path and heat maps eye gaze analysis. Then results from both studies were compared to answer this pilot study's hypothesis.

3.1   Participants

The population used in the study was taken from a Public University in Cyprus (age range 18 - 28). The participants were initially categorized into 7 FD, 6 FI and 3 FN/FM learners using the Hidden Figures Test (HFT).

3.2   Procedure

The study was conducted in two parts:

Part A - Hidden Figure Test - Participants level of field independent was measured with the use of the Hidden Figures Test developed by Witkin et al. [23]. Participants' had a 30 minutes time limit to complete the test.

Part B - User Evaluation: Cognitive Abilities - Users' interaction behavior was examined using eye tracking as a tool to assess their cognitive abilities. Participants were placed in front of an eye tracker and asked to complete a task on 9 Web pages that were preselected. Nine fact-finding tasks or known- item search task (tasks in which the information is located in a particular place of a Webpage) were defined in the experiment in searching for a specific information. Participants' had to click on the finding task as to indicate their response. All 9 Web pages were analysed using the ViCRAM algorithm, and visual complexity score was given for each page. Due to the number of pages used, complexity was described in three categories: Simple, Medium and Complex.

3.3   Materials

The researchers' administered the HFT from the Educational Testing Services kit for cognitive factors designed by Witkin et al. [23] to measure participants' cognitive ability and classify them into a field type. It consists of 32 questions divided equally into two parts. The test presents five simple figures and asks learners to find one of the 5 simple figures embedded in a more complex pattern. Those possessing a score 10 or below they were defined as FD, while FI scored 16 or higher and FN scored from 11 to 15.

The stimuli used during the eye tracking study contained 9 Web pages with a range of visual complexity from 0 - 10 (0 visual simple and 10 visual complex) based on the ViCRAM tool. For the data analysis, Complexity categorization was used which was retrieved based on the algorithm rankings (see Table 1). The content of the Web pages retrieved from five different categories: Shopping, Government, Leisure-Social, Education and News.

Table 1. Web Pages Used: Category and Complexity Level

Page ID	Category	Complexity Level
P1	Government	Simple
P2	Leisure/Social	Simple
P3	Education	Simple
P4	Leisure/Social	Medium
P5	Education	Medium
P6	Education	Medium
P7	News	Complex
P8	News	Complex
P9	Government	Complex

4   Results and Discussion

Eye movements were recorded during task processing with the aid of the eye tracker iViewX model software. The Web stimulus recording mode of the BeGaze 3.1 analysis software was used to capture not only the eye movements, but also mouse clicks as a way of detecting users' task time completion. Participants' visual attention was measured and analyzed based on the scan path and heat maps eye gaze analysis. Finally, users' cognitive dimensions as retrieved from the HFT and task completion time and were statistically analyzed with the use of the SPSS. The findings of the study are discussed with respect to how FD, FM, and FI learners behave within simple, medium and complex pages.

4.1   Hidden Figure Test

As previously mentioned, the Hidden Figure Test (HFT) was used to determine users' main current cognitive occupation (e.g. field dependent, field independent and field neutral/mixed) in terms of their level of field independence. Their score on the test was calculated as the difference between the number of questions answered correctly minus the number answered incorrectly. Taking into how other researchers' determined the cut-off scores of the test [24, 25], participants were classified as 7 Field Dependence, 6 Field Independence, and 3 as Field Mixed learners. The testing activity involved in the HFT has been described as perceptual disembedding and is a reliable and widely used approach for determining FD-I [26]. Kuder-Richardson reliability coefficient of the Hidden Figure Test reflects the degree of .76 [27].

4.2   Task Completion Time

Participants' had to click on the finding task by indicating their response and thus identifying the amount of completion time of each participant per task. This variable was taken into account since researchers were aiming to examine how subjects' cognitive trait with respect to time task completion affects visual complexity. Since the number of participants was small and this being a pilot study, a comparison between the average completion time for each complexity categorization and cognitive ability was calculated. Therefore, for the statistical test, for each complexity level (simple, medium, complex) the average completion time was calculated, ending up with three completion times. Then Levene's test equality of variances was performed to examine the relation between cognitive abilities and time completion.

The results of this test (see Table 1) indicated that completion time is significantly different in complex pages between the FD and FI users, [t(12)= 2.34, p =.04], as the first group produced significantly higher time completion means (M= 157.33, SD = 72.60) than the FI group (M = 84.70, SD = 38.53). The same pattern was observed in the medium pages, showing a significant difference in terms of time task completion between the two groups, [t(6.82)=3.82, p=.007] with the FD group

(M=101.84, SD=34.46) outperforming the users' of the FI group (M = 50.45, SD = 9.01). Additionally, in the simple pages no statistical differences appeared. A possible assumption might rely on the fact that people behave the same or perhaps any differences in the behavior are less likely to have an effect on a simple complexity page, since, the layout of the pages does not impede users' navigation and Web search. Comparisons between the FN group and the other two groups were not statistically significant at $p < 0.05$.

Table 2. Independent sample T-test with regard to users' cognitive ability scores and webpages' visual complexity

Levene's Test Equality of Variances		F	Sig.	t-test for Equality of Means		
				t	df	Sig. (2-tailed)
a) Complex	Equal variances assumed	3.821	0.074	2.338	12	0.038*
	Equal variances not assumed			2.338	9.132	0.044
b) Medium	Equal variances assumed	7.028	0.021	3.817	12	0.002
	Equal variances not assumed			3.817	6.816	0.007*
c) Simple	Equal variances assumed	3.601	0.082	1.407	12	0.185
	Equal variances not assumed			1.407	7.461	0.200

*The mean difference is significant at the 0.05 level.

In line with these results, a study by Nisiforou and Laghos [2] found a large variation in task completion time among the FD-I cognitive groups. Similar findings were observed in the work conducted by Burnett et al [28], as the FI learners' outperformed FD learners in terms of time taken to respond correctly to a problem-solving task. Other studies stated that FI individuals face less difficulty in separating the most essential information from its context than FD subjects do [29].

4.3   Cognitive Abilities and Visual Complexity

Users' cognitive behavior based on their field dependent-independent dimension was analyzed through gaze plots (scan path) and attention maps (focus map, heat map).

The results revealed that although participants were engaged in the same online environments of viewing activity, they tend to demonstrate different attention patterns. The stimulated data indicated that users' cognitive abilities with respect to visual attention show a significant impact on gaze behaviour. The emerged results were discussed in view of common and different Web navigation behaviour with regard to the three cognitive ability categories. According to Figure 1 users' common behavior within a simple page is revealed without taking into account their level of field independent. This observation supports the previous results, since no statistical differences exist in the simple pages among the three cognitive groups.

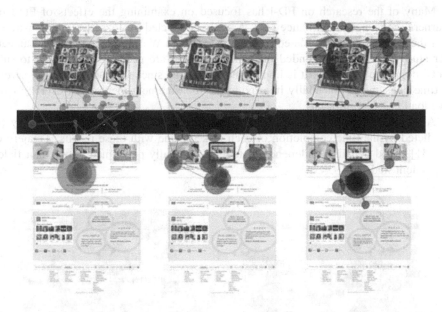

Fig. 1. Gaze Plot/Scanpaths demonstrating the common behaviour on simple pages FI, FD and FN (from left to right)

On the contrary, Figures 2 and 3 demonstrated evidence on how users' cognitive characteristics affect their Web navigation according to medium and complex pages respectively. Besides, FD users' scan paths appeared to be more disoriented and scattered on visual complex pages in contrast to FI subjects' that displayed a more oriented and organized scan paths. Similar results were reported in a study conducted by Harper et al. [6]. In line with this, Michailidou [4] found that visually complex pages generate users' disoriented navigation while, visually simple pages produce the opposite perspective.

Since the perception of complexity is correlated with the variety in the visual stimulus a visual pattern may also look complex if its parts are difficult to identify and separate from each other [3]. Data analysis revealed that users' cognitive ability has a significant impact on user gaze behavior and that this influence is detectable through a variety of eye tracking metrics.

The results also highlight the importance of designing environments that reflect individuals' cognitive characteristics. The environments could be e-learning or any Web pages and interfaces in general for which a user can adapt based on their characteristics. These outcomes are in line with Toker et al. [22] that investigated the relationship of users' such characteristics along with their attention patterns. Individuals that are located towards the FD dimension have difficulty in separating incoming information from its contextual surroundings, and are more likely to be influenced by external cues and to be non-selective in their information uptake. FI individuals on the other hand, are more likely to be influenced by internal than external cues and therefore, be selective in their information input [28, 29].

Many of the research on FD-I has focused on examining the effects of FD-I on learners' computer performance [14]. A study conducted by Jozsa [30] demonstrated that the cognitive style is related to differences in the Web searching tasks. In an earlier study, it was recommended that further studies are needed with respect to subjects' cognitive style [24]. It is important to note that since the completion of surveys is time consuming; potentially improving the measurement methods of users' cognitive load is also significant.

Additionally, the results suggest that the cognitive ability classification may be predicted by the time completion of each task. In line with these results, Tinajero et al. [31] found that field independent students generally performed better than field-dependent students.

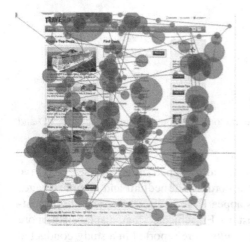 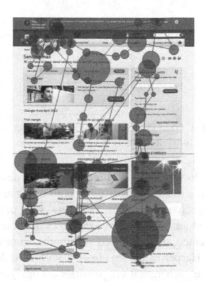

Fig. 2. Scanpaths showing the non-common behaviour of FD (orange) and FI (blue) subjects in a medium page

Fig. 3. Scanpaths indicating the different behaviour between FD (green) and FI (red) users in complex page

The complexity algorithm was explicitly used in this study as a tool that allowed the investigation between eye tracking technologies and cognitive abilities. Specifically, with both these technologies (algorithm and eye tracking) this pilot study identified that: 1) Field dependency could be determined with the use of eye tracking technology, 2) Visual complexity prediction tools could be used to evaluate an interface in order to help in the interface adaptation, 3) Designers will have an additional tool for validating their interface in order to design environments that not only assist users with disabilities, but all users that would like to interact with interfaces that meet their learning and interaction style.

5   Conclusions

This study is a pilot investigation towards a project that aims to formulate a framework and suggest guidelines in designing adaptive environments by understanding how users of different cognitive types interact with different tasks [2]. It supports the view that individual differences exist in terms of cognitive abilities that should provide insight to users' navigation in assessing and perusing digital information. This demonstrates that the differences among the behavior of the FD and FI cognitive groups, in terms of the time taken to complete the given tasks in the complex and medium complex Webpages should be taken into consideration.

Cognitive style ultimately has implications for the design of hypertext instructional systems and the development of personalized user models. The use of eye tracker technology as a measure of noticing users' cognitive ability during visual processing gives an understanding on how this information and cognitive overload affects user ability to interact. The link between eye tracking and cognitive modeling is extremely intuitive and fruitful area of research. It is important, therefore, to understand precisely what the eyes reveal in order to model human behavior by designing suitable and adaptive environments based on the assumption that individuals interact differently. Developing a new measurement method to test the cognitive behavior of humans, instead of solely relying on questionnaires, is of paramount importance. This can lead to solutions that improve users' Web experience. Finally, the results of the study demonstrate a necessity for emerging solutions that will reflect the user's cognitive ability and can, however, improve users' Web experience through the design of innovative interfaces.

In addition, further research is under progress that will take the above study on its next stage using neuroimaging methodologies such as Electroencephalography (EEG). EEG is a tool that allows us to detect the location and the changes in the brain activity while it is performing a cognitive task. Hence, the design of guidelines will be conducted to be used by developers in order to create simpler Web pages to allow interaction for all cognitive abilities. The findings should provide insights that enable the development of models that better predict and stimulate human performance in evaluating cognitive load.

References

1. Lindgaard, G., Fernandes, G., Dudek, C., Browntilde, J.: Attention web designers: You have 50 milliseconds to make a good first impression! Behaviour & Information Technology 25, 115–126 (2006)
2. Nisiforou, E.A., Laghos, A.: Do the eyes have it? Using eye tracking to assess students' cognitive dimensions. Educational Media International 50, 247–265 (2013)
3. DaSilva, M., Courboulay, V., Estraillier, P.: Image complexity measure based on visual attention. In: IEEE International Conference on Image Processsing, ICIP 2011, pp. 3281–3284 (2011)
4. Michailidou, E.: ViCRAM Visual complexity Rankings and accessibility Metrics. PhD thesis, The University of Manchester (2009)

5. Furuta, R., Frank, M., Shipman, I., Marshall, C.C., Brenner, D., wei Hsieh, H.: Hypertext paths and the world-wide web: experiences with walden's paths. In: HYPERTEXT 1997, pp. 167–176. ACM, New York (1997)
6. Harper, S., Michailidou, E., Stevens, R.: Toward a definition of visual complexity as an implicit measure of cognitive load. ACM Trans. Appl. Percept. 6, 1–18 (2009)
7. Germanakos, P., Tsianos, N., Lekkas, Z., Mourlas, C., Samaras, G.: Eye-tracking users' behavior in relation to cognitive style within an e-learning environment. In: ICALT 2009, pp. 329–333 (2009)
8. Solso, R.L., MacLin, M.K., MacLin, O.H.: Cognitive Psychology, 7th edn. Allyn & Bacon (2004)
9. Messick, S.: The nature of cognitive styles: Problems and promise in educational practice. Educational Psychologist 19, 59–74 (1984)
10. Hayes, J., Allinson, C.W.: Cognitive style and the theory and practice of individual and collective learning in organizations. Human Relations 51, 847–871 (1998)
11. Workman, M.: Performance and perceived effectiveness in computer-based and computer-aided education: do cognitive styles make a difference? Computers in Human Behavior 20, 517–534 (2004)
12. Dragon, K.: Field dependence and student achievement in technology-based learning: A meta-analysis. Master's thesis, University of Alberta (2009)
13. Burnett, W.C.: Cognitive style: A meta-analysis of the instructional implications for various integrated computer enhanced learning environments. PhD thesis, Indiana University of Pennsylvania (2010)
14. Hercegfi, K.: Event related assessment of hypermedia based e-learning materials with an HRV-based method that considers individual differences in users. International Journal of Occupational Safety and Ergonomics 17, 119–127 (2011)
15. Ford, N., Miller, D., Moss, N.: Web search strategies and human individual differences: Cognitive and demographic factors, Internet attitudes and approaches. Journal of the American Society for Information Science and Technology 56, 741–756 (2005)
16. Oliva, A., Mack, M.L., Shrestha, M., Peeper, A.: Identifying the perceptual dimensions of visual complexity in scenes. In: 26th Annual Meeting of the Cognitive Science Society, Chicago (2004)
17. Rayner, K.: Eye movements in reading and information processing: 20 years of research. Psychological Bulletin 124, 372–422 (1998)
18. Ivory, M.Y., Sinha, R.R., Hearst, M.A.: Empirically validated web page design metrics. In: CHI 2001, pp. 53–60. ACM Press, New York (2001)
19. Germonprez, M., Zigurs, I.: Causal factors for web site complexity. Working Papers on Information Environments, Systems and Organizations 3 (2003)
20. Tuch, A.N., Bargas-Avila, J.A., Opwis, K., Wilhelm, F.H.: Visual complexity of websites: Effects on users' experience, physiology, performance, and memory. Int. J. Hum.-Comput. Stud. 67, 703–715 (2009)
21. Jacob, R.J.K.: Eye tracking in advanced interface design. Oxford University Press Inc., NY (1995)
22. Toker, D., Conati, C., Steichen, B., Carenini, G.: Individual user characteristics and information visualization: connecting the dots through eye tracking. In: CHI 2013, pp. 295–304. ACM Press, NY (2013)
23. Witkin, H.A., Moore, C.A., Goodenough, D.R., Cox, P.W.: Field-dependent and field-independent cognitive styles and their educational implications. Review of Educational Research 47, 1–64 (1977)

24. French, J.W., Ekstrom, R.B., Price, L.A.: Kit of reference tests for cognitive skills. Educational Testing Services, Princeton (1963)
25. Angeli, C.: Examining the effects of field dependence–independence on learners' problem-solving performance and interaction with a computer modeling tool: Implications for the design of joint cognitive systems. Computers & Education 62, 221–230 (2013)
26. Rittschof, K.A.: Field dependence–independence as visuospatial and executive functioning in working memory: implications for instructional systems design and research. Educational Technology Research and Development 58, 99–114 (2010)
27. Study, N.E.: An overview of tests of Cognitive spatial ability. Paper presented at 66th Midyear Meeting Proceedings. ASEE, Galveston (2012)
28. Guisande, M., Pramo, M., Tinajero, C.Y., Almeida, L.: Field dependence-independence (fdi) cognitive style: An analysis of attentional functioning. Psicothema 19, 572–577 (2007)
29. Zhang, L.: Field-dependence/independence: Cognitive style or perceptual ability? validating against thinking styles and academic achievement. Personality and Individual Differences 37, 1295–1311 (2004)
30. Jozsa, E., Hamornik, B.P.: Find The Difference! Eye Tracking Study on Information Seeking Behavior Using an Online Game. Journal of Eye Tracking, Visual Cognition and Emotion 2, 27–35 (2012)
31. Tinajero, C., Pramo, M.F.: Field dependence-independence and academic achievement: a re-examination of their relationship. British Journal of Educational Psychology 67, 199–212 (1997)

Making Web Pages and Applications Accessible Automatically Using Browser Extensions and Apps

Ignacio Peinado and Manuel Ortega-Moral

Fundosa Technosite, Madrid, Spain
{ipeinado,mortega}@technosite.es

Abstract. Web accessibility depends on three factors: the semantics of the web contents, the assistive technologies (ATs) and the capabilities of the web browsers (Fernandes, Lopes, & Carriço, 2011). Moreover, the widespread implementation of Rich Internet Applications (RIAs) poses new challenges for ensuring the equality of access to dynamic web content. This paper presents the development of a solution that will automatically activate the accessibility features and the available ATs in two web browsers that take more than 50% of web browsers market share, and depending on the expressed needs and preferences of the user. The two extensions presented will take advantage of the infrastructures developed in CLOUD4all and APSIS4all in order to inject CSS and JavaScript in any web pages, as well as activating non-out-of-the-box ATs, and hence guaranteeing access to both static HTML pages and Rich Internet Applications.

Keywords: e-Accessibility, Web accessibility, ATs, adaptation of accessibility features, CLOUD4all, APSIS4all.

1   Introduction

People use interactive systems every day. Nowadays, we need technology for performing common activities such as withdrawing money from an ATM, attending online courses or performing administrative duties. These activities can be performed on a plethora of devices and environments: on the same day; we might withdraw money from an ATM, buy a train ticket from a Ticket Vending Machine and then read our mail in our mobile phone on our way to work, where we might then use a computer to perform our daily activities. Nevertheless, many of these technologies do not fulfill the needs and preferences of people with special needs, preventing them from fully participating in relevant activities such as e-Government or e-Learning.

Electronic Accessibility or e-Accessibility has been defined by the World Health Organization as referring to "the ease of use of information and communication technologies (ICTs), such as the Internet, for people with disabilities" (World Health Organization, 2013). The International Organization for Standardization (ISO)

C. Stephanidis and M. Antona (Eds.): UAHCI/HCII 2014, Part IV, LNCS 8516, pp. 58–69, 2014.
© Springer International Publishing Switzerland 2014

broadens the scope defining accessibility as "the usability of a product, service, environment or facility by people with the widest range of capabilities" (ISO, 2008). Problems that people with disabilities encounter when using interactive systems range from minor annoyances to critical flaws that prevent any use of the system at all.

Web accessibility depends on three factors: web page semantics, assistive technology (AT) and Web browser capabilities (Fernandes, Lopes, & Carriço, 2011). The Web Content Accessibility Guidelines (WCAG) 2.0 provides a wide range of recommendations for making web content more accessible (World Wide Web Consortium, 2008). Additionally, User Agent Accessibility Guidelines (UAAG) provides guidelines for designing user agents – i.e. media players, assistive technologies and, especially, web browsers – that lower barriers to Web accessibility (World Wide Web Consortium, 2013). Moreover, the emergence of Rich Internet Applications (RIAs) has posed new accessibility challenges. RIAs use client-side scripting languages, such as JavaScript, or asynchronous communication technologies such as AJAX to enrich the interactivity of web pages. Since ATs need to interact with this dynamic content, new guidelines had to be developed in order to ensure that all content is properly presented to users. The WAI-ARIA, the Accessible Rich Internet Application Suite, defines a way to make Web Content and Web Applications more accessible to people with disabilities. WAI-ARIA provides a framework for adding attributes to identify features for user interaction, how they relate to each other, and their current state (World Wide Web Consortium, 2014).

Popular web browsers like Mozilla Firefox or Google Chrome have implemented several accessibility features such as keyboard shortcuts, page zooms or mechanisms to control web content (Using Google products: How to use accessibility features, 2014) (Accessibility features in Firefox - Make Firefox and web content work for all users, 2014). Plus, browser extensions and apps permit the provision of accessibility features that are not built-in in the browser. For instance, Google has developed extensions such as ChromeVis[1] or ChromeVox[2] that provide users with out-of-the-box accessibility features. Unfortunately, many users are not aware of the accessibility features provided by their browsers or of the existence of extensions and apps that might fulfil their needs.

This paper presents the development of two extensions for Google Chrome and Mozilla Firefox that will take advantage of the infrastructure developed within the CLOUD4all and APSIS4all FP7 projects. These browser extensions with provide users with the automatic activation of the accessibility features available both in the browser and in third-party browser extensions, depending on their expressed needs and preferences.

---

[1] https://chrome.google.com/webstore/detail/
chromevis-by-google/halnfobaneppemjnonmmhngbfifnafgd
[2] https://chrome.google.com/webstore/detail/
chromevox/kgejglhpjiefppelpmljglcjbhoiplfn

1.1 Automatic Personalization of Accessibility Features: The APSIS4all and CLOUD4all Approaches

Many researchers and developers have proposed solutions for facilitating the configuration of devices, platforms and applications depending on the preferences of the users. Many of these approaches rely on the construction of user models (INREDIS (INREDIS Consortium, 2010), VUMS cluster (Peissner, et al., 2011)) or on the dynamic generation of optimal UIs (Cameleon Framework (Calvary, et al., 2002), SERENOA (SERENOA project Consortium, 2013)). The approach adopted by APSIS4all and CLOUD4all is slightly different: both projects do not perform user modelling, but capture in a generic form the needs and preferences of the users when interacting with technology. Thus, instead of characterizing a user as 'low vision', both systems will define concrete interaction preferences such as 'high Contrast activated' or 'font size: big'. This permits for much more flexible configuration capabilities, allowing users outside any cluster to define individual parameters for individual situations.

The APSIS4all project is an ICT-PSP project led by Technosite[3] and partially funded by the EC that is developing mechanisms for allowing end-users to overcome the accessibility barriers of public digital terminals (PDTs) such as automated teller machines (ATMs) or ticket vending machines (TVMs). APSIS4all has developed a set of accessible, usable User Interfaces (UIs) that will provide end-uses with an easy way for describing their needs and preferences when interacting with technology. Once users have configured their preferences through a web tool, the UIs of any APSIS4all-compatible PDTs will be able to automatically adapt their UIs to these expressed needs and preferences, therefore facilitating the interaction. APSIS4all has adopted two approaches for enhancing the interaction with PDTs: a 'direct interaction' approach, where users can interact with machines that get adapted; and an 'indirect interaction' approach, where users circumvent the use of non-accessible PDT with an accessible mobile web that represents the machine. Preferences are stored according to specification EN 1332-4, a standard for coding interaction needs. Because the coding of preferences is based on standards, the PDT can retrieve the user's needs and preferences regardless of the service provider, and provide the most suitable UI for that specific set of needs and preferences. The web tool for collecting the needs and preferences of the user is currently online[4]. More than 1000 ATMs from "la Caixa", one of the most important banks in Spain, are APSIS4all-compatible. Although the results from the APSIS4all project have been really promising, it is only limited to the adaptation of the UIs of compatible PDTs, hence lacking generality.

CLOUD4all is another EC-funded project from the 7th Framework Programme led by Technosite that moves one step forward from the work of APSIS4all. CLOUD4all is part of a greater effort - the Global Public Inclusive Infrastructure (GPII) - that aims at developing a complete new paradigm in accessibility by extending the concept of

---

[3] http://www.technosite.es
[4] http://cajerofacil.apsis4all.eu

automatic configuration of the accessibility features from specific devices to any technology that users encounter during their daily lives. CLOUD4all uses cloud technologies to activate and augment any natural (built-in) accessibility or installed access feature, or recommends the appropriate third-party solutions that better fit the user s' needs. In this sense, CLOUD4all aims at overcoming two important accessibility barriers: 1) users will be recommended with the ATs that better suit their needs and preferences, and 2) users will not need to configure the settings of any CLOUD4all-compatible device they use.

Within CLOUD4all up to 19 proof-of-concept implementations of the auto-configuration capabilities are being developed for different devices, platforms and applications. To this point, it can be installed in desktop computers with Windows 7 and Fedora with Gnome, and in Android smartphones; third-party AT solutions such as Mobile Accessibility for Android (developed by Code Factory)[5], Read&Write Gold (by TextHelp)[6] or Maavis (by OpenDirective)[7] have been modified in order to become CLOUD4all-compatible. On top of that, cloud-based AT solutions such as WebAnywhere[8] or SAToGo[9] can be launched and set up automatically. In order to launch and configure these solutions, some CLOUD4all modules need to be installed in the host device, and solution implementers had to provide access to the settings and the process launchers. However, the experience showed that the access to the device is not always possible or applications do not allow other applications to change the settings on-the-fly. Hence, how can we provide auto-configuration from preferences in those situations?

This paper presents an approach to auto-configuration for web content using CLOUD4all and APSIS4all preferences. This proof-of-concept implementation will permit both Mozilla Firefox and Google Chrome users to change their access features in any platform (Windows, Mac OS X and Linux), and in any desktop computer, regardless the GPII is installed or not.

Section 2 presents an overview of the architectural solutions that support the auto-configuration process in both CLOUD4all and APSIS4all; then, section 3 presents the actual implementation of the auto-configuration capabilities for web browsers using the CLOUD4all and APSIS4all infrastructures. Finally, section 4 presents some conclusions and discuss some future work.

2   Architectural Solutions

As mentioned before, the extensions developed rely on the architectural solutions that support the auto-configuration process in both the CLOUD4all and APSIS4all projects.

---

[5] http://www.codefactory.es/en/products.asp?id=415
[6] http://www.texthelp.com/North-America/readwrite-family
[7] http://maavis.fullmeasure.co.uk/
[8] http://webanywhere.cs.washington.edu/
[9] http://www.satogo.com/en/

2.1   The CLOUD4all Architecture

The CLOUD4all architecture has been designed to work across platforms and devices, including desktop computers, mobile devices (both feature phones and smartphones) and cloud-based and web applications (Clark, Basman, Zenevich, Mitchell, & Strobbe, 2013). The main components of the CLOUD4all architecture that take part in the auto-configuration process are listed next:

- The **User Listeners** are responsible for starting the auto-configuration process, and provide a set of extensible tools and techniques that will allow users to share their token easily, i.e. via a USB key, a QR code, a NFC card or a text input where users might type their token.
- The **Flow Manager** is the central point of the architecture, and is responsible for orchestrating the personalization workflow.
- The **Preferences Server** is where preferences are stored. Within CLOUD4all, the preferences are formatted according to the ISO-24751 standard, in a platform-agnostic format. No personal information about the users is stored in the preferences.
- The **Device Reporter** provides information about the device (OS, technical features) and about the solutions installed in the platform running CLOUD4all.
- The **Matchmakers** are where the main intelligence of the system resides. The Matchmakers will get information about the preferences of the user, the accessibility features present in the device, the solutions available – taken from the Solutions Registry–, and the context where the interaction is taking place, and will calculate the most appropriate settings for the solution, for that specific user and in the current conditions.
- The **Lifecycle Managers** and the **Setting Handlers** perform the actual launching and setting of applications and access features.

The CLOUD4all architecture is based on web standards, and has been designed to support cloud-level scalability, extensibility and long-term growth. Many of the components of the architecture have been designed to be able to reside locally or in the cloud, or both. Therefore, instances of the flow manager, the matchmakers or the preferences server can be available either on the device, on the cloud or in both places simultaneously. This ubiquity will make it possible to maintain the auto-configuration process even in low-bandwidth connections or no connection at all. On the other hand, modules such as the user listeners, the device reporter and the setting handlers are device-bound, as they provide information about the specific device that will be auto-configured.

2.2   The APSIS4all Architecture

The APSIS4all architecture has been developed with a mix of technologies to support the specific features of each machine. It is distributed both locally (in ATMs and TVMs) and in the cloud, and is based in four main modules:

- **Preference wizard:** a java-based web application that guides users through a questionnaire optimized to maximize the information recovered with a minimum number of questions.
- **Coding system:** Preferences gathered with the wizard are exported from the encrypted database to a XML version of EN 1332-4. They are stored in the cloud and copied to personal contactless cards. Additionally these preferences can be shared with applications with permissions through two protocols: SFTP and XMLHttpRequest.
- **Multimodal interface manager:** a system deployed in ATMs and ticket vending machines able to read cards with preferences coded inside and transform user interfaces appropriately.
- **Monitoring system.** This part of the architecture is in charge of collecting logs and statistical information in order to debug the system and create automatic reports of use.

Whereas the Preference wizard is coded in Java, contactless cards (MiFARE) use private operating systems to store and communicate information with machines. The multimodal interface manager is developed basically in Flash in ATMs while TVMs use a mixture of C++ technologies in the machines and XSLT transformations over theXML UI template to produce the final UIs. Monitoring systems work both locally and in the server-side.

3   Implementing the Auto-personalization from Preferences in Web Browsers

By January 2014, the combined use of Google Chrome and Mozilla Firefox adds a total of the 52.4% of the web browser market share (Awio Web Services LLC, 2014). In Google Chrome, an extension is a zipped bundle of files that adds functionality to the browser[10]. Unlike packaged apps, Google Chrome extensions make it possible to interact with web pages and servers or with browser features such as bookmarks and tabs. In Mozilla Firefox, extensions can add new features to the browser, such as different ways to manage tabs, and they can modify web content to improve the usability of particular websites[11]. Traditional - XUL-based - extensions are more powerful, allowing for instance to change the browser's chrome -, but in most cases they require restarting the browser. On the other hand, add-on SDK (JetPack) extensions provide a set of high-level APIs that permit to develop restartless extensions.

Several extensions providing accessibility features for web pages have been developed and are available via the proprietary extension repositories for both platforms. For instance, Accessibility Evaluator for Firefox[12] allows a page author or user to view a list of navigation landmarks. Google developers have developed Chromevox, a browser extension that implements a screen reader. Most of the extensions currently

---

[10] http://developer.chrome.com/extensions/overview.html
[11] https://developer.mozilla.org/en-US/Add-ons
[12] http://firefox.cita.illinois.edu

available provide information and cues to web developers for improving the accessibility of their websites (generally checking against WCAG 2.0 guidelines) or focus on specific disabilities (i.e. Chromevox, ChromeVis). The browser extensions presented in this paper will inject CSS and JavaScript into any web pages that are displayed in the browser in order to activate or deactivate the accessibility features of the browser and the available ATs. Moreover, the synchronization capabilities provided by both browsers will permit this personalization to happen in any browser instance with these extensions installed regardless of the platform.

All the personalization process will take advantage of the Cloud infrastructure provided by CLOUD4all, whose main elements were presented in the previous section. The user listener and the lifecycle handler will reside in the background page of the extension. Background pages do not have access to the actual content of the websites, and run in a different process than the content scripts that will inject code in the web pages. The background page will get the token and will scan the defined preferences servers in search for a valid set of needs and preferences. An XMLHttpRequest will be sent to the online flow manager, comprising an object that includes the token of the user and the identifier of the solution. The online flow manager will then make a request to   Needs and Preferences Server. If the N&P server stores a set of needs and preferences that corresponds to the token requested, it will respond with an error 500; otherwise, the needs and preferences of the user (in the form of 24751 terms) will be sent to the Matchmakers, that will transform this set into application-specific preferences (ASP). Simultaneously, the XMLHttpRequest to the APSIS4all needs and preferences server will get a set of needs of preferences in EN1334 format or an error 500. I case the request successes, the transformation process will be replicated within the browser. In both cases, the application-specific preferences will be stored using the storage functionalities provided by the browser APIs (storage for Google Chrome, simple-prefs for Mozilla Firefox). The background page will capture any changes in the stored preferences and will communicate them to the content script, that will inject the appropriate CSS or JavaScript to the pages displayed in the browser. The modules involved in the auto-configuration process, as well as the communication amongst them, are presented in figure 1.

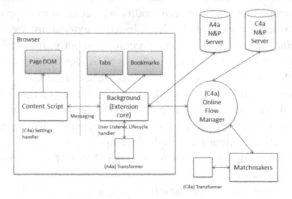

Fig. 1. Arquitectural description of the auto-configuration process

The JavaScript injected in the DOM of the visited web pages will allow us to perform a level of UI remoulding. UI remoulding denotes the configuration of the UI that results from the application of one or several transformations on all, or parts, of the UI (Coutaz & Calvary, 2009), including aspects such as the suppression of UI components that become irrelevant in the given context or the substitution of UI components. In its current state, the extensions support the following customizations:

- Activate / Deactivate the default screen reader (only in Google Chrome).
- Change the font-size of the pages ("medium", "large" and "extra-large").
- Magnification (100%, 200% or 300%).
- Apply high contrast themes ("black on white", "white on black", "yellow on black" or "black on yellow").
- Invert Colors. Applies a CSS filter to invert all colors of the web page.
- Simplifier. The simplifier injects a JavaScript script that removes all unnecessary elements from a webpage and presents them as they will be accessed by a common screen reader.

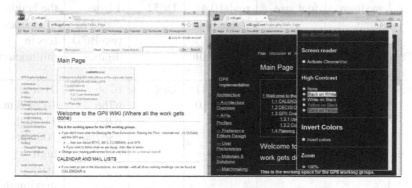

Fig. 2. Google Chrome screen before and after adaptation

The extension core receives the user preferences either in a ready-to-use format (Application specific Preferences) or may need to transform them. The transformer is responsible of taking the terms, expressed in different formats, and transforming them into application-specific terms that can be understood by browser. The extensions are able to interpret and adapt websites based on two user preference formats: EN 1332-4 and ISO 24751 part 2. As mentioned previously, APSIS4all is using the draft revised version of standard EN 1332-4. This European Standard defines the data objects to be stored within an integrated circuit(s) card and exchanged with terminals to identify specific user interface preferences. The preference information may be used by terminals to configure appropriate methods of communicating with the user during a transaction process (IST/17, 2007). CLOUD4all uses a set of common terms based on ISO 24751 part 2 (International Organization for Standardization, 2008). ISO 24751-2 provides a common information model for describing the learner or user needs and preferences when accessing digitally delivered resources or services. The approach is to split needs and preferences into three categories: 1) the display describes the presentation and structure of resources, 2) the control focuses on how resources are to be controlled and operated; and finally 3) the content describes supplementary or alternative resources to be supplied. The following tables show the rules to translate standards into Application Specific Preferences (ASP). These rules define the way user preferences are used to remould UIs. Table 1 compares tags that are equivalent or similar in meaning whereas Table 2 shows the equivalence took up by the system presented in this paper.

Table 1. Comparison of standard tags and value spaces

ASP		ISO 24751- 2		EN 1332-4		
Tag	Values	Tag	Values	Tag	bits	Values
Screen reader	Boolean	screen reader: usage	required, preferred, optionally use, prohibited	DF61	b1	1/0
Font-size	medium, large, x-large	font size	real(10,4) range (0.0 .. *)excluding (0.0)	DF51	1 byte coded as two BCD digits	the height of characters in millimetres
Magnification	100%, 200%, 300%	magnification	real(10,4) range (1.0 .. *)	DF64	b7b6 b7b6 b7b6 b8b7b6 b8b7b6	01:low 10:medium 11: high 100:very high 101: maximum
High contrast themes	black on white, white on black, yellow on black, black on yellow	foreground colour	RGB plus Alpha	DF52	b4b3b2	000:white,0 01:red,010: orange,011: yellow, 100:green, 101:blue, 110:purple, 111:black
		background colour	RGB plus Alpha	DF52	b7b6b5	000:white, 001:red, 010:orange, 011:yellow, 100:green, 101:blue, 110:purple, 111:black

Table 1. (*continued*)

Invert Colours	Boolean	invert colour choice	Boolean	-	-	-
Sim-plifier	Boolean	content density	overview, detailed	DF5 D	b4b3	01: Simplified text required 10: Very simplified text required

Table 2. Equivalence of standards and value spaces

APfP	ISO 24751-2	EN 1332-4
Screen reader = True	screen reader -usage = "required" OR "preferred"	DF61[b1] = '1'
Font-size = medium	font size < 14pt	'X'< DF51 <'Y'
Font-size = large	14pt < font size < 18pt	'X' < DF51 < 'Y'
Font-size = extra-large	18pt < font size	'X' < DF51 < 'Y'
Magnification=100%	Magnification=1.0	DF64[b7b6]='01'
Magnification=200%	Magnification=2.0	DF64[b7b6]='10'
Magnification=300%	Magnification=3.0	DF64[b8b7b6]='100' OR '101'
High contrast themes=" black on white"	background colour = black AND foreground colour = white	DF52[b7b6b5b4b3b2]='000111'
High contrast themes=" white on black"	foreground colour = white AND background colour = black	DF52[b7b6b5b4b3b2]='111000'
High contrast themes=" yellow on black"	foreground colour = yellow AND background colour = black	DF52[b7b6b5b4b3b2]='111011'
High contrast themes=" black on yellow"	foreground colour = black AND background colour = yellow	DF52[b7b6b5b4b3b2]='011111'
Invert Colours = True	invert colour choice = True	-
Simplifier=True	content density = "overview"	DF5D[b4b3]='10' OR '01'

The notation used in this table is explained with these examples:

- DF5D[b4b3]='10' OR '01' means data object DF5D has the value '10' or '10' it its bits 4 and 3. The APfP system will understand that text simplification is required.
- Screen reader -usage = "required" OR "preferred" means that when attribute usage in container Screen reader takes values "required" or "preferred", then the APfP system activates the screen reader.

Although further work has been done to establish equivalences between EN 1332-4 and ISO 24751-2, this is out of the scope of this paper.

4   Conclusions and Future Work

Browser extensions and apps provide a great opportunity to improve the accessibility of web browsers, as well as to provide personalized access solutions for people with special needs. The auto-personalization capabilities the approach presented in this paper allow us to enhance at least two of the three aspects of web accessibility as defined in (Fernandes, Lopes, & Carriço, 2011): 1) the injection of CSS and JS into web pages provides an enhancement of the accessibility features of the web browsers by allowing the activation of styling features such as magnification or application of UI themes; and 2) the possibility of activating non-out-of-the-box ATs. Regarding the semantics of the web content, the injection of more complex JavaScript algorithms will also permit to enhance the semantics of the pages, both by direct action – i.e. adding WAI-ARIA roles to the appropriate components - or providing recommendations to developers about web practices. Also, more complex JavaScript functionalities will permit UI remoulding by removing elements or adding new ones depending on the preferences of the users. The development of packaged apps in Google Chrome or traditional, XUL-based, extensions in Mozilla Firefox in combination with common applications APIs can be used to enhance the overall user experience when using common applications such as Gmail, YouTube or Picasa, even providing capabilities to adapt the browser's chrome to the needs and preferences of the user.

To sum up, it seems clear that the auto-adaptation of the accessibility features of web browsers has the potentiality to provide access to web content to people with special needs. The capability to read different standards makes the system more compatible and easy to integrate with technologies coding user preferences. Finally, these extensions broaden the scope of APSIS4all project from just public digital terminals to personalize any device where a web browser is running.

Acknowledgements. The research leading to these results has received funding from the European Union Seventh Framework Programme ([FP7/2007-2013]) under grant agreement n° 289016 (CLOUD4all) and by European Union's ICT Policy Support Programme as part of the Competitiveness and Innovation Framework Programme. GA 270977 (APSIS4all).

References

1. Accessibility features in Firefox - Make Firefox and web content work for all users (2014), http://support.mozilla.org/en-US/kb/accessibility-features-firefox-make-firefox-and-we?redirectlocale=en-US&redirectslug=Accessibility (retrieved from Mozilla support)
2. Awio Web Services LLC. Web Browser Market Share (2014), http://www.w3counter.com/globalstats.php (retrieved February 20, 2014)
3. Calvary, G., Coutaz, J., Bouillon, L., Florins, M., Limbourg, Q., Marucci, L., et al.: The CAMELEON reference framework (2002)
4. Clark, C., Basman, A., Zenevich, Y., Mitchell, J., Strobbe, C.: D105.1.1. System Architecture V1. Deliverable, Cloud4all project (2013)
5. Coutaz, J., Calvary, G.: HCI and software engineering: Designing for user interface plasticity. In: Human-Computer Interaction: Development Process, p. 211 (2009)
6. Fernandes, N., Lopes, R., Carriço, L.: On web accessibility evaluation environments. In: Proceedings of the International Cross-Disciplinary Conference on Web Accessibility, p. 4. ACM (2011)
7. Gajos, K.Z., Weld, D.S., Wobbrock, J.O.: Decision-Theoretic User Interface Generation. AAAI 8, 1532–1536 (2008)
8. INREDIS Consortium (2010), INREDIS website http://www.inredis.es/default.aspx (retrieved)
9. International Organization for Standardization. ISO/IEC 24751-2:2008. Information technology – Individualized adaptability and accessibility in e-learning, education and training – Part 2: "Access for all" personal needs and preferences for digital delivery. ISO/IEC, Genève, Switzerland (2008)
10. ISO. ISO 9241-171: 2008. Ergonomics of human-system interaction - Part, 171 (2008)
11. IST/17. BS EN 1332-4: 2007. Identification card systems. Man-machine interfaceCoding of user requirements for people with special needs. BSI (2007)
12. Peissner, M., Dangelmaier, M., Biswas, P., Mohamad, Y., Jung, C., Wolf, P., et al.: D6.4. Interim Report on VUMS cluster standardization. Deliverable, MyUI (2011)
13. SERENOA project Consortium (2013), SERENOA project website: http://www.serenoa-fp7.eu/ (retrieved)
14. Using Google products: How to use accessibility features (2014), Google Accessibility: http://www.google.es/accessibility/products/ (retrieved)
15. World Health Organization. What is e-accessibility? (September 2013), WHO website: http://www.healthinternetwork.com/features/qa/50/en/ (retrieved)
16. World Wide Web Consortium. Web content accessibility guidelines (WCAG) 2.0 (2008), W3C Website: http://www.w3.org/TR/WCAG20/ (retrieved February 2014)
17. World Wide Web Consortium. Web content accessibility guidelines (WCAG) 2.0 (2008)
18. J. Allan, K. Ford, K. Patch, J. Spellman (eds.): World Wide Web Consortium. User Agent Accessibility Guidelines (UAAG) 2.0 (2013), http://www.w3.org/TR/UAAG20/ (retrieved February 19, 2014)
19. Craig, J., Cooper, M. (eds.): World Wide Web Consortium. Accessible Rich Internet Applications (WAI-ARIA) 1.0 (2014), W3C website: http://www.w3.org/TR/wai-aria/ (retrieved February 19, 2014)

The German Web 2.0 Accessibility Survey

Empirical Findings and Recommendations

Michael Pieper

Fraunhofer Institute for Applied Information Technology – FIT
Schloss Birlinghoven, 53754 Sankt Augustin, Germany
michael.pieper@fit.fhg.de

Abstract. The German BIENE award (**B**arrierefreies **I**nternet **E**röffnet **N**eue **E**insichten / Accessible Internet Provides New Insights) happened to be a best practice competition for accessible websites organized by the social association "Aktion Mensch" and the endowment "Digitale Chancen". For the last 2010 competition 224 web pages have been checked for their barrier free accessibility. Web applications that facilitate interactive sharing of *user generated content* have been of particular importance. In this respect it soon turned out, that Web 2.0 services cannot only be made accessible by applying common design guidelines and ad-hoc adaptations. In addition to conventional software ergonomic verification procedures, accessibility validation has to rely on sociological reasoning about unique Web 2.0 entities and corresponding usage obstacles. Empirically these considerations have been conceptualized by an online survey amongst 671 respondents with all kinds of different disabilities, carried out by "Aktion Mensch".

Keywords: Accessibility, Usability, Human-Computer Interaction, Web 2.0.

1 Introduction

The German BIENE award (**B**arrierefreies **I**nternet **E**röffnet **N**eue **E**insichten / Accessible Internet Provides New Insights) happened to be a best practice competition for accessible websites organized by the social association "Aktion Mensch" and the endowment "Digitale Chancen". For the last 2010 competition 128 contributions out of originally 224 additionally went through a special ergonomic test procedure of process-oriented interaction with competitors' web pages. Accessibility was analyzed on the basis of on-line transactions like purchase, money-transfer or public authority form-filling dialogues. However, of special importance in this respect are transactions that facilitate interactive sharing of user generated content, when it comes to Web 2.0 technologies. Special attention has to be paid to the technological evolution step concerning the offer and the accessibility of the World Wide Web to a web with which not any more the pure spreading of information or product sales are in the foreground, but the participation of users and the user-centered generation of other additional use. In this respect it soon turned out, that Web 2.0 services cannot only be made accessible through common methods such as the application of conventional design

C. Stephanidis and M. Antona (Eds.): UAHCI/HCII 2014, Part IV, LNCS 8516, pp. 70–76, 2014.

guidelines and/or ad-hoc adaptations. In addition to more or less software ergonomic verification procedures, accessibility validation has most basically to rely on sociological reasoning about unique Web 2.0 entities and corresponding usage obstacles.

2   Sociological Issues of Inclusive Web 2.0 Design

Inclusive Design is a way of designing products and environments so that they are usable and appealing to everyone regardless of age, ability or circumstance. Amongst other issues it follows the concept of working with users to remove barriers in the social, technical, political and economic obstacles to overcome digital divide. As user participation is at stake inclusive design or Web 2.0 accessibility for all becomes a purely sociological issue. The actualization of topical contents continuously occurs through intensive user participation, so that websites become more dynamic and more adapted to user needs, especially to the needs of disabled end users. On account of the immediate participation of the users it is often spoken also of the "democratization" of the net, because the contents of the web are no longer influenced any more by only the operators of the websites, but by the users as well. "We see through a range of already very well-known websites (…), that networks are taking shared responsibility for the construction of vast accumulations of knowledge about themselves, each other, and the world. These are dynamic matrices of information through which people observe others, expand the network, make new 'friends', edit and update content, blog, remix, post, respond, share files, exhibit, tag and so on. This has been described as an online 'participatory culture' [1] where users are increasingly involved in creating web content as well as consuming it" [2]. The (social) role of website operators has changed in web 2.0 in this respect, as that they are responsible, primarily, for the supply of a properly designed platform suitable for interactive and collaborative use as well as for its administration. Finally, the success of a platform provided by the operator or better designer appears in the intensity of its use which generally correlates with the quality of the contents in terms of "customer use" ("Usefulness"). Only in this respect, quality of contents correlates secondarily with the highest possible absence of usage barriers ("usability") [3], [4]. Avoidance of usage barriers in turn depends on a specific execution of certain (social) roles of website developers in general. As Web 2.0 is primarily associated with the term "user generated content" the crucial questions thus arises, in how far end user content generation coincides with low or barely existent usage barriers. Equally the question has to be answered in which way website developers support end users to generate barrier-free content.

2.1   Social Roles of Website Developers and Barrier-Free User Content

Four types of usage obstacles can be distinguished with respect to (social) roles of website developers. These roles can be derived from certain areas of responsibility for website operability, i.e. the responsibility to minimize or remove defined barriers [5].

1. Techno-functional barriers:

— relate to insufficiently applied software technologies or programming and hard- and software restrictions by assistive technologies

- examples are CAPTCHAS (non machine-readable graphics code[1]), accessibility of Flash-players, missing form identifications etc.
- area of responsibility: Web programmer and service provider

2. Editorial and content barriers:

- relate to insufficient editorial or structural preparation and implementation of **content** (poor CMS)
- examples are difficult language, missing text-structure (e.g. CSS), missing desc. txt etc.
- area of responsibility: Web editors

3. User interface design barriers

- relate to insufficient software **ergonomic** design
- examples are low contrast, confusing background pictures, non readable fonts etc.
- area of responsibility: Web designer

4. Organizational barriers

- related to insufficient organizational **circumstances** and environment
- examples are missing budget or missing demands for alternative website regeneration and assistive technologies (e.g. speech output for the blind, font size and contrast modification for the vision impaired etc.)
- area of responsibility: Customers

Due to not always clearly defined areas of responsibility overlapping between these four usage barriers is possible. Such as the responsibility for an adequate web appearance of pictures or Wiki applications in principle lies with the editor, it may partially as well lie with the designer or even with the programmer, when declarative programming statements are needed.

In a two factorial design different role responsibilities of web programmers, service providers, editors, designers and customers interfere with distinguishable content generating and content perceiving usage patterns of end users, thus revealing further refined insights into Web 2.0 usage obstacles. Three kinds of usage patterns can be distinguished:

1. Simple form-based usage (e.g. user registration, processing of user profiles, commenting, reading in Wiki-applications and Weblogs)
2. Extended form- or editor-based usage (e.g. writing in Wiki-applications and Weblogs)
3. Media-intensive usage (e.g. uploading and viewing of pictures, videos, hearing of podcasts)

---

[1] ...which cannot be processed by screen readers and is thus not accessible for vision impaired or blind end users.

Table 1. Accessibility problems by type of usage barrier and usage pattern

Usage Barrier / Usage Pattern	Techno-functional barriers	Editorial and content barriers	User interface design barriers
Simple form-based usage	Captchas, indications for form-fillings and buttons, accessibility of Flash-players…	Intelligibility of explanation texts, expected input and error messages…	Design of forms…
Extended form or editor based usage	Graphic editors, font sizes in editors, problems with Java script, accessibility of Flash-players		Design of forms, Perceptibility of editor functionality…
Media-intensive usage	Media upload/download	Quality (Resolution), size and contrast of media, sign-language videos, Podcasts, desc. txt	Controllability of players, Quality (Resolution), size and contrast of media

3   Empirical Findings and Recommendations

Empirically these considerations have been conceptualized by an online survey amongst 671 respondents with all kinds of different disabilities, carried out by "Aktion Mensch" [5]. Respondents' age was between 14 and above 70, amongst them 293 female and 378 male respondents.

The online survey itself was realized free of barriers. Participants with most different impediments were moved with the help of different aids into the position to perceive the survey and to navigate and understand the forms. According to the results of previous BIENE test procedures, all survey contents have been processed accessible for screen readers, by sign language videos and in simple language. The "Aktion Mensch" thus conducted the first truly accessible online survey among people with disabilities. Five complexes of unique Web 2.0 usage obstacles and corresponding recommendations to eliminate these barriers could be attributed to the results of this survey.

3.1   Elimination of Barriers to the Use of Wiki-Applications

To increase the accessibility of Wiki-applications, especially the content has verbally to be elaborated. Comprehension problems caused by complicated language stand in the foreground. The online survey revealed that about one-third of affected end users with limitations in the understanding of written language - amongst them users with reading disability and dyslexia, learning and cognitive disabilities, and deaf end users - had problems in reading Wiki pages. Missing videos in sign language impeded comprehension for deaf end users. Motor-impaired respondents indicated problems in navigating and controlling search fields by speech recognition. Missing values in writing or commenting Wikis indicate that none of the respondents experienced problems caused by their disability. Most of the barriers lie therefore, on the one hand, in the intelligibility and orientation on the GUI of Wikis and to the other in applying the mostly graphic editors and forms to write and annotate content. For the blind, the flow of text for screen readers is partly disrupted due to the large number of links, since these are always especially announced.

Table 2. Barriers by Disability (5)

Barriers \ Disability	Vision impaired (n=133)	Blind (n=124)	Hard of hearing (n=96)	Deaf (n=260)	Motor impaired (n=75)	Dyslexia/ reading disability (n=41)	Cognitive/learning disability (n=46)
Barriers total[2]	48%	82%	21%	26%	34%	23%	44%
Non-specified barriers in general	13%	42%	5%	8%	8%	3%	9%
Missing tags/Captchas	5%	39%	1%	-	-	-	3%
Orientation problems	15%	8%	-	2%	6%	10%	12%
Information overload	9%	9%	3%	3%	8%	10%	9%
Missing subtitles and gesture language	2%	-	5%	10%	-	-	-
Understanding problems	2%	1%	5%	6%	6%	-	3%
Problems with Flash	3%	8%	3%	-	3%	-	3%

3.2 Elimination of Barriers to User Registration and Editing of User Profiles

Most problems appear in the perceptibility, controllability and orientation during user registration or editing user profiles. In many Web 2.0 offerings user registration is the prerequisite for the productive use of the services. It should therefore be very thoroughly examined and adapted in terms of accessibility. Particularly critical in this respect is the programming of forms and captchas. Improvement should also be carried out concerning the intelligibility of explanations, expected inputs and in particular of error messages. Programming of error messages should as well be checked for compatibility with different assistive input and output devices. In particular, visually impaired and blind end users have massive problems with user registration. Nearly half of the blind end users are able to carry out a user registration independently. The most frequent problems in this respect originate on the basis of security and spam

---

[2] Because multiple barriers have been taken into account for single barrier values, they do not sum up to total barrier value.

defensive measures from Captchas which are discernible neither from screen readers nor by enlargement software. Unless it is not alternatively offered by audio files this non machine-readable graphics code for access authorization is also hardly accessible for the vision impaired. It can be assumed that roughly two third of the partially sighted and blind end users abort registration processes, leave corresponding applications and are thus excluded from a large variety of Web 2.0 services.

3.3   Elimination of Barriers in Dealing with Pictures (Photos), Videos and Podcasts

Many contents on the Internet are multimedia, which basically leads to disability-caused usage barriers on the side of partially sighted and blind users regarding the visual - and with the hard of hearing and deaf users regarding the auditive share of web offers. Differently than with purely text-based websites screen readers can offer a solution for blind end users only with an appropriate design of multi-media contents (e.g. appropriate 'desc. txt'). To the vision impaired, multimedia web offers are often too small and badly dissolved. Subtitles and sign language videos which could lift the barriers for auditively impaired users do normally not exist with most of the web offers. For uploading and embedding photos and videos, instruction forms are often problematic, since their design is neither clear and concise nor are certain form elements (e.g. buttons) sufficiently distinguished from each other. Additionally, visually impaired end users often get disoriented, because enlargement software limits the view area and complicates thus the allocation of multimedia content. Especially previewing of pictures may no more be recognizable. Even with downloading of podcasts download buttons are often not marked unambiguously. Often Java scripts impede a smooth download of podcasts by assistive technologies (e.g. screen readers). In summary barriers in dealing with multimedia content have therefore to be reduced by improved programming of upload and download forms. For instance, an offer to provide own multimedia content should encourage the user additionally to indicate content descriptions to the media to be uploaded, so that access to all end users can be granted regardless of their perceptive abilities. These additional descriptions can also be recorded by forms and added to the uploaded medium as an appropriate alt attribute. Barriers due to Captchas, Java-script or Flash elements can be minimized by programming alternatives. Inclusion of assistive technologies can thus be simplified.

3.4   Elimination of Barriers to Commenting Functions and Weblogs

Again, using commenting forms and related Captchas is particularly difficult for vision impaired and blind end users of assistive technologies. Input pages are mostly poorly structured and screen readers do not adequately read form fillings in editing fields and therefore do not forward it readably to a braille display. Users with cognitive and learning disabilities experience disability related barriers in dealing with written language by filling out input boxes. End users with dyslexia and reading disability are more likely inhibited by personal self-assessment and public biases in the use of weblogs and commenting functions. In writing web log entries technical as well as linguistic barriers likewise appear. Blind and vision impaired respondents report about problems to completely monitor and control formatting and representation options. Here again usability of editors depends on their controllability by assistive technologies. Thus, the amount of links in a Weblog leads to disorientation and navigation problems, because - if at all - it takes a while for a screen reader to display an entire list of links. As usage of weblogs and commenting functions is mostly form-based, accessibility problems again arise from insufficiently structured form-filling dialogues. To reduce these difficulties, the available elements of the applied descriptive language and a logical sequence of end user operations should hence be put into effect.

3.5   Eliminating Barriers in Dealing With Social Networking Sites (SNS)

So far at least between 15% and 29% of differently handicapped survey respondents use SNS. They only mention a few problems, which have partially appeared in the perceptibility and usability of executable functions and the perspicuity of the overall website. Most of the difficulties stem from the multiplicity of functions, information overload and from advertising banners disturbing website access by assistive technologies like screen readers. Also forms, graphic menus and buttons are often not properly designed. Especially for the blind and visually impaired respondents accessibility is a nevertheless particular factor to consider. As 91% of the blind respondents use a screen-reader, compatibility between speech processing software and readability of the web application is of crucial importance to usability. Despite low use of social networks, even the quite low problem values for cognitively and reading impaired survey respondents at least in tendency point out to the fact, that usability apart from raised requirements for media competence is also relevant for this user group. One non neglectable reason for relatively low user rates could also stem from previously indicated barriers of user registration, treatment of user profiles and photos or videos, which are often a precondition for activities in SNS applications.

References

1. Jenkins, H., Clinton, K., Purushotma, R., Robinson, A.J., Weigel, M.: Confronting the challenges of participatory culture: Media education for the 21st century. MacArthur Foundation. (2006), http://www.digitallearning.macfound.org/
2. Beer, D., Burrows, R.: Sociology and, of and in Web 2.0: Some Initial Considerations. Sociological Research Online 12(5), 17 (2007), http://www.socresonline.org.uk/12/5/17.html
3. Davis, F.D., Bagozzi, R.P., Warshaw, P.R.: User acceptance of computer technology: A comparison of two theoretical models. Manag. Sci. 35, 982–1003 (1989)
4. Ma, Q., Liu, L.: The technology acceptance model: A meta-analysis of empirical findings. J. of Organizational and End User Computing 16, 59–72 (2004)
5. Berger, A., Caspers, T., Croll, J., Hoffmann, J., Kubicek, H., Peter, U., Ruth-Janneck, D., Trump, T.: Web 2.0 / barrierefrei: Eine Studie zur Nutzung von Web 2.0 Anwendungen durch Menschen mit Behinderungen. Aktion Mensch e.V., POB, 53175 Bonn (2010)

Automated Accessibility Evaluation Software for Authenticated Environments

A Heuristic Usability Evaluation

Elisa Maria Pivetta, Daniela Satomi Saito, Carla da Silva Flor,
Vania Ribas Ulbricht, and Tarcísio Vanzin

Post-graduate Program in Knowledge Engineering and Management,
Federal University of Santa Catarina, Florianópolis, SC, Brazil
elisa@cafw.ufsm.br,
{daniela.saito,carla.flor,vrulbricht,tvanzin}@gmail.com

Abstract. Web accessibility has been the subject of much discussion regarding the need to make Web content accessible to all people, regardless of their abilities or disabilities. While some testing techniques require human intervention, accessibility can also be evaluated by automated tools. Automated evaluation tools are software programs that examine the code of Web pages to determine if they conform to a set of accessibility guidelines that are often based on the Web Content Accessibility Guidelines Version 2.0 (WCAG 2.0), developed by the World Wide Web Consortium (W3C). In this context, the purpose of this study is to analyze an automated software program for evaluating authenticated environments and verify the usability of this tool, since automated systems require precision and reliability in terms of both results and use in any type of environment. With this in mind, this paper aimed at evaluating the ASES software by means of a heuristic evaluation carried out by three experts. The analysis revealed major accessibility problems, as well as improper functioning of available tools and inconsistency of results. Furthermore, ASES was found to have problems of efficiency, interaction, validity, and reliability in the results presented. Considering that this is an open-source accessibility testing tool that can be found on a government web site, the correction or improvement of the system's deficiencies identified in this study is highly recommended, as there is a lack of software available to evaluate authenticated environments.

Keywords: Automated evaluation tool, heuristic evaluation, usability.

1 Introduction

Web accessibility has been the subject of much discussion regarding the need to make web content accessible to all people, regardless of their abilities or disabilities. According to the W3C [1], web accessibility refers to allowing all people to perceive, understand, navigate, interact with and contribute to the web.

C. Stephanidis and M. Antona (Eds.): UAHCI/HCII 2014, Part IV, LNCS 8516, pp. 77–88, 2014.

In this context, accessibility evaluation encompasses a range of procedures aimed at detecting known accessibility problems, such as violations of guidelines, system failures, errors, or user performance indicators [2]. Several approaches have been used to assess the accessibility of a site. Automated evaluation tools, for example, are software programs that test virtual environments for accessibility by analyzing their code to determine how well they meet the guidelines established for the inspection.

According to [3], evaluation methods differ in terms of their validity, usefulness, reliability, and efficiency. With these considerations in mind, the purpose of this study was to analyze automated software designed to evaluate authenticated environments in order to verify its usability precision and reliability. The software selected for analysis is referred to as ASES (Site Accessibility Evaluator and Simulator) [4]. The criteria used for tool selection focused on the compliance with the WCAG 2.0, subscription to the open-source philosophy, and validation of an authenticated environment – in this case, Moodle [5]. In an initial survey, seven automated accessibility evaluation tools were identified, but only two were selected: WAVE and ASES.

The objective of the first phase of this study was to evaluate WAVE, and the results are described in [6]. The present paper reports on the second phase, which centered on the examination of the ASES software. The analysis was performed by three experts, as suggested by Nielsen [7], and consisted of conducting a heuristic usability test founded on the ergonomic criteria presented in [8]. Each of the experts analyzed the tool according to criteria based on a severity scale. After the individual evaluations were completed, each evaluator verified the arguments used by their colleagues in order for them to reach a consensus and assign a collective score. In doing so, errors found individually could be assessed and reassessed by all experts.

2   Automated Evaluation Software

Automated evaluation software, also known as validator, evaluator and online validator, scans the code of a web page and checks its content for accessibility. These tools help determine if a given interface was developed according to accessibility standards [9].

Some of the automated accessibility validation software tools available online for free meet the minimum requirement for selection – i.e., compliance with the recommendations of both WCAG 1.0 and WCAG 2.0. The initial plan was to choose from the pool of programs suggested by WAI, but the list was found to be outdated[1], as none of the tools singled out adhere to the standards for accessibility set forth in WCAG 2.0. Thus, we used the programs picked out by [10] in addition to other tools identified by the authors of the present work. Table 1 presents the selected tools.

---

[1] http://www.w3.org/WAI/ER/tools/complete

Table 1. Automated Evaluation Tools

Software	Description
Access Monitor	It generates an accessibility report and a summary of results with an evaluation score that sums up and measures the level of accessibility achieved [11]. WAI Conformance Levels: A, AA, AAA.
AChecker (Public)	The results are grouped into three categories: known, likely, and potential problems [12]. WAI Conformance Levels: A, AA, AAA.
ASES 2.0	It is a tool designed to support compliance with existing accessibility guidelines in government web sites. Conforms to the standards proposed in the WCAG 2.0 [9] and e-MAG 3.0 [13]. WAI Conformance Levels: A, AA, AAA.
TAW3	It presents three categories of accessibility violations: problems, warnings, and not reviewed [14]. WAI Conformance Levels: A, AA (AAA: commercial).
WAAT	Java application [16]. WAI Conformance Levels: A, AA, AAA.
WAVE	It offers four types of reports as follows: errors, features and alerts; reading order and structure of the page; page display in text-only format; and identification of page headings [17]. WAI Conformance Levels: A, AA, AAA.
Worldspace FireEyes	Add-on for the Firefox browser, it tests static and dynamic content [18]. WAI Conformance Levels: A, AA.

Among the tools listed in Table 1, Worldspace FireEyes [18] and TAW3 [14] were excluded from analysis for testing for accessibility in only two of the three levels of compliance – A and AA.. It is noteworthy that the success criteria adopted for each level are determined according to the degree of difficulty individuals with disabilities are likely to experience when accessing information on the web, as compared to other audiences. Thus, the the A, AA, and AAA levels are relevant to the verification.

The next step was to run the other software tools and evaluate them with a Moodle environment being used for the testing. Some of the programs failed the evaluation process, proving to be only suitable for use in areas in which access is open. Only two of the tools listed in Table 1 obtained successful results in authenticated environments: WAVE [17] and ASES [4].

Then, the research process was divided into two parts: the first phase consisted of a study of the WAVE tool, as presented in [6]; the second phase, described in this paper, centered on the examination of the ASES software. The analysis was found to be opportune, as ASES was designed to evaluate the accessibility of web pages and is offered for download on a government web site.

A search was conducted using the CAPES[2] database and the search engine Google.com to take stock of the state of the art in the area. The results obtained called for an evaluation of ASES, for the only existing work on the subject was conducted by [19] and consisted of a review of the Lattes Platform[3] using the ASES software. No studies providing an evaluation of the tool were found.

---

[2] http://www.periodicos.capes.gov.br.ez47.
periodicos.capes.gov.br/
[3] A Plataforma Lattes integra bases de dados de currículos, grupos de pesquisa e instituições brasileiras. http://lattes.cnpq.br/

2.1   ASES Software

ASES, the Portuguese acronym for Site Accessibility Evaluator and Simulator, is a Web site designed to support the adoption of accessibility guidelines by government agencies. It is free software released under the GNU Lesser General Public License (LGPL), and its features are described both on the web site [4] and in the software manual. ASES offers the following functions:

- Accessibility Evaluator – examines the source code of web pages to determine their level of adherence to established practices presented in the WCAG 2.0 [9] and e-MAG 3.0 [13] documents;
- CSS Validator – checks whether the CSS code conforms to the accessibility standards devised by the W3C;
- HTML (4.01 and XHTML) Validator – inspects HTML/XHTML syntax to ensure it complies with the W3C specifications;
- Screen Reader Emulator – calculates the shortest amount of time a screen-reader user would take to reach a certain point of a Web page;
- Low Vision Simulator – simulates conditions or disabilities that impair vision, such as hyperopia, myopia, color blindness, cataracts, glaucoma, and retinopathy;
- Visual Descriptor - associates images with their textual equivalents;
- Systematic Analysis of Images – checks the lack of text-alternatives to the same image on several different pages;
- Alternative Content for Script Tags – provides alternative content for script tags;
- Alternative Content for Object Tags – provides alternative content for object tags;
- Label Placement – helps ensure all form controls have descriptive labels;
- Insert DocType – assigns DocTypes (headers at the top of HTML documents) to the desired pages;
- Form Filler – helps fill in the blanks on a form;
- Device-Dependent Event Handler – points out events that require the user to have any specific input device that is missing, such as "onMouseClick" and "onMouseOver". It also allows users to edit events to call a JavaScript function;
- Redundant Links for Image Maps – provides redundant links to image maps.

The first part of the evaluation process consisted of installing the ASES software and verifying its functionality in order to, later, analyze the tool according to the guidelines and recommendations of the WAI [15].

3   Evaluating the ASES Software – Methodology

Heuristic evaluation was the usability inspection method used to evaluate ASES. In a heuristic evaluation, experts can either put their knowledge of typical user behavior to use throughout the evaluation process [20], [21] or examine specific aspects of inter-faces. Heuristics act as mnemonics for the evaluator's existing knowledge that can be applied to the analysis of usability and accessibility issues.

For this type of testing, [22] suggests using from 3 to 5 reviewers to achieve a favorable benefit-cost ratio. Thus, the selected software tools were evaluated by three experts: two of them completed both their Bachelor's and Master's degree in Computer Science, and the third graduated with a degree in Design and holds a Master of Science in Knowledge Engineering and Management. The three evaluators are doctoral candidates and participate in a research group on web accessibility.

In this context, the evaluation process was performed using the steps adapted from [20] and [21]:

1. Study Design – definition of the heuristics to be used and their form of evaluation;
2. Evaluation Script – a guide is prepared to take the experts through the process;
3. Evaluation Period – each expert spends 1-2 hours independently inspecting the product, using the heuristics as guidance;
4. Findings and Problem Identification – by using the heuristics as the evaluation framework, the aspects that are not in line with the established practices are detected and recorded as problems;
5. Analysis, Evaluation, and Reporting – once identified, the problems are rated according to their severity level, and experts propose solutions to be presented in a report.

4   Evaluation Process

This section is intended to describe the methodological steps in conducting the evaluation of the ASES software.

4.1   Study Design

In view of the steps described for the first part of the evaluation process, we developed a set of heuristics for the accessibility testing using the ergonomic criteria proposed by [8] as a reference. They are as follows:

1. Guidance – refers to the means available to advise, orient, inform, and guide the users throughout their interactions with a computer (messages, navigation, alarms, etc);
2. Workload – concerns all interface elements that play an important role in reducing the users' cognitive and perceptual load and increasing the dialogue efficiency;
3. Explicit control – concerns both the system processing of explicit user actions, and the control users have on the processing of their actions by the system;
4. Flexibility – refers to the means available to the users to edit or customize the interface according to their needs;
5. Error Management – refers to the means available to prevent or reduce errors and to recover from them when they occur;
6. Homogeneity/consistency – refers to the way interface design choices are maintained in similar contexts, and are different when applied to different contexts;

7. Significance of codes and names – refers to how clear and meaningful the codes and names are to the users of the system;

8. Compatibility – refers to the match between the system and the users' expectations and needs when performing a task. It also concerns the coherence between environments and between applications;

9. Help and Documentation – relates to the ease of access to the system. The easier a system is to use, the smaller is the need for help or documentation. When required, Help should be easily accessible;

10. System Status – concerns the provision of information about what is going on with the system and of appropriate feedback within reasonable time.

When evaluating the heuristics presented above, a severity scale was used by the evaluators to estimate each problem's severity and frequency of occurrence, as well as the level of difficulty in overcoming it [23]. By doing so, it was possible to determine the scale values shown in Table 1.

Table 2. Scale used for rating severity of problems identified

Value	Evaluation	Description
0	I don't agree that this is a usability problem at all	This value may be obtained from the evaluation of an expert about a problem pointed out by another expert
1	Cosmetic problem only	Need not be fixed unless extra time is available
2	Minor usability problem	Fixing this should be given low priority
3	Major usability problem	Important to fix, so should be given high priority
4	Usability catastrophe	It is imperative to fix this

Source: Adapted from [23].

4.2 Evaluation Script

The script is a description of the procedures to be adopted by each of the experts in the evaluation process. It contains the instructions to conduct the testing and details the steps 3 and 4 of the methodology, namely, evaluation period and findings and problem identification, respectively. Each of the experts participating in the evaluation process was provided with the following information and recommendations:

1. Introduction to the ASES software;
2. Overview of the evaluation objectives;
3. Definition of the evaluation context – Moodle was considered a convenient environment for being a platform, used in a public universities, in which access is authorized via user authentication;
4. Time required to complete the task;
5. Criteria for use – outline of the heuristics to be used in the evaluation;
6. Rating scale – severity levels to be assigned to each dimension evaluated.
7. Recommendations as to the conduction of the evaluation process:

(a) Evaluating all of the software tools available – Accessibility Evaluator (evaluation of guidelines, contrast and screen reader), Source-code Checker (CSS, HTML 4.01 and XHTML), Tag Analyzer (Image and Object), Editors (Doctype and Events);

(b) Inspecting each area of the software at least twice:
   (i) In the first inspection, evaluators should work separately and avoid interaction with one other, assigning scores and taking notes of observations about the problems and errors found. This procedure is crucial for ensuring independent and unbiased reviews;
   (ii) In the second inspection, experts come together to discuss their scores and share their findings. Following peer review, evaluators may assign a new score if they wish to do so.

4.3   Evaluation Period

Evaluations were supposed to be completed within the recommended time frame of 1–2 hours, but, due to implementation problems, this time restriction was removed and experts were allowed to take as much time as necessary to conduct their analyses. The tests were performed on four computers, with some variations in the configuration of the equipment, as specified below:

- Windows Seven, 32 bit, 2 Gb RAM, 10-inch screen monitor;
- Windows Seven Professional, 64 bit, 2Gb RAM, 13-inch screen monitor;
- Windows Seven, 64 bit, 8 Gb RAM, 14-inch screen monitor;
- Windows Seven Professional, 64 bit, 4Gb RAM, 14-inch screen monitor;

A virtual learning environment based on the Moodle platform was selected for testing the program, so as to verify the scope and quality of an evaluation conducted on a web site in which users are allowed access via user authentication. In order to do so, a password was required to provide access to Moodle and inform ASES about the internal address of the environment, i.e., the URL (Uniform Resource Locator) to be tested.

4.4   Findings and Problem Identification

Initially, the analyses were conducted individually by each expert, as described in the evaluation script. Subsequently, once problems had been identified and notes had been taken, the results were discussed by the group so that each participant could review the scores assigned to the tools. Final evaluations were obtained by calculating the mean of the individual scores and the ratings determined by consensus between the evaluators.

Table 3 presents the results regarding to Accessibility Evaluator tool. The table below shows the mean rates of severity assigned by the experts to each heuristic evaluated and the observations describe the results of their analyses.

Table 3. Mean ratings and observation by experts

Heuristics	Mean rate	Relevant observations by Experts
Guidance	3	- Moving between open windows is confusing. - Some items only work by double-clicking on them, rather than by single-clicking, which is the default method. - When a report is being generated, there is an option to view in detail the page evaluated. However, there is no clear indication of this possibility, which may prevent the user from accessing the window for a "detailed view of the evaluation."
Workload	4	- In the "Save As" dialog box, the default file type for documents is not a valid format. - Switching between the Default Source and Edit Source tabs makes correction difficult, especially when a large number of errors are found. Note: the errors of the WCAG are only visible in the Default Source tab.
Explicit Control	4	- It is not possible to verify if the error or warning of the WCAG was corrected after editing the code. - Each time the source code is edited, the system asks if changes are to be saved. The user should be able to save the changes only when editing is completed. - The user is not able to capture the colors of the Web site evaluated using the contrast checker. - No feedback is given regarding the action being executed.
Flexibility	3	- The system allows users to increase or decrease font size and change color contrast options, but the shortcut keys are reversed. - Users are not able to search through the source code. - It does not allow users to adjust the layouts for code visualization (Default Source and Edit Source).
Error management	3	- The error message shown when the Accessibility Evaluator was accessed ("unable to access page content") does not provide any explanation to prevent the error from happening or help the user correct it.
Homogeneity/consistency	4	- Inconsistency between the number of errors presented in the summary report and those found in the detailed view of each page, in which only the eMAG-related errors could be visualized. - The features available in "Edit Source" and "Default Source" are not consistent with the other software functions. - The available formats in the "Save" and "Save As..." functions are not consistent with the other software features. - The "Save PDF Report" option does not provide information about what type of report is to be saved, but in the version in the ASES format this information piece is provided by the system. - There is no standardization of window messages. - Inconsistency and differences as far as icons and messages are concerned – that is, sometimes they appear and at other times they do not.
Significance of codes and names	2	- Use of unclear and/or unexpressive terms and abbreviations. - "Open URL" in the CSS Validator does not specify whether the URL should be a CSS or HTML file.

Table 3. (*continued*)

Compatibility	4	- The tool did not provide a complete evaluation of the authenticated area.
		- In the detailed view of the accessibility evaluation of pages, the only visible tab is Edit Code, which does not show the errors to be corrected. In order to visualize and correct the errors, it is necessary to switch between the Default Code and Edit Code tabs, rendering the completion of the task counterproductive.
Help and documentation	3	- Not all of the tools are working as indicated in the manual. - The manual is incomplete.
System status	4	- The system crashes. - The accessibility evaluator does not respond when reports are being generated and no feedback is given, as if no function was being run. - The results presented refer to the first Web site evaluated. - The low vision simulator does not work and no message is displayed when clicking on it.

4.5   Analysis, Evaluation and Reporting

This section presents the analysis and evaluation of the features available in the ASES software. In general, basic accessibility problems were identified in the interactions with the program, mostly because ASES did not show much flexibility. The enter and tab keys did not work when replacing the mouse. In this regard, it should be noted that navigation and tool usage via keyboard shortcuts is a basic accessibility requirement for software items. The options of increasing and decreasing font size and adjusting the contrast of the screen allowed for greater flexibility, but these functions were not available within all software areas.

Even with these problems, the scores assigned by the experts were similar for most of the heuristics, as evidenced in Table 2. As far as the divergences are concerned, in order to reach a consensus, the heuristics were reviewed and a new evaluation of the problems detected was jointly conducted.

Regarding the final results obtained, the problems associated with workload, homogeneity/consistency, compatibility, and system status were considered critical and in need of urgent solution.

The workload was affected by the improper functioning of window error messages and source-code warnings, which did not show pertinent data, thereby impairing the efficiency of the inspection task performed by the user.

The lack of homogeneity and consistency was observed in multiple areas of the software. There was no standardization in the system in terms of icons and windows, and save options presented different formats even when they had the same function.

As for compatibility, ASES was not found to be fully supported in authenticated environments, which was one of the assumptions of this study. In certain situations, the tool produced the error report when the authenticated URL was inserted, but when the source code was analyzed, the user was recognized by the system the user as a visitor, rather than as an authenticated user.

The system status was affected by constant system crashes, forcing a reboot of the operating system. The Accessibility Evaluator tool showed different behaviors when used by the experts. With the first expert, the system tested one URL and then stopped working. With the second and third experts, the results of the attempts to evaluate other URLs were reported in the reviews of the first address tested. However, after changing computers, the third expert was only able to conduct the check once, and then the tool did not work anymore. All experts tried to perform their tasks by closing down and restarting the software. However, they were not successful in this strategy. Other issues such as lack of feedback and system malfunctions of the Low Vision Simulator were also pointed out.

Still concerning the status of the system, the Alternate Content for Script Tags evaluation tool ran smoothly, but provided no feedback, i.e., it did not show whether or not there were errors. In this situation, it was not possible to know if the lack of response means that no errors were found. Ideally, a message should be sent as feedback whenever possible. For instance, in the Label Placement tool, when the site evaluated was correct, messages such as "Congratulations" were generated by the system. Another observation is that this tool, unlike the others, did not show the original source code, only the editable code.

Although not rated at a level of severity as high as that assigned to the previous heuristics, issues related to guidance, error management, flexibility, and help and documentation were considered relevant problems that should be given high priority, requiring corrections to improve software usability.

The guidance framework for software structure and navigation between open windows and tools was considered confusing. Apart from that, some functions only worked by double-clicking and the system did not provide any visual indication to inform the user that another window could be accessed from a certain moment on.

Regarding error management, no messages appeared to indicate when the tool was unable to access certain content. In addition, experts also noted the lack of possibilities for correction and provision of solutions when problems occurred. In the CSS Validator, the Doctype element was not recognized as a CSS document, which is true. However, the system defined it as an error, and this is neither an accessibility problem nor an error on the page.

With respect to help and documentation, ASES presented a detailed but incomplete manual and the Redundant Links for Image Maps tool, which could not be found when using the software.

Difficulties related to explicit user control were reported when using the Contrast Checker, since this tool only allows users to enter the values referring to the background and foreground colors of the page to be tested, not allowing them to pick colors from web pages through the feature known as eyedropper. For this reason, users are forced to use a graphics software program and have it installed on their computer. Problems related to Save options, the checking of errors, and WCAG warnings also posed difficulties to tool management.

Finally, the Significance of Codes and Names was considered a minor problem. With respect to this heuristic, the CSS Validator had a confusing denomination for the

"Open URL" feature, as, although it was possible to insert any hyperlink in the form, the tool only evaluates CSS files.

5   Final Remarks

This study evaluated the usability of automated accessibility evaluation software for an authenticated virtual environment. Software programs in this category present different approaches, formats, features, and benefits, and some perform a number of tests while others underestimate the problems on a web site. The ideal choice for a tool depends on a set of functions and on how the evaluator defines the priorities of the site to be tested. In this sense, the following validation criteria adopted, this study aimed to test the ASES automated evaluation software based on WCAG 2.0.

As previously discussed, experts identified the problems associated with the Workload, Explicit Control, Homogeneity/Consistency, Compatibility, and System Status criteria as the most critical ones. The analysis showed that the tool is not easy to use and has several problems that hamper access for users. The instability of the tool was found to be an obstacle to its usability, and the frequent errors, with no possibility of correction, revealed an inconsistent system.

Regarding the Guidance, Error Management, Flexibility, and Help and Documentation criteria, the results point to the need of having correction as a high priority. On the other hand, the errors relating to the Significance of Codes and Names were regarded as a minor problem that should be given low priority.

When testing an authenticated environment, ASES not always performs the analysis starting from the authenticated page, which prevents the use of this tool for projects of this kind. Moreover, the program may give not-so-attentive users the impression that the testing was performed on the URL address provided, leading to false expectations about the results of the analysis. In order to better understand the indications of errors and warnings of ASES, it is important that the users have some knowledge of computing. Also, because the automated evaluation tools give more technical results, a bit of coding knowledge is required.

We suggest that this accessibility evaluation tool be adapted to conform to the guidelines developed by the WAI, considering its four basic principles – perception, operation, understandability, and robustness, so that error reports, warnings, and other items can be classified within these categories. Adjustments to the problems identified are also recommended, mainly due to the lack of software able to assess authenticated environments.

Based on the results of the evaluation of ASES, we conclude that the software is not stable and the functionality of its tools depends on the performance of the system in which they operate. Thus, in order for the results of accessibility evaluations performed by ASES to be reliable, the system's interface should be redesigned and adaptations should be made with a view to achieving greater usability.

Finally, this analysis was not intended to promote, support, or degrade the software listed in this paper; rather, it aimed at encouraging the development of more usable accessibility evaluation tools.

References

1. World Wide Web Consortium, http://www.w3.org/
2. Brajnik, G.: Beyond conformance: The role of accessibility evaluation methods. In: Hartmann, S., Zhou, X., Kirchberg, M. (eds.) WISE 2008. LNCS, vol. 5176, pp. 63–80. Springer, Heidelberg (2008)
3. Brajnik, G.: Web Accessibility Testing: when the method is the culprit. In: Miesenberger, K., Klaus, J., Zagler, W.L., Karshmer, A.I. (eds.) ICCHP 2006. LNCS, vol. 4061, pp. 156–163. Springer, Heidelberg (2006)
4. ASES - Avaliador e Simulador para a Acessibilidade de Sítios, http://www.governoeletronico.gov.br/acoes-e-projetos/e-MAG/ases-avaliador-e-simulador-de-acessibilidade-sitios
5. Moodle.org, http://www.moodle.org
6. Pivetta, E.M., Flor, C., Saito, D.S., Ulbricht, V.R.: Analysis of an automatic accessibility evaluator to validate a virtual and authenticated environment. International Journal of Advanced Computer Science and Applications 4, 15–22 (2013)
7. Nielsen, J.: Why You Only Need to Test with 5 Users (2000), http://www.nngroup.com/articles/why-you-only-need-to-test-with-5-users/
8. LabUtil: Laboratório de utilizabilidade: critérios ergonômicos, http://www.labiutil.inf.ufsc.br/CriteriosErgonomicos/LabIUtil2003-Crit/100conduc.html
9. Web Content Accessibility Guidelines 2.0, http://www.w3.org/TR/WCAG20
10. Al-Khalifa, H.S., Al-Kanhal, M., Al-Nafisah, H., Al-soukaih, N., Al-hussain, E., Al-onzi, M.: A Pilot Study for Evaluating Arabic Websites Usign Automated WCAG 2.0 Evaluation Tools. In: Proceedings of the 2011 International Conference on Innovations In Information Technology. IEEE Computer Society, Saudi Arabia (2011)
11. UMIC - Agência para a Sociedade do Conhecimento, http://www.acessibilidade.gov.pt/accessmonitor/
12. AChecker, http://achecker.ca/checker/index.php
13. e-MAG – Modelo de Acessibilidade de Governo Eletrônico – versão 3.0 (2011), http://www.governoeletronico.gov.br/biblioteca/arquivos/e-mag-3.0/download
14. TAW, http://www.tawdis.net/
15. Web Accessibility Initiative, http://www.w3.org/WAI/
16. Web Accessibility Assessment Tool, http://www.accessible-eu.org/
17. Web Accessibility Evaluation Tool, http://wave.webaim.org
18. Worldspace FireEyes, http://www.deque.com/products/worldspace-fireeyes
19. Barbosa, G.A.R., Santos, N.S.S., Reis, S.S., Prates, R.O.: Relatório da Avaliação de Acessibilidade da Plataforma Lattes do CNPq sob a Perspectiva de Deficientes Visuais. In: Anais Estendidos do IHC 2010, Belo Horizonte, Minas Gerais, pp. 139–150 (2010)
20. Paddison, C., Englefield, P.: Applying heuristics to accessibility inspections. Interacting with Computers 16, 507–521 (2004)
21. Preece, J., Rogers, Y., Sharp, H.: Design de Interação - Além da interação homem-computador. Bookman, Porto Alegre (2005)
22. Nielsen, J.: Topic: Heuristic Evaluation (1997), http://www.nngroup.com/topic/heuristic-evaluation/
23. Prates, R.O., Barbosa, S.D.J.: Avaliação de interfaces de usuário: conceitos e métodos. In: XXIII Congresso Nacional da Sociedade Brasileira de Computação, SBC, Rio de Janeiro, pp. 1–43 (2003)

High-Literate and Low-Literate User Interaction: A Comparative Study Using Eyetracking in an Emergent Economy

Letícia Régis Di Maio[1], Ney Wagner Freitas Cavalcante[1], Simone Bacellar Leal Ferreira[1], José Luiz dos Anjos Rosa[2], and Aline Silva Alves[3]

[1] Departamento de Informática Aplicada, Universidade Federal do Estado do Rio de Janeiro, Rio de Janeiro, Brazil
{leticiaregis,ney.cavalcante,simone}@uniriotec.br
[2] Centro Universitário Estadual da Zona Oeste, Rio de Janeiro, Brazil
jrosa@uezo.rj.gov.br
[3] Fundação Oswaldo Cruz, Rio de Janeiro, Brazil
aalves@fiocruz.br

Abstract. The information technology including, increasingly, the services offered to citizens, this necessitates the development of web pages accessible to everyone, regardless of education level. Whereas a significant portion of the Brazilian population is within the low literacy profile, the objective of this research was to analyze the different forms of navigation among users of high and low literacy. Data were collected through user testing through eye tracking. The experiences of interaction were performed from two tasks initiated in the Google search engine and completed in two popular sites. At the end, some suggestions were proposed interface improvements.

Keywords: Accessibility, Low-Literate Users, Eyetracking, Interface.

1 Introduction

The frequent use of technology is growing worldwide. Currently, there is a gradual migration of daily routines, to the electronic mean and the Web tools became part of everyday life [17] and perform a social role especially for users with disabilities [10].

Access to information should be facilitated and guaranteed, so this migration brings new challenges to researchers and systems developers, since their interfaces need to be accessible to all users' profiles.

To help users to retrieve web content, search engines are often used: 80% of the access to Web pages comes from these tools [20]. Search involves analyzing different types of media, so it is a mentally exhausting activity that requires focus and attention [7],[13]. But there are users who have limitations related to literacy that can jeopardize the interaction mainly because the available content on the Web is mostly textual [10], [12]. The most usability problems on the Web are related to finding, reading and understanding information [17]. People with low reading skills have these problems

C. Stephanidis and M. Antona (Eds.): UAHCI/HCII 2014, Part IV, LNCS 8516, pp. 89–100, 2014.

magnified due to lack of language skills, so it is characterized also as an accessibility issue. The lack of these skills affects the way people interact with computer interfaces as search engine [9],[6], used to retrieve Web content, that is predominantly textual [7].

Users with low reading skills have peculiarities that should be considered on the design and development of sites, such as content perception limitations and search strategies [6],[9]. So, they use the web in a different way from those users whom have high reading skills [3],[10],[14]. The aim of this research was observed and analyze users, with two different profiles (high-literate users and users with low reading skills), toward to identify their experience and interaction details, during queries formulations on search engine, Google, and the desired information from two different popular commercial sites.

The United Nations Educational, Scientific and Cultural Organization (UNESCO) [14] considers as functionally illiterate, persons lacking in reading, writing, calculation and science skills, whose level of schooling is equivalent to less than four years of school attendance. This classification, adopted by the National Institute of Education Studies and Research Anísio Teixeira (INEP) and the Brazilian Institute of Geography and Statistics (IBGE) [21], [8] was utilized. According to the Brazilian agency, the rate of functional illiteracy at the year 2013 in Brazil was estimated at 20% of the total.

To observe the users interactions, it was adopted the eyetracking method to collect data. It was used the Tobii T120 eye tracker equipment from Tobii Technology [19]. To investigate the relevance between text and image in the information available on the sites analyzed, the pattern of saccadic movements and fixations was used.

For the tasks execution, ten users were observed, five for each profile. This number was defined taking in account the recommendations proposed by Nielsen [18]. As the number of users increases, the information that is collected tends to repeat itself, providing a smaller amount of news information. According to research, five users are able to detect 85% of usability problems [18]. To select and define the users' profile, the volunteers answered to a questionnaire [1].

During the tests, the participants perfomed two queries on a search engine (Google) and completed the determined tasks on two different commercial sites, selected based on the familiarity with their physical stores. The time complete the tasks was established among researchers, but unknown by users to promote naturalness during the interaction.

Besides the eyetracking, direct observation method (in which researchers observes the path followed during navigation) and thinking aloud verbal protocol were adopted.

The tests were conducted in a controlled laboratory environment. After responding the questionnaire and signing a consent term, the eyetracking equipment was introduced to each participant. After calibration, tasks, printed on sheets, were presented to the users. A short questionnaire was filled by users at the end of each task, to verify the difficulties around the task, and find out interface improvement suggestions.

2 Literacy in Brazil

Literacy can be analyzed by different perspectives and conceptualized in different ways. A common understanding about literacy involves oral, reading and writing skills, besides abilities with logic, mathematics, symbolic analysis (images and sounds) and text interpretation [21]. In fact, the concept of functional illiteracy varies from region to region. Nowadays it is a common approach to consider that these skills must be contextualized and they are not developed equally among different individuals. Besides, literacy concept also considers functional aspect that means the ability to apply oral, reading and writing on different areas of daily life, as in computing, ecology, health and other areas [21].

The United Nations Educational, Scientific and Cultural Organization [14],[21] considers as functionally illiterate people between 15 and 64 years old, which lack mastery of skills in reading, writing, calculations and science, corresponding to an education of less than four years of study [4],[14]. This classification, adopted by the National Institute of Education Studies and Research Anísio Teixeira (INEP) and the Brazilian Institute of Geography and Statistics (IBGE) [21] was utilized in the present work. A research performed by IBGE showed that 29 million people in Brazil are functional illiterate that means more than 20% of the total population [14]. In this work, we adopt this concept but we call the participants as "low literate users", once one of the protocols used to guide the study recommended not to call them functional illiterates [3].

There are other criteria that could be used instead of considering only age and years of study on formal education. There are institutions that developed specific literacy and numeracy tests, with levels of difficulty and punctuation, to evaluate people's skills in reading, writing, calculations and science. However, these tests are private, so there are no public tools that allow us to classify users this way [3].

2.1 Eyetracking and Tests with Users

Eyetracking is the technology that allows tracking ocular movements of the observer by means of infra-red rays, recording both the course taken by the eye and its focus point [2]. Once it has tracked the course taken by the user's eyes, it can support the development and improvement of the interface, which, if well designed, can become a source of motivation or, conversely, become a decisive factor in rejecting the system [5].

Within the web context, it is important to consider the functionally illiterate as potential users and propose accessible technological solutions for this group, taking into consideration the accessibility guidelines [16]. One of the drawbacks for low-literacy users is text comprehension. Intelligibility is the word used to describe the characteristic of a text that is easy to read and understand. Easy texts can compensate for low levels of prior knowledge, poor reading skills, or lack of interest or motivation [2].

Thus, the proposed solutions should be made adequate to the more learned public, while guaranteeing that it can be easily read and understood by functional illiterates as well [3].

2.2   Related Works

In his research studies, Barboza [2] put together an interesting bibliographical survey on usability and on the plain and simple language used on government websites for those with high or low literacy, where he also mentions the use of eye tracking. However, he did not apply tests to the above mentioned users.

In his work, Lukasova [11] used eyetracking in conjunction with Functional Magnetic Resonance tests to investigate changes in behavior and neural functioning in children and adults with the aim of contributing to future studies for specific clinical groups, such as developmental dyslexia, autism and schizophrenia. Despite the relevance of this work, the author did not use adults with any type of deficiency or learning difficulty.

3   Research Method

The current research study, of an exploratory nature, is based on the qualitative method of data collection consisting of four stages, as described below:

a. Selecting the profile of users to take part in the study: ten adults were chosen, forming two distinct groups. The first group was composed of 5 adults with at most three years of schooling, i.e., less than 4 years of completed formal studies in accordance with the UNESCO [21] classification. The second group, composed of 5 fully literate adults, had 5 years or more of schooling. All participants have at least three months of practical knowledge of web browsing and are between the ages of 18 and 64.

b. Selecting sites and defining tasks: two commercial sites for popular Brazilian stores were chosen according to the profile of the users. In the first store - "Casa Show," which sells construction materials, - the user was supposed to look up the price of a certain item. In the second store - "Óticas do Povo", which sells eyeglasses, - the user was supposed to find the address of a specific shop location.

c. Case Study: a case study was set up for the two groups showing their performance of the required tasks (details in section 4).

d. Data analysis: Eyetracking technology generates complementary results to those of traditional usability tests, with reports on user web browsing [19]. The data provided by this type of test come in various formats (quantitative, statistical, with images and videos), showing the path covered sequentially during browsing, indicating the duration at each focus point of the participant's eyes, and capable of detecting where there was more cognitive effort or likely problems of non-explored usability. The results of the use of eyetracking tests are presented in section 5 of the Data Analysis.

3.1   Limitations

It was necessary to categorize users and so the UNESCO classification was chosen, which has been adopted by the Brazilian Institute of Geography and Statistics (IBGE). If other tests had been chosen to assess reading and writing abilities of users, other results might have been obtained. Despite the wide range of ages adopted as a criterion, users having the same level of schooling and similar computer skills were chosen, so as to minimize a possible bias caused by the age criterion.

4   Case Study

Preparation of Test Environment: Initially, researchers defined user profiles and classified them in two distinct groups, with 5 participants in each, being that the first group contained members with little schooling and the second, members with higher schooling. Then invitations to join the research study were sent out to associations, universities and community centers outlining the educational profile of the users in question. Eleven users were willing to join the study, being that one of them was selected for the pilot test.

Implementation of Tests: One of the users was given a pilot test which was comprised of two tasks to be performed on two commercial sites of popular Brazilian shops, and only then was the test given to the remaining 10 users. All users signed an informed consent form in order to partake of the study which was read out loud by the researchers. Further clarification about the research work at hand was also provided at this time. Afterwards participants replied to a printed questionnaire, which had been used for the profile classification according to each one's declared schooling time.

Next, the Eyetracking equipment was introduced and each participant had his eyes calibrated by the machine, besides receiving the necessary information about posture and concentration in order to avoid possible loss of registration by the tracking device. The number of tasks required on the test was outlined, as well as the freedom and the expected autonomy each user would have to perform said tasks, before seeking help from the researchers. To assure anonymity of participants, their names were entered in code as follows: LL_01, LL_02, LL_03, LL_04 e LL_05 for the low-literacy group and HL_01, HL_02, HL_03, HL_04 e HL_05, for high-literacy users. Table 1 shows the profile of each participant and the total time needed to perform each task.

In order to understand better the logical and strategic content that led each user to make a decision while undertaking a task, be it due to error, misapplication or distraction, participants were requested to verbalize their thoughts after the assessment session, i.e., a protocol of consecutive verbalization was adopted. Simultaneous verbalization was not chosen because according to the "Web Accessibility Assessment Protocols for Functional Illiterates" proposed by Capra [3],[4], simultaneous verbalization is a barrier for low-literacy users.

Table 1. Users profile

Basic users data				
User	Age	Formal Education	Execution time task 1	Execution time task 2
LL_01	59	3 years of schooling	06 min e 50s	05min e 22s
LL_02	64	3 years of schooling	04min e 05s	10min e 03s
LL_03	58	3 years of schooling	02min e 42s	06min e 55s
LL_04	62	3 years of schooling	02min e 22s	06min e 49s
LL_05	59	3 years of schooling	05 min e 31s	05 min e 26s
HL_01	36	PhD	01min e 49s	34s
HL_02	35	Graduate	01min e 02s	36s
HL_03	38	PhD	51s	36s
HL_04	40	PhD	57s	44s
HL_05	33	PhD	46s	39s

Application of Tests: After initial adjustments, the 10 users began taking the tests, which contained the same tasks as the pilot test. A video of the tests was recorded by the tracker whilst researchers took notes using the direct observation technique in sync with the recordings. Each task was oriented with positive comments in order to encourage users to continue the test. Each task was to take 10 minutes, though researchers could only offer their help after the 5 initial minutes had passed. At the end of each task, a questionnaire about the performance of the task was filled out and a quick interview with the user ensued, focused on the interaction process with the sites and the functionality of the tasks. Once the reports had been written, a survey of the data using certain collected metrics during web browsing of participants was made for later comparison with reports generated by eye tracking, model TOBII T120. Ocular tracking equipment can generate the most varied types of reports according to the metrics needed by researchers. Because of this, once the tests had been completed, the Areas of Interest (AOI) that would be relevant for the research were determined. Then quantitative data was extracted, with image and video of each participant showing not only the path taken during browsing, but also the behavior of the user.

5   Data Analysis

In order to analyze the data, the following ocular tracking metrics were adopted: First Fixation Duration (FFD), the duration in seconds of the first fixation on an AOI; Fixation Count(FC), the number of times a participant fixates on an AOI; Mouse Click Count (MCC), the number of times a participant clicks the mouse on an AOI; Time To First Fixation (TTFF), the time elapsed from the stimulus onset to the first fixation on an AOI; and Time To First Mouse Click (TTFMC), the time elapsed until the participant first clicks the mouse on an AOI.

The areas of interest were chosen based on the heat map resource that registered the areas that most caught the attention of participants, as well as interface elements that would receive user interaction in order to finish tasks. The following areas of interest were selected: "Google search button"; "lower Google search button"; "Google search engine on inner page"; "Google search engine"; "upper Google search engine";

"link to the initial site page"; "first Google-sponsored link"; "search suggestion in text area"; "Casa Show search area"; "Casa Show hydraulics menu"; "small water tank image"; "large water tank image"; "Óticas do Povo menu"; "Óticas do Povo central banner"; "Óticas do Povo lower banner"; "Óticas do Povo image map"; "Óticas do Povo text map"; "Óticas do Povo shop address" and "Óticas do Povo Ctrl + F".

5.1   Observations Made during the First Task

During the first task, users were to start at the Google site, then locate the site for the Casa Show shop and consult the price for a 1000 liter Fortlev water tank. On average, the time needed to complete the first task was 258 seconds for low-literacy users, and approximately 65 seconds for high-literacy participants.

1st Step (Searching the Google site): Associating FC metrics (Fixation Count) to the area of interest (AOI) "Google search engine", it was observed that before entering, nine users clicked on the search engine and only one (LL_01) clicked on the "Google search" button. This user commented during consecutive verbalization that he had needed to "turn on" Google by clicking on the button, before initiating the search.

Based on TTFMC metrics (Time To First Mouse Click) in connection with the area of interest (AOI) "Google search engine," one can affirm that on average low-literacy users took 38.8 seconds to click on this field while those of high-literacy took 3.6 seconds.

Regarding the association of MCC metrics (Mouse Click Count) with the AOI "Google search button," it was observed that all participants disregarded the Google search Button and opted to use the ENTER key, with the exception of the first low-literacy user.

The scroll bar resource was used by all low-literacy users, unlike the other group that preferred to use the (Ctrl + F) shortcut, or search fields to the sites.

As regards the association of FC metrics (Fixation Count) and MCC (Mouse Click Count) with the AOI "suggestion of Google search auto-completion," it was possible to note that of the three high-literacy users who read the Google suggestions, only one took advantage of this resource. In contrast, all low-literacy users ignored the suggestions. This behavior had already been ascertained during the study. Capra [4] states that low-literacy users behave differently from high-literacy users. The user's context, such as his country, culture, language, level of schooling, age and experience with computers, also reflects his mental models [5]. Users with less knowledge are less flexible in their search strategies and tend not to resort to new approaches [15].

In relation to the association of the FFD metrics (First Fixation Duration) and TTFMC (Time To First Mouse Click) with the AOIs "link to the initial site page of the task" and "Google sponsored link", it was seen that all low-literacy users became confused with the sponsored links to competitors' sites, in detriment to the attention they should have been paying to links to initial pages of the site proposed in the task. Thus all of them had to reinitiate the task. The tendency to abandon the search was also perceived when they became satisfied with their search results, even though they had not obtained the best or the most correct result, which coincides with the research studies of Modesto [15].

Now the majority of high-literacy users disregarded the sponsored links, paying much more attention to the objectives proposed in the tasks.

The Google search engine site displays search results in two lines: the first as a link (underlined), taking users to another page, and the second (positioned under the link), as a URL of the visited site. Knowing that the link is composed of key words of the search conducted by the user and that not always does the URL associated to the link correspond to the address awaited by the user, it was perceived that the low-literacy participant would get confused with this analysis of results.

As low-literacy participants have difficulty in quickly transferring their attention from one subject to another without getting lost, they could only keep their focus, when typing, either on the text entry field or on the keyboard. The resource had no influence on searches when they were about supplying feedback more quickly to the user [15]. This observation can be confirmed based on the path taken by the eyes (gaze plot) which shows there were more fixations on the links than on the URLs (positioned under each link of the search results.)

2nd Step (Searching the Casa Show site): The initial "Casa Show" site page was visited by 8 participants, 4 of each profile, as shown by TTFF metrics (Time To First Fixation) with the AOI "Casa Show hydraulic menu", being that the behavior of each profile of participants was distinctive. Those at low-literacy levels would browse starting from the vertical site menu, aided by the scroll bar, but only one of them realized that the sub item on the menu containing the option "Hydraulics" would lead to the "water tank" product proposed in the task, which can be proven by FC metrics (Fixation Count) with the above mentioned AOI.

Based on the TTFC metrics (Time To First Fixation) with the AOI "small Casa Show water tank image" it was seen that within those in the low-literacy profile, 3 complied with the task by image fixation, differently from the other 2, who did so by text analysis, as the value of this metric (TTFF) with regard to the area of interest resulted in zero.

Of the 4 high-literacy users who browsed the initial page, only one located the inner page with the product by clicking on the "Hydraulics" option, according to the association between MCC metrics (Mouse Click Count) with the area of interest (AOI) "Casa Show hydraulics menu." The analysis of the MCC metrics (Mouse Click Count) and the AOI "Casa Show search field" allowed researchers to observe that 2 participants of this profile found the inner page with the help of the Casa Show site search field. The other high-literacy user used the site images, according to data obtained by the association between MCC metrics (Mouse Click Count) and the area of interest (AOI) "small water tank image."

By means of the association between FC metrics (Fixation Count) and the AOIs "small water tank image" and "large water tank image" it is possible to state that low-literacy users, before interacting with images related to the researched product, had 3 times greater fixation on the texts than did high-literacy users. To accomplish the task, low-literacy users undertook lengthy reading of the greater part of the information in the texts and only then did they compare this to the images in order to interact with the interface. However, high-literacy participants browsed in a more objective way and perhaps due to greater experience with the Internet, used resources to optimize the search, often disregarding both the menus and the images.

5.2   Observations Made during the Second Task

During the second task, participants were to start at the Google site, then locate the Óticas do Povo site to find the store address in the neighborhood of Campo Grande. The time needed to complete the second task was 415 seconds for low-literacy users, and 38 seconds for high-literacy participants, i.e., the latter were on average eleven times faster.

1st Step (Searching the Google site): With reference to TTFF metrics (Time To First Fixation) and TTFMC (Time To First Mouse Click), one can observe that in order to perform the first step (arrive at the initial "Óticas do Povo") site page, low-literacy users took, on average, 356 seconds, while the high-literacy users took 26 seconds, i.e., the latter were on average 13.6 times faster.

The date in which the 2nd task was performed, the AOI "Google-sponsored link" corresponded to a competitor's site to the one that should have been searched. Thus, related to the FFD metrics (First Fixation Duration) and MCC (Mouse Click Count) it was possible to note that in this AOI, low-literacy users paid less attention and spent less time, fixating their eyes on this link for 0.11 seconds, on average. However, high-literacy users displayed fixation duration on average of 0.32 seconds and did not click on the competitor's site, opting for the link of the expected site for the task. This might justify the fact that the majority of low-literacy users became confused with competitors' sites, feeling the need to restart the task. By virtue of the greater time of fixation for the AOI "Google-sponsored link", it was seen that high-literacy users were not dispersive with the link of a competitor's site and were able to focus better on the task.

2nd Step (Searching the Óticas do Povo site): Based on the association of the TTFF metrics (Time To First Fixation) and TTFMC (Time To First Mouse Click) with the AOI "Óticas do Povo stores menu", one can state that the time frame between arriving at the initial site page and clicking on the "Stores" menu was greater for low-literacy users (94 seconds, on average) as compared to the time taken by high-literacy users (2 seconds, on average). One can thus affirm that low-literacy users are more susceptible to interface problems, such as the lack of legibility of the "Stores" menu, caused by the small font size and by little color contrast. This was confirmed during the post-test interview when participants were questioned about suggestions for improving the site, even though they had already written on the questionnaire that they had none. During the interview, however, they said that the size of the letters could be enlarged and that they were unable to see clearly due to the colors.

One characteristic that may have contributed to this longer period of time is low legibility of the "Stores" menu that displayed reduced font size and little color contrast.

As regards FC metrics (Fixation Count), one could observe that, although the tracker registered seventeen fixations on the "Stores" menu on the part of low-literacy user LL_04, he was unable to associate the menu label with the task objective. In addition, this same user, when associating the FC metric (Fixation Count) to the AOI "lower Óticas do Povo banner", which corresponds to a promotional link (with images of eyeglasses), made 28 fixations, believing this was the path to the store addresses. His intentions were made clear during the consecutive verbalization, when user LL_04 stated: - I was trying to "enter" the store by going through the shop window. The addresses should have been "inside." When the user clicked on this link, he was sent to a page of offers, becoming even more frustrated as he did not find the store addresses there. When 5 minutes of the test had passed (more than half the time given to perform the task), this user received help from the researchers and went back to browsing the upper horizontal menu so that he was finally able to interact with the "Stores" menu to finish the task. This same promotional link received on average 6 fixations from the other 4 low-literacy users, but was ignored by users of the other group.

6   Suggestions for Improving the Interface for Low-Literacy Users

Owing to the study, some common behaviors and difficulties for low-literacy users were perceived:

Labels used for interface elements, such as buttons and menu items, among others, should be objective and clear so as not to induce the user to error. One such example occurred with the "Google Search" button, which caused two participants to select this button before actually typing something into the search field, believing that only by this means could they initiate the Google search.

Interfaces should be designed using simple language in order to facilitate browsing for this type of user, since they do not have the ability to read and write to a full extent.

As this type of user does not normally make use of search tools on commercial sites, preferring to navigate the menu, these should not contain too many sub-items and should be labeled in a simple way. The use of unusual or technical words can lead to loss of time and user withdrawal. The word "Hydraulics", present on the site of the first task, can be used as an example of this. A low-literacy participant could hardly be expected to know this word, which could be replaced by "pipes and water". For the site of the second task, "Stores" on the menu could be replaced by "Addresses".

One should seek to use only images that contribute to the understanding of the task. Gazeplot showed that one of the low-literacy participants was distracted by the photo of a famous Brazilian model, thus taking longer to accomplish the task.

Care should be taken with the use of images so that they do not cause ambiguities or confuse users.

Due to the time and difficulties low-literacy users had to conclude the second task, one might suggest the use of a search filter by alphabetical order.

7   Conclusion

The aim of this research work was to assess the interaction of low-literacy Brazilian users with web system interfaces, focusing on accessibility and usability characteristics, by means of eyetracking. Low-literacy and high-literacy user behavior was analyzed during browsing. In order to do this, Tobii T120 equipment was used during test application with video recording, in addition to questionnaires and interviews.

Researchers were able to determine metrics and areas of interest of participants and, after the conclusion of tests, the tracker produced navigation reports for each user with a large amount of data. This resource allowed the study to make use of fine details that only observation or even recording of users would not have shown.

Eyetracking results point to differences in navigation of users having distinctive literacy profiles. By means of eye-tracking metrics, mainly due to the quantity and duration of fixations, it was possible to measure the degree of difficulty that low-literacy users have when navigating, showing that this profile user reads the entire text on pages so as to be sure to make the right decisions and that images, when not contextualized, may be dispersion factors.

Recommendations for improving interface need validation though they were based on earlier work already mention in section 2.3. It is hoped that these suggestions can contribute to the development of accessible interfaces for this type of user.

It is recommended for future work that a larger number of users be used in order to perform a statistical treatment of the data.

References

1. Associação Brasileira de Empresas de Pesquisa. Critério de Classificação Econômica Brasil CCBE 2013 (2014), http://www.abep.org/new/criterioBrasil.aspx
2. Barboza, E.M.F.: A linguagem clara em conteúdos de websites governamentais para promover a acessibilidade a cidadãos com baixo nível de escolaridade. Revista do Instituto Brasileiro de Informação em Ciência e Tecnologia (2011)
3. Capra, E.P., Ferreira, S.B.L., Silveira, D.S., Modesto, D.: Evaluation of Web Accessibility: an Approach Related to Functional Illiteracy. Publicado em: Procedia Computer Science 14, 36–46, http://www.sciencedirect.com/science/journal/18770509/14 ISSN 18770509
4. Capra, E.P.: "Protocolos de Avaliação de Acessibilidade Web com Analfabetos Funcionais" Programa de Pós Graduação em Informática – Dissertação de Mestrado - Departamento de Informática Aplicada da Universidade Federal do Estado do Rio de Janeiro (UNIRIO) – Eliane Pinheiro Capra (2011)
5. Ferreira, S.B.L., Nunes, R.R.: e-Usabilidade. LTC, Rio de Janeiro (2008)
6. Gupta, N.K., Rosé, C.P.: Understanding Instructional Support Needs of Emerging Internet Users for Web based Information Seeking. Journal of Educational Data Mining 2, 38–82 (2010)
7. Hearst, M.A.: Search User Interfaces. Cambridge University Press, New York (2009)

8. Instituto Brasileiro de Geografia e Estatística: Síntese de Indicadores Sociais: Uma Análise das Condições de Vida da População Brasileira (2010), http://www.ibge.gov.br/home/estatistica/populacao/condicaode vida/indicadoresminimos/sinteseindicsociais2010/SIS_2010.pdf (2012)

9. Kodagoda, N., Kahan, N., Wong, W.: Identifying Information Seeking Behaviors of Low and High Literacy Users: Combined Cognitive Task Analysis. In: Proceedings of NDM9, the 9th International Conference on Naturalistic Decision Making, pp. 347–354. The British Computer Society, London (2009)

10. Kodagoda, N., Wong, B.: Effects of Low & High Literacy on User Performance in Information Search and Retrieval. In: Proceedings of the 22nd British HCI Group Annual Conference on People and Computers: Culture, Creativity, Interaction, pp. 173–181. The British Computer Society, Swinton (2008)

11. Lukasova, K.: Movimento ocular em crianças e adultos: estudo comparativo com uso integrado de RMf e Eyetracking. Tese de Doutorado. Faculdade de Medicina da Universidade de São Paulo. Programa de Radiologia, São Paulo (2012)

12. Marshall, P.: The importance of reading comprehension, No Date (2013), http://www.k12reader.com/the-importance-of-reading-comprehension/

13. Modesto, D.M., Ferreira, S.B.L.: Guidelines for search features development – a comparison between general users and users with low reading skills. In: Paper published in Proceedings of the 5th International Conference on Software Development for Enhancing Accessibility and Fighting Info-exclusion (DSAI 2013), University of Vigo, Vigo (November 2013), http://www.sciencedirect.com/science/journal/18770509/14 ISSN 18770509

14. Modesto, D.M., Ferreira, S.B.L., Alves, A.S.: Search Engine Accessibility for Low-Literate Users. In: Kurosu, M. (ed.) HCII/HCI 2013, Part III. LNCS, vol. 8006, pp. 324–331. Springer, Heidelberg (2013)

15. Modesto, D.M.: Acessibilidade de Recursos em uma Interface de Motor de Busca com Foco em Usuários com Baixo Letramento - Programa de Pós Graduação em Informática – Mestrado - Departamento de Informática Aplicada da Universidade Federal do Estado do Rio de Janeiro (UNIRIO) – Débora Maurmo Modesto (2012)

16. Melo, A., Piccolo, L., Ávila, I., Tambascia, C.: Usabilidade, Acessibilidade e Inteligibilidade Aplicadas em Interfaces para Analfabetos, Idosos e Pessoas com Deficiência. In: Resultados do Workshop do VIII Simpósio Brasileiro sobre Fatores Humanos em Sistemas Computacionais 2009 (2014), http://www.cpqd.com.br/file.upload/1749021822/resultados_workshop_uai.pdf

17. Nielsen, J., Loranger, H.: Usabilidade na Web: Projetando Websites com Qualidade. Elsevier, Rio de Janeiro (2007)

18. Nielsen, J.: Why You Only Need to Test With 5 Users, 2000b (2008), http://www.useit.com/alertbox/20000319.html

19. TOBII (2013), http://www.tobii.com/en/eye-tracking-research/global/products/hardware/tobii-t60t120-eye-tracker/

20. Thurow, S., Musica, N.: When Search Meets Web Usability. New Riders, Berkeley (2009)

21. United Nations Educational, Scientific and Cultural Organization: Understandings of Literacy. In: The Education For All Global Monitoring Report: Literacy for Life, 2006, pp. 149–159 (2012), http://www.unesco.org/education/GMR2006/full/chapt6_eng.pdf

Accessibility Driven Design for Policy Argumentation Modelling

Dimitris Spiliotopoulos[1], Athanasios Dalianis[1], and Georgios Kouroupetroglou[2]

[1] Innovation Lab, Athens Technology Centre, Greece
{d.spiliotopoulos,t.dalianis}@atc.gr
[2] Speech and Accessibility Lab, Dept. Informatics and Telecommunications
University of Athens, Greece
koupe@di.uoa.gr

Abstract. This paper discusses the design of a web interface for policy argumentation modeling. Given the complexity of the interface the WAI-ARIA descriptions were used to ensure that the data were accessible and the visual-heavy presentation was simplified. Conclusions were drawn as to the usefulness of the WAI-ARIA guidelines to an elaborate design of user interaction with highly dynamic content.

Keywords: web interface, policy modeling, WAI-ARIA, accessibility.

1 Introduction

Recent advances in user interface design and approaches on handling complexity have led to wide adoption of data visualization techniques along the spectrum of web applications. With semantic web clearly in position to harvest, analyze and provide metadata for large-scale applications, such as opinion mining, brand monitoring, and others, data visualization is a key feature of research interest. The dynamic nature of data visualization, the dense amount of information represented and the raw number of connections between data renders such task difficult to model.

Since quite some time, graphs have been identified as a formidable tool to navigation and data exploration [1]. Recent studies verify the effect in perceived usability of graph visualization [2]. It is also argued that it is the efficient access of information through visualization that helps improve usability of traditional data exploration interfaces [3]. Usability-driven techniques are applied directly to web interfaces in order to reveal patterns and shortcomings in information accessibility [4]. Usability is also affected during the interaction with graph visualizations because the context is affected, taken out of focus [5]. That is more profound in visualization tools that exhibit high hidden dependencies [6]. On the interaction level, the semantics of the interactions can also be used to generate user interfaces [7].

Complex data semantics can be visualized using appropriate structures, like graphs, that come in several varieties. Interactive graphs aid usability since users are able to interact with the data they see, rather than triggering visualizations by clicking elsewhere on the interface. Building interactive user interfaces that heavily depend on information visualization necessitates that the design of the interaction also be focused in the visualization techniques and approaches.

WAI-ARIA is a W3C recommendation that has been recently drafted in order to describe semantic assignments that can be used in user interfaces to aid accessibility [8]. This recommendation tries to address the latest changes that semantic web has introduced to the way that information is presented and accessed. The web page centric design has been abandoned for the more distributed approach that uses multiple interaction elements and very high interactivity. The main objective of the WAI-ARIA suite is to ensure or improve web interface accessibility. Studies show that the WAI-ARIA specification can be used to adjust existing Web 2.0 interfaces to a more accessible format [9]. However, that is accomplished by defining a number of methods that essentially improve the usability, as well. That is an interesting additional value that can be used in the design as an additional set of tools for maximizing the user experience. Core design methods, such as prototyping, personas and storyboarding may use accessibility guidelines to create W3C compliant interfaces [10].

The WAI-ARIA recommendations have also been applied to the social web to improve both accessibility and usability [11, 12]. Social web is a major source of large amounts of data that are analyzed and visualized. It is, therefore, clear that semantic web and accessibility guidelines based on semantics can be part of a clean user interface design. In the cases when dynamic content that is not covered by the WAI-ARIA guidelines, other remedies may be submitted [13]. However, for the most part, the WAI-ARIA guidelines provide enough technical competence to significantly improve usability.

This work focuses on the WAI-ARIA authoring practices [14] and applies them on top of the usability-driven design and methods for designing a highly interactive information visualization web interface for policy argumentation modeling. This work identifies the intentions behind the suggested practices and includes them in the user-driven design of the NOMAD authoring interface that is entirely graphical. The paper starts by introducing the problem and then describes a pilot experiment with expert users and the resulting web interface prototype based on their feedback.

2   Requirements and Problem Specification

As part of the NOMAD[1] EU-funded project, policy makers and political scientists create domains and policies for web and social web collection of arguments of the citizens. The final policy model for a specific policy is, then, fed to the NOMAD system for collection of data, analysis and visualization. Creating an ontology domain is a meticulous task that requires specialized tools not only for testing the completeness of the data but also for evaluating the correctness of the relations between the data types.

---

[1] NOMAD - Policy formulation and validation through non-moderated crowdsourcing, www.nomad-project.eu

In order to study the broadness of the latter, a common initial design approach is to allow only tree-based structures to be created. That simplifies both the available space for the assignment of relations as well as the interaction required by the end users. However, there are instances where the complexity of a domain may only be fully expressed by a proper graph representation. Potentially, an unconstrained graph may be a quite complicated structure requiring high effort and cognitive load for the user to visually parse and verify the data and their relations. It is also far more complex, on the interaction level, to create such structure compared to simple tree representations.

For such rich technological basis, it was decided to study the WAI-ARIA authoring practices in order to create interactive prototype views of a graph-based authoring web interface. The requirements were simple:

1. Users need to open and edit ontology domains and policy models. In order to do that, they also need to navigate through the available domains. Domains have unique title names, spanning from one work to a long sentence.
2. To edit a domain or a policy model, insertion and deletion of nodes as well as naming and renaming are the main tasks. A different, in terms of design, is the task to apply or delete connections between the nodes.
3. Entities, norms and arguments are the three types of data that can exist on the ontology and consequently on the any visual structure.
4. Graphs may contain tens or hundreds of nodes with a relatively high amount of connections.

The challenging aspects of the task were to be able to maintain a constant level of comprehension for the users towards their data. That would minimize unnecessary looking back or zooming out on the interface in order to put the data back into perspective. One other step towards a usable interface was the need for full access to all the information at any time, unconstrained editing, yet with minimal effort by the users.

3   Tree-Based Interaction Draft Prototype

In order to be able to understand the way that experts construct a policy model, an authoring environment with tree-based representation of the ontology domains was made available (Fig. 1). Expert users created their own policy models and domains as well as revisited to check the system output. The system performs a targeted crawling process based on the policy model description and the analyzed data become an additional source of data on the policy model.

The original requirements suggested that a simple tree hierarchy of terms was sufficient for the representations of the policy models. The mind map overview (fig. 1, centre) and the hierarchy tree (fig. 1, right) could be used interchangeably for editing the models. At the early stages, the user interaction was observed in order to establish a baseline for the type of interaction needed for creating policy models. Indeed, there were several approaches that were also different, to a degree, from the traditional ontology creation process.

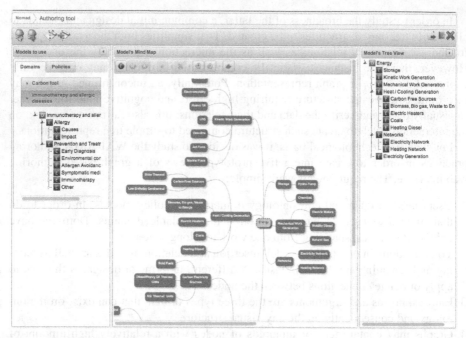

Fig. 1. Tree-based representation (initial interactive prototype for policy domain authoring)

Ten participants evaluated the interaction during the first design iteration. The purpose was twofold. The innovation of the NOMAD approach necessitated a visual modeling of policies that would be used for the data collection and the linguistic analysis. In that respect, this evaluation was designed to examine the steps that the policy experts follow and the required functionalities to achieve the goal via their interaction. Moreover, the participants copy-pasted, drag-and-dropped nodes in order to create and edit the policy models as represented by a hierarchy tree or a mindmap.

The WAI-ARIA authoring practices document includes sections on trees and drag-and-drop support. The guidelines contained in the two sections as well other general ones were used for the construction of questionnaires for the user feedback. The following is a partial list of items that were examined during the evaluation.

1. Structural navigation: clear identification of logical structure
2. Nesting: Clear role of hierarchy tree
3. Nesting: Clear role of mindmap
4. Nesting: Distinctions and differences between trees and mindmaps in interaction
5. Focus: Clear identification of items in focus
6. Labeling: Nodes labels accessibility
7. Describing: Types of data (nodes) identification
8. Dynamic changes: Live regions implementation
9. Drag-and-drop support: Purpose of drag-and-drop (duplication, editing, etc.)
10. Drag-and-drop support: Drag source and drop destination clearly marked
11. Drag-and-drop support: Cancelling drag-and-drop

12. Drag-and-drop support: Testing of functionality for between-tree-mindmap actions
13. Presentation: all data elements focusable, selectable, accessible, editable, consistent

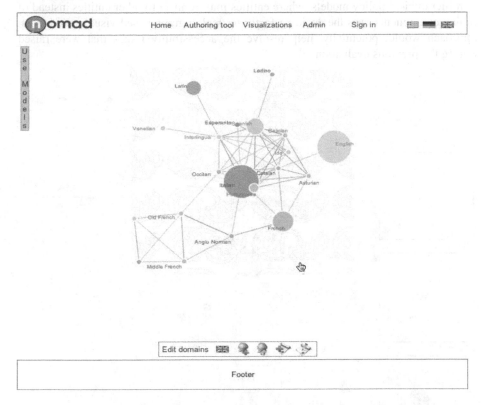

Fig. 2. Graph-based representation (mockup)

The feedback clearly favoured the more graphic of the two layouts. In the usability feedback, the tree structure was deemed more straightforward for editing, viewing the full model without having to zoom out and in clear representation of the data types (due to larger area available for the mindmap). For the above accessibility-based questions, the users identified the key points of attention:

1. Colour must be used to differentiate data types. Entities, arguments and policy components should be clearly identifiable and distinguishable from one another.
2. When a user selects an item, the linked items should be easily discoverable (mindmap).
3. Drag-and-drop between the tree and mindmap is a good approach since it allows pre-arranged actions.
4. Mindmaps and trees may be more suitable for small models, larger ones lead to unwanted need to zoom in and out, mindmaps grow too large and trees too long for larger models, making them harder to navigate.

4   Graph-Based Visual Authoring of Policy Models

As the user requirements were updated in the next iteration, the same participants evaluated the graph-based visualization approach. The core requirements for larger non-hierarchical policy models, where entities may connect to other entities instead of policy components, was the deciding factor to deploy graph-based visualization. That approach would, potentially, help resolve the accessibility issues that were raised during the previous evaluation.

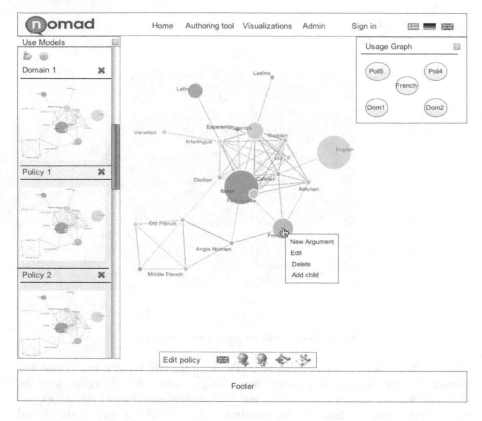

Fig. 3. Graph-based multiple representation of policy models (mockup)

At this point, the WAI-ARIA derived design specifications discussed in the previous section would serve as the guide for the interaction design. In effect, the user feedback served as hypotheses as well as additional interaction requirements for the updated design. The hypotheses were formulated automatically and were evaluated on the usability improvement over the earlier results. Figure 2 shows one of the several mockups that were designed for this approach. In order to test the parameters thoroughly, the mockups were designed to go beyond the user suggestions and also explore the WAI-ARIA derived specifications to more extensive paradigms.

The policy authors evaluated colour representation of possible actions, foci status, and data types through multiple mockups. Additionally, visual ways of ensuring that navigation information was clearly presented on the graphs were investigated. The desired result was to be able to design the same process for navigation using both mouse/trackpad and keyboard as input devices.

The feedback from the participants was very encouraging in some cases, such as the visual feedback for node selection, but also revealed that more work was needed for certain tasks that, although did not seem very complicated, were found to be quite difficult to decide on an optimal way to complete. Such task is shown in figure 3. In that example, the policy model author was trying to insert a policy component and its connected nodes to the model that was being edited. Selecting a node for drag-and-drop from an existing policy model, off a list of policy models currently showing was too complicated to do using the keyboard because of two active navigation-enabled areas at the same time.

5   Conclusion

This work investigated the recently release WAI-ARIA accessibility guidelines as a potential design specification for designing user interaction elements for accessible and usable dynamic content. The test bed was the NOMAD policy modeling authoring environment during the first two iterations of the design and testing. The traditional usability evaluation was enriched with specific accessibility-derived design considerations in order to evaluate accessibility along with usability for an accessibility-aware user driven approach.

The unavoidable complex approach, on the concept level at least, of policy modeling using a visual user interface was a serious test case for a semantically rich web application with highly dynamic content. Policy components, entities and arguments as the basic ingredients of a policy model and that was the first time that the visual modeling of a policy was experimentally investigated.

That usability evaluation session revealed that the initial hypothesis that the WAI-ARIA specific guidelines can serve as specification for the design of a complicated visual approach to a web interface was verified. It also revealed that, for highly dynamic content, the adoption of the WAI-ARIA authoring practices is not a straightforward task as was previously claimed in other works [15].

There was strong indication that additional effort is required for a fully usable and accessible web interface design for the more complex interaction functionalities. For example, spoken interaction can be used to quickly find the data in graphs, wither by title or even in tags (semantic or otherwise) that can be used for grouping and filtering. The authors believe that spoken interaction for navigation and editing tasks as well as respective visual dynamics to correspond to the input commands warrants a further investigation.

Acknowledgements. The work described here was partially supported by the EU ICT research project NOMAD, FP7-ICT-288513.

References

1. Leblanc, B., Marshall, M.S., Melancon, G.: Graph Visualization and navigation as an interface to data exploration. In: VSST 2001, Barcelona, vol. 2, pp. 279–284 (2001)
2. Mazumdar, S., Petrelli, D., Elbedweihy, K., Lanfranchi, V., Ciravegna, F.: Affective Graphs: The Visual Appeal of Linked Data. In: Semantic Web – Interoperability, Usability, Applicability. IOS Press (to appear, 2014)
3. Paulheim, H.: Improving the Usability of Integrated Applications by Using Visualizations of Linked Data. In: Proc. Int. Conf. on Web Intelligence, Mining and Semantics, WIMS 2011, Article 19. ACM, New York (2011)
4. Chi, E.H.: Improving Web Usability Through Visualization. IEEE Internet Computing 6(2), 64–71 (2002)
5. Herman, I., Melancon, G., Scott Marshall, M.: Graph Visualization and Navigation in Information Visualization: A Survey. IEEE Transactions on Visualization and Computer Graphics 6(1), 24–43 (2000)
6. Kuhail, M.A., Lauesen, S., Pantazos, K., Shangjin, X.: Usability Analysis of Custom Visualization Tools. In: Proc. SIGRAD 2012, Sweden, November 29-30, pp. 19–28 (2012)
7. Mayer, S., Tschofen, A., Dey, A.K., Mattern, F.: User Interfaces for Smart Things - A Generative Approach with Semantic Interaction Descriptions. ACM Transactions on Computer-Human Interaction (to appear, 2014)
8. Craig, J., Cooper, M.: Accessible Rich Internet Applications (WAI-ARIA) 1.0, W3C Proposed Recommendation (February 6, 2014), http://www.w3.org/TR/wai-aria/ (retrieved February 28, 2014)
9. Mori, G., Buzzi, M.C., Buzzi, M., Leporini, B., Penichet, V.M.R.: Collaborative Editing for All: The Google Docs Example. In: Stephanidis, C. (ed.) Universal Access in HCI, Part IV, HCII 2011. LNCS, vol. 6768, pp. 165–174. Springer, Heidelberg (2011)
10. Green, S., Pearson, E., Gkatzidou, V., Perrin, F.O.: A community-centred design approach for accessible rich internet applications (ARIA). In: Proc. 26th Annual BCS Interaction Spe-cialist Group Conference on People and Computers (BCS-HCI 2012), pp. 89–98. British Computer Society, Swinton (2012)
11. Buzzi, M.C., Buzzi, M., Leporini, B.: Web 2.0: Twitter and the blind. In: Proc. 9th ACM SIGCHI Italian Chapter Int. Conf. on Computer-Human Interaction: Facing Complexity, pp. 151–156. ACM
12. Buzzi, M.C., Buzzi, M., Leporini, B., Akhter, F.: Is Facebook really "open" to all? In: IEEE International Symposium on Technology and Society (ISTAS), pp. 327–336 (2010)
13. Borodin, Y., Bigham, J.P., Dausch, G., Ramakrishnan, I.V.: More than meets the eye: a survey of screen-reader browsing strategies. In: W4A 2010, p. 13 (2010)
14. Scheuhammer, J., Cooper, M.: WAI-ARIA 1.0 Authoring Practices, W3C Working Draft (March 7, 2013), http://www.w3.org/TR/wai-aria-practices/ (retrieved February 28, 2014)
15. Lele, Y., Kariya, C., Kale, N., Nandgaonkar, A., Phatak, M.: Human Computer Interaction for Visually Impaired Users in Web Based Applications. International Journal of Scientific & Engineering Research 4(8) (August 2013)

Practical Eye Tracking
of the Ecommerce Website User Experience

Wilkey Wong, Mike Bartels, and Nina Chrobot

Tobii Technology, AB, Danderyd, Sweden
{wilkey.wong,mike.bartels,nina.chrobot}@tobii.com

Abstract. Eye tracking is a productive tool in researching the user experience of ecommerce websites. Because information throughout the online path to purchase is communicated visually, gaze behavior is among the most effective and informative means of testing the extent to which a given ecommerce site facilitates a smooth transaction. The process of analysis typically involves examining the characteristics and patterns of visual attention during the online shopping process. Eye-tracking metrics are used in conjunction with data-based visualizations and traditional usability techniques to answer a variety of questions about the online shopping process. Principles of appropriate design, execution and analysis of an ecommerce eye-tracking study are discussed, along with relevant case examples.

Keywords: eye tracking, ecommerce, usability, user experience, visual behavior analysis, heat map.

1   The Challenge of Ecommerce

The advent of the internet has completely transformed the means by which products and services are bought and sold. Today's consumer has the ability to purchase virtually anything at any time from any place with only the click of a mouse or the tap of a finger. For businesses, this technological evolution has resulted in dramatic improvements in efficiency, communication, productivity, research and scalability. There is little doubt that as access continues to spread and bandwidth continues to grow, ecommerce will become an even more powerful force in the global economy [1].

However, for any business that hopes to realize the promise of ecommerce, a number of challenges exist. First and foremost, an ecommerce site must perform the complex task of convincing a user to execute a financial transaction without a human sales presence. That means there is no agent to promote the product, answer questions or help facilitate the purchase, and if the user does not respond to the site's "pitch," an entire internet worth of competition awaits. To further complicate this already daunting market scenario, an ecommerce website must address a number of technical considerations, including security, privacy, usability, navigation, logistics, multi-platform use and customer support [2]. The delicate practical balance between marketing, customer relations and computer science required to sell products online is a difficult one to achieve.

C. Stephanidis and M. Antona (Eds.): UAHCI/HCII 2014, Part IV, LNCS 8516, pp. 109–118, 2014.

The challenge of implementing and maintaining a successful ecommerce site is evident in the relevant literature. In a study of online shopping behavior, Loveday & Neihaus [3] found that 60% of intended online purchases are never completed. The Baymard Institute [4] aggregated ecommerce interaction data from a range of different industries and concluded that 68% of online shopping carts were abandoned before a transaction was made. Consumer attitudes research suggests that online shoppers experience frustration and dissatisfaction [5], [6]. And yet, ecommerce continues to expand as a proportion of the overall economy [7]. For this reason, it is more important than ever that businesses optimize their online sales capabilities and close the gap between shopping online and buying online.

The internet offers a wide array of web analytics for evaluating the performance of an ecommerce site, such as page views, unique visitors, active time, click paths and exit rate. These metrics are valuable as descriptors of online activity, but they reveal very little about the underlying drivers of site performance. Why is Product A selected for purchase more often than Product B? What causes the high exit rate on a particular page in the signup process? These questions are difficult to answer with web analytics alone. Understanding the complex interplay of cognitive, emotional and behavioral processes that defines the shopper journey requires a bottom-up research approach. To this end, eye tracking is a very effective tool.

2   Eye Tracking as an Ecommerce Research Methodology

In nearly all human-computer interactions, the most basic point of connection between an interface and its user is the eye [8]. In the context of online shopping, goods are presented, explained, promoted and processed almost entirely through information and imagery perceived by the shopper's visual systems. Products that are not seen will not be bought. Information that is not read will not inform the purchase decision. Steps in the transaction that are ignored may result in errors and, potentially, abandonment. Therein lies the essential motivation for including eye tracking in the study of ecommerce

By eye tracking shoppers' visual behavior – from that very first glance on the landing page to the instant they click on the "buy" button – UX researchers are able to uncover both barriers and affordances in the shopper journey. This may include discovering unintended patterns of attention, quantifying the attractive power of key interaction elements, identifying the attentional or cognitive mechanisms behind missed opportunities and differentiating the performance of design variants. In a domain that is so intensely visual, it makes eminent sense to include a methodology that naturally connects visual behavior to the outcomes that matter most in ecommerce: increased sales, satisfaction and loyalty [9].

An added benefit of the eye-tracking approach to ecommerce research is its universality. Because visual attention is so basic to online interactions, it can be applied to almost any shopping context – clothing, music, insurance, childcare, etc. There are essentially no limitations on the type of shopping experience that can be examined through eye tracking. This universality also applies to the shopping medium.

Whether the ecommerce site is accessed via tablet, smartphone, laptop, desktop or other system, the primary and oftentimes sole modality for communicating information, value, and relevance is screen-based. In today's UX research, eye tracking is used to collect data on a multitude of consumer device formats and a wide range of different types of ecommerce sites.

3   Developing an Eye-Tracking Study for Ecommerce

3.1   Logistical Considerations

Ecommerce user experience studies including eye tracking have many of the same considerations as non-ecommerce studies. These include the number of tasks that can be reasonably executed during the session, order of presentation of stimuli, whether the study will be between-subjects or within-subjects and what types of people should be recruited to take part in the research. There are, however, additional questions specific to ecommerce studies. Participant privacy is an important consideration, as most eye-tracking software automatically captures hardware-generated events such as loading of website URLs, mouse clicks, and keystrokes as a non-modifiable part of its normal operation. Thus, researchers who engage in studies that require actual user logins should establish a protocol or policy regarding data access, storage, and retention similar to those in use at academic research institutions that engage human subjects.

Another important decision for the researcher is how to facilitate a 'purchase' in the testing environment. Options include (1) allowing the participant to complete real transactions during the session, (2) halting the task immediately before a transaction is completed and (3) setting up a 'trapdoor' scenario in which simulated transactions are immediately nullified. Each of these options has benefits and drawbacks that must be weighed on a case-by-case basis. The appropriate logistical approach for a given study is the one that replicates as closely as possible an authentic shopping process, while ensuring that accurate eye-tracking data can be captured and meaningfully applied to research objectives.

3.2   Asking Appropriate Research Questions

A sound methodological framework is a useful first step in designing a study, but the real challenge is in developing appropriate research objectives. Ecommerce websites are often dynamic and intricate, with the capacity for highly variable user behavior, compared with other types of consumer research materials (e.g., packages, advertisements, signage). Added to that is the challenge of realistically simulating the online shopping process with participants who may not be willing or able to make an actual purchase during the testing situation. To put it simply, the test stimuli are complex, the behavior of the user is unpredictable and the testing scenario is not entirely naturalistic. For these and other reasons, it is essential that suitable research objectives are developed before the start of data collection.

Examples of unsuitable research objectives include, "I want to know where people look," "I'd like to add eye tracking to my study," and "I need a heat map."

Such statements are not uncommon in our experience. However, studies based on such requests tend to fail for three reasons:

A. They are not specific with respect to the research insight sought. The desire to "know *where people look*" is an incredibly broad starting point. It is instead preferable to focus on specific visual activities.
B. The requests do not relate to measurable behaviors (e.g., order of looking, duration of looking, context in which looking occurs).
C. It is unclear how these statements relate to business priorities. Without an understanding of the relationship between performance metrics and relevant indicators, it is exceptionally challenging to broach the issue of return on investment of the research.

The most fruitful eye-tracking research objectives are the ones that focus on specific questions about the user experience. For example, "are product imagery, special offers, and reviews salient and in a visible location?" "How readily are calls to action seen and processed?" "What elements of the checkout tend to be ignored?" Because websites are primarily visual media, the questions that can be addressed through eye tracking are myriad. Defining and prioritizing these questions is the key to developing a successful study with actionable results.

3.3   A Practical Example of Appropriate Research Objectives

A simple illustration of the aforementioned approach to eye-tracking ecommerce is now provided. It begins not with the general question of "where do people look on the site," but rather by examining a specific component of the transactional process and associated visual behaviors. Figures 1 and 2 on the following page illustrate the gaze behavior of two groups of participants as they consider the purchase of headphones on the target.com website (simulated data). Group A (fig. 1) viewed the product on a product display page and was more likely to purchase the product. Group B (fig. 2) viewed the product in a quick look product display window and most often chose not to purchase the product.

In this example, standard web and sales analytics would offer a wealth of information about these user experiences, including when pages were visited, how long the pages were visited, where the user subsequently navigated and whether or not the product was purchased. Obviously, these data are valuable in describing the behavior of online shoppers, but eye tracking adds the potential for several further layers of analysis: Do shoppers see the image right away? Where is attention most heavily concentrated? Which product details tend to be ignored? As highlighted in the figures, one potentially important distinction between these two heat maps is that shoppers who tended to purchase the product also tended to view the 5-star customer rating. In contrast, the shoppers who did not purchase generally failed to see the ratings. Is this conclusive evidence that inattention to star-ratings causes shopper abandonment? Of course not, and yet it does provide a concrete jumping off point to explore this aspect of the shopper experience in detail.

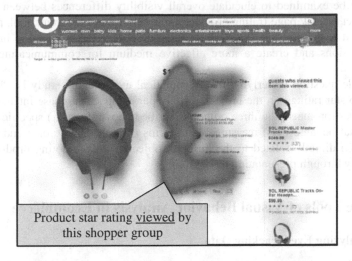

Fig. 1. Group A: Heat map of fixations for users viewing headphones on a target.com product display page. This user group most often chose to purchase (simulated data).

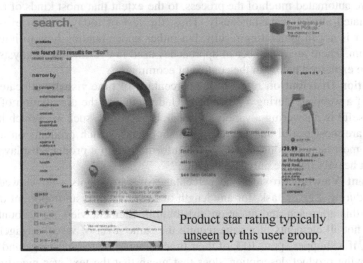

Fig. 2. Group B: Heat map of fixations for users viewing headphones on a target.com *Quick View* window. This user group most often chose *not* to purchase (simulated data).

The next step is to determine whether or not the anecdotal evidence in these figures is representative of the population at large. The researcher might prepare a follow-up study, comparing attention to star ratings among a large sample of purchasers and non-purchasers on a comprehensive list of different product types. Additionally, it might be of interest to examine the impact of attention to high vs. low star ratings on purchase intent. And of course there is the visual salience of the star rating itself, which may be examined to elucidate overall visibility differences between the standard product display page (rating provided on the right) and the quick look page (rating provided at the bottom). Analyses such as these have the potential to inform site design decisions and create a more effective medium for communicating product value.

The basic question underlying this hypothetical eye-tracking study is, "how does attention to star ratings on the product display page impact purchase intent?" Notice that this question meets the three criteria described above. It is (A) specific to a particular visual behavior, (B) measureable in terms of both the eye data and the sales data and (C) directly related to the business objective of promoting products more persuasively through presentation of star ratings.

4   The Tools of Visual Behavior Analysis in Ecommerce

4.1   Analyzing Eye-Tracking Data

At its core, eye-tracking data consists of a time-ordered sequence of pixel coordinates. The primary task of the analyst is to extract meaningful behaviors, trends, and tendencies from this fundamental information stream. Recent advances in eye-tracking software have automated much of the process, to the extent that most kinds of results can be calculated almost instantaneously. Thus, the test of today's adept eye- tracking researcher is not in generating results, but rather understanding how to interpret and apply them. There are a number of approaches used in eye-tracking analysis, three of which are explained below in the context of ecommerce.

Attention Distribution refers to the percentage of time visually allocated to each feature of a webpage during a given task. Understanding the distribution of attention can be useful in answering a variety of research questions, such as: Which homepage features are most useful and interesting to shoppers? Which products on a category page are most heavily considered? Which information on a product display page factors most heavily into the purchase decision?

Element Viewing provides the percentage of participants who viewed a given element during a given task, for any length of time. There is an important distinction between this approach and attention distribution. Element viewing accounts for the fact that not all elements of a page require the same level of visual engagement. For example, if a shopper spent 10% of their time viewing a product image and the other 90% viewing product description, does that mean that the text was nine times more important to shoppers? The more probable explanation is that an image can be processed very quickly, whereas a block of text requires more detailed perceptual and cognitive processing. An analysis of the percentage of the total sample that fixated the image and text at least one time would be a better assessment of the level of interest in these elements.

Perceptual Flow is the typical order in which page elements are first seen? Understanding the shopper journey is not just a matter of *where* attention lands; it is also a matter of *when* attention lands. By analyzing the time to first viewing of elements, it is possible to map the perceptual flow of the page. Is the price of an expensive item seen after the selling points? Is the upsell for a product seen in time to convince someone to take advantage before adding to cart? To answer such questions it is important to understand the typical sequence of visual behavior.

The list of other eye-tracking approaches commonly applied to research includes length of scan path, number of fixations/visits and duration of fixations/visits to name a few. The experimental design and objectives of the study should be taken into account when determining which approaches to data analysis will be most fruitful.

4.2   Visualizing Eye-Tracking Data

The numerical results described above are very useful in demonstrating trends in shopper visual behavior, although in many cases images can be more impactful than numbers. For example, it may be difficult for some clients to conceptualize the following hypothetical research finding: "Users take an average of 17.5 seconds to notice the hotel offers on the lower part of an car rental homepage (based on time to first fixation)." The eye-tracking metric proffered in this case is quite clear, but what does it actually mean in the context of web interaction? To provide perspective, one might include a gaze video example of a user demonstrating this behavior alongside the metric. The combination of data results and visual illustration can be singularly effective in presenting the findings of an ecommerce study. Three of the most commonly used eye-tracking visualizations and relevant ecommerce examples are provided below.

- **Heat maps** are, for better or worse, eye tracking's signature visualization. This graphical representation of visual behavior data renders gaze or fixation points of one or more participants in a color-coded intensity plot of visual behavior (see Figures 1 & 2 above). As a snapshot of aggregated visual attention, this graphic is efficient and useful. However, it is important to keep in mind two limitations: (A) attention to page elements that require little time to process will be deemphasized in a heat map, and (B) a heat map does not take into account the time-course of the visual interaction.

- **Gaze plots** present the position and sequence of fixations/gaze points of a given participant viewing a given page (see Figures 3 and 4 below). While these visualizations are not as clear or intelligible as heat maps when multiple participants' data are aggregated, they are useful in illustrating noteworthy individual gaze behaviors.

- **Gaze replay videos** consist of screen recordings from the eye-tracking sessions with the participant's point of gaze overlaid on the video. These visualizations can be used to illustrate the visual behavior on dynamic content (drop downs, video, etc.) or across multiple pages (category page → PDP → shopping cart). For example, one might present a video clip of a user watching a promotional product video.

The visualizations described above are not unique to ecommerce. They are employed in virtually every commercial and scientific field of eye tracking. Nonetheless, we submit that evaluation of ecommerce extracts greater utility from such visualizations than most other applications. This is because the UX researchers who typically conduct eye-tracking studies rarely have the authority or know-how to make unilateral changes to the site. Recommendations from eye tracking must be approved or at least communicated across multiple departments, a list that may include sales, marketing, creative, support, consumer insights and technology, among others. Subsequently, recommended changes must be clearly expressed to developers or software engineers. Thus, the UX researcher is faced with the difficult task of conveying study results and suggested revisions to a large number of colleagues from many different backgrounds, most of whom have no experience with eye-tracking research. In this scenario, visual results (heat maps, gaze plots, gaze replays, etc.) can be far more intuitive and compelling in communicating the gist of a complex finding than charts and tables alone.

4.3   A Comprehensive Approach to Analysis

Eye tracking is rarely, if ever, the sole methodology included in a study of ecommerce sites or apps. As previously discussed, these sites are often complex and dynamic, and shopper behavior can be highly variable. In order to fully evaluate and characterize the user experience, it is important to include additional data streams, such as clicks, key presses, page visits and task time. Most eye-tracking software captures this information automatically, so there is no impact on the technical or methodological setup. In terms of analysis, this additional data pairs nicely with the eye data, which often anchors the spatial context from which an analysis of these events can be carried out. The visual and navigational components of user interaction are inextricably linked. It, therefore, makes sense to evaluate these related processes in parallel.

The other data stream that is typically incorporated into eye-tracking ecommerce research is direct user feedback. While the thoughts, perceptions and expectations of users are difficult to probe during the online shopping experience, post-testing interviews and questionnaires are able to explore the cognitive and emotional experience of the user in ways that visual and navigational data cannot. This is especially true when using the Retrospective Think-Aloud (RTA) technique, in which a screen recording with gaze and click data is replayed for the participant as the moderator conducts the interview. The video serves as a useful memory aid for the interviewee, as he or she attempts to recall the experience of interacting with each page in the shopping process.

4.4   A Practical Example of a Multi-Dimensional Eye-Tracking Study

A recent case study involving research conducted by Valsplat illustrates the use of eye tracking alongside other data streams to diagnose usability issues and recommend changes to an ecommerce website. KLM airlines was the subject of this study, specifically the online booking tool. In 2009, KLM launched a redesign of this feature, and utilized eye tracking, click/navigation and qualitative results to inform design decisions. The study consisted of multiple rounds of iterative testing. A Tobii T120 eye tracker was used to collect visual behavior data from participants as they booked a flight for an upcoming trip. In post-testing interviews, the RTA technique was employed.

Among other elements of the booking tool, the study sought to understand the user experience on the Select Flights page. Figure 3 below demonstrates the visual behavior of a user attempting to choose a flight. Notice that there are two separate areas of concentrated attention (on the far left and on the far right). In this version of the booking tool, the price and flight times were placed on opposite sides of the page. This resulted in a somewhat unwieldy visual experience, as users were forced to constantly look from one side of the screen to the other to find a suitably priced and scheduled flight. This finding was supported by the navigational and qualitative data (i.e., users often abandoned the purchase and expressed frustration).

Fig. 3. Initial design of *Select Flights* page. Flight times and pricing are on opposite sides of the page, which results in a suboptimal pattern of visual attention.

These results were taken into account in the redesign of the Select Flights page. Figure 4 illustrates the visual behavior of a user interacting with an updated version of the Select Flights page. Since the pricing and schedule for each flight have been moved closer together on the new page, the data suggest that users enjoy a less taxing visual interaction. Without the eye-tracking data, it may have been difficult to pinpoint this minor flaw. When the new booking tool was launched with this change implemented, sales data demonstrated a 30% increase in conversion rate. KLM offered much of the credit for this success to the use of eye tracking in prelaunch testing.

Fig. 4. Redesign of *Select Flights* page. In this version, flight times and pricing appear side-by-side, which results in a more efficient, less effortful pattern of visual behavior.

The case above encapsulates many of the best practices described in this paper. The KLM ecommerce study approached a complex online shopping process in an intelligent way. The methodology was naturalistic and yet carefully controlled, while also integrating other data streams. The research objectives were focused, straightforward, measurable and relevant to business objectives. Finally, the analysis provided actionable conclusions in support of specific site modifications.

5   Summary

Online transactions or ecommerce is becoming an ever more prominent subject of study in user experience research. Because the primary channel of communication at the interface is visual, an investigative technique based on characterizing and interpreting visual behavior can be a powerful tool in understanding and optimizing the user experience. Eye tracking is a method that is useful and unique in the insights it provides regarding the processes of buying and selling online. When deployed in a structured methodology – including a suitable research question, appropriate metrics and visualizations, and framing of actionable insights in the context of articulated business goals – eye tracking is capable of returning tangible and substantial value.

References

1. DeLone, W., McLean, E.: Measuring E-Commerce Success: Applying the Delone & McLean Information Systems Success Model. Int. J. Electron. Comm. 9(1), 31–47 (2004)
2. Luo, J., Ba, S., Zhang, H.: The Effectiveness of Online Shopping Characteristics and Well-Designed Websites on Satisfaction. Mis. Quart. 36(4), 1131–1144 (2012)
3. Loveday, L., Niehaus, S.: Web Design for ROI. New Riders, San Francisco (2007)
4. Baymard Institute, http://baymard.com/lists/cart-abandonment-rate
5. ForeSee Results, Inc., http://www.waafiles.org/whitepapers/online-retail-satisfaction-index-u.s.-holiday-2012-foresee.pdf
6. Chatham, B.: Exposing Customer Experience Flaws. Forrester Tech Strategy Report (December 2002)
7. Brown, J., Dant, R.: The Role of E-Commerce in Multi-Channel Marketing Strategy. In: Martinez-Lopez, F. (eds.) Handbook of Strategic E-Business Management, pp. 467–487. Springer Verlag (2014)
8. Jacob, R.: Eye Tracking in Advanced Interface Design. In: Barfield, W., Furness, T. (eds.) Virtual Environments and Advanced Interface Design, pp. 258–288. Oxford University Press, New York (1995)
9. Romano Bergstrom, J., Schall, A.: Eye Tracking in User Experience Design. Morgan Kaufmann, Burlington (2014)

An Accessible CAPTCHA System for People with Visual Disability – Generation of Human/Computer Distinguish Test with Documents on the Net

Michitomo Yamaguchi[1,3], Toru Nakata[2], Takeshi Okamoto[3], and Hiroaki Kikuchi[1]

[1] Department of Mathematical Modeling, Analysis and Simulation,
Graduate School of Advanced Mathematical Sciences, Meiji University,
Tokyo, #164-8525 Japan
[2] Research Institute for Secure Systems, National Institute of Advanced Industrial Science
and Technology (AIST), Ibaraki, #305-8568 Japan
[3] Graduate School of Technology and Sciences, Tsukuba University of Technology,
Ibaraki, #305-8521 Japan
yama3san@meiji.ac.jp, toru-nakata@aist.go.jp,
ken@cs.k.tsukuba-tech.ac.jp, kikn@meiji.ac.jp

Abstract. We propose a new scheme of CAPTCHA that does not become a perceptual barrier for disable people. Our CAPTCHA system generates the tests in verbal style, so its use is not limited in specific perceptual channels. The tests are composed of several phrases and there are two kinds of tests: Human users try to (1) distinguish a phrase of strange meaning from others, and (2) identify the common topic among them. In our test we utilize open documents for material. Note that there is quite a large amount of documents on the net, so we can generate brand-new tests every time. One may say that adversaries can look for the phrases over the Internet and get several hints. Our system hides the sources by substituting the consonants of the phrases against such an attack. The mechanism is designed to imitate the phenomenon called "consonant gradation" of natural languages.

Keywords: universal design, aid for the visually-impaired, verbal interaction, information security.

1 Introduction

Demand for New Turing Tests for the Visually-Impaired. The purpose of this paper is to construct an accessible CAPTCHA system specially for people with visual disability.

The challenge-response tests of CAPTCHA [1] (Completely Automated Public Turing test to tell Computers and Human Apart) are widely used to differentiate humans from software agents. Typically, the systems challenge the user to read distorted letters. Artificial intelligence (AI) problems, which is easy for humans but difficult for current AI, are frequently employed for the purpose.

C. Stephanidis and M. Antona (Eds.): UAHCI/HCII 2014, Part IV, LNCS 8516, pp. 119–130, 2014.

There exists a big social problem that most of the visually-impaired cannot pass current CAPTCHAs. Several researchers [2–4] have pointed out that state-of-the-art audio CAPTCHAs are too difficult for them. A recently study [5] shows that five Japanese subjects with visual impairments have tried 10 times to pass Google's audio CAPTCHA, but nobody have succeeded even one. For those reason, audio CAPTCHAs do not work for a substitution of visual ones.

We reconfirm requirements for CAPTCHA system as follows.

Accessibility. Tests depending on the specific perceptual ability should not be used as CAPTCHA anymore.

Ability as a Turing Test. Tests must distinguish humans from software agents.

Ability of Auto-generating New Tests. The system must generate brand-new tests without limitation on amount.

Related Work. Maintaining the quality of the tests is also a hard problem.

The test system of Holman et al. [6] shows pairs of a picture and a sound to a user and test that the user can understand the situation of the materials. This scheme needs to collect a myriad of pictures and sounds data. We deem it difficult to collect them enough for practice.

Contextual cognition and theory of mind have been widely studied in cognitive science. Sally-Anne test [7] is to distinguish one's sphere of knowledge from others' one. In Dick's novel, he showed an idea of Voigt-Kampff [8], which submitted eccentric phrases and checked fluctuations of one's feeling. These tests will work as a Turing test but it is difficult to generate them automatically.

There are already CAPTCHA-like tests in verbal style. Contextual cognition test is the most typical verbal test. Only the humans can evaluate naturalness of the phrases. We can feel difference between natural human-made phrases and machine-translated phrases (Yamamoto et al. [9]) or machine-synthesized phrases with moderate randomness (*KK12* system of Kamoshida et al. [10]).

Regarding information security, the system has to generate brand-new tests for every time, or the adversaries can pass the tests when the system set old ones again. Unfortunately, conventional schemes leverage strings of private documents in order to prevent adversaries from finding out their sources. It is a serious problem for us to use such schemes as a CAPTCHA since the amount of private documents is finite. The system cannot limitlessly generate brand-new tests.

Our Approach. We summarize our approach as follows.

- We utilize contextual cognition tests as a part of the accessible CAPTCHA system.
- Our system collects phrases from a large amount of documents on the Internet to generate unbounded amount of tests.
- Using public documents is not safe, because adversaries may find out sources of phrases by using search engines and utilize them to break the tests. As a countermeasure, our particular system employs substitutes the consonants of the phrases.

The substitutes makes harder for adversaries to look for the sources of original phrases from such erroneous ones. The mechanism is similar to the phenomenon called

Test of detecting machine-synthesized semi-random phrases:
Q. Which phrase is generated by computer?
A) The world will little note, nor long remember what we say here.
B) Now we are dedicated in a larger people.

Test of detecting common topic:
Q. What is the topic common to the following sentences?
– Twitter is an social networking service.
– Vector processors are used for parallel computing.
A) Computer, B) Sports, C) Culture.

Example of Consonant Substitution:
Original: London, Paris, and Rome.
After distorted: Wonton, Pawi, and Home.

(a) Simple Example of Our Verbal Turing Tests.

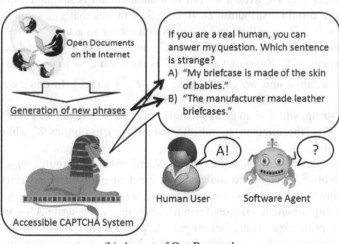

(b) Aspect of Our Proposal.

Fig. 1. Sketch of Our Proposal

"consonant gradation" of natural languages. We expect that most humans can interpret the erroneous phrases to some extent due to linguistical ability.

Our Contributions. We show the brief sketch of our proposal in Fig. 1.

We propose two methods to generate contextual cognition tests. One is test of detecting machine-synthesized phrased generated by Markov chain. It is based on the scheme of *KK12*, and we try to redeem its weakness around discrete co-occurrence of terms. The other method is to generate topic detection tests. The system shows several phrases and challenges the user to answer the topic common to them.

We then implement them as CAPTCHA programs, and evaluate their performances in three points: 1) ability as a Turing test, which must be easily solved by humans, 2) generation of new tests without limitation on amount, and 3) ability of hiding the sources of the phrases appeared in the test.

2   Mechanism of Our System

2.1   Notations

Let X be an operation. We write $x \leftarrow X$ to indicate that x is assigned by X. Let i, j be integers. We denote an integral element x from i to j by $x \in [i, j]$. Let $\{x_i\}$ be a finite set of $x_0, x_1, \ldots$. We write $x \overset{D}{\leftarrow} \{x_i\}$ to indicate that x is sampled randomly from $\{x_i\}$ following a certain distribution D. If $D = \$$, it means that x is sampled uniform-randomly from $\{x_i\}$. We use the same notation of a set for an array.

We will use a multi-associative memory C and write $key \in C$ to indicate that key is a registered key of C. Suppose that, e.g., C is the form $C = \{(key, val_0), (key, val_0), (key, val_0), (key, val_1)\}$ and we pick a value c as $c \overset{D}{\leftarrow} C(key)$. In this case, c will be substituted by val_0 with 75% and by val_1 with 25%.

Let k be a string, which is an array of characters. We denote the length of string k by $|k|$. We write $\mathcal{K} \leftarrow$ **thesaurus**(k) to indicate that a thesaurus outputs $\mathcal{K}$, which is the set of synonyms of k.

Let $\mathcal{M}$ be a stock of documents, which is utilized as the source of k. We write $\{m_i\} \leftarrow$ **search**$(+k, -\mathcal{K}, \mathcal{M})$ to indicate that a set of phrases $\{m_i\}$ is retrieved from $\mathcal{M}$ by searching with keyword k, without the words in $\mathcal{K}$.

We need morphological analyses for our experiments. We write $A \leftarrow$ **ma**(k) to indicate that a morphological analyzer outputs A, which is the array of morphemes of k and the last element of A is a terminal symbol. We denote a concatenation string of each element in A by **concat**(A). We write $\{(seg_{M,i}, seg_{R,i})\} \leftarrow$ **da**(m) to indicate that a dependence analyzer outputs two segments of documents, which are retrieved from document m. For instance, **da**("I hit the ball with the bat.") outputs $\{(seg_{M,i}, seg_{R,i})\} = \{($"hit", "the ball"$), ($"hit", "with the bat"$), \ldots\}$.

2.2   Overview of the System

We begin by showing a framework of our system. Let $\mathcal{V}$ be a *verifier*, i.e. CAPTCHA system and $\mathcal{P}$ be a *prover*, who tries to pass the test. $\mathcal{V}$ determines whether $\mathcal{P}$ is human or not as follows.

1) $\mathcal{V}$ runs a program $\mathcal{G}$ which generates AI problems using the contextual cognition if $\mathcal{V}$ needs to differentiate human from software agent.
2) $\mathcal{G}$ collects phrases from source documents $\mathcal{M}$, analyzes morphology of them, and generate/update corpora. We use open documents in the Internet $\mathcal{M}$.
3) $\mathcal{G}$ generates a pair of (z, a) with the corpora, where z is a problem and a is its answer. The phrases in z have a certain property such as contextual naturalness.
4) $\mathcal{V}$ repeats the steps 2)–3) N times and outputs $\{(z_i, a_i)\}$ to $\mathcal{P}$ as a test. $\mathcal{P}$ can recognize the test by his/her favorite perception since it consists of textual information.
5) $\mathcal{V}$ receives the answers $\{a_i'\}$ from $\mathcal{P}$. $\mathcal{V}$ checks whether $a_i = a_i'$ or not for all i. If the number of correct answers is greater than t, $\mathcal{V}$ judges $\mathcal{P}$ as a human.

Note that we may skip the step (2) in the case of updating if $\mathcal{G}$ can generate brand-new problems in high ratio.

2.3 Basic Components of the Process

We introduce several functions which are the building blocks of our AI problems.

Generation of Corpora. We generate two kinds of corpora: a n-th-order Markov chain modeled corpus (C_0) and a pre-post-state modeled corpus (C_1). They are multi-associative memories. The key of C_0 is a morpheme n-gram and its values are co-occurrence of it. The value of C_1 is a morpheme and key is a couple of morphemes before and after it.

We write $C_0 \leftarrow \mathbf{cpsgen}_0(\{m_j\}, n)$, e.g.: $\{("I hit", "the"), ("hit the", "ball"), \ldots\} \leftarrow \mathbf{cpsgen}_0(\{"I hit the ball with the bat."\}, 2)$, to indicate the following procedure for all m_j.

1) Compute $mor_j \leftarrow \mathbf{ma}(m_j)$. Assign $C \leftarrow \emptyset$ and $i \leftarrow 0$. C is a local variable, whose data structure is the same as C_0.
2) If $i + n < |mor_j|$, go to the step (3). Otherwise, output C as C_0 and finish this process.
3) Assign $key \leftarrow (mor_j[i], \ldots, mor_j[i + n - 1])$, $val \leftarrow mor_j[i + n]$, and $C \leftarrow \{C, (key, val)\}$.
4) If $mor_j[i]$ is an independent morpheme, tags it.
5) Go to the step 2) after computing $i \leftarrow i + 1$.

We write $C_1 \leftarrow \mathbf{cpsgen}_1(\{m_j\})$, e.g.: $\{("I the", "hit"), ("hit the", "the"), \ldots\} \leftarrow \mathbf{cpsgen}_1(\{"I hit the ball with the bat."\})$, to indicate the following procedure for all m_j.

1) Compute $mor_j \leftarrow \mathbf{ma}(m_j)$. Assign $C \leftarrow \emptyset$ and $i \leftarrow 1$. C is a local variable, whose data structure is the same as C_1.
2) If $i + 1 < |mor_j|$, go to the step 3). Otherwise, output C as C_1 and finish this process.
3) Assign $key \leftarrow (mor_j[i - 1], mor_j[i + 1])$, $val \leftarrow mor_j[i]$, and $C \leftarrow \{C, (key, val)\}$.
4) Go to the step 2) after computing $i \leftarrow i + 1$.

Generation of Synthesized Phrases. We generate synthesized phrases by Markov chain of order n. Let ℓ_L be the minimum length of them and ℓ_H be the maximum one. We write $s \leftarrow \mathbf{mcpgen}(n, \ell_L, \ell_H, C_0)$ to indicate the following procedure.

1) Pick $\ell \overset{\$}{\leftarrow} [\ell_L, \ell_H]$.

2) We generate the beginning of a synthesized phrase. Pick key uniformly and randomly from tagged keys in C_0, $val_0 \overset{D}{\leftarrow} C_0(key_0)$, and assign $ary \leftarrow (key_0, val_0)$.

3) If val_0 is a terminal symbol or $\ell < |\mathbf{concat}(ary)|$, output $\mathbf{concat}(ary)$ as a synthesized phrase and finish this process. Otherwise, go to the step 4).

4) Assign $key_0 \leftarrow (ary[|ary| - n], \ldots, ary[|ary| - 1])$. Pick $val_0 \overset{D}{\leftarrow} C_0(key_0)$ and assign $ary \leftarrow (key_0, val_0)$. Go to the step 3).

2.4 Countermeasures against Breaking the Test by Software

Extraction of Discrete Co-occurrence Features. In a linguistic sense, co-occurrence is interpreted as an indicator of semantic proximity or an idiomatic expression. We call *discrete co-occurrence* to indicate a fixed pattern of terms that often appear together with keeping several distance each other. For example, phrase of "not only . . . , but also . . ." is a discrete co-occurrence pattern.

We generate unnatural phrases by Markov chain of small order n. However, in that case, it is difficult for us to generate phrases which have a feature of discrete co-occurrence. Because each term of the phrases only depends on the last n terms. We are afraid of adversaries to use this shortcoming.

Therefore, we extract the feature as $\hat{C}_0$ and append it to C_0. We write $\hat{C}_0 \leftarrow \mathbf{dcogen}(\{m_j\}, n, C_1)$ to indicate that, for all m_j, the following procedure.

1) Compute $\{(seg_{M,i}, seg_{R,i})\} \leftarrow \mathbf{da}(m_j)$. Assign $C \leftarrow \emptyset$. C is a local variable, whose data structure is the same as C_0 and $\hat{C}_0$.

2) For $(seg_{M,i}, seg_{R,i}) \in \{(seg_{M,i}, seg_{R,i})\}$, we do as follows.

   2-1) Compute $mor_{M,i} \leftarrow \mathbf{ma}(seg_{M,i})$ and $mor_{R,i} \leftarrow \mathbf{ma}(seg_{R,i})$.

   2-2) Assign $key_1 \leftarrow (mor_{M,i}[|mor_{M,i}| - 1], mor_{R,i}[0])$. If $key_1 \in C_1$, pick $val_1 \overset{D}{\leftarrow} C_1(key_1)$. Otherwise, we assign an empty string to val_1.

   2-3) Assign $ary \leftarrow (mor_{M,i}, val_1, mor_{R,i})$, $key_1 \leftarrow (ary[0], \ldots, ary[n - 1])$, $val_1 \leftarrow (ary[n], \ldots, ary[|ary| - 1])$, and $C \leftarrow \{C, (key_1, val_1)\}$. If $key_1[0]$ is an independent morpheme, tags it.

3) We output C as $\hat{C}_0$ and finish this process.

The reason why we insert val_1 between $seg_{M,i}$ and $seg_{R,i}$ is that because of randomness. The phrase which consists of $seg_{M,i}$ and $seg_{R,i}$ only cannot be used as a part of an unnatural phrase.

Consonant Substitution to Hide the Document Source. To protect the tests from attacks using search engines, our system hides the sources by substituting the consonants of the phrases in them. Let s_p be a string without consonant substitution and s_a be a string with one. Let r_L be a the minimum number of the substitution and r_H be a maximum one. We write $s_a \leftarrow \mathbf{cogd}(s_p, r_L, r_H)$ to indicate the following procedure.

1) This is an initialize step.
   - Let $\mathcal{L}_L$ be a set which includes all kinds of a group of Japanese consonant, that is, $\mathcal{L}_L = \{\text{"}group - a\text{"}, \text{"}group - ka\text{"}, \ldots\}$.

- Convert kanji (Chinese characters) of s_p into hiragana (Japanese syllabary characters) and output the result as s_m.
- Pick $r \xleftarrow{\$} [r_L, r_H]$.

2) We check the consonant of s_m.
- For each letter of s_m, check which the group of consonant is and output the result as an array L_{s_m}, whose element is a kind of the group of Japanese consonant. For example, we get ("$group-a$", "$group-sa$", "$group-ga$", "$group-a$") from the term "a-sa-ga-o".
- If $|L_{s_m}| < r$, compute $r \leftarrow |L_{s_m}| - 1$.
- If $r > 0$, go to the step (3). Otherwise, output s_m as s_a and finish this process.

3) We substitute the consonants of s_m.
- Pick $u \xleftarrow{\$} L_{s_m}$ and $v \xleftarrow{\$} \mathcal{L}_L \backslash u$.
- Check an index i of the element u in the array L_{s_m}.
- Replace the i-th letter in s_{s_m} by a letter of the same group of vowel in v
- Go to the step (2) after computing $r \leftarrow r - 1$.

The output of **cogd** is similar to the phrase which includes several "mistakes" such as misprint and mishearing. We expect that human can correct them by interpreting contexts and his/her experience [11–13].

2.5 Detail of Generation of Our CAPTCHA

We show two kinds of AI problems concerning contextual cognition.

Markov-Chain Phrase Problem. Markov-chain phrase problem is that a prover selects the most unnatural phrase among several synthesized phrases.

We use *word salad* as a synthesized phrase by Markov chain. Word salad usually keeps grammatical correctness to some extent and stands for certain meanings. The naturalness of their meanings differs in respect to the order n of the generation algorithm i.e. the synthesized phrases become more unnatural as n is small, vice versa.

We give an account of an algorithm $\mathcal{G}_0$, which generates a Markov-chain phrase problem. Let p be the number of choices and $\mathcal{M}$ be phrases of source documents. Let n_{NP} be the order of Markov chain to generate natural phrases and n_{WS} be one to generate word salad. Let ℓ_L and ℓ_H be the minimum/maximum length of synthesized phrases, respectively. Let r_L and r_H be the minimum/maximum number of substituting consonants, respectively. We require $p > 1$, $n_{NP} > n_{WS} > 0$, $\ell_H > \ell_L > 0$ and $r_H > r_L > 0$. $\mathcal{G}_0$ is inputted p, n_{NP}, n_{WS}, ℓ_L, ℓ_H, r_L, r_L and $\mathcal{M}$, then outputs (z, a) as follows.

1) The system collects phrases $\{m_j\}$.
- Pick $\{m_j\} \xleftarrow{\$} \mathcal{M}$.

2) The system generates corpora for Markov chain.
- Compute $C_{0,NP} \leftarrow$ **cpsgen**$_0(\{m_j\}, n_{NP})$ to generate natural phrases.
- Compute $C_{0,WS} \leftarrow$ **cpsgen**$_0(\{m_j\}, n_{WS})$ to generate word salad.
The system extracts discrete co-occurrence and append them to $C_{0,WS}$.
- Compute $C_1 \leftarrow$ **cpsgen**$_1(\{m_j\})$.
- Compute $\hat{C}_{0,WS} \leftarrow$ **dcogen**$(\{m_j\}, n_{WS}, C_1)$.

- Assign $C_{0,WS} \leftarrow \{C_{0,WS}, \hat{C}_{0,WS}\}$.

3) The system generates a word salad and natural phrases by Markov chain.

- Pick $x \xleftarrow{\$} [0, p-1]$.
- Compute $s_x \leftarrow$ **mcpgen**$(n_{WS}, \ell_L, \ell_H, C_{0,WS})$.
- For $i \in [0, p-1] \backslash x$, compute $s_i \leftarrow$ **mcpgen**$(n_{NP}, \ell_L, \ell_H, C_{0,NP})$.

4) The system substitutes consonants of the synthesized phrases.

- For $i \in [0, p-1]$, compute $z_i \leftarrow$ **cogd**(s_i, r_L, r_H).

5) The system outputs a problem.

- Assign $z \leftarrow (z_0, \ldots, z_{p-1})$ and $a \leftarrow x$.

Topic Detection Problem. Topic detection problem is that a prover selects the most related keyword with submitted phrases from choices.

We try to generate the phrases which do not include strings of the choices by using a thesaurus. Moreover, we append a phrase which is not related with the keyword to ones which are related with it.

We give an account of an algorithm $\mathcal{G}_1$, which generates a topic detection problem. Let q be the number of submitted phrases and $\mathcal{K}$ be a set of keyword. We require $p > 1$, $q > 2$, $n_{NP} > 0$, $\ell_H > \ell_L > 0$ and $r_H > r_L > 0$. $\mathcal{G}_1$ is inputted $p, q, n_{NP}, \ell_L, \ell_H, r_L, r_L$, $\mathcal{K}$, and $\mathcal{M}$, then outputs (z, a) as follows.

1) The system chooses a keyword key_t used as a correct answer and generate a set $\hat{\mathcal{K}}_t$, whose element is a synonym of key_t.

- Pick $key_t \xleftarrow{\$} \mathcal{K}$ and compute $\mathcal{K} \leftarrow \mathcal{K} \backslash key_t$.
- Compute $\hat{\mathcal{K}}_t \leftarrow$ **thesaurus**(key_t).

2) Let $\mathcal{K}_d$ be a set of a dummy keyword and $\hat{\mathcal{K}}_d$ be a set, whose element is a synonym of the corresponding element of $\mathcal{K}_d$. Assign $\mathcal{K}_d \leftarrow \emptyset$ and $\hat{\mathcal{K}}_d \leftarrow \emptyset$. To generate $\hat{\mathcal{K}}_d$, repeat the following steps if $|\mathcal{K}_d| < p - 1$.

- Pick $key_d \xleftarrow{\$} \mathcal{K} \backslash \mathcal{K}_d$.
- Assign $\mathcal{K}_d \leftarrow \{\mathcal{K}_d, key_d\}$.
- Compute $\hat{\mathcal{K}}_d' \leftarrow$ **thesaurus**(key_d) and assign $\hat{\mathcal{K}}_d \leftarrow \{\hat{\mathcal{K}}_d, \hat{\mathcal{K}}_d'\}$.

3) The system extracts phrases, which are related with key_t but do not include strings of the choices.

- For $\hat{key}_t \in \hat{\mathcal{K}}_t$, $\{m_j\} \leftarrow$ **search**$(+\hat{key}_t, -\{key_t, \mathcal{K}_d\}, \mathcal{M})$. For simplicity, we assume that $\{m_j\}$ in this step includes the results for all $\hat{key}_t$.
- Compute $C_{0,NP} \leftarrow$ **cpsgen**$_0(\{m_j\}, n_{NP})$.
- Pick $x \xleftarrow{\$} [0, q-1]$. For $i \in [0, q-1] \backslash x$, compute $s_i \leftarrow$ **mcpgen**$(n_{NP}, \ell_L, \ell_H, C_{0,NP})$.

4) The system extracts phrases, which are related with a dummy keyword $\hat{key}_d$ but do not include strings of the choices.

- Pick $\hat{key}_d \xleftarrow{\$} \hat{\mathcal{K}}_d$.
- Compute $\{m_j\} \leftarrow$ **search**$(+\hat{key}_d, -\{key_t, \mathcal{K}_d\}, \mathcal{M})$ and $C_{0,NP} \leftarrow$ **cpsgen**$_0(\{m_j\}, n_{NP})$.
- Compute $s_x \leftarrow$ **mcpgen**$(n_{NP}, \ell_L, \ell_H, C_{0,NP})$.

5) The system substitutes consonants of the extracted phrases.

- For $i \in [0, q-1]$, compute $z_i \leftarrow$ **cogd**(s_i, r_L, r_H).

6) The system outputs a problem. The choices consist of key_t and the elements of $\mathcal{K}_d$.

- Assign $z \leftarrow (z_0, \ldots, z_{q-1})$ and $a \leftarrow key_t$.

3   Experiment

3.1   Tools and Parameters

We implemented an evaluation program (hereinafter referred to as the **EvaPro**) to evaluate our proposals. We used MeCab [14] to analyze morphology, Cabocha [15] to analyze dependence, and Weblio thesaurus [16] to get synonyms of queried terms.

We show several parameters of our AI problems in **EvaPro**.

Markov-Chain Phrase Problem ($\mathcal{G}_0$). We employed "Aozora Bunko [17]" as $\mathcal{M}$. We then set $p = 4$, $n_{NP} = 7$, $n_{WS} = 1$, $(\ell_L, \ell_H) = (40, 80)$, and $(r_L, r_H) = (2, 5)$.

Topic Detection Problem ($\mathcal{G}_1$). We employed documents which is collectable by GAPI [18] as $\mathcal{M}$. We then set $p = 4$, $q = 5$, $n_{NP} = 7$, $(\ell_L, \ell_H) = (30, 60)$, $(r_L, r_H) = (2, 5)$, and $\mathcal{K} = \{$"*sport*", "*weather*", "*economy*", "*meal*"$\}$. In fact, we set $\mathcal{K}$ in Japanese.

Note that we determine the range of substitution degree (r_L, r_H) and the minimum phrase length ℓ_L the following reason. Let s be a phrase and $\hat{s}$ be a phrase to which the consonant substitution is applied. We assume that adversaries try to restore $\hat{s}$ to its original string s and output s'. If $s' = s$, adversaries can get several hints of our problems to query on s'. Therefore, the number of a prospective for s', that is, $\sum_{i=r_L}^{r_H} \binom{\ell_L}{i}$ should be large. In fact, the number of the prospective for s' is about 1.5 billion under the condition of $\ell_L = 30$ and $(r_L, r_H) = (2, 5)$. It takes about 11 days to find s by using a computer which can operate at 1.8 million per second. (In fact, it is difficult for adversaries without the knowledge of s to confirm whether $s' = s$ or not because several prospective for s' may natural but $s' \neq s$.)

Consequently, it is difficult for adversaries to find s by brute-force attacks.

Meanwhile, we determine ℓ_H owning to an availability. We suppress the amount of phrases by ℓ_H.

Table 1. Results of our Subjective Experiment

(a) Results of Markov-Chain Phrase Test.

Sight	w/o Consonant Substitution		w/ Consonant Substitution	
	Average Accuracy Rate [%]	Capability [%] as a Turing Test	Average Accuracy Rate [%]	Capability [%] as a Turing Test
Totally Blind	89	86	73	57
Low Vision	78	82	49	41
All	85	83	60	46

(b) Results of Markov-Chain Phrase Test.

Sight	w/o Consonant Substitution		w/ Consonant Substitution	
	Average Accuracy Rate [%]	Capability [%] as a Turing Test	Average Accuracy Rate [%]	Capability [%] as a Turing Test
Totally Blind	71	86	81	100
Low Vision	67	71	60	71
All	69	75	70	79

3.2 Experiment on Test's Performance for Real Humans

We evaluate four kinds of tests: Markov-chain phrase test with/without consonant substitution and Topic detection test with/without one. We show our process of the subjective experiment as follows.

1) **Preprocessing.** For each AI problem, **EvaPro** collects phrases from $\mathcal{M}$, analyzes morphology of them, and generates a corpus.
2) **Generate tests.** **EvaPro** generates four kinds of tests. Each one consists of ten AI problems and includes the alternative answer choices, which consists of four items. Finally, **EvaPro** outputs them as a text. Note that this process is completely automated, that is, we do not modify anything in the text without appending several explanations.
3) **Distribute tests.** 24 subjects participate the experiment. Seven subjects of them are the totally blind, recognize the tests by their auditory sense with a screen reader. Seventeen subjects are the weak-sighted, recognize them by sight (and hearing, partly).
4) **Check results.** The subjects answer the tests without any training. We check them as follows.

   Average accuracy rate. This is an average of the rate how subjects correctly answer every a problem.

   Capability as a Turing test. The rate is that subjects correctly answer at least t times among N problems. In this case, we set that $(N, t) = (10, 7)$.

Note that we determine a threshold t to the following effect. We assume that a verifier judges a prover as a human by at least t correct answers among N problems. If there exists an adversary $\mathcal{P}^*$ who solves an AI problem by the probability of P, the success probability of brute-force attacks to the test by $\mathcal{P}^*$ is $\sum_{i=t}^{N} \binom{N}{i} P^i (1 - P)^{N-i}$. Burzstein et al. [19] claim that a CAPTCHA system is unuseful if there exists an adversary who solves it by the probability of 1% more than. Hence, we set $t = 7$ corresponding to $N = 10$ and $P = 1/p = 0.25$.

Results and Discussion. The results appear in Tab. 1. (Data from out previous work [20].) The rate of Markov-chain phrase test is lower than one of topic detection test. In my understanding, the reason why differences of naturalness between natural phrases and word salad becomes small is that phrases with consonant substitution are more unnatural than without ones. In fact, an influence of the consonant substitution in Markov-chain phrase test is significant by our statistical test but is not significant in topic detection test.

To compare our proposal with a conventional system, we also show our results [20] of experiment for Google's audio CAPTCHA of the version at November 2013. The capability as a Turing test was only 7%. Moreover, there were only five among 24 Japanese who can answer correctly at least one in ten challenges.

Consequently, our system is better suited for the visually-impaired.

3.3 Experiment on Performance against Cracking

We consider adversaries with search engines and generation rate of new phrases.

Attacks Using Search Engines. Straightforward attack is that adversaries convert documents on the Internet into ones written in hiragana and they seek source documents of our problems. However, this approach needs vast amounts of memories. Thus, we employ a typically and easily-implemented attack as follows: suppose that there are phrases written in hiragana and their consonants are swapped, adversaries repair several "mistakes" in the phrases with conventional tools, and convert them into the ones which includes several kanji-characters.

We show the following experiment as such an attack.

1) Extract 100 natural phrases from M and swap their consonants in the same manner as Sec. 2.5.
2) Convert them into sound files with Microsoft Speech Platform 11. They are 48KHz-16bit mp3 files in stereo.
3) Convert them into text files with Dragon Speech 11, which is software of speech recognition. Conversion to kanji-characters and restoration are done in this process.
4) For each one, we check whether it includes a source of the corresponding substituted phrase to less than top ten affairs. If it includes, we consider that adversaries find the source of the phrase. By checking all the results of the samples, we calculate a detection rate against attacks by search engines.

Generation Rate of New Phrases. Let Z be a multiple set, whose element is a generated phrase in each test. We call $z \in Z$ new phrase if $z' \notin Z \backslash z$, where $z' = z$. For each test, we generate it 10000 times under the same condition of the subjective experiment, assign generated phrases to Z, and check they are new phrases or not.

Results and Discussion. Attacks Using Search Engines. The detection rate by Yahoo! is 9% under the condition of $(r_L, r_H) = (2, 2)$ and 1% under the condition of $(r_L, r_H) = (2, 5)$. In our subjective experiment, the number of choices by a problem is four, thus the success probability of brute-force attacks is 25%. The four sums of detection rate, that is $1 \times 4\%$, is lower than this probability. Therefore, an advantage of adversaries does not increase by such attacks.

Generation Rate of New Phrases. We collected phrases of 1717 lines, 87260 letters, and 4361 kinds of morphemes in Markov-chain phrase test. Moreover, we collected phrases of 1209 lines, 109042 letters, and 9726 kinds of morphemes in topic detection test. The rate of Markov-chain phrase test and topic detection test is 99.94% and 99.65%, respectively.

Each test generated new phrases with a small amount of documents at a high rate. Therefore, we have only to collect materials for test at any time in case of update. This means that our system can dispose old phrases and generate new ones.

4 Conclusion

We constructed an accessible CAPTCHA system, which generates two type of AI problems using the contextual cognition. We showed that our system could differentiate humans from software agents with high probability compared with conventional Google's audio CAPTCHA, generate new phrases as problems without limit by using phrases on the Internet, and have a tolerant against adversaries by existing search engines.

References

1. von Ahn, L., Blum, M., Hopper, N.J., Langford, J.: Captcha: Using hard ai problems for security. In: Biham, E. (ed.) EUROCRYPT 2003. LNCS, vol. 2656, pp. 294–311. Springer, Heidelberg (2003)
2. Bigham, J.P., Cavender, A.C.: Evaluating existing audio captchas and an interface optimized for non-visual use. In: CHI 2009, pp. 1829–1838. ACM (2009)
3. Bursztein, E., Bethard, S., Fabry, C., Mitchell, J.C., Jurafsky, D.: How good are humans at solving captchas? a large scale evaluation. In: SP 2010, pp. 399–413. IEEE Computer Society (2010)
4. Shirali-Shahreza, S., Shirali-Shahreza, M.H.: Accessibility of captcha methods. In: AISec 2011, pp. 109–110. ACM (2011)
5. Yamaguchi, M.: A generating method of accessible verbal questions with online documents for substitution of captcha-like tests. Verbal Interface & Interaction 15(4), 337–352 (2013) (Japanese)
6. Holman, J., Lazar, J., Feng, J.H., D'Arcy, J.: Developing usable captchas for blind users. In: Assets 2007, pp. 245–246. ACM (2007)
7. Wimmer, H., Perner, J.: Beliefs about beliefs: Representation and constraining function of wrong beliefs in young children's understanding of deception. Cognition 13(1), 103 (1983)
8. Dick, P.K.: Do androids dream of electric sheep? (1968)
9. Yamamoto, T., Tygar, J., Nishigaki, M.: Captcha using strangeness in machine translation. AINA 2010, 430–437 (2010)
10. Kamoshida, Y., Kikuchi, H.: Word salad captcha - application and evaluation of synthesized sentences. NBIS 12, 799–804 (2012)
11. Miller, G.A., Licklider, J.C.R.: The intelligibility of interrupted speech (1950)
12. Rawlinson, G.: The Significance of Letter Position in Word Recognition. University of Nottingham (1976)
13. Saberi, K., Perrott, D.: Cognitive restoration of reversed speech. Nature 398(6730), 760 (1999)
14. Kudo, T.: Mecab: Yet another part-of-speech and morphological analyzer, http://mecab.sourceforge.net/
15. Kudo, T., Matsumoto, Y.: Japanese dependency analysis using cascaded chunking. In: CoNLL 2002, pp. 63–69 (2002)
16. Weblio-Thesaurus, http://thesaurus.weblio.jp/
17. Aozora-Bunko, http://www.aozora.gr.jp/
18. GAPI. Net-0.5.0.1, http://gapidotnet.codeplex.com/
19. Bursztein, E., Martin, M., Mitchell, J.: Text-based captcha strengths and weaknesses. In: CCS 2011, pp. 125–138. ACM (2011)
20. Yamaguchi, M., Okamoto, T.: An evaluation of a captcha for the visually impaired using questions of context interpretation. National University Corporation Tsukuba University of Technology Techno Report 21 (2014) (Japanese)

Design for All in the Built Environment

City – Mass Communication Space – Access to Information in Relation to the Composition of the City

Agata Bonenberg

Faculty of Architecture, Poznan University of Technology,
Nieszawska 13C, 61-021 Poznan, Poland
agata.bonenberg@put.poznan.pl

Abstract. Streets and squares in the cities were created so that they could constitute public space – space of a social integration. Important social binding agent is a common, direct access to information, ability of passing it on and undertaking actions appropriate to its response. In an era of information revolution, new information and communication technologies enriched social contacts. Access to information no longer requires direct interpersonal contact due to which the contact became less related to city space. The subject of the article is the evolution of city space with relation to the access to information. The cotemporary closing of which is the phase of multimedia mass communication and city spaces designed for information society.

Keywords: City, mass - communication space, access to information, urban composition.

1   Introduction

Stepping into the center of the Roman Capitol Hill leading from via Sacra, the visitor of the city will find himself standing in front of a prow of the antique Rostra. A site of paramount meaning, the heart of the Roman Republic, the heart of the Roman Empire, from which decisions of the governing bodies and news were announced and spread throughout the then world. It was located in the most significant place in the layout of the Roman Forum. In truth, the gravity of the place and the prominence of its function were emphasized by prows of conquered ships – both via Sacra as well as the Rostra were raised to a rank of a symbol – the heart of the ancient Empire.

Spaces of streets and squares in the cities, from the very beginning of settlements' development documented history was demarcated so that they could create public space – social integration space. The primary role of, task and reason for the existence of common spaces in the city is the necessity of creating society – the reason behind which is to improve political organization of its residents [1]. The common bond of the society is joint access to information, possibility of easy dissemination thereof and undertaking actions based on the received feedback. The building and maintain close ties between the city's inhabitants is the basic factor enabling social, economic, political and cultural development of the city environment. Absence of social integration

C. Stephanidis and M. Antona (Eds.): UAHCI/HCII 2014, Part IV, LNCS 8516, pp. 133–142, 2014.
© Springer International Publishing Switzerland 2014

would eliminate the chance of acting as a collective body – there never would come to existence complex social ties characteristic of modern relations.

2   City as a Mass Communication Space

In ancient time, access to information was interpersonal, direct and contributed to stabilizing one of the basic human qualities – man as a social being together with all the psychological and behavioral consequences. In our nature lies the need to live in a community. Technological inventions: printing (XV century), telegraph (XVII century), telephone (XIX century), radio (XX century), television (XX century), internet network (XX century) made access to information both global as well as local ceased to be based on interpersonal contact. The nature of social contacts changed and enriched with new tools. During centuries, access to information was becoming increasingly less bound with direct contact between people. In this context, the next step being the building of information society, in a certain sense is a critical moment in history: work, relaxation and enjoyment, functioning in society and even building a relationship with another person – with quite a significant limitation of direct personal contact. Questions on the role of direct contacts in a social organization are justified. To what degree will progress its self-limitation? How far will we go to replace meeting with another person using other forms of communication including the use of mass media communication? Will participation in mass communication fulfill human social needs?

Pondering the subject of space in an information society a question should be posed, what future awaits the city? What will happen with its public spaces? Will there be a necessity of designing public spaces in new projects?

The temptation of closing oneself off in virtual contacts exists; there also exist possibilities of work, free time exclusively through the internet. At the same time, attention should be turned to the value of direct interpersonal contacts as a factor building human ties and relations and as a therapeutic element. Therefore, it is most probable that in order to achieve satisfaction and happiness in live, personal contact with others is vital. Carrying this postulate over to spatial design a need and mission appears to build social integration space – also for the information society. Yet, while conversing, it is the non-verbal communication that outweighs the impact of verbal message, and it is this that is most difficult to pass on through digital communication sources (even when using image transmission).

In „Life between buildings", Jan Gehl writes about three categories of activities of city dwellers in public spaces: necessary activities, optional activities, and social activities [2]. Necessary activities in public space are those, which are required to carry out. Optional activities are those that users of public space pursue only in certain optimal conditions, most frequently in places having high space layout and viewing attributes.

Social activities are all activities that depend on the presence of others in public spaces. (…) Social activities occur spontaneously, as a direct consequence of people moving about and being in the same spaces. This implies that social activities (indirectly supported) whenever necessary and optional activities are given better conditions in public spaces (Gehl, 2009).

Public and semi-public spaces have a basic leading meaning for creating neighborhood societies: within them, the flow of information has local characteristics. This fact directly reflects on building a relation with a specific place, creating a bond with the surrounding environment as it pertains to its joint usage, management and maintenance.

Mass media communication has a different effect on a completely different scale. It plays an important role in social integration, despite the fact that it pertains to phenomena on a larger scale and higher organization levels: national, ethnic groups, religion and cultural. It is associated with creating and building collective identity of nations and even inhabitants of an entire continent. Mass communication as opposed to direct communication does not contribute to creating a bond between the user with his work or living space[1]. Quite the contrarily, mass communication is associated with the disintegration of traditional neighborhood communities [3] (neglecting public spaces), as it is viewed as a competition with traditional direct contacts. The natural need to function in society, the feeling of being a part of a community is satiated by participation in mass media. Social integration always takes place on many levels: neighborhood and even family integration may lose its meaning to belonging to a much wider group [4]. Propagating various models of behavior, bringing geographically distant places closer, mass communication eliminates fear and anxiety ensuing from the idea of migration. This loosens a person's attachment do a known environment and intensifies his mobility.

The historical, increased percentile of society's participation in the circulation of mass information is presented by the curve of social reach of information (diagram no. 1). With time, access to information encompassed increasingly wider range circles. The social reach of information curve includes four (4) main development phases of mass communication processes: the elite phase, popularization phase, specialization phase and multimedia phase [5]. As much as the elite phase is communicating within the circle of the highest social classes, the multi-media phase signifies an unlimited access to mass communication report.

The placement of the curve with typical layout of cities in different historic periods may suggest the occurrence of the following dependencies: with the growing access to mass information, a gradual polycentrism and loosening of city structure. Simultaneously, architecture is losing communication properties: individualized detail, codification using symbols and allegories expressed in sculptures and frescos.

There is no doubt that the access to information issue is only one of many factors affecting the evolution of city and architectural space. Additionally, the basic issue was increase in population, function specialization, political issues, espoused culture and many others. However, attention should be turned to consolidating meaning of access to information in historical cities. Architecture was a very important information medium about a place, about social and economic relations. It may be said that

---

[1] An exception being multi-million metropolises, in which the issuers of local mass media: regional television programs, radio stations, internet portals and printed press.

what once was communicated through architectural form and it hierarchy as well as layout in a city, today it can be passed on using other communication sources. The primary aim of the created graphs is the observation of the direction of this transformation and a diagnosis of modern space tendencies. Characteristic of space urbanization taking place in the era of information society is quite significant, that is at a multimedia phase of mass communication.

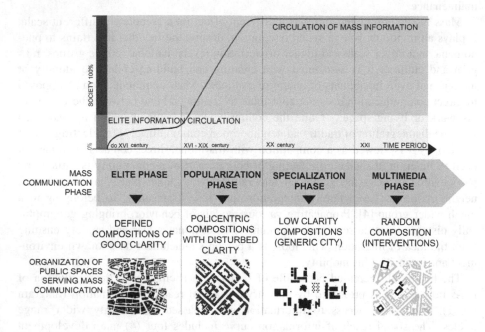

Fig. 1. The diagram illustrates relations between legibility of city space and phases of mass communication

2.1   Elite Phase – Cohesive and Clear City Composition

In the first, elitist phase of access to information, participation of a mass user was minimal. The time periods here are fluid due to non-uniform development of common education in Europe – which was the condition for receiving mass information in a printed form (XVI – XVII centuries). Prior to this, illiteracy of a considerable part of society constituted barriers in information circulation and general access to global and local information took place in public city spaces. Social and political order expressed through city's urban composition as well as architecture of buildings was understood to the recipients. Legibility of city space was based on a basic, common to all people level of recognition that is on associations and emotions: impressive, tall buildings were important (church, city hall); detail on the facades of tenement houses indicated the source of fortunes of wealthy merchants. The expression of artistic, decorative, sculptural elements in architecture was literal, and the scale of individual objects in the city tissue reflected its rank.

Public places: stages for rituals and interaction[2] are deserving of special attention among public spaces. They were consciously created with thought given to particularly meaningful activities related to culture and ritual.

As the effect on associations and emotions is the most basic method of influencing the collective, the historic city tissue, to this day is very positively perceived by general public of inhabitants. Referring to simple reflexes and associations is the most communicative method of designing city composition. Popularity of historic city centers as its prestigious trade districts, entertainment, and tourism centers fully supports this theory. These spaces also favorable contribute to traditional and direct social integration.

2.2   Popularization Phase

In the popularization phase of mass communication, mass communication and access to information commenced to be differentiated and better organized. This related to a development in the XVIII century of technologies such as telecommunication, print and transportation network, and prior to that with a better access to education. On the market began to appear subject magazines, catalogues, books and daily newspapers. Access to information, admittedly in a small degree, but started to cease being the direct consequence of participation in public and social life: through the postal service, it independently reaches a growing number of people.

The demographic and spatial development of European cities caused partial decentralization and the establishment of mutually competing local central points. Societies accumulated around local city squares, gardens and parks – access to local information was tied with exiting the indoors in the outdoor space of the nearest neighborhood. In this phase, public and social integration spaces became even more diversified and hierarchized. A significant time period for general access to information in city space is the XIX century, when the voice of social organizations educating also the most poverty-stricken society classes was heard. These organizations funded reading rooms and libraries (e.g. People's Education Society and People's Reading Rooms Society in the Wielkopolska region of Poland).

Specialization phase in industrial cities of the XX century – specialized systems and the loss of legibility of city structures.

The specialization phase of mass communication development process marks the period of increased social awareness of citizen rights, educations and facilitation of initiating mass social movements. Education of the society, increase of personal wealth, possibility of free disposal of time off from work, knowledge of the right to rest and recreation had an effect on the city space layout. It is therefore, natural, that the specialization phase of mass communication is linked with industrial city concepts and segregation of functions within its boundaries. As a result, areas and city districts are crated with the same uniform functionality – specialized. Industrial terrains, recreation, residential areas and trade and administration centers are being allotted their own space and thus separated in urban design.

---

[2] Especially significant areas: squares, city centers as opposed to streets, ports and other specifically utilization spaces have additional cultural meaning (Kostof, S. 1992).

In shopping and administration centers, transmission of information is of great importance as it relates to the proper function of sales and services as well as government administration. Organization in the specialized phase of mass communication is based on simple telecommunication tools (telephone, telefax) – and thus the quantity of remote data transfers between businesses and administrations is limited. Establishing a business in a good location (city center) is conditioned by access to clients, government administration and in that sense, also a condition of operation. Limited information and communication technologies up to the 1990's of the XX century were a factor in consolidating new investments and agglomeration of building development.

A significant factor in social reception and clarity of the city in the industrial age was the fact of their tie to the intellectual culture of the European elite. Renowned urbanists and architects were commissioned with city planning, and this related to the advanced specialization of business management groups and project designers of new communities as well as with urban designing development theory. The consequence of expanding a theoretical, research and scientific database is acceptance of spatial solution, the justification of which has scientific, intellectual character or expressing ideological contexts. The source of information about the designation of a building was neither a clear form nor significance placement of it in the city tissue. Knowledge is the condition for comprehension of intellectual layer – for people lacking knowledge, space loses its communicative properties (so well developed in the elitist phase of mass communication).

3   Multimedia Phase of Mass Communication – Urban Spaces of Information Society

In the last, multimedia phase of mass communication, attention should be turned to the fact of "pulling away" the relay of mass information as well as of economic development from factual space. The internet network, expansively developed data communication infrastructure, technical infrastructure, hardware equipment enable considerably large capacities of information reach the recipient outside the city space. Therefore, the relay of information ceases to be, in this phase, a central creative element consolidating building development, the meaning of real spaces lessens for social and political organization, as this organization becomes possible through information and communication technologies. In a hypothetical situation, in which the only city composition shaping parameter would be information flow, the city urban composition in the multimedia phase may be defined as a "cloud" of project intervention: unorganized collection of architectural objects. However, in reality, the appearance of new project designing plans may depend on factors unrelated to information access and signify expansion of creative freedom:

- may be a representation of abstract elements with artistic meaning,
- may concentrate on relations with the context of nature,

- may constitute a group of new functions "place on" the historic city space – using it without significant integration into the existing city tissue,
- may be inspired by personal interests and beliefs of the city's residents.

The last, multimedia phase of mass communication takes place under conditions of considerable breaking up of the city structure, in part as a consequence of the development of cities of the industrial era but also as a consequence of decentralization deepened by the general access to information and communication technologies.

Development of a European city at the multimedia mass communication phase may be describes as a "cloud" of interventions taking place in an existing, relaxed structure. It is based on revitalization, reclassification of the designation of city terrains, repair activities that result from moving away from traditional production of goods and replacing it with creative activity based on access to information. The dominating problematic issue in the plans of newly design projects of residential communities and suburban city districts are the widely understood environmental issues. The said projects frequently exhibit the natural conditions of the location.

In intensely urbanized Europe and America, interest in utilizing historic structures, investing in costly renovation and revitalization of architectural objects having material culture of past generations is a testimony to the maturity of societies and access to knowledge, which enables appreciation and enjoyment of this heritage. Together with the longing for human scale architecture and urban planning, returns the desire to use space subjected to adaptation or renewal – as unique, the only and the original. In this cultural change can be seen the popularity of lofts and every kind of non-standard living spaces.

Many parameters and many variables are the decisive factors in location intervention. Many to the degree that the map of city newly designed projects or objects appear to be unorganized and accidental. The deciding factors about the investment site are the following: technical state of the existing building development, issues of ownership, accessibility of non-developed lot, social premises, and political interests. Moreover, the financial and spatial scale of interventions may be greatly diversified. They may be a social, public or private undertaking. Characteristics of these activities have much in common with the notion of acupuncture of the city, the author of which is Brazilian urban planner, Jaime Lerner [6], which is expressed as a group of activities aimed at activation and improvement of city space in the smallest scale. The effects of interventions both when they pertain to the scale of urban planning (planning of communities but also development of a city square or greenery square) as well as architectural interventions have a common positive quality: new and old elements in urban structure are not standing in opposition to each other, on the contrary, they may base on a good, neighboring relations and the existing natural and cultural environment. Here dominates holistic approach and agreement to multi-motif approach to the composition of the city. The described above position of acceptance and drawing from resources is valuable. The opinion of the author is that in differentiation to the concept of industrial cities, in partially valid postulates in the Athens Charter, the city spaces of an information society may be directed at emphasized exhibition of cultural and social resources [7].

Monumental conceptual projects, for example Le Corbusier's plan for Paris was a manifest of the coming revolution – a new order. The tool to achieve the goal – tearing down and cutting off from the situation found. The revolution was a voice of discord on the subject of future order, emotionally packed concept full of rebellion against the low living standards in historic cities. City space project concepts for the information society are not based on revolution. Their basis is standard improvement, urban and architectural interventions. Also, the leading principle behind them is a collective diversification giving the users a choice of how and where to live. This allows some residents to realize their fascination with the past, hence the numerous adaptation and renewals of the historic building tissue. For other users, it enables closeness with nature – in projects geared at widely understood ecological values. The significance of the economic cost in a world living in the shadow of fuel crisis does not go unnoticed as well as awareness of the meaning of power-saving solutions for the natural environment. In comparing both assumptions, an industrial city treated the user of city spaces in a more object-like manner, not providing them with the above said choice. This approach tied to the rest, to the social order ensuing precisely from industrialization: collective work in the industry or office work.

A wide range of possibilities opens to the project designers based on the following foundations: ecology, respect of nature, reference to traditional and historic architecture (expansion of the vernacular movement definition) as well as application of advanced computational[3] project designing methods. When the boundaries of a single city or metropolis we find and appreciate the multiple motifs building development: from architecture of advanced solutions of traditional and even archaic concepts. From environments fully controlled electronically, all the way to ground building projects created by hands of future users. Thanks to this, the city structure is becoming multithreaded and rich. The user of city space, "creative class" representative will understand this order and will enjoy the multithreaded city tissue. It is vital to keep in mind, that it is dynamics and ability to innovate, which are the greatest positive value in information society. The multithreaded city space may either draw it out or become its final result.

Using the existing buildings city tissue ties with the necessity of improving the quality of public space, which surrounds it. It may lead to tearing down buildings or intensification of the building development. The goal is to achieve an acceptable, high standard of architectural and city spaces. One of the best improvement methods is introducing attractive recreation areas and greenery into the urbanized space.

An example of celebrating the city lifestyle thanks to city greenery project is High Line Park in New York. The subject of the project is adapting the unused industrial seaport railway remaining in Manhattan into atypical park of elongated shape: with high quality greenery, small architecture as well as artistic installations tied thematically to the surroundings. Historic city structure elements, during the renewal process

---

[3] Computational project designing enables generating an architectural form using a digital optimization method, in which the architect controls the form using a software program code.

may become valuable space attracting and concentrating members of the creative class.

Simultaneously with the New York project, in London, a park was created having much greater natural character and much larger space. It was built on post-industrial areas, torn down and destroyed still during WWII. Attention should be drawn to the pro-social characteristic of this city investment – directed at raising the living condition standards in a multi-cultural, multi-ethnic and not wealthy city district of Mile End Park. Both investments constitute an intervention into city space, the aim of which is not to allow its degradation while at the same time creating and maintaining social public space. Singular, scattered changes in the city tissue have a limited impact radius and do not disturb the fragmentation level of city space[4]. A significant improvement in how the city is perceived, its functional integration can be obtained through appropriate investment coordination. This type of planning is a frequent practice. The aim is to mark a meaningful to the city location, create corridors or activation axis, which will enable the impression of space integration.

4   Conclusions

The essences of the scientific achievement presented in the publication is based on the formulating and analysis of a relation between mass media communication, information society, spatial behavior of people and city composition. The direction of spatial transformations in the city is becoming a medium visualizing cultural, economic and social changes. The establishment of a society based on access to information shapes and changes spatial behavior. Due to this, taking on the subject combining the phenomenon of knowledgeable society as well as spatial development is substantiated.

The analysis this of scientific problem has been performed in the context of cultural, social and technical conditions. The accessibility to information and communication technologies influences the directions for spatial transformation the characteristics of which are following:

- Possibility of using information and communication technologies in resource management, a better and more complete use of architectural space. The ongoing internet communication constitutes a tool, thanks to which setting up a group meeting or establishing the order of space usage is possible [9].
- Building spaces supporting creativity and innovative activities through raising the quality of the surroundings, the level of individualization, and openness to the cultural and nature context of architectural solutions.
- Building society integrating spaces in physical space and not only in virtual reality. An open attitude towards neighborhood activities – in an era of distance work, era of *"freelancers"*, it is the quality of interaction with others and quality of space is a

---

[4] The issue of city fragmentation is related to the growing tendency of spatial, social, economic, cultural and political divisions in the cities. A socially harmful phenomenon, as it emphasizes the differences between the residents – generating conflicts and also, usually, increase of crime [8].

deciding factor where people will settle – distance from the place of employment is becoming a second rate factor.

- Positive perception of diversity, multithreaded tissue and motif both in the area of city culture as well as spatial area.

References

1. Kostof, S.: The City Assembled, p. 194. Thames & Hudson, Londen (1992)
2. Gehl, J.: Life Between Buildings, pp. 9–12. Wydawnictwo RAM, Kraków (2009)
3. Goban-Klas, T.: Media i komunikowanie masowe, p. 119. Wydawnictwo Naukowe PWN, Warszawa (2009)
4. Goban-Klas, T.: Media i komunikowanie masowe, pp. 119–121. Wydawnictwo Naukowe PWN, Warszawa (2009)
5. Mrozowski, M.: Media masowe, władza rozrywka i biznes. Oficyna Wydawnicza ASPRA-JR, Warszawa (2001)
6. Lerner, J.: Acupuntura urbana. Editora Record, Rio de Janeiro (2003)
7. Bonenberg, W.: Emotions Ergonomics in the Network Society. In: Vink, P. (ed.) Advances in Social and Organizational Factors, p. 798. CRC Press, Taylor & Francis (2012)
8. Graham, S., Marvin, S.: Splintering urbanizm. TJ International Ltd., Padstow (2001)
9. Bonenberg, A.: Design for the Information Society. In: Stephanidis, C. (ed.) Universal Access in HCI, Part I, HCII 2011. LNCS, vol. 6765, pp. 12–19. Springer, Heidelberg (2011)

Brand Visual Identity in Architecture

Wojciech Bonenberg

Faculty of Architecture, Poznan University of Technology
60-021 Poznan, Nieszawska 13C, Poland
wojciech.bonenberg@put.poznan.pl

Abstract. The article presents brand visual identity research results in architectural designing. Architectural brand concept has been presented, the key visual features of architectural forms building the brand have been discussed. The method of creating the architectural brand visual model and the measurements of the brand power in exemplary locations have been presented. The research is aimed at answering the following questions:

- What actions should be taken for an architectural form to shape a strong brand i.e. so that the brand is noticed and appreciated as a significant element of the city attractiveness?
- What should be done to improve the quality of architecture as a brand i.e. the ability to create competitive advantage of the location?

Keywords: architecture, brand, visual identity.

1   Problem

The city brand is created by many features such as the city appearance, life quality in the city, citizens' income, public space standard, municipal transport, services and cultural attractions offered by the city. The article focuses on a significant brand element, namely the appearance of architecture creating the city visual identity.

The research presented is based on the assumption that the architectural surroundings visual identity builds the strong city brand.

The research is aimed at the identification of architecture visual features which have impact on strong city brand.

Landscape research from architectural-urban perspective is most frequently identified with the analysis of visual assets of landscape interiors. Most of this research is based on landscape perception theories originating from the 19th century gestaltism (Gestalt psychology). The emphasis is placed on such landscape features as the degree of diversification, simplicity and the complexity of landscape forms, rhythm, harmony, contrast, composition axes and dominant features, plan view sequence. Attention should be paid to the attempts of landscape quality measurement based on the view analyses. Teledetection analysis of landscape forms may serve as an example [1]. Photos are used here for visual qualitative interpretation of photomorphic units (PMU). Picture analysis relates to such picture features as shape, size, contrast, colour, texture and interconnecting relations. This direction of landscape research has

C. Stephanidis and M. Antona (Eds.): UAHCI/HCII 2014, Part IV, LNCS 8516, pp. 143–152, 2014.
© Springer International Publishing Switzerland 2014

developed extensively on the basis of intuitive assessments of photographic image, consisting in the selection of hierarchically linked qualitative features. SBE Scenic Beauty Estimation by Terry and Boster [2], used for the assessment of natural landscapes, may serve as an example. VAC Visual Absorption Capacity [3] and LS Landscape Sensitivity [4] techniques are developed on similar assumptions. The LPR Landscape Pattern Recognition method presents an interesting approach [5].

In the above mentioned research landscape visual quality is the combination of the communicative (informational) function and meaning-related (symbolic) function. The landscape brand (brandscape) may be a trigger of reflections and emotions of a person watching the landscape - it may inspire cognitive processes, allow for finding something more than registered by the eye only, for finding identity in the elements of architectural narrative. Elaborating on Arnheim observations [6], visual identity may be considered a method existing between image presentation of space and experiencing its uniqueness. The motif of visual identity appears in works on mediatization of contemporary reality. From this perspective architecture has the power of visual promotion, building identity by strong media impact [7]. The attempt of new insight into visual identity which could be referred to as the photo vision machine is worth noticing [8]. Here emotional dimension of the message, based on "visual thinking" described by Arnheim matters in particular [9]. It includes not only architecture but also film arts, multimedia and graphics. From this perspective the visual identity is a metaphysical symbol describing the space structure, investigating relations between culture, history and space. Therefore, significant visual features of architectural brand may be distinguished:

- visual categorization - assigning symbols to a defined group of messages,
- visual hierarchization - creating a defined structure of ontological dependencies.

Visual identity may thus be a synthesis of knowledge about the world where architectural brand serves the function of a special space quantifier. Two elements make the brand function understood this way:

- the collection of symbols which characterize the urban landscape in a unique way,
- visual features of architectonic forms being the scenery of landscape interiors.

The purpose of the study is to demonstrate that visual features of architecture may be an effective tool creating the city brand owing to the combination of informative function with expression, persuasion, interpretation of cultural and social specifics of the city.

The area of research query comprises central area of the city of Poznan, most characteristic districts: Wilda, Jezyce, Nowe Miasto and Solacz.

Municipal marketing promoting beneficial image of the city is most often identified with the creation of less or more effective tourism promotions, press and TV advertisements. Visual quality of urban landscape is one of the most effective marketing tools. The attractive appearance of architectural surroundings allures tourists, new citizens and investors. Ugly architecture, composition chaos and repelling views - scare people away. Poor city landscape brand lowers real estate prices and discourages investors.

From marketing perspective, architectural form is a clear sign, the meaning of which corresponds with the product brand. Branded products are distinguished by one of a kind visual features which create their unique identity. One clear analogy between architectural facilities and other products intended for consumer market (such as cars, clothes, furniture etc.) may be noticed in this respect. The appearance of architectural facilities is significant for the following reasons: promotion (it attracts the attention of potential tourists, citizens and customers), value (it presents unique assets connected with tradition and culture), identification (it allows for distinguishing themselves against the competition).

Strong brand gives competitive advantage, it helps to create a positive market image, it wins customers, it helps to identify and recognize a product. All these features refer to an architectural form as a brand giving competitive advantage to the space in which it is located. Thus the appearance of architectural surroundings builds the city brand. Architecture characterized by identity acquires specific nature as a kind of promotional message which is supposed to attract tourists', citizens' and investors' attention. The architecture stemming from the tradition and culture is the evidence of the value of the place in which it was built. Therefore, it is so important to create one's own, unique architecture image as a brand connected with the location. The brand identity in architectural designing inheres in this.

2   Method

The research method comprises:

a) Architectural brand identity analysis - the creation of the brand model for city of Poznan.

b) Architectural - urban query used for the assessment of brand power on the basis of a representative sample.

c) Comparison of the as is condition with the brand model.

d) Conclusions and recommendations.

Defining architectural brand identity distinguishing Poznan metropolitan area is the starting point for the proposed research model.

Brand identity is, above all, the reflection of the mental brand image connected with the location. It presents the values which space should offer to a person. Brand identity is thus connected with aspirations, personality, system of values, citizen culture. In also involves symbolic and emotional values [10].

The next research step is the visual brand identification. Visual brand identification is connected with the set of architectural form attributes which create the surroundings visual image.

The next stage of research is the measurement of relations between the brand identity and architectural visual brand identification. This stage is used for creating the model of architectural brand for a defined location.

The gap between the brand identity and the brand visual identification attests to the failure to match architecture with the location context. The effect is poor architecture brand.

The most important features building architectural brand identity include:

C_1) *Uniqueness* – distinction of local architecture from competitive equivalents. Exposing such values as the place tradition, the atmosphere of urban interiors, unique expression. Individualization of architectural details, characteristic proportions of urban interiors, intimate scale, interesting merging with local surroundings may serve as an example.

The uniqueness connected with local tradition is a potential source of new creative inspirations which may be interpreted in an innovative manner, enriching the contemporary appearance of the space, giving an individualized nature to it.

C_2) *Familiarity* – shaping architectural surroundings through the prism of habits and experiences of recipients (consumers). Familiarity is significant for social acceptance of architecture, it evokes citizens' strong relations with a house, street, district and city. The feeling of familiarity has a beneficial impact on strengthening of social bonds, safety condition, care for common good.

C_3) *Personification* – the possibility of using architectural surroundings bearing the hallmarks of one's own tastes and systems of values. It is the expression of difference and original likes of citizens.

Characteristic appearance of such architectural elements as fences, entries to buildings and flats, pedestals, cornices, balcony decorations, facade colours etc. are the display of architectural personification, the expression of aspiration, taste and ambition of citizens, owners of houses, shops, cafes.

Personification displays itself in:

the style referring to citizens' preferences,
architectural forms referring to likes and sensitivity of local community.

C_4) *Prestige* - subjective feeling of satisfaction connected with interacting with "branded" architecture, giving the feeling of pride, importance and respect.

C_5) *Legibility* - the essence of legibility is enabling people clear and precise image of space, owing to architectural forms, combining composition and functional assets in an orderly manner. Within this meaning, architectural facilities are recognizable elements of spatial structure. Legibility means good orientation in the surroundings and it allows for recognizing the role and importance of a particular architectural form in urban structure.

It is directed at friendly and comprehensible perception of spatial impressions. Legible architecture creates a more comprehensible environment, providing a bigger number of emotional stimuli.

C_6) *Cultural identification* - the system of symbolic and emotional values, being the result of identification with culture, tradition, history and collective memory of the location. Cultural identification is an important element of stylistic autonomy in architecture,

C_7) *Fashion* - the wish to attract attention by "being in vogue". At first impulse, the willingness to distinguish oneself from surroundings is a stimulus creating fashion. This is a stage of *distinguishing* and it comprises a small group of pieces of art designed by the elite of worldwide architects. This is owing to them that some architectural forms become fashionable. Next, elite fashion is copied more and more extensively and it becomes mass fashion. Imitation results from subconscious desire for identification with fashionable patterns. Finally, mass fashion gets out of date, people turn away from previously fashionable patterns, they search for new fashion.

The importance of the above mentioned factors for building architectural brand identity at the area of Poznan metropolitan area was determined by questionnaire surveys.

The surveys covered the group of 50 respondents: architects, developers, real estate agents. The question referred to which factors give competitive advantage and thus have impact on long-lasting increase in the space value. Each expert was asked to indicate three, in his/her opinion, most important factors building architectural brand, from amongst seven listed possibilities.

The applied survey procedure was based on standard methods of qualitative measurements of brand image (*freelist*), broadly described in the reference literature [11], [12]. Table 1 presents survey results.

Table 1. The ranks of architecture brand identity building features at the area of Poznan

Feature that builds the identity of an architectural brand		Wilda District		Jezyce District		Nowe Miasto District		Solacz District	
		Number of indications	Feature significance	Number of indications	Feature significance	Number of indications	Feature significance	Number of indications	Feature significance
C_1	Uniqueness	80	67,23	108	100,00	30	66,67	91	75,83
C_2	Familiarity	78	65,55	96	88,89	18	40,00	105	87,50
C_3	Personification	65	54,62	71	65,74	27	60,00	120	100,00
C_4	Prestige	25	21,01	45	41,67	13	28,89	89	74,17
C_5	Legibility	76	63,87	58	53,70	36	80,00	95	79,17
C_6	Cultural identification	119	100,00	94	87,04	12	26,67	89	74,17
C_7	Fashion	18	15,13	25	23,15	45	100,00	15	12,50

The research was conducted with respect to four districts of the city of Poznan: Wilda, Jezyce, Nowe Miasto and Solacz. These districts distinguish themselves with characteristic urban landscape which is the reflection of unique tradition and history. Thus in each district the importance of partial elements influencing the place identity is different.

3   Brand Visual Identification

Brand visual identification is aimed at answering the question what makes some arc-hitectural facilities considered branded ones and others not? What visual features prejudge that we can say of a given building that it is distinguished by strong brand identity? Visual features of a building emphasize its *Uniqueness* (C_1), *Familiarity* (C_2), *Personification* (C_3), *Prestige* (C_4), *Legibility* (C_5), *Cultural Identification* (C_6), *Fashion* (C_7). Therefore, it is about the assessment which visual attributes make a building have strong brand. The answer to this question comes from the theory of construction of architectural forms and research linking these forms to the location.

Based on reference literature [13], [14] 20 standard visual attributes of a building regarding colour, material, texture, scale, articulation, roof shape, cornices and balco-nies, composition structure were distinguished. These features are significant ele-ments of architectural design.

The following visual features of buildings were taken into account:

- color of the facade consistent with the background,
- color of the facade in contrast with the background,
- material: brick,
- material: wood,
- material: plaster,
- material: glass + aluminum,
- material: stone,
- flat roof,
- sloping roof,
- bay windows and balconies,
- dominant cornice,
- elevation devoid of ornament,
- ornament on the façade,
- rhythmical façade,
- horizontal articulation,
- vertical articulation,
- small scale,
- large scale,
- traditional detail,
- modern detail.

Next, the measurement of relations between the building visual attributes and fac-tors shaping brand identity was made. The expert assessment comprises 140 inter-factor relations. Standard qualitative measurement methods based on Likert scale [15] were used for the research. As a result (Fig. 1), diagrams showing which visual attributes of buildings exert a bigger impact on brand identity in particular districts of Poznan were obtained. These diagrams constitute a kind of architectural brand mod-els, determined for districts subject to research.

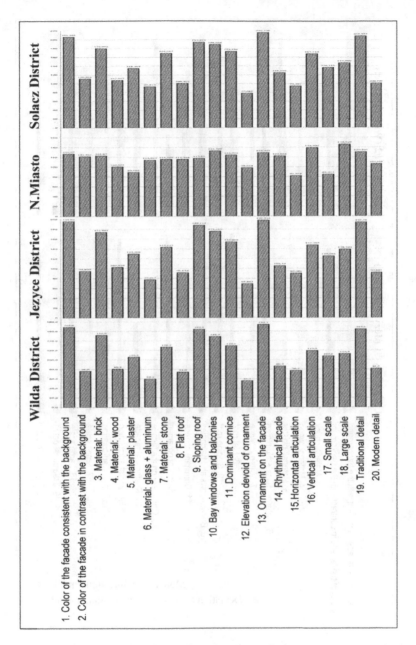

Fig. 1. Model of architectural brand for the examined districts of Poznan: Wilda District, Jezyce District, Nowe Miasto District, Solacz District. Diagrams show which visual attributes of buildings exert a bigger impact on brand identity in particular districts.

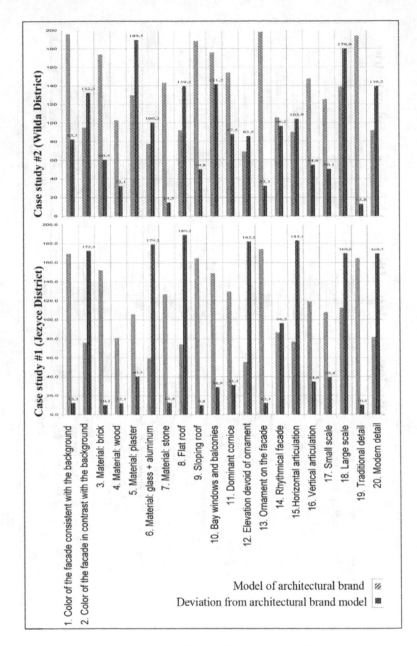

Fig. 2. Deviation from the model of an architectural brand. Results of measurements comparing visual identity of new developments executed over the past 10 years with architectural brand model.

Then visual features of newly built buildings were compared with the brand model in order to determine whether new architecture contributes to the creation of urban landscape (cityscape) visual identity of particular districts of Poznan.

Figure 2 presents the results of measurements comparing visual identity of new developments executed over the past 10 years with generated brand model. The result analysis allows to assess whether and to what extent visual features of new architectural designs build cityscape brand identity in particular districts of Poznan.

4   Conclusions

The brand model prepared was used for the assessment of visual identity of architectural brand of new developments in selected districts of Poznan. Research showed that a substantial majority of new developments is placed within the average and low value.

In particular districts new developments are standardized with respect to style, specific visual features connected with local traditions, characteristic colours and unique materials are disappearing.

New developments cause standardization of urban landscape, the fading of visual diversity influencing architectural brand identity. These are the factors reducing the city attractiveness for tourists, new citizens and investors. For this reason, research conducted should be used by designers, investors and self-government authorities in order to improve the landscape brand (brandscape) of Poznan.

References

1. Antrop, M.: The "Natural" way of visual image interpretation for landclassifi cation and landscape planning. In: Actes du Symp. Intern. de la Comm. VII de la Soc. Intern. de Photogramm. et de Télédétection. Intern. Archives of ISPRS, Toulouse, vol. 24-VII/1, pp. 897–906 (1982)
2. Terry, D.C., Boster, R.S.: Measuring Landscape Esthetics: The Scenic Beauty Estimation Method. Research Paper RM-167. Rocky Mountian Forest and Range Experiment Station, U.S. Dept. of Agriculture, Fort Collins (1976)
3. Amir, S., Gidalizon, E.: Expert-based method for the evaluation of visual absorption capacity of the landscape. Journal of Environmental Management 30(3), 251–263 (1990)
4. Thomas, D.S., Allison, R.J.: Landscape Sensitivity. John Wiley and Sons, Chichester (1993)
5. Motloch, J.L.: Introduction to Landscape Design. John Wiley and Sons, New York (2001)
6. Arnheim, R.: The Two Authenticities of the Photographic Media. The Journal of Aesthetics and Art Criticism 51(4), 537–540 (1991)
7. Bonenberg, A.: Facades and Multimedia Screens in Contemporary Architecture – Ergonomics of Use. In: 4th AHFE International Conference, Advances Social and Organization Factors, pp. 122–127. CRC Press, Taylor & Francis Group, New York (2012)
8. Virilio, P.: The Vision Machine. British Film Institute and Indiana. University Press, London (1994)
9. Arnhem, R.: Myślenie wzrokowe. Wyd. Słowo/Obraz Terytoria, Gdańsk (2011)

10. Upshaw, L.B.: Building Brand Identity: The Strategy for Success in a Hostile Environment. John Wiley and Sons, London (1995)
11. Rosch, E.: Principles of categorization. In: Rosch, E., Lloyd, B.B. (eds.) Cognition and Categorization, pp. 27–48. Lawrence Erlbaum, New York (1978)
12. Weller, S.C., Romney, A.K.: Systematic data collection. Sage, Newbury Park (1988)
13. Koos, U., Richter, K.: The Book of Design. Keiser Verlag, Neusass (2001)
14. Meiss, P.: Elements of Architecture. From Form to Place. Chapman and Hall, London (1992)
15. Kall, J., Kłeczek, R., Sagan, A.: Zarządzanie marką. Oficyna Ekonomiczna, Krakow (2006)

Technical Progress and Ergonomics
in Contemporary Domestic Kitchen

Jerzy Charytonowicz and Dzoana Latala-Matysiak

Wroclaw University of Technology, Department of Architecture
53/55 Prusa Street, 50-317 Wroclaw, Poland
jerzy.charytonowicz@pwr.wroc.pl,
dzoanalatala@wp.pl

Abstract. Technical progress, thanks to which the contemporary kitchen achieved the current shape, initiated changes going towards adapting the kitchen equipment to widely understood needs of the user. The whole of current studies concerning the ergonomics of the kitchen area in apartment is insufficient, it doesn't fulfill contemporary designing requirements. Verifying and updating previous research, supplementing them and presenting in the form of designing criteria is essential. Taking into consideration all needs of contemporary family, diverse by age, fitness and agility, it is necessary to provide optimal and widely understood quality of kitchen area.

Keywords: domestic kitchen, technical progress, ergonomics.

1 Introduction

Domestic kitchen has changed during the last thirty years – from a closed work area it has evolved to an open, functionally most important area in apartment.

Small laboratory kitchen, which was invented in 1926, became a standard kitchen solution, especially in a common block of flats, till almost late 80's of 20th century. However, narrow kitchen, limited space and the isolation of a housewife during kitchen works soon met with criticism [1]. That resulted with changes in the functional layout of new and renovated apartments - the outcome was the open kitchen, partly or entirely connected with a living room.

The opening of the kitchen was determined by technical progress as well, among others by inventions like kitchen electric hood [1]. The kitchen area was no longer a neglected, hidden part of the flat. The appearance of contemporary kitchen and its specialized equipment more and more encourages to share kitchen works with family members and to spend time together during preparing and having meals. Technical progress, thanks to which the contemporary kitchen achieved the current shape, initiated changes going towards adapting the equipment to widely understood needs of the user. The lifestyle has changed in many ways – the television promotes collective, family cooking, and it gives impression of participation, satisfying a subconscious and deeply coded (in a man) need to stay in family circle, group of relatives or

C. Stephanidis and M. Antona (Eds.): UAHCI/HCII 2014, Part IV, LNCS 8516, pp. 153–162, 2014.

friends during the food preparation and dining [1]. The open kitchen model is conducive to social and family integration process, and it's a solution used more and more often as a visible sign of changing image of domestic kitchen, which comes back to the primary central location against a background of the house or apartment – like a prehistoric bonfire or centrally situated hearth in primitive civilizations [2].

2   What the Technical Progress Caused

The technical progress was an unquestionable, contributory cause of changes in the kitchen area. It manifested by bringing into the residential area new equipment and appliances, new technologies, production engineering (in the kitchen it's a food preparation process). So called technical novelties still occur, thanks to whom the domestic kitchen is changing not only by its appearance, but also in relation to functional and applied features. An aspiration for improvement of appearance and quality of kitchen equipment details is an effect of those changes, and implementation of solutions which raise a prestige of a kitchen space, simultaneously increasing the comfort of its everyday usage. The kitchen area is the most intensely used, highly filled with mechanized, electric equipment. It's a multimedial and technologically advanced area, where a lot of dangerous activities connected with food preparation processes take place – it's like a laboratory, where high temperatures, chemical detergents, sharp utensils, electricity and water can cause life hazard [1]. It is necessary to admit that it's a side effect of technical progress, mostly because of electrical equipment and huge variety of chemical substances and materials.

The domestic kitchen has evolved from closed work area to an open and the most important functional area in the apartment. It's more and more often designed as an open kitchen, connected with a living room, creating one multifunctional and united area, which is pro-social and generally ensuring the family comfort of performing kitchen works. The kitchen can also be solved as so called kitchen room – a closed, separated room, which looks, despites of its character, like a representative room: a living room. The kitchen furniture doesn't look like kitchen ones, but more like furnishing of the living room. It doesn't have to be closed area of course, but can be connected with living room, so that is really hard to notice where the kitchen area begins [2].

Technical progress, thanks to which the contemporary kitchen achieved the current shape, initiated changes going towards adapting the equipment to widely understood needs of the user. Therefore the kitchen is more and more often user-friendly, which means it's adapted to individual needs of diverse users, fit and disabled, old and with different level of agility and efficiency [2]. The technical progress caused the entry of mass media into the kitchen area. All kind of equipment connected with the Internet and also devices equipped with response systems, are able to choose and take up previously programmed functions and perform intelligent reactions in specific cases as well. Thanks to so called the intelligent systems, efficient managing of the entire household and controlling the individual devices efficiency is possible [2]. Some innovative kitchen equipment, more frequently used lately, is equipped with devices such as   saving water or electricity, which makes the kitchen ecological. The technical progress takes care of an environment and also reduces overall costs, letting the user to save money. By using the "safe in use" kitchen equipment it is possible to reduce or even eliminate accidents and health hazard. There are lots of kitchen tools and devices equipped with all kinds of security systems, especially childproof. Ergonomic shapes, easy to use and intuitive control panels, are only examples of technical progress influence, connected with amplified care of the user and wide knowledge about consequences that the progress brings into the daily life, and also a need to design with care for the users' safety with special needs (disabled and advanced in years) [2]. So called   the island kitchen, both open and closed, is an attractive solution, ensuring very good conditions for all kitchen works and also conducive to tightening the social and family bounds. The island kitchen is more and more common element of kitchen equipment, and it can establish some kind of border between two areas: the kitchen and the living room, creating one shared multifunctional room. The kitchen island (furniture and equipment) takes most functions of the kitchen line, including with function of equipment and food storage in lower area of the kitchen island body [2]. Enormous variety of kitchen equipment and kitchenware gives unlimited possibility of choice and individualization in the kitchen area, however it's necessary to be guided by ergonomic criteria of kitchen designing to make this choice optimal.

3   Ergonomics in Domestic Kitchen

Intuitive nature of facilities, which were introduced in the kitchen area from the beginning of mankind till almost 19th century, confirmed the need of conscious shaping the work environment in household, especially in the kitchen area [1]. The progress of ergonomics science took place through a wide range of research conducted by psychologists, physiologists and anthropologists for the military services during the World War II [3]. Discontinuous by warfare research were continued and although a lot of kitchens didn't fulfill standards of the time, research were aspiring to implementing those standards. Till the end of the first half of 20th century the research were run in a lot of European countries to the wide scale [4]. Soon the ergonomics issues appeared in workplaces, universities and in the industrial design studios. The ergonomics science was developing together with technical progress. Unfortunately the whole of current studies concerning the ergonomics of the kitchen area in apartment is insufficient, it doesn't fulfill contemporary designing requirements, mainly with regard to sudden technological development of the kitchen equipment and due to secular trend [5]. To sum up the results of previous results of research, relating to domestic kitchen area it is possible to pull the following conclusions out:

- the whole of current studies concerning the ergonomics of the kitchen area in apartment is insufficient, it doesn't fulfill contemporary designing requirements, mainly with regard to sudden technical progress, which took place at the turn of 20th and 21st century. It is connected with increasing number of technologically and materially advanced kitchen devices

- the efforts of kitchen equipment manufacturers to provide widely understood ergonomic quality of their products are most often confined to specific solutions, but they don't guarantee integrated kitchen equipment; that's conductive to health hazard in the kitchen area
- improper spatial arrangement and limited kitchen area also generates health hazard, limited motor and manipulative space in small kitchen requires special attention and careful arrangement
- existing and still used apartments in blocks of flats built in 70th of XX century need the ergonomic correction in order to adapt to contemporary needs of the users
- with regard to rapid technological development of kitchen equipment, its computerization, introduction of intelligent technologies, multimedia, the Internet, and due to secular trend, the whole of current studies concerning the ergonomics of the kitchen area in apartment is insufficient, it doesn't fulfill contemporary designing requirements

Because of above mentioned, verifying and updating previous research, supplementing them and presenting in the form of designing criteria, fulfilling the present requirements, especially ergonomic directives, is well grounded and necessary.

3.1   Ergonomic Designing Criteria

Among others, the kitchen area is the most intensively used area in apartment. More and more often multifunctional, should be well equipped with devices and furniture which are comfortable and safe to use, in order to carry out the meal preparing process and to facilitate comfortable consumption. As the functional area, which should integrate the family, the kitchen should enable necessary works to all users, regardless of their age, sex and level of psychophysical efficiency. That's why it's so important for the kitchen to be flexible, mobile and possible to adjust to diverse and changeable in time needs of the users. The kitchen area designing should provide for necessary space designed both for equipment and its usage. Equally important issue is to ensure the motion area, which should enable collision-free moving and walking in the kitchen.

3.2   Specific Spatial and Motor Requirements of Individual User

Kitchen designing and optimal selection of comfortable and safe kitchen equipment should be preceded by defining specific spatial and motor requirements of individual user. For designing the kitchen area one should use an anthropometric atlas, however the data concern to phantoms in static positions, without consideration the body position change during movement or free position (not standing on attention); those are closer to natural body positions, typical of man ready to take action. Therefore the anthropometric atlases require widening the range of data. It was proper to analyze particular elements of kitchen equipment and functional areas by means of extreme planar percentile phantoms of man and woman (defined as C5 and C95) in dynamic positions during housework. The motion area (walking path) and maneuver space should be set according to features and motion possibilities of a high person – by 95 percentile (95C) male phantom, because it enables comfortable walking and working for all kitchen users. The outreach and grasp scope should be set down individually for a very high man (95C) and for a very short woman (5C) [5].

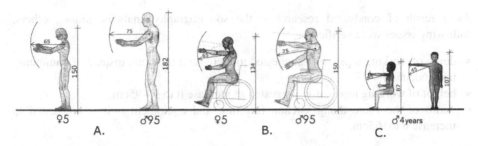

Fig. 1. The comparison of heights and outreach of phantoms: A. a woman 5C and a man 95C, B. a woman on a wheelchair 5C and a man on a wheelchair 95C, C. 4 years old child (Source: own work)

The motion area and maneuver space is different for disabled users. The most space is required for people on wheelchairs with regard for size and the way of wheelchair drives. To take into consideration the sitting position of work - the space of operation and outreach is significantly different (Fig. 2).

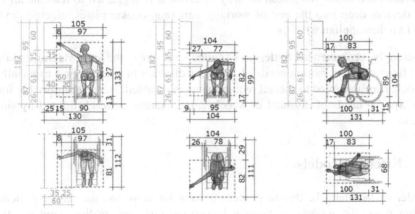

Fig. 2. An example of carried out analysis: the usage of typical kitchen cabinets by disabled wheel-chaired phantom of a very short woman (5C) (Source: own work)

Children also belong to the group of people of temporary limited efficiency (fitness) connected with age – a characteristic reduced body proportion and of course different spatial and motor requirements. It is necessary to pay attention that not every device should be adapted to children motion requirements, and more - some should be protected against them, preventing the uncontrolled use of those electric and dangerous ones.

3.3   Conclusions

As a result of conducted research – the somatography analysis, among others, following issues were verified:

- depth of working tops – it is suggested to increase it to 80cm, instead of commonly used 60cm
- height of working tops – it is suggested to increase it to 90-95cm
- width of the route along kitchen furniture and equipment – it is suggested to increase it to165cm.

The research complemented existent recommendations; it has been noticed that, among others:

- raising of devices location level eliminates the necessity of assuming the uncomfortable body positions and also reduces the service area
- the use of all kind of drawers and systems which let to slide out the inside of device (e.g. oven, fridge drawer, lover cabinets drawer) is a solution which reduces the uncomfortable body positions and enhance the visibility
- it is necessary to locate dangerous kitchen equipment aside from the children outreach and to use integrated security systems. It is suggested to relocate all kind of devices deep into the end of working tops (e.g. cooker plates, electric devices and kitchen appliance)

It is strongly recommended to design so called spare area –the area which is enlarged to the functional and motion needs of the user– disabled in wheelchair – especially as the kitchen area adapted to special requirements of disabled, is also comfortable for fit users. Special needs of disabled in wheelchairs concerns outreach limited by sitting position.

4   Kitchen Models

In order to facilitate the design process of new kitchens and the rearrangement of existing ones, the models of kitchen layouts in different quality standards (low, medium or high) were suggested:

- low standard kitchen area – equipped with necessary devices and kitchen equipment, with minimal working and maneuver space, addressed to small family (young childless couple, couple with grown children etc.)
- medium standard kitchen - equipped with standard devices and kitchen equipment, with average working and maneuver space, addressed to a family with three or four members (couple with one or two children etc.)

- high standard kitchen - equipped with all kind of devices and the newest kitchen equipment, with increased working and maneuver space, addressed to a family with three, four or more members (couple with two, three or more children, plus grandparents etc.).

Designed classification of above mentioned kitchen standards follows the assumption about family members (number of the kitchen users). The kitchen standard is also connected with brand and quality of kitchen equipment, which often comes of users finances and their personal preferences. However the dimensions of kitchen devices or furniture, as well as their choice, should be dependent on area and space which they take up. The L-shaped kitchen model scheme in three quality standards shows the main differences in kitchen designing (Fig. 3, 4, 5).

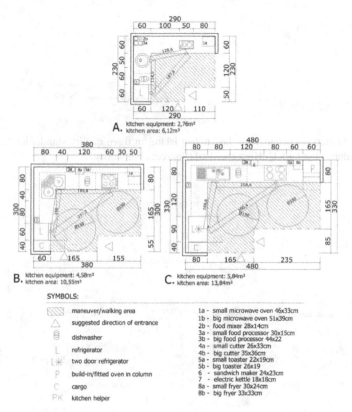

Fig. 3. The L-shaped kitchen in three quality standards: A. Low standard, B. Medium standard, C. High standard   (Source: own work)

The conducted spatial and motor analysis were used to prepare twenty four model schemes of kitchen, which can be connected with dining area (in low standard: twenty four combinations). Depending on chosen area standard, the model schemes can be used as well as to design and rearrange kitchen areas. With regard to special requirements of disabled, concerning the dining area, eighteen kitchen models with dining area were proposed.

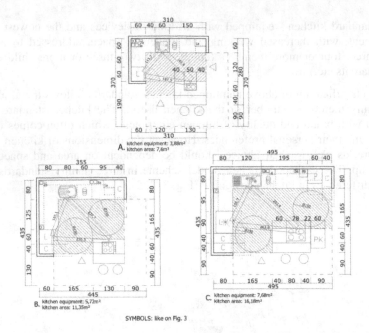

Fig. 4. The L-shaped kitchen with the kitchen island in three quality standards: A. Low standard, B. Medium standard, C. High standard (Source: own work)

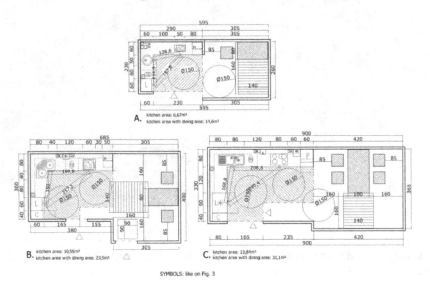

Fig. 5. The L-shaped kitchen with dining area in three quality standards: A. Low standard, B. Medium standard, C. High standard (Source: own work)

The location of dining kitchen area in relation to work kitchen area has an influence on the shape of the whole kitchen. It is necessary to take into consideration that the presence of the kitchen island is not an excuse from obligation to design comfortable dining area – like a table with chairs, at least only for whole family members.

It is possible to connect the kitchen island with the dining table, which can be actually advantageous because of the nearness of the table and the cooker, so that ready meals don't have to be carried from long distance – can be placed directly on the table and served. The kitchen users can accompany or participate in the meal preparing process. It also uplifts the cooking and make it a social event. It is recommended to design the island kitchen which is opened or arranging the multifunctional kitchen area together with the dining area.

The island kitchen connected with the dining area is an optimal solution, which can be regarded as a model (Fig. 6).

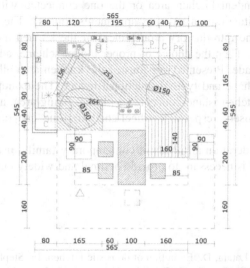

Fig. 6. The L-shaped kitchen with the kitchen island and dining area in high standard (Source: own work)

During the analysis it turned out to be essential to compare the length of individual working triangle sides in those kitchen models, which enabled setting the new recommended lengths between a refrigerator, sink and a stove - on the basis of the spatial-motion requirements of extreme planar percentile phantoms, kitchen equipment dimensions and applied exact area standard (low, medium or high) and particular kitchen layout, previous lengths of working triangle and the length of working tops were verified. The new dimensions are:

- the low standard: fridge – sink 115-181cm, sink - cooker: 125-226cm, cooker - fridge: 132-265cm,
- the medium standard: fridge – sink: 136-167cm, sink - cooker: 170-238cm, cooker - fridge: 197-359cm,

- the high standard: fridge – sink: 156-211cm, sink - cooker: 163-253cm, cooker - fridge: 182-445cm.

The sum of kitchens working triangle sides, regardless of the kitchen standard, comprises between 364-890cm.

5   Summary

The technical and technological progress, which took place in a field of an apartment infrastructure and kitchen equipment, is a continuous process, thereupon in the kitchen some new solutions appear,   which require constant verification – that's why the ergonomic research would be the most appropriate.

The proposed model schemes of kitchen layouts can be used as "ready-to-use" templates of independent kitchen area or the one connected with the dining area, depending on the situation (in existing apartments/houses). The designing process should begin with the introductory arrangement of the kitchen area against a background of the house. Then the choice of proper model scheme, adjusted to the other rooms, should be made. Presented versions of the kitchen area allow to make quick decision about the shape and type of functional layout. The example of high quality kitchen area with kitchen island connected with the dining area, adjusted to requirements of disabled users (especially wheel-chaired), one can consider as optimal solution.

Taking into consideration all needs of contemporary family, users diverse by age, fitness and agility, it is necessary to provide optimal and widely understood quality of kitchen area.

References

1. Charytonowicz, J., Latala, D.: Evolution of domestic kitchen. In: Stephanidis, C. (ed.) Universal Access in HCI, Part III, HCII 2011. LNCS, vol. 6767, pp. 348–357. Springer, Heidelberg (2011)
2. Charytonowicz, J., Latala, D.: Desirable features of contemporary domestic kitchen. In: Vink, P. (ed.) Advances in Social and Organizational Factors, pp. 3–11. CRC Press (2012)
3. Tilley, A.R.: The measure of man and woman, p. 9. John Wiley & Sons, Inc., New York (2002)
4. Grandjean, E.: Ergonomics of the home, pp. 24–26, 29–31, 33, 36. Arkady, Warsaw (1978)
5. Charytonowicz, J.: Principles of creating laboratory workstands. Scientifics Papers of the Institute of Architecture and Town planning of the Technical University of Wroclaw, p. 16. Publishing House of Wroclaw University of Technology, Wroclaw (1994)

A Virtual Dressing Room for People with Asperger's Syndrome

A Usability Study to Realise Design Goals

Line Gad Christiansen[1], Anthony Lewis Brooks[1],
Eva Petersson Brooks[1], and Torben Rosenørn[2]

[1] Department of Architecture, Design and Media Technology
Aalborg University, Campus Esbjerg, Niels Bohrs Vej 8, 6700 Esbjerg, Denmark
(lgc,tb,ep)@create.aau.dk
[2] Department of Learning and Philosophy
Aalborg University, Campus Esbjerg, Niels Bohrs Vej 8, 6700 Esbjerg, Denmark
tur@learning.aau.dk

Abstract. Using the Virtual Dressing Room[1] (VDR) system, which is created as a research project between different companies and universities in Denmark and funded by the Danish National Advanced Technology Foundation, a usability study has been conducted with people with Asperger's Syndrome (AS), the initial aim was to determine if the people with AS would use the VDR system and understood it, as a second aim, the findings was used to determine a set of design goals. Seven teenagers with AS participated in the study, in the age range from 15 to 17 years old. A questionnaire was used before the study, to determine the target groups interests and how/if they purchase clothes. Through observations and video recording of the usability study, a qualitative interaction analysis provided a set of design goals to be used when designing for this target group. The goals emphasized the importance of an easy accessible and consistent solution with a limited amount of options and the importance of the user's own preferences.

Keywords: Asperger's Syndrome, Autism, Design Goals, Usability Study, Virtual Dressing Room, Virtual Environment, Questionnaire.

1 Introduction

A Virtual Dressing Room (VDR) is a solution enabling people to virtually check if a pieces of clothes fits in size. The VDR system used for this study is a part of a cross-disciplinary research project funded by the Danish National Advanced Technology Foundation, including Aalborg University in Esbjerg, Commentor A/S and Virtual

---

[1] The Danish National Advanced Technology Foundation:
http://hoejteknologifonden.dk/projektgalleri/
6_juni_2011_17_nye_investeringer/det_digitale_proeverum/

C. Stephanidis and M. Antona (Eds.): UAHCI/HCII 2014, Part IV, LNCS 8516, pp. 163–170, 2014.

Lab A/S as partners [1, 2]. The VDR targets a decreased amount of returned clothes purchased online. Through the usability study conducted for this research, the VDR also showed potential in other areas such as ADL for people with Asperger's Syndrome (AS), which is a condition under the autism spectrum disorder [3]. When being impaired by autism, social activities can be difficult [3, 4].

For people with AS, their intelligence level is normal to high, but their social competences and their ability to deal with changes is low [4]. They do not have the skills of putting themselves in the place of others, also called Theory of Mind, and hence they cannot understand why the people around them act as they do [5]. People with AS often perceive activities within social contexts, as challenging [4]. Attwood [6] further argues that people with AS can suffer from sensory overload and that daily activities can be challenging, which can affect situations such as shopping for clothes. This study addresses the question of designing a Virtual Dressing Room (VDR) targeting people with AS.

2   Asperger's Syndrome

The gender spread in the diagnostics of autism is 1 female to (at least) 6 males [7], and in the case of teenagers with autism, the girls often have it more difficult in relation to unknown situations and social context, they are more restricted to try out new things or enter new experiences than boys [6]. When introduced to new things, such as settings or people, individuals with AS perceive the world through a bottom-up mental model [4], meaning that they have difficulties generalizing sensory information, e.g. having to perceive all the information consciously before making an interpretation. This affects both their social life, their ability to interpret situations and, also, how comfortable they feel in new surroundings.

Attwood [6] stated that a person (especially when being young) with AS can over-compensate in social situations, by e.g. denying that there are any problems. The person believes or pretends that he never makes mistakes, never is wrong and that he must be listened to because of his high intelligence. In an effort to avoid looking stupid, the person with AS denies his social limitations which can result in behaviors such as dominance and arrogance [6].

According to Dautenhahn [7], when designing for children with autism, the differences between people with autism in a specific age need to be considered. Therefore, before initiating the design activity, the target group should be defined very clearly and the individual needs taken into account. The environment has to be safe, motivating and give the user a sense of being in control. People with autism have difficulties with having a holistic view on a situation (e.g. having different perspectives on one thing and consider all the perspectives before making a decision) [7].

2.1   Shopping and AS

Louis [8] argues that people with autism generally finds shopping situations uncomfortable, which is in line with results from a netnography study by the forum

Wrongplanet.net, where several people with AS reported that they found shopping stressful and challenging. According to the netnography study, aspects such as lighting, sounds, smells and the open areas with a large amount of shoppers increased the stress level for people with AS. Hence a short shopping trip demanded a lot of energy from the person, with the result of them needing solitude the rest of the day.

Baas & Raaij [13] researched how AS affects exploratory consumer behavior. They hypothesized that AS would affect consumer behavior negatively. Through a comparative study they concluded that their results supported their hypothesis [13]. They found that people with AS tend to:

• Repeat the same behavior more frequently
• Know and buy less new products and services
• Take fewer risks and be less adventurous
• Have a low preference for exploratory shopping behavior
• Communicate less with others about purchases
• Change brands less often with as the primary reason a preference for less change and variety   [13, p.476]

Clothes shopping are in this study is considered as an aspect of the Activities of Daily Living (ADL) [9]. According to Smith et al. [9], ADL for people with autism, including AS, can be difficult, especially in the area of personal care skills [10]. A to a pre-questionnaire, conducted before the usability study, including 13 participants, showed that people with AS enjoy using computers and consoles, which is in line with Chen & Bernard-Opitz's study [11] and Putnam & Chong's [12] survey. These preferences in technology are used as a basis for choosing the VDR as a possible solution for increased ADL. In this regard, the paper will, in particular, focus on the VDR as a safe and joyful virtual environment and will conclude with a set of design goals targeting users with Asperger's Syndrome (AS).

2.2   Technology and AS

Putnam & Chong [12] did a survey to determine what people with autism want in relation to software and technology. They found that the people who responded to their survey (who were both people with autism and parents to children with autism), had three main areas that they wanted software and technology to support: (1) social/communication; (2) academic/school help (3) and scheduling/organization [12]. According to the authors, the development of a system should consider sensory integration and motivation. Furthermore, the majority of the responses from the target group indicated a main interest in computers and technology. Using a computer was also considered as a general strength for the people with autism [12].

3   Method

A usability study of the VDR system was conducted with the aim of both providing insights to the interactions with the system and what a designer should consider when designing towards this target group. A questionnaire responded by 13 participants, was send out before the usability study in order to determine the target groups interests and preference. Analysis of the usability study was compared to both the questionnaire and existing literature to generalize the findings.

3.1   Technology

For the usability study, a prototype of the VDR system that is being developed within the VDR research project was available and used. This prototype was an iteration of the front-end of the VDR, which is the part that the users are exposed to. However, it suffered from not being well functioning, e.g. it was difficult for some participants to navigate the system.

3.2   Participants

The usability study of the VDR system included seven teenagers, 15 to 17 years of age, with AS. The participants came from a Danish school, and knew each other before the study was conducted. The participants were joined by three teachers and pedagogues, which the participants knew from their daily routines at the school. Two of the participants were female and the remaining five subjects were male. According to the teachers accompanying the participants, they all suffered from Asperger's Syndrome in different degrees.

3.3   Procedure

In order to come up with a set of design goals a usability test of the VDR in a controlled environment was carried out, focusing on possibilities and constraints when people with AS were using the VDR system. Observations and video recordings were used for the data gathering, but as ethics was of a great concern, the interactions with the VDR were purely done on the participants' terms, e.g. in relation to how and when during the day that they wanted to interact with it and how long time they used interacting with the VDR. As people with AS has social impairments, easily get sensory overloads and experience new environments in another way than typically developed people, the ethics were prioritized. All the participants were presented with the VDR system at the same time in the morning of the day of the study, and they could then interact with it as they pleased in a time period of three hours, they were not forced in any way and all agreed to participate in the study beforehand. Parental information was sent out one week before the study.

The unit of analysis was the actions and interactions when using the VDR. In line with Petersson [14, 15, 16], the preference was to design the shopping activities that most likely will lead to a desired shopping experience. The possibilities and constraints that can occur when designing these activities are all relative to the need of a more holistic view on this complex situation. In order to consider this complexity, we used interaction analysis [17], focusing on two aspects: (1) the attributes of the VDR; in what way the participants enhanced or decreased the (inter)action, and (2) the process and outcome when using the VDR; how the design enhanced or decreased the shopping experience.

Before the usability test, a questionnaire with 13 participants was used to determine what interests people with AS have and how they perceive shopping, both online and in stores. The respondents were both some of the participants for the usability study and people with AS from schools and living facilities in Denmark.

4   Results

4.1   Questionnaire

In the questionnaire used before the usability study, 10 out of the 13 participants were male, the majority of these were between the age of 15 and 19. The results from the questionnaire showed that the participants generally preferred to use computers in relation to their interest, e.g. for gameplay and other activities, such as watching movies. They dislike buying clothes, over 75 percent answered that buying clothes is one of the activities that they preferred the least. Seven out of the 13 participants mainly shops online for clothes, but does so rarely (less than one time per month). The main reason for buying clothes online are that it is quick, they do not have to buy the clothes from people and that you do not have to walk around in the shop, but all 13 participants responded that they need the sensation of the clothes and that this is the weakness of online shopping. This fits in line with Attwood [6] who states that people with AS suffers from sensory overload, and according to feedback from the test, the reason they need to feel the clothes is due to that a lot of fabrics used for clothes, tend to be itching for people with AS.

4.2   Usability Study

Throughout the usability study, the seven participants interacted with the VDR system as they pleased. They all entered the system, but only two of the participants tried the system multiple times, the others responded that they did not find clothes interesting, they disliked the clothes options, they found the system to be boring and not functioning well. The female participants mainly observed from a distance, which is in line with Attwood [6] who stated that girls with AS are more reluctant to try new things. After the study, the participants gave feedback about the system, 6 out of the seven participants replied that the system was boring.

5   Discussion and Conclusions

Due to the amount of participants, the study is explorative and conducted purely with a qualitative approach. Combined with the differences within the target group [7], the design goals extracted from the study can be restricted and not applicable to everyone with AS. As the participants were in a specific age group (teenagers), the design goals might differ if the study was conducted with another age group.

As the female participants where reluctant and did not participate much, the design goals are mainly aiming towards the male participants, but as the gender ratio are 1:6, the findings could be generalized as the majority of the people with AS, are mainly male.

Speculations are that a participatory design of the interface and content, or a more user centred approach for the VDR, could show other tendencies and demands from the target group. It could also increase the level of interaction from the participants.

The results showed that the VDR system included both possibilities and constraints. It was found that too many options of clothes decreased the participants' willingness to interact with the VDR. However, being a technological alternative to an otherwise stressing situation was perceived as a positive opportunity for the participants, but they also reported that they required feedback targeting the sensation of the fabrics.

- One of the main aspects for designing for people with AS is that too many options and choices can become confusing. In this case, the clothes were not appealing and there were too many options of clothes for them to make a decision, resulting in the participants leaving the system. This was confirmed by one of the teachers when giving feedback to the system, stating that some of the participants had difficulties with deciding the clothes they wanted to choose; hence they chose the clothes that were shown in the system when they entered the system. One male participant entered the system after observing others trying the system, when he entered the clothes shown was a dress, and he did not change to another piece of clothes, resulting in a girl teasing him.
- The people with AS are very different from each other, both in behavior and interests, meaning that the system should accommodate the different interests in some way, unless only targeting a narrow group within the target group. This is in line with the findings from Dautenhahn [7].
- The content has to be concrete and easy accessible. The content should be concise as it could demotivate the user with AS otherwise. For the VDR system, the application did not fill out the screen and around it; there were different information and options not related to the VDR available, it was observed through the usability study that this had a negative effect on the user experience, in the way that they lost focus on the system.
- Consistency within the content of a system should be considered. People with AS are detail oriented [6], and through the usability study if was observed that even small inconsistencies would remove the users attention from the system and unto the inconsistency, such as small breaks in the system, the buttons being influenced by graphic noise in the room etc.
- There should be a possibility of changing the interaction or going back in the system at any point during the interactions with a system. For instance, when the picture button was activated, the user could not avoid for the picture to be taken, resulting in a lot of the participants leaving the field of interaction and then returning when the picture was taken.

As the VDR system is a prototype and hence a work in progress, when developing a more finalized system, these findings could be implemented and another usability test conducted.

Acknowledgements. It should be acknowledged that the Danish National Advanced Technology Foundation contributed to this work, as did the Virtual Dressing Room project by providing a prototype of the front-end VDR system.

References

1. Gao, Y., Petersson Brooks, E.: Designing Ludic Engagement in an Interactive Virtual Dressing Room System – A Comparative Study. In: Marcus, A. (ed.) DUXU 2013, Part III. LNCS, vol. 8014, pp. 504–512. Springer, Heidelberg (2013)
2. Kristensen, K., Borum, N., Christensen, L.G., Jepsen, H.W., Lam, J., Brooks, A.L., Brooks, E.P.: Towards a Next Generation Universally Accessible 'Online Shopping-for-Apparel' System. In: Kurosu, M. (ed.) HCII/HCI 2013, Part III. LNCS, vol. 8006, pp. 418–427. Springer, Heidelberg (2013)
3. Attwood, T.: Strategies for improving the social integration of children with aspergers syndrome. Autism 4(1), 85–100 (2000)
4. Beyer, J.: Autisme i et Udviklingsperspektiv. Autismebladet 3 (2010)
5. Baron-Cohen, S., Leslie, A., Frith, U.: Does the autistic child have a "Theory of mind"? Cognition 21(1), 37–46 (1985)
6. Attwood, A.: The Complete Guide to Asperger's Syndrome. The Complete Guide to Asperger's Syndrome. Jessica Kingsley Publishers, London (2006)
7. Dautenhahn, K.: Design Issues on Interactive Environments for Children with Autism. In: Proceedings of ICDVRAT, 3rd International Conference on Disability, Virtual Reality and Associated Technologies, pp. 153–161 (2000)
8. Louis, M.M.: Walking the Walk: My Autistic Son and the Scholarship of Empathy. Womens Studies in Communication 31(2), 233–239 (2010)
9. Smith, L.E., Maenner, M.J., Seltzer, M.M.: Developmental Trajectories in Adolescent and Adults with Autism: the Case of Daily Living Skills. Journal of the American Academy of Child & Adolescent Psychiatry 51(6), 622–631 (2012)
10. Pierce, K.L., Schreibman, L.: Teaching Daily Living Skills to Children with Autism in Unsupervised Settings Through Pictorial Self-management. Journal of Applied Behavior Analysis 27(3), 471–481 (1994)
11. Chen, S.H.A., Bernard-Opitz, V.: Comparison of Personal and Computer Assisted Instruction for Children with Autism. Mental Retardation 31(6), 368–376 (1993)
12. Putnam, C., Chong, L.: Software and Technology Designed for People with Autism: What do users want? In: Proceedings of the 10th International ACM SIGACCESS Conference on Computers and Accessibility, pp. 3–10 (2008)
13. Baas, T.H., Raaij, W.F.: Familiar or Risky: the Asperger Syndrome Affects Exploratory Consumer Behaviour. Journal of Economic Psychology 31(3), 471–477 (2010)
14. Petersson, E.: Non-formal Learning through Ludic Engagement with in Interactive Environments. Doctoral dissertation, Malmoe University, School of Teacher Education, Studies in Educational Sciences (2006)

15. Petersson, E.: Editorial: Ludic Engagement Designs for All. Digital Creativity 19(3), 141–144 (2008)
16. Brooks, E.P.: Ludic Engagement Designs: Creating Spaces for Playful Learning. In: Stephanidis, C., Antona, M. (eds.) UAHCI 2013, Part III. LNCS, vol. 8011, pp. 241–249. Springer, Heidelberg (2013)
17. Jordan, B., Henderson, A.: Interaction Analysis: Foundations and Practice. The Journal of the Learning Sciences 4(1), 39–103 (1995)

MoviBed - Sleep Analysis Using Capacitive Sensors

Maxim Djakow[1], Andreas Braun[2], and Alexander Marinc[2]

[1] Hochschule Darmstadt, Darmstadt, Germany
maxim.djakow@stud.h-da.de
[2] Fraunhofer Institute for Computer Graphics Research IGD, Darmstadt, Germany
{andreas.braun,alexander marinc}@igd.fraunhofer.de

Abstract. Sleep disorders are a wide-spread phenomenon that can gravely affect personal health and well-being. An individual sleep analysis is a first step in identifying unusual sleeping patterns and providing suitable means for further therapy and preventing escalation of symptoms. Typically such an analysis is an intrusive method and requires the user to stay in a sleep laboratory. In this work we present a method for detecting sleep patterns based on invisibly installed capacitive proximity sensors integrated into the bed frame. These sensors work with weak electric fields and do not disturb sleep. Using the movements of the sleeping person we are able to provide a continuous analysis of different sleep phases. The method was tested in a prototypical setup over multiple nights.

Keywords: Capacitive proximity sensor, sleep analysis, smart furniture.

1   Introduction

Sleeping is the single most time-consuming activity of our lives - on average we spend approximately a third of our lives sleeping. It is peculiar that our knowledge regarding this very important activity remains limited. However, its importance becomes apparent as soon as sleep deprivation sets in. Work performance, well-being, concentration are negatively affected almost immediately, and may lead to severe long-term consequences if the situation is not remedied [1].

Sleep can be distinguished into different phases, their frequency and duration forming the basis for measuring the sleep quality of an individual person [2]. A popular method to distinguish those phases is based on recognizing the movement of a person throughout the night, a so called actigraphy [3]. The advent of small accelerometers based on microelectromechanical systems (MEMS) has made it possible to perform this type of screening at home, e.g. using wristbands or smartphones [4]. However, it still requires either a body-worn device or an external unit that is attached to the bed.

Capacitive proximity sensors allow detecting the presence of a human body by means of weak oscillating electric fields. They have been applied to various applications for body parameter sensing in fields such as human-computer interaction or smart furniture, creating different interaction devices, or furniture that is able to sense occupation and posture [5–7].

C. Stephanidis and M. Antona (Eds.): UAHCI/HCII 2014, Part IV, LNCS 8516, pp. 171–181, 2014.
© Springer International Publishing Switzerland 2014

In this work we present MoviBed, an extension to one of our earlier prototypes [8]. This earlier prototype allowed detecting position and posture of one or two persons on a bed, based on static analysis of capacitive proximity sensors data. MoviBed allows the detection of sleep phases based on movement registered by an array of capacitive sensors that is attached to the bed frame. It uses dynamic data analysis to gather a measure of overall movement to detect sleep phases, as well as additional data regarding single movements. The system was installed in an extended prototype and evaluated for both detection of different movements and the analysis of different sleep phases.

2   Related Works

The most common method and "gold standard" for determining sleep phases is producing a polysomnogram in a sleep laboratory. These devices are monitoring a large number of body activities, the most common being electrical brain activity (EEG), electrical muscle activity (EMG), eye movement (EOG), hear rate (ECG), breathing rate, acoustic detection of snoring, body posture, leg movement and blood oxygen levels. The result is a graph as shown in Fig. 1. It allows a precise analysis of various sleep disorders and distinguishing the different sleep phases. However, the equipment is quite invasive and requires the sleeping person being attached to numerous measuring instruments.

The recent advent of mobile technology has spawned numerous smartphones equipped with MEMS systems and microphones that can be used to detect movement in the sleep [4, 9]. The phone is usually placed on the mattress, e.g. below the pillow

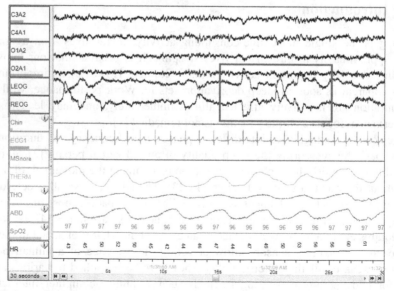

Fig. 1. Polysomnogram of a person in REM sleep (Source: http://en.wikipedia.org/wiki/File:Sleep_Stage_REM.png)

Fig. 2. Zeo sleep manager with electrode headband, base station and smartphone running the associated application

and tracks movement either by vibrations of the mattress or sounds the user generates when moving. A variety of personal health applications are available on all modern smartphone operating system, one example being WakeApp, providing an improved wake experience by adjusting alarm time according to the currently detected sleep phase [10].

A final category is made up of devices specifically designed for personal sleep analysis. Those provide a middle ground between intrusive laboratory environment and light-weight analysis by smartphones. One example is the Zeo Sleep Manager shown in Fig. 2. This device is comprised of an electrode headband that provides EEG measurements, a base station that is receiving and analyzing those signals and various applications for PC and smartphone that provide user interfaces for personal sleep analysis. Additionally there is a social networking component that allows comparing the individual sleep quality with other users of the system.

3   Sleep Phase Recognition

The most reliable way to track sleep phases is by using an electroencephalography (EEG); that is measuring the electrical activity of the brain by placing electrodes on the scalp. Various different types of neural oscillations can be distinguished - the most important for sleep phase detection are alpha waves, theta waves, delta waves and sleep spindles. The American Academy of Sleep Medicine (AASM) distinguishes three different phases of non-rapid eye movement sleep (NREM) and REM phase [11].

- Stage 1 - occurs mostly in the beginning of sleep. It has slow eye movement, alpha waves disappear and the theta wave appears.
- Stage 2 - dreaming is very rare and no eye movement occurs. The sleeper is quite easily awakened. EEG recordings have a tendency for characteristic "sleep spindles"

- Stage 3 - was previously divided into stages 3 and 4. It is slow-wave sleep (SWS) or deep sleep. Stage 3 used to be the transition between stages 2 and 4 where delta waves began to occur, while delta waves are dominant in stage 4.
- REM sleep - is a phase of sleep characterized by random and rapid movement of the eyes. It is considered the lightest phase of sleep and occurs all through the night but gets longer close to morning.

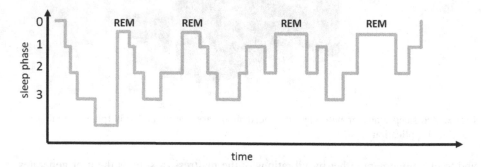

Fig. 3. Example of human sleep phases throughout the night

A typical distribution of sleep phases throughout the night is shown in Fig. 1. It can be easily scene that the sleep is distributed into different cycles, whereas the sleeping person is moving through the different sleep phases until having a REM phase and then going back to deep sleep. If the only available data is body movements it is becoming more difficult to reliably determine the sleep phase. Studies have shown that the magnitude of movement is typically associated to the following phases in decreasing order: wake, stage 1, REM, stage 2, stage 3 [12]. Another method is distinguishing between awake phase, active sleep and quite sleep and takes into account the order of those phases. This information allows to correlate the actual sleep phases with good certainty [13]. We have chosen this method for our system.

4   Movement-Detection Using Capacitive Sensors

Capacitive proximity sensors enable us to detect the presence of suitable object and their relative proximity to the electrode. Consequently a moving object will cause a change of sensor values. If we aggregate these data deviations from an array of sensors we get a reliable measure of objects moving above the electrodes. In the case of MoviBed we can assume that there is a limited number of persons moving on top of the sensors and thus it is possible to associate the sensor values to movement. In the following we will present a suitable method to achieve a reliable detection of the movements of a sleeping person. We are following a similar approach as Salmi and Leinonen [13].

At any given time t a set of the latest values of all n sensors can be stored as a tuple in the following form:

$$\overrightarrow{s_t} = \begin{pmatrix} s_{1_t} \\ s_{2_t} \\ \vdots \\ s_{n_t} \end{pmatrix} \tag{1}$$

As capacitive proximity sensors are particularly susceptible to external influences, such as temperature, humidity and other electric fields it is necessary to apply filtering on the sensor values. A suitable candidate is a median filter - a low-pass filter method that selects the median object of a sorted set of values, thus discarding outliers and strongly deviating values. This is particularly suited if transmission errors may occur.

If a person is moving on the bed the value of all sensors in detection distance of the moved body parts will change accordingly, the most relevant example in our case being a person moving in its sleep. We can generate a measure of movement intensity by comparing the values at time t with those at time t-1 resulting in:

$$\overrightarrow{d_t} = |\overrightarrow{s_t} - \overrightarrow{s_{t-1}}| = \begin{pmatrix} |s_{1_t} - s_{1_{t-1}}| \\ |s_{2_t} - s_{2_{t-1}}| \\ \vdots \\ |s_{n_t} - s_{n_{t-1}}| \end{pmatrix} \tag{2}$$

In subsequent calculations we will use $\overrightarrow{d_t}$ as combined measurement. For distinguishing between wake, active sleep and quiet sleep we are solely interest in the most intense movement. Thus we are testing for the largest value over a set of m samples, generating the value b_t.

$$b_t = \max{(\overrightarrow{d_{t1}}, \overrightarrow{d_{t2}}, ..., \overrightarrow{d_{tm}})} \tag{3}$$

The value b_t is affected by changes in the speed of movement. Therefor as a final step we generate a centered average value of order $2q$-1:

$$\overline{b_t} = \frac{1}{2q-1} \sum_{i=-q}^{q} b_{t-i} \tag{4}$$

The resulting value $\overline{b_t}$ allows us to quantify the intensity of movements over a given period. In order to extract an actual body movement from this value we have to quantify a threshold $s(t)$ that is determined by the average of q previous values of $\overline{b_t}$ multiplied with a factor f that has to be evaluated individually for each configuration of bed and sensors. This threshold $s(t)$ allows us to identify a movement m at any time t. This behavior is denoted in the following equations:

$$s(t) = \left(\frac{1}{q} \sum_{i=1}^{q+1} \overline{b_{t-i}}\right) * f \;, \quad m_t = \begin{cases} 1, & if \; \overline{b_t} > s(t) > \overline{b_{t-1}} \\ 0, & else \end{cases} \tag{5}$$

As previously mentioned it is difficult to determine sleep phases solely by monitoring the movement. Instead following the example of Salmi and Leinonen and distinguish three phases - wake, active sleep and quiet sleep [13]. These are determined by dividing the sleep time into a three-minute epochs e_{i_a} and qualify these as active or quiet by counting the number of movements occurring in those intervals and comparing it to the average amount of movements in all epochs $\overline{e_a}$ determined by the following equations:

$$e_{i_a} = \sum_{e_{i_{Start}}}^{e_{i_{End}}} m_i \ , \quad \overline{e_a} = \frac{1}{n}\sum_{i=0}^{n} e_{i_a} \tag{6}$$

In consequence we determine the status of any epoch with this final equation:

$$e_{i_a} = \begin{cases} active, & if\ e_{i_a} > \overline{e_a} \\ quiet, & if\ e_{i_a} \leq \overline{e_a} \end{cases} \tag{7}$$

These active and quiet periods can be semi-autonomously interpreted by humans in order to determine the actual sleep phases. For example initial activity for 20 to 40 minutes followed by a quiet period can be attributed to a person falling asleep. Following quiet phases are a good indicator for deep sleep phases.

5   MoviBed Prototype

The Prototype uses existing hardware that has been created by Braun et al. [8] that uses the CapToolKit [14] to read from eight capacitive sensors and send their values to a PC using USB. Each of the sensors uses thin copper-foil as electrodes that are attached to the slatted frame of the bed, as shown in Fig. 4. On each bedside is one electrode placed below the head-area, two below the top and bottom torso-area and one below the feet. This way the whole body can interact with the sensors and most motions can be detected. The computer besides the bed runs a Java-program which reads the character-string encoded sensor-values via the RXTX library from the serial interface and processes the data in the way described in the previous chapter. To be read and analyzed later by this or other programs, all processed data of a recording can be saved in a comma-separated-file, together with its associated time and date, detected motions and epochs. For further investigation by a human gets the processed data in a simple GUI visualized.

Fig. 4. MoviBed prototype [8]

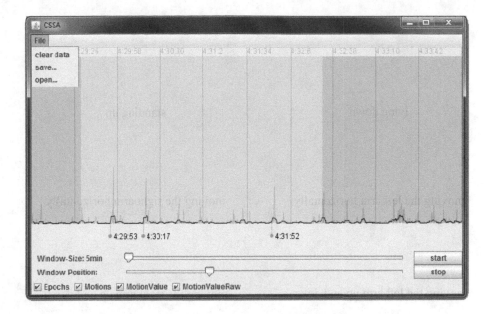

Fig. 5. Graphical user interface of the prototype

All movement-data are displayed in real-time in a linear graph, each detected motion is marked and labeled with its time and the epochs are visualized as coloring of the graphs background, in which active phases are shown in green and quiet phases in blue. This way the whole recording can be analyzed at one glance or in smaller time-windows for a more detailed analysis.

6   Evaluation

We have performed two different evaluations of MoviBed. The first part is a test of the detection precision regarding different movements. The test person was performing the following chain of events: (1) Lying down and standing up again, (2) moving the left and right arms away from the body horizontally, (3) moving the arms up and down, (4) moving the left and right leg away from the body horizontally, (5) lifting the left and right leg, (6) rotating the head, (7) rotating the whole body. The test person was asked to perform this sequence waiting 15 seconds between each event. Distinct values b_t were recorded over time and plotted to get a measure for the detected movement intensity.

Fig. 2 gives an overview of some example sensor activities caused by (1) moving an arm and (2) moving the head alone. It can be observed that the head is causing a considerably smaller output compared to the arm. This can be attributed to the fact that the head is a smaller object and the movement does barely alter the shape of the body with respect to the sensor electrodes. Therefore we can group the movements into three different categories based on how distinct the sensor response is:

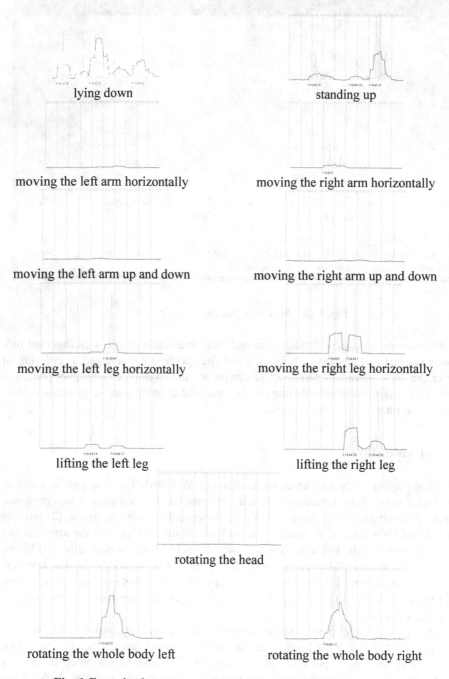

Fig. 6. Examples for movements and their associated value b_t over time

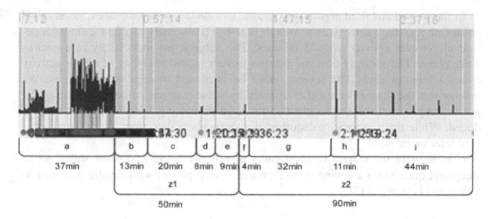

Fig. 7. Movement data over three hours in night one

- Strong response - lying down and standing up (1), rotating whole body (7), horizontal leg movement (4)
- Medium response - horizontal arm movement (2), lifting legs (5)
- Weak response - lifting arms (3), rotating head (6)

The second evaluation we performed was detecting movements in the sleep of a single person over three nights. Fig. 3 gives an example of three hours of the first night. We follow the methods presented by Salmi and Leinonen [13] to group the epochs and analyze the resulting data set. The exemplary analysis for the three hours shown in Fig. 3 results in the following sleep phases: (a) very active wake phase of 37 minutes, (b) fallen asleep and spending 13 minutes in NREM phases 1 and 2, (c) about 20 minutes of deep sleep, (d) going back to phases 2 and 1, (e) first REM phase of 9 minutes, (f) approximately 4 minutes of light sleep, (g) deep sleep phase, (h) potential REM phase of 11 minutes, (i) potential light sleep and REM sleep.

The cycles $z1$ and $z2$ denote full sleep cycles with the person moving from deep sleep to REM and back again. The first has a duration of 50 minutes and the second of 90 minutes.

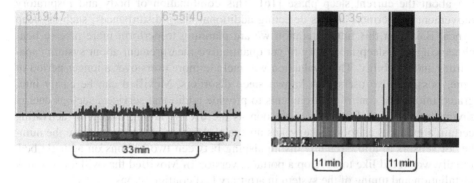

Fig. 8. Anomalies in the second (left) and third (right) night

In the second and third night we were able to monitor some anomalies; i.e. atypical phases of very high activity as shown in Fig. 4. The anomaly of night 2 shows a period of constant activity over 33 minutes. The subject was most likely in a restless wake phase. The anomaly of night 3 shows to very intensive phases of sensor activity over 11 minutes each. The severity can't be attributed to regular movements. We assume that the sensors were either affected by some external influence, e.g. irregular power supply or there was an error in the data processing that could not be reproduced. While this temporarily disturbed the sleep phase detection, the system recovered later in the night.

Conclusively the system in most cases to reliably discern between wake, active sleep and quiet sleep allowing us to reproduce sleep phases with similar accuracy as Salmi and Leinonen [13].

7   Conclusion and Future Work

On the previous pages we have presented MoviBed, a sensor-equipped bed for personal sleep analysis. Based on a platform for capacitive proximity sensing MoviBed is able to detect movement on the bed and associate it to different phases of sleep. We have presented a method to calculate movement measures from raw capacitive sensor values in order to associate different periods of time to phases of wakefulness, active sleep and quiet sleep. We have tested this method in an extended prototype both for the capability to distinguish different movements, as well as for sleep phase recognition. We were able to reproduce the results of Salmi and Leinonen that introduced this method of movement-based sleep phase recognition, without requiring disturbing measurement devices typically used in full-scale sleep laboratories. Therefore MoviBed marks an important step in enabling regular customers to apply some minor sleep analysis in their own homes.

Nonetheless MoviBed is but an intermediate step in this direction. We plan to rebuild the prototype using the OpenCapSense capacitive proximity sensing toolkit, that provides higher precision compared to the CapToolKit used in the current iteration [15]. We expect that this allows us to more precisely distinguish different movements and in addition get an idea about respiratory movements that allows additional reasoning about the current sleep phase [16]. This combination of body and respiratory movement furthermore allows detecting additional sleep disturbances, such as sleep apnea. Based on this future iteration we are planning to perform more precise benchmarking in a sleep laboratory to get quantitative measurement about system capabilities and reliability. This evaluation will include more users over a longer period of time, possibly also users with known sleep disorders. MoviBed can be easily integrated into home control environments to provide additional services, such as energy saving by shutting of appliances as soon as the user is falling asleep, or activating certain appliances as soon as he wakes up again. Another idea is to increase the number of sensors to allow reliably distinguishing between two persons on a single bed. Finally we would like to develop a portable version of MoviBed that will allow quick installation and tuning of the system in arbitrary bed configurations.

Acknowledgments. We would like to thank all volunteers that participated in our study and provided valuable feedback for future iterations. This work was partially funded by EC Grant Agreement No. 610840.

References

1. Pilcher, J.J., Huffcutt, A.J.: Effects of sleep deprivation on performance: A meta-analysis. Sleep J. Sleep Res. Sleep Med. 19, 318–326 (1996)
2. Moser, D., Anderer, P., Gruber, G., Parapatics, S.: Sleep classification according to AASM and Rechtschaffen & Kales: effects on sleep scoring parameters. Sleep (2009)
3. Littner, M.M., Kushida, C.: Practice parameters for the role of actigraphy in the study of sleep and circadian rhythms: an update for 2002. Sleep (2003)
4. Jones, C., Campbell, S., Zone, S.: Familial advanced sleep-phase syndrome: A short-period circadian rhythm variant in humans. Nat. Med. (1999)
5. Zimmerman, T.G., Smith, J.R., Paradiso, J.A., Allport, D., Gershenfeld, N.: Applying electric field sensing to human-computer interfaces. In: Proceedings of the SIGCHI Conference on Human Factors in Computing Systems - CHI 1995, pp. 280–287. ACM Press, New York (1995)
6. Braun, A., Hamisu, P.: Using the human body field as a medium for natural interaction. In: Proceedings of the 2nd International Conference on PErvsive Technologies Related to Assistive Environments - PETRA 2009, pp. 1–7. ACM Press, New York (2009)
7. Große-Puppendahl, T.A., Marinc, A., Braun, A.: Classification of User Postures with Capacitive Proximity Sensors in AAL-Environments. In: Keyson, D.V., et al. (eds.) AmI 2011. LNCS, vol. 7040, pp. 314–323. Springer, Heidelberg (2011)
8. Braun, A., Heggen, H.: Context recognition using capacitive sensor arrays in beds. Technik für ein selbstbestimmtes Leben - 5. Deutscher AAL-Kongress. VDE VERLAG GmbH, Berlin (2012)
9. Krejcar, O., Jirka, J., Janckulik, D.: Use of mobile phones as intelligent sensors for sound input analysis and sleep state detection. Sensors (2011)
10. AppZoo GmbH, http://thewakeapp.com/ (retrieved January 27, 2014)
11. Schulz, H.: Rethinking sleep analysis. J. Clin. Sleep Med. 4, 99–103 (2008)
12. Wilde-Frenz, J., Schulz, H.: Rate and distribution of body movements during sleep in humans. Percept. Mot. Skills (1983)
13. Salmi, T., Leinonen, L.: Automatic analysis of sleep records with static charge sensitive bed. Electroencephalogr. Clin. Neurophysiol. 64, 84–87 (1986)
14. Wimmer, R., Kranz, M., Boring, S., Schmidt, A.: A Capacitive Sensing Toolkit for Pervasive Activity Detection and Recognition. In: Fifth Annu. IEEE Int. Conf. Pervasive Comput. Commun. PerCom 2007, pp. 171–180 (2007)
15. Grosse-Puppendahl, T., Berghoefer, Y., Braun, A., Wimmer, R., Kuijper, A.: OpenCapSense: A Rapid Prototyping Toolkit for Pervasive Interaction Using Capacitive Sensing. In: IEEE Int. Conf. Pervasive Comput. Commun. (March 18-22, 2013)
16. Guerrero-Mora, G., Elvia, P.: Sleep-wake detection based on respiratory signal acquired through a Pressure Bed Sensor. Engineering in Medicine and Biology Society, EMBC (2012)

Contribution of Augmented Reality Solutions to Assist Visually Impaired People in Their Mobility

Benoît Froissard[1,2], Hubert Konik[2], Alain Trémeau[2], and Éric Dinet[2]

[1] Laster Technologies, Courtabœuf, France
benoit.froissard@laster.fr
[2] Laboratoire Hubert Curien, Université Jean Monnet, Saint-Étienne, France
{hubert.konik,alain.tremeau,eric.dinet}@univ-st-etienne.fr

Abstract. The study is dedicated to analyze opportunities of augmented reality eyewear solutions for visually impaired people in a context of mobility. In order to perfectly understand the needs of low vision individuals, their expectation towards visual aids, and to clearly define crucial requirements, an experimental study has been carried out in a re-adaptation clinic. 58 patients with different visual pathologies have been carefully selected by vision-care professionals. During experiments and interviews, professional techniques developed for teaching patients to efficiently use their visual residual capabilities have been analyzed. One of the main objectives was to show the usefulness and the importance to put in the loop all actors to be able to derive relevant knowledge essential to success in the design and in the development of new visual aids dedicated to facilitate mobility of low vision people. The first results are encouraging and they tend to demonstrate the interest to use embedded augmented reality systems in order to propose helpful solutions easily adaptable to the specificities of the different visual troubles affecting mobility.

Keywords: Visual impairment, augmented reality, virtual reality, eyewear, residual capability, handicap compensation, optometry, mobility aids.

1   Introduction

Visual media are becoming more abundant in our daily life and a core constituent of information and communication technologies. This leads the emergence of new needs, changes in behavior, consumption patterns and distribution practices. Today people are less and less refractory for new technologies like smartphones or other embedded systems. Such elements motivate the study presented in this paper. This study is dedicated to analyze opportunities of augmented reality eyewear solutions for visually impaired people in a context of mobility. By adopting credible tools, acknowledging the importance of significantly improving visual impaired condition, mobile visual aid systems answer a critical societal problem.

There are around 285 million of visually impaired people in the world. Aged related Macular Degeneration (AMD) is for example one of the most important visual disease in occidental countries. The forecasts of the World Health Organization

C. Stephanidis and M. Antona (Eds.): UAHCI/HCII 2014, Part IV, LNCS 8516, pp. 182–191, 2014.
© Springer International Publishing Switzerland 2014

highlight a major risk it is necessary to face. In this context, developing adapted tools is urgent. Nowadays, the only primary aids offered to visually impaired people for independent mobility consist of different types of canes. Even if electronic travel aids exist and even if they were initially designed to replace canes, they are ultimately used as secondary aids. The main reason of the low success of assistive technologies in the context of navigation is the lack of significant additional information provided by electronic aids to low vision individuals. During the past years many research teams proposed different assistive technologies or solutions to compensate visual troubles. Meanwhile, few researches have been conducted on wearable systems exploiting the residual vision of visually impaired people to assist them in mobility. However, professionals working in the field of low vision agree to say that it is important to stimulate the residual vision early in the sight-loss process.

Many new technological devices such as cell phones, smartphones and augmented reality eyewear are being developed to give to anybody new information and new way to access to information. These devices could be used to help visually impaired people in their daily life by providing salient useful information or enhancement of targeted information.

In the following, a state-of-the-art of works using augmented reality for visually impaired people is presented in Section 2. Section 3 overviews the main visual needs of low vision individuals. Section 4 presents a first work on edge enhancement that we have implemented and tested on an augmented reality device in order to provide additional useful information to visually impaired people. Results obtained during experiments carried out in a re-adaptive clinic are summarized and discussed in section 5. The last part of the paper is dedicated to a brief conclusion and to put into perspective this work in the context of mobility.

2   Related Work

Nowadays some systems take into account the needs of visually impaired people but always in a specific context. For example, the virtual reality solution named "sightmate" is mainly devoted for reading and watching television. This solution exploits low level image processing methods such as edge detection, enhancement, or MPEG modification introduced by Peli et al. [1]. Such a tool seems to be useful but only for patients with enough visual residual capabilities from 20/70 to 20/200.

Many studies in neuroscience demonstrated that contrast is a very important low level feature for human visual system. The main problem with contrast is the large number of definitions (e.g. physical contrast, perceived contrast, etc.). According to Peli et al., virtual reality systems should measure, enhance, and adjust contrasts of virtual scenes or natural images in order to help visually impaired people [2]. In some visual activities such as reading, image processing is very useful for individuals with low vision, for instance when text is enhanced [3].

In a general way, low level image processing is used to enhance low visual information in 2D images such as edges or colors, whereas 3D computer vision can be used for object recognition and depth perception. Such an approach can significantly contribute to improve the visual perception of low vision people but must be carefully managed to not trouble their residual visual capabilities. Some studies have shown that virtual reality and augmented reality could create inattentional blindness [4]. By multiplexing too much data, there is a risk to mask a more or less important proportion of real information. In such a case, observers can face some troubles to perceive their environment as it is in comparison with direct observation.

In [5], Balakrishnan et al. proposed to use a head mounted display coupled to a stereo camera system in order to enhance in real time the visual perception of low vision people. One of the main advantages of this type of device is that it allows an access to information regarding the surrounding environment and the location of scene's elements. According to Chauvire et al., optical see-through eyewear should be used as a visual aid [6]. Peli et al. also demonstrated that optical see-through eyewear should help visually impaired people by modifying edges [7-9]. However, they noticed that their edge detector [10-11] is unfortunately not well-adapted to this kind of use because it needs black and white to enhance edges [12].

3   Visual Needs of Low Vision People

Most of visually impaired people are elderly. According to Newell et al. [13], these people have more troubles than others to correctly use new technological devices and are not always self-confident in their manipulation. Therefore, it is essential to adapt new technologies by taking into account the habits and the reflexes acquired from interfaces that are now obsolete. To achieve such a goal, Newell et al. [14] proposed to put in the loop the users for developing new solutions or new methodologies. The point of view of visually impaired people is very important for researchers to know what should be the main functionalities, how to design an ergonomic visual assistive device, how to imagine a convenient and friendly user interface, how to improve the acceptation of visual aids by users. These questions were studied and analyzed by Shinoara et al. in [15].

In order to understand the needs of visually impaired people, their expectation towards visual aids, and to define the essential requirements, an objective experimental study has been conducted in a re-adaptation clinic. 58 patients with low vision have been carefully selected by vision-care professionals. One of the main goals of this study was to put in the loop both patients and vision-care professionals in order to understand what are the visual needs of visually impaired people and how specialists work with them. One of the main objectives of this paper is to show that from the collected data and the derived knowledge, we could design and develop visual aids correlated to the needs and expectations of visually impaired people. Re-adaptation methods used by vision care professionals could inspire the development of solutions adapted to each user and to his/her residual visual capabilities. Vision-care professionals such as orthoptists, opticians, ergo-therapists or locomotion instructors explained the methods and approaches they use with patients. Their practices differ according to their medical specialty:

- Orthoptists analyze the residual visual capabilities and eye-oculomotor fluency of patients. The objective is to train patients to autonomously use their residual capabilities to compensate their visual problem. Generally, after a training period, visually impaired people are able to extract more information from real world by themselves and they can achieve all, or quite all, of their daily tasks with more abilities than before. In this context, augmented reality displays or any type of optical or electronic devices can help low vision individuals into their daily life activities.
- Ergo-therapists analyze movement of patients during near and middle vision tasks such as cooking, eating, as well as for domestic and professional activities. For professional activities, ergo-therapists precisely analyze the working environment to accordingly adapt the residual visual capabilities. The objective is to train patients to better know how using their own capabilities to understand the world, and how to interact with their direct environment.
- Locomotion instructors analyze mobility capabilities of low vision people and how they can find useful information to walk freely and confidently. Patients learn how to: extract information; analyze their surrounding environment; know where they are and how they can go to a targeted destination. These kinds of tasks are very important for patients, especially when they need to navigate by their own inside their home. Patients also learn how to analyze information from canes, sounds, and other signs to have access to complementary information from the world. In outdoor environments, visual information from the surroundings as zebra crossing, traffic ways or number of ways are essential for visually impaired people to navigate freely and safely. Locomotion instructors advise and help low vision patients to use assistance solutions to facilitate their mobility.

To sum up, different categories of vision-care professionals can help visually impaired patients by learning how to exploit different types of features, especially visual features. Visual features are very informational for low vision people but they are sometimes not enough perceptible by them. Therefore, one of the main functionalities of a visual aid is to enhance these visual features to make them more informational and more discriminative. After discussion with vision-care professionals, we conclude that visual aids must only enhance the most important visual features to avoid a counterproductive overrepresentation. We also conclude that visually impaired people must exploit their residual visual capabilities when they use such aids and that they should not be totally assisted. Some orthoptists strongly insisted on this last point.

We interviewed patients and asked them to answer to binary questions related to: a particular need (e.g. recognizing faces or reading), the possibility to perform one daily task in autonomy (e.g. walking or cooking), expectations regarding the use of any future assistive solution (e.g. virtual reality or augmented reality), etc. As an example, here is one specific question: "Are you able to walk alone for a short unknown pathway in full self-confidence?" Questions were asked in the mother speaking language of patients to avoid any misunderstanding problem. Table 1 presents an overview of data collected from 24 visually impaired patients. This table summarizes the ratios of the answers of patients to several questions about daily tasks performed in full autonomy.

Table 1. Results related to particular daily tasks

Tasks performed in autonomy	Can do it (%)	Cannot do it (%)
Doing a short known walk	66.7%	33.3%
Doing a short unknown walk	41.7%	58.3%
Doing a long walk	50.0%	50.0%
Shopping in a supermarket	66.7%	33.3%
Recognizing faces	25.0%	75.0%
Reading	33.3%	66.7%

Table 1 shows that mobility activities -long walk and walk onto unknown pathway-cannot be performed in autonomy with self-confidence by many visually impaired people. It is difficult for these people to adapt to new environments. According to our interviews the expectation of low vision individuals is to have access to additional information in order to overcome this issue. For a walk in a well-known area, only 33.3% of patients face some difficulties; on the other hand for a walk in an unknown area, 58.3% of patients face difficulties. Unknown areas are very challenging for patients. Two other main activities which need aids to be performed in autonomy are face and people recognition as well as reading. Face recognition is a very difficult visual task, only 25% of patients can achieve it easily.

4   Edge Enhancement for Low Vision People

Several studies have shown that edges are one of the main visual features useful for low vision people. Consequently, in our experiments we firstly tested the hypothesis that edge enhancement can help visually impaired people to better perceive their environment. The main questions we addressed in this study were what do we mean by edges, by edge enhancement, and by improving visual perception from edge enhancement?

Depending on the observers and on their residual visual capabilities, depending on the visual task to carry out or depending on the task to perform, edges are not perceived in a same way and the expectations of users in term of edge enhancement are not identical. In the everyday life the content of scenes may vary as well as the ambient light conditions. Sometimes under direct illumination there are some spot lights and shadows, sometimes under dim light objects are not well contrasted. Consequently, that does make sense in this context to use an adaptive edge detector. We could for example consider an edge detector invariant to photometric changes but this type of detector will not satisfy all expectations of all users. We could consider another edge detector, for example, more robust to image changes but once again this will not satisfy expectations related to semantic features. All these observations suggest that the visually impaired people should be able to interact with the edge detector in order to easily adjust edge detection and edge enhancement, according to the context and in function of the expectations of the moment.

In order to evaluate the relevance of different techniques of edge enhancement, we asked to selected patients to compare original images with their enhanced versions. Patients have been divided in two groups because this experiment was performed during two different periods. For this experiment, we considered a set of 48 images of indoor environments, offices or home interiors. All pairs of images (original and enhanced images) were displayed in a random order on a calibrated display. The first objective of this experiment was to validate the hypothesis that edge points superimposed to real world data improve the visual perception of people with low vision when they analyze a scene.

For each pair of displayed images, patients were asked to answer to the following question: "Among the two displayed images which one is easier to analyze?". During a training phase, the meaning of the question was explained to participants in order that they perfectly understand the relation with recognition and interpretation tasks. Patients could display as many times as they want the two versions of images forming each pair. Observers were allowed to move freely their head and eyes during the experiment. The duration of an evaluation session was about 30 minutes on average.

Few elderly people participated to this experiment (13 out of 58). In general, elderly people face some troubles with new technology devices [15]. However, most of elderly observers involved in the experiment (10 out of 13) were able to perform the evaluation session without any help. When necessary, we assisted patients by switching images when they required.

Fig. 1. Examples of edge detection: respectively Sobel, Canny, and the pyramid-based method that we have introduced. Let us note that the quality of images of most of micro cameras used by see-through eyewear systems is very low. Here the resolution of each image is 640 × 480 pixels.

Many studies conducted in neuroscience demonstrated that contrast is a very important low level feature for non-disabled observers and also for people with low vision. In [16], Haun *et al.* reported that "the perceptual impact of an image, and the way its contrast is interpreted by an observer, is dependent on the structure of the image, thereby suggesting that perceived contrast of complex imagery is not an entirely passive process". As mentioned above, the main problem with contrast is that there are numerous definitions and numerous computing formulas. In our experiment we compared four standard edge point detection methods (Fig.1): Sobel, Canny (computed either from grey levels only or from color) and a pyramid-based method we developed for our experimental protocol [17-21]. The pyramid-based method uses a real-time multi-scale framework for the selection of the most contrasted edges.

In our experiment, extracted edge points were superimposed to the original image. Four different colors of edges were used during the display (yellow, green, red and blue) and 4 thicknesses were considered. Edge thickness was adjusted according to the visual acuity of patients: the thinner for 10/10, the thicker for 1/20 and two intermediate values for 3/10 and 1/10.

5   Data and Results

5.1   Statistics on Visually Impaired Patients Who Participated to Experiments

Group 1 was composed of 28 visually impaired patients: 2 were less than 40 years old, 5 were between 41 and 60 years old, 14 were between 61 and 80 years old, 7 were over than 81 years old. 82% of these patients were retired. The experiment carried out with this group took place in a re-adaptation clinic for people with low vision. Group 2 was composed of 30 visually impaired patients: 1 was less than 40 years old, 10 were between 41 and 60 years old, 13 were between 61 and 80 years old, 6 were over than 81 years old. 63% of these patients were retired. We classified these patients according to their visual acuity (see Table 2) and according to their pathology (see Table 3). One group performed the experiment in a dark room with images displayed on a CRT device, while the other performed the same experiment under normal light conditions (300cd/m2) with images displayed on a LCD device. Let us note that no statistical disparities were found between the data collected from these two experiments.

Table 2. Classification of patients according to their visual acuity measured for both eyes

Far visual acuity	Group 1	Group 2
Higher than 5/10	4	12
Between 1/10 and 5/10	23	24
Between 1/50 and 1/10	15	15
Lower than 1/50	14	9

Table 3. Classification of patients according to their pathology

Visual pathology	Percentage of patients
Scotoma	67.2 %
Tunnel vision	29.3 %
Eccentricity	6.9%

5.2   Statistics on the Gain Resulting from Edge Enhancement

82 % of people with low vision preferred the enhanced images whereas 17% preferred the original ones. Only 1% had no preference. Whatever the image shown and whatever the pathology and the residual visual capabilities of observers, most of them preferred enhanced images (see Table 4). However, when we consider one by one

Table 4. Improvement rate due to edge enhancement with edge thickness adapted to the visual acuity of patients

Visual pathology	Does edge enhancement help people with low vision to better analyze images?
Patients with a scotoma	Yes for 77%
Patients with tunnel vision	Yes for 68%

Table 5. Preference rates for each edge detection method

Edge detection method	Patients with a scotoma	Patients with tunnel vision
Edges	79 %	87 %
Sobel	59 %	67 %
Canny	47 %	47 %
Color-Canny	32 %	53 %
Pyramid-based approach	65 %	67 %
Pyramid-based vs Sobel	86 %	88 %
Pyramid-based vs Canny	94 %	100 %
Pyramid-based vs Color-Canny	89 %	88 %

each pair of images, there are some subtle differences between results. It appears that the answers depend on various parameters, such as the content of the scene, the lighting conditions under which the image of the scene has been captured, the recognition task, the interpretation task, etc. Most of observers explained that they prefer to see local edges enhanced only on certain areas rather than on the whole image.

According to Apfelbaum *et al.* [12], for visually impaired people, the edge detection is the crucial step before the edge enhancement step. To confirm this assumption, for each edge detector tested we analyzed the percentage of enhanced images for which all patients expressed a preference in comparison with the images without enhancement and in cross-comparison with the other edge detection methods. The first row of Table 5 illustrates the proportion of observers who expressed a preference for enhanced images (whatever the method used) rather than for non-enhanced images. The following rows illustrate the relevance of each specific method by cross-comparison with the other methods. The improvement due to edge enhancement is clearly demonstrated. Moreover, these results demonstrate that the pyramid-based approach outperforms the others. Whatever the pathology, there is a clear difference between the percentages of enhanced images for which all patients expressed a preference for the pyramid-based method.

6   Discussion

According to the conclusion of reference [12], a development of a dedicated edge detector for visually impaired people is necessary. In our study, we have proved that the quality of edge detection plays a pivotal role in edge enhancement and in image improvement for low vision people. We have also shown that the quality of edges depend on various factors which vary in function of many parameters.

From the surveys we conducted and from the discussions we had with visually impaired patients and vision-care professionals, we can argue that augmented reality optical see-through eyewear could be a relevant solution to improve the visual perception of low vision people and that this type of system could be efficiently used as a visual aid. The experiment performed in this study contributes to prove that additional information multiplexed with real scene is beneficial for visually impaired people and could help them in their daily life, for object recognition (e.g. in kitchen, office), for environment understanding (e.g. localize doors in a corridor, stairs in a building), as well as for basic visual tasks (e.g. reading, watching TV). Our experiment relied on multiplexing real visual data with low level features based on edges.

We also developed a real-time edge detector for videos. Corresponding experiments with low vision patients will be carried out to test it in real mobility conditions. The main constraint in this domain is to obtain the required authorizations from accredited authorities to develop the experimental protocol. At short term, in the context of mobility, we aim to validate: (a) the edge detector and the multiplexing technique that we have defined, (b) the usability of the augmented reality eyewear system that Laster Technologies has designed, (c) the relevance of the interactive software solution that we have developed specifically for visually impaired people.

Other parameters, out of the scope of this paper, such as technological characteristics (e.g. the consumption and the autonomy of the system) or ergonomic parameters (e.g. the weight of the system) have to be taken into account to ensure the success of assistive technologies in the context of navigation. These additional parameters will be studied during new interviews of both low vision patients and vision-care professionals.

Acknowledgments. Firstly authors would like to thank Laster Technologies, one of the funders of this research work. The study is also funded by the French technology research agency (ANRT). Authors are very grateful to all visually impaired patients who spent time during experiments. Patients always accepted with an enormous kindness to answer to numerous questions, helping to better understand needs and expectations for new generations of visual aids. Authors would like also to thank the teams of Vision & Recherche and of AGE ARAMAV for their respective efficient collaboration.

References

1. http://www.vuzix.com (last visited on March 03, 2012)
2. Haun, A.M., Peli, E.: Measuring the Perceived Contrast of Natural Images. SID Symposium Digest of Technical Papers 42(1), 302–304 (2011)
3. Fine, E.M., Peli, E.: Enhancement of text for the visually impaired. Journal Opt. Soc. Am. A 12(7), 1439–1447 (1995)

4. Apfelbaum, H.L., Apfelbaum, D.H., Woods, R.L., Peli, E.: Inattentional blindness and augmented-vision displays: effects of cartoon-like filtering and attended scene. Ophthalmic and Physiological Optics 28(3), 204–217 (2008)
5. Balakrishnan, G., Sainarayanan, G., Nagarajan, R., Yaacob, S.: Wearable Real-Time Stereo Vision for the Visually Impaired. Engineering Letter (May 2007)
6. Chauvire, C., Charbonnier, S., Swital, M., Le Brun, J., Petit, J.-P., Villette, T., Chaumet-Riffaud, P., Mohand-Said, S., Sahel, J.-A., Safran, A.B.: Improved Vision with a Novel Enhanced Reality Non-Immersive Head-Mounted Device (HMD) for Reducing Low Luminance Dysfunction (LLD) in Patients with Age-Related Macular Degeneration (AMD). In ARVO (2011)
7. Peli, E., Luo, G., Bowers, A., Rensing, N.: Applications of augmented vision head mounted systems in vision rehabilitation. Society for Information Display 15(12), 1037–1045 (2007)
8. Peli, E., Vargas-Martin, F.: Augmented-view for restricted visual field: Multiple device implementations. Optometry & Vision Science 11, 715–723 (2002)
9. Vargas-Martín, F., Peli, E.: P-16: Augmented view for tunnel vision: Device testing by patients in real environments. SID Symposium Digest of Technical Papers 32(1), 602–605 (2001)
10. Peli, E.: Wide band image enhancement US patent 7,280,704 (2007)
11. Peli, E.: Wide band image enhancement US patent 6,611,618 (2003)
12. Apfelbaum, H., Apfelbaum, D., Woods, R.L., Peli, E.: 41.2: The effect of edge filtering on vision multiplexing. SID Symposium Digest of Technical Papers 36(1), 1398–1401 (2005)
13. Alm, N., Gregor, P., Newell, A.F.: Older people and information technology are ideal partners. In: International Conference for Universal Design (2002)
14. Newell, A.F., Gregor, P.: User sensitive inclusive design. In: Proceedings on the 2000 Conference on Universal Usability, pp. 39–44 (2000)
15. Shinohara, K., Wobbrock, J.O.: In the shadow of misperception: assistive technology use and social interactions. In: Proceedings of the 2011 Annual Conference on Human Factors in Computing Systems, pp. 705–714 (2011)
16. Haun, A., Peli, E.: Measuring the perceived contrast of natural images. In: SID Symposium Digest of Technical Papers, pp. 302–304 (2011)
17. Heath, M., Sarkar, S., Sanocki, T., Bowyer, K.W.: A robust visual method for assessing the relative performance of edge-detection algorithms. IEEE Trans. Pattern Anal. Machine Intell. 19, 629–639 (1997)
18. Heath, M., Sarkar, S., Sanocki, T., Bowyer, K.W.: Comparison of edge detectors: A methodology and initial study. Comput. Vis. Image Understand. 69(1), 38–54 (1998)
19. Basu, M.: Gaussian-based edge-detection methods - A survey. IEEE Trans. Sys., Man, Cybern. 32(3), 252–260 (2002)
20. Pellegrino, F.A., Vanzella, W., Torre, V.: Edge detection revisited. IEEE Trans. Sys., Man, Cybern. 34(3), 1500–1518 (2004)
21. Nadernejad, E., Sharifzadeh, S., Hassanpour, H.: Edge detection techniques: evaluations and comparisons. Applied Math. Sciences 31(2), 1507–1520 (2008)

The Evolution of Public Hygiene and Sanitary Facilities in the Context of Urbanization Processes and Social Conditions

Anna Jaglarz

Wroclaw University of Technology, Department of Architecture
St. Prusa 53/55, 50-317 Wroclaw, Poland
anna.jaglarz@pwr.wroc.pl

Abstract. The evolution of public places and facilities for personal hygiene is directly related to the history of urbanization and to people awareness of public health and its relationship to sanitation. Throughout history, this awareness has varied extremely both between cultures and periods and produced widely disparate responses in spite of virtually identical needs. Availability of technology, variable over the centuries, was dependent on the social and cultural requirements of the times. On the one hand, the new technologies developed in order to meet the growing needs, on the other technological achievements were ignored and not used by years. An example can be a legacy and the inheritance from civilizations such as the Cretans and Romans who accomplished amazingly great feat as regard engineering and the production of hygienic and sanitary facilities, with supplying the warm and cold running water, flushing systems, steam rooms and a lack of such appliances centuries later, when because of the civilization development the basic technology would seem to be far more advanced. It is possible to say that the form of hygienic and sanitary environment of man has always been reflecting the social and economic aspects, which are a consequence of widely understood, changeable, both individual and social needs, and of the cultural and technical progress of civilizations resulting from them. Experiences and achievements of previous generations are a base of the contemporary model of the societies life. Understanding and analysis of the contemporary needs related to public hygiene and sanitary area and possibilities of its shaping should be based on an analysis of earlier experiences in this field.

Keywords: public health, public hygiene, public bathing, hygienic practices, public hygienic-sanitary facilities, public bath, public toilet, public restroom, public bathrooms design, development of public hygienic-sanitary spaces, history of urbanization.

1 Introduction

Hygienic procedures have been known for centuries, however their purpose is changed. Our ancestors washed themselves mainly in order to cool the body. Removal of natural smell from the skin have become the most important for us. It is a insistent

C. Stephanidis and M. Antona (Eds.): UAHCI/HCII 2014, Part IV, LNCS 8516, pp. 192–203, 2014.
© Springer International Publishing Switzerland 2014

desire to get rid of one of the animal features, because none of animals would not want to give up this basic distinctive identification, confirming a separate identity and the membership of the specific group. Yet there is a certain inconsistency in the proceedings of human. On the one hand he removes his personal smell, on the other he willingly uses of perfume and toilet waters, so he still wants to stand out with exactly a smell.

Attitude to hygiene and health over the centuries was associated with the formation of moral rules and standards. Introduction of physical distance and assimilation of standards concerning morality and shame followed gradually. Human sensibility changed. The expansion of the culture into the intimate space of the man followed. Also awareness of health and medicine increased. The approach towards hygiene and ideas of it changed and evolved with the social modifications of behaviors and customs and with the expansion of medical awareness, leading to the contemporary aseptic model of the cleanness and the contemporary forms of public hygiene and sanitary facilities.

History of the body cleanliness and public hygiene shows primarily the changeability of hygiene and sanitation habits and practices or even ideas related to water over centuries, and the gap between the past and the present.

2   Shaping the Concept of Hygiene and Methods of Its Appreciation over the Centuries

In ancient Greece and Rome the care of the body cleanness and hygienic procedures taking place in public scenery and the recreational circumstances were a visiting card of the free citizen. In no other civilization, public bathing was not so great social significance as in Ancient Rome, where the public baths were a main center for cultural and social life. Bath houses held the same positions that in other societies, institutions such as restaurants, urban squares, spas, sports and recreations centers. In the thermal baths people discussed, rested, played, created poems and philosophical treatises. Public baths were above all a place of socializing for the Romans.

In the Middle Ages, public bath houses were very popular, but they were not the institutions of hygiene. They were a sources of many pleasures. Medieval swimming and bathing establishments played the role of entertainment and fun places. Erotic bath prevailed over bath for washing. Water as a environment of physical delights and a source of sensual pleasures attracted more than a process of cleansing and care of the skin condition. A wine, a food, a music and alcoves with curtains were an indispensable elements supplementing the medieval bath.

From the end of the Middle Ages, when the liquidation of the public baths was ordered due to epidemics, and the baths were considered as harmful to health, while water was recognized as a dangerous cause of diseases, up to the mid-eighteenth century, hygiene, was held in fact, without the use of water. Cleanliness was unknown to the body except the face and hands, the only visible parts of it. Hygienic treatments were focused on what has been noticeable. The neatness of clothes, emphasized particularly by the collar and cuffs was a real indication of the purity. The adoption of the above assumptions was associated closely with the concept of hygiene, which rejected water as dangerous, having the ability to penetrate everywhere substance. Hygienic processes were to be held "dry", therefore, they have been limited to perfuming and wiping.

The situation changed at the end of the eighteenth century. Skin contact with the water was recommended as a result of healthcare argumentation. Water stimulated and washed the areas covered by clothes in order to strengthen them. The appearance was not so important as the hardening of the body and taking care of fitness and vigor. The cleanness had a specific physical usefulness and its scientific justification was possible. Cleaning provided the health care, strengthening the body and correct functioning of the organism. The cleanness, which was an expression of aesthetics in the seventeenth century, has become functional. The concept of public cleanliness had appeared as a origin of what was supposed to develop in the nineteenth century. People began to notice the connection between the lack of cleanliness and diseases. First projects connected with urban spaces and water supplies came into existence in this time. The idea of water available for each became more and more real. Public baths offering also hydrotherapy were willingly built. Spas objects having a medical approval and a social prestige, have become very popular. These institutions acted the significant part in the legitimization of water.

The word "hygiene" came into common use at the beginning of the nineteenth century. It didn't define health only, but all funds, abilities and skills used to maintenance of health. People wanted to be healthy and at the same time were convinced that to achieve this they must take care to maintain the purity of the body. Hygiene handbooks which have appeared, persuaded to certain practices, for example using of soaps. Washing has come to mean the aseptic, which had a great relationship with discoveries made by Pasteur. Microorganisms, bacteria, viruses have become a cause of the real turning point in the purity criteria.

Widespread fear of the water reigning from the Renaissance to the late nineteenth century led to equality between social classes when it comes to hygiene. This equality started to walk away into oblivion along with the "hygiene and health awareness". The threat of diseases caused that the widening gap between rich and poor, was not only unpleasant but also dangerous. Public baths and laundries were built in order to cope with difficult-task of improvement the sanitary conditions the poor lived in which. But the large public bath complexes that came into being was intended not only for the lower classes. Public bathing establishments were also popular in the first half of the twentieth century, and in some cultures, a strong tradition of public baths have remained to this day and still supports a common, social ablutions.

3   The Evolution of Public Hygienic and Sanitary Spaces, Buildings and Facilities

3.1   Ancient Times

The first evidence of the actual functioning of hygiene and sanitary facilities for public use are derived from the Cretan Knossos, and their history dates back to around

1700 BC. These objects turn out to be surprisingly sophisticated in their design and technology, while in many respects different from ones functioning today. Most of the large cities in the ancient world were similarly advanced when it comes to availability of hygienic and sanitary facilities, both intended for the local population, as well as accessible to tourists. They were intended primarily to broad application and popularization of municipal objects, which were to replace and complement deficiency in the field of private bathrooms.

The history of public baths began in Greece in the sixth century BC. The attitude of Greeks to the bath was rather practical, without mystical references. They took a bath and showers for keeping the purity of body, for refreshing themselves in heat, after the journey, after the fight, after the gymnastics and exercises. However, the bathing wasn't for them only the simple relax after the muscle effort, but it was also helpful in keeping the mind and body in harmony. Cold baths were closely related to sports and military exercises. Warm baths were practiced only if they were prescribed by Hippocrates, because it was suspected that they caused the delicate and effeminate body, while cold water caused that body was forceful and prepared to fight. Cold water tempered both body and character.

Louterion - shallow, circular basin based on a pedestal, reaching to about the hip was the first form of public baths. It was located in the open air, in the shade of olive trees, near *palestra* - a place for gymnastics and *exedra* - a place for philosophical debates. The woman rinsed herself with water, when man - the gymnast - washed himself before exercises. Next he covered his body with oil and sand. After exercises he scraped off it along with the dirt and sweat that was the result of his efforts, using a small, curved tool made from iron or bronze called *strigil*. A bit later, when *palestra* was converted into the appropriate room of exercises, baths became their essential part. Delphi baths consisted of at least ten marble basins, hung on poles over the heads. The whole was surrounded with jaws of lions, from which water leaked. It was a kind of shower. Special hangers were designed on the clothes. When physical training had become even more significant part of the life of the Athenians, the baths adjacent to the gymnasium became larger and more sophisticated. Baths were covered and equipped with a typical bath with a depth of about 20 cm. Their bottom was slightly sloping, which aided the outflow of water. The Greeks used them in the following way - sitting on a small stool in the water up to the calf, poured over themselves with trickles of water using the special spoon or the sponge. This bath has been reserved for occasions when a man was particularly tired. The Greeks also used large, shallow, circular pool, with rows of degrees surrounding the edge, in which they could rinse itself with the help of the sponge. It was the perfect place to sit and relax in the water before the learning of philosophy.

In the days of the Roman Empire the bath wasn't only hygienic procedure, but also a pleasure. In Rome, as in Greece, the cold water was a symbol of the health, stimulated the body, proved the masculinity and the hardness of character. The Romans didn't treat their body as the object of the aspiration to the ideal of the beauty, didn't derive satisfaction from it, in contrast to the Greeks. They meant rather the health care, keeping the purity and, most important, experiencing of the pleasure.

Ancient Rome and Roman amazing baths can be regarded as a basic pattern, on which the development of the contemporary forms and technologies of public hygienic and bathing services is based. Baths, originally intended as municipal institutions available to all for free or for a small fee, with increasing prosperity of societies began to develop in the direction of separation of the individual services and facilities. In every Roman town was at least one public bath and, if necessary, aqueduct, which supplied bath and public wells. The real era of public baths began actually in 19 BC, along with the construction of the thermal baths by Agrippa. Thermal baths were a kind of recreation center equipped with the stadiums and swimming pools, but also gardens and promenades. There were also eateries and rooms for rest and relaxation. Libraries and theatres provided pleasures connected with the culture. Thermal baths were a place of entertainment, games, social events, as well as political, literary and artistic debates.

Public baths were designed for simultaneous using by thousands of people. Everyone used them - the rich and the poor, women and men, slaves, thieves, prostitutes. Roman baths built by successive rulers were larger and grander than ever before. Building such large complexes would not be possible without new technologies and significant progress in Roman architecture. Plan of the bathing structure was a combination of regularity and diversity. Rectangular shaped main room, *cella media*, was covered with the cross vault, however surrounding them smaller, round or polygonal rooms, were covered with domes. Brick and cement structures were being covered inside with decorative, smooth or relief, facings. The walls and some floors, and even the bottom of the pools were decorated with mosaics. They presented the forms of fauna and flora, marine deities and human figures. Marble was dominant finishing material , but gold, precious stones and ivory were also used. The walls were decorated with figures of nymphs, monsters, warriors and athletes. Seats and bases of washbasins were richly carved. The water gushed from silver taps. Numerous oblong, rectangular and oval, marble baths were available for bathers. Water was supplied by the aqueduct. *Hypocaustum* was applied for the heating

In the second century AD in Rome were built many public latrines. Impurities from them flowed down channels to the Tiber. The oldest of them, the channel *cloaca maxima*, is functioning until today. Every latrine was equipped with about twenty marble seats situated side by side, surrounded by grooves with continually flowing water. Consoles, usually in the shape of dolphins, were supports for hands and simultaneously were partitions between the seats. Even the majestic latrines in the imperial palace were equipped with three adjacent seats. There were also latrines in the form of a trough, along which from both sides wooden seats were attached.

The real example of the urban public sanitary equipment designed for men, urinal, called *pissoir* or *Vespasienne*, appeared for the first time in ancient Rome. In the first century AD the Roman Emperor Vespasian decided, as part of a recovery plan of the city, to build urban urinals for the public convenience. In contrast with public latrines, for the use of earthenware jug, placed in front of fulling workshops (urine collected in them was a valuable raw material used for felting, dyeing and cleaning of fabrics), the Romans didn't need to pay. However owners of workshops had to pay the tax on the unpleasant smell imposed on them by the emperor. It was an effective way allowing to assure both continuity of production for workshops, as well as making rich the emperor's treasure trove, and at the same time dissuading citizens from urinated in the random places.

3.2   The Middle Ages

Comparing medieval Europe to the Mediterranean lands from the period of greatest development of Greece and Rome, it is easy to notice the backwardness of Europe in terms of the sanitation. While focusing on Europe, it can be observed that the era of the Middle Ages was however a remarkable period, when it comes to hygiene.

Up to times of the Middle Ages people inhabiting Europe were largely primitive, characterized by an underdeveloped economy and technology. But even then certain needs to keep hygiene existed and were practiced.

The Middle Ages is very long period, during which the general development followed, so the formation of states and the development of art, technology, improving the standard of living. Thanks to the enlargement of the settlements and the cessation of migration became possible to build long-lasting buildings, also public baths. Of course, washing or bathing is the most important aspect of hygiene. In the Middle Ages the bath was nothing special, it was applied not only to hygienic purposes, but also for pleasure. Its health benefits were also appreciated. People walked to the baths with their families, took clothes off already at home in order to avoid its destruction or theft, walked on the streets only in towels. Separate bath buildings were built at each of the castle. They were also common in most towns and villages. These facilities were a places of rest, where in addition to body washing was the ability to refresh themselves, conversations and plays. Steam baths, acquired from Scandinavian nations, were very popular in Poland and Russia. Fireplace, which from time to time was being poured with water in order to create steam, was placed in one of the corners of the wooden room sealed with resin. The excess of the smoke could get away through the openings in the roof. These baths were willingly visited by both the Polish rulers of the Piast and Jagiellonian dynasties, as well as their lieges, even the poorest, because in many such institutions one day a week was appointed as a free bath for beggars.

The population inhabiting cities took a bath primarily in the public baths. In the country the practice of the bath was not less popular than in the city. In order to wash, the person squatted in the small wooden tub with hot water placed at home or outside the house, under expanded bed sheet, what imitated the bath room. The bath was usually taken collectively - in two or more persons. Hospitality and social custom favored keeping rituals, such as shared bath of growers or bath preceding the wedding day (the groom was taking it among his companions, the bride, accompanied by her friends). Villagers also used open bodies of water, gushing sources or hot springs called either natural or wild. Some villages had a public baths, where baths were supplemented by medical treatments. At the end of the Middle Ages custom of taking a bath, whether water bath or steam bath, at home or in the public bath, became a universal phenomenon in almost all social environments. In the Middle Ages the both public and private bath took place in wooden tubs with round and oval iron rings.

They were placed in the bedrooms. Metal bathtubs came into use in the fourteenth century. Water heating methods have been improved - the wooden tub was filled using the tube linked to the boiler with hot water standing on small stove. Metal bathtubs were also placed directly over the heat source.

In the Middle Ages, amongst the universal ignorance, as regards the sanitation, lack of interest in the development of assistive devices for meeting physiological needs such as urination and defecation was noticeable to about 1500. Development of cities such as London and Paris took place without appropriate channel systems. Municipal sewage flowed in gutters into the rivers, which were the source of drinking water for the people. Public latrines were also placed directly by the rivers. People used the chamber pots called *lasana* or chairs with a holes called *sellae petrusae*, which were emptied into vats or the pit under the staircase. The content was often poured out the window directly into the street, to the detriment of passers-by. This habit outlasted quite a long time in Paris. For comparison, in the medieval Hanseatic Gdansk, latrine was located near every house, in the corner of the yard. Hanseatic cities were planned precisely and the problem of garbage collection and disposal was resolved by sanitary regulations. In Gdansk backyard privy was a part of the architectural plan - the first latrines appeared there along with the first residents. But not everywhere it was a rule. In Plock, or the Norwegian Bergen and Oslo latrines were built much later. Initially, no one cared too much about hygiene and outbuildings were used as latrines.

It is no wonder that medieval cities were horrible stinking. Unpaved streets were dirty, because people didn't refrain from pouring filth out the window. In order not to get bogged down in the mud, people walked on the boards, which were placed every few years anew. Level of the streets was rising quickly - in some cities, streets layers from the thirteenth century there were at least four meters below today's street level. Cesspits placed in the courtyards of medieval houses filled up within a couple of years, after which they had to be emptied. The structure of the latrine, depending on conditions and materials from which it was built, could be used for 150-200 years. Earlier latrines were generally smaller than later. They were mostly wooden structures, but sometimes latrines were made of brick and stone. The shape of the stone latrine could be resembling a well - it happened that exactly wells converted into latrines. Conventional latrines and privies, however, were made of wood. Hay and moss were used as a toilet paper.

3.3   Early Modern Period – From 16th to 18th Century

From the beginning of the sixteenth century, both practices - bath at home and bath in the public baths - started to disappear gradually. It was related with characteristic fear of epidemic and disease transmission by the water. Rejection, or "condemnation" of bath became all the more distinct, that this practice had earlier own institutions and a methods. Within the following years failure of hygiene took place in entire Europe. Public baths began to disappear from the towns and villages, and the ones that remained had a bad reputation of debauchery places and the sources of all diseases. Baths disappeared, and with them practice of the communal bathing. By the start of the reign of Louis XIV in France functioned only two public bath establishments, which were officially registered. But these specialized in therapeutic steam baths recommended by doctors, in the hair removal treatments, and assisted informal social meetings. In England a hundred years later there were several public baths in London offering similar services.

Bathing enthusiasts could also use river bathing or spas and thermal springs. Around 1750, the first in aristocratic circles, water was slowly reintroduced as an essential element of maintaining bodily hygiene. This was the first step in the process that ultimately led to the reactivation of the public bathing. There were also opinions from a growing number of doctors convinced of the positive effects of regular hot and cold baths.

Development of public sanitary facilities, just as of hygienic devices and practices, didn't have its continuation in the large part of the Western World for a long time. They didn't exist at all, or their role was fulfilled by appointed places of manure storage or very primitive latrines. Wealthy passengers used special chamber pots being a part of carriages equipment. Appropriate chamber pots occurred also in new latrines. They were in common use. Depending on the social class of the user they were ordinary made of copper or faience, or silver, richly decorated. Unfortunately, scruffy habit of pouring their contents directly into the street still remained. Similarly the habit of public meeting the physiological needs such as urination and defecation was impossible to eradicate. In Versailles, which in the seventeenth century did not have a sewage system, but was equipped with three hundred portable "closed stools - toilets", hygiene of urination and defecation was still ignored. We should pay attention to the social problem of using the toilet. On the analysis basis of earlier social behaviors associated with it, it is easy to notice, that the idea of the privacy and intimacy of meeting personal physiological needs such as urination and defecation turns out to be quite modern phenomenon. In the time of Louis XIV, the residents of Paris and surrounding areas impatiently waited for dusk to take advantage of the open space. The view of streets reminded of human weaknesses. Unfortunately such a situation was a serious impediment for the ones who preferred privacy and a place to sit. Recommendations on these issues didn't appear until the late sixteenth century.

It should be noted that the sixteenth century was a turning point in terms of the development of private and public toilets. In France in 1519, the Norman government imposed on citizens an obligation to have a toilet in every house. In India, the Mughal Jahangir king ordered to build a public sanitary devices for more than a hundred residents of Alwar. However such actions didn't become a principle, and what's more, belonged to rare exceptions. In addition, to emphasize the contrast between then Europe, and the Arab World in this respect, it is worth mentioning that while the Hindu palace residents used the marble flush toilets, London until to 1700 didn't have running water, and the majority of European citizens still counted on chamber pots and "holes in the open air."

At the end of the eighteenth century, after a period of obvious avoidance essential for the present devices, clockmaker from London, Alexander Cummings, patented flushed toilet and proved to be a precursor of the present toilet model. Then it was improved by the English manufacturer of furniture, Joseph Bramah, which began production of a large number of toilets, in the form of cast iron toilet bowls. However, the majority of cities still wasn't equipped with the sewage system. People used latrines and chamber pots.

3.4   Modern Era – 19th and 20th Century

In the early nineteenth century in Paris alone, the services associated with hygiene, as well as with pleasures, were provided by the staggering total of seventy-eight public baths. However only the second-half of the nineteenth century brought evidence of the recovery of social awareness about the problem of public hygiene and sanitation in the cities.

An imposing bathing establishment called the Thermes Parisiens was opened in Paris in the 1850. A wide range of various baths and treatments available in the shared and private rooms was advertised in brochures. Guests could enjoy the communal Russian sauna, private rooms with hot air for the dry bath, Turkish bath with the Byzantine decor, numerous studies with beds for massage, relaxation rooms, swimming pool replenished with a constant supply of hot and cold water gushing from a fountain. All of this was available in richly decorated interior with the majority of marble, glazed ceramics, mosaics and stucco.

The emphasis on luxury and physical pleasure as essential elements accompanying caring for personal hygiene contributed to the success of public baths, which were also supported by the rapid development of swimming pools in the same period. The revival of public baths allowed once again to appreciate forgotten blissful feeling resulting from contact of the skin with the water. By far the most popular bathing institutions proved to be those that were equipped with a swimming pool, allowing to combine pleasure of games and fun with the requirements of personal hygiene, which became more and more respected and encouraged. In combining with the hygienic function of the use of water, swimming baths helped to support the passion for swimming, kind of sport recommended by doctors and educators. One of the unique places in this regard was the Parisian Gymnase Nautique des Champs-Elysees, founded in 1850 in a park amid gushing fountains. The pool was in the shape of a long rectangle with a picturesque island in the middle, linked to either edge by means of little wooden carved bridges. Two tiers of galleries, divided into boxes with balconies, hidden from view by decked drapes and curtains were located on both sides of the pool. The building was covered with huge glass roof which provided excellent illumination of the interior. The roof was partly decorated with climbing plants. In very sunny and hot days the roof could be covered with white curtains. A billiard room, places for reading and conversation, rooms with beds and individual bathrooms complemented all the attractions.

The development of the public baths intended for a wide range of users started with the arrival of private bathrooms in wealthy households. These hygienic establishments became places for the masses. The bath in the tub had been replaced by the shower bath which was more practical, quicker and made possible of using less water than bathtub. About 1900 public baths with showers became the institutions intended for the working classes. In the United States the history of public baths had a similar course to European countries - France, England and Germany. Even before the end of the nineteenth century, experts in health and public hygiene commenced their action directed at popularizing the cleanness. They demanded a public bath, the use of which would be free of charge. Such objects appeared in New York in the early twentieth century. They were equipped with showers, and the costs for upkeep and running costs were kept to the minimum in order apart from the bath they could provide even soap and towels for free. However in spite of these conveniences, increasing possibilities of a bath in private bathroom in own home resulted in less and less interest in public hygiene institutions. For this reason public baths were closed down.

As regards public sanitary facilities, about 1840 the public urinal regained its rank, this time on the Parisian streets. In 1860 in Paris, there were also special toilet pavilions for women, enclosed and lockable, in contrast with usually opened or only partially shielded men's urinals. In the '80s similar pavilions, public restrooms, have already been designed for both sexes, and were also equipped with a toilet bowl. We can say that in many ways these objects didn't differ much from some of contemporary public toilets. In the '80s, there was also a return of an itinerant seller of public convenience, albeit in a more refined form of vehicle equipped with a water. It was a special horse carriage, which looked like a wagon and consisted of several sections - toilet cabins. Such vehicles were running on the main streets of major cities and were offering the possibilities of meeting the physiological needs for a fee.

In England, the sudden development and increase of the public toilets number was associated with the event of the World Exhibition in London in 1851, for the purpose of which toilets was designed and installed in such an amount that they could accommodate the crowds of visitors. Their equipment was supposed to reflect the quality and aspiration of exhibition. The introduction of facilities for tourists, especially visitors, traveling Europe by rail was another consequence of the great London exhibition and other similar events. Newly built stations and terminals were equipped with complete sanitary facilities, and the standard of their equipment was adapted to the class of the transport. In many ways, it was a pronounced beginning of the availability of this type of public facilities on a large scale. However a few years later, the project of sanitary engineer responsible for the installation of toilet facilities in the Crystal Palace, George Jennings, of the construction of underground toilets in subway stations in strategic locations of London was rejected by the authorities. Jennings suggested fully-fitted objects, with all the comforts and with the additional service which could receive a small fee for using them. Paradoxically his offer was rejected by the English gentlemen, who preferred to expose their wives and daughters to unpleasant visual impression associated with view of corners used by some people for certain physiological needs, as well as unpleasant bodily feelings as a result of the lack of ability of meeting own needs than to agree to the construction of facilities providing favorable conditions, privacy and intimacy.

4   Summary

Long-term development of public hygienic-sanitary facilities over the centuries and the final battle about their availability lasting in the late nineteenth and early twentieth century ended successfully and eventually they became widely available in most major cities. Most of them was designed with allocating for use of pedestrians and tourists. With a sense of spatial order and spatial composition they were entered in the development plans of cities and located, for example, in the traffic circles or at the streets dividing shopping centers. The demand for public hygienic-sanitary facilities serving urban pedestrian traffic decreased significantly since most commercial institutions and services was obliged to provide this type of facilities for the society. On the other hand, because of the condition of many municipal public toilets, people stopped using them. Despite the insignificant upgrade, some objects have survived until today in many places, and although little is needed to have their equipment again was useful, however, they are no longer available as once. Similarly, some of the former bathing institutions - when they were not longer needed, public baths were converted into museums and their previous functions would seem to have been relegated firmly to the past, along with the pleasure of using them. However, in some Western cities - New York, London, Geneva, Brussels, Amsterdam and many cities in Germany - in response to new social needs, these objects are starting to work anew, offering to the possibility of using the bathtub and the shower for affordable price or even for free. The purpose is not only providing possibilities to maintain personal hygiene to people who do not have their own bathrooms, but also opportunities for social integration, which disappeared along with the public baths because of the availability of private bathrooms in the second half of the twentieth century.

References

1. Bonneville (de Bonneville), F.: The Book of the Bath, pp. 19–60. Rizzoli International Publication Inc., New York (1998)
2. Goldman Rubin, S.: Toilets, Toasters & Telephones, pp. 3–27. Browndeer Press Hacourt Brace & Company, Nowy Jork (1998)
3. Historia higieny, http://www.kolo.com.pl
4. Historia zapisana w latrynach, Swiat nauki, Proszynski Media sp. z o.o., Warszawa, 1 (2006)
5. Ouley, G. (ed.): Historia zycia prywatnego. T. 2: Od Europy feudalnej do renesansu. Ossolineum, Wroclaw (1998)
6. Chartieus, R.: Historia zycia prywatnego. T.3: Od renesansu do oświecenia. Ossolineum, Wrocław (1999)
7. Hryn – Kusnierek, R.: Tam gdzie krol piechota chodzi, pp. 96–99. Focus, Axel Ganz, Andreas Tilk G+J Gruner + Jar Polska, 5 (2005)
8. Jacques, R., Jean Charles, S.: Historia epidemii. Od dzumy do AIDS. Wydawnictwo W.A.B., Warszawa (1996)
9. Kira, A.: The Bathroom, pp. 193–199. The Viking Press, Nowy Jork (1976)
10. Kopalinski, W.: Opowiesci o rzeczach powszednich. Instytut Wydawniczy Nasza Ksiegarnia, Warszawa (1990)
11. Krzeminska, A.: W wodzie, winie i blocie. Polityka, Polityka Sp. z o. o. S.K.A., Warszawa, 32 (2006)
12. Lebrun, F.: Jak dawniej leczono. Lekarze, swieci i czarodzieje w XVII i XVIII wieku. Oficyna Wydawnicza Volumen, Dom Wydawniczy Bellona, Warszawa (1997)

13. Mitrowska, M.: Po co nam kapiel? Focus, pp. 12–16. Axel Ganz, Andreas Tilk G+J Gruner + Jar Polska, 10 (2000)
14. Sokolowska, M.: Myc sie czy wietrzyc. Dramatyczne dzieje higieny od starozytnosci do dzis, pp. 6–90. Wydawnictwo Dolnoslaskie, Wroclaw (1999)
15. Szubert, M.: Leksykon rzeczy minionych i przemijajacych, Muza SA, Warszawa (2003)
16. Vigarello, G.: Czystosc i brud. Higiena ciała od sredniowiecza do XX wieku. Wydawnictwo W.A.B., Warszawa (1996)
17. Vigarello, G.: Historia zdrowia i choroby, Od sredniowiecza do wspołczesnosci. Oficyna Wydawnicza Volumen, Niezalezna Oficyna Wydawnicza, Warszawa (1997)

Tradition and Innovation in Architectural Education

Some Reflections on Architectural Design Teaching with the Computer in the Background

Nina Juzwa[1] and Katarzyna Ujma-Wasowicz[2]

[1] Lodz University of Technology, Institute of Architecture and Urban Planning,
90-924 Łódź, Al. Politechniki 6, Poland
nina.juzwa@polsl.pl
[2] Silesian Unicersity of Technology, Faculty of Architecture,
44-110 Gliwice, ul Akademicka 7, Poland
katarzyna.ujma-wasowicz@polsl.pl

Abstract. The presentation is devoted to the problem of introducing computers into the educational process during the last semester of architectural studies for a master's degree. Non-linear structures become almost the principle of design through modifying the traditional, orthogonal image of architecture. Students are open to the creation of concepts which modify the traditional orthogonal spatial system of architecture.

The two-level system of teaching at the course of graduate studies results in students with varying degree of preparation being admitted. This fact in conjunction with large exercise groups and a relatively short time allocated for the project require methodical preparation of the classes. The shaping of the future form of an object can be presented using a freehand sketch, mock-ups or computer models. These tools correspond to the subsequent three phases of the development of the project: exploration of ideas and the context of the environment, working out variants for decisions on functional solutions, spatial and aesthetic concretization of design solutions. In the opinion of the authors of the paper extending the discussion in the first two phases of the teaching process, that take place without the use of computer drawing, leads to a higher originality of the solutions and to an increased efficiency in their preparation.

The above thoughts, supported by examples, are the subject of this presentation.

Keywords: architectural design, teaching in architecture, sketch, mock-up, computer model, idea, concept, dialog in architecture.

1 Introduction

Architecture has accompanied mankind for thousands of years. It creates a spatial frame of life, expresses different contents, different sense of the relationships of humans with their environment. Maybe this is the reason why we are instinctively inclined to look for richer meanings in architectural objects than just information about

C. Stephanidis and M. Antona (Eds.): UAHCI/HCII 2014, Part IV, LNCS 8516, pp. 204–214, 2014.
© Springer International Publishing Switzerland 2014

their utility. Architecture expresses the relationship of individuals with their home, town or generally with the space surrounding them.

Architectural design of buildings and urban planning of districts, urban quarters, or generally speaking complexes of objects together with their environment has two dimensions: functional and cultural. Both are also subject to quality assessment of the proposed solutions. Functionality means that the building/urban complex should meet the pragmatic requirements of the program assumptions or ideas (social, psychological, architectural, economic, environmental, etc.). The cultural dimension means that the shape of the designed/implemented space expresses not only the excellent quality of the technical process, but above all the creation of a new non-material quality of the material environment. Gothic cathedrals, or the earlier antiquity buildings, perfect in proportions medieval and renaissance squares, illusory baroque palaces and gardens, modernism of Le Corbusier, buildings-sculptures and sculptures – Gaudi gardens, classic in their modernity buildings of R. Maier, as well as the revitalized spaces of the historical centres of Warsaw, Glasgow, Lyon – to mention a few places from many – lead to the reality of the architectural/urban planning allowing us to feel our humanity more fully. The expression of these places in the development of thought and culture means more than an increasing technical perfection, it also signifies the changing forms of human existence. This, in turn, is the essence of activities forming the culture and history of the place. Currently, the two dimensions of solutions, the functional excellence and the achieved aesthetics of form articulate the importance of the design of built environment for a technical society at the beginning of the new millennium.

This problem, which is extremely important, poses questions of fundamental importance: "How should we teach?" and "What should we teach?". The topicality of these questions in the international academic world of architects makes the discussion about the hierarchy of needs, the range of knowledge necessary for practicing the profession, etc. increasingly widespread. The variety of tasks posed by the architectural profession triggers different strategies for directions of development and ways of teaching.

Considering the teaching process of architectural design this means a reference to:

- the transfer of multi-faceted knowledge related to architectural design
- the concept of the teaching process itself.

Acting in a consumer society architecture, as well as other types of human activity, is subject to conditions of development of technology and civilization, changing social values and trends. One thing is certain – architecture is never neutral nor devoid of relationships with its environment. This cannot be changed even by such icons of architecture as Rem Koolhaas who encourage to ignore the context. These relationships, although expressed in realisation concepts should also emerge in the conception of the teaching process itself. Thus, the qualifications of architects and, consequently, the reality created by them, are equally a result of the development of the tradition and culture of the local population, as well as of the teaching process. Regarding the contemporaneity of actions in the architecture a very interesting observation was made by Ł.Zagała, a Polish designer of the younger generation, who wrote that today we can confidently state that architecture is lagging behind the rapidly changing life-style of people and rapid technological development. This temporal changeability, as a factor of the present day has to influence the space and architecture, as well as its design methodology. He noticed that we still build in the same manner, but we live increasingly differently. Contrary to appearances, we are building warmer, more transparently and economically, while the general principles, apart from a few specta-cular experiments, have not changed significantly [1]. And so it sometimes happens – modern architecture responds to changes and passing time. Buildings similarly to other everyday devices do not always have to be characterized by long lifetime. Maybe we are moving toward a situation where all modern objects have a short life-time, similarly to modern consumer goods (cars, washing machines, refrigerators, etc.). Examples include sports facilities built for the Summer Olympics held in Lon-don in 2012 (additional grandstands of the Aquatics Centre, Basketball Arena, Olym-pic Shooting Venue).

Today both economics and energy efficiency associated with the use of the object, closely connected with the technique and technology of solutions, enter the sense of architectural design issues. Turner [2] in studies of relationships between economic efficiency and the concept of spatial (architectural) solution distinguishes five com-ponents in the structure of a building: the foundation, structure, enclosure, mechanical devices and finishing elements – each of them brings about, a variable in time, partic-ular set of technical and construction problems.

The publication is based on the experience in teaching architectural design devel-oped within the framework of course exercises conducted at the masters degree level of studies, diploma supervision and workshops for students of the Faculty of Archi-tecture of the Silesian University of Technology in Gliwice (Poland). The subject are utility objects for science, production, trade, sports, offices, etc. The paper focuses on problems which transposed onto the process of teaching can be expressed in three stages, which are also the three terms of evaluation of the learning progress of stu-dents during the semester. These are:

- exploration of ideas and the context of the environment – an idea often expresses a symbol of the concept presented in the form of a graphic sign, drawing, graphics, colour;
- generation of solutions of architectural and constructional concept, in which of particular importance is the ability to present a range of variants of spatial, struc-tural and aesthetic decisions;
- concretization of design decisions.

This allows you to implement the concept of architecture, which departs from the Cartesian idea of immovable networks and stability. The architecture of the informa-tion age, creating a space seemingly chaotic, often "ecstatic", co-creates the contem-porary culture of desire and admiration fever [3]. Today's students are participants and followers of such culture.

2   Architectural Design – Complexity, Interdisciplinarity, Creating Variants

Architecture, however still perceived as an art whose task is the symbolic expression of the role of objects in space, and sometimes even the ability to create a "decoration " for construction and installation solution, is seen as an activity at the interface of theory, applied sciences and practical knowledge. The reasons lie probably in the directions/trends of modern architecture, in which, generally speaking, we can distinguish:

- traditional design based on the realization of human/user's needs,
- design aiming at creating environmentally friendly architecture,
- design, in which computers are widely used [4] [5] [6].

Lately, this trend has been actively pursued in the form of parametric design, in which a prominent role, next to the architect, is played by the computer with modern software and technology associated with the implementation of the undertaking at hand and is usually a matter of interest of students. The technique, which increasingly enters various aspects of life in large, complex projects often results in shifting the role of the architect in the direction of interdisciplinary activities, combining theoretical knowledge with experience and practical engineering knowledge. Similar observations can be made in the current pro ecological trend – the so-called "zero energy architecture".

The most striking feature of architectural design, as well as an ergonomic design, is its complexity and interdisciplinarity. The easiest explanation of it is that each project is a response to a given functional program in a material form (drawings, visualization) and offering a uniform architectural vision. This principle may be expressed in different ways:

- architectural concepts, using a "simple" idea merge knowledge coming from the different areas of expertise (within ergonomics, ecology, social conditions, etc.);
- architecture is associated with signs and symbols, and therefore with emotions developed on many levels, its "language" is the form of the object, which inspires to pose existential questions, but its function descends into the background in this design phase;
- design that uses knowledge about modern technologies implements solutions simple in form and spatial organization, while developing complex construction-technical systems.

The issues of the economics of solutions, closely connected with technology and technique, enter the centre of design and teaching architecture. Its definition is: „economics" is a social science that studies how rational individuals, groups, and organizations manage scarce resources which have alternative uses, to achieve desirable ends [7]. When speaking of economics dealing with the laws governing the economy it should reached also into its other aspect of meaning, which says that economics is a skill of rational use... or the ability to cost-effective use of...

When teaching issues related to architectural design are discussed, the interpretation of problems connected with economy, in the opinion of the authors of the paper, focuses mainly on two issues: construction in conjunction with materials and energy efficiency. The first, concerning questions about the relationships between the spatial, construction and installation structure, and cost of materials of an object makes one think about the impact of the changing techniques and technologies on the spatial shape of architectural solutions. The second involves the general global preference for activities leading to the sustainable use of natural resources. The most common reason to seek new implementation opportunities, even the most ephemeral ones, are decisions about the new possibilities of techniques and technology concerning their effectiveness - although this effectiveness is not always "right away" or "directly" expressed.

Teaching at a school of architecture is a simultaneous game of reality, hence the huge receptivity to changes in the given project and receptivity to changes in design and teaching. New trends are born together with spatial and social changes. The educational system should also evolve within the schools of architecture under their influence.

3   Idea, Concept, Project

Architectural design is a process of creation related to transformation or to formation of the new reality. Methodically speaking there are two formulas functioning next to one another: thinking of a project which leads from the details (functional and technical solutions) to an overall layout concept and a geometrical form. The second approach leads the designer differently. The first step is a thought – an overall picture. Detailed solutions are the second step. In each case there are three stages of action:

- analysis – synthesis – evaluation
- synthesis – analysis – evaluation

Both models are consistent and form symmetrically different approaches to the design process. But they split architects, of which almost 90% is on the first side, and 10% on the second side – this situation is somewhat the effect of inborn abilities and somewhat the effect of the teaching methodology. The ideal model is to be able to conduct detailed analysis at the beginning of the design task and to create an overall shape of the object as a summary (according to modernists' rule "form follows function") as well as to be able to visualize the whole object in the first place and (in time) to lead to solutions related to function, structure and technology. An important aspect of the learning process is to teach both skills.

Both models are consistent and form symmetrically different approaches to the design process. But they split architects, of which almost 90% is on the first side, and 10% on the second side – this situation is somewhat the effect of inborn abilities and somewhat the effect of the teaching methodology. The ideal model is to be able to conduct detailed analysis at the beginning of the design task and to create an overall shape of the object as a summary (according to modernists' rule "form follows function") as well as to be able to visualize the whole object in the first place and (in time) to lead to solutions related to function, structure and technology. An important aspect of the learning process is to teach both skills.

We deal with ideal designers when they can equally success in beginning the concept design with details and ending up with a whole, or the other way round: beginning with an overall idea of a building form which leads to the details. From the didactic point of view it is essential to teach the students both skills.

At the level of teaching as well as during the professional work, each practicing architect and each student should start the design process with lining their conceptual path according to the following rule: idea – solution alternatives – architectural concept – project. The mentioned stages should be referring to the methods of visualizing – presenting the developing thought.

- Idea – one needs an idea to be able to hypothesize. An idea helps to form criteria and provides a framework of evaluation possibilities in the architectural creation.
- Solution alternatives – alternating teaches how to move freely around the two formulas of the teaching process: "from the particular to the general" and "from the general to the particular" which is particularly important in the phase of concept creation.
- Architectural concept – the search for solution alternatives should lead to clarifying one concept picturing the new architectural object and/or the new urban plan.

The design course conducted by the author pursues the first two phases to be performed as a freehand sketches or watercolors. In the next phase a draft is also required but in the form of a model. The last phase of the design in architectural teaching is the time of generating a digital project – creating the visualization and the technical documentation.

Summarizing:

- Idea and solution alternatives – freehand drawing or watercolor
- Chosen object concept – draft model
- Deciding on the object shape (project) – digital visualization (Fig.1) (Fig.2)

4   Case Study – Students' Feelings

In order to justify our argument (uncertain about the outcome), a survey was conducted at the end of the course among the students (60 persons) of the 3rd semester of extramural master's degree course (and thus a paid course)

The exceptionality of this group lies in the fact that:

- as teachers we meet them in classes only on Sundays, and the schedule of meetings is very scant;
- among the mentioned students we have many from outside of the Faculty of Architecture at the Silesian University of Technology;
- a few of them are from other Polish regions;

- almost all students are employed in architectural firms, and so they often think of themselves as having sufficient knowledge to design independently.

The more, the answers they gave us were for us, the university teachers sometimes regarded as excessively conservative, very encouraging.

During the first few classes (whose a total maximum is 9-10 per semester, and the real contact with the student, allowing us, the teachers, to transfer knowledge, experience, and conduct discussions on the project is limited to 3-4 meetings) we required from students freehand drawing and preparing mock-ups reflecting the idea and concept of the designed facility. At that time the students did not have positive opinions about such approach – they were irritated by our requirements, they rebelled against such "restrictions". They treated our requirements as a necessary evil on the grounds that nowadays projects are generated using computers and there is no need to "waste" time on manual search for solutions. At that time they did not accept the argument that the computer is only a tool to a relatively quick and neat drawing of the ready/selected concept.

A total of 26 persons aged 25-36 years participated in the study: 18 men and 8 women. Only 2 of the respondents do not have a job.

In the prepared questionnaire four questions were posed (three of a closed character and one open). The table below shows the questions with the percentage of responses (Table 1).

Table 1. The results of the survey conducted among the students

L.p.	Question	YES	NO
1.	In your opinion, is freehand drawing/sketching needed by the architect in the creation of the first idea about the object?	95 %	5 %
2.	In your opinion, does a mock-up facilitate conceptual thinking?	85 %	15 %
3.	In your opinion, does a computer „library" restrict creative thinking?	60 %	40 %
4.	In your opinion, which computer software you are familiar with can successfully substitute CREATIVE THINKING? Please, specify.	AutoCad, SketchUp ArchiCad,,,Photoshop RevitArchitecture, Atlantis, 3DMax	none
	% of answers given	65 %	35 %

The interpretation of the conducted survey is clearly positive. At the end of the class a very small percentage of students, despite the initial resistance and irritation, considered our requirements as impractical and without future. The survey revealed that it was agreed that an architect seeking an initial concept/thought about an object should, or maybe has to, search for it using hand drawing. Also, the perception of the teaching method, involving the obligation to prepare a working mock up (more time-consuming way of reflecting one's mind) has gained approval.

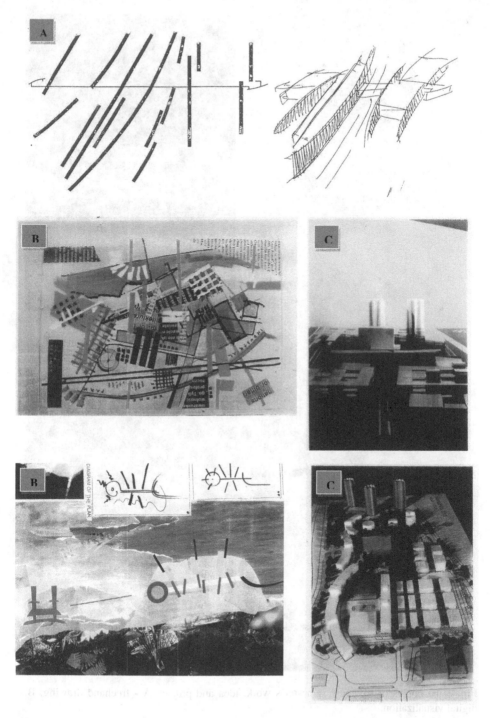

Fig. 1. Examples of students' semester's work: idea and chosen object concept. A - freehand drawing; B – watercolor; C - draft model.

Fig. 2. Examples of students' semester's work: idea and project. A - freehand drawing; B - digital visualization.

There exists, however, a significant group of people who believe that computer software can replace the logic and culture of design and that many software packages meet their and the investors' expectations, accelerates the process of creating documentation, creates forms which are a response to the aspiration of present times and future.

5   Conclusions

An architect/ an urban planner presents a graphic solution of a given problem. In the beginning the architect doesn't know either the final outcome or the range of complexity of the undertaken task – the awareness of both evolves during the design process. The reasons are of course the complexity and interdisciplinarity of the task as well as the instability spread in time and uncertainty of the final result. The design process is therefore a form of a game, or maybe more a form of a dialogue between the problem and the solution. Dialogue is here a keyword which allows establishing an agreement between the architect and the drawing, the architect and the client, the drawing and the client, the developer/investor and the user etc. In this dialogue the designer uses the practical knowledge drawing from professional experiences, theoretical knowledge, occurring facts and values. These direct relations between spontaneously used theoretical knowledge and an experience most probably influenced the popularity of expressions: Knowing in Action; Reflection in Action; Reflection on Action [8] – these expressions are aiming to highlight the creative use of knowledge, reflection, the ability to compare and the use of experiences of others in solving similar design issues.

In presenting the discussed problems other issues should be emphasized as well – the issues of facility management and qualitative surveys of buildings. K. Fross notes that during preparing an architectural project in the traditional way the idea and inspiration are still used as dominant elements. Rarely are performed pre-design analyses, calculations of the capacity of the plot, investigations of user groups and their needs, matrices and diagrams of functional links, surface calculations, "work carpets", defining the characteristics of the image fitting for the given organization, case studies, assessment of the object in various fields, surveys, interviews etc. [9]. It is hard not to agree with this point of view, especially when we are referring to engineering students. However, it seems that the main task of the educational process at the next stage of teaching in higher education, at the master's degree level, primarily should be the emphasis on deepening the passion for creative thinking. Otherwise such architects become the usual technocrats.

Of course the discussed issues are open. In the era of an easy access to modern technologies and mental changes of societies everything is dynamically changed. The question is: Will the computer captivate the humankind and limit its intellectual possibilities? Or maybe it will develop these possibilities? Will we live matrix lives?

References

1. Zagała, Ł.: Architektura i prędkość – refleksja nad stanem architektury w dobie rewolucji informatycznej (Architecture and speed condition of architecture in age of information revolution – reflection). In: Architektura i Urbanistyka, Cyberprzestrzeń nr 1/2007. Silesian University of Technology, Gliwice (2007)
2. Turner, R.G.: Construction Economics and Building Design. Van Nostrand Reinhold Company, New York (1986)
3. Rewers, E.: Postpolis, wstęp do filozofii ponowoczesnego miasta (Postpolis, introduction to the philosophy of the postmodern city). Universitas, Kraków (2005)
4. Juzwa, N., Ujma-Wasowicz, K.: Large scale architecture. Design human factors and ergonomics aspects based on state-of-the-art structures. In: AHFE International 2012, Conference Proceedings 4th International Conference on Applied Human Factors and Ergonomics, San Francisco (2012)
5. Juzwa, N., Gil, A.: The construction in architectural design teaching. Mock-ups as tools for schaping an architectural idea. In: Proceedings of EAAE Conference, Barcelona (2005)
6. Ujma-Wasowicz, K., Gil, A.: Projektowanie architektury w wirtualnej rzeczywistości. Przyszłość, czy tylko wybór? (Architectural designing in virtual reality. Future or choice?) In: Architektura i Urbanistyka. Cyberprzestrzeń" nr 1/2007. Silesian University of Technology, Gliwice (2007)
7. http://en.wikipedia.org/wiki/Economics
8. Schon, D.: Educating the reflective practitioner. Jossey-Bass, San Francisco (1988)
9. Fross, K.: Badania jakościowe w projektowaniu architektonicznym na wybranych przykładach (Quality evaluation in architectural design on selected examples). Silesian University of Technology, Gliwice (2012)

Specch.io: A Personal QS Mirror
for Life Patterns Discovery and "Self" Reshaping

Alessandro Marcengo, Luca Buriano, and Marina Geymonat

Telecom Italia – Research & Prototyping Department,
via Reiss Romoli, 274, 10148 Torino, Italy
{alessandro.marcengo,luca.buriano,
marina.geymonat}@telecomitalia.it

Abstract. This paper describes the process that led to the design of the *Specch.io* framework. *Specch.io* is a platform for seamless data collection, mash-up, visualization and exploration of personal data. The project is part of an internal research track focused on the usage of technology to promote and foster individual well-being from a biopsychosocial (BPS) perspective. The objective of *Specch.io*, is to reveal and raise awareness on individual life patterns, generating integration and meaning about aspects of the "self" that can hardly be captured from a subjective point of view.

Keywords: Quantified Self, Personal Informatics, Self-Ethnography, Self-Experimentation, Life-logging, Ubiquitous Computing, Human-Computer Interaction, Info visualization.

1 Introduction

As a research group at a leading Telco, we began to work on this project having observed and developed the awareness that being "hyper-connected" and "always on" does not generally make peoples' lives better in terms of quality of life. The aim was therefore to think of a new way of being always connected: a "service" vision of the future Internet in which the labels "being wired" and "smart life" will mean to return to and recover the real and tangible dimension of existence, however assisted by highly valuable but invisible technological aspects; in other words, a phenomenon of technological re-humanization similar to that seen in other sectors, such as in mobility and urban planning towards a vision of a smart city, or nutrition and energy towards a vision of sustainable consumption.

To undertake this direction, we focused on recent research within the fields of the quantified self (QS) and personal informatics (PI). These strands contain the initial elements of a different meaning, a new interpretation on the technological aspect of being "always on", putting into foreground peoples' awareness of their patterns and specificities, thereby giving "hyper connectivity" a positive role. The purpose of collecting personal information in different areas of people's lives (i.e. location, mood, food, fitness, money, digital usage, health, etc.) has become in these approaches a means to improve knowledge about patterns of action, consequently improving

C. Stephanidis and M. Antona (Eds.): UAHCI/HCII 2014, Part IV, LNCS 8516, pp. 215–226, 2014.
© Springer International Publishing Switzerland 2014

self-awareness and promoting change towards a higher level of personal well-being, albeit typically limited to only a few discrete aspects.

Our project embraced this approach by integrating it with a broader theoretical and technological perspective that not only included a concept of physical well-being, but also (and mostly) took into account psychological and social well-being. On the other hand, it also promoted different forms of possible "change". In actual fact, most of the literature in the areas mentioned above (QS and PI) merely address potential behavioral change oriented to correcting basic parameters (e.g. weight, calories, activity, etc.). We believe change can take many forms (i.e. cognitive reshaping), and can have different levels of depth both in terms of its impact on the structure of the person, as well as on duration (behavioral changes usually have an impact on a superficial level and do not last for a long time). Our project has been to build a platform that allows access to an integrated view of the person, and is directed at improving knowledge of one's own life patterns, increasing one's overall awareness through the emergence of significant causal or space-time correlations, and hence facilitating change (whether environmental, behavioral, or cognitive) towards a higher level of personal biopsychosocial well-being. In this work, we intend to describe the basis on which we began to build what we think might be a transparent and integrated system as a generator of new meanings for the end user. We started from the literature and various experiments made in the last twenty years, and considered the relevant literature about change that surpass the behavioral standpoint. This analysis and our own personal backgrounds has led to the choice of a theoretical framework based on a constructivist and post-rationalist perspective [19] that in our opinion overcomes the shortcomings of behaviorism and cognitive rationalism. Moreover, we involved a panel of people involved in self-logging practices in order to gather requirements from which to start to develop our system. On the basis of this knowledge, we have developed a concept and a prototype in our laboratories that give shape to our idea, and these allow us to further investigate all the technological and human aspects involved. Thus was born Specch.io.

2   Related Works and Theoretical Framework

We analyzed the pertinent literature of different scientific fields (Computer Science, Psychology, Sociology, Anthropology) for some macro themes concerning our work. At first we adopted an historical perspective examining some well-known lifelogging projects [14] identifying value aspects and obstacles within them. We considered some pioneering work of which we cite as examples MyLifeBits [4] [16], Total Recall and the LifeLog Project as well the limitations that characterized them. In addition to the obvious constraints in terms of technological availability [21],[31], storage [13], data collection and information management [1],what interested us most was the emergence of non-technological aspects fundamentally related with ethical [25] and privacy [2] issues. We then reviewed some Personal Informatics works in light of Li's [24][23] definition, examining emerging opportunities and new limitations in comparison to the first lifelogging projects. Consistent with our vision, it is clear from these works that an inherent aim is the notion of change. However, this is primarily related to behavioral economics models or, as in the case of Li [23] or He [20] to a specific model of behavioral change like the transtheoretical model of change (TTM) [34]. A topic of specific interest for our project was the analysis of issues related to the ease of personal data collection [36] and the possibilities of integration between different data sources. Both are partly advocated by the relevant literature [23] and partly developed in different projects [29] and different trials [5], although never fully accomplished and always a source of difficulty [47]. We then focused on the contact stage between the system and the user: the interface that provides visual access to personal data, which should foster sense-making for the person. In this sense, we have examined the fundamental works of Tukey [45] Tufte [44] and Card [7] in addition to the complete works of Ware [46] and Few [15]. We then focused on studies of big screens starting our review from ambitious [6],[38] and futuristic [11] projects to the latest applications [30] in this field. Furthermore the specific functional or perceptive limits of some solutions [42] have allowed us to choose an appropriate hardware configuration for our project. Last but not least we carried out an extensive analysis on the human change issue and the limitations of purely behavioral change [9],[10],[12],[35]. As we mentioned above our motivation to start this project did not draw on the themes of persuasive technology intended to change patterns of dysfunctional behavior, but rather on a vision aimed at creating a "tool" for enabling higher levels of integration and well-being [26] in the sense of Siegel [39]. We therefore considered that the current outlook was too limiting for us and out of our scope. We therefore retraced the last decades of cognitive psychology from Skinner [41] and Miller [27] passing through the Lewin's fundamental advances on the role of the context [22] to Bandura's more recent models on cognitive-emotional processes [3]. The theoretical reference framework was identified in the constructivist and post rationalist view [17],[18].This effectively expresses concepts further emphasized by Ricoeur [37] and Morin [28] about the relativity of individual reality captured through a reading lens that is in a large part subjective, and in which emotional and affective components are even more critical than rational ones. Beside the literature analysis, we further developed our concept by adding a collection of requirements gathered through interviews with a panel of users already oriented to the collection of personal data, which will be described in the next section.

3   Panel Interviews

The purpose of the interviews was to collect design requirements from interested parties who have significant experience of self-logging, and who are thus accustomed to using logging tools during their daily activities. This allowed us to obtain results based on the actual and consolidated experiences of loggers, which is fundamental to integrating theoretical aspects. As a cross-cultural generalizability of other studies is equivocal, this work was also motivated by the fact that there is no research on this topic in the context of Italian culture.

Recruitment. As an industrial project, it has been important to preserve the confidentiality of the work. People were therefore selected internally. Owing to the availability of a large database containing the names of colleagues willing to participate in experimental activities, an email was prepared in which the potential subject had the possibility to easily discriminate their suitability to participate in the interviews. The discriminant included the use of at least one web or mobile application, or wearable object for at least three months in the last 12 months (a list of commercial products with three examples for each category was given as an example, together with an empty field to list unexpected logging strategies). We obtained forty-six responses. The respondents were then asked to complete a more specific questionnaire about the type of logging activities performed. On this basis, we selected 12 subjects (10 men and 2 women) deemed suitable to participate in the interviews. We excluded all subjects who carried out logging on their digital life (e.g. *Twitter, Facebook, Klout,* etc.), because potentially biased towards the aims of the project. The final participants' areas of logging concerned daily physical activity (8/12), the duration and quality of sleep (3/12), health aspects (4/12), emotional aspects (1/12), weight (10/12), food (4/12), productivity (1/12), energy consumption (3/12), and location (9/12). Of the total, the majority (9/12) of the participants tracked more than one aspect in their life.

Procedure. The 12 selected colleagues were invited to a meeting room for an hourlong interview entitled *"Current experience of logging and future projections"*. The semi-structured interview was recorded. The purpose of the interview was explained to each participant as a means to collect requirements for a future system of Quantified Self / lifelogging. The first 15 minutes of the interview focused on the current use of lifelogging strategies with reference to the aims and limitations encountered. The remaining 45 minutes were focused on the "future" of lifelogging, and in particular on three aspects: data collection means, usage, utility and purpose of data collection, and return/rendering and interaction with these data. No compensation was provided.

Results. The results were derived from the subjects' most significant statements in a proper recording grid according to the three categories of investigation highlighted above. We then added an extra area of requirements which spontaneously emerged out of our investigation boundaries.

— **Data collection.** The data collection emerged as particularly critical. It has been underlined by all participants as currently any kind of data collection requires a large investment in both motivational and cognitive terms. Even the applications referred to as minimally invasive or with very low maintenance levels (e.g. *Jawbone* for sleep cycles or *Expereal* for emotional states) still require a certain level of "obsessiveness" to be used perpetually, especially when the novelty effect decreases. Also, it became apparent that not all types of data require the same level of commitment in the collection procedures. For instance, recording personal location through apps like *Moves* does not require much cognitive investment, whereas the collection of emotional states (via *MoodPanda, T2, Expereal,* etc.) becomes very annoying and invasive after the first few days. In order to justify the widespread adoption of lifelogging activities, the relationship between investment and benefit was judged insufficient by all of the respondents, with the exception of a few specific tasks. As such, the need for greater simplicity and cognitive economy in data collection is emphasized.

— **Usage, utility, and purpose of data collection.** The purpose of self-tracking was not clearly verbalized in the context of the semi-structured interviews, but rather expressed as *"control over what I do"*, *"learn some things about me"*, *" motivates me to..."*. The literature's focus on behavioral change did not appear to be evident, even if the emergence of a desire for "change" (not just limited to the personal behavior) arose as unifying factor. The relative satisfaction with systems dedicated to very specific activities (e.g. pedometers) emerged in this area; however, there was significant dissatisfaction with the possibility of correlating different variables (for example: *"what determines the quality of my sleep?"*,*"I always wonder if there is a correlation between what I eat and my headache?"*). Answers to this kind of question are not easy, unless extensive motivational investment is made in personal data management. Most of the respondents (8/12) expressed an unfulfilled need to be able to understand the relationship between variables as an indispensable element of knowledge. During the interviews, some loggers showed an implicit schema to organize the correlation between variables: a plot based on two primary variables (space and time *"what the moment was, and where I was?"*) to "host" any kind of secondary variables (mood, activity, food, etc.). This plot seems to provide a context in which all other data looks more manageable.

— **Rendering and interaction with data.** Most of the participants (10/12) were generally satisfied with the data rendering provided by the tools used (web and mobile apps). All the loggers stressed the importance of the aesthetic aspect (beside the functional one) as an element of satisfaction in the exploration of their data (*"It's so cool, when..."*). The aspect that generated dissatisfaction with over half (7/12) of the users was the in/ability to interact with the data. The preselected views and data aggregates were in fact seen by half of the users as facilitative (*"it is probably the best way to see my sleeping pattern"*), whereas the other half saw them as limiting additional levels of knowledge (*"I wish I could sum up my amount of deep sleep, eliminating incomplete measures"*).

— **Further aspects.** Some unsolicited, although somehow predictable, aspects of partial dissatisfaction with existing logging tools were highlighted during the interviews. The initial issues that emerged were privacy concerns about possible usage, actual confidentiality, and the management of personal data by third parties. This topic has been the subject of various interventions well beyond our expectations. Total control over personal data and its confidentiality was deemed an indispensable aspect for a wider adoption of personal informatics (*"what if these data are then sold to my medical insurance?"*).The second relevant issue has been the realtime topic, such as the fruition of personal data while it is generated. We believe that this issue has been prompted by the considerable recent media attention given to Google Glasses (spontaneously cited by half of the respondents). A possible personal data-driven scenario was mentioned extemporaneously by a few of the loggers, although with unclear formulations (beside sports performance).

These data allowed us to identify a number of key design principles that we tried to imprint with a single guide sentence favoring the strength of the message rather than the accuracy of the requirement.

- Seamless Data Collection
- Foster Change
- Variables' Relationships
- Context: space-time plot

- Promote Data Interaction
- Privacy First
- Beautiful Appearance
- Real-Time Insight

From these pillars, we started to develop all the components of the Specch.io technological framework, from data collection means to the integration platform and the data interaction interface.

4   The "Specch.io" Framework

From the scientific literature analysis briefly summarized above, as well as the requirements gathered during the interviews, we proceeded to develop a concept and a prototype integrating the knowledge collected from these two inputs. This represented an artifact that is able to collect personal data in a seamless (without any explicit user action) or semi-seamless (with a slight friction in daily activities) way; a platform capable of integrating these data and highlight correlations; and an object able to render personal life patterns in a beautiful, integrated, and rich manner.

Data collection and integration modules are still ongoing; as a result, we will focus on the description of the final rendering object, the one closest to the end user, and the one with the most theoretical and methodological implications.

5   "Specch.io": A Personal Data Renderer

We designed a tool for data rendering and interaction by starting with the requirements collected from lifeloggers and an analysis of the relevant literature, in particular on the functioning of our semantic memory, and the mechanisms of meaning generation and change derived from the recent literature in the field of cognitive sciences. A sort of personal "magic mirror", which we called *Specch.io* ("specchio" is the italian word for "mirror"). The metaphor of the mirror to access personal data suggests an intimate space for self-reflection, where we can spot things about our lives that we cannot see from a subjective point of view, comparable to the way in which we cannot see a mark on our nose if not by using a mirror. We know that as humans we are neither good recorders of our lives (human memory is a highly plastic and generative process), nor good interpreters of what happens to us (each reading is always biased by our interpretive schemes).

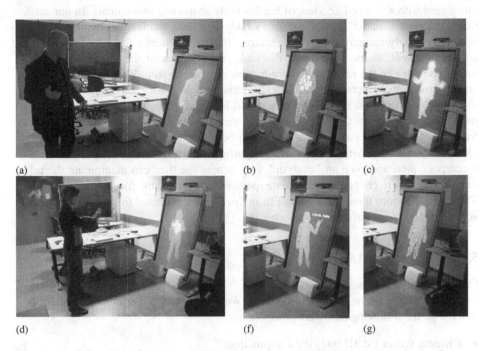

(a)   (b)   (c)

(d)   (f)   (g)

Fig. 1. Rendering and interaction with personal data in the "evocative" view. In the first sequence (a-b-c) the user access two different data set (a and c) activating and then "pushing" the squares on his body shape (b). In the second sequence (d-f-c) a different user "selects" a data set (d), then activates via gestures (f) a timeline in order to move backward to previous days data (g).

The idea to use such a powerful metaphor as the mirror was also drawn from a shared cultural imagination. Across time and cultures, the idea of a magic mirror is a recurrent theme in legends, fairy tales, and literary fiction. These fictional mirrors typically allow their users to see beyond mere reflected images, for example, by showing the true nature of oneself, revealing hidden knowledge, or opening portals for travelling to other worlds. Some well-known examples include the evil queen in the fairy tale Snow White who owns a magic mirror capable of giving a true answer to her questions; in Lewis Carroll's Through the Looking-Glass, and What Alice Found There [8], Alice, driven by curiosity, steps through a mirror to an alternative world; in J.R.R. Tolkien's The Lord of the Rings [43], Galadriel owns a magic mirror consisting of a basin filled with water, allowing her to see images from past, present, and future. These examples – among countless others – substantiate the magic mirror idea as a powerful, archetypal metaphor for the process of gaining insight into ourselves and raising self-awareness. Following these perspectives, the goal of Specch.io is the creation of an information visualization framework where personal data about the user can be shown in conjunction with a visual representation of the user's body in a seamless and immediate way. Placing her/himself in front of a device that behaves like a (magic) mirror, the user will see real-time visualizations of her/his data, integrated with a mirror-like view of her/his body shape and movements. In our intentions, the joint visualization of the user's body and data should feel natural enough, and immediately recognizable and evocative, to give the user a feeling of immersion and engagement; at the same time, the look and behavior of the visualization's elements shouldn't be too realistic and predictable in order to stimulate a sense of wonder and curiosity about personal data. Ideally, this "magic mirror" should fulfill a role, like in fictional stories, of a portal to a world in which personal data visually reveals itself, and thus prepare the user to access more analytical data views. In fact, starting from this "evocative" vision (which can also be *per se* exhaustive) it would be possible to access a "synthetic" view where significant correlations are highlighted on a time/space plot, and even an "analytic" view where the user can manipulate the relationship between channels and create personal experiments for self-ethnography. There are therefore three levels of depth in *Specch.io* connected to different modes to access and use personal data.

5.1   Hardware and Software

Computational Framework

For our experiments on Specch.io concept, we've assembled a computational framework with the following hardware components:

- a Kinect sensor for 3D body data acquisition;
- a Sharp PN-L602B monitor standing in portrait orientation, for a mirror-like integrated display of body and personal data;
- a set of computational nodes for data processing and visualization (currently a single PC, which will evolve into a set of networked PCs).

The software components of the framework consist of a set of applications coordinating the data processing flow, which run the data analysis and visualization algorithms that embody our "magical mirror" concept. These applications are currently written in Processing [33], a programming language and development environment for creating images, animations and interactions. Some tasks are performed via the body data acquisition and analysis capabilities of the OpenNI and NITE libraries [32], which are wrapped into the simple-openni library [40] for their use within the Processing environment. A personal data feed component completes the magic mirror framework, providing access to the user's data. This data channel, currently implemented as a local database, will evolve into a networked data feed.

Data Processing Flow

A typical data processing flow in our "magic mirror" prototype unfolds as follows:

- The 3D sensor (Kinect) acquires information about the scene in front of the mirror in the form of a depth-map, i.e. a representation of the objects in the scene as a set of points in a 3D space;

- A scene analysis is performed (via the OpenNI and NITE libraries) in order to filter out all the depth-map points not belonging to humanoid shapes, thus keeping only the points belonging to the body of the user in front of the mirror (called "user map" in the following);
- A "skeleton" representation of the body is extracted (via the OpenNI and NITE libraries) from the user map in the form of a set of data encoding the position and orientation of the body's joints and limbs (called "user skeleton" in the following);
- An "outline" representation of the body is computed (via our framework's algorithms) in the form of a linked list of 2D points, delineating the body's outline from a 2D projection of the (3D) user map (called "user outline" in the following);
- Personal data about the user are retrieved from the personal data feed;
- A visualization is generated (via our framework's algorithms) from the user map, user skeleton, user outline and personal data; the visualization is rendered and displayed on the large monitor in front of the user.

Each of these steps (except for the personal data retrieval) is performed in real-time with a frame rate in the order of tens of frames per second, giving a fluid visual feedback that can be perceived by the user as a mirror-like experience.

Interaction and Animation
The Specch.io visualizations can often benefit from the presence of interactive features, exploiting user skeleton information for limb position detection (e.g. hand position detection) and gesture recognition. Natural movements allow the user to focus on specific visualization elements chosen from among various different personal data sets and visualization designs, and switch between the "evocative", the "synthetic", and the "analytic" view.

Moreover, the real-time nature of the framework makes animation an interesting feature, both as an informative visualization element and as a transition effect.

An example of the joint use of interaction and animation is the set of ways of leaving the mirror we're experimenting with. In one of these, when the user suddenly opens wide her/his arms, the gesture is recognized as the intention of leaving the "evocative" view. This triggers an animation effect that penetrates the visualized body shape, simultaneously fading the screen to black and preparing the emerging of the "synthetic" view. The reverse animation – re-integrating the body's shape – can be used when the "evocative" view is requested back.

6   Future Works

As a technological framework Specch.io is evolving to integrate different data feeds from both Quantified Self gadgets already on the market today (Fitbit, Jawbone, etc.) both from channels that are currently not collected in a sufficiently seamless manner (i.e. mood, heart rate, etc.) and for which we are developing ad hoc collection techniques. An additional roadmap concerns the data integration platform, and the inclusion of reasoning processes able to provide significant correlations between events.

As a data rendering interface, *Specch.io* will involve the envisioning and implementation of a specific set of InfoVis designs and algorithms on the three levels of data interaction ("evocative", "synthetic", and "analytic" view). Due to the peculiar nature of the *Specch.io* concept, a common and important aspect of these designs will be the interplay between the visualization of personal data, and the rendering of the user's body shape and movements. Several possibilities will be explored concerning the possible rendering of data in the visualized body:

1. "Tattoo" behavior: where the position of InfoVis elements closely follow the body's movements, as though they were tattooed or painted on the body surface.
2. "Projection" behavior: where InfoVis elements independently "live" and move in their own space, and appear as if they were projected on the body's surface.
3. A behavior somewhere in-between the previous two, where, for example, the InfoVis elements behave a bit like they were projected, but are also constrained to stay within the body's outline.
4. More complex behaviors, with a deep interplay between the shape/movements of the body and shape, position, and movements of InfoVis elements. This will be the most challenging case.

7   Conclusions

Many users are already familiar with Quantified Self and Personal Informatics applications in emerging vertical sectors directed to specific tasks, such as Nike+, Fitbit, Moodscope, Mint, etc. The scenario for tomorrow's Quantified Self instead aims at something beyond this: a possible integration between different aspects of life that are now discrete (e.g. location + mood + sleep + fitness + health + food + work), thanks to the ever-increasing possibility of sensing, seamless logging, and evolution of intelligent systems able to examine correlations between vastly different data sets. A scenario in which being connected becomes an implicit and imperceptible task generating value, meaning, and knowledge for the user. The purpose of the Specch.io framework is just that: to go from numbers to patterns, from "how" to "why".

References

1. Abigail, S., Whittaker, S.: Beyond total capture: a constructive critique of lifelogging. Communications of the ACM 53(5), 70–77 (2010)
2. Allen, A.L.: Dredging-up the Past: Lifelogging, Memory and Surveillance. University of Chicago Law Review 75(1), 47–74 (2008)
3. Bandura, A.: Social Foundations of Thought and Action. Prentice-Hall, Englewood Cliffs (1986)
4. Bell, G., Gemmell, J.: A Digital Life. Scientific American Magazine (February 18, 2007)
5. Bentley, F., et al.: Personal Health Mashups: Mining significant observation from wellbeing data and context. In: Proceedings of CHI 2012 Workshop on Personal Informatics in Practice: Improving Quality of Life Through Data (2012)

6. Canada, C., et al.: La Cueva Grande: a 43-Megapixel Immersive System. In: Proceedings of Virtual Reality Conference 2006 (2006)
7. Card, S.K. (ed.): Readings in Information Visualization: Using Vision to Think. Morgan Kaufmann, San Francisco (1999)
8. Carroll, L.: Through the Looking-Glass, and What Alice Found There. Evertype (2009)
9. Consolvo, S., et al.: Flowers or a Robot Army? Encouraging Awareness & Activity with Personal, Mobile Displays. In: Proceedings of the 10th International Conference on Ubiquitous Computing: UbiComp 2008, pp. 54–63 (2008)
10. Consolvo, S., McDonald, D.W., Landay, J.: Theory- Driven Design Strategies for Technologies that Support Behavior Change in Everyday Life. In: CHI 2009, pp. 405–414 (2009)
11. Cruz-Neira, C., et al.: Surround-screen projection-based virtual reality: The design and implementation of the cave. In: Proceedings of ACM SIGGRAPH 1993 (1993)
12. Di Clemente, C.C., Marinilli, A.S., Singh, B., Bellino, E.: The Role of Feedback in the Process of Health Behavior Change. American Journal of Health Behavior 25(3), 217–227 (2000)
13. Dix, A.: The ultimate interface and the sums of life? Interfaces 50, 16 (2002)
14. Dodge, M., Kitchin, R.: Outlines of a World Coming into Existence: Pervasive Computing and the Ethics of Forgetting. Environment & Planning B: Planning & Design 24, 431–445 (2007)
15. Few, S.: Data visualization past, present and future. Innovation in Action Series (2009)
16. Gemmell, J., et al.: MyLifeBits. A Personal Database for Everything. Communications of the ACM 49(1), 88–95 (2006)
17. Guidano, V.F., Liotti, G.: Cognitive processes and emotional disorders. Guilford, New York
18. Guidano, V.F.: Complexity of the Self. Guilford, New York (1987)
19. Guidano, V.F.: The self in process. Guilford, New York (1991)
20. He, A.H., Greenberg, S., Huang, E.M.: One Size Does Not Fit All: Applying the Transtheoretical Model to Energy Feedback Technology Design. In: CHI 2010, pp. 927–936 (2010)
21. Hodges, S., et al.: SenseCam: A Retrospective Memory Aid. In: Dourish, P., Friday, A. (eds.) UbiComp 2006. LNCS, vol. 4206, pp. 177–193. Springer, Heidelberg (2006)
22. Lewin, K.: Field theory in social science; selected theoretical papers. Harper & Row, New York (1951) (Cartwright, D. (ed.))
23. Li, I., Dey, A.K., Forlizzi, J.: Understanding My Data, Myself: Supporting Self-Reflection with Ubicomp Technologies. In: UbiComp 2011, pp. 405–414 (2011)
24. Li, I., Dey, A.K., Forlizzi, J.: A Stage-Based Model of Personal Informatics Systems. In: CHI 2010, pp. 557–566 (2010)
25. Mayer-Schönberger, V.: Delete: The Virtue of Forgetting in the Digital Age. Princeton University Press, Princeton (2009)
26. Marcengo, A., Rapp, A.: Visualization of Human Behavior Data: The Quantified Self In book: Innovative Approaches of Data Visualization and Visual Analytics. IGI GLOBAL (2013)
27. Miller, G.A., et al.: Plans and the structure of behavior. Holt, Rhinehart, & Winston, New York (1960)
28. Morin, E.: La Méthode: L'humanité de l'humanité - l'identité humaine (t. 5). Le Seuil, Nouvelle Èdition, coll. Points, Paris, France (2003)

29. Moore, B., et al.: Assisted Self Reflection: Combining Lifetracking, Sensemaking, & Personal Information Management. In: Proceedings of CHI 2010 Workshop - Know Thyself: Monitoring and Reflecting on Facets of One's Life (2010)
30. Ni, T., et al.: A Survey of Large High-Resolution Display Technologies, Techniques, and Applications. In: Proceedings of the IEEE Conference on Virtual Reality (2006)
31. O'Hara, K., et al.: Memories for life: a review of the science and technology. Journal of the Royal Society Interface 3, 351–365 (2006)
32. OpenNI, http://www.openni.org
33. Processing, http://processing.org
34. Prochaska, J.O., Velicer, W.F.: The Transtheoretical Model of health behavior change. American Journal of Health Promotion 12(1), 38–48 (1997)
35. Ramirez, E.R., Hekler, E.: Digital Histories for Future Health. In: Proceedings of CHI 2012 Workshop on Personal Informatics in Practice: Improving Quality of Life Through Data (2012)
36. Rawassizadeh, R., et al.: UbiqLog: A Generic Mobile Phone based Life-Log Framework. In: Personal and Ubiquitous Computing. Springer, London (2012)
37. Ricoeur, P.: Oneself as Another. University of Chicago Press, Chicago (1992)
38. Sandstrom, T., et al.: The hyperwall. In: Proceedings of the Conference on Coordinated and Multiple Views in Exploratory Visualizations 2003 (2003)
39. Siegel, D.J.: The Developing Mind: How Relationships and the Brain Interact to Shape Who We Are. Guilford Press (2012)
40. Simple-openni, https://code.google.com/p/simple-openni/
41. Skinner, B.F.: Science and human behavior. Macmillan, New York (1953)
42. Thelen, S.: Advanced Visualization and Interaction Techniques for Large High-Resolution Displays. In: Middel, A., et al. (eds.) Visualization of Large and Unstructured Data Sets - Applications in Geospatial Planning, Modeling and Engineering (IRTG 1131 Workshop), VLUDS 2010. OASICS, vol. 19, pp. 73–81 (2010)
43. Tolkien, J.R.R.: The Lord of the Rings. Harper Collins Publishers (2005)
44. Tufte, E.R.: The Visual Display of Quantitative Information. Graphics Press, Cheshire (1983)
45. Tukey, J.W.: Exploratory Data Analysis. Addison-Wesley (1977)
46. Ware, C.: Visual Thinking: for Design. Morgan Kaufmann, San Francisco (2008)
47. Whittaker, S., et al.: Socio-technical lifelogging: Deriving design principles for a future proof digital past. Human-Computer Interaction 27, 37–62 (2012)

Analysis of Natural Lighting with Regard to Design of Sustainable Office Buildings in Poland

Dariusz Masły and Michał Sitek

The Silesian University of Technology, Faculty of Architecture,
ul. Akademicka 7, 44-100 Gliwice, Poland
{dariusz.masly,michal.sitek}@polsl.pl

Abstract. The study was a part of a larger research project which was devoted to simulation-based design analysis for daylit office spaces in Southern Poland. The paper consists of two main parts. The influence of various facade systems, lightshelves and fixed shading systems on daylight factor in the analysed office space is presented in the first part. These introductory analyses allowed to identify the optimal facade for an office building. The second part of the project included the comprehensive analysis of selected best performing architectural solutions. These analysis examined how lighting conditions were changing during typical time of an office work throughout the year. Illuminance levels and visual comfort were analysed. New issues like the performance of external retractable venetian blinds were added. This paper also investigates how state of the art simulation technology can be used to integrate natural lighting design strategies into the early stages of architectural design process.

Keywords: natural lighting design strategies, daylight analysis, sustainable office buildings, indoor environment quality.

1 Introduction

This project is devoted to simulation-based design analysis for daylit spaces. There were two main aims of the study and they are reflected in the structure of the project. So this paper consists of two main parts.

The first aim was to answer the question what facade system would be optimal for an office building in Southern Poland. Therefore the first part is devoted to the influence of various architectural solutions on daylight availability. The influence of various architectural solutions on luminous environment in the analysed office space was identified through computer simulations. This study examined the performance of various facades, lightshelves and fixed shading systems. The influence of various solutions on daylight factor was analysed, therefore the selected design solutions were examined only for overcast sky conditions and on December 21st, at midday.

The second part of the project included the comprehensive analysis of selected architectural solutions that were best performing in the first part of the study. These analysis examined how lighting conditions were changing during typical time of an office work throughout the year. The aim was to estimate how the changing position

C. Stephanidis and M. Antona (Eds.): UAHCI/HCII 2014, Part IV, LNCS 8516, pp. 227–236, 2014.
© Springer International Publishing Switzerland 2014

of sun would affect lighting conditions in the office – the daylight availability and visual comfort, and whether selected architectural solutions would meet the expectations throughout the whole working time.

In recent years many researches have proved that occupants react positively to daylight. Properly daylit offices can improve the overall well-being of their occupants. The healthy daylit indoor environments are linked to gains in productivity, increased occupant satisfaction and improved employee morale. The correlation has been well substantiated [5].

The Typical Sustainable, Energy-Efficient Office Building of the Twenty–First Century. During the whole twentieth century the common certainty was that technologically advanced systems, mainly ventilation, air-conditioning and electrical lighting systems, would cause an increase in efficiency, happiness and comfort of office workers. They were believed to solve all problems resulting from low light and air quality both inside and outside buildings [2]. Today air-conditioned office buildings with deep floor plates, containing large interior zones and large glazed surfaces are the most common type of building in centres of cities in developed world [17]. Still they are the symbol of high quality office space around the world. But outcomes of many researches confirm that the buildings do not meet the actual needs of their users [6], [8], [11], [18], [20]. At the beginning of the 21st century it became apparent that the sealed, air-conditioned, high-rise offices didn't realise hopes put on them. First of all they contradicted the concept of sustainable development.

So what kind of an office building should be analysed? A state–of–the–art intelligent office building should be environmentally friendly. This means that it is expected mainly to use less energy. A new model of sustainable development is based on reducing energy demand and on improving building performance and process [1]. The prevailing components of operating costs in an intelligent office building are the costs of mechanical ventilating, air-conditioning and artificial lighting [12]. The costs of air-conditioning of sealed, glass, high-rise office buildings with deep floor plates are particularly high. The annual HVAC energy consumption of a typical office building varies between 650 kWh/m^2 and 400 kWh/m^2 [10], [12], [17]. However the energy demand in the most modern offices has been reduced by 30 – 40% and even 70% reduction of energy demand has been achieved in state–of–the–art sustainable office buildings. Examples of these offices include Energon in Ulm (Germany) (81 kWh/m^2), and Manitoba Hydro Place (Canada) (100 kWh/m^2). The characteristics of the state–of–the–art, highly efficient offices are [13]:

- these buildings are as far as possible naturally ventilated and daylit,
- their facades are designed to prevent risk of overheating,
- they are typically designed with a narrow floorplate, so daylight can be effectively distributed,
- the buildings are also extended along the east-west axis, because it is much easier to manage heat gain and daylighting on north and south exposures. The east and west exposures are usually reduced. Quite often sustainable office buildings are organised as a series of a few south-facing office wings.

The office building designed for the analysis was about 77 m long and 15m wide. The building had a total area of about 4 600m². It had 4 storeys and was about 19 m high. The study focussed on the open-plan space. The analysed floor area was situated on the second floor and it was 10.8m in width and 9.0m in depth. It gave an area of 97.2m². The width of an office module was 2.7 m, therefore the space was 4 cellular office modules wide and 3 office desks plus corridor deep. A view from the top shows the analysed office room, see Figure 1. The building was assumed to have a floor-to-floor height of 4.2 m. The office space was 3.0m high, above the level there was a suspended ceiling and a concrete slab. The analysed office space faced south.

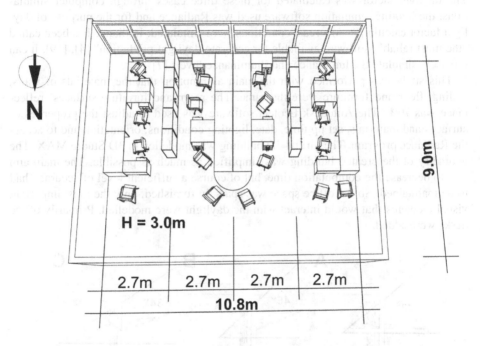

Fig. 1. A view from the top showing the analysed office room

2   Part I - The Analysis of the Influence of Various Architectural Solutions on Daylight Availability

The daylighting problem can be divided in three issues: daylight availability, visual comfort and energy use [14], [16]. During the first part of the study the daylight availability was analysed. The room was only illuminated with daylight, no electric lighting was included. When we use traditional side windows we experience the problem of uneven distribution of natural light. The illuminance is highest close to the facade, and then decreases quickly as one move further into the room [3], [4]. Therefore, sidelighting systems were proposed to reduce excessive daylight levels near the windows and increase them in the area of the room away from the facade. The aim was to achieve a more balanced daylight distribution throughout the room. Three devices were proposed, see Figure 2:

- the classic lightshelf (A) – it consisted of 90cm deep external sunshade and 60cm internal shelf,
- the advanced lightshelf 60 (B) – the collecting external part was 90cm deep and the internal reflecting part's depth was 60cm,
- and the last device was the advanced lightshelf 120 (C) – the internal part was deeper, 120cm.

The daylight factor was calculated for these three cases through computer simulations, the lighting simulation software used was Radiance and for the purpose of daylight factor calculations overcast conditions were simulated. Radiance has been called "the most reliable software available for accurate daylight prediction" [4], [19], it can precisely simulate the luminance and illuminance levels [7].

This study was performed with the main assumption that the materials of walls, ceiling, floor and furniture were the same. The room and furniture surfaces' reflectance was 70%. The Autodesk Ecotect software was used to adjust the properties of surfaces and materials, set up time, date, lighting conditions, orientation and to access the Radiance program. The virtual 3D building was modelled in 3D Studio MAX. The geometry of the created building was simplified as much as possible. The main aim was to decrease the computation time, but of course a sufficient level of accuracy had to be maintained. So the office space was sparsely furnished, only the most important visual elements that would interact with the daylight were modelled. Primarily office desks were added.

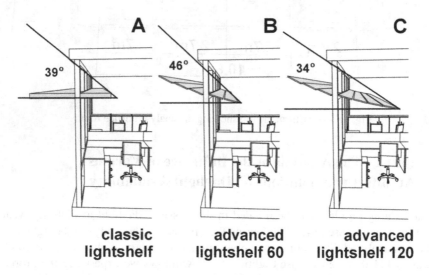

Fig. 2. Three devices were proposed to achieve a more balanced daylight distribution throughout the room

To calculate daylighting metrics an analysis grid was defined in Autodesk Ecotect. The "virtual sensors" were located on a plane 80cm above the floor. That was approximately at a height of a standard office desk. Radiance calculated DF values for these sensor points.

It should be highlighted that in fact lightshelf almost always reduces the amount of light received in the interior relative to a conventional, non-shaded window, but it also gives a more balanced daylight distribution throughout the room. The lowest light levels are for the case with classic lightshelf (A), but it also has the best ratio of DF near the windows to DF at depth of 8.5m which is 5.8. For the case with advanced lightshelf 120 (C) it is 7.1 and another advanced lightshelf – 6.6 (B). For the facade without any lightshelf the ratio is 8.

Bearing in mind that the aim for many designers of sustainable offices today is to achieve a minimum DF of 2% near every workplace, this can be said that the best solution is advanced daylight 60. In the part I of this study it was also analysed how the glass area of the facade would influence daylight penetration. Two different facades were compared, one with full height glazing and second where the windows constituted 73 percent of the facade area. The sill was at height of 80cm. The visual transmittance of the double glazing was 64%.

The ideal of an all-glass building has been pursued by architects for the past 100 years. And this approach, I purposefully do not name it a strategy, has not been effective. While we compare the highly glazed office space to the more moderately glazed one we see that the difference in the level of Daylight Factor is not considerable. However, in central Europe it must be remembered that against potential positive impacts including higher DF the negative impacts of heat gain and loss need to be considered. The increased glass areas lead to many problems. For example, due to lower thermal insulation of glazed facades poor thermal comfort is common in the winter time. We can also expect higher winter and night time heating requirements, and higher risk of overheating and increased cooling loads, when the intensity of the solar radiation becomes higher in the spring and summer [4]. It is much more economical to use transparency strategically. Therefore, for the further studies the 73% case was selected.

3   Part II - The Comprehensive Analysis of Lighting Conditions Throughout the Year for Selected Architectural Solutions Used in an Example Office Building

In the part II of the analysis a hypothetical building situated in Cracow in the southern part of Poland was examined (longitude: 20° E, latitude: 50° N). The footprint of the analysed building was designed along the east-west axis, but it was slightly rotated towards East. The angle of rotation was 19 degree. To properly design shading devices the effective solar heights have to be taken into account, therefore both the solar height and the azimuth angle must be known. While a building faces south at equinox the effective solar height is equal all working day (between 8 a.m. and 4 p.m.). For this latitude it is 40 degrees. Such building is the easiest case to shade. But the analysed building was rotated towards East. The effect of turning the office brought about difficulties with lower solar heights. At 8 o'clock the effective solar height was only 27 degrees, at 10 o'clock 35 degrees, and for example at 4 hour p.m. it was 76 degrees (these hours represent true solar time).

Sunny conditions were studied for two days of the year: 21st of June (summer extreme regarding solar heights) and 21st of March (the midpoint of the year). During the study the influence of various shading systems on daylight availability was simulated. While the shading devices were being designed, the aim was to protect office space through working hours. In all cases, the basic assumption was that the office was occupied between 8 a.m. and 4 p.m.

The effect of shading devices on solar transmittance must be well known at the design stage, because the knowledge is crucial if we want to properly protect building from excessive heat gains during summer and properly design the energy-efficient HVAC system.

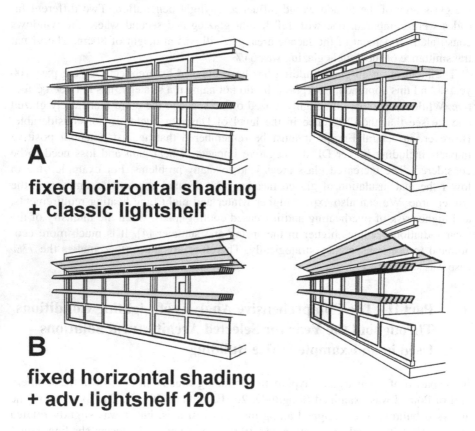

A
fixed horizontal shading + classic lightshelf

B
fixed horizontal shading + adv. lightshelf 120

Fig. 3. Two selected shading devices were designed to protect south facade from the 21st march to the 21st September

The two selected best solutions were, see Figure 3:

- A: the classic lightshelf (60cm internal shelf, 100cm deep external sunshade) and the fixed horizontal shading,
- B: the advanced lightshelf 120 and two surfaces of fixed horizontal shading.

The selected shading devices were designed to protect south facade from the 21st March to the 21st September.

At the stage of the analysis of natural lighting two questions were asked:

- How do these various solutions affect the daylight availability in analysed office open-plan space?
- Does the advanced lightshelf really perform better than the classic one under sunny conditions?

Horizontal shading with classic lightshelf performs better than the advanced light-shelf with louvers. But the most important result is that both shades take away a considerable amount of the important diffuse light from the sky when compared to the facade with only the advanced lightshelf 120.

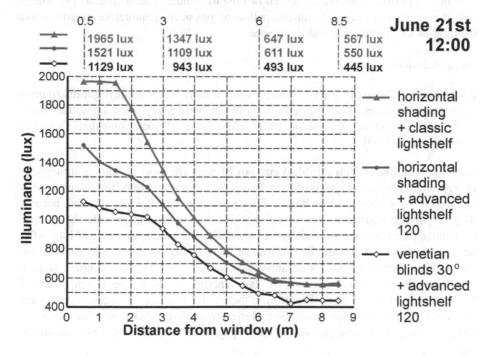

Fig. 4. Illuminance at summer solstice for three selected alternative designs (June 21st at 12.00)

Illuminance levels analyses and visual comfort analyses were done for three days: summer and winter solstice and equinox (see Figure 4). Three selected alternative designs were thoroughly investigated - two previously presented cases with external fixed horizontal louvers and one new. The new one was a facade with external retractable venetian blinds and advanced lightshelf 120. The angle of venetian blinds was 30 degrees. The idea of adding a new case was to verify how venetian blinds would influence the illuminance levels if external fixed shading devices were taking off so much daylight. The illuminance levels for venetian blinds case are apparently lower. But we have to take into consideration also the risk of glare. The results of visual comfort analyses showed that the luminance on the window plane in the case A exceeded the recommended maximum value of 2000 cd/m2, whereas the venetian blinds reduced it to about 1000 cd/m2. In the case A the risk of glare occurred, while the case with venetian blinds represented the acceptable level of luminance [4], [15]. To achieve a glare free environment in the case A for example interior curtains or blinds could be added, but the illuminance levels would go down significantly as a consequence.

4   Conclusions

It should be emphasised that we still do not exactly know when people feel comfortable in a lit environment. We do not know how to evaluate visual comfort [4]. Therefore the study was limited to an estimation of physical, quantitative measures like daylight factor, illuminance and luminance.

The conclusions are:

Lightshelves. The use of lightshelves provides a more balanced daylight distribution throughout the room. The classic lightshelf performs really good on south facade while for the north side the use of specially designed, advanced lightshelf should be taken into consideration.

Exterior Automated Retractable Venetian Blinds. The most promising strategy for energy efficiency and visual comfort in Polish offices appears to be the use of exterior automated retractable venetian blinds. They provide a very flexible solution, because they respond to variations of solar heights, can be adjusted to provide the window luminance preferred by user, and can be retracted to let maximum daylight into office space under overcast conditions. But it must be remembered that the decisive factors are occupant behaviour, and what automated systems can do. The common story is that a building has large windows but the venetian blinds are permanently closed. Occupants don't retract them. Therefore if there is the risk that automated systems can be inefficient the best solution will be to design fixed external shading. The protection against solar gains will be guaranteed and daylight factor values will be still relatively high.

Glazed Facades. The best solution is glazing from table height up to a suspended ceiling. 100% glazed office does not provide significantly more daylight at the height of office desk than the suggested case.

Fixed shading Systems. If the office faces south, higher solar heights are experienced so fixed shading systems perform best of all. Moreover the lighting conditions inside a narrow-plan office building are equally good on south and north side.

References

1. ARUP, Sauerbruch Hutton, Experientia, & Galley Eco Capital: C_life. City as living factory of ecology, Manual. In: Proc. of the Low2No Design Competition, Jatkasaari, Finland (2009), http://www.low2no.org
2. Bauman, F.S.: Giving Occupants What They Want: Guidelines for Implementing Personal Environment Control in Your Building. In: Proc. of the World Workplace 1999 Conference, CA, USA, October 3-5 (1999)
3. Boubekri, M.: Daylighting, Architecture and Health. Building Design Strategies. Architectural Press, Elsevier Ltd., Oxford, UK (2008)
4. Bulow-Hube, H.: Daylight in glazed office buildings. A comparative study of daylight availability, luminance and illuminance distribution for an office room with three different glass areas. (Report EBD-R–08/17). Department of Architecture and Built Environment, Division of Energy and Building Design, Lund University, Faculty of Engineering, Lund, Sweden (2008)
5. Choi, J., Beltran, L.O.: Study of the Relationship between Patients' Recovery and Indoor Daylight Environment of Patient Rooms in Healthcare Facilities. In: Proc. of the 2004 ISES Asia-Pacific Conference, Korea, October 17-20 (2004)
6. Cole, R.J., Brown, Z.: Reconciling Human and Automated Intelligence in the Provision of Occupant Comfort. Intelligent Buildings International 1 (2009)
7. Galasiu, A.D., Atif, M.R.: Applicability of Daylighting Computer Modelling in Real Case Studies: Comparison between Measured and Simulated Daylight Availability and Lighting Consumption. A report of IEA (International Energy Agency) SHC Task 21/ IEA ECBCS Annex 29: Daylight in Buildings (November 1998)
8. Harrison, A., Loe, E., Read, J.: Intelligent Buildings in South East Asia. E & FN Spon, Routledge, UK (1998)
9. International Energy Agency: Daylighting in Buildings. A Source Book on Daylighting Systems and Components. A Report of IEA Solar Heating & Cooling Task 21/Energy Conservation in Buildings and Community Systems Annex 29. Lawrence Berkeley National Laboratory, USA (July 2000), http://gaia.lbl.gov/iea21/
10. Kuwabara, B., Auer, T., Gouldsborough, T., Akerstream, T., Klym, G.: Manitoba Hydro Place. Integrated Design Process Exemplar. In: Proc. of the PLEA 2009 - The 26th Conference on Passive and Low Energy Architecture, Canada (2009)
11. Mierzwiński, S.: Wentylacja hybrydowa w budownictwie zrównoważonym (Hybrid Ventilation in Sustainable Buildings). In: Jędrzejewska-Ścibak, T., Sowa, J. (eds.) Problemy Jakości Powietrza WewnęTrznego w Polsce 2003 (Issues of Indoor Air Quality in Poland 2003), Wydawnictwa Instytutu Ogrzewnictwa i Wentylacji Politechniki Warszawskiej, Poland (2004)
12. Odyjas, A.: Systemy klimatyzacji i ogrzewania niskoenergetycznego budynku biurowego (Low-Energy HVAC in Office Buildings). Chłodnictwo & Klimatyzacja 9/2009 (134) (September 2009)
13. Perepelitza, M.: Integrated Facades. BetterBricks (2010), http://betterbricks.com (accessed February 12, 2010)

14. Reinhart, C.F.: Daylighting Dashboards – from Evaluating Performance to Suggesting New Forms. In: Proc. of the 4th VELUX Daylight Symposium, Rolex Learning Center, EPFL, Switzerland, May 4-5 (2011)
15. Reinhart, C.F., Petinelli, G.: Advanced Daylight Simulations Using Ecotect, Radiance, Daysim – Getting Started. National Research Council Canada, Institute for Research in Construction (2006)
16. Reinhart, C.F., Wienold, J.: The Daylighting Dashboard – A Simulation-Based Design Analysis for Daylit Spaces. Building and Environment 46, 386–396 (2011)
17. Utzinger, M.: Hybrid Ventilation Systems and High Performance Buildings. In: Proc. of the PLEA 2009 - The 26th Conference on Passive and Low Energy Architecture, Canada (2009)
18. Vischer, J.C.: Workspace Strategies. Environment as a Tool for Work. Chapman & Hall, Wilson & Hedge, USA (1987)
19. Ward Larson, G., Shakespeare, R.: Rendering with Radiance. The art and science of lighting visualization. Booksurge (1998)
20. Wilson, S., Hedge, A.: The Office Environment Survey: A Study of Building Sickness. Building Use Studies Ltd., UK (1987)

Induction Machine Faults Leading to Occupational Accidents

Beata Mrugalska

Faculty of Engineering Management,
Poznan University of Technology,
Poznan, Poland
beata.mrugalska@put.poznan.pl

Abstract. In order to obtain high performance and safety degree in machine operation it is necessary to identify potential machine faults. Such faults may have an effect on the machine itself but may also lead to accidents at work. Thus, the activities aiming at the identification of the relation between the failure causes and their effects seem to be necessary to be undertaken. With this purpose, the first part of the paper concerns the analysis of machine faults. In order to achieve it, induction machines are chosen and are widely discussed. In the next part of it the issues of occupational risk are presented, in particularly statistical data about accidents at work in Polish enterprises. It allows to determine the problem of faults and their influence on workers' safety in industrial environment.

Keywords: induction machine, occupational accident, machine fault.

1 Introduction

Recently, design methods are perceived as well-developed fields which cover consumer products, machinery, software, architecture and arts. Not only do they allow to find simple solutions to existing problems but also to interrelated with one another (Anggreeni & Voort, 2013). In order to perform a set of functions, which solves these problems, various product robust design methods are applied (Phadke, 1989; Mrugalska & Kawecka-Endler, 2012; Mrugalska, 2013a). Furthermore, numerous approaches for fault detection of the product or its components have been built up (Ding, 2008; Isermann, 2005; Mrugalski & Witczak, 2012; Mrugalski, 2014). These methods are very crucial and vital in the case of complex products as they allow early fault detection of their components which may help to limit the range of the fault and resulting economic losses (Hughes et al., 2012, Mrugalska & Arezes, 2013). However, regardless of increasing know-how it is still compulsory to remember about assuring safety of machinery and people operating them (Gambatese, 2000; Ridley & Pearce, 2006; Butlewski, 2012; Górny, 2012; Górny & Mrugalska, 2013; Mrugalska & Arezes, 2013).

C. Stephanidis and M. Antona (Eds.): UAHCI/HCII 2014, Part IV, LNCS 8516, pp. 237–245, 2014.

As every day, 6,300 people die due to occupational accidents or work-related diseases, what constitutes more than 2.3 million deaths per year, this problem has become one of the most important ones in contemporary world. It is particularly visible in developing countries, where a huge part of the population is at risk resulting from being engaged in hazardous activities, such as agriculture, fishing and mining (Safety at work, 2013). It is worth to emphasize that even in some countries where the development of technology, application of protection on work stands, control of the course and realization of processes and implementation of preventive actions are on high level, the number of accidents is also high. In most cases it results from the fact that the process of risk identification and assessment and implementation of risk control strategies is obeyed or not done properly. Moreover, there is sometimes even lack of awareness of existence of potential accident risk from both points of view: workers and also employers. Such state requires taking radical and efficient actions leading to upgrading working conditions and to raising the awareness and culture within the range of not following security (Hankiewicz, 2012; Kawecka-Endler, 2003; Kawecka-Endler & Mrugalska, 2011; Tytyk, 2008).

In this paper a particular attention is paid to occupational accidents which are caused by machine faults in industrial environment. The presented data concern Polish enterprises in years 2008-2012.

1.1   Machine Faults and Their Causes

Machine faults are a major area of concern for the contemporary manufacturing industry as they result in production downtime. Data show that half of the cost related to manufacturing operations is connected with maintenance (Hughes et al., 2012). Thus, an increasing demand has appeared to diagnose systems as it can help to reduce machine downtime by determining the root causes of faults after they happen. It is advisable to do on-line monitoring of the machine variables by taking measurements to diagnose the state of the machine when it enters into the fault mode (Ding, 2008; Isermann, 2005; Mrugalski & Witczak 2012; Mrugalski, 2013). It is shown that "the sooner the cause can be determined the sooner a corrective measure can be implemented and the machine put back online" (Hughes et al., 2012).

Machine fault (or a machine failure) can be defined as "any change in a machinery part or component which makes it unable to perform its function satisfactorily or it can be defined as the termination of availability of an item to perform its intended function" (Jayaswal et al., 2008). However, before the final fault takes place it is possible to notice incipient fault, distress, deterioration, and damage (Bloch & Geitner, 2005), what makes their part or component unreliable or unsafe for continued use (Mrugalska & Kawecka-Endler, 2011). In practice there are many reasons why machine faults can occur, for instance design faults, improper assembly, material defects and exceeding the initial design conditions during operation (Hughes et al., 2012). Their range may be minor or catastrophic. However, two types of the most often appearing faults can be differentiated: internal and external, as presented in Table 1.

Table 1. Categorization of induction machine faults (Adapted from (Singh & Kazzaz, 2003; Casimir et al., 2005)

Type	Subtype	Examples
Internal	Electrical	bar breaks, dielectric failure, insulation fault, magnetic circuit failure
	Mechanical	bearing faults, coil and sheet steel motion, contact between stator and rotor, rotor strikes, static or dynamic eccentricity
External	Electrical	noisy network, voltage fluctuations, unbalanced voltage
	Environmental	cleanliness, humidity, temperature
	Mechanical	assembly fault, pulsating load, overload

Table 2. Exemplary causes of induction machine faults (Adapted from (Kazzaz & Singh, 2003; Stack et al., 2005; Trigeassou, 2011))

Machine element fault	Subcategory of machine element fault	Causes of machine element fault
Bearings	Ball bearing	excessive load, increased noise level and vibrations, leakage current induced by multilevel inverters, lubricant contamination, variations in the torque load
Rotor	Conductor displacement	frequent starting, shock, winding vibration
	Connector failure	conductor pressure, excessive vibration
	Fault between coils and the stator frame	angular points in the slots, bad insulation, coil pressured by the frame, shock, thermal cycle
	Frame vibration	bad installation, coil vibration, contact with the rotor, magnetic imbalance, overload, power supply imbalance
	Insulation fault	extreme temperature condition, frequent starting, insulation damage during installation
	Inter-phase short-circuit	high temperature, imbalanced supply, insulation failure, slacking of coils
	Inter turn short-circuit	excessive temperature, high humidity, over-voltage, vibration
Stator	Bar breaks	high temperature, lack of cleanliness, loss of lubricant, magnetic imbalance, overload, thermal fatigue, unbalanced load
	Bearing fault	bad installation, high temperature, lack of cleanliness, loss of lubricant, magnetic imbalance, overload, unbalanced load
	Bearing lubricated badly	bad quality of lubricant, excessive temperature
	Magnetic circuit failure	manufacturing fault, overload, thermal fatigue
	Mechanical imbalance	alignment problem, short-circuit ring movement
	Misalignment	bad installation, bearing failure, magnetic imbalance, overload

As it can be seen external faults concern environmental disturbances which can result from natural causes or derive from the activities of humans (Mrugalska, 2013b). Moreover, both internal and external faults refer to components of electrical and/or mechanical part of the motor. It is worth to emphasize that it is investigated that more than 40% of induction machine failures concern mechanical subtype (Trigeassou, 2011). They are mainly bearing, rotor and stator failures (Akin & Rahimian, 2013; Choi, 2013; Thorsen & Dalva, 1995; Bonnett & Yung, 2008). The exemplary of them and their causes are shown in Table 2.

2   Materials and Method

The purpose of this study was to analyse and determine the most popular induction machine faults and their causes. This knowledge is very crucial and vital as it may provide data about possible working conditions of operators. For this aim, three primary activities were undertaken: a review of the literature, an investigation of failures for a chosen group of machinery such as induction machines and analysis of data about working conditions in the European Union countries, particularly in Poland. On the basis of statistical data, the problem of faults, which may have the major effect on workers' health and safety, was emphasized.

3   Results and Discussion

In Poland frequency rates of job-related fatalities and occupational diseases are much higher than registered in the 15 former traditional EU states (Eurostat, 2012). For example, in 2011, the overall number of individual and mass accidents at work amounted to 96573 that account 0.4% of the total number of accidents. On the other hand, the number of people injured in mass accidents at work amounted to 1,078 persons what comprise 1.1% of the total number of the injured. It should be emphasized that after a significant decrease in the total number of persons injured in 2009, in 2010 an increase (8.2% compared to the previous year) in the number of injured persons in accidents at work was notified, and then in 2011 a further increase (3.2%) was identified (Central Statistical Office, 2012). The causes of occupational accidents in Polish national economy in years 2008 - 2012 are shown in Figure 1.

As it can be noticed more than half of causes of accidents, in the successive years after 2007, comprised a group of incorrect employee action. This group encompass inadequate concentration on a performed activity, a surprise with an unexpected event, lack of knowledge about hazards and regulations concerning occupational health and safety and inappropriate pace of work and lack of experience. Another cause of accident was inappropriate general organization (ca. 11%). In this group it was taken into account inappropriate organization of work in which dominated: inappropriate co-ordination of collective work, tolerance of violation of occupational health and safety regulations by supervisors, work performed by too small number of

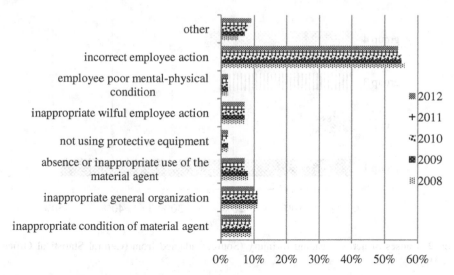

Fig. 1. Causes of actions leading to injury (Source: adapted from (Central Statistical Office, 2009; 2010; 2011; 2012; 2013))

people and inappropriate organization of a working place which most often caused accidents due to inappropriate passages and routes leading towards a working place or storing and not removing dispensable objects and substances around a working place as well as lack of a personal protection. A less numerous group, however, the most important for the aim of this paper, was inappropriate condition of material agent (ca. 9%). In these statistics material agent includes:

- "material agent connected to the specific physical activities performed by the victim at the moment of accident is a machine, tool or other object used by the victim at the moment when the accident occurred;
- material agent connected with the deviation in a machine, tool, other object or environmental factor that is directly connected to the deviant event;
- material agent that is a source of injury comprise machine, tool, other object or environment factor the contact with which caused injury (physical of psychical)" (Central Statistical Office, 2012).

Analysing in details material agent four groups of causes can be identified as follows:

1. constructional defects or inappropriate technical and ergonomic solutions of a material agent,
2. faults of material agent,
3. inadequate quality of the material agent manufacturing mainly failing to comply with required technical parameters or appliance of substitute materials,
4. inappropriate exploitation of a material agent, i.e. overexploitation, insufficient conservation and inappropriate maintenance and repairs.

The data concerning them from 2012 are presented in Figure 2, respectively.

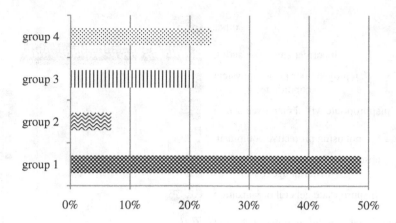

Fig. 2. Causes of actions leading to injury (Source: adapted from (Central Statistical Office, 2013))

The most numerous group of inappropriate condition of material agent (which was identified in 15651 cases) constituted constructional defects or inappropriate technical and ergonomic solutions of a material agent (48.7% of causes), faults of material agent (6.8% of causes), inadequate quality of the material agent manufacturing mainly failing to comply with required technical parameters or appliance of substitute materials (20.8% of causes in this group). A significant part of this group constituted causes linked to inappropriate exploitation of a material agent (23.6% of causes in this group). On the basis of these data it is possible to assess the size of the problem of faults leading to accidents. Moreover, it is worth to emphasize that in 2012 total cost of disability and family pensions, single compensations, sickness benefits, rehabilitation benefits (financial) and other benefits paid from accident budget of the Social Insurance Institution due to occupational disease, accidents at work, on the way to work and home was about 5.2 milliard zloty (PAP, 2013).

4   Conclusions

Huge complexity of production systems and their interaction with environment is clearly visible in modern industrial practices. Changing economical/economic conditions (European and global), in which Polish industrial companies also have to operate, are very demanding not only as far as quality is concerned but also modernity of production processes. Providing good working conditions is the determinant of these requirements. In order to achieve it, it is advisable to pay attention to a material agent and its faults which are crucial factors in industrial environment. As statistical data indicate they lead to almost 9% of accidents at work. Thus, their appropriate identification and diagnosis must be undertaken to reduce machine downtime and assure an appropriate safety level at work stands.

References

1. Akin, B., Rahimian, M.M.: Faults in Induction and Synchronous Motors. In: Toliyat, H.A., Nandi, S., Choi, S., Meshgin-Kelk, H. (eds.) Electric Machines: Modeling, Condition Monitoring, and Fault Diagnosis, pp. 9–26. CRC Press, Taylor & Francis Group, Boca Raton (2013)
2. Anggreeni, I., Van der Voort, M.: Tracing the Scenarios in Scenario-Based Product Design. A Study to Support Scenario Generation (2013), http://eprints.eemcs.utwente.nl/11231/01/TR-CTIT-07-70.pdf
3. Bloch, H.P., Geitner, F.K.: Machinery Component Maintenance and Repair. Elsevier, Oxford (2005)
4. Bonnet, A.H., Yung, C.: Increased Efficiency Versus Increased Reliability. IEEE Industry Applications Magazine, 1077–2618 (January-February 2008)
5. Butlewski, M.: The Issue of Product Safety in Contemporary Design. In: Salamon, S. (ed.) Safety of the System. Technical, Organizational and Human Work Safety Determinants, pp. 112–120. Publishing House of Czestochowa University of Technology, Częstochowa (2012)
6. Casimir, R., Bouteleux, E.S., Yahoui, H.R., Clerc, G., Henao, H., Delmotte, C., Capolino, G., Houdouin, G., Barakat, G., Dakyo, B.R., Didier, G., Razik, H.S., Foulon, E., Loron, L.R., Bachir, S.R., Tnani, S., Champenois, G., Trigeassou, J., Devanneaux, V., Dagues, B., Faucher, J.R., Rostaing, G., Rognon, J.: Synthese de Dlusieurs Methodes de Modelisation et de Diagnostic de la Machine Asynchrone a Cage en Presence de Defauts. Revue Internationale de Genie Electrique 8(2), 287–330 (2005)
7. Central Statistical Office.: Accidents at Work in 2008, Warszawa (2009), http://www.stat.gov.pl/gus/5840_1817_PLK_HTML.htm
8. Central Statistical Office: Accidents at Work in 2009, Warszawa (2010), http://www.stat.gov.pl/gus/5840_1817_PLK_HTML.htm
9. Central Statistical Office: Accidents at Work in 2010, Warszawa (2011), http://www.stat.gov.pl/gus/5840_1817_PLK_HTML.htm
10. Central Statistical Office: Accidents at Work in 2011, Warszawa (2012), http://www.stat.gov.pl/gus/5840_1817_PLK_HTML.htm
11. Central Statistical Office: Accidents at Work in 2012, Warszawa (2013), http://www.stat.gov.pl/gus/5840_1817_PLK_HTML.htm
12. Choi, S.: Introduction. In: Toliyat, H.A., Nandi, S., Choi, S., Meshgin-Kelk, H. (eds.) Electric Machines: Modeling, Condition Monitoring, and Fault Diagnosis, pp. 1–8. CRC Press, Taylor & Francis Group, Boca Raton (2013)
13. Ding, S.: Model-based Fault Diagnosis Techniques: Design Schemes, Algorithms, and Tools. Springer, Heidelberg (2008)
14. Eurostat: Health and Safety at Work Statistics (2012), http://epp.eurostat.ec.europa.eu/statisics_explained/index.php/Health_and_safety_at_work_statistics#Main_tables
15. Gambatese, J.A.: Safety in a Designer's Hands. Civil Engineering 70(6), 56–59 (2000)
16. Górny, A.: Minimum safety requirements for the use of work equipment (for example of control devices). In: Arezes, P., et al. (eds.) Proceedings Book of the International Symposium on Occupational Safety and Hygiene - SHO 2013, pp. 164–165. Sociedade Portuguesa de Seguranca e Higiene Occupacionais, Portugal (2013)
17. Górny, A., Mrugalska, B.: Application of SMART Criteria in Planning Improvements to the Operating Conditions of Machinery. In: Stephanidis, C. (ed.) HCII 2013, Part II. CCIS, vol. 374, pp. 494–498. Springer, Heidelberg (2013)

18. Hankiewicz, K.: Ergonomic characteristic of software for enterprise management systems. In: Vink, P. (ed.) Advances in Social and Organizational Factors, pp. 279–287. CRC Press, Boca Raton (2012)
19. Hughes, K., Szkinyk, G., Surgenor, B.: A System for Providing Visual Feedback of Machine Faults. In: ElMaraghy, H.A. (ed.) Enabling Manufacturing Competitiveness and Economic Sustainability, pp. 305–309. Springer, Heidelberg (2012)
20. Isermann, R.: Fault-Diagnosis Systems: An Introduction from Fault Detection to Fault Tolerance. Springer, Heidelberg (2005)
21. Jayaswal, P., Wadhwani, A.K., Mulchandani, K.B.: Machine Fault Signature Analysis. International Journal of Rotating Machinery, Article ID 583982 (2008), http://www.hindawi.com/journals/ijrm/2008/583982/
22. Kawecka-Endler, A.: Work Conditions in Assembly as a Determinant of Achieving a Good Quality of Work. In: Strasser, H., Kluth, K., Bubb, H. (eds.) Quality of Work and Products in Enterprises of the Future, pp. 785–789. Ergonomia Verlag oHG, Stuttgart (2003)
23. Kawecka-Endler, A., Mrugalska, B.: Contemporary Aspects in Design of Work. In: Karwowski, W., Salvendy, G. (eds.) Advances in Human Factors, Ergonomics and Safety in Manufacturing and Service Industries, pp. 401–411. Taylor and Francis Group, Boca Raton (2011)
24. Kazzaz, A.S., Singh, G.K.: Experimental Investigations on Induction Machine Condition Monitoring and Fault Diagnosis Using Digital Signal Processing Techniques. Electric Power Systems Research 65, 197–221 (2003)
25. Mrugalska, B.: Design and Quality Control of Products Robust to Model Uncertainty and Disturbances. In: Winth, K. (ed.) Robust Manufacturing Control. Lecture Notes in Production Engineering, pp. 495–505. Springer, Heidelberg (2013a)
26. Mrugalska, B.: Environmental Disturbances in Robust Machinery Design. In: Arezes, P., et al. (eds.) Occupational Safety and Hygiene, pp. 229–236. Taylor and Francis Group, London (2013b)
27. Mrugalska, B., Arezes, P.: Safety Requirements for Machinery in Practice. In: Arezes, P., et al. (eds.) Occupational Safety and Hygiene, pp. 97–102. Taylor and Francis Group, London (2013)
28. Mrugalska, B., Kawecka-Endler, A.: Machinery Design for Construction Safety in Practice. In: Stephanidis, C. (ed.) Universal Access in HCI, Part III, HCII 2011. LNCS, vol. 6767, pp. 388–397. Springer, Heidelberg (2011)
29. Mrugalska, B., Kawecka-Endler, A.: Practical Application of Product Design Method Robust to Disturbances. Human Factors and Ergonomics in Manufacturing & Service Industries 22, 121–129 (2012)
30. Mrugalski, M.: Advanced Neural Network-Based Computational Schemes for Robust Fault Diagnosis. SCI, vol. 510. Springer, Heidelberg (2013), J. Kacprzyk (ed.)
31. Mrugalski, M.: An Unscented Kalman Filter in Designing Dynamic GMDH Neural Networks for Robust Fault Detection. International Journal of Applied Mathematics and Computer Science 23(1), 157–169 (2013)
32. Mrugalski, M., Witczak, M.: State-Space GMDH Neural Networks for Actuator Robust Fault Diagnosis. Advances in Electrical and Computer Engineering 12(3), 65–72 (2012)
33. PAP: Coraz Więcej na Wypadki (2013) (in Polish), http://www.stefczyk.info/wiadomosci/gospodarka/coraz-wiecej-na-wypadki,7314907636
34. Phadke, S.M.: Quality Engineering Using Robust Design. Prentice Hall/Englewood Cliffs, New York (1989)

35. Ridley, J., Pearce, D.: Safety with Machinery. Elsevier, Butterworth-Heinemann, Oxford (2006)
36. Safety at work (2013),
    http://www.ilo.org/global/topics/
    safety-and-health-at-work/lang-en/index.htm
37. Singh, G.K., Kazzaz, A.S.: Induction Machine Drive Condition Monitoring and Diagnostic Research - a Survey. Electric Power Systems Research 64(2), 145–158 (2003)
38. Stack, J.R., Habetler, T.G., Harley, R.G.: Experimentally generating faults in rolling element bearings via shaft current. IEEE Transactions on Industry Applications 41(1), 25–29 (2005)
39. Thorsen, O.V., Dalva, M.: A Survey of Fault on Induction Motors in Offshore Oil Industry, Petrochemical Industry, Gas Terminals, and Oil Refineries. IEEE Industry Applications Magazine 31(5), 1186–1196 (1995)
40. Trigeassou, J.C. (ed.): Electrical Machines Diagnosis. ISTE Ltd. and John Wiley & Sons, Inc., London and Hoboken (2011)
41. Tytyk, E.: Management of Work Conditions Quality Through Ergonomic Designing of Work Condition Sources. Foundations of Control and Management Sciences 11, 107–116 (2008)

The Controversy between the Human Factors and Ergonomics Demands and the Current Designing Rules of Contemporary Stadiums

Zdzislaw Pelczarski

Bialystok University of Technology, Bialystok, Poland
pelczarski.z@wp.pl

Abstract. The research concerns determining factors of the development of architectural form of modern stadiums and leads to conclusion that the size and shape of the field of game, which is the field of observation, is derivative of the game rules, with no any regard to the factors defining visual comfort of spectators. These game rules, having been invented over one hundred years ago, had not account for the entertaining character of the action on the pitch, nor for the need of co-existence between the field and huge spectator stands.

The interiors of future stadiums should be shaped considering correct relationship between the needs of spectators and arena. The appropriate standards of the visibility, adjusted to anatomical features of human eye perception, should have the supreme priority in these relationships, consequently causing, as an outcome of these corrected standards, changes in the shape and size of the arena.

Keywords: human factors, ergonomics, contemporary stadium, designing.

1   Introduction

The architectural form of contemporary stadiums is the result of evolutionary development lasting about a hundred years. The most important element that initiated this process was the playing field, in particular its size and shape. Rules of the Game, including the football pitch parameters, have been specified in the code known as the Cambridge Rules, which final version was established in 1863 at the University of Cambridge, shortly before the first meeting of The Football Association. These rules played a significant part in developing the contemporary football.

In the first paragraph of this document saved to establish that the length of the ground shall not be more than 150 yds. (137 m) and the breadth not more than 100 yds. (91 m). It was a field of game much larger than the rectangle with dimensions of 105 m x 68 m, required today by FIFA. Notable is the fact that the creators of the rules of the game have not took into account the huge number of fans who, like it soon turned out, became an inseparable and key part of the football phenomenon.

Already the first years after the creation of football league in England had proved that thousands of supporters of their club teams started to participate massively in all

C. Stephanidis and M. Antona (Eds.): UAHCI/HCII 2014, Part IV, LNCS 8516, pp. 246–256, 2014.
© Springer International Publishing Switzerland 2014

Fig. 1. Football match being played on Monkmoor Race-course in Shrewsbury. The match took place as part of the celebrations for Queen Victoria's Golden Jubilee in 1887. [Author: unknown, Document reference: PH/S/13/M/13, Shropshire Archives, Castle Gates, Shrewsbury, SY1 2AQ, http://www.archivezone.org.uk/subjects/sport-and-entertainment/f; admittance: 26.01.2014]

Fig. 2. Archive image shows match at the Fallowfield Ground in Manchester for the 1893 final between Wolves and Everton. Fallowfield had an official capacity of 15,000, but 45,000 turned up to watch. [Author: unknown, File in the Public Domain, Wikimedia Commons, http://en.wikipedia.org/wiki/File:FA_Cup_Final_1893_Wolves_Everton.jpg; admittance: 26.01.2014]

matches, including these played outside of their place of residence (Fig.1., Fig.2.). For example, over 114,000 people watched match Tottenham Hotspur versus Sheffield United in the 1901 Football Association (FA) Cup on Crystal Palace Stadium in London. It has been estimated that a large percentage of these football supporters travelled by the railways. In 1923 the FA Cup was moved to Wembley. The ground had been built for the British Empire Exhibition and had excellent railway links. Over 270,000 people travelled in 145 special services to the final that featured West Ham United and Bolton. The facts, as reported above, show that already in the early stages of the football stadium development, it turned out, that as important as field and rules of the game are needs of numerous observers of the action ongoing on the arena. From that moment until today, the architects have focused attention mainly on the activities related to the enlargement and quality improvement of the spectators' zone - but adjusting it in the same time to the constant size and shape of the enormous playing field, defined by the rules of game in 19th century. Soon they realized however, that increasing the capacity of the stadium stands has strict limitations, caused by the anatomical range of vision of human eye.

A dominant influence on a form of the modern football stadiums have great world organizations, such as FIFA or UEFA. Acting in new reality of the commercial sport they define and control the utility standards, deciding about the minimum allowable values of their parameters. They also have an impact on regulations issued by the International Committee for Standardization. These standards are not always the result of a premise to ensure the highest operational parameters for the entire audience watching mach.

2   Limites of the Range of Human Sight

For the human eye the critical angle of seeing of two points as separate objects equals $0°1'$ (0,017°), [1]. European Standard EN 13200-1 specifies two values of maximum range of sight for soccer stadiums: 190m, as a maximum value and 150m, as recommended one [2]. In case of the first, angular height of the retinal image of soccer ball is $\psi=0°4'$ (0,067°), what means only four time more than critical minimal angle of view. In case of the second one its value rises up to $0°5'$. In consequence of these regulations the limited distance of farthest row of the audience to the farthest point of playing field is determined by calculating the distance at which the ball, is seen in the angular size equal to the minimum viewing angle (ψ). For the ball of soccer, with a diameter of 22 cm, this distance is 190m (Fig.3). The boundaries of the field for maximum range of view at football stadium is determined by drawing arc lines, which are a set of points in space behaving just this distance from each of the corners of the rectangular pitch (Fig.4.),[3]. This parameter determines the spatial size of the spectators' zone, its capacity and shape. This in turn translates into qualities of usability, communication and evacuation routes, as well as the construction cost of stadium stands and canopies.

3   Dependence of Size of Retinal Image on the Distance from the Observed Object

The size of retinal image is usually expressed in the angular value, as so called viewing angle. It is the angle between two rays of view running from the extreme points of

Fig. 3. The maximum range of vision of football (Lmax = 190m) determined by the elevation height of points of the eye in the top row and minimal angle of view of the ball ($\psi = 0°4'$). *Stadion Slaski* in Chorzow, Poland 2005; (photo: P. Oles, WOSiR Achieves)

the observed object, intersecting at the geometric center of the eye lens. Viewing angles decrease with increasing distance of the object from the eye of the observer (Fig.5., Fig.6.). As mentioned above the dynamics of changes in the size of the vertical viewing angle of a player figure depend on the distance from the observer. In zone of small distances (5-35m) occurs a sharp drop in angular height of retinal image of the object, from 20° to 3° (with average decline rate 0,57°/1m). In zone 35-100m can be noticed the reduction of this height is 3° to 1° (with average decline rate 0,03°/1m). Zone 100-190m is characterized by the decrease of height of image of observed object from 1° to 0.5° (average rate of decline 0.006°/1m) [4].

As shown in Fig.5. the largest distances between any place in the stands and the furthest point of the pitch are equal to longest lines of vision and the smallest viewing angles, achieved from this place. They are always lines of vision of the pitch furthest corner. For the first row of seats the shortest line of vision of furthest corner (Ls1) belongs to central place (Pe1) and is equal 90m. The longest sight lines (Ln) belong to points of eye lying on arc line with a radius of 190m with the center in the furthest corner of the pitch. It means that the angular heights of players figures seen on the pitch in these critical points (pitch corners) of field of vision for all the viewers, regardless of the place occupied, are in the range of very low values, such as 0,54° - 1,15°. This is due directly to the dimensions of the playing field, defining, in fact, the vast field of observation, which considerably exceeds the capabilities of the human eye in range of full and qualitatively satisfying visual perception.

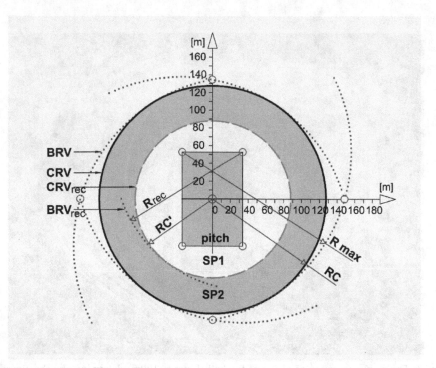

Fig. 4. Field of maximum range of view of the soccer pitch (according to the European Standard: EU-13200-1); R max = 190m, recommended: R rec = 150m; (author)

Legend:; *BRV=190m - Boundary of the field of maximum range of view of soccer pitch, angular height of a player ap = 0,54°; BRVrec =150m - Boundary of the field of recommended range of view, ap = 0,69°*

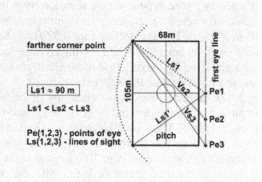

Fig. 5. Analysis of the view lines length from the first row of seats when observing the farthest corner of the playing field, (author)

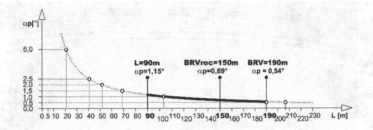

Fig. 6. Dependency graph of the angular height of the footballer on the distance of the observer; (author)

*Legend:; αp –Angular height of a player; L -Distance of the observer; **L = 90m**- Closest possible distance between the observer and the furthest player on the pitch,(ap = 0.69°); **BRV=190m** - Boundary of the field of maximum range of view of soccer pitch, angular height of a player αp = 0,54°; **BRVrec=150m** - Boundary of the field of recommended range of view (αp = 0,69°)*

4   The Readability of Informational Signs and Symbols

One of issues tightly associated with a range of visibility in the interior of a mod-ern stadium is a system of the identification of players. It is based on use of signs of numbers, placed on their sports clothing (Fig.7). The fundamental parameter which allows the identification of individual players, considering the distance between an observer and the playing field, is readability of the numbers, which each of them have been marked by.

According to Rules of the International Federation of Football Associations (FIFA), since the year 2005 dimensions of basic number have been increased. Currently its height should be in the range 25-35cm [5]. From the point of view of the requirements of ergonomics the readability of informational graphic characters requires that the angular size of their outer contour should achieve a minimum value equal 0°5' [6], [7]. According to the calculations for a distance specified by the limits of maximum range of vision (190m), the minimum character height should be not less than 28cm.

Limit values for viewing angles are reliable only with ideal conditions. When they do not guaranty proper lighting and transparency of the air the increase of the character size of 1.5 to 2 times is required. It should be emphasized however, that in the ergonomically practice to provide the reliable readability of letters and numbers the optimal viewing angle ψ=0°18' ought to be applied. As seen it is more than three times larger than the minimum angle (ψ=0°5') [8].

Similar results as those obtained by using the above-mentioned optimal viewing angle can be achieved using the algorithm H=L/200, where H is the height of the letters and L is the distance of the observer [9]. This confirms the reliability of both methods and at the same time proves that the reliance on a minimum angle does not provide a readability graphic characters.

Fig. 7. Spatial relationships between the vast pitch and the spectators' zone in the interior of a typical contemporary soccer stadium. The image was taken from the highest row of the stand. Viewers are separated from the arena by a safety net, which impairs the vision quality; (photo: author).

These facts lead to the conclusion, that accepted by FIFA values meet only the minimal anatomical conditions of visual perception and in very limited extent. The practical experience shows that they are not sufficient to ensure full comfort of observation and the readability of informational signs and symbols.

5   Ancient and Contemporary Amphitheatric Buildings

The differences and similarities between ancient and contemporary amphitheatric buildings have been visualized on Fig.8. The main feature that differentiates these two architectural forms is the size of the arena. The dimensions of the rectangular normative arena of modern football stadium may not be less than 130m x 90m.It houses the pitch with dimensions 105m x 68m, which requires grassy outer bands along the outside lines of the playing field as well as a proper space for maintenance services of the arena. Overall dimensions of this vast field increases even more, when in the addition to a football field, it must also accommodate the athletics track.

The arena of Colosseum was much smaller, of an oval shape similar to an ellipse, which the long axis was 76m, and the short one just 47m, wherein the depth of the zone for the 50.000 spectators stretched itself until 54m. Terraces for the audience reflected the elliptical shape of the arena, creating a visibility profile with a slope similar to the profiles of today's stadiums. The elevation of the last row of seats were also similar to those of nowadays. All mentioned parameters caused that the visibility of objects in the arena, but also the visual and acoustic contact of the viewers with an audience situated on opposing site of field of the arena were far superior in quality than those achieved in the interiors of our stadiums.

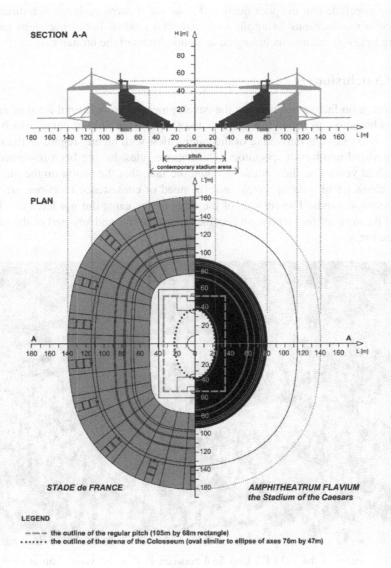

Fig. 8. The comparative analysis of shape and size of the arenas and the spectator zones of ancient Colosseum and contemporary stadium (Stade de France); (author)

In summary, it is clear that the ancient Romans through centuries of practical experiences in the construction of the objects of this type were able to define the most appropriate relationship between shape and size of the arena and space for the audience. With this knowledge, on the one hand, the best visibility conditions, and on the other hand, the biggest capacity of viewers zone, have been achieved. Equally can be firmly conclude that the poor quality of vision at modern stadiums is a direct consequence of the decisions fixing the huge size of a football field - decisions undertaken long time ago without including an anatomic limits of the human eye.

6   Conclusions

The research on factors determining the development of architectural form of modern stadiums leads to conclusion that the size and shape of the field of game, which is the field of observation, is derivative of the game rules, with no any regard to the factors defining visual comfort of spectators. These game rules, having been in-vented over one hundred years ago, did not take account the fact, that the action on the pitch has, in fact, character of great spectacle, nor the need of coexistence be-tween arena and huge spectator stands. The creators of the rules of the game did not have any knowledge of the army of fans who soon became an inseparable and key part of the football phenomenon.

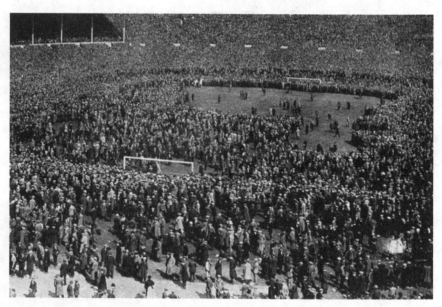

Fig. 9. The scenes at the 1923 FA Cup final between Bolton and West Ham at newly built Wembley Stadium. The official attendance is 126,047, but some estimates suggest 300,000 showed up for the first ever football match at the stadium. [File from the Wikimedia Commons. Public Domain, http://en.wikipedia.org/wiki/File:Whitehorsefinal.jpg; admittance: 26.01.2014]

Already in the early stages of the football stadium development, it became obvious, that as important as field and rules of the game are needs of numerous observers of the action ongoing on the arena (Fig.9.). From that moment until today, the architects have focused attention mainly on the enlargement and quality improvement of the spectator's zone - but adjusting it in the same time to the constant size and shape of the enormous playing field, defined by the rules of game in half of 19th century.

Soon they realized however, that increasing the capacity of the stadium stands has strict limitations, caused by the anatomical range of vision of human eye.

For the human eye the critical angle of seeing of two points as separate objects equals 0°1' (0,017°). European Standard EN 13200-1 specifies two values of maximum range of sight for soccer stadiums: 190m, as a maximum value and 150m, as recommended one. In case of the first, angular height of the retinal image of soccer ball is $\psi=0°4'$ (0,067°), what means only four time more than critical minimal angle of view. This parameter determines the spatial size of the spectator's zone, its capacity and shape. This in turn translates into qualities of usability, communication and evacuation routes, as well as the construction cost of stadium stands and canopies.

The lengths of sight lines of the furthest objects situated at the pitch are different for each place of the spectator zone and are in the range from 90m to 190m. From such a distances are seen the ball and the players, located in the farthest corner of the playing field. The angular heights of players figures seen on the pitch in critical points of field of vision (pitch corners), for all the viewers, regardless of the place occupied, are in the range of very low values, such as 0,54° - 1,15°. This is due directly to the dimensions of the playing field, defining, in fact, the vast field of observation, which considerably exceeds the capabilities of the human eye in range of full and qualitatively satisfying visual perception.

Fig. 10. Interior of The Azteca Stadium (Mexico), one of the world's largest contemporary football stadiums (115.000 seats). Its construction and opening in 1966 marked the beginning of a new architectural generation of football venues. [Author: Jymlii Manzo, Wikimedia Commons, Creative Commons Attribution 2.0 Generic license, http://commons.wikimedia.org/wiki/File:Estadio_Azteca_07a.jpg, admittance: 26.01.2014]

Ancient Romans were those who had knowledge of how to define the most appropriate relationship between shape and size of the arena and proper space for the audience. With this knowledge they were easily achieving, on the one hand, the best visibility conditions, and on the other hand, the biggest capacity of viewers zone. Analysis of these ancient achievements authorizes firmly to the conclusion that the poor quality of vision at modern stadiums is a direct consequence of the decisions fixing the huge size of a football field - decisions undertaken long time ago without including an anatomic limits of the human eye.

All mentioned above facts lead to the conclusion that accepted by football au-thority's values of parameters associated with visibility meet only the minimal ana-tomical conditions of visual perception and in very limited extent. The practical expe-rience shows that they are not sufficient to ensure full comfort of observation of the moving objects and the readability of informational signs and symbols (Fig.10.).

The results of the presented studies evoke many reflection of the architectural nature and among them main guidelines for the future development of stadiums. According to the author the interiors of future stadiums should be shaped considering correct relationships between the needs of spectators and arena. The appropriate standards of the visibility, adjusted to anatomical features of human eye perception, should have the supreme priority in these relationships, consequently causing, as an out-come of these corrected standards, changes in the shape and size of the arena.

References

1. Lapaczewska, K.: Pole widzenia. Badania modelowe. Prace i Materialy, Zeszyt 102, 7–16 (1986)
2. EN 13200-1: The European Standard which has the status of a Polish Standard (2003), PN EN 13200-1: Spectator facilities - Part 1: Layout criteria for spectator viewing area – Specification (2005)
3. John, G., Sheard, R.: Stadia. A Design and Development Guide, 105–120 (1997)
4. Pelczarski, Z.: Widownie współczesnych stadionów. Determinanty i Problemy Projektowe 90, 152–154 (2009)
5. FIFA: Equipment Regulations. Regulations Governing the Sports Equipment at FIFA Competitions, Zurich, p. 13 (2005)
6. Neufert, E.: Podrecznik Projektowania architektoniczno-budowlanego. Ed. III, pp. 37–38. Arkady, Warszawa (2005)
7. Nixdorf, S.: Stadium ATLAS. Technical Recommendations for Grandstands in Modern Stadiums, pp. 130–137. Ernst & Sohn, Berlin (2008)
8. Ziobro, E.: Ergonomia, wybrane zagadnienia, pp. 144–145. Politechnika Wrocławska, Wroclaw (1989)
9. Rosner, J.: Ergonomia, pp. 164–170. Panstwowe Wydawnictwo Ekonomiczne, Warszawa (1985)

Living without Boundaries: A Brazilian Observatory

Alexandra Pereira-Klen[1], Edmilson Rampazzo Klen[1], Tatiana Capitanio[2], and Filippe Barros[2]

[1] Federal University of Santa Catarina, EGR – Graphic Expression Department, Brazil
erklen@cce.ufsc.br, xandaklen@gmail.com
[2] Data4Good, Brazil
{tatiana,fbarros}@data4good.com.br

Abstract. This paper introduces the project: "Human Diversity: a lens on the Program Living without Boundaries". The project "Human Diversity", financed by the Brazilian Social Development Ministry, puts the "Design for All lens" on the Program in order to conduct studies and research with the aim to support the assessment as well as to help conducting and indicating adjustments to improve the Program's implementation. In this work the focus is put on the tools, techniques and approaches that are being used to build up the "Brazilian Accessibility Observatory".

Keywords: Universal Design, Brazilian National Plan, Accessibility Observatory.

1 Introduction

"I have no legs,
But I still have feelings,
I cannot see,
But I think all the time,
Although I'm deaf,
I still want to communicate,
Why do people see me as useless, thoughtless, talkless,
When I am as capable as any,
For thoughts about our world." [1]

This poem written by little Coralie Severs when she was aged 14 sounds as a kind of wake-up call. Do we all have "...thoughts about our world"? And more: does the world have thoughts about everyone? In this sense everyone meant as the widest range of people possible: with and without disabilities.

"...thoughts about the world":
What are the governments doing with this regard?
What is the society doing with this regard?
What are the companies doing with this regard?
In sum: what are we doing with this regard?

C. Stephanidis and M. Antona (Eds.): UAHCI/HCII 2014, Part IV, LNCS 8516, pp. 257–266, 2014.

Motivated by all these questions the project "Human Diversity: a lens on the Program Living without Boundaries" intends to put the "Design for All lens" on the Brazilian National Plan on the Rights of Persons with Disabilities – also known as the "Program Living without Boundaries". By carrying out studies and specific research on the theme the final aim of the project is to support the assessment as well as to help conducting and indicating adjustments to improve the Program's implementation.

In this paper the Brazilian Program will be presented in section 2 followed by some similar initiatives in other countries in section 3. The project "Human Diversity" will be outlined in Section 4 with focus on the tools, techniques and approaches that are being used to build up the "Brazilian Accessibility Observatory". The Final Remarks in Section 5 will highlight some stakeholders' expectations and will provide information in how to access the interim results of this project.

2   Rights of Persons with Disabilities

According to the United Nations (UN) [2] about 10% of the world's population, approximately 650 million people, live with a disability. They are the largest minority in the world and about 80% of them live in developing countries. Among the poorest people in the world, 20% have some type of disability. Women and girls with disabilities are particularly vulnerable to abuse. People with disabilities are more likely to be victims of violence or rape, and less likely to get help from police, legal protection or preventive care. About 30% of boys and street girls have some kind of disability and in developing countries 90% of disabled children do not attend school.

For at least the last three decades the UN is undergoing an effort to set the needs and rights of people with disabilities as a priority on their agenda. More recently and as a concrete result, after years of efforts, the UN Convention on the Rights of Persons with Disabilities and its Optional Protocol was adopted in 2006 and entered into force on May 3, 2008. Since then countries around the world are being asked to ratify the Convention.

In Brazil, on 17 November 2011, the federal government reinforces the commitment of the country to the prerogatives of the UN Convention and launches the **Brazilian National Plan on the Rights of Persons with Disabilities** – also known as the **"Program Living without Boundaries"**.

The Brazilian National Plan is supported by 15 Brazilian Ministries as well as by the National Council on the Rights of Persons with Disabilities – "CONADE" - and has the main goal to ensure to all Brazilian citizens, without discrimination, the right to development and autonomy. Furthermore the Program has as a fundamental reference the finding that, although the condition of disability is present in different social groups and different ages, there is a close relationship between extreme poverty and the worsening of the disability. Motivated by these indicators, the Program pays special attention to people who are in extreme poverty.

With an investment of approximately US$ 3,2 billion by 2014, the Brazilian National Plan focus its policies on the access to education, social inclusion, attention to health and accessibility. The main goals on these four areas are presented in tables 1-4 [3].

Table 1. Access to Education Goals (2011-2014)

Access to Education	Rooms with Multifunctional Resources (RMR)	Rooms with Multifunctional Resources -Implemented	15.000
		Upgrade Kits for the RMR	30.000
	Accessible School	Schools supported with money for accessibility	42.000
	Accessible School Transport	Accessible School Vehicles	2.609
	Pronatec - National Program of Access to Technical Education and Employment	Training-scholarship for persons with disabilities	Priority for persons with disabilities
	Inclusion	Federal Universities with accessibility projects	100%
	Bilingual Education	Sign Languages teachers, translators and interpreters hired	690
		Sign Language courses created	27
		Pedagogy courses created in bilingual perspective	12
	Benefit of Continued Provision of social assistance (BPC) in the school	Expand the amount of BPC beneficiaries (aged 0 to 18) enrolled in the school	72.000

Table 2. Access to Social Inclusion Goals (2011-2014)

Social Inclusion	Benefit of Continued Provision of social assistance (BPC) - Work	BPC beneficiaries inserted in social-assistance networks	50.000
	Inclusive Homes	Inclusive Homes	200
	Reference Day-Centers	A place to help, during the day, persons with disabilities in situations of dependency	27
	Benefit of Continued Provision of social assistance (BPC) - Changes	Normative modified	Carried out

Table 3. Accessibility Goals (2011-2014)

Accessibility	My Home, My Life II	Hired Adaptable Housing	1.200.000
		Installed Adaptation Kits	20.000
	Guide-dogs centers	Training Centers of instructors and trainers for guide-dogs	5
	National Program of Innovation in Assistive Technology	Creation of economic subsidy for innovation in Assistive Technology	Funding already available
		Creation of reimbursable funding for innovation in Assistive Technology	Funding already available
		Creation of economic subsidy for Innovation in Paralympic Sports Equipment	Funding already available
	National Reference Center for Assistive Technology	National Reference Center for Assistive Technology	Opened in July 2012
		Interdisciplinary Groups of Assistive Technology	20
	Microcredit	Creation of a credit line for the acquisition of assistive technology products	Funding already available
	Tax Cut	Published Normative	Carried out

Table 4. Attention to Health Goals (2011-2014)

Attention to Health	Early identification and intervention of deficiencies	Neonatal triage implanted (in Federal States)	27
		Hospitals equipped for neonatal hearing triage	175
		National information system in neonatal triage - implanted	1
	Therapeutic Guidelines	Published therapeutic guidelines	10
	Specialized center for rehabilitation	Specialized centers for rehabilitation - in operation	45
		Accessible vehicles acquired	88
	Orthopedic Workshops	Fixed orthopedic workshops	6
		Itinerant orthopedic workshops (terrestrial)	7
		Itinerant orthopedic workshops (fluvial)	6
		Qualified orthopedic workshop2	60
		Prosthetics and orthotics trained	660
	Dental Care	Centers of dental specialties	420
		Equipped surgical centers	27
		Trained oral health teams	6.000

3   What Other Countries Have To Say

According to the Organization for Economic Cooperation and Development/Development Assistance Committee (OECD-DAC) over 85% of people with disability are unemployed and just 4% of minors with disabilities have access to formal education. The UN Convention defined people with disabilities as those "who have long-term physical, mental, intellectual or sensory impairments". Today 158 countries are signatories of the UN Convention. What can we learn with some of these countries?

The United States has a federal legislation covering the aspects of accessibility, as infrastructural requirements and web accessibility for instance (only applied to federal government agencies however). Each state in the country has its own policies and guidelines. According to the Annual Disability Statistics Compendium the US has a poverty rate, in 2012, of 29.2 percent among the population of disabled people ages 18 – 64; and the employment rate (in the same population) is of 32,7 percent. These data shows that despite the efforts made, there is still much to do.

Japan established its first national action plan in 1982, "The Long-Term Plan of Measures for Persons with Disabilities". Nowadays the Basic Programme for Persons with Disabilities is based on the concept of "rehabilitation and normalization" and is a guide providing the basic directions of measures for persons with disabilities to be implemented in ten years (2003-2012).

However, as stated by Tomoko Otake [4], Japan – like the US - appears to be experiencing difficulties with accessibility and social participation on the parts of people with disabilities, despite some attempts at increasing the accessibility in some areas of society. Otake goes further affirming that like the American goals, the Japanese government appears to have lofty goals in relation to people with disabilities, with mediocre results. This makes us think! The Plans are surely necessary. But...

"...thoughts about the world":

How can we transform visions into actions and reality?

How deep is the impact of external factors in these Plans?

The President of the European Consortium of Foundations on Human Rights and Disability said that Europe is seeing a weakening of economic, political and social structures, referring to the current economic crises. In Portugal for instance the government national plan "Estratégia Nacional para a Deficiência (ENDEF I 2011-2013)" has suffered with the crises. Statistics [5] show that the population with disabilities in Portugal has a poverty rate 25% higher than the population with no disabilities. It also states that social security, technical support, technology services and funding programs also suffered cuts.

"...thoughts about the world":

What is priority?

Who is priority?

4   Human Diversity: The Project

The on-going project "Human Diversity: a lens on the Program Living without Boundaries" started officially in December/2013 and will last for 18 months. The project is intended to support the 'Brazilian Ministry of Social Development and Fight against Hunger' in analyzing the implementation of the National Plan also called "Program Living without Boundaries". The Brazilian government wants to make sure that the vision of the National Plan can indeed become true. They want to make sure that the proposed goals (Tables 1-4) for the timeframe 2011-2014 are achievable and if not they want to prepare themselves and take the necessary corrective steps and measures.

In order to comply with these needs the Human Diversity Project is organized in 5 Work Packages (Figure 1) as follows:

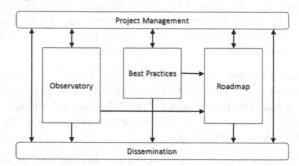

Fig. 1. Work Packages and their Inter-relations

- Observatory: which main objective is to structure a "Brazilian Accessibility Observatory" reflecting the survey held about the Program Living without Boundaries as well as its implementation throughout Brazil. Sub-section 4.1 presents the data collection and analysis tool as well as the Infographics technique that are being used to build up the "Brazilian Accessibility Observatory
- Best Practices Mapping: a one-stop-shop for best practices carried out in the accessibility world.
- Roadmap: which goal is to propose short/medium/long term actions based on the Design for All principles. This Roadmap will indicate necessary adjustments to the Program Living without Boundaries and will serve to assist the Brazilian Ministry of Social Development to conduct its implementation. The roadmap will comprise short-medium-and long-term actions.
- Dissemination: its objective is to increase the impact of the project by means of specific actions such as: the development of an accessible website for the project, the participation in meetings organized by the Ministry as well as by using techniques and tools, such Infographics (see sub-section 4.1), which allow us to exercise our belief that information generates change.
- Project Management: this work package is intended to carry out the activities needed to successfully achieve the expected results. The project follows the PMI[1] practices.

---

[1] PMI: Project Management Institute (www.pmi.org).

4.1   Observatory: Tools, Techniques and Approaches

Data Collection and Analysis. The project will carry out a web-survey (online survey) with exploratory study characteristics in order to collect sample data. The sampling will include between 70 and 100% of the municipalities that have joined the Program Living without Boundaries. By the date, the total number of municipalities was 935, distributed as follows:

South Region: 192 municipalities

Center-West Region: 183 municipalities

Southeast Region: 107 municipalities

Northeast Region: 381 municipalities

Northern Region: 72 municipalities

The survey research technique allows obtaining data or information about features, actions, or opinions of a particular group of people, representing a target population - in this case the municipalities that joined the Brazilian National Plan.

For better understanding the technique adopted for collecting and analyzing the project's data, it will be presented below the online platform used in the project: Google Form, pointing out the macro-environmental context that allowed the emergence of this tool as well as the advantages of its use against other existing options.

From the 90s decade, with the internet network popularization, the society began to experience a new democracy within the ways of human communication and expression. According to Schmidt and Cohen (2013, p.3) the internet is among the few things that the human being has created and yet does not understand fully, and that today is configured as an infinitely multi-faceted exchange of energy and human expression channel.

Lévy (1999, p. 120) shows as a definition of this new scenario for communicating and exchanging based on networks, the concept of "universality", in which as much as the cyberspace expands, it becomes more universal. Schmidt and Cohen (2013, p.3) define this moment as the most anarchic experiment in history, in which the greatest impact of the spread of these communication technologies is their help in decentralization of power and control over the messages, transferring the control from institutions and government to individuals [6].

Within this universal communication context made possible by the network, many online surveys, free and collaborative tools have emerged. Their usage is increasingly common among researchers, due to their reduced costs, quick collection of data, ease audience segmentation and the automation of the results tabulation. Moreover this option also presents itself more convenient to the respondent who can choose the time, place and time dedicated to responding to the survey [7].

In order to select Google Form as the research tool to be used in this project, we evaluated eight different tools (SurveyMonkey, Obsurvey, Flisti, Insightify, Vorbeo, Polldaddy, Eval & Go and Google Form), considering the following criteria: easy usage, question formats, questions limit, answers limits, sending out format and data export formats.

Google Form was selected for being the only cost-free platform, with superior limit of questions (255) and answers (200,000). Moreover, among all analyzed tools, Google Form was the only one to allow exporting the data directly into a spreadsheet, an essential factor to increase work productivity [8].

The creation of a research form is done online, by using the address www.docs.google.com/forms, where nine different types of questions are available: text, short text responses; paragraph text, long text responses; multiple choice, single choice; checkboxes for multiple selection of responses; dropdown menu answer; scale, for the classification of items in a numerical scale; grid, for selection of a point in a two-dimensional grid; date, to select a date on a calendar; and schedule for selecting a time of day or period [8].

When configured online the tool allows you to send the form by e-mail, social media or an online published address. Each respondent may access the form at the time they wish to provide their answers, which will be recorded in an online electronic spreadsheet. The owner of the form can follow responses in real time accessing the online spreadsheet, where you will also find an option of viewing the summary of responses, already presented with graphs and summary texts. If the researcher prefers, it can also be downloaded as a csv file format for viewing and manipulating data in another spreadsheet program [8].

Having said that, due to its democratic and universal nature of collecting and analyzing information, it was decided to use an online form to carry out the survey. Additionally considering the ease to manipulate the tool, the extension of limits of questions and answers as well as the diversification of export data formats, the online form tool selected to carry out the survey to set up the "Brazilian Accessibility Observatory" is Google Forms.

Infographics. In order to allow a better understanding of the way that the data will be displayed and disseminated in the project, the information graphic (infographic) format will be briefly presented pointing out some key drivers for its adoption.

To contextualize the adoption of infographics it is important to highlight that if one wants to influence decision-making, the way a information is presented is as important as its content [9]. A good presentation can be the first step to influence a perception.

According to Ramírez, Mas and Marzal [10], different ways of representing a product may affect the way concepts and aesthetic, symbolic and emotional attributes are transmitted to the target audience. Additionally having a memorable display is the first step to creating effective presentations of data [11].

Therefore to have a memorable way of showing this project's data and to ensure its proper perception, the infographic was chosen as the language format which can be operationally defined as a visual representation of data, information and knowledge in a graphical format through signs, symbols, tables, maps, among others. In doing so it is possible to give a complex message to the public in a creative, informative and neat way. [12,13,14]. Furthermore the infographic ensures that the image is not merely illustrative, but part of the information itself interacting with the verbal text which means that this format facilitates the information understanding by sending on a simple and objective way to the audience without compromising the credibility of the content [12,15]. Another relevant issue about the infographic's format is the new way to read that they enable. If the verbal text is read in a linear way, the infographic communication enables the reader to determine where to start reading, even if influenced by an entry point of look [12]. Finally infographics allow a better space usage as they are characterized by the power of synthesis and simplification, becoming even more attractive to diverse audiences [12].

As for the conclusion, the choice of infographics format is justified by its enunciation autonomy and its role as messages simplifier, making them more attractive, objective and informative to the interlocutors.

5   Final Remarks

The "Human Diversity" Project team has partners which represent several segments of persons with disabilities. It is interesting to perceive how they are aligned considering their expectations about the Program Living without Boundaries.

Their "...thoughts about the world"?

Actions to help persons with disabilities realize their rights.

Besides the "Brazilian Accessibility Observatory", the project will also carry out a mapping of best practices and will provide a roadmap to the Brazilian Ministry of Social Development. This roadmap will reflect where we are (the Observatory), where we wish to go (best practices) and how we intend to get there (Roadmap with short-medium and long-term actions). All these results (including the Infographics) will be available at the project web-site: www.niide-u.ufsc.br . Everyone is invited to visit the site, to share the project results and to spread the word.

Acknowledgments. The authors would like to thank the NIIDE-U (Interdisciplinary Center for Innovation in Universal Design) team for the joint work, especially Mr. Otávio Esser Vieira and Ms. Fernanda Roder Moreira for their contributions.

This work was financially supported by the Brazilian National Council for Scientific and Technological Development (CNPq) and by the Brazilian Ministry of Social Development and Fight against Hunger through the CNPq Call 24/2013.

References

1. The Victor Pineda Foundation: It's About Ability – An Explanation of the Convention on the Rights of Persons with Disabilities. UNICEF (2008)
2. http://www.onu.org.br/a-onu-em-acao/
   a-onu-e-as-pessoas-com-deficiencia/
3. Viver sem Limites – Brazilian National Plan on the Rights of Persons with Disabilities
4. http://www.disabled-world.com/news/asia/japan/japan.php
5. newspaper Expresso has published on November 2013, Portugal
6. Schmidt, E., Cohen, J.: Nova Iorque: Alfred A. Knopf (2013)
7. Walter, O.M.F.C.: Análise de ferramentas gratuitas para condução de survey online. Produto & Produção 14(2), 44–58 (2013)
8. http://www.docs.google.com/forms (accessed on February 05, 2014)

9. Pitt, M., Stahl-Timmins, W., Anderson, R., Stein, K.: Using information graphics in health technology assessment: Toward a structured approach. International Journal of Technology Assessment in Health Care 25(4), 555–563 (2009)
10. Ramírez, M.A.A., Mas, J.A.D., Marzal, J.A.: Influence of the mode of graphical representation on the perception of product aesthetic and emotional features: An exploratory study. International Journal of Industrial Ergonomics 38, 942–952 (2008)
11. Borkin, M.A., Vo, A.A., Bylinskii, Z., Isola, P., Sunkavalli, S., Oliva, A., Pfister, H.: What Makes a Visualization Memorable? IEEE Transactions on Visualization and Computer Graphics 19(12), 2306–2315 (2013)
12. Módolo, C.M.: Infográficos: características, conceitos e princípios básicos. In: XII Congresso Brasileiro de Ciências da Comunicação da Região Sudeste (2007)
13. Módolo, C.M., Gouveia Junior, A.: Estudo quantitativo dos infográficos publicados na revista Superirnteressante nos anos de 1987 a 2005. In: XXX Congresso Brasileiro de Ciências da Comunicação (2007)
14. Liu, Y., Hao, L.: Information Graphics as a Visual Language. In: IEEE 11th International Conference on Computer-Aided Industrial Design & Conceptual Design (CAIDCD), vol. 1, pp. 757–761 (2010)
15. Teixeira, T.G.: Inovações e desafios da linguagem jornalística: o uso dos infográficos na cobertura de Ciência, Tecnologia e Inovação. IV Encontro Nacional de Pesquisadores em Jornalismo - SBPJOR (2006)

Impact of New Design Techniques on Environmental Orientation of Architectural Form-Finding

Romuald Tarczewski

Faculty of Architecture, Wroclaw University of Technology, Poland
romuald.tarczewski@pwr.wroc.pl

Abstract. The paper presents problems related with influence of new techniques of building modeling on creation of architectural form. Short historical context is presented, which allows reader to became familiar with some oldest issues related to the exchange of information in the investment process. It is followed by study of architect-structural engineer relations and changes caused by new paradigms of aesthetics, referred to as "free-form design".

Keywords: free-form modeling, organic forms, spatial structures, shell and spongy structures, 3D modeling.

1   Introduction

The Baroque era was a breakthrough in the development of the form in art. Its eccentric redundancy and noisy abundance of details contrasted the clear and sober rationality of the Renaissance and Antiquity. This was reflected also in the architecture. However, technical limitations did not allow the use in buildings equally free-form as, for example, in sculptures. The technological revolution in the construction and design methods has opened new possibilities for shaping architectural forms. In the late nineteenth and early twentieth centuries the process of developing architectural forms appropriate to the new design possibilities was palpably under way. An example of a building whose form became a symbol of change, even against the background of contemporary Art Nouveau style, is Gaudi's Casa Mila.

A hundred years later, the situation appears to be reversed than was previously. There is a need to develop methods of shaping structural systems which not only meet the challenges posed by new forms of geometry but are a source of inspiration for the creation of new forms. A set of trends, often referred to collectively as 'free-form design' established a new paradigm of aesthetics in architectural design. Designers use means of expression such as: large span, organic forms, randomness, discontinuity of the structural system. These trends developed on the basis of new methods of computer generation of geometric forms. Such tools give designers almost unlimited freedom to create and change to some extent a way of thinking, free from the orthogonal preferences associated with the use of traditional drawing boards.

C. Stephanidis and M. Antona (Eds.): UAHCI/HCII 2014, Part IV, LNCS 8516, pp. 267–278, 2014.

2 The Investment Process as the Process of Generation and Exchange of Information

When a man, sheltering from the weather conditions went from the initial phase of search for a refuge in natural places and the construction of primitive huts, to the phase of construction of objects that can be called (according to our present terminology) houses – construction as one of the important areas of human activity was born. Then appeared specialized craftsmen engaged in building not only for their own purposes, but primarily for the needs of others. Almost immediately, appeared the problem, which we would call today "the modeling of building objects". The investor had to clearly communicate his expectations to contractor, so that he could build an object corresponding to the contract. It was also important in order to set the price for the work.

2.1 Building Modeling from Antiquity to the Renaissance

As long as the activity concerned common, well-known and accepted technologies and solutions, "model" of the building could be very simple. A simple residential building could be described simply by the amount of chambers. In the case of the palace and sacred buildings, more complex descriptions were used, including drawings.

Building modeling dates back to ancient Mesopotamia. It is represented: "… with examples of building specific documentation across a broad spectrum of types: existing plans, plans and elevations, models, quantities, contracts for supply, reports of work-in-progress, workshop records, metrological texts, dedicatory inscriptions and contracts for sale of buildings" [4]. Construction and information technologies of the time were clay-based – about five thousands of clay tablets of this type have been excavated. Until today survived around 30 tablets with floor plans of buildings, houses, temples and ziggurats. The tablets have plans of elevations, combined plan-elevations and annotation. Some of the plans give dimensions, and some give room names. "Many tablets show walls as a pair of parallel lines, with doorways shown as a break in the wall. Some show walls as single lines, with openings marked by strokes across the lines" [4].

The text descriptions, especially bills of quantities, were one of the most important documents describing the building. Their importance is largely the result of the fact that they allowed to estimate the cost of construction of the building. Ancient Mesopotamians developed a series of standard coefficients to convert floor areas to the number of bricks, depending on the size of the brick. Among the oldest documents for the construction of the building is bill of quantities for the Greek fleet arsenal in Piraeus, dating from about 300 years BC [10]. Use of the building models, both descriptions and drawings, allowed to link the agreement between craftsmen and investors with current legal system. The Code of Hammurabi provided a very severe punishment, including decapitation, for the perpetrator of construction disaster. Vitruvius, in the introduction to the tenth chapter of his book De Architectura libri decem, describes the customs in Ephesus, regarding reward and punishment of architects who kept or exceeded the planned investment costs.

It is not difficult to see that most of the buildings, which originated in ancient times disclose largely orthogonal preferences. They are just the result of modeling of buildings. Both the transmission of information between the contractor and the investor, and the modeling of the structural system, allowed operating only a limited number of means of expression. Since the design methods of complex structural systems were unknown – mostly simple, pole-beam structures were constructed. A development occurred in Roman times, when arches and vaults began to be commonly used. The Hypostyle Hall of the Temple of Amun in Karnak, Egypt is a good example of this approach.

Fig. 1. Hypostyle Hall, Temple of Amun, Karnak, Egypt (photo: Wikimedia, CC license)

2.2   Modeling of Buildings in Modern Times

The term technology of information exchange includes both its physical media, and concepts of the its producing, notation and presentation. Progress in this area took place continuously throughout the centuries, but rapidly accelerated since the Renaissance. Table 1 presents a comparison of the periods of emergence and use of the key information exchange techniques.

Table 1. Evolution of techniques of information exchange in the investment process [3]

Century	13	14	15	16	17	18	19	to 1950	to 2000	beyond 2000
Parchment	■	■								
Abacus	▒	▒	▒	▒	▒					
Arabic numerals	▒	▒	▒	▒	▒	▒	▒	▒	▒	▒
Cotton-based paper	■	■	■	■	■	■	■	■		
Spectacles		▒	▒	▒	▒	▒	▒	▒	▒	
Standardized imperial measurement		▒	▒	▒	▒	▒	▒	▒		▒
Perspective			▒	▒	▒	▒	▒	▒	▒	▒
Orthographic triad to same scale			▒	▒	▒	▒	▒	▒	▒	▒
Modern drawing instruments			■	■	■	■	■	■		
Printing press			▒	▒	▒	▒	▒	▒	▒	▒
Movable type			▒	▒	▒	▒	▒	▒	▒	▒
Graphite pencils					■	■	■	■		
Graduated rules	▒	▒	▒	▒	▒	▒	▒	▒	▒	▒
Linen-based paper					■	■	■	■		
Pattern books					▒	▒	▒	▒	▒	▒
Metric measurement						▒	▒	▒	▒	▒
Modern 'lead' pencils						■	■	■		
Wood-based paper							■	■		
Colour pencils							▒	▒	▒	▒
Tracing paper							▒	▒	▒	▒
Reliable drawing boards							▒	▒	▒	
Tee squares								▒	▒	▒
Published standards								▒	▒	▒
Typewriter								■	■	
Mimeography								■	■	
Blueprints								■	■	
Photocopiers								■	■	▒
Technical pens								■	■	
Felt-tip pens									■	■
Polymer pencils									■	■
Plastic paper									■	■
Computers									■	■
Adult literacy		2,5%					25%	75%	90%	95%

There can be identified several milestones in the formation of the conventions for the representation of architectural works and projects. The sketchbook of Villard de Honnecourt on parchment (1230-35) and the plan of the Abbey of Saint Gallen (~820) show the roots of modern architectural representation. Others are: invention of perspective by Brunelleschi (~1410), introduction of Modern "lead" pencils by N.-J. Conté (1795), W.F. Stanley's invention of tee squares (1860) and reliable drawing boards (1870), introduction of technical pens (1932) and invention of felt-tip pens by Rotring (1952). The recent revolutionary step in this way was the introduction of computers into the common use, in the eighties of the twentieth century. An idea of the scale of these changes gives a comparison of drawing instruments from the sixteenth and eighteenth centuries, Fig. 2.

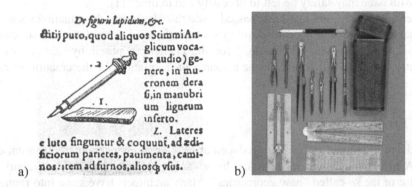

Fig. 2. The old drawing instruments: a) the oldest known drawing of a pencil (1565) and b) draftsman's pocket toolbox (1782) [5]

Major changes covered also the structural design. Starting from the seventeenth century are developing new areas of knowledge: structural mechanics and strength of materials. It became possible to use structural systems much more complex and achieve far greater values of parameters such as the span and height. Structures have become considerably lighter in comparison with those of the previous periods - example on Figure 3. After World War II, appeared a new method of calculating structures that dominated the structural design: Finite Element Method. Its uniform, universal approach to solving various problems has provided designers with completely new, previously unavailable capabilities.

Fig. 3. Grand Palais, Paris (photo: Wikimedia, CC license)

In this way, a new building modeling techniques have opened for designers a new window of opportunity. The problem is now not just the design of a particular form but to find new and original one.

3   New Paradigms of Aesthetics

In 1915 American architect, Claude Bragdon, noted that: "modern architecture, except on its engineering side, has not yet found itself: the style of a building is determined, not by necessity, but by the whim of the designer; it is made up of borrowings and survivals". The author of these words added that "the development of new architectural forms appropriate to the new structural methods is already under way, and its successful issue may safely be left to necessity and to time" [1].

After a hundred years that have passed since this statement, the situation seems to be reversed. There is a need to develop such methods of formulation of structural systems, which not only "keep up"'" for the challenges posed by new forms of geometry, but they will be able to be a source of inspiration for the creation of new forms.

3.1   Free-Form Design

The advent of computers has not produced at once great changes in architectural design. A breakthrough was made when the advanced software has allowed relatively easy use of the so-called "new geometries". Many architects have gone into raptures with new design tools. They began to design forms that could not been previously possible to define – available modeling techniques did not allow for it. Thus was born the group trends in architectural design often referred to as "free-form design". It established a new paradigm of aesthetics in architectural design. Designers use means of expression such as: large span, organic forms, randomness, discontinuity of the structural system. These trends developed on the basis of new methods of computer generation of geometric forms. Such tools give designers almost unlimited freedom to create and change to some extent a way of thinking, free from the orthogonal preferences associated with the use of traditional drawing boards. An example is the use of flexible surfaces defined by several control points – NURBS. This approach also allows the use of techniques that are seemingly far from the architectural modeling, known for example of in movie animation. An example would be the use of Autodesk Nucleus module that allows simulation the movement of soft objects. Assuming a flat surface fabric with the desired properties, and then leaving it for a few placed below rigid spheres of different diameter, one can obtain a new, smoothly curved surface. Similar surface has been applied for shaping concrete roof shell in Kakamigahara Crematorium in Japan, designed by Toyo Ito and Mutsuro Sasaki, Fig. 4.

Fig. 4. Kakamigahara Crematorium by Toyo Ito [9]

3.2   Reintegration of Architectural Form and Structural System

These trends were initially contested by structural engineers. Indeed, these geometrical forms could be difficult to achieve with structures of a simple static schemes. This led to the inevitable tensions in relations between architect and engineer and often caused need to enter the far-reaching changes to the original idea. Today, many engineers began to see in the use of new techniques of designing a chance to introduce qualitative changes in the development of structural systems. This is a completely new concept not only in technical solutions but also in the organization of design. The architectural form can no longer be formed independently of the structural design, which is "added" to it later. Its development is the simultaneous exploration of aesthetic expression and the efficiency of the structural system, on a common geometrical base.

So far, it was possible to adapt structural solutions developed over the centuries to the new aesthetic criteria. But now, forms so different from previously used arise, that the current understanding of the logic of structural system becomes useless. An example is the Taichung Metropolitan Opera located in Taiwan, designed by Toyo Ito. This project uses a plurality of curved surfaces, catenoids stretched on cuboidal net of vertices, that passing smoothly into one another, both in the vertical direction and in the horizontal, creating an unusual form of the object, Fig.5. One should also mention the Tandanor Performing Arts Center located at Buenos Aires waterfront, designed by Monad Studio as a composition of sweeping forms and intricate spatial trajectories.

Fig. 5. Taichung Metropolitan Opera in Taiwan, arch. Toyo Ito [11]

This type of buildings commonly referred to as "organic" must be designed as a whole, without separation of structural system design and architectural "rest". Taichung Opera is a wonderful example of this unity.

Similar design recently appeared also as a MSc Diploma project at Faculty of Architecture, Wroclaw University of Technology [8]. This is W. Tunikowski's *MoS (Museum of Sexuality) in the estuary of life.*

274   R. Tarczewski

The building was designed to be a bit shapeless embryo-like structure. Located on the bay, close to the historic monastery of Mont Saint-Michel, is surrounded and periodically flooded by high tide waters of the sea, Fig. 6.

Fig. 6. MoS (Museum of Sexuality) in the estuary of life – general view

The unity of architectural form and structural system is even more evident here than in the case of Taichung Opera House. The branches - "tentacles" of the main body are used not only for creation of additional space, but are also main elements of the building anchorage in the ground, Figure 7. Author claims that the building "creates urbanistic space of cult connected with search of human's existential identity". Adopting this type of aesthetics by young designers who are just starting their career, proves that it is a trend, the glory days of which are yet to come.

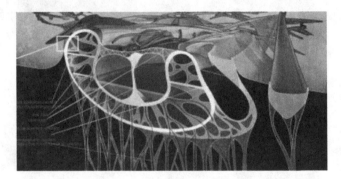

Fig. 7. Mos (Museum of Sexuality) in the estuary of life – section

In the architectural design of such forms, two sources of inspiration are used: natural and geometric, or rather topological. Both are related to the evaluation of the structural properties of achieved forms. In the forms inspired by the natural sources it is possible to direct conclude about the structural properties on the basis of observation of the analyzed objects. In the case of geometrical forms there are the tools that allow assessing and prediction of their properties.

4   Geometrical and Structural Basis for Organic Forms

Geometrical basis for organic forms is provided by the theory of polyhedra, especially saddle polyhedra. The first mathematical attempt to these structures was done in 1890 by H.A. Schwartz. He developed theory of "triply periodic minimal surfaces". The next step was made by H.S.M. Coxeter in thirties last century, who discovered infinite regular polyhedra, and then by A.H. Schoen and M. Burt in sixties – who worked over saddle polyhedra and infinite saddle polyhedra. Such polyhedral compounds are called 'sponges' or 'labyrinths'.

Another inspiration comes from nonorientable closed surfaces with Euler characteristic $\chi = 0$. From the large family of geometrical realizations of this abstract (topological) object, immersed in $\mathbb{R}3$, one can focus his attention on the original geometric construction called Klein bottle. Further continuation of this idea leads to the real projective plane. This is a large group of objects, such as Steiner's roman surface or Boy's surface, which are characterized by a variety of forms that can be used in shaping architectural forms.

Overview of geometric methods shaping organic forms and natural prototypes of structural forms can be found in [6,7].

Structural properties of organic forms i.e. forms based on infinite saddle polyhedra comes from their connection with minimal surfaces. Rigidity of double curved surfaces spanned on non-trivial contour (contour which cannot be immersed in a planar surface in $\mathbb{R}2$) is related to their Gaussian curvature. It applies also to stress distribution. For any closed edge curve there is at least one stable minimal surface. However, there can exist more of these surfaces, provided that they satisfy the Euler-Lagrange equation. Their shape is inter alia result of the external conditions of the medium in which they are located (e.g. loads) and state of stress in them. In the Nature it enables a self-optimization of structures by maintaining a constant state of stress on the surface of a biological component. In the case of engineering structures, constant stress condition cannot be fulfilled for all possible load cases. Thus, structural shaping of such structures becomes interaction of architectural and optimization factors.

A systematic description of a large number of topological objects that may occur in space, and their expected properties and then application to the creation of structural forms, became possible by their systematization in the periodic table, similar to Mendeleev table used in the chemistry. This systematization was proposed by M. Burt in [2]. It is based on statistical characteristics, such as average valency, average sum of angles and genus. These simple characteristics combined with general relations, first of all – Euler's formula, allows not only description of the "polyhedral world" in the currently known extents, but also prediction of new forms, that are of importance for structural shaping.

The close relation between polyhedral geometry and its structural properties has been studied, on the basis of periodic table of polyhedra, in [9]. Figure 8 presents distribution of structural properties due to the potential stability of infinite polyhedra for genus $g = 0$ and $g = 3$. It includes two types of structures: lattice structures, where edges of the polyhedra are materialized as bars, pin connected in vertices (without filling of faces), and plate structures, where faces are realized as plate elements, hinge connected along edges. There are four distinct zones:

zone A – hiperstable lattice and plate structures
zone B – unstable lattice structures and hiperstable plate structures
zone C – unstable plate structures and hiperstable lattice structures
zone D – unstable lattice and plate structures

Hiperstability and unstability is here referred to as the number of the edges of polyhedra higher/lower than resultiong from Möbius/Maxwell equations. It may be noted that the border polyhedra between areas A and D are self-dual polyhedra. For genus $g = 0$ it is a polyhedron 3^3 – tetrahderon. Based on the graph in Figure 8, one can specify to what extent it is possible to apply bar structures, and to what extent - plate or mixed structures.

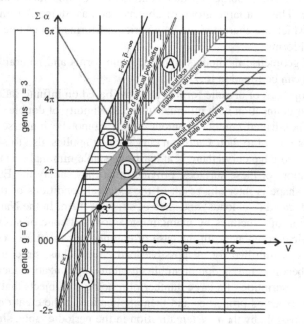

Fig. 8. Distribution of structural properties in relation to potential stability of polyhedra, for genus $g = 0$ and $g = 3$

5   Final Remarks

This paper focuses only on the aesthetic and structural aspects of the creation of architectural forms. Of course the environmental compatibility of buildings covers a much wider range of issues. However, the two mentioned above are particularly important because of the public perception of architecture.

Modeling of buildings is a specific, problem-oriented way of their presentation. Models are created e.g. for architectural and structural design. They differ substantially from each other and contain different sets of information. Models can be created for different purposes, for example for the preparation of financial analyzes, the building management or for exchanging information between the participants of the investment process. Unfortunately, despite the efforts of many companies and institutions, despite the many international programs undertaken, has still not been possible to develop a single, coherent way of modeling which would allow using such model in all necessary aspects and applications. Limitations in modeling capabilities fundamentally affect the created objects in every respect.

As conclusion it should be emphasized, that all new non-traditional design strategies open new window of possibilities for both architectural and structural form finding. Initially the freedom to determine the geometry threatened with a dangerous thoughtlessness and carelessness. Today it is an inspiring challenge. It is difficult at this moment to predict all the consequences of this, but it seems that dominate rather the positives. After a long period of imitations and not very successful postmodern exploration, there is a chance for a real breakthrough.

The new paradigm of aesthetic blurs the differences between the structure and the purely architectural filling. Similarly, should be approached to seek new forms - by combining aspects of design, structural performance and aesthetic. The results of these studies can be obviously different. The mere use of complex, previously impossible to model, forms – does not guarantee a positive aesthetic effect.

Fig. 9. Guggenheim Museum in Bilbao: a) façade [12], b) structural system [13]

Shown above in Figure 9, the Guggenheim Museum in Bilbao designed by Frank Gehry, impresses with its complex form. At the time it was built, it was a kind of "shock" for modern architecture. But, can this form be considered as environmentally compatible? How much more one can say it about the objects whose form is much simpler, but at the same time remarkable and perfectly complementary to their natural surroundings, such as shown in Figure 10: Oceanarium in Valencia designed by Félix Candela and Salginatobel Bridge designed by Robert Maillart.

Environmental orientation of architectural design has many aspects: energy, climate, etc. This paper focuses on the form-finding. The reasonable use of innovative organic forms, fully integrated with the structural system, is – according to the author – a deep meaning for environmental compatibility of the buildings.

Fig. 10. Two positive examples of environmentally compatible structures: a) Oceanarium in Valencia [14] b) Salginatobel Bridge [15]

Acknowledgements. Author wishes to thank arch. Wojciech Tunikowski for making available drawings from his diploma thesis [3].

References

1. Bragdon, C.: Projective Ornament. The Manas Press, Rochester (1915)
2. Burt, M.: The periodic table of the polyhedral universe. Technion, Haifa (1996)
3. Gelder, J.: Specifying architecture: a guide to professional practice. Construction Information Systems, Australia (2001)
4. Gelder, J.: Building project documentation in ancient Mesopotamia. Forum 5/1 (September 2002)
5. Hambly, M.: Drawing Instruments, 1580-1980. Sotheby's Publications, London (1988)
6. Tarczewski, R.: Topology of structural forms. Natural and man-made prototypes of structural forms. Oficyna Wydawnicza Politechniki Wrocławskiej (2011) (in Polish)
7. Tarczewski, R.: Natural and geometrical prototypes of organic forms in architecture. In: Obrębski, J.B., Tarczewski, R. (eds.) Beyond the Limits of Man. Proceedings of the IASS 2013 Symposium, Wrocław, Poland, September 23-27 (2013)
8. Tunikowski W.: MoS (Museum of Sexuality) in the estuary of life. MSc Thesis at the Faculty of Architecture, Wroclaw University of Technology (Nominee to the RIBA President's Medals Student Awards), Wroclaw (2012)
9. Wester, T., Burt, M.: The Basic Structural Content of the Polyhedral Universe and the Plate-Lattice Duality. In: Proceedings of the IASS Symposium on Shell and Spatial Structures, Singapore, vol. 1, pp. 187–196 (1997)
10. Ziolko, J.: Byggesaksdokumenter. Norske standarder og bruk av EDB-methoder. Universitetsforlaget, Oslo (1991)
11. http://www.toyo-ito.co.jp
12. http://www.guggenheim-bilbao.es/en/the-building/
13. http://www.guggenheim-bilbao.es/en/the-building/the-construction/
14. http://en.wikipedia.org/wiki/File:Valencia_Oceanografic.jpg
15. http://en.wikipedia.org/wiki/File:Salginatobel_Bridge_mg_4080.jpg

Kitsch in Architecture – Contemporary Polish Hotels

Elzbieta Trocka-Leszczynska and Joanna Jablonska

Faculty of Architecture, Wroclaw University of Technology, Poland
elzbieta.trocka-leszczynska@pwr.wroc.pl, aska@stalwol.pl

Abstract. Kitsch has become embedded in the landscape of Polish cities and villages and is especially well represented in the architecture of hotels. It portrays society's relentless yearning for the wealth and tradition of extensive old-style mansions combined with economical building materials, restrictions of computer aided design and the desire to pander to mass tastes. In effect, there are produced over-scaled, not ergonomic, cheap accommodation facilities, filled with plastic and gypsum ornaments, which are unfamiliar to local culture. Drawing on a number of case studies this paper investigates the causes of kitsch manifestation and its effect on the surroundings and proposes methods of protecting the urban and rural landscape from devastation.

Keywords: Design for Quality of Life Technologies, kitsch in architecture, contex desig, computer aided design.

1 Introduction

The Polish urban and rural landscape is peppered with kitsch architecture and detail. The areas surrounding traditional or contemporary settlements are drastically changing due to questionable design choices and short-sightedness of investors and others members involved in the investment process. The problem especially concerns hotels, whose owners are mainly focused on attracting vast numbers of clients by choosing simple, fun and usually mediocre architectural designs. This strategy, combined with an economical approach towards investments, very often produces a styleless building decorated with pitiful imitations of what used to be good architectural solutions. Kitsch hotels are not by any means a new or only Polish phenomenon. There are many other examples, such as "Cesar's Palace", the "Mirage", "the Venetian", "Luxor Hotel and Casino", "Circus Circus Hotel & Casino" or many other resorts in Las Vegas. This study, however, focuses only on the local problems, which is driven by the need to preserve the contemporary and historical landscape of Polish urban organisms, in an organized, clear and aesthetical form.

1.1 Definitions

The term "kitsch", which is often related to artistic disciplines, is very hard to identify and describe. Definitions fluctuate from mass produced everyday items to achievements of pop-art and other self-aware implementations (so called "camp" – defined

C. Stephanidis and M. Antona (Eds.): UAHCI/HCII 2014, Part IV, LNCS 8516, pp. 279–290, 2014.
© Springer International Publishing Switzerland 2014

by Susan Sontag [1]). In order to define the frames of this concept, authors tend to study the etymology of this word. Moles connects it to the lack of "style" in style and dates the first use of the term "kitsch" in its contemporary meaning to about 1860 in Munich. He relates this notion to German words: "kitschen" and "verkitschen" – which respectively meant: careless work and dishonest trade. Banach [2], on the other hand, refers to art schools in Munich during the 1870s , which used the word "kitsch" to describe objects of low value. The author also recalls another concept, which is derived from the English expression "sketch" or German "die Skizze" to describe something unfinished, preliminary to the actual masterpiece, unworthy of selling. But he is more fond of term "Kitt", which means a kind of glue that can connect different things. [2] [3] Based on these ideas, kitsch may be defined as something cheap, shoddy, not worth having, created form mismatched parts or patterns or even deceptive.

At this point, the aforementioned trend does not seem excessively harmful or dangerous to true beauty or aesthetics. But Osęka [4, p. 11] states very strongly that (quotation): "Kitsch – is not a funny two-headed calf, but a serious, grim, and tragic disease that is spreading throughout the world with such force that it can be compared to environmental contamination." The popular perception that kitsch is a form of entertainment tends to overshadow the problem, and therefore Osęka's criticism may come as a shock to the general public. But even authors who have closely studied the kitsch phenomenon, tend to perceive it as a "playful companion" of everyday life. Take Banach [2] for example, who labels kitsch as "the enemy", as it creates an untrue, short, and empty experience. On the other hand, he also highlights the role of kitsch in the mythologizing of down-to-earth life or in helping to fulfill one's needs in a cheap way. Although the threats posed by ugly paintings or an odd-looking cup may sound irrelevant, such an indulgence is unacceptable as far as architecture is concerned. Architecture influences many people, their social life and taste, the urban context, and the spatial order of an urban, rural or natural landscape.

According to Moles [3], the popularization of the aforementioned trends is a direct consequence of the growth of the middle class and their material needs. He stresses that the need to develop relations between huge numbers of people, which is common in cities, is no longer based on emotions or feelings towards other human beings, but is driven by creating, selling and buying products, which are as artificial in nature as the process of their constant consumption. [3] [4] This "artificiality" cheapness, fictitiousness and unfamiliarity, will be used to identify the qualities of kitsch for the researched cases.

1.2   Methodology

The scope of work includes Polish hotels situated in small and medium towns as well as villages. The scale of the buildings is represented by the number of beds, ranging from 50 to 2000. The examples chosen for this study cover different aspects of architecture, and include the following: urban solutions of different scale and form, concepts of façades, small architecture, interior design, and architectural detail. Since the focus of this study is on contemporary issues, the choice of buildings was limited to those erected within the last 20 years. It should be noted that this paper does not address the results of conscious and deliberate artistic activity, which is a different subject. The study adopted the following research methods: literature study, case study, analysis, graphical analysis, critical analysis, synthesis, and comparative synthesis.

2   Discussion

2.1   Causes

When we look at hotels in the context of the aforementioned definitions, it seems that such facilities are designed to please users by creating an illusion of "luxury" and "wealth", but in a very economical way, and with disregard for aesthetics, quality and durability. As Moles [3, p. 35] states (quotation): "In the adaptations of the surroundings to the needs of man one can see a 'recipe for happiness'. Kitsch is the art of happiness and each attempt to bring happiness to civilization is also an attempt aiming at kitsch. This is why kitsch is universal, for can it be imagined, that one would not be driven by this basic aspiration?". This statement makes it so much easier to understand why recreation and leisure units, especially contemporary Polish SPA and Wellness facilities, as well as wedding hotels, use a very questionable mixture of styles.

Such an outbreak of "kitsch infection" is exacerbated by the fact that designers often pander to the wishes of investors. This theory was also proposed by a well-known Polish architect Piotr Szaroszyk [5], who states that the criticism of unsuccessful buildings should be addressed to the clients of architects. A closer look at this problem reveals that investors, hoping for a rapid income, tend to praise what they understand as "the tastes of the masses". Architects and interior designers are also driven by the desire for profit, which allows them to neglect some aesthetic aspects. Moreover, in a number of cases, they are confident about their solutions because of their own understanding of architecture. At this point it should also be stressed that investors themselves often introduce many "improvements" to the hotels at the stage of "interior design".

The aforementioned issues are closely connected with another cause of kitsch popularization in the Polish landscape, i.e. the complete lack of architectural criticism from professionals and independent observers. As noticed by Tokajuk [1], kitsch is also a social phenomenon and as such must be evaluated from different points of view. Szczepanik-Dzikowski [6] remarks that the public only notices unique buildings, while mediocre implementations remain invisible for the society. In most Polish small and medium cities, an overwhelming number of dull buildings have been erected in recent years. It is also not surprising that national architectural and social magazines or television programs are not interested in exposing these eyesores, for they are focused on attracting and intriguing their audience. For this reason kitsch criticism appears only on the Internet, where the whole problem is addressed with a touch of black humor. Due to the fact that anyone can publish their opinion in the form of a comment, these websites often resemble a second-rate public gathering, rather than a source of constructive criticism. Only by engaging in a constructive debate can the public awaken to the threat of kitsch and learn about the importance of aesthetics, spatial order and the role of context. Such discussions are helpful in investigating which solutions are dangerous to the built and natural landscape.

2.2 Imitations of Traditional Architecture

In order to be a background for joy, celebration and comfort, kitsch architecture must reproduce forms that are recognized by masses. One group of such solutions is based in traditional wooden buildings, which evoke childhood memories of holidays in the countryside, whereas the second group is a symbol of great status and wealth. Interestingly enough not only Polish history is taken into account, and many elements are borrowed from different European cultures. SPA and Wellness hotels are usually inspired by ancient Greek and Roman or contemporary Turkish baths. The needs of clients to feel like bygone emperors are catered for in plastic pillars, plaster imitations of expensive stones immersed in swimming pools, which are finished with simplified mosaic patterns to match mass-production standards. At the same time, all of the swimming pools are usually fitted with stainless steel balustrades and covered by asymmetric, arched roofs, which are supported by glulam beams, due to structure and durability requirements. This odd set of mismatched elements seems to be indifferent to both architects and users.

Another example of kitsch-based units are wedding hotels. The experience of celebration is usually complemented by enormous portions of food and loud music and is short enough to fulfill the need for joy and fun. Fake architecture seems to be a proper frame for whole event. Brides, grooms and their guests must be photographed against the background of floral ornaments, classical pillars or sculptures. The picture is completed by rich architectural details made of foam polystyrene and gypsum, incompetently imitating agoras and temples of ancient Rome, historic Polish mansions or famous European buildings. Hotel gardens are filled with simplified forms of Italian and French fountains, plastic animals and sheds – a symbol of the "carefree" Polish country.

Both examples share the kitsch aspects listed by Moles [3, p. 96] (quotation): "accumulation as a factor of madness, the fantastic romanticism, comfort and culture mosaic". According to the same author, these features can be extended to: the need to feel safe and comfortable, self-acceptance based on possessions, cultivate daily habits and maintain the same standard of living – at least the same as that of the neighbors. These reasons could be easily explained by a phenomenon that took place in Poland in the communist period after the second world war. During that time, due to the demise of a great number of Polish Intelligentsia, cities had to be filled with villagers. Although they came willingly in search for accommodation and labor, they had problems with adapting to new standards. It is needless to stress that post-war housing mainly consisted of modern prefabricated apartment buildings, which were unfamiliar both to villagers and city-dwellers. As a result, the impoverished members of society, who lived in substandard conditions, started to search for ways to manifest high social status, emphasize their noble descent, and fulfill the longing for their former lifestyle. Initially these phenomena could be observed mostly in the interiors of apartments, but with time it spread to general architectural aesthetic. The process of economically-driven migration between the village and the city is still ongoing in Poland and, moreover, people have become convinced that a cheap way of demonstrating their social status is something positive and desired.

3   Case Studies

However the problem of contemporary kitsch in hotel architecture is not limited to the combination of unfortunate forms and styles, or 'the lack of styles'. It also lies in the thoughtless transformation of historic elements or detail into simplified and easy-to-produce hybrids that look like a cross between the general understanding of 'what old ornaments looked like' and a cheap computer aided design or industrial technology. The artificial and standardized nature of particular features of the overall design combined with their availability and door-to-door distribution, allows for a quick and almost unlimited spread of what Osęka [4] defines as a disease. In addition, the near-desperate search for the individualization of cheap standardized technologies resulted in buildings with peculiar aesthetic qualities. Representative examples of such practices include the hotel in Prusice (Fig. 1, 180 – max. no. of guest in conference room), whose exceptionally vast, horizontal, two-story cubature has a form of simple rectangular barracks covered with flat roofs.

Fig. 1. Hotel in Prusice (on the left) and wedding resort near Rawicz (on the right) are examples of the over-scaled, chaotic search for individual form, which is disconnected form surroundings, tradition or culture (fot. E. Trocka-Leszczynska, 2014)

In order to improve the general perception of the building, parts with large window-openings and vertical pillars were added. These sections have also been decorated with strange slopes designed next to the windows and on attic-wall areas. A similar problem can be noticed in the wedding hotel near Rawicz (Fig. 1), where the first floor was pushed back withdrawn from the from façade the line of the ground floor so as not to highlight the magnitude of the building. Moreover, the inexpressive walls, which are   lined with standardized widows, have been split by glass tubes that might be the result of the search for individual architectural expression. Though such cylinders originally might have been interpreted as allusions to the world's famous contemporary buildings, in their current surroundings and with such an economical approach, they are at best mediocre.

Venturing further into the   topic of "creative" inspiration in Polish hotels, it is important to mention two other examples. The architecture of the first one, situated near

Lipno (Fig. 2, with 27 rooms, a wedding hall, and a restaurant), seems to be a combination of multi-family housing and industrial forms, complemented with a windowless, low-rise tower. An amalgamation of square forms, triangles, rectangles and slopes is covered with a combination of gables and flat roofs. The exterior was finished with plaster painted in yellow and orange horizontal stripes. The roof was covered with ceramic red tiles and the entrance front as well as the front wall of the restaurant were glazed. These materials do not work well together, they seem to be "borrowed" form different functions and styles.

The hotel in Leszno (Fig. 2) seems a little bit more compact (with a multifunctional hall for up to 80 people), and its architecture seems to be vaguely inspired by ships. Though the building looks much simpler, it has a complicated plan with straight and obtuse angles, an additional tower, which is adjacent to the main building along a diagonal axis, and at least seven different types of windows. While the front façade features varied architectural articulation methods, the rear of the hotel consists of a blank plastered wall, painted in two colors. This architectural diversity of the building, and the aforementioned accumulation of unusual forms, is also observed in other examples (Fig. 3, Fig. 4).

Fig. 2. Hotels near Lipno (right) and in Leszno as examples of the search for contemporary forms based on industrial forms or ship-inspired architecture (fot. E. Trocka-Leszczynska, 2014)

Probably one of the most glaring examples of kitsch is the recently built hotel in Karpacz (Fig. 3). The hotel with 906 rooms was partially opened in 2010 and is a part of a country-wide network of hotels. Since it offers a variety of attractions and services, such as a water park, SPA&Wellness center, a conference center, a night club, restaurants, playgrounds, etc., it required a great volume. Despite many protests from the local community, resistance from local authorities (the project was incompatible with the land-use plan) and criticism from the architectural community, the building was erected in an over-scaled form, and now dominates the surrounding vernacular architecture.

At first glance it may seem that its features could serve as an inspiration for new designs, but a closer examination reveals that this architectural style is similar for all facilities built by this chain, regardless of their location. The volume of individual modules, their varied roof types, forms of balconies, widow types (especially curved large openings), stand out in the surroundings. The wood-like paneling of chosen details can hardly be considered as a reference to the tradition of the region as the dominating part of the facades is covered with painted plaster. Such economical solutions, combined with PCV and steel sheets, appear in all the examples presented in this paper. These components are very cheap, and although they age really fast and ugly, they have successfully replaced all the other local and regional materials, such as different types of bricks and stones, ceramic tiles or wood.

Fig. 3. Enormous hotel in Karpacz: on the left – view of different cubic volumes covered with a variety of roof forms, in the middle – details of the façade, on the right: main hall (fot. J. Jablonska, 2013, E. Trocka-Leszczynska, 2014)

There is also another issue connected to the aforementioned problems. Similarly to other professionals, architects tend to use computers and dedicated software in their design work. One of the advantages of computer aided design is easy access to libraries with pre-defined 2d and 3d models of products available in mass production. In most cases, such software is a very useful tool as long as the designer uses typical and standardized solutions. Any customizations require additional knowledge, more time, extra effort and sometimes might be impossible to perform. It could be the case that the constant pressure of time and these virtual tools are contributing to the decline of creativity and, consequently lead to randomness in architecture. The wedding house in Rydzyna (Fig. 4) seems to be a good example of a diverse, but accumulation of typical forms. In front of the building there is a circular driveway, flanked by the two wings of the hotel, which were erected on a polygonal plan. The wings are connected with a curved stairway, and gable-roofed, glazed oriel. All this is complemented by a Bauhaus-like side entrance, atop a curved and organically-shaped staircase with an iron balustrade, half-circle dormers and windows in straight PCV frames.

Fig. 4. The "house of weddings" in Rydzyna – an example of an accumulation of forms based on standardized solutions, easy to create using computer-aided-design software (fot. E. Trocka-Leszczynska, 2014)

What is interesting, the interiors in most of the studied examples are usually disconnected from exteriors in terms of form and style (Fig. 5). Due to the low quality of
design and economical approach towards selecting building materials, wedding hotels
are usually a disproportionate composition of very simple blocks. These solids are
covered by gable roofs, which in most cases do not fit in well with anything, but are
required by local spatial regulation. The forms, shapes and materials of pseudo-
traditional slopes do not match any other detail in the building. The quality of this
solution is usually lowered even more by the cheapest building materials on the market used for finishing, i.e. steel sheets or bituminous tiles. Architectural accents are
implemented in the forms of small, inappropriately-shaped oriels, mismatched secondary roofs over the entrances, large openings only next to ballrooms and terraces,
which looks like additional extension. The windows and doors are usually made of
vinyl imitation wood. Walls in such hotels are finished with plaster and painted in
random colors.

Due to these economical standards of design, it is impossible to distinguish buildings from each other or to define their architectural style. This disproportion is clearly
visible in another wedding hotel (with 105 rooms) situated near Poznan (Fig. 5). The
property is a wide, horizontal single story building covered by a gable roof. Walls
are finished with painted plaster (unsurprisingly) and accentuated with brick-like
ceramic tiles. Simple sloping roofs are covered with steel-sheet tile and fitted with
flat, rectangular skylights. The dominating element of the architectural design is the
polygonal oriel with large openings. It is surrounded by secondary roofs over entrances, which are supported by simple pillars. The interior of this simple building,
resembles a palace, rather than a single-story country house. Large public spaces and
halls have been filled with simplified classical and baroque columns, cantilevers and
circular suspended ceilings made from gypsum boards, and stretch ceiling. The walls
are covered by patterned tapestry and decorated with richly ornamented mirror
frames. The palatial character is also accentuated by crystal chandeliers (Fig. 6).

Fig. 5. The wedding hotel near Poznan, as an example of architectural disconnect between the
building's exterior and the interior. On the left – a village-like exterior, on the right – interior
hall with a mixture of details – distant borrowings from classical and baroque style. (fot.
J. Jablonska, 2013)

Fig. 6. The wedding hotel near Poznan, as an example of palatial architecture to express status and tradition (fot. J. Jablonska, 2013)

Similar solutions can be observed in the interiors of the aforementioned hotel near Rawicz. The main hall is bright in color with cylindrical pillars crowned by diagonal capitols, and is decorated with hanging strings of beads, art-deco chandeliers, golden frames of a mirror and a strange, quilted detail on one of the walls (Fig. 7). These elements could well represent the "glamour style" – which has recently become quite popular among Polish interior designers – but the floor paneling and gypsum-board celling are inconsistent with this assumption. The restaurant is a darker, club-like place, and adopts two contrary approaches to designing. One is historically-based with stylized tables and chairs, made from dark wood and patterned upholstery, supplemented with pinned curtains, sculpted plaster on walls and gypsum cornices (Fig. 7, 8) and lamps with crystal beads (Fig. 9). The other resembles a discothèque with aggressive green lights, asymmetrically-shaped mirrors and large aquariums. This stylistic puzzle is finished with the same floor paneling as in the hall, and glass partitions in very cheap and unstylish PCV frames. Moreover the dramatic connections between plastic ornaments, gypsum details, plain walls, and tiled floors, tend to bring out the senselessness of such solutions.

Fig. 7. The wedding resort near Rawicz, as an example of the connection between contemporary materials and "historically based" forms: on the left – round columns and ceiling made of cheap gypsum-board, on the right stylized entrance to restaurant (fot. E. Trocka-Leszczynska, 2014)

Fig. 8. The wedding wedding resort near Rawicz – interior details: on the left – aquarium in gypsum form illluminated by "crystal" chandeliers, on the right – mirrors in polygonal frames made from tinted mirror glass, with a stylized hanger and palatial, textile window decoration in the background (fot. E. Trocka-Leszczynska, 2014)

Fig. 9. The wedding hotels in detail: on the left – "crystal" chandeliers made from textile and plastic, on the right – plastic espalier covered with flaky paint and surrounded by artificial flowers (fot. E. Trocka-Leszczynska, 2014)

Details artificial in form and material were noticed in most of the studied examples, and they were present not only in the interiors (Fig. 9) but also in the form of landscaping features in the surrounding gardens or outdoor public spaces (Fig. 10). Small fountains used as a setting for photography, typically made of concrete, were supposed to resemble ancient Roman, Greek or baroque sculptures, though nothing in vicinity would justify such choices, e.g. a nymph placed in the corner of two plain walls. The most peculiar example found during this investigation, was an enormous installation of an insect in one of the wedding facilities.

Fig. 10. Landscaping features in wedding hotels: on the left and in the middle – concrete fountains inspired by ancient culture and baroque, on the right – giant insect installation (fot. E. Trocka-Leszczynska, 2014, J. Jablonska 2013)

The study resulted in a list of the most common elements in Polish kitsch architecture of hotels. It includes the following – for exteriors: neglected context, unstylish building structures merely adjusted to the land-use plan, incorrect proportions, lack of architectural expression, strange inspirations, unjustified references, accumulation of diversified details, the cheapest building materials, finishing made from plaster, paint, steel sheets or ceramic tiles – for interiors: significant discrepancy between the style of the exterior and the interior, contradicting ideas and assumptions or lack of concept in the designs, lack of clear functional and formal zoning, thoughtless choice of colors, textures, patterns, ornaments, fabrics, tapestry, etc.

4   Conclusions

What is interesting in the studied cases is that historical allusions are usually made to ancient, renaissance, baroque styles or to traditional country housing. Roman and gothic architectural features seem to be purposely omitted. In Poland these two styles are culturally connected to sacral architecture of churches. This phenomena perfectly shows the strong connection between kitsch and needs for entertainment or possessions. But owning even the most beautiful artificial chandeliers, concrete fountains and plastic columns neither enriches a person nor architecture. A civilization of happiness cannot be built on the basis of fraud, for it will not last. Moreover, creating and erecting any monumental building, which is correct in form, is possible today with the use of archeological, historical and conservatory knowledge, and with the implementation of proper building materials and technologies. The question is whether the contemporary Polish landscape needs Persian temples or Roman theaters? Although the nonsense of such a concept seems obvious to the whole society, it is constantly repeated in the architectural designs of hotels. The validity of both arguments against kitsch should be particularly stressed in all public debates and discussions on spatial order of urban and rural context in Polish historical and cultural regions.

Polish architecture has great potential to be exceptional and original. It should be based on traditional urban development and regional architecture. Inspiring ideas can be found in local materials and building technologies, both contemporary and historical. The scale and proportions of cities and villages are already adjusted to human proportions and needs, so their further growth must be harmonious with the existing structure. Hotels, as a service for both citizens and guests, should be erected in the architecture style which is representative of the country and which highlights the advantages of building culture. International or historic inspirations are also needed in the buildings but "borrowings" and connections should be of high quality and must be introduced with respect towards aesthetics and the overall educational role of architecture in everyday life of users.

References

1. Tokajuk A.: Piękno, oryginalność, kicz i estetyka drugiej kategorii w architekturze współczesnej. In: Czasopismo Techniczne z. 13. Architektura z. 6-A, Wydawnictwo Politechniki Krakowskiej, pp. 438–442 (2007)

2. Banach, A.: O kiczu. Wydawnictwo Literackie, Kraków, pp. 9–10, 18, 340–341 (1968)
3. Moles, A.: Kicz czyli sztuka szczęścia. Studium o psychologii kiczu. In: Szczepańska, A., Wende, E. (trans.) Państwowy Instytut Wydawniczy, Warszawa, pp. 13–18, 20–24, 35, 96, 101 (1978)
4. Osęka, A.: Introduction for "Kicz czyli sztuka szczęścia. Studium o psychologii kiczu". In: Szczepańska, A., Wende, E. (trans.) Państwowy Instytut Wydawniczy, Warszawa, pp. 5–11 (1978)
5. Szaroszyk, P.: Krytka czasem krzywdzi, ale nie wolno się obrażać. Architektura 11(17), 66 (2000)
6. Szczepanik-Dzikowski: Jaka architektura taka krytyka. Architektura 11(17), 66 (2000)

Day-Lighting and Sun Protection in Hospital Facilities – Assessment of the Used Solutions

Joanna Tymkiewicz and Magdalena Jamrozik-Szatanek

The Silesian University of Technology, Faculty of Architecture, Gliwice, Poland
joanna.tymkiewicz@polsl.pl,
magdalena.jamrozikszatanek@gmail.com

Abstract. The paper is a recapitulation of research into hospital buildings, focused on defining the advantages and disadvantages of the applied sun-
protection systems and indication of the types of benchmark solutions. Proper
selection of sun-protection systems in health care units is very important, because it contributes to creating the conditions of day lighting and their impact
on patients' physiology. Moreover, sun protection systems influence the
architecture of buildings - their external image and aesthetics of the interiors,
ergonomics of rooms, providing comfort for the main groups of users: patients
and medical staff, and contributing to energy-efficiency of buildings. The scope
of the presentation is to draw particular attention to the complexity of this issue
from users' perspective.

Keywords: day-lighting, hospital, sun protection, sun blinds.

1 Statement of the Objective and Significance of the Proposed Presentation

Exterior walls and facades should secure access of natural light to the interiors, protect from excessive sunlight, or increasing natural light distribution into rooms of
bigger depth. These functions are served by facades equipped with technical solutions, including, for example, movable sun-protection shields. Hospital buildings are
structures of specific requirements concerning natural lighting conditions and sun-
lighting of rooms. The quantity, size, proportions and arrangement of windows are of
great importance. Nevertheless, the selection of appropriate sun protection is equally
important, as it exerts an impact on the psychological comfort of patients and the
comfort of their stay at hospital. However, the selection of appropriate sun protection
is equally important, as it exerts an impact on the psychological comfort of patients
and the comfort of their stay at hospital. Modern technologies offer many visually
attractive systems of sun-protection devices, but not all of them may be used in hospital facilities, not only because of efficiency but also due to the fact that the effects

C. Stephanidis and M. Antona (Eds.): UAHCI/HCII 2014, Part IV, LNCS 8516, pp. 291–302, 2014.
© Springer International Publishing Switzerland 2014

such as shading and contrasts in the interiors, or changes of colors of the light may contribute to wrong assessment of the patient's health condition or hinder such assessment. The objective of the described research is to analyze the advantages and disadvantages of various sun protection systems in view of their applicability to hospital facilities, and to indicate preferred solutions that should be proposed at the design stage, or solutions that may be implemented in the course of the performance of the facilities. The scope of this paper is to draw attention to the importance and essence of these issues.

2   Description of Methods

Nowadays, computer simulations are used to evaluate the effectiveness of sun protection systems, but the authors of this paper have adopted a different approach- from users', human perspective. Thus, in the course of the research the methods typical for environmental studies were used:

- In-situ tests and observations conducted in hospital buildings in Poland,
- Pilot interviews with users of hospitals (children aged 3-12, youngsters aged 13-18, parents, medical, technical and administrative staff),
- Participative studies; assessment of experience, knowledge and needs of hospital users – at three stages:

— Stage I – precise preparation of the studies;
— Stage II – focus meetings, analyses conducted with the participation of users (workshops for children and young people, surveys/interviews, AEDET and ASPECT questionnaires, photographic analyses;
— Stage III - meeting, recapitulation of the collected data.

The theoretical bases of the conducted research were analyses of professional literature evaluating the state of knowledge of the discussed issue, which revealed that the publications devoted to sun- protection systems mostly focus on office facilities (for more information – see: [6-8]); whereas, as far as the architecture of health care buildings is concerned, the issue of sun-protection shields is only marginally discussed, and, mainly in the context of the influence of sun-protection systems on the aesthetics and colors selection of the interiors, or as one of details of building facades.

3   Definition of the Scope of Research

Short descriptions and photographs of the researched hospital units are presented below. The majority of the studied medical facilities are pediatric hospitals which consented to the cooperation in the research. In Poland, the following hospitals were involved:

Fig. 1. Entrance area to children's hospital in Radziszow (photo. Magdalena Jamrozik-Szatanek)

CHILDREN'S REHABILITATION CENTER IN RADZISZÓW. Situated in the suburban area in Wieliczka Foothills and surrounded by greenery. Divided into segments, the shell of the building preponderates over the local environment, a part of the building is suspended. It is colourful and its horizontal character is enhanced by balconies of hospital beds units (see also [4]).

Fig. 2. The North wing of the pediatric oncology hospital in Chorzow (photo. Magdalena Jamrozik-Szatanek)

PEDIATRIC AND ONCOLOGY CHILDREN'S CENTER IN CHORZÓW. The hospital is located in the very centre of the city. Surrounded by compact urban settlements, it is shaped as the "H" letter, inside which the entrance to the building is placed. The shell of the building comprises mansard roofs covered with brick tiles, and white walls.

Fig. 3. Western façade and the main entrance (photo. Magdalena Jamrozik-Szatanek)

PEDIATRIC CHILDREN'S CENTER IN SOSNOWIEC. Located in the vicinity of the housing estate and the park, surrounded by tall trees. The shell of the building is divided into multi-colored segments, and the entrance zone highlighted. There is a greenery courtyard inside the building site.

For the sake of comparison, studies of selected hospitals in Italy were carried out, in consideration of the climatic differences, reflected in the applied sun-protection systems. The selected hospitals include:

Fig. 4. Courtyard and the main entrance to Children's Hospital in Florence (photo. Magdalena Jamrozik-Szatanek)

MEYER CHILDREN'S HOSPITAL IN FLORENCE is situated in the suburban zone and embedded in the green hills of Toscana. The hospital complex consists of historical buildings perfectly adjoined to the modern architecture of the entrance hall and patients' beds unit. The roofs have skylights formed as "Pinocchio" caps.

Fig. 5. The main entrance to Sandro Pertini Hospital (photo. Magdalena Jamrozik-Szatanek)

SANDRO PERTINI HOSPITAL IN ROME is located at the 8 km distance from the very centre of Rome. Due to its two-storey structure it has a friendly and inviting scale. The facades are rhythmically partitioned by semi-circular pilaster. Inside the hospital site there are two courtyards with greenery, playgrounds and recreation spaces.

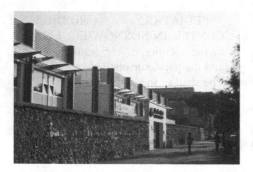

Fig. 6. The main entrance to the new Bambino Gesu Hospital unit in Rome (photo. Magdalena Jamrozik-Szatanek)

BAMBINO GESU CHILDREN'S HOSPITAL IN ROME. This low hospital facility, surrounded with stone walls, is situated next to the Basilica of Saint Paul Behind the Walls. The facades of the Hospital are divided by vertical pillars and the spaces between them filled with glass and white panels. They also have sun-breakers that protect the Hospital from excessive sunlight.

The objective of making the comparison between the pediatric hospital facilities in Poland and Italy was to demonstrate the wide range of sun-protection solutions applied in hospital buildings.

4   Discussion of the Results

4.1   Factors Considered in the Assessment

The studies and observations of hospital facilities in Poland revealed that usually only internal protection solutions are used, including: vertical blinds and shades, or, in few cases- venetian blinds. From the users' perspective, they have an important advantage – ease of control and adjustment to individual needs; however, such protection systems are often insufficient. In consequence, on sunny days of the hot seasons the users (patients and medical staff) feel discomfort caused by dazzle and overheat inside the hospital (including patients' rooms). This is very disturbing, as the interiors of Polish hospitals are rarely air-conditioned. Whereas, in Italy, due to different climatic conditions and the resulting excess sunlight, external shields are most popular (roller blinds, awnings, shades, sun-breakers, etc.). Interior blinds are used as elements supporting sun protection systems, commonly in the spaces and rooms that require isolation from the external environment, for example: patients' rooms, staff rooms (doctors' duty rooms, nurse duty rooms). Furthermore, the protection solutions entail more than single elements and give a possibility of choice. For example, in the patients' rooms in Mayer Children' Hospital, children can shield the window with venetian blinds, curtains, and, in addition, their beds are isolated by hangings (the main function of which is separate the patient from other roommates, but they may also serve as additional sun-protection devices, etc.).

The outcome of the research has been compiled in tables that contain the characteristics and assessment of sun-protection systems, their advantages and disadvantages in view of a specific nature of hospital facilities.

4.1.1   Exterior Blinds

The place of mounting sun protection elements is important to their effectiveness. The exterior blinds are more effective, but also more expensive, because they should be constructed in a manner that prevents their damage caused by atmospheric factors, including pollution, temperature differences, to prevent thermal expansion of the material, which, in turn, may lead to damaging paint coatings on the bottom of slats, or permanent deformation of metal lamellas. Also, wind power may also damage or destroy the elements of the exterior sun-protection system. Therefore, it is recommended to use automatic control of putting up and down the blinds, depending on the impact of the wind. The use of movable blinds with altering angle of the slats is really effective.

Table 1-4. Hospital buildings - advantages and disadvantages of exterior sun protection systems (elaborated by the authors on the bases of [1-3], [5-8])

Table 1.

	Awnings Made of the material covered with impregnate that has antifungal and antistatic properties. Example of use: **Fig. 7.** Sandro Pertini Hospital in Rome (photo. Magdalena Jamrozik-Szatanek)
Advantages	Disadvantages
They provide shading, reduce excess heat and sunlight of the rooms, and partly protect from rain or snow falls but also, to a certain degree, from the wind.	In the case of stronger wind blows they should be folded, to prevent their damage; they give insufficient protection against rainfalls and often get dirty.

Table 2.

	Façade louvers – " sun breakers" They have the form of pergolas, canopies, screens on the facade, shields adjoined to the walls, they may be movable or immovable, automatically controlled. Example of use: **Fig. 8.** Bambino Gesu Children's Hospital in Rome (photo. Magdalena Jamrozik-Szatanek)
Advantages:	Disadvantages:
• They contribute to clear, modern external image of the building, shade, to a certain degree, partly control sun dazzle, and redirect sunlight (but are not completely self-sufficient, usually aluminum slats can be replaced by photogalvanic cells).	• Heated air may be transferred, due to the set-up of the slats, directly to the glazing, which intensifies the excess heat in the rooms, • They do not provide thermal insulation in the winter season, • They may limit the view from the window, • In the case of metal blinds and holders unpleasant noise effects may occur (rasps, clangs), under the changing atmospheric conditions lamellas should be cleaned regularly, to maintain their property of light reflection.

Table 3.

	**Exterior roller blinds** The blinds curtain consists of slats made of aluminum or aluminum tape filled with polyurethane foam; the slats may be glazed or have ventilation openings. Example of use: **Fig. 9.** Sandro Pertini Hospital in Rome (photo. Magdalena Jamrozik-Szatanek)
Advantages:	Disadvantages:
• They protect the windows and doors from the external impacts (rain, wind, sun rays, noise), • They prevent the cooling of rooms in the autumn and winter seasons, because when they are closed, there is the space filled with air between the shell and the pane, providing good insulation, • They constitute important elements of protection people and their possessions (if installed for such purpose, it is essential to strengthen their profiles and use special mounting technology,, • The blinds may be manually operated, or operated by electric drives, also, there is an option of solar energy drives.	• The system is not very efficient as far as sun protection is concerned, • They provide visual isolation, because, when rolled down, they obscure the whole surface of the window; therefore, it is necessary to provide an option of manual rolling up the blinds, as in case of electricity failure (fire), they may make it impossible to evacuate people from the building.

Table 4.

	**Exterior louvers** The slats are made of aluminum, steel, glass, and constitute an important decorative element of the façade. Example of use: **Fig. 10.** Sandro Pertini Hospital in Rome (photo. Magdalena Jamrozik-Szatanek)

Table 4. (*continued*)

Advantages:	Disadvantages:
• They provide insulation from thermal and solar radiation, • They shade the interiors in an effective way, • They improve light dispersion, and, when properly set-up, offer the possibility of unhindered airing and visual contact with the exteriors, • They may be automatically controlled or operated by electric drives, • Glass louvers do not obscure the view from the window, and, at the same time, reduce the dazzle effect, • They may be equipped with photo-galvanic cells, although such solution is still expensive.	• They contribute to the generation of streaky shadows, which, in turn, may cause disorientation and contrast in the field of vision, • There are problems with maintaining the cleanliness of the horizontal slats, due to settling of dust, • Unpleasant noise may be generated when the set-up of the slats is being changed.

4.1.2 Interior Blinds

Interior systems are not effective in terms of thermal protection, but investors prefer this solution because of cost-efficiency and the fact that they are not exposed to damaging atmospheric impacts. They are also popular among users, because they are flexible and may be adjusted to individual preferences, offer easy access and operation. They are important elements of the aesthetics of the interiors, but, as such, are also subject of hygienic and sanitary requirements. In the case of glass facades and double pane windows, it is possible to fit various types of movable blinds (venetian blinds, roller blinds) into the sealed space between the panes. In comparison with interior shields, such solution is more durable and it is easier to maintain cleanliness, because the material of the blinds or the slats , or other accessories are protected against dust, dirt and other pollutants.

Tables 5-8. Hospital buildings-advantages and disadvantages of interior sun protection systems (elaborated by the authors on the bases of [1-3], [5-8])

Table 5.

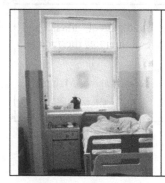

Interior roller blinds
They are made of fabrics of varying light permeability, from partly transparent, to completely opaque; they come in different colours and patterns, resistant to the impact of sun rays; in one colour, multi-coloured, with overprints, Jacquard, etc. Moreover, the market offers attested, antiseptic, antibacterial, anti-allergic fabrics.
Example of use:

Fig. 11. Pediatric And Oncology Children's Center In Chorzów (photo. Magdalena Jamrozik-Szatanek)

Table 5. (*continued*)

Advantages:	Disadvantages:
• They constitute important elements of interior design, but also aesthetic elements of glazed surfaces visible from the outside, • Roller blinds with runners reduce the circulation of heated air and, to a certain extent, protect against cooling the rooms at cold nights (at daytime, the blinds are usually rolled up to let in sun-light), • There is an option of using inflammable fabrics.	• Less effective than exterior sun protection systems, because the heat partially remains between the fabric and the pane, • At a low angle of sun rays infiltration, discomforting dazzle may occur, or the necessity of rolling down and using artificial light, • The blinds made of materials in strong colors may evoke disrupted reception of colors in the interior space, which may be detrimental for the psychical condition of patients, but may also make it difficult for doctors to assess the condition of the patient (for example: apparent paleness or skin flush).

Table 6.

	**Venetian blinds** Lamellas are made of various materials: aluminum, wood, or wood-like materials, in a wide range of colors. Example of use: **Fig. 12.** Mayer Children's Hospital in Florence (photo. Magdalena Jamrozik-Szatanek)

Advantages:	Disadvantages:
• They provide moderate light distribution- it should be taken into account that the blinds as such should not function as secondary source of dazzle, • In the summertime they may contribute to temperature reduction in the interior space by 5-7°C, whereas, in the wintertime temperature increase by 2°C, • For the sake of energy-efficiency, automatic control of the blinds is recommended in synchronization with darkening fluorescent lamps.	• They limit the view from the exteriors, and, partially, from the interiors, • At sunny days they may generate disturbing streaky/patterned shadows, • Pollutants can easily settle on horizontal lamellas and their cleaning is very time-consuming.

Table 7.

Vertical blinds
They make it possible to shade glazed surfaces with big dimensions, the rails are mounted to the ceiling or the wall and may be bend into an arch according to specified and customized dimensions. A wide range of colors, textures and materials- fabrics, PVC, with different properties.
Example of use:

Fig. 13. Children's Rehabilitation Center in Radziszow (photo. Magdalena Jamrozik-Szatanek)

Advantages:	Disadvantages:
• Rotary vertical lamellas may be easily and precisely adjusted to achieve the required quantity and direction of the incoming sunlight, • They constitute an important interior design element , yet, when used on big glazed surfaces may essentially influence the aesthetics of the facade colour-lines.	• Due to considerable weight of long material strips, mounted only at the top, damages to the chain mechanism may occur at frequent use, also, similarly to roller blinds made of colourful materials, they may have a negative impact on the assessment of colours of interiors.

Table 8.

Hangings
They are fabrics hinged without restraints and can be moved along the mounting rail and their important quality is the decorative function.
Example of use:

Fig. 14. Mayer Children's Hospital in Florence (photo. Magdalena Jamrozik-Szatanek)

Advantages:	Disadvantages:
• If the material is property selected, they may contribute to the deadening of sounds and partly reduce heat losses from glazes surfaces, their main function is to separate patients from other room-mates; they are usually hung up on frame constructions by the beds, but not in front of the windows.	• They are less flexible as far as sun-light protection is concerned, as when drawn, they cause complete visual isolation along the entire height of the window.

5   Conclusions

In consideration of a specific nature of hospital buildings, each of the above mentioned systems should be assessed in consideration of: possibility of a compromise between the required, for sanitary and hygiene reasons, sun lighting and sun protection, possibility of providing visual contact with the external environment; color schemes of the material which may change due to temperature (vertical blinds and roller blinds); generation of annoying contrasts and patterned shades (venetian blinds or imprints on glass); maintaining cleanliness; potential for creating the aesthetics of the interiors and facades; energy-efficiency and effectiveness in providing a feeling of comfort in the interiors.

After the recapitulation of professional literature studies and the research performed by the authors of the paper in hospital buildings, it may be stated that none of the discussed solutions is perfect. In view of the effectiveness of sun-protection, exterior systems seem to be the best solution, but, the demand for interior blinds is bigger. Roller blinds or vertical blinds are preferred by patients, because they provide an option of individual adjustment. However, special attention should be given to the selection of the materials, and preference given to fabrics in pastel colors, without imprints, inflammable, antiseptic and anti-allergic. As far as hospitals are concerned, systems difficult to adjust should be avoided, especially, if they restrict the view from the windows (for example: big-size vertical blinds). Likewise, systems generating streaky/ patterned shadows (venetian blinds, glass with imprints) or other patterns are undesirable. Technical and accessory rooms located at lower parts of the building façade may be protected by anti-break systems, but this solution is not recommended in patients' rooms. It seems that the best compromise is to choose sets of double-glazed windows with sun protection shields placed in the sealed space between the panes. Such solution combines the advantages of interior blinds, as they have an aesthetic potential, are more efficient as far as sun-protection is concerned, and, provide the insulation against the impact of pollutants (both internal and external). This may be a reference or benchmarking solution for hospital solutions. The entire positive effect of sun-protection systems may be achieved by adjusting different configuration of panes in sets (protection against sunlight, low-emission, sound-proof, self-cleaning), operated manually or by electric drives.

References

1. Altomonte, S.: Daylight and the occupant. Visual and physio-psychological well-being in built environments. In: Plea 2009 - 26th Conference on Passive and Low Energy Quebec City, Canada (June 22-24, 2009)
2. Boyce, P., Hunter, C., Howlett, O.: The Benefits of Daylight through Windows. Lighting Research Center, Renssellaer Polytechnik Institute, Troy New York (2003)
3. Daylight in Buildings. A source book on daylighting systems and components, the International Energy Agency (IEA) Solar Heating and Cooling Programme, Energy Conservation in Buildings & Community Systems, A report of IEA SHC Task 21/ ECBCS Annex 29. Lawrence Berkeley National Laboratory, Berkeley (July 2000)

4. Jamrozik – Szatanek, M.: Research on Social Space in rehabilitation hospital for children in Radziszow, ACEE Architecture, Civil Engineering, Environment No. 2/2013, the Silesian University of Technology, Gliwice, pp. 5–11 (2013)
5. Sawali, D. (ed.): Vademecum of Sun-shading Techniques. Consortium Publisher. Wydawnictwo Konsorcjum: Somfy, Anwis, heroal, Hörmann, Dragon (2009) (in Polish)
6. Tymkiewicz, J.: Functions of the Exterior Walls of Buildings in View of Quality Analyses. The Impact of Architectural Design Solutions of Facades on the Quality of Building. Publishing House of the Silesian University of Technology, Gliwice (2012) (in Polish), http://repolis.bg.polsl.pl/dlibra/docmetadata?id=17876
7. Tymkiewicz, J.: Sun-shading Systems – Advantages and Disadvantages of Various Solutions. Technical Journal 2-A/2/2011, 213–220 (2011) (in Polish), https://suw.biblos.pk.edu.pl/resources/i5/i4/i6/i9/r5469/TymkiewiczJ_SystemyOslon.pdf
8. Tymkiewicz, J.: Guidelines for Programming and Modernizing Facades as a Follow up of Users' Needs Analyses, ACEE Architecture, Civil Engineering, Environment No. 1/2008, the Silesian University of Technology, Gliwice, pp. 37–46 (2008), http://www.acee-journal.pl

Notheime – Ergonomically Designed Crisis Houses of the Building Cooperative "Schlesische Heimstätte"[*]

Jadwiga Urbanik

Wrocław University of Technology, Faculty of Architecture,
Institute of History of Architecture, Arts and Technology
jadwiga.urbanik@pwr.wroc.pl

Abstract. In Germany after World War I in years 1918-1923 inflation was a decisive negative economic factor. Since 1923 the inflation process started to increase suddenly. Since July 1923 German currency lost its function of means of payment. Cash was changed into valuables as quickly as possible. Economic development was totally crippled.

In Wrocław need for flats was enormous. It was much bigger than in other German cities. In June 1919 building cooperative "Schlesische Heimstätte", provinzielle Wohnungsfürsorgegesellschaft m.b.H (Silesian Homestead, provincial company supporting housing construction, Ltd.), was founded in Wrocław as part of Prussian housing act. It acted under the aegis of Ministry of Social Care.

In the first years after WWI, at the time of great postwar crisis, Ernst May - a young architect beginning his career, was appointed as a manager of "Schlesische Heimstätte". The company was to supply people of modest means with healthy and properly furnished flats at low prices.

In the first half of the twenties so called crises houses (*Notheime*) were proposed. The propositions of the smallest houses were introduced in 1919-1920. They were dwelling summer houses with a room, small barn and toilet. They were to be enlarged or replaced with new buildings after the economic situation would have improved.

Because of the lack of building materials after WWI, building cooperatives used substitute materials. Traditional natural materials were recommended in all designs – walls built from bricks and plastered, wooden truss and roof covered with tile. In order to find cheap solutions old local building materials were used. Walls could be built from dried clay blocks, limestone, calcareous slag or wood. Shingled or even thatched roof houses were suggested.

A lot of attention was paid for economically and ergonomically designed layout of crises houses. They were to solve the enormous dwelling problems in Wrocław and Silesia.

Keywords: interwar period, "Schlesische Heimstätte", dwelling houses, crisis houses, *Notheime*.

---

[*] Text is based on Research Project funded by National Science Centre, Poland; Project no. 2011/01/B/HS3/00753.

C. Stephanidis and M. Antona (Eds.): UAHCI/HCII 2014, Part IV, LNCS 8516, pp. 303–313, 2014.
© Springer International Publishing Switzerland 2014

1   Introduction

In years 1918-1923 inflation was in Germany a decisive negative economic factor. Since 1923 the inflation process started to increase suddenly. Since July 1923 German currency lost its function of means of payment. Cash was changed into valuables as quickly as possible. Economic development was totally crippled.

In Wrocław need for flats was enormous. It was much bigger than in other German cities. Although a number of flats built here was as large as in, for example, Berlin, it was still not enough. Wrocław municipality gave an account of the worst housing conditions.

In June 1919 building cooperative "Schlesische Heimstätte", provinzielle Wohnungsfürsorgegesellschaft m.b.H (Silesian Homestead, provincial company supporting housing construction, Ltd.), was founded in Wrocław as part of Prussian housing act. It acted under the aegis of Ministry of Social Care. [1-5] It existed till 1941.

The partners of this company were: Prussian state, Silesian province, almost all country second levels of local government administration, a lot of districts and building cooperatives as well as Schlesische Landgesellschaft. In 1925 construction office employed about 40 people and had its branches in Jelenia Góra (former Hirschberg), Legnica (former Liegnitz) and Wałbrzych (former Waldenburg).

It specialized in building small and functional houses for people of modest means and worked out a catalogue of ready designs

In 1919 Ernst May, was appointed as a manager of "Schlesische Heimstätte". May was under big influence of movement for protection of native lands (Heimatschutzbewegung). He simply paid attention to traditional architecture. [4] The company was to supply people of modest means with healthy and properly furnished flats at low prices. Own house with a garden, was the long - awaited ideal and was connected with a possibility of growing own food. In hard economic times occupants - to - be quite often helped to build their future houses.

Architectural and urban planning concepts were to draw inspirations on Silesian countryside buildings. The buildings were to remind old houses and agricultural homestead.

After 1918, in order to lower construction costs, standardization and streamlining of construction processes were propagated. Standardization turned out to be a superior feature of "Schlesische Heimstätte" company's construction despite its traditional, often rural look.

In construction office of "Schlesische Heimstätte", a catalogue of one - and multi - family houses were worked out.

May put emphasis on rational, functional and economic lay out of a flat where kitchen consisting of a dwelling part and cooking niche, was a central place. This type of flat was very common in Silesia.

Because of the lack of building materials after WWI, building cooperatives used substitute materials. Traditional natural materials were recommended in all designs – walls built from bricks and plastered, wooden truss and roof covered with tile. [6] In order to find cheap solutions old local building materials were used. Walls could be built from dried clay blocks, limestone, calcareous slag or wood. Shingled or even thatched roof houses were suggested. [7]

2   Model Houses from the 1921 and 1922 Breslau Fairs

In Germany, after the First World War, prices in the housing industry raised 40 – 50 times compared to the pre-war period. Small residential houses, self-constructed by the estate owners were seen as a solution to the housing shortage problem. Many such houses were built in the immediate post war period, especially in the countryside. It was seen as its duty by Schlesische Heimstätte to support this movement in any way necessary.

"Schlesische Heimstätte" company presented a house with centring roof covered with clay shingle at Wrocław Building Fairs in 1921. [8-9] Three walls of the house were erected in "Schima" construction from fired airbrick which, because of larger size and smaller weight, allowed to build faster than from traditional brick. The fourth wall was made from clay hollow bricks produced by "Schlesische Heimstätte" company. The company constructed a machine to produce such bricks. With its help it was possible to make use of the clay being on side. [4]

Fig. 1. Model Schlesische Heimstätte house from the 1921 Breslau Fairs (Source: Schlesisches Heim, 2, no.5, p.114)

The Schlesische Heimstätte exhibition pavilion in the 1922 Breslau Technical Fair was redesigned according to the DIY ethos. Architectural consulting was seen as the company's main field of activity. The quest for more efficient solutions was dictated by constantly raising costs of construction materials and transport. A DIY house was designed to be basic and simplistic. All the necessary construction work should have been possible to accomplish by non-specialist workers.

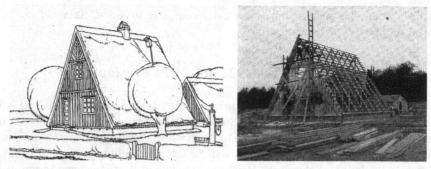

Fig. 2. Model Schlesische Heimstätte house from the 1922 Breslau Technical Fair (Source: Schlesisches Heim, 3, no.5, p.110)

The 10000% rise in the roof tiles' costs forced constructors to eliminate such expensive materials and substitute them with more readily available ones. The DIY house from the Technical Fair was erected without any outer walls – mainly as a wooden structure.

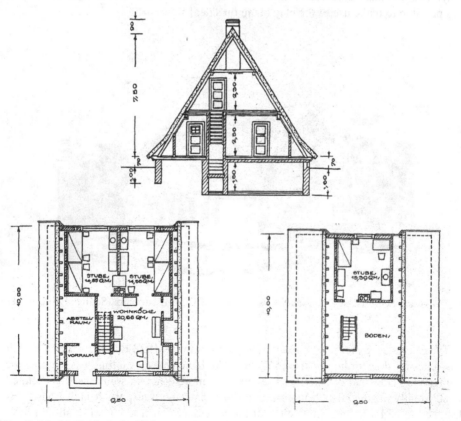

Fig. 3. Model Schlesische Heimstätte house from the 1922 Breslau Technical Fair (Source: Schlesisches Heim, 3, no.5, p.111)

The beam which held the gable roof was supported on the first floor level by the low foundations made of field stone, crushed stone, bricks, concrete etc. This solution had a great advantage: it completely eliminated the need for costly materials for the outer walls. The house was painted with saturated colours. The intended roof covering was made from clay and straw thatch (clay shingles) and assembled by the owner.

The collar beams on the first and second floor level supported the rafter to prevent it from collapsing. They served as a construction holding the ceiling and propped the attic floor (under the ridge). A system of pillars and purlins made of roughly hewn logs complemented the rafter. The roof covering made of clay soaked thatch (clay shingles) was put on this structural frame. The walls between the wooden construction poles were made of straw cemented with clay (if it was available near the construction site). Such walls were pasted with straw and clay from the inside and then reinforced with reed or wood and plaster. The gables were covered with bituminous felt and wooden facing made of unplaned planks. To improve the durability of the building, wooden parts were coated with karbolineum. The roof was covered with clay shingles. The main room in the house was a traditional living room-kitchen (Wohnküche) connected with two double bedrooms. Besides, there were also stairs leading above to the attic and one additional living room. [10,11].

3 Crisis Houses – Notheime

The extreme price increase after the WWI (over 8 times for a m2) brought about the search for more economic methods of house building. The easiest way to cut the costs was size reduction. They took pattern from the small traditional cottage houses (sized 4x6 m) of the Riesengebirge (Karkonosze) region. Another source of inspiration was the social housing complex founded in the XVI century by Jacob Fugger in Augsburg. The lodgings of the Fuggerei consisted of only the most basic chambers. Architects of the time drew their ideas from the above mentioned examples to design the crisis house – Notheime. [12].

The proposals of the smallest houses were introduced in 1919-1920. They were crisis houses (dwelling summer houses) with a room, small barn and toilet. They were to be enlarged or replaced with new buildings after the economic situation would have improved. [7]. However, they were never mass-produced. [4]

The VI group's 7a type building has been suggested for the country environment. It was situated further back, 10-12 m from the building line. In better economic situation, the house could have been transformed into a utility building with a proper residence built by the street. The 7a type was intended to be a temporary residence for a 5 member family.

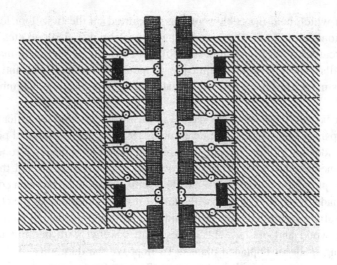

Fig. 4. The dwelling estate plan with crises houses, group VI, type 7a (Source:Schlesisches Heim, 1, no.2, p.3)

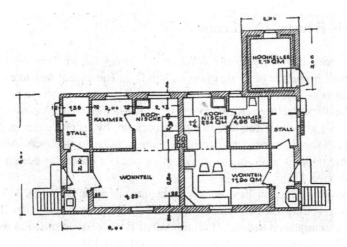

Fig. 5. Crises house, group VI, type 7a (Source: Schlesisches Heim, 1, no.2, p.2)

Fig. 6. Crises house, group VI, type 7a (Source: Schlesisches Heim, 1, no.2, p.3)

Tiny hall of 2m2 served as a vestibule and a passage leading to the toilet and barn (for goats, rabbits and chickens). It was also connected with the basement of 9m2. The main room was the living room-kitchen of 17m2, divided between the living room section and the kitchen niche. The living room section contained parent's bed and dining space. A furnace, kitchen stove, sink, food locker and a folding table filled in the kitchen niche.

Fig. 7. Crises house, living room-kitchen (Wohnküche), group VI, type 7a (Source: Schlesisches Heim, 1, no.2, p.4)

Fig. 8. Crises house, kitchen niche, group VI, type 7a (Source: Schlesisches Heim, 1, no.2, p.4)

Ship cabin and sleeping car patterned children bedroom contained two or three bunk beds, big wardrobe and a folding table. It was accessible from the kitchen niche. Such layout allowed the space to be easily warmed and illuminated. The attic, accessible by the outer staircase and the door in the gable was used for storing the crops and drying clothes. Particular furniture, specifically adapted to such small spaces has been also designed.

Fig. 9. Bed room in crises house (Source: Schlesisches Heim, 1, no.3, p.16)

The III group, type 4 crisis house served for residential purposes only. In this case the dimensions of the interior space were also minimized. It was primarily aimed at families with children, but could also be inhabited by young couples, singles, disabled or retired people. It was possible to join the buildings into rows to use the terrain more economically. It was specifically utilized in urban environment, on 200m2 parcels. Small vestibule was connected with habitable kitchen and tiny bedroom. There was also utility space situated in the back of the house.

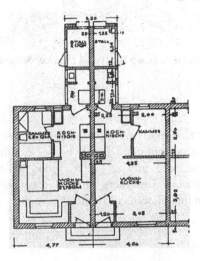

Fig. 10. Crises house, group III, type 4 (Source: Schlesisches Heim, 1, no.2, p.6)

Fig. 11. Crises house, street view, group III, type 4 (Source: Schlesisches Heim, 1, no.2, p.8)

Fig. 12. Crises house, garden view, group III, type 4 (Source: Schlesisches Heim, 1, no.2, p.8)

4   Conclusions

The crisis houses project from post-war years in Breslau and Silesia province was a reaction to the, so called, tenement multi-family houses existing in the big cities. Single-family house, even reduced in size, was a good alternative for narrow and crowded tenement apartments. Designers utilized ergonomic methods in interior planning suitable for the minimal needs of future inhabitants.

References

1. Kononowicz, W.: Wrocławskie dokonania urbanisty i architekta Ernsta Maya w latach 1919-1925 – etapem w drodze do funkcjonalnego Frankfurtu. Kwartalnik Architektury i Urbanistyki 55, 3–38 (2010)
2. Ludwig, B.: Osiedla mieszkaniowe w krajobrazie wałbrzyskiego okręgu górniczo-przemysłowego (1850-1945). Oficyna Wydawnicza Politechniki Wrocławskiej, Wrocław (2010)
3. Ludwig, B.: Ochrona wartości krajobrazowych w projektach osiedli autorstwa spółki "Schlesisches Heim" pod kierunkiem Ernsta Maya na Dolnym Śląsku. Kwartalnik Architektury i Urbanistyki 56, 3–22 (2011)
4. Störtkuhl, B.: Ernst May i Schlesische Heimstätte. In: Quiring, C., Voigt, W., Cachola Schmal, P., Herrel, E., (eds. German edition), Ilkosz, J. (ed. Polish edition) Ernst May 1886-1970, pp. 23–31. Muzeum Architektury in Wrocław, Wrocław (2012)
5. Urbanik, J.: Schlesische Heimstätte. In: Eysymontt, R., Ilkosz, J., Tomaszewicz, A., Urbanik, J. (eds.) Leksykon Architektury Wrocławia, p. 1020. Via Nova, Wrocław (2011)
6. Lübbert: Eine billige Bauweise. Schlesisches Heim 1(6), 2–4 (1920)
7. May, E.: Können wir noch bäuerliche Siedlungen treiben? Schlesisches Heim 1(9), 4–7 (1920)
8. Ausstellungshaus des Schlesischen Heimes auf der Breslauer Messe. Schlesisches Heim 2(5), 114–119 (1921)

9. May, E.: Der Lehmbau Brandprobe eines Lehmschindeldaches anläßlich der technischen Messe in Breslau am 5.Juni 1921. Schlesisches Heim 2(6), 168–170 (1921)
10. May, E.: Das Ausstellungshaus der Schlesischen Heimstätte auf der Breslauer Technischen Messe. Schlesisches Heim 3(5), 109–112 (1922)
11. Schlesisches Heim 4(1) (1923)
12. May, E.: Notheime. Schlesisches Heim 1(2), 1–10 (1920)

Ergonomic Solutions of Facilities and Laboratory Work-Stands at Universities

Programming of Ergonomic Technological Lines – Case Study

Dorota Winnicka-Jasłowska

Department of the Theory, Design and History of Architecture
Faculty of Architecture, Silesian University of Technology
Akademicka 7, 44-100 Gliwice
Poland
Dorota.Winnicka-Jaslowska@polsl.pl

Abstract. The scope of the paper is the design of laboratories in consideration of modern technologies and modern manners of work: ways of shaping and arranging laboratory facilities, depending on the equipment and process technology. Following the introduction, the functional and spatial programming process of laboratory stands at the Faculty of Bio-Medical Engineering, Silesian University of Technology, devised by the author of this paper will be discussed.

Keywords: laboratory work-stand, universities, ergonomic solutions.

1 Introduction

Didactics, experience and research and development activities require new space. University R&D facilities are used for analyses on the didactic level, as well as research, development works and experiments conducted by the research and teaching staff. These functions are served by laboratories, located in faculty buildings and generally constituting a detached spatial zone, or in a separate building designed for research, development and laboratory works. The laboratory functions are usually essential for the following engineering disciplines: biology, chemistry, physics, but also biotechnology, bioengineering, medicine and related fields of science. Computer and telecommunication workshops frequently support specialist laboratories.

Modern laboratories look different than older facilities. Laboratories are generally associated with typical work- stands connected into technology lines and set in a specific sequence. In the face of technological and technical evolution and the advancement of new fields of science, modern labs have undergone a revolutionary metamorphosis, so their image is not the same as in the past.

C. Stephanidis and M. Antona (Eds.): UAHCI/HCII 2014, Part IV, LNCS 8516, pp. 314–321, 2014.
© Springer International Publishing Switzerland 2014

2   Modern Laboratories

2.1   Principles of Arranging Laboratories

Each discipline of knowledge and science has its own specific qualities, characterized by process technology of research and experimental works, special equipment and apparatuses and work procedures. The methods of laboratory work have a significant importance to the arrangement of laboratories; therefore, nowadays linear technology layout of the work-stands is not as popular as in the past.

There are three essential types of work applicable to laboratories:

- interactive work - involving teams and supported by computers
- experimental and individual work performed by one or two researchers at one work-stand, and
- experiment - empirical work carried out by students divided into groups and using one or several work-stands.

Hence, laboratory space should be adjusted to the type of activity and cooperation in the performance of specific tasks. The main objective of the design of laboratories is the provision of safety and efficiency of work at laboratory stands.

Modern R&D activity is nowadays supported by on-line computers, run concurrently with the performance of research work. Accordingly, contemporary lab stands must be enlarged to accommodate hardware. Likewise, modern specialist apparatuses and other equipment are very technologically advanced and used at all levels of research: starting with teaching tasks and leading up to well-developed R&D projects. Thus, in the phase of spatial and architectural programming of laboratories, the provision of sufficient place for apparatuses and supporting installations should be taken into account.

As already mentioned above, computers are indispensible tools of all types of laboratory space, including: generally accessible space of the laboratory, seminar rooms for instruction classes preceding or following laboratory experiments, and the space for specific R&D labs. Computers are used to control the operation of other equipment and apparatuses, to insert the data derived from the experiments, and to on-line cooperation with other work-stands.

Laboratories devoted to R&D projects may be placed in science teaching buildings or grouped in separate laboratory facilities. The space required for research is different from the teaching space, as it is destined to individual or small team work. Yet, the requirements for the mechanical and electrical equipment are very similar for both types of laboratories.

However, research laboratories vary, depending on the disciplines of science. For example, chemical labs require work-stands for each researcher equipped with fume tools. Biological laboratories need a proper stand with easy access to various types of apparatuses. Physical laboratories should have the equipment mounted to the floor and designed in consideration of enabling easy access to electricity and water.

Research laboratories should be adjusted to tasks performed by research teams under the supervision of the project manager, in terms of sufficient floor area. The teams should include 4-8 members. It is also important for the laboratory module to be reproductive and flexible to enable rearrangements of space.[1]

2.2   Supporting Space

Didactic and research works require highly specialized apparatuses and equipment for analytical and experimental tasks. This means that it is essential to provide supporting space in a room adjacent to the lab.

The requirements that such supporting rooms should meet depend on the discipline of science. For example, a chemical lab should be provided with the space for apparatuses placed on desks or on the floor. For the discipline of biology, rooms should accommodate large- size apparatuses, as well as additional desks for smaller equipment. Moreover, biological labs need rooms for cultivation or culture of bacteria, plants, etc. and prep rooms, as well as rooms for controlling the microclimate.

Currently, teaching syllabuses and the tasks that students are to perform need more space for research and education, not to mention space for the equipment frequently used in classes. Usually, such equipment is kept in storage rooms.[1]

The programming of supporting space is only possible when the design architect knows and understands the processes that take place in a laboratory, and insight into the manner of operating apparatuses and equipment to be used. In addition, it is important to consider the microclimate conditions for the supporting rooms.

3   Detailed Regulations Concerning the Architectural Desing of Laboratories in Poland. Work Safety and Hygiene

Buildings containing laboratory facilities should be constructed and maintained in compliance with specific technical and building regulations – and, in particular, as far as safety and hygiene of work is concerned.[3] Laboratory rooms should have identifiable safety exits to secure the evacuation from the building in case of safety hazards. They should be marked with symbols stipulated by the provisions of the Polish Standards.[4]

Laboratories should be supplied with the equipment preventing contamination or pollution with chemical substances. The provided installations should enable safety of operation and should not expose workers to electric shocks, fire hazards, explosion hazards and other detrimental impacts. The rooms in which hazards may occur should be clearly marked with warning signs – in compliance with the Polish Standards.

Laboratory work rooms should offer both natural and artificial light, appropriate temperature, air exchange and precautions against humidity, adverse heat conditions and excess sunlight. The height of laboratory rooms should not be lower than 3.3 m. The rooms where hazardous reagents and elements posing a threat to health and safety, should make use of the technical solutions that prevent their penetration to other parts of the laboratory. Work-stands should be protected against uncontrolled heat emission caused by radiation, conduction, convection, and the influx of cold air from the outside. Measuring and testing equipment that may release hazardous gases, vapors and dust should be air-tight. If this is impossible, they should at least have local exhausts. If substances hazardous to health may be released in the course of processes and if there is a possibility of ventilation failure, a warning system should be used. If mechanical ventilation with air circulation is installed, the quantity of fresh air should not be lower than 10 % of the total volume of the exchanged air. However, air recirculation should not be installed in work rooms where hazardous biological or chemical substances pose the hazards stipulated in the regulations on safety and hygiene of work concerning the presence of chemical reagents or materials emitting unpleasant or noxious smells, instant increase of the concentration of hazardous substances or threats of explosion.

4   Functional and Floor Area Design Program for the Laboratories of the Biological Engineering Faculty, Silesian University of Technology – Case Study

4.1   Objectives of the Architectural and Programming Task

The Faculty of Biomedical Engineering, Silesian University of Technology, was founded a few years ago. Initially, it occupied some buildings of the University campus. The creation of the new Faculty and new engineering disciplines of study was planned to be provided in modern laboratories and workshops; hence, the Faculty authorities applied for acquiring a new building, and ordered a programming study for new laboratories. The author of this paper devised initial functional and spatial program of the new laboratories.[2] The introduction to the task were pre-design analyses to define users' needs in consideration of a definite nature of the Faculty, specialization of its Departments and technologies of laboratory processes. As a result, ergonomic "ideal" models were created and model solutions for all the laboratories and workshops specified by the Faculty authorities, with the main focus on the principles of ergonomics, technologies of R&D processes and the planned equipment.

4.2   Description of Date Collection Method and Elaboration of the Design Project

The grounds and input for the research is the identification of basic groups of users and their organizational and social needs. The description of the Faculty's organizational structure with division into organizational units and the number of their users provided supportive material. Next, the users and their activity types were depicted, as well as their organizational needs and, what is of special importance nowadays: their social needs.

In the past years this factor was not taken into account in the design of university buildings. These days other fields of science, such as sociology and environmental psychology offer better insight into social issues and support architects in their design solutions, especially as far as human requirements, such   as the needs of privacy and territoriality, isolation and cooperation are concerned. Students constitute the biggest group of university buildings users, with their specific needs that change the image of a modern university facility. An important element in the conducted research work was the consideration of students' organizational and social needs.

In the case of any design that will house an institution, it is essential to understand the objectives of its activity, modes of operation and planned or predicted organizational and technical and technological changes. Organizational changes are of great importance and they should translate into the manner in which space is shaped. Forecasts of further development of organizations such as university units, faculties etc. have an impact on design assumptions. Yet, it is spatial solutions that determine the efficiency of current and future functionality of a given organizational structure.

It is also vital to assume the number of users of the designed building. The quantity of the users is subject of change in the whole life cycle of the building: it may increase or decrease and change its proportions. Nonetheless, an approximation is important as it enables the formulation of a strategy of efficient space management of the facility, for example, if the number of students' declines, some class rooms, lecture rooms or even parts of the building may be leased.

On the other hand, if the number of students or teaching staff increases, some space reserves should be available, so that the surplus of space that occurred in some periods of the functional life of the building could be rented or utilized for organizing such events as conferences or exhibitions.

Another cognitive step in the discussed research is to determine appropriate teaching and learning conditions. The starting points are the curricula and knowledge of the manner in which classes, lectures and workshops for students are conducted. It should be remembered that every university, and even its particular faculties, have specific spatial requirements and functional types of facilities; beside class rooms, lecture rooms or seminars, there are others specific to a given field of study, such as laboratories or studios equipped with devices and aids typical of a given faculty.

In the case of the Bio-Medical Engineering Faculty these are laboratories and work rooms used by students during instruction hours and by the research and teaching staff. Each of the four Faculty Departments has its specialist equipment set-up in a specific technology line and having specific dimensions, which is very important in designating the size and proportions of rooms. Therefore, it was necessary to conduct the site inspection of the existing specialist facilities.

For each of the inspected facilities photographic inventory was carried out as well as general physical measurements taken. The required data included: basic dimensions- length and width, examination of the equipment and technology line, as well as information on the type of activity and manners of equipment use and operation.

The information was collected from interviews with the users (both university staff and students) and from the in-situ inspection with participation of all parties concerned. In each room photographic documentation was taken, which was helpful in making records of the equipment and its arrangement. The interviews also involved the assessment of the facilities in terms of size, functionality and equipment, enabling the formulation of conclusions valuable for devising an ergonomic model of an "ideal 'new room. The information obtained from university staff also included functional connections among laboratories and the sequence of their use in the teaching process typical of a certain study line, for example: seminars that introduce students to laboratory classes, in order to consider the functional need of their proximity.

During the in-situ inspection data on specific requirements and technical conditions that the facilities should fulfil was also collected: micro-climate, lighting conditions (exposure to sunlight or location oriented to the north due to the need of providing lower temperature and elimination of the access of sunlight, or additional lighting of work-stands, etc.), allowable noise emissions levels and vibrations (evoked by some equipment, as well as their potential negative impact on other precise apparatuses, for example on electronic microphones), allowable ambient temperature, ventilation, air-conditioning, etc.

Detailed interviews with the teaching and research staff were conducted to obtain information necessary for designing new laboratories and work rooms, to enable precise determination of the technological aspects of work stands and the space required.

After the analytical and data collection phase, the next step was focused on devising ergonomic models of "ideal" new rooms. On the grounds of information and criticism derived from the staff it was possible to devise best solutions concerning the spatial arrangement and square area of the planned facilities, taking into account the modularity of the facilities to facilitate the transformation of schematically drawn solution to specific design solutions.

Next, focus meetings were arranged with the university staff to discuss the proposed solutions of laboratory functions. Such meetings are held in small groups consisting of carefully selected people who can contribute to the rectification of the proposed solutions. Staff members representing the four Faculty Departments also actively participated in the process of devising model solutions concerning office space and facilitating the adoption of the most suitable ones in terms of the Faculty's organizational needs. Stage I was finalized by correcting the drawings and schemes and preparing the draft of the program.

4.3   Results of the Analyses

The final elaboration included Check-Lists for each laboratory in view of: the inventory of the existing conditions, specific requirements and graphic model solutions.   In the case of completely new laboratories, the Check List contained complete information on the apparatuses, with their dimensions and photographs and graphic presentations of model solutions. Thus, the elaboration comprised a set of the preferred laboratories, and input material for the subsequent design concept. Before the concept emerged, the elaboration helped the new Faculty to decide whether the new laboratories could be arranged in the buildings offered by the University authorities and adjusted for the needs of the Faculty of Biomedical Engineering. Accordingly, thanks to the elaboration the optimal surface area of the laboratories was defined.

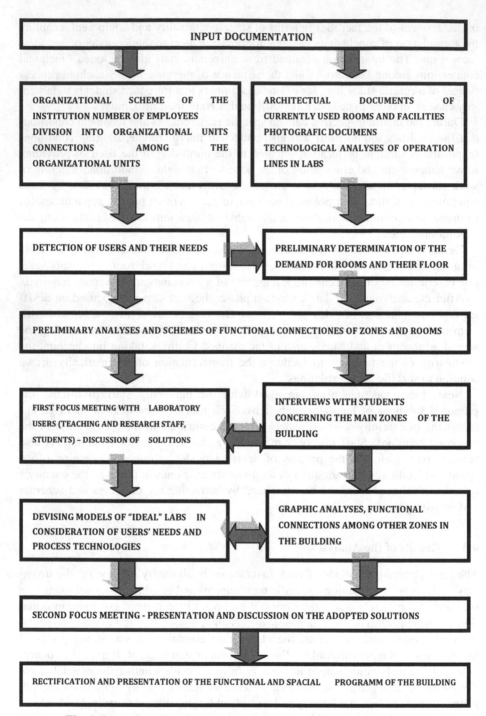

Fig. 1. Research Project Diagram. (Author: Dorota Winnicka-Jasłowska)

5   Conclusions

The detection of the functioning rules of a future building in consideration of didactic, research and development and social processes that it houses contributes to the formulation of elaborate functional and spatial program for the newly designed building. The complexity of laboratory technologies utilized by particular Departments requires profound pre-design analyses, without which it would be practically impossible to design the research and laboratory zones that make up essential parts of the Faculty building. The visits and in-situ inspections in the existing Departments explicated and enabled the understanding of the essence of the processes involved in the teaching and research activities of the Faculty staff. Interviews with the Faculty staff also indicated different modes of student instruction in comparison with, for example, the Faculty of Architecture, specific to the field of study, which, surely, have a definite impact on the shape of the interior space and functional solutions (for example: location of seminar rooms in the vicinity of laboratories. Accordingly, it may be concluded that every type of a university and its particular faculties should fulfill the requirements specific to a given field of study. Thus, design templates cannot be used. This applies to the majority of functional zones and types of rooms in university facilities, as substantiated by all analyses of existing university buildings carried out by the author of this paper, revealing frequently occurring errors in the understanding of specific features, field of study and the associated activities. The pre-design analysis discussed in the paper was also made to "try out" data collection and processing methods and to propose and select best solutions.

References

1. Neuman, D.J., Kliment, S.A.: Series Founder and Editor: Building Type Basics For College and University Facilities, pp. 121–133. John Wiley & Sons, Inc. (2003)
2. Winnicka-Jasłowska, D.: Creating a Functional and Space Program for New Building of Faculty of the Biomedical Engineering Building, Silesian University of Technology. In: Ajdukiewicz, A. (ed.) ACEE-Architecture, Civil Engineering, Environment, vol. 5(3), pp. 41–50. Gaudeo, Gliwice (2012), http://www.acee-journal.pl
3. http://www.bhp.abc.com.pl
4. e.g. PN-N-01256-5:1998: Znaki bezpieczeństwa – Zasady umieszczania znaków bezpieczeństwa na drogach ewakuacyjnych i drogach pożarowych (Safety Signs - Principles of Safety Signs for Escape Routes and Fire Road)

Global Access Infrastructures

PGA: Preferences for Global Access

Richard Schwerdtfeger [1], Gregg C. Vanderheiden[2], Jutta Treviranus[3], Colin Clark[3],
Jess Mitchell[3], Lisa Petrides[4], Lisa McLaughlin[4], Cynthia Jimes[4], Jim Tobias[5],
Sheri Trewin[1], and Michelle Brennan[3]

[1] IBM, Austin TX, USA
{schwer,trewin}@us.ibm.com
[2] Trace R&D Center Madison Wi & Raising the Floor – International, Geneva, Switzerland
Gregg@raisingthefloor.org
[3] Inclusive Design Research Center, OCAD University, Toronto, Ontario, Canada
{jtreviranus,cclark,jmitchell,mbrennan}@ocadu.ca
[4] Institute for the Study of Knowledge Management in Education, Half-Moon Bay CA, USA
{lisa,lisam,cynthia}@iskme.org
[5] Inclusive Technologies, Matawan NJ, USA
tobias@inclusive.com

Abstract. This paper highlights the research for year one of the Preferences for
Global Access (PGA) project whose long term goal is to define a cross-platform
preference acquisition system to acquire a user's needs and preferences for accessing Information and Communication Technology (ICT) as part of a cloud-
based Global Public Inclusive Infrastructure (GPII).

Keywords: accessibility cloud GPII inclusive.

1 Background and Need

Each year, our daily activities are increasingly mediated in some way by digital technologies -- from point-of-sale devices, to self-service kiosks, to Internet-based services, to name a few. Access to these technologies has gone from optional to essential as
more traditional ways of doing things are replaced with devices having digital interfaces: Agents are becoming kiosks, books are becoming eBooks, and parking meters
are becoming digital fare stations. As such, the ability to use digital technologies is all
but required for full participation in commercial, cultural, recreational and social
activities. Yet today, millions of people are not able to access these technologies.

While there have been advances in accessibility features embedded in native platforms and websites, and while advocacy toward accessible user interfaces and content
design continues, most applications and products are designed as one-size-fits-all
solutions. For example, if users are blind pictures are replaced with text, and if users
do not use a mouse, keyboard navigation is activated. This approach fails to recognize
the heterogeneity of individuals and the different contexts they operate. Access issues
arise for multiple reasons, including breakdowns between the technology's interface
and a user's ability to engage with it, and compatibility of access solutions with a

C. Stephanidis and M. Antona (Eds.): UAHCI/HCII 2014, Part IV, LNCS 8516, pp. 325–336, 2014.
© Springer International Publishing Switzerland 2014

user's device or with a user's context or setting. Additionally a user's functional disability may be temporary or permanent, stable or progressive. This means that a user may have shifting needs over time that move within or between certain diagnoses. In sum, accessibility solutions designed for people with a specific disability diagnosis are not fully inclusive, and only provide support for individuals whose problems can be described as "typical" for that diagnosis. The result has been a limited set of solutions that work for some, but exclude many.

The predominant one-size-fits-all approaches not only affect the "goodness of fit" and thereby effectiveness of the solutions, but also remove the ability of individuals to control the interfaces they must use. Whether embedded in the design of products or services, or embodied in the clinical interventions that arrogate such decisions to certified authorities, current solutions potentially deny agency—the sense of autonomy made concrete by action—to users. In doing so, these solutions can serve to disempower the person who is theoretically best positioned to make his or her own personalization decisions and to learn from those decisions.

The result of factors such as these is that many users are dissatisfied with their assistive technology (AT) systems (Hastings Kraskowsky & Finlayson, 2001), and many report underutilizing or abandoning their systems altogether (Reimer-Weiss & Wacker, 2000). In attempting to mitigate these factors, this project seeks to replace a one-size-fits-all, "inoculation model" of accessibility—one assessment and prescription for all time—with an approach that is more accurately developmental and attuned to technological churn. We seek to enable users with sensory or physical limitations, cognitive constraints, unique learning affordances, or other barriers to discover and articulate their needs and preferences for specific contexts, in an unobtrusive yet helpful way. Enabling users to explore preferences and to learn how to improve their experience with technology can have a significant impact on users' ability to remove the barriers to access that they experience.

2   PGA Project Objectives

The PGA project is a multi-year project. Within the scope of this project, preferences are defined as functional descriptions of how users prefer to have information presented, how they wish to control any function in the technology application, and settings or commands that are stored (or that will be stored) for them. Preference sets are groups of preferences, which may apply to different contexts or devices. One user may have multiple preference sets, such as preferences for home, for school, for their desktop, or for their mobile device.

This project is focused on creating, refining and maintaining preference sets for users in order to support **access to information communication technology (ICT)**, including technologies, tools, devices and resources; **ease of use of ICT** by all users, including non-technical users; and **increased participation** by individuals in all of the activities that require ICT or that ICT can enable, including the activities that establish their needs and preferences.

The specific objectives of this project (Year One and beyond) are to:

1. Provide a knowledge base on proposed user preference gathering systems for people with disabilities, including expert judgment on how best to assist users in specifying the appropriate aspects of these preferences.

2. Develop a system of tools and technological architecture that supports creation of user preferences for people with disabilities, is operable as a Web application or system of applications that reflects expert judgment, and supports continuing evolution of the content of user preferences and of the means of assistance provided to users. These tools should:

   ▪ Allow users to create initial preference sets and preference sets for different contexts;

   ▪ Encourage users to manage their preference set(s) through direct manipulation/editing, and by responding to suggestions created by inference engines monitoring their use and contexts—the aim being to support users over time, as their needs and preferences change, and as they develop increased understanding of what they require and what works best for them through the use of the tools;

   ▪ Engage users, reduce the time it takes them to acquire their preferences, and allow them to quickly make changes to those preferences throughout the lifecycle of interacting with ICT; and

   ▪ Be appropriate to different user groups—from power users to those who have limited experience with technology; to users who may not know what they want and need; to users of different ages, in different environments, and who utilize different technologies.

3. Aggregate and refine knowledge regarding what works for specific needs and preferences from a variety of knowledge sources including professionals, user feedback, and usage metrics, so that this can be used to guide the user in selecting preferences

4. Encourage ongoing development of preference tools within the community at large

3 Challenges

In addition to the challenges in Section 1, there are a number of complicating factors that make the creation of preference tools particularly difficult to do well.

3.1 Diversity of the Users

In considering all of the different types and degrees of disability that an individual may have, it is apparent that complex patterns of user needs occur even within a single disability type. The needs of someone who is completely blind, for example, are different from someone who has low vision and can see but cannot read text. And the needs of the individual who cannot read text are different from an individual who requires screen magnification for readability. Furthermore, individuals can and often do have one or more disability concurrently—including a combination of both physical and cognitive disabilities. At the same time, individuals vary in terms of their technological self-efficacy, and some may not use computers at all. Accessibility solutions must be flexible and responsive enough to balance the need to overcome serious barriers to entry with the need to showcase diverse preference possibilities to users who are interested in them. Ultimately, accessibility solutions must meet the unique needs of each user.

3.2   Cognitive Access

Cognitive needs potentially impact the widest number of users; however, accessibility standards and solutions have not done an adequate job of addressing this group of users (Hudson et al., 2004). This is due to several factors, including the complexity and wide variation in the realm of cognitive needs, that there is a lack of developer education on the needs of cognitively impaired users, and that there is a lack of a single vehicle for capturing cognitive needs. When solutions do exist, they are either specialized stand-alone solutions with limited scope or are limited to a single application or web browser. In some cases, a limited focus on necessary requirements to specific cognitive constraints ignore their incongruence—and in some cases incompatibility—with preference solutions for other disabilities.

There is also an inherent paradox: some of the solutions intended to support individuals with cognitive needs, such as the timing and modality of reminder messages, may be beyond the cognitive ability of the user to comprehend and accurately select these preferences. This raises the potential role of assistance or helpers in preference collection.

3.3   Personalization

Research has shown that when users are provided with the opportunity to change their preference settings, they rarely do so (Iyengar et al., 2000; Trewin, 2000; Forrester, 2004; Spool, 2011). Trewin (2000) discusses barriers to personalization of preferences for less experienced users in particular, including lack of awareness of available options, lack of knowledge of how to change settings, difficulty identifying the solution to meet a given preference or need, and a lack of control over the unconfigured interface. This presents a challenge, especially in light of the fact that assistive technology (AT) solutions do not provide "session support"—a way for users to easily explore and get assistance if needed when creating or changing settings. A recent study by the Pew Research Center found that 63 percent of non-Internet users would need assistance in getting started on the Internet (Zickurh, 2013). And an earlier study by Pew identified people with disabilities as 27 percentage points less likely to use the Internet than their non-disabled peers (Fox, 2011).

However, the fact that it is difficult for users to understand or configure technology to meet their needs should not be confused with the critical importance of being able to do so. Bridging this gap is one of the key goals of this project.

3.4   Solution Readiness and Awareness

Beyond the complicating factors listed above tied to user-centered design, this project seeks to address the complexities involved in creating scalable software architecture. The creation of globally accessible and highly personalizable solutions require that the software is designed to be easily understood, extended, and adapted for use across many platforms and contexts. One-size-fits-one solutions, which this project seeks to build upon and create, are in the early stages of readiness for mainstream consumption. We foresee that in some cases, challenges may arise due to unwillingness on the part of proprietary platform providers to adopt open source solutions, in other cases, developers may not have a clear understanding of the concepts or systems used to build and implement tools. We must also address interoperability and platform dependency challenges, find ways to support non-experts in understanding and integrating tools into their software systems in a scalable way, and recognize and attempt to address the cost and time intensive implementation processes.

4   PGA Results Year One

The PGA team delivered three critical outputs in the field of accessibility that will have a transformational impact on this project and the industry as a whole: 1) We deepened understanding of the diversity of user preferences, including cognitive access and advocacy momentum to guide new forms of support for users with cognitive impairments; 2) we created the Preference Tool Ecosystem, which is a set of concepts and paradigm-shifting maps for software development toolkits for preference acquisition; and 3) we designed specifications for the Preference Framework—an architectural framework capable of supporting exchange of preference tools and data across platforms and networks.

4.1   Preference Matrix and Cognitive Preferences

The Preferences Matrix, developed as part of our knowledge building work, contains an extended list of disabilities and to include cognitive needs, contextual needs, and individual learning styles with examples of their functional equivalents, or preferences that move beyond existing work in the accessibility and special education literature.

In compiling the preferences matrix our work revealed that although cognitive needs, in particular, potentially impact the widest number of users, accessibility standards and solutions have not done an adequate job of addressing this group of users. The PGA team produced a concise inventory of requirements needed to support users with cognitive impairments that revealed opportunity spaces for advancing the field such as awareness of the deep inadequacy of current digital math solutions capable of serving users with cognitive constraints, insights around the potential impact of widespread use of well-known technological supports like breadcrumbs on access for users with cognitive constraints, and guidance for where to get started in an area long-regarded as too difficult to design for.

4.2   Establishment of Guiding Concepts

In order to successfully build the tools to support preference gathering in line with the PGA project goals and challenges, it was critical to develop ways for understanding how users enter into and move around in preference environments, how to efficiently capture preferences, and which interaction methods and design strategies are most suitable to engage and support users. Thus, to lay the groundwork for the Preference Tool Ecosystem, the team created concepts and conceptualizations around user activity spaces, interaction methods, inference methods, and tool design.

Conceptualized User Activity Spaces. Considering the diversity of users, it became clear in our work that users would require different points of entry into preference collection activities. They would need to choose how, where, and when they engage with the tools, all in light of their context, diverse experiences, attitudes, and access to support. From this foundation of user and contextual diversity, the team identified the activities users would potentially require for meaningful engagement with preferences, and created names for various "activity spaces" users would inhabit.

The five activity spaces developed by the PGA team include:

1. **First Create** - This activity space is essential for users who are not already computer users. When in this activity space, the novice user is supported in determining what is needed in order to be able to use the computer (or other devices) at all. (If users can already use the computer, then they could use *Capture* to start with the settings they already use. From there, they could go into an *Explore* activity to find out what really works for them.   If the user has no useful ability to operate the computer – then First Create would be used. After First Create, that user would likely then use Explore.)
2. **Capture** – If users are already using a computer, their current settings can be used as a starting point, understanding that default settings should not be presumed to serve the user well. Capture can also be used at any time to capture a particular set of settings – for example to capture a new set to be used for a particular context such as a set of preferences that work well for that user in libraries.
3. **Explore** - In the Explore activity space, users who have at least basic access, are encouraged to try new configurations, find new transformations, and discover new preferences without fear of permanently losing their current level of access.
4. **Adjust** - This activity involves providing the user with the ability to easily adjust a single preference, or adjust multiple preferences.
5. **Manage** - Manage covers a wide range of advanced activities involving the viewing, editing, and/or re-organizing of preference sets.

It is important to note that within this conceptualization, users will not necessarily move through the five activity spaces in a linear progression, but rather the activity spaces represent different ways that users may interact with preference tools in different contexts.

Identified Interaction Methods. Interaction methods are the techniques for presenting and providing preference features to users. The aim is to offer appropriate methods within each activity space to engage the user to discover, explore, and adjust preferences—toward the ultimate goal of increasing user engagement and success in completing the preference process. The following interaction methods were identified:

- **Prompt & Ask** - The most direct method is to explicitly prompt the user to make a selection for a preference.
- **Tasks & Rewards** - These may include game-like interactions that are highly engaging and stimulating, or more straightforward questions or a combination of both.
- **Show** - The user may wish to have the system show specific preferences or types of preferences that are available, as well as the specific adjustments that are available for each preference.
- **Randomize & Try** - When not much is known about the user, a preset or common selection of customizations (or selections predicted from other information gathered about the user) could be presented for the user to preview. They could try the customizations offered or ask for a new set of choices.
- **Infer & Recommend** - To reduce preference gathering time it is beneficial to infer and recommend preferences and let the user to decide whether to add them to their profile.

Identified Core Design Requirements. We identified nine concrete requirements for preference tools if they are to meet users where they are, rather than expecting them to adapt to yet another system with unfamiliar interactions. The preference tools should cumulatively:

1. Encourage exploration and experimentation
2. Demonstrate the chosen preference
3. Ensure that users are informed
4. Ensure that users are allowed to control preference selections.
5. Integrate preference management into user workflow
6. Enable continuous refinement
7. Integrate usable decision support wisdom, by providing feedback to the user on what preferences have worked in similar circumstances for others or by communication with other users
8. Provide a range of interfaces, ranging from ultra-simple to full-featured
9. Where possible, infer and suggest user needs by monitoring their interaction with the system to improve the user experience.

4.3   The Definition of a Preference Tool Ecosystem

The Preference Tool Ecosystem is composed of three general categories of tools: initialization tools, exploration tools, and editors. Within each of these categories, we have identified specific tools aligned to each of the user activity spaces. The ones which we will cover in greater detail will be First Discovery and Exploration tools as these tools are the most critical in assisting the user in acquiring their needs and allowing them to get through the preference gathering process with the greatest speed and with ongoing refinement by engaging the user.

First Discovery Tools. The role of *First Discovery Tools* is to find out what the basic needs of a person are, needs that, if they are not met, would prevent the person from using the ICT at all. First Discovery and addressing access to single sign form the key components necessary to getting a user "in the door" to any ICT system and then on to any preference gathering tool to enhance their access. Until we know these basic needs we cannot begin to give the user an *Explore* tool because we do not know what would be within their ability to perceive or understand. Most users who use a First Discovery tool will then be guided toward a tool to Explore. First Discovery tools are only used with people who do not currently use ICT and therefore do not already have settings or AT that can be captured and used as a starting point.

A First Discovery tool is probably one of the most challenging tools since it must start without any assumptions about the user and slowly establish what types of input and output a user is able to interact with, before moving into a space of preference setting activity.

Within First Discovery, all of the underlying complexity of the preference exploration and preference management tools exists. However, additional complexities must also be accommodated. These include: determining what can be used for input or response from the user when the user cannot operate one or all of the traditional computer input devices (keyboard or mouse or touchscreen), and determining what can be used to present information to the user when the user cannot perceive or understand one or all of the traditional computer output (audio, video, braille display, etc.).

First Discovery must therefore employ a different strategy from the other preference gathering tools. With First Discovery we need to turn on many of the accessibility features, critical to getting the user in the door, such as text to speech and then begin to systematically remove settings. Other preference tools are more often than not additive, enhancing existing settings as the user goes through the preference gathering process.

We expect First Discovery to primarily rely on the following interaction methods:

- **Prompt & Ask:** First discovery tools are particularly challenging because they must have an interface that is operable by everyone no matter what their disability or combination of disabilities. This means that they must have parallel presentations (visual, auditory, tactile) and accept a wide variety of different response modes (voice, keyboard, touchscreen, pointing device, alternate input devices), especially in the initial moments. The system may need to try several different types of prompts or questions. For example, this might mean presenting an initial prompt in textual, audio, and visual formats (icon and sign).
- **Infer & Recommend:** Based on user input in response to prompts, questions, tasks and games, we expect the systems will need to infer which presentation modes are

perceivable and understandable and usable for the user, but constantly check and confirm any inferences. Inference can be very important in helping to guide the discovery tool in efficiently trying different strategies in the early stages where effective communication with the user has not yet been established. The tool then needs to adapt all of its inputs and outputs to those modes

The key goal of this First Discovery process is to determine the limits beyond which the individual cannot perform (e.g., font sizes that will be too small for them to read, keys that are too small for them to hit, and controls that they cannot operate), and a rough estimate of their preferences along these basic parameters (e.g. approximate font size they like).

From here the user would likely proceed into an exploration tool to refine their preferences. They may do this directly or after they have had a chance to use their new access for a while.

Capture and Create Tool. As discussed previously, users who are already using access technologies (AT or built-in access features) can more easily create a first Needs & Preferences set by simply using a Capture and Create tool that would capture their current settings and preferences and create their first Needs & Preferences set from that versus going through the Discovery process. From there they can move on to the *Explore* tools to find out if there are better settings for them.

Exploration Tools. Exploration Tools provide a means for users to explore ways to personalize their experience in the context of a task they are performing. They are intended to expand the user's understanding of the possibilities of personalized interfaces. Different exploration tools can support exploration and experimentation for different groups (by age, interest, ability, subject matter, task). We anticipate that the ecosystem will provide these contextualized tools, and that the role of the PGA project is to facilitate that by developing toolkits and providing exemplars.

Exploration Tools allow users to explore and play with content transformations and adaptations in context. Exploration tools may provide their own context, or they may allow the user to choose their own context (web page or task) and explore the effect of the different settings on that context. To operate in this latter form, a tool would need to be built so that it can be integrated into either web based or native applications.

As a part of our work in this area – a prototype Exploration Tool was developed. This tool provides users with presets, which are logically grouped selections of preferences with default settings.

Preferences Management Tools (PMTs) and Mini-PMTs. Preferences Management Tools (PMTs) are web-based tools that give users the ability to see and edit their preferences for any device, application, or context. As a concept, these tools are web based to provide cross-platform compatibility, ease of adaptability, and re-use of code. These are robust tools that provide the user with the ability to customize preferences for one or many devices. They allow the user to change and apply global preferences or define and edit preferences for different specific devices and contexts.

Personal Control Panels (PCPs). Personal Control Panels (PCPs) provide users with an easy means to directly adjust the device's/software's settings on the fly. A PCP allows the user to quickly choose "for the moment" settings they may need from a short list of features they feel the need to have quick and constant access to. (This list of settings can be chosen by the user from her preference set, or pre-populated with settings the user might find useful). PCPs can also give users the option of saving settings for later use on that device or on other devices. That is, they can have preference saving capability – or they can launch a preference tool to do this.

- PCPs for a single person can be different in different contexts
- PCPs can launch Preference Tools
- A PCP could also have an embedded PMT

4.4   The Preferences Framework: Architecture Design

The Preferences framework architecture, designed to support PGA will be based on the following principles:

- *Reusable Components* Including: flexible UI components designed for adaptation to support preference creation and management; Pluggable personalization service to support transformation and delivery; web and native platform services building off Clour4All and Flexible Learning Object Environments (FLOE) work; robust scalable frameworks
- *Adaptable UIs vs transcoding* capable of supporting features such as highcontrast, text-to-speech, and layout simplification
- *Web and Native platform accessibility features*
- *Support for security and privacy*
- *Open Source code and documentation*

The preference framework architecture is illustrated in Figure 1.0. Figure 1, below, illustrates the components that are offered within the Preferences Framework, as well as some of the services and tools they interact within in the broader GPII ecosystem. The Preferences Framework offers: 1) Views and Adjusters, which provide reusable widgets and controls with which users can edit their preferences; 2) Enactors, which do the work of transforming the user interfaces based on these preferences; 3) Data Stores, which provide persistence for the user's preferences; and 4) Recognizers, which provide activities to help infer new preferences and settings. These components typically interact with both web content and a suite of native/server-side GPII transformation services, including the Flow Manager, which is responsible for configuring and launching native access solutions.

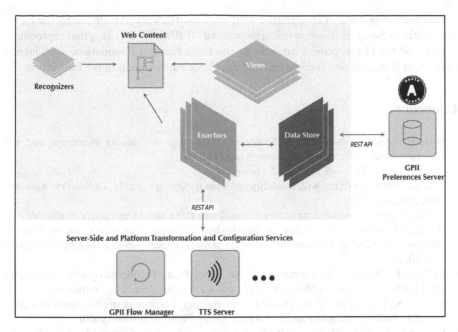

Fig. 1. The Components of the Preferences Framework

5   Conclusion

A Preference Tool Ecosystem and Preferences Framework has been created that takes a functional approach to determining personal preference sets, acknowledges the importance of self-awareness and self-determination while also facilitating guidance from a variety of knowledge sources. These models acknowledge that there can be no one authority or initiative that can support this hugely complex domain and that any system or infrastructure must support collaborative, collective, distributed input and development in order to be sustainable and scalable.

The next stage of the project requires the engagement of the broad spectrum of users, potential developers, knowledge sources and implementers in the participatory design and development process. In collaboration with other GPII efforts, the PGA initiative will create the necessary architecture to support the creation of the ecosystem of preference tools delineated in the first phase of the project and PGA will also create exemplars and models of the range of tools that can be implemented and tested with a special emphasis on first creation and inference.

Acknowledgements. This research was funded by the National Institute on Disability and Rehabilitation Research, US Dept of Education under contract ED-OSE-12-D-0013 (Preferences for Global Access). The opinions and results herein are those of the authors and not necessarily those of the funding agencies.

This work was done in cooperation with the Cloud4all project funded by the European Union's Seventh Framework Programme (FP7/2007-2013) grant agreement 289016 and the FLOE project funded by the Flora Hewlett Foundation, the Ontario Ministry of Research and Innovation, and the Canadian Foundation for Innovation.

References

1. Forrester Research. Accessible technology in computing—examining awareness, use, and future potential. Online Forrester research report (2004),
   `http://go.wisc.edu/1g87i5` (retrieved)
2. Fox, S.: Americans living with disability and their technology profile. Online Pew Research Center report (2011),
   `http://pewinternet.org/Reports/2011/Disability.aspx` (retrieved)
3. Hastings Kraskowsky, L., Finlayson, M.: Factors affecting older adults' use of adaptive equipment: Review of the literature. American Journal of Occupational Therapy 55(3), 303–310 (2001)
4. Hudson, R., Weakley, R., Firminger, P.: An Accessibility Frontier: Cognitive Disabilities and Learning Difficulties (2004), `http://go.wisc.edu/6z0i2g` (retrieved)
5. Iyengar, S., Lepper, M.: When choice is demotivating: Can one desire too much of a good thing? Journal of Personality and Social Psychology 79(6), 995–1006 (2000)
6. Reimer-Weiss, M.L., Wacker, R.R.: Factors associated with assistive technology discontinuance among individuals with disabilities. Journal of Rehabilitation 66(3), 44–50 (2000)
7. Spool, J.: Do users change their settings? Online article (2011),
   `http://www.uie.com/brainsparks/2011/09/14/do-users-change-their-settings/`
8. Trewin, S.: Automating accessibility: the dynamic keyboard. In: ASSETS 2004: Proceedings of the 6th International ACM SIGACCESS Conference on Computers and Accessibility, Atlanta, Georgia, pp. 71–78. ACM, New York (2004)

Federated Databases and Supported Decision Making

Denis Anson[1] and Yao Ding[2]

[1] Misericordia University, Dallas, Pennsylvania, 18612 USA
danson@misericordia.edu
[2] Trace Center, University of Wisconsin-Madison, USA
ding@trace.wisc.edu

Abstract. Currently, information required to make informed choices of appropriate assistive technology products is scattered among broad, general-purpose databases and narrow, focused databases. The vocabulary used to describe features has not been standardized, and can be very hard to interpret by end-users of assistive technology. The described project will create a federated Unified Listing of assistive technologies for information and communication technologies, and develop a Shopping Aid, using information provided by the individual to filter products and services from the Unified Listing to those that are relevant to the individual. By examining needs information across users, the Shopping Aid will be able to suggest additional needs that are common among people like the user, and to make recommendations for upgrading choices when the probably benefit exceeds the individual's cost of change.

Keywords: GPII, Supported Decision Making, Federated Database, Shopping Aid.

1 Introduction to the Problem

The conventional computer interface is designed by and for young, healthy adults, with normal movement, senses, and cognitive skills. While this group includes a majority of the workforce, and especially the computer and software development workforce, it does not include many of the people who require computer access in the modern world. Computer use is becoming virtually ubiquitous in modern society. In 1999, virtually all businesses in the state of Kentucky used computers in some way [1]. By 2011, 75.6 percent of American households included a computer, and 71.7 percent had in-home internet access [2]. However, people with disabilities and the aging have significantly lower access to computers and the Internet than do their younger, healthier associates. In Australia, in 2011, 96% of 18-24 year olds reported computer and internet access, compared with less than half of those 65 years or older. Just over half of adults with disabilities reported having access to computers [3]. As computers become a mainstream means of access to education, commerce, government services, and medicine, access to computers becomes increasingly essential to participation in society.

C. Stephanidis and M. Antona (Eds.): UAHCI/HCII 2014, Part IV, LNCS 8516, pp. 337–347, 2014.
© Springer International Publishing Switzerland 2014

Almost from the introduction of the personal computer, it was applied to the needs of individuals with disabilities [4, 5]. However, many of the early computer applications were special, adapted programs for people with disabilities[6, 7], which did not provide access to the same programs and services enjoyed and used by able-bodied computer users. Not until the advent of the Adaptive Firmware Card for the Apple II [8, 9] could a person with a disability have access to the same programs as his/her non-disabled peers. Since then, some hundreds to thousands of methods of providing access to information technologies have been developed and marketed.

Given the wide range of available accommodations, why are elderly and/or disabled people only half as likely to be using computers as their able-bodied peers? While the cost of accommodation may be a factor, very functional examples of on-screen keyboards, magnifiers, and screen-readers, among other accommodations, are available at no cost. A more common contributing cause is the lack of appropriate information about available accommodations for those who need them most. Many providers of assistive technology services work in the school or medical systems. However, many of those who would benefit from access accommodations are not enrolled in schools, or do not have access to advanced medical systems. While it is possible to obtain information through skilled Internet searches, the people who need computer accommodations don't have advanced computer skills!

1.1   Distributed Information about Accommodations

A person who needs accommodation to successfully use information technologies has two fundamental problems to address before a solution can be found. First, the individual must determine what sort of accommodation might be required. This requires an explanation of the difficulty experienced in using an information appliance. In many cases, the individual has neither the insight to characterize his/her experience nor the vocabulary to explain it to an AT specialist. Since the individual does not know what the "normal" experience might be, s/he cannot easily describe how his/her experience is not normal. Lacking training in human performance, s/he may not be able to accurately describe the experience. Most non-professionals, in discussing visual deficits, for example, may describe problems as having "double-vision" or "out of focus" (needing glasses), but has no way to describe visual field cuts, reduced sensitivity of the retina (it's dark!), or astigmatism. Second, because most AT listings are based on the function of the device, the individual must have some idea that it is possible to address this problem, and what the solution might be in order to begin the search.

The next problem involves finding a potential solution to the problem being experienced. Information about computer access technologies is currently available from a wide range of sources in varying degrees of detail. The European Assistive Technology Information Network (EASTIN) maintains an online database of assistive technologies (http://www.eastin.eu/en-GB/searches/products/index) organized broadly on ISO codes. AbleData (http://www.abledata.com), funded by the U.S. Department of Education through the National Institute on Disability and Rehabilitation Research, also provides a broad ranging database of almost 40,000 products, organized by life skill. In both cases, the information about a specific product is very limited, and does not readily support decision-making. More focused assistive technology databases such as The Toolbox (http://www.agrability.org/toolbox/), a database of farm related technologies, or the product databases maintained by Microsoft or the American Foundation for the Blind are much narrower in focus, but may provide more information about the included assistive technologies. None of the available databases provides sufficient information to support product selection about a wide range of products.

2   Federating Data Sources

Federation is a process, often political, of bringing independent entities together into a common group, while continuing to allow independent operation. The Global Public Inclusive Infrastructure (GPII) Unified Listing is a federated database combining information from a wide range of sources into a single shared database. The information sharing of the Unified Listing is bidirectional. While the Unified Listing replicates content from contributing sources, it also allows those sources to replicate Unified Listing records that are relevant to the audience of those sources. The database of the American Foundation of the Blind, for example, may replicate records in the Unified Listing that have been contributed by other organizations who are concerned with providing access to blind consumers, but would not be interested in adaptations contributed by Microsoft related to on-screen keyboards from Windows 8.

2.1   Challenges of AT Federation

There are two primary difficulties in combining information from diverse sources about assistive technology. Different groups or manufacturers may use different terms to mean the same thing, and in other places, use the same word to mean different things.

As an example of how different terms are used for the same thing, consider the rate at which speech synthesizers produce speech. Speech synthesis is used for Augmentative and Alternative Communication devices, where the requirement is to be understood by naïve listeners, and in screen readers, where the requirement is to provide blind users familiar with the voice with reading speeds that are commensurate with those of sighted colleagues. An objective measure of speech rate would be the number of words spoken from a standard source in one minute. Without a standard source, however, words spoken per minute can be variable. Unfortunately, manufacturers may use neither the same terms, nor the same scales. JAWS for Windows, for example, includes an adjustment for "Rate," which slides from 40 to 150. The normal speech rate seems to be around 70 on this scale, while 150 appears to be many hundreds of words per minute. ZoomText 8.1 also has a Rate: adjustment, which ranges from 50 to 250, and appears to be approximately words per minute spoken. OS X, on the other hand, has an adjustment for "Speaking Rate" which scales, like Windows, from "Slow" to "Fast," with "Normal" at midscale. It is unclear whether these scales are linear, logarithmic, or merely scalar.

An example of the same word being used to mean different things is provided by the example of "word prediction." Early assistive technology attempted to "guess" the word that the user was typing based on the first few letters that had been typed. This feature was termed either "word completion" or "word prediction," with the latter term being used most often. As the technology advanced, it became possible to guess not only the word being typed, but the word or words most likely to follow. With this expansion of capability, some AT professionals began referring to predicting the current word as "word completion," reserving the term "word prediction" for the ability to predict the most likely word following the current word. However, "word prediction" continues to be used for both processes by manufacturers and practitioners in the field.

The issue of different (unique) terms being used for the same feature can be resolved by developing an assistive technology thesaurus. This will involved developing a canonical listing of terms to describe features of assistive technology and user interface adjustments, then matching variants to those canonical terms. The issue of the same term being used for different features will require developing standard "operational definitions" of each of the features and settings for assistive technology that can be used to match individual product functions.

We have to determine how best to handle data conflicts between different sources. Some of these data conflicts will arise from errors made during data entry. If the same device resides in three or more databases, it may be possible to rectify much of the data by "majority rules," since it is unlikely that the same typographical error will occur in more than one database. In cases where errors cannot be easily resolved, it will be necessary to flag the record for review. Another type of data conflict may arise from different applications of a product. Many of the needs of a person with low-vision are similar to those of a person with learning disabilities when consuming text content. Some products may be used in both populations, but be described differently, based on the orientation of the individual describing the product. The easiest way to control for this type of data conflict would be for the GPII Unified Listing database to focus on objective measurements, and not attempt to include measures of suitability for any type of disability. This would conflict with the needs of the Shopping Aid (described below), suggesting that another solution must be found, possibly requiring flagging conflicts for resolution by human staff.

3   Decision Support – The GPII Shopping Aid

The Unified Listing will attempt to contain information about all assistive technology products and all device settings that affect the usability of information and communication technologies, and usability adjustments of consumer electronic devices. This will make the information necessary to make a decision about product selection available to the user of the Unified Listing. Unfortunately, it will also make a vast amount of unnecessary information available. The result of this wealth of information could be severe information overload.

The concept of information overload has been recognized since the 1960s, though it has been suggested much earlier [10-15]. The problem is that, when presented with a choice between a small set of options, individuals may be able to make a meaning-ful choices. When presented with many options, the ability to make choices is li-mited. The individual cannot process all of the available choices, so becomes unable to select any of the offerings. In order to make meaningful choices between options, most people do not require more information; they require more focused, relevant information, and less information about inappropriate topics. The challenge is to differentiate relevant from inappropriate information for each individual.

The GPII Shopping Aid, an on-line decision assistance tool, attempts to limit over-load by pre-filtering information based on what the individual has communicated, so that the choices are both fewer and more relevant to the individual user.

There are three routes of access to the GPII Shopping Aid Decision tool. First, the individual may use the Discovery Aid, an access evaluation tool that can be used ei-ther independently or with the assistance of an assistive technology professional to identify access needs. The Discovery Aid will identify components of the technology interface that present barriers, but will not attempt to find solutions. On completion of the Discovery Aid, the needs profile will be transmitted securely to the Shopping Aid. Alternatively, for those individuals who are able to work with an AT profes-sional, the clinician can select the desired AT functions after evaluation to produce a functional profile of the individual. Finally, the sophisticated user may directly de-scribe functional needs to the system.

In each case, the Shopping Aid will draw from the Unified Listing those products that address the identified needs of the user. These can be sorted by the number of needs addressed, or by the match to user preferred (not necessary) features.

3.1   The Language of Assistive Technology Intervention

One of the challenges in assistive technology provision is that different groups think about intervention in different ways. Three key groups to be addressed by the GPII Shopping Aid are device/system manufacturers, AT specialists and clinicians (who may not be AT specialists), and end-users of assistive technology. Each of these groups thinks about assistive technology in different ways.

Device manufacturers may, in product development, think about the functional needs of their products, but this quickly is translated into product feature descriptions. For example, the introduction of ZoomText 10[1] describes that product as having five new features, including "Background Reader, ZoomText Recorder, ZommText Cam-era, Enhanced WebFinder, and Read from pointer." A competing product, MAGic[2]

---

[1] AI Squared, 130 Taconic Business Park Road, Manchester Center, Vermont 05255,
    Phone +1 (802) 362-3612.
[2] Freedom Scientific, 11800 31st Court North St. Petersburg, FL 33716-1805,
    Phone: 1-877-775-9474 (within US).

describes its features as including "change how colors appear on your screen, apply tinting, make your screen display in monochrome, and invert the brightness and color of the display." As products develop, much of the development occurs by the addition of new features, so that more mature products have a large and diverse features set.

Assistive Technology providers and clinicians who may provide assistive technology on occasion do not select products based on the feature set of any product, but on the functional needs of a specific client. After evaluating a client, the AT practitioner may determine that this person would benefit from a word prediction program that provides in-line prediction, and which presents the words in alphabetical order. While a product that includes word prediction as one of many features may be among the products considered, the complexity of controlling a wide range of features may make it less desirable to the AT user than more focused, but easier to configure, products. For AT providers, the inclusion of a wide range of features does not necessarily increase the desirability of a product. The practitioner considers primarily the feature or features that match the needs of a specific individual.

End users, in the majority of cases, have little experience in the range of variation that is available in user interfaces, either natively or through add-on assistive technology. The primary awareness of the end user is that certain tasks on certain devices are difficult or impossible. The thinking of the typical end-user is needs or difficulty based: I need to perform this task and can't, or this operation is difficult for me. Most consumers of assistive technology will not be able to describe why a task is difficult, only that it is.

While it may be reasonable to expect AT practitioners to learn how assistive technology features work, and the language that is used to describe them, the same is not true of the clinician who only recommends assistive technology sporadically, and even less so for individuals who need assistive technology for their own use. Some means of addressing the needs of different audiences must be found.

3.2   The Janus Interface

Janus, the Roman god of transitions, is depicted as having two faces, so that he looks to the future and the past at the same time. The GPII Shopping Aid will have multiple faces, looking toward specific user groups.

For technology developers and manufacturers, the Aid will allow navigation by features. A manufacturer might search, for example, for all assistive technologies that offer in-line word prediction. Another might seek products that read text from the screen, and that highlight each word as it is spoken. This search would allow a developer to direct limited resources into the likely most-profitable features, or to determine if a "new" feature had already been developed by someone else.

For assistive technology providers, the GPII Shopping aid will have a function oriented interface. Using this interface, the AT provider will be able to provide a set of desired functional abilities, and receive a listing of product that provide one or more of the functions needed. When the provider selects a product from the list, competing products that provide the same functionality are subtracted from the list, allowing the user to easily select the set of products (one or more) that provide the functional capabilities require by the client.

For the end user, a very different interface is required. Here, the GPII Shopping Aid allows the individual to indicate the tasks that are difficult, or features that are desired. In this interface, the user will be able to describe features that are required, and those that are desired. For example, a user might indicate that words on the computer screen are too small to read, and it would be helpful if they were a different color. Using this information, the GPII Shopping Aid can provide a list of products with the required features, ordered by the number of desired features that are included.

In keeping with the requirement to avoid cognitive overload, each interface will allow the user to select a broad category of requirements, and drill down to specific features. In this way, no user will be confronted with the hundreds of potential accommodations. Each user will see the few accommodations that are relevant to a specific search.

Additional interfaces may be developed to meet the unique needs of different user groups. For example, library staff members are often asked to assist patrons in setting up computers within a library. These staff may or may not have functional limitations themselves, but are unlikely to have the level of understanding of disability and assistive technology of a clinician who even rarely provides AT services. For such users, an interface with different types of requirements, using a different vocabulary may need to be developed. However, once the basic mechanisms of the Janus Interface are realized, adding additional interfaces will be easier.

3.3   Auto-suggest Features

Historically, recommendations of assistive technologies have been based on at most the experience of a single AT provider. There has been no way to combine the experience of practitioners around the world, or to compare potential solutions for the individual. The unique structure of GPII allows a level of understanding of individual human-computer interaction and interface accommodation that has not previously been possible. This understanding arises spontaneously from the portability features of GPII.

Each user of GPII has a personal preference file that is stored in the cloud, and delivered to the device being used on demand. This file includes the needs profile of the user as well as the specific licenses owned by the user, and the devices and settings that are preferred. This information allows GPII to configure each system the individual uses to match the specific needs of that person. The stored needs profile also allows the individual to return to the Shopping Aid to find new solutions if a selected product proves unsatisfactory over time. The combined information of many GPII preference files makes unique information available.

Assistive Technology Syndromes and "People Like You". In medicine, collections of signs and symptoms that tend to occur together are identified as syndromes. If a person shows a number of the indicators of a syndrome, this can predict the occurrence of other symptoms of the syndrome that may be covert. For example, the flattened face, upward slant of the eyes, and low muscle tone of a newborn are indicators that the child may have Down syndrome, and may also indicate the presence of cardiac abnormalities that frequently accompany that condition.

It is probable that there are analogous patterns of assistive technology need. For example, a person who lives with Type II diabetes may have visual changes that require the use of enlarged print, or in extreme cases, a screen reader. Such a person may also require keyboard accommodations because of reduced sensation and mobility in the hands. The visual changes of normal aging (presbyopia) are often accompanied by changes in hearing (presbycusis) as well. Beyond these trivial associations it is likely that there are more complex interactions of needed accommodation.

The GPII preference files offer the opportunity to identify patterns of needs that occur among users of assistive technology. If such patterns can be identified, we will be able to match the individual needs identified by GPII users to the identified patterns of common needs. When an individual uses the Shopping Aid to select assistive technologies, they may have identified a portion of a common pattern, but failed to consider a developing issue, or one which they had not identified as outside the norm. In these cases, the Shopping Aid may ask, "Many people like you also indicate that they also have difficulty with [additional need]. Would you be interested in looking a products that make that task easier?" If the user does not have the identified additional need, they can ignore or dismiss the suggestion. But if they do, they may find use of information and communication devices much easier.

Goodness of Fit and Improved Solutions. In many cases, the assistive technology solutions selected by an individual with functional limitations provide necessary access, but not equivalent access. In some cases, assistive technology does not currently exist to meet the specific needs of the individual. In other cases, there may be compatibility issues between "best case" solutions. In these, and other cases, it will be possible to create a "goodness-of-fit" metric to describe the extent to which an individual's current assistive technology solutions meet the identified needs of that individual's personal preference profile.

Over time, new assistive technology products are introduced, or existing products are updated to provide additional functionality. Matching the new capabilities of assistive technology over time will allow prediction of improvements in this goodness-of-fit that are available, and to suggest to the user that they may wish to look at new or updated versions of their assistive technology solutions.

Few things in ecommerce are more annoying that the constant barrage of emails generated by on-line vendors. After purchasing a product, a customer receives a stream of emails saying, "We saw that you were looking at this product. You might be interested in these…" These email contain a variety of products, often including the item just purchased or other products with exactly the same functionality. Often the recommendations are for incompatible models of the device purchased. The purchaser of a Nikon lens might receive suggestions for Canon lenses of similar focal length. From a vendor viewpoint, only a very small "hit rate" makes these emails cost effective, since the cost of generate a custom email is very low. But for the customer, they can be very distracting and counter-productive.

To avoid this constant annoyance, we plan to develop a companion to the goodness-of-fit metric, which we are calling "Changeability." Some individuals, commonly known as "early adopters," enjoy trying new approaches to tasks, and are happy to be notified of new things to try. For others, the energy expended in integrating an assistive technology into their activities is substantial, and they are loath to change. In still other cases, a person may be very busy with their daily tasks, and simply not have the time to invest in learning a new accommodation, even if, over the long term, it produces savings in time that exceed the investment.

We propose to develop a "Changeability" metric for users of GPII. This metric will indicate the willingness to try new approaches given an expected return. This may be a multidimensional metric, or as simple as a slider ranging from "You're bothering me" to "Why didn't I know about this sooner!" Ultimately, the Changeability metric will translate into a threshold change in goodness-of-fit. When new versions or new products would allow a configuration of assistive technologies to exceed that of an individual's current selections, they will be notified that better solutions now exist, and they may wish to consider them.

To minimize the risk of hounding GPII users excessively, we can monitor response to these suggestions. If an individual ignores two or more alerting messages, it is likely that the current setting for Changeability is too high, and it can be incrementally decreased. If the individual repeatedly responds to alerting messages with visits to the Shopping Aid, even if they do not change their technology, this can be taken as an indication that they are not satisfied with their current solutions, and are willing to change. Additionally, if the individual clicks a "Why didn't I know about this?" button, that can be an indication of willingness to try new things. In either case, the Changeability setting might be incrementally increased. Over time, the frequency and probable impact of messages will adapt to the level that is desired by each individual user.

4   Conclusions

Currently, an individual seeking access solutions faces daunting challenges. Manufacturers describe their products through their features. Different manufacturers may use different words for the same feature, or the same word to describe different features. Assistive technology practitioners and clinicians must translate the manufacturing terminology into functions that match the needs of their clients. End users may not have access to assistive technology professionals (indeed, may not even know that such exist), may not be able to effectively describe their experience, and lack the vocabulary to make effective selections from the available products.

The Global Public Inclusive Infrastructure (GPII) is a world-changing approach to providing accommodations for individuals who have difficulty using the standard interface of information or communication technologies. With GPII, the individual can determine the type of interface that works for them in one location, and those same accommodations can follow them wherever they go. For this to work, the individual needs an effective way to tell the system what assistive technologies they prefer to use, and how those technologies should be configured.

Together, the Unified Listing and the GPII Shopping Aid provide an entry point to use of the GPII. The Unified Listing, a federated database of accommodations for information and communication devices, provides an encyclopedic view of available accommodations. Combining the information that is currently available in both broad and specialized databases of AT solutions into a single source allows the GPII to meet the needs of virtually any individual for whom a solution currently exists. The GPII Shopping Aid filters this knowledge to provide the information that is relevant to the individual, and at each step, to hide the information (cognitive noise) that is not relevant to the individual's needs.

As the number of users of GPII increases, the accumulated information will allow development of two enhanced features. First, we will be able to generate information about "people like you," allowing recommendations for needs that the user did not mention, either because they were not aware of the need, or aware that solutions were possible. Second, through a "goodness-of-fit" metric and "personal changeability" measure, we will be able to recommend possible improvements in the assistive technology solutions of a user only when the potential benefit is large enough to be worth the effort for that individual.

References

1. Allen, S.N.: Computer and Internet Usage at Businesses in Kentucky. Center for Business and Economic Research, located at the University of Kentucky, Gatton College of Business and Economics (1999)
2. U.S. Census Bureau. Computer and Internet Use in the United States. In: Bureau USC (ed.) U.S. Census Bureau (2013)
3. Schollum, P.: Household Use of Information Technology. In: Statistics ABo (editor), Australia. Australian Bureau of Statistics, Canberra (2010-2011)
4. McDonald, J.B., Schwejda, P., Marriner, N.A., Wilson, W.R., Ross, A.M.: Advantages of Morse code as a computer input for school aged children with physical disabilities. Computers and the Handicapped. National Research Council of Canada, Ottawa (1982)
5. Gibler, C.D., Childress, D.: Language anticipation with a computer-based scanning communication aid. In: IEEE Computer Society Workshop on Computing to the Handicapped, Charlottesville, VA, pp. 11–5 (1982)
6. Brandenburg, S.A., Vanderheiden, G.: Communication, Control, and Computer Access for Disabled and Elderly Individuals - Resource Book 3: Software and Hardware. Little, Brown and Company, Boston (1986)
7. Borden, P.A., Vanderheiden, G.: Communication, Control and Computer Access for Disabled and Elderly Individuals - Resource Book 4: Update to Books 1, 2, and 3. Trace Research and Development Center, Madison (1988)
8. Schwejda, P., Vanderheiden, G.C.: Adaptive-Firmware Card for the Apple II. Byte 7, 276–314 (1982)
9. Anson, D.: Apple II Alternative Input Systems. In: Clark, E.N. (ed.) Microcomputers: Clinical Applications, pp. 37–45. Slack, Thorofare (1986)

10. Bridenbaugh, C.: The great mutation. American Historical Review 68, 315–331 (1963)
11. Streufert, S., Suedfeld, P., Driver, M.: Conceptual structure, information search, and information utilization. Joural of Personality and Social Psychology 2, 736–740 (1965)
12. Bartlett, C.J., Green, C.: Clinical prediction: Does one sometimes know too much? Journal of Counseling Psychology 13, 267–270 (1966)
13. Malhotra, N.K.: Information Load and Consumer Decision Making. Journal of Consumer Research 8, 419 (1982)
14. Palme, J.: You have 134 Unread Mail! Do You Want to Read Them Now? In: Smith, H.T. (ed.) Computer Based Message Services, pp. 175–176. Elsevier, North Holland (1984)
15. Wallace, D.F.: The Tsunami of Available Fact. In: Wallace, D.F. (ed.) The Best American Essays 2007. Mariner, New York (2007)

Common Terms Registry

Tony Atkins[1] and Gregg C. Vanderheiden[1,2]

[1] Raising the Floor – International, Switzerland
`tony@raisingthefloor.org`
[2] Trace R&D Center, University of Wisconsin – Madison, USA
`gv@trace.wisc.edu`

Abstract. This paper will focus on the rationale behind and the work to date on the Common Terms Registry, a database that improves the ability to articulate Assistive Technology needs and solutions by providing a common vocabulary of clearly defined terms.

Keywords: assistive technologies.

1 Introduction

The growing networked and technologically advanced society in which many of us participate is not all-inclusive. Most mainstream devices, applications, materials, media and web sites make dozens of assumptions about their users. For example, most assume that users can see and hear well, and have the ability to operate a mouse, keyboard or touch screen with high precision.

For users who do not meet these assumptions, the simplest tasks can be difficult or even impossible. These users rely on assistive technologies (AT) to meet their needs. These solutions close the gap between the assumptions made by mainstream developers and manufacturers and the reality in which users with disabilities live [1].

When a need is first identified, AT users and the people who support them (therapists, caregivers, family members, etc.) must find the right combination of tools, adaptations and adapted materials/devices/software for each individual. Users and the people who support them need tools and a common language or vocabulary to help find solutions to meet their needs [2].

The process of selecting solutions to meet a user's needs is not a one-time event. With the rapid development cycles and short working lifetimes of modern technologies, a user can expect to replace or at least upgrade their educational materials, resources or assistive technologies every few years [3]. Even minor changes can make for a painful adjustment. Users need tools to translate their existing needs and preferences for use with new technologies.

Users can also expect to encounter technology in public areas in their daily life (such as library computers or airline self-check systems). As a result, users need to continually reassess their needs against what is available that will either be able to meet their needs directly or to adapt media, materials and devices so that they are able to use them.

This matching process is enormously aided if the people identifying the user's needs and the people creating solutions can use a common vocabulary. This is the role of the Common Terms Registry.

C. Stephanidis and M. Antona (Eds.): UAHCI/HCII 2014, Part IV, LNCS 8516, pp. 348–357, 2014.

Each of these needs continues to grow. The concept of disability is expanding beyond health conditions alone to include a wider range of mismatches between individual needs and the constraints imposed by their physical and societal environment [4]. The global population is also aging, which increases the number of people affected by age-related disabilities [5].

2   The GPII

The Global Public Inclusive Infrastructure (GPII) exists to address these growing needs. The GPII is creating an infrastructure to simplify the development, delivery and support of access technologies and to provide users with a way to instantly apply the access techniques and technologies they need, automatically, on any computers or other ICT they encounter [6].

The Cloud4All project, a project funded under the European Union's FP7 program is working to build the GPII and meet its objectives. The Common Terms Registry and Unified Listing support the goals of the Cloud4All project by bringing together existing data sets regarding needs and solutions, and by standardizing the vocabulary used to describe needs and solutions.

Another challenge is the high cost of producing Assistive Technologies. The Prosperity4All project, another European Union funded project, is working to lower the costs of producing AT and to expand the ability of AT manufacturers to reach a wide enough base of global customers to scale their business models and provide affordable solutions. The Common Terms Registry and Unified Listing support the goals of the Prosperity4All project by helping users find AT solutions and by helping AT producers find customers.

This paper will focus primarily on the rationale behind and the work to date on the Common Terms Registry. We will also discuss the future of both the Common Terms Registry and Unified Listing.

3   Common Terms Registry and Use Cases

The Common Terms Registry (CTR) is a database of common terms related to user needs and AT solutions. Each common term can have many aliases, translations, and transformations (see section 2.1 for definitions). A common vocabulary has many applications, which will be described in more detail in this section.

Imagine that you as an end user currently own a screen magnifier on your personal computer, which you use with programs that do not provide large enough fonts. For programs that provide large enough fonts, you prefer not to use a screen magnifier, which limits how much of the user interface you can see at a single time. You want for that preference respected on every new device or public resource you use, and for it to be applied as intelligently as possible.

To make this possible, you first need to be able to clearly describe the fact that a program (or operating system feature) provides the ability to magnify the screen. You also need to clearly describe whether the currently running program has the ability to change the size of the fonts onscreen, to describe the current font size, and to describe the maximum font size available. In all cases, you need a single way of describing the underlying concept (a *term* in the Common Terms Registry), and an awareness of the way in which the term is described within the application (an *alias* in the Common Terms Registry).

To decide whether to change the font size or to use the screen reader, you would need some way of describing the conditions under which to use each solution (a series of *operators* in the Common Terms Registry, such as "greater than").

If the font size common term is described as being measured in pixels and your program uses ems, you need some way to convert from "16 point" to "1.3 ems" (a *transformation* in the Common Terms Registry).

Once we have a way to represent the needs and preferences of a user and the features and settings of an application, things like a matchmaker to help users find new solutions or a preferences service that configures public resources to adapt to user's needs and preferences are possible. Those are the core use cases required by the GPII (finding solutions, and representing user preferences in various contexts).

These are by no means the only use cases for this common vocabulary. The Common Terms Registry is ultimately a resource owned by its community. Beyond any initial or planned use case, the Common Terms Registry will grow to meet the changing needs of AT users, caregivers, researchers, manufacturers, and anyone else who wishes to contribute.

3.1   Proposed Data Structures

In its initial state, the Common Terms Registry contains the following records:

- Terms
- Aliases
- Translations
- Transformations
- Operators

Record: All records have the following common fields.

Table 1. Fields common to all record types in the Common Terms Registry

Field	Description
Type	The type of record, i.e. term, alias, translation, transformation, operator.
Permanency	An indication of how likely a field is to change over time.
NameSpace	The namespace to use in combination with the UniqueID to construct a URI that refers to the record.
UniqueId	A completely unique identifier for this record.
Notes	Any additional information associated with this record.
Status	The review status of this record.

Term. A term is a single canonical way of describing a need or solution. For example, users who require high-contrast schemes may be concerned about the ability to set a high-contrast background and foreground color. Each of these would be a common term, identified by a persistent ID such as backgroundColor or foregroundColor. In addition to the common fields described above, term records have the following fields.

Table 2. Fields used by the "Term" record type in the Common Terms Registry

Field	Description
ValueSpace	A description of the values allowed for this term.
TermLabel	A short label for this term as it would appear in a menu or listing.
Definition	A description of the term.
ApplicationUniqueFlag	Whether this term is unique to a particular application.
Uses	A description of other systems that use this term and how they use it.

Alias. An alias is another name for a standard term, with no other differences. When describing system settings and other user preferences, the difference may be simply a matter of formatting. For example, one program might have a registry entry or setting for max.volume and another might have a registry entry or setting called max_volume. Other examples may simply be a matter of alternate wording. For example, one developer may use "loudness" instead of "volume" when describing their settings. In addition to the common fields described above, alias records have the following fields.

Table 3. Fields used by the "alias" record type in the Common Terms Registry

Field	Description
AliasOf	The uniqueID of the parent record this record is an alias of.
TermLabel	A short label for this term as it would appear in a menu or listing.
Uses	A description of other systems that use this term and how they use it.

Translation. A translation is representation of a term in another language with no other differences. For example, in US English, the preference for a particular background color might be presented as "backgroundColor". In Commonwealth countries, that might be presented as "backgroundColour". In addition to the common fields described above, translation records have the following fields.

Table 4. Additional Fields used by the "translation" record type

Field	Description
TranslationOf	The uniqueID of the parent record this record is a translation of.
ValueSpace	A translation of the terms used in the parent record's value space.
TermLabel	A translation of the short label for the parent record as it would appear in a menu or listing.
Definition	A translation of the definition of the parent record.
Uses	A description of other systems that use this term and how they use it.

Transformation. Translations and aliases present a term using different words or formatting, with no meaningful difference in the values used to describe a user's needs or preferences. For example, two devices may have a volume control that can be set from 0 to 10 in increments of 1. If those two devices have the same maximum volume and each of their corresponding volume levels are the same loudness, then a user who prefers (or requires) for the volume to be set to 10 would have the same experience in having that preference applied to each device. It wouldn't matter if one device called the control "volume" and the other called the control "loudness". On the other hand, if two devices have a different maximum volume, are adjustable using different increments, or have a different perceived loudness when set to the same value, then something else is required.

For these cases, the Common Terms Registry provides a transformation. A transformation provides a bidirectional lossless algorithm for converting from one way of describing preferences and needs to another. To continue the previous example, the common term describing volume preferences might be expressed using a decibel scale. For an implementation that uses 0-10 to indicate volume, the transformation record would provide an algorithm for converting from decibel to 0-10 values and from 0-10 values to decibel values. In addition to the common fields described above, transformation records have the following fields.

Table 5. Additional fields used by the "transformation" record type in the Common Terms Registry

Field	Description
ValueSpace	A bidirectional lossless algorithm for converting to and from the values used by the common term.
TermLabel	A translation of the short label for the parent record as it would appear in a menu or listing.
Uses	A description of other systems that use this term and how they use it.

Operator. There are some preferences that are conditional, and depend on the environment and the content an AT user is interacting with. For example, an AT user may wish to have two different color schemes, one for daylight hours, and one for nighttime.

Operators are terms that can be used to clearly identify what settings should be applied under what circumstances. For example, "greater than", "less than", and "in the following range" are all operators. The conjunctions "and", "or" as well as the adverbs "not" and "only" are also operators. Operators can be combined to describe complex conditions.

In addition to the common fields described above, operator records have only one additional field.

Table 6. Additional fields used by the "operator" record type in the Common Terms Registry

Field	Description
Definition	A clear definition of the operator.

Relationships. Terms and Operators are unique records that do not refer to another record implicitly. All other record types (aliases, translations, transformations) must refer to a single parent term (see the aliasOf, translationOf, etc. fields proposed above).

3.2   Proposed Review Structure

The Common Terms Registry is an open registry. Its operation and the process for accepting and curating new terms will be defined by the currently-under-revision ISO/IEC 24751. Anyone can sign up for an account that will allow him or her to submit new entries for the Registry; the only requirement is a valid email address. There are currently three types of users defined: Contributors, Moderators and Administrators.

When users sign up for a new account, they become Contributors. Contributors can create new records, which are stored as "unreviewed" records. These unreviewed records are only visible to the Contributor who created them and to moderators.

Contributors can submit, view and edit their own entries (only) until the entries are "passed" by a moderator to the "Candidate" status. At this point, the contributor is no longer able to edit the record.

Moderators have all of the abilities of Contributors but are able to see all contributions. In addition, Moderators can view "unreviewed" records and use annotations (comments) to engage in a back and forth discussion with the Contributor submitting the record. When Moderators involved in a review are satisfied with the quality and completeness of a record, they can change its status to "candidate". Moderators can also promote Contributors to become additional Moderators as a part of the "meritocracy" model of the Common Terms Registry review process.

Administrators have all of the abilities of Moderators and Contributors. In addition, Administrators have final approval of changes to the database. An administrator can promote a "candidate" record to and "active" record, at which point it becomes visible to the public. Administrators can also directly edit active records (a history and audit trail of changes is stored).

The database includes both canonical terms and terms that are used by individual manufacturers. A single Administrator can move a manufacturer's term for a concept into the Registry. Deciding and dubbing a term as the canonical term for the concept is only done after considerable study and action by an Editorial Team.

In addition to the curation role(s) above administrators also provide oversight over all levels of the community. For example, they can promote Contributors to Moderators and Moderators to Administrators. They can also demote Administrators or Moderators based on feedback from the community. This kind of oversight is common to community-managed sites and is part of the meritocracy mode of the Registry.

The curation process is only tentatively defined and partially implemented (as the 24751 revisions is still in process). Currently the editorial group is working as a committee of the whole to clean up existing entries and create the technical mechanisms for submission of new entries. As the community of contributors grows, the workflow will be formalized so that the progression from "unreviewed" to "candidate" to "active" record will be enforced. The full range of permissions and user classes will also be implemented.

3.3   Provenance and Information Flow

The Common Terms Registry and particularly the Unified Listing will be updated based on information found in a number of existing sources. A key goal of both projects is to make clear the source of information, and to preserve the flow of information between systems. Value added by an upstream authority or community should be incorporated into the federated record wherever possible. Value added by contributors to the Common Terms Registry and Unified Listing in updating federated records should be fed back to the original sources wherever possible.

4   Current Status and Work Plan

The initial data set used to populate the Common Terms Registry was taken from the ISO/IEC 24751 standard augmented by all of the terms used by different companies in building solutions as part of the Cloud4all project. During this project the need for

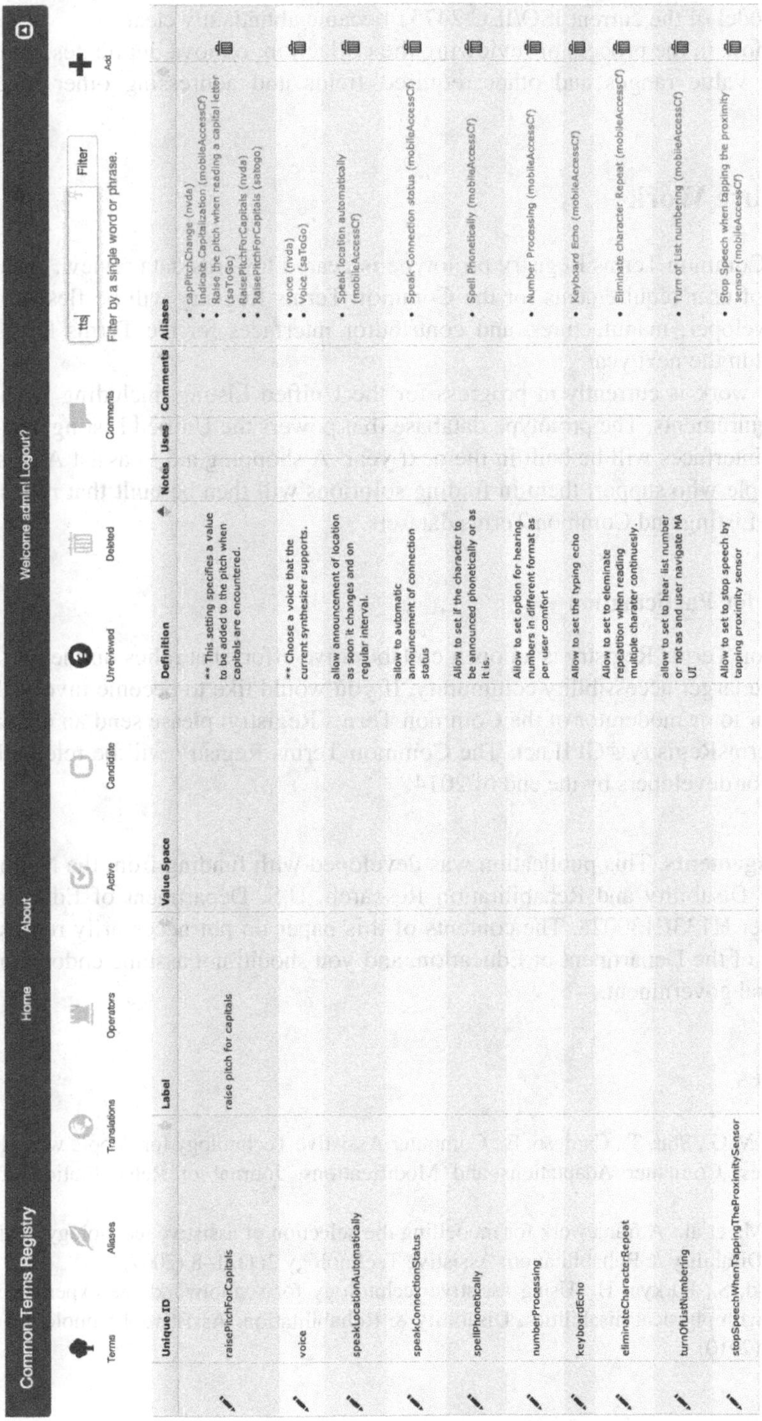

Common Terms Registry

Terms | Aliases | Translations | Operators | Home | About | Active | Candidate | Unreviewed | Deleted | Welcome admin Logout?

Filter by a single word or phrase. | tts | Filter

+ Add

Unique ID	Label	Value Space	Definition	Notes	Uses	Comments	Aliases
raisePitchForCapitals	raise pitch for capitals		** This setting specifies a value to be added to the pitch when capitals are encountered.				• capPitchChange (nvda) • Indicate Capitalization (mobileAccessCf) • Raise the pitch when reading a capital letter (saToGo) • RaisePitchForCapitals (nvda) • RaisePitchForCapitals (saTogo)
voice			** Choose a voice that the current synthesizer supports.				• voice (nvda) • Voice (saToGo)
speakLocationAutomatically			allow announcement of location as soon it changes and on regular interval.				• Speak location automatically (mobileAccessCf)
speakConnectionStatus			allow to automatic announcement of connection status				• Speak Connection status (mobileAccessCf)
spellPhonetically			Allow to set if the character to be announced phonetically or as it is.				• Spell Phonetically (mobileAccessCf)
numberProcessing			Allow to set option for hearing numbers in different format as per user comfort				• Number Processing (mobileAccessCf)
keyboardEcho			Allow to set the typing echo				• Keyboard Echo (mobileAccessCf)
eliminateCharacterRepeat			Allow to set to eliminate repeatition when reading multiple character continuesly.				• Eliminate character Repeat (mobileAccessCf)
turnOfListNumbering			allow to set to hear list number or not as and user navigate NA UI				• Turn of List numbering (mobileAccessCf)
stopSpeechWhenTappingTheProximitySensor			Allow to set to stop speech by tapping proximity sensor				• Stop Speech when tapping the proximity sensor (mobileAccessCf)

Fig. 1. Screen shot of the initial "review" interface to the Common Terms Registry

an expandable model (which is proposed for the ISO/IEC 24751 standard) rather than the fixed model of the current ISO/IEC 24751 became abundantly clear.

We are now in the process of reviewing the collection, remove duplicates, adding definitions, value ranges and other required fields and addressing other quality concerns.

5   Future Work

The initial Common Terms Registry prototype is geared towards data review. A more mature set of user requirements for the Common Terms Registry will be fleshed out and the developer, manufacturer, and contributor interfaces for the Terms Registry will be built in the next year.

Planning work is currently in progress for the Unified Listing, including fleshing out user requirements. The prototype database that powers the Unified Listing and the initial user interfaces will be built in the next year. A shopping aid to assist AT users and the people who support them in finding solutions will then be built that relies on the Unified Listing and Common Terms datasets.

5.1   Call for Participation

The Common Terms Registry is an open collaborative effort that relies on the participation of the larger accessibility community. If you would like to become involved as a contributor to or moderator of the Common Terms Registry, please send an email to CommonTermsRegistry@GPII.net. The Common Terms Registry will be released as a resource for developers by the end of 2014.

Acknowledgements. This publication was developed with funding from the National Institute on Disability and Rehabilitation Research, U.S. Department of Education, grant number H133E130028. The contents of this paper do not necessarily represent the policies of the Department of Education, and you should not assume endorsement by the federal government.

References

1. Brodwin, M.G., Star, T., Cardoso, E.: Computer Assistive Technology for People who Have Disabilities: Computer Adaptations and Modifications. Journal of Rehabilitation 70(3) (2004)
2. Scherer, M., et al.: A framework for modelling the selection of assistive technology devices (ATDs). Disability & Rehabilitation: Assistive Technology 2(1), 1–8 (2007)
3. Murchland, S., Parkyn, H.: Using assistive technology for schoolwork: the experience of children with physical disabilities. Disability & Rehabilitation: Assistive Technology 5(6), 438–447 (2010)

4. Leonardi, M., et al.: The definition of disability: what is in a name? The Lancet 368(9543), 1219–1221 (2006)
5. Treviranus, J., et al.: Leveraging Inclusion and Diversity as Canada's Digital Advantage
6. Vanderheiden, G.C., Treviranus, J., Gemou, M., Bekiaris, E., Markus, K., Clark, C., Basman, A.: The evolving global public inclusive infrastructure (GPII). In: Stephanidis, C., Antona, M. (eds.) UAHCI 2013, Part I. LNCS, vol. 8009, pp. 107–116. Springer, Heidelberg (2013)

Evaluating the Global Public Inclusive Infrastructure: Cloud4all Evaluation Framework

Eleni Chalkia[1], Juan Bautista Montalva Colomer[2],
Silvia de los Rios[2], and Ivan Carmona Rojo[3]

[1] Centre of Research and Technology Hellas/Hellenic Institute of Transport (CERTH/HIT),
Thessaloniki, Greece
hchalkia@certh.gr
[2] Universidad Politécnica de Madrid (UPM), Madrid, Spain
{jmontalva,srios}@lst.tfo.upm.es
[3] Technosite - Fundación ONCE, Madrid, Spain
icarmona@technosite.es

Abstract. Moving rapidly into digital economy expands the need for accessibility coming from the growing number of people with disabilities, in various contexts. Additionally, ubiquitous computing has amplified the need for interactive systems to be able to adapt to their context of use, enhancing their utility while preserving usability. Cloud4all project [0] aims to develop a complete new paradigm in accessibility, by replacing adaptation of individual products and services, with auto-configuration of any mainstream product or service, using cloud technologies to activate and augment any natural accessibility the product or service has, based upon a set of the user's Needs & Preferences (N&Ps). In order to assess this goal, Cloud4all has developed an evaluation framework, as part of the User Centred Design (UCD) iterative process. This paper provides an overview of the 1st pilots' evaluation framework, together with ideas and plans about the general framework of the pilot test.

Keywords: Accessibility, evaluation framework, auto-configuration, scenario, usability, user experience, Cloud4all.

1   Introduction

In order to be useful, ubiquitous systems need to be designed following user centered design, so that the users' Needs & Preferences (N&Ps) are taken into account in the entire design and development process [2]. The goal of this user centered design (UCD) is to create tools and products that satisfy the user who is willing to use them due to their increased utility, ease of use, and pleasure provided by the interaction with them. However, the evaluation of pervasive computing systems and their influences on users is quite difficult because it requires analysis of real users in a real context [3].

User centered design is enhanced by the involvement of real users in a real context, doing multiple evaluations of the products under development during the development

C. Stephanidis and M. Antona (Eds.): UAHCI/HCII 2014, Part IV, LNCS 8516, pp. 358–367, 2014.
© Springer International Publishing Switzerland 2014

cycle. User's evaluation planning itself though, has been a very critical point in the development process, since it includes various aspects to be examined, which are yet not clearly defined by the literature. Terms like usability, accessibility and user experience are heavily involved in the evaluation of systems under development.

Usability is an overall term that covers aspects of a system as user friendliness and ease of use, and has been nominated with various definitions over time [4, 5, 6, 7, 8, 9] which are rather complementary than contradictory. ISO standards for software quality refer to broad view of usability as quality in use, as it is the user's overall experience of the quality of the product [10]. Thus, usability is related to the users, the goal and the contexts of use that are appropriate to the particular circumstances.

Nevertheless, while using new technologies, users are not necessarily seeking to achieve a task, but also to amuse and entertain themselves. Therefore the term user experience, initially popularized by Norman [11], covers the components of users' interactions with systems that go beyond usability studies. User experience, the newest term in the set of criteria against which a system should be evaluated, is a multidimensional concept and a commonly accepted definition is still lacking. According to Hassenzahl and Tractinsky [12], user experience attempts to go beyond the task-oriented approach of traditional Human Computer Interaction (HCI) by bringing out aspects such as beauty, fun, pleasure, and personal growth that satisfy general human needs but have little instrumental value. Therefore, when compared to basic usability, enjoyability and the hedonic quality [12, 14, 15] play an essential role.

The features of ubiquitous systems and products and the context of use affect the human's experiences and preferences about their use, utility and usability. Thus, user experience in user-product interaction, usability of the product and its utility, are terms closely linked to each other, which have to be evaluated. In Cloud4all, a European co-funded project, there will be 3 consecutive test iterations, to enhance the user centered design, as the project and its developments evolve. This paper presents the framework that has been developed for the 1st iteration of Cloud4all tests that focuses on the usability of the tools under development, and also provides some ideas, based upon the lessons learned from the 1st iteration for the next iteration phases.

2   Evaluation Framework Applied within Cloud4all

Cloud4all project aims to develop a complete new paradigm in the domain of HCI accessibility, by replacing adaptation of individual products and services for a person, with auto-configuration of any mainstream product or service users' encounter, using cloud technologies to activate and augment any natural (built-in) accessibility the product or service has, based on a set of the user's Needs & Preferences (N&Ps). The scope of Cloud4all is to provide to the users a seamless experience when changing platforms; having their settings transferred and transformed from one platform to the other in such a transparent to the user way, that he/she will not have to interact at all with the specific device settings.

In the core of this auto-configuration, the user has to assess this scope and evaluate the achievements of Cloud4all towards its objectives. In order to assess this goal, Cloud4all has developed an evaluation framework, as part of the User Centred Design

(UCD) iterative process that is twofold. On the one hand, the scope is to evaluate the usability and user experience of tools that are developed in Cloud4all and require human machine interaction to achieve their goal. And on the other hand, to validate the usability and the utility of the auto-configuration, that actually does not create UIs but triggers the procedure of already existing UIs to auto-configure themselves based on the user that uses them each time.

In this context, we addressed the following questions:

1. How will the auto-configuration affect the user with disabilities experience executing common tasks every day, in familiar devices and platforms?
2. Will users feel more confident using technology and devices and platforms that they are not familiar with when the auto-configuration exists?
3. Will the developers be willing to include their application to the Cloud4all concept and enrich the solutions repository?

In Cloud4all we have developed a common framework for evaluating the project developments addressing the above research questions. It is obvious from the questions above that the target groups of users of Cloud4all address both users with disabilities and the developers of Assistive technologies and mainstream solutions that want their products to be used by people with (or without) disabilities. The scope of the tests with each group is totally different, but they are both included under the umbrella of Cloud4all/GPII [17] concept. More details on the users involved and the scope of the evaluation are available in the following sections.

Due to the complexity of the study and the need for gathering feedback from the users in a very early stage of the project, as part of the UCD, preliminary tests have been planned in early phases of product development. Thus, 3 consecutive pilot iteration phases have been planned, starting from an early stage of the project. In each of the 3 iteration phases a different experimental plan will be developed, since the tools under evaluation will be evolving and the scope of the testing will also evolve. All 3 experimental plans though will be designed using the same patterns and including the same components of the evaluation framework. Thus in all 3 experimental plans the following evaluation framework will be defined:

- Scope of the evaluation (what to evaluate, goals of the study, research questions).
- Participants' details and recruitment (disability groups, participants per site).
- Research hypothesis.
- Pilot scenarios.
- Techniques and tools (what to measure and why, how to measure).
- Indicators and metrics per scenario.
- Test protocol (exact agenda, tasks).
- Results analysis tools and communication of the results with the developers.

At this point we have to highlight that Cloud4all testing goes beyond strict usability testing, since in its context both tools that are actually used by the users in order to achieve a goal, but also tools that are backend and don't have interface for the users, have to be evaluated. Thus, we have used various applications (desktop, mobile, tablet) as the means for the evaluation of tools that don't have an interface for the user and not as the target of the evaluation. This means that the actual target of the testing is not to evaluate the applications that are actually used, but use them in order to have an interface to evaluate the auto-configuration features of Cloud4all. Facilitators' role is very important in this perspective, since confusion to users could and has been quite obvious and could lead to biased results.

3   Specificities of Cloud4all 1st Evaluation Phase

3.1   Scope of Tests

The conducted experiment was planned in order to address these research questions. The first 2 questions refer to the users with disabilities, while the last question refers to developers. Starting from the first 2 questions, we can see that the core of the testing with the users with disabilities is the auto-configuration. The auto-configuration is consisted of various components which are connected to each other in such a way to create a complex architecture.

The scope of Cloud4all 1st pilots' iteration is three fold. Firstly, the goal was to introduce the concept of Cloud4all to users and get their general reaction feedback on this. At this phase, since not all the architectural components were ready to work with each other and a live demonstration of the Cloud4all vision is not possible, the users were presented with a video of a case study of Cloud4all and were asked to provide some general information about their opinions on this vision.

Additionally, the users were presented with scenarios that demonstrated the ability of the basic infrastructure to automatically launch and set up access solutions for users according to their preferences. Specific applications that have been connected to the Cloud4all architecture using specific user N&P sets (personas) were used to demonstrate this and prove to the users the extendability of Cloud4all vision.

Finally, very early testing of the auto-configuration scenario took place, using specific tools developed for the pilots. The goal of this testing was the evaluation of some components of the architecture, as well as the identification of the usability and the utility of the auto-configuration scenario from different types of users.

Regarding the part of the evaluation with the developers, the scope was to introduce them to the Cloud4all concept and the tool they can use in order to join Cloud4all/GPII and gather their initial feedback about acceptance and usability aspects.

3.2   Participants' Details and Recruitment

Three different types of users are included in the pilots of Cloud4all: developers, stakeholders and end users. Each user group tested different scenarios which were addressing their needs.

Cloud4all has established three pilot sites where all the evaluation activities will take place: Spain, Greece and Germany; covering, this way, geographically Europe, which will allow for cross-relation to cultural and socioeconomic issues.

In each one three iteration phases and for three pilot sites, the user groups above will actively participate. For that reason, the active recruitment of users for the activities that involve them directly (i.e. pilot tests, online user forum, demonstrators) has to be supported by other dissemination activities included in the project. Therefore, the attendance to workshops, conferences and other forums, as well as the social networks, can also be invited to participate in the pilot activities. In this way, new end-users, people with disabilities, experts and developers interested in the aim of the project can participate in the evaluation phases by entering in the pool of candidates to participate in the sites.

It is crucial to follow a proper procedure in the liaison with and involvement of users groups. Recruiting and retaining volunteers is an essential process that will guarantee a reliable outcome regarding users input in the concept validation, co-design and design stages as well as in all the evaluations and testing activities that need to be carried out during the project.

To that end, in each evaluation phase, some quotas for participation and selection criteria for these activities are established previously. In the first evaluation phase, the selection criteria for the end users with disabilities were the following:

- Type of disability;
- Gender;
- Age;
- Educational background;
- Operating system used

The selection criterion for experts (stakeholders) was the type of disability in which each one has experience, which is directly linked to the beneficiaries of each solution, and for developers, it was agreed to involve different profiles according to their expertise (mobile, desktop, web, AT).

Regarding the users with disabilities, the project initially did a classification of the profiles that will be involved in the different phases of the Project in order to try to represent as much as possible the wide range of problems, needs and preferences of the users in the different environments where Cloud4all will work. According to this classification, those are the profiles of users involved in this first iteration:

- Blind users
- Low vision users
- Users with dyslexia
- Cognitive impaired users
- Low literacy Users
- Elderly users

Specifically in the 1st iteration phase in the three sites 140 beneficiaries participated: 93 users with disabilities, 30 developers and AT providers, and 17 key stakeholders.

3.3   Pilot Scenarios

The pilot scenarios have been the first part of the pilot framework that was drafted in Cloud4all, and have been used as a basis on knowing what we have ready to test, and why and how we should test it. The pilot scenarios are actually stories of tasks the users have to perform in order to achieve a goal. The achievement of the goal and the execution of the tasks, as well as the users' experience while executing the tasks are the feedback that we gathered at this phase. The methodology of the pilot scenarios is the continuation of the methodology used for the identification of the use cases of Cloud4all, which is based on Rosson & Carroll's "Scenario based Design" [16]. According to Rosson & Carroll, 2001b and also in Cloud4all, the most important issue in the pilots' evaluation is the usability parameters. The feedback received from the 1st evaluation phase will help to re-define the "problem" and the "problem scenarios" and, successively, the use cases application interaction and pilot scenarios. This feedback will help us to guide the 2nd phase development and evaluation and so on [16].

Two are the main scenarios tested in this iteration phase. The first one is the auto-configuration scenario, which is depicted at the figure below. Before the auto-configuration scenario started, the specific preferences of the user where gathered from the pilots facilitators, for a specific platform (Platform A), and a N&P set of the users was created, together with a user token that includes all the information. The user was asked to perform a specific task in platform A which was configured with the settings that the user defined. Then the user was asked to go to another platform (Platform B), log in with his/her token and perform the exact same task, while the UI has been auto-configured. Afterwards, the user was asked to define his/her settings from Platform B, from scratch, log out and log in again with the new N&Ps set to Platform A.

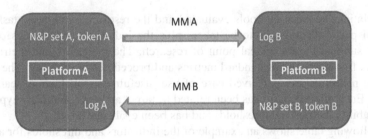

Fig. 1. Auto-configuration scenario

Moving forward to the tests with developers, in this pilot phase the scenario for the developers was focusing on getting feedback for the usability of the tool that the developers will use to add their application in Cloud4all/GPII and the developers where explicitly asked to perform the following tasks:

1. Add a new solution or common term: Adding a new solution/setting to the solutions ontology (without previous experience in cloud4all) /proposing a new term in the common terms registry.
2. Edit an existing solution: Changing the preferences in a solution that already exists on the ontological framework and the registry.
3. Search the ontology: Searching (by a free text and /or by categorization lists) for solutions, settings, etc., stored in the solutions ontology.

3.4   Experimental Plan

The techniques used in the Cloud4all pilots are divided in two categories based on the number of users and the interactions involved (i.e. between, among). Individual techniques are usually associated with in depth data gathering and group techniques have to do with breadth and diversity in data gathering.

Thus, the following individual participation techniques were used:

- Structured and semi-structured interviews.
- Contextual interviews.
- Usability and accessibility testing.
- Observations, including Think-Aloud Protocol Analysis.
- Paper mock up.
- Click demo.
- Wizard of Oz.

In addition, focus groups with experts and creativity sessions took place as group participation techniques.

Objective and subjective evaluation tools were used to accomplish and allow carrying out the evaluation techniques designed to assess each solution to be tested in Cloud4all pilots. To this end, subjective tools, such us, questionnaires, forms or service diaries, together with objective tools like timed tasks, video/sound/screen recording, whenever possible, were applied for the validation of Cloud4all applications with end-users.

The relations between the tools evaluated and the research hypothesis, tasks to be performed per tool, measures to be taken, plus the indicators and metrics used per tasks and sub-tasks are a critical point of research. The indicators and metrics used during this first iteration are standard metrics and procedures in usability. The general subjective measures are: perceived ease of use, usefulness, satisfaction, learnability and trust. Each pilot scenario has been related to target audience, research hypothesis, scope, usability metrics and thresholds and has been evaluated so.

The following table shows an example of the indicators and thresholds for a task of the scenario for the developers; "The user opens the semantic alignment tool to search the ontology".

Table 1. Indicators and thresholds for task "The user opens the semantic alignment tool to search the ontology"

Indicators	Metrics	Success thresholds
Timing measure	Minutes & Seconds	< 1' 30'' sec
Task completion	Binary (Yes, No)	Yes
Errors	Number	[< 2]
Help requests	Number	[< 2]

Since the environment has a great role in the pilots' realization and in Cloud4all, as mention above, we have pilot sites in 3 different countries in Europe (Greece, Spain and Germany), we tried to be as detailed as possible in order to keep a standard baseline among the different sites. Thus, a common agenda has been created with detailed steps of the procedure to be followed by the pilots' facilitators. Even if some small details have changed from one site to the other, this would not create important bias in our study. Nevertheless, the variety of the pilot sites and the complexity of the study in relation to the deferent environments and cultural issues may bias the trials, but this was an issue that was not taken into account in this first evaluation phase. Results of this phase allowed us to gain some conclusions for the next phases.

3.5 Results Analysis Tools and Communication of the Results with the Developers

The purpose of using data collection instruments (e.g. questionnaires, facilitator's diary) is to expedite the collection of necessary data for meeting the objective of each iteration phase. Good collection tools are simple, concise, and reliable. Similarly, good analysis tools assist analysis and reporting in all evaluation phases. According to Rubin & Chisnell [17], data analysis falls into two different types. The immediate (preliminary) reporting of problems aims to quickly ascertain any arising issues. Main patterns and trends identified within each pilot site were reported in users.gpii.net. Recommendations based on identified problems and bugs should be swiftly reported, in order for members of the development teams to be able to implement any changes on time. These issues should include only obvious problems (i.e. evaluators should be cautious and sometimes report less than more). In addition, any consequent changes at the tools to be tested should be in agreement with pilot site leaders to avoid using- and therefore testing -different versions in different sites.

The second level of analysis is the overall evaluation for each iteration cycle. It is a thorough analysis which aims to provide a comprehensive and in depth analysis leading to a concise report of main results and findings, and their diffusion mechanisms to interested parties within the project in the form of specific recommendations for the next stage of development.

As the level of complexity within the Cloud4all evaluation framework is rather high and potentially increases in the next iterations, two perspectives for data analysis were adopted and presented: data source-wise (driven by metric type) and tool-wise (driven by tool tested) with consideration and account for the inevitable overlap between the two perspectives.

Statistical analysis entails three separate steps and is associated with two reporting stages:

- Data compilation;
- Creating summaries;
- Data analysis;
- Creating a detailed account of recommendations for the second iteration phase based on a common template;
- Produce the first iteration evaluation report.

Chosen analysis path depends on data types. Subjective data from questionnaires were quantified based on a unified coding scheme and will be treated as ordinal. Objective data are easily quantifiable and mostly treated as continuous.

4   Conclusions

This paper describes the pilot evaluation framework for the 1st evaluation phase of Cloud4all project. It depicts the main highlights of the testing, providing to the reader an overview of the research questions to be addressed in Cloud4all in general and continues with specific details of the plans for the 1st iteration tests. The main scenarios performed by the users, the participants details, the experimental plan and the results analysis tools follow to give to the reader a holistic idea of the Cloud4all pilots testing.

This 1st iteration phase of pilots of Cloud4all was an important lesson for the facilitators and the developers of the project. The results of this evaluation where gathered and distributed to the developers, following a feedback loop that was very helpful for the updated of the various tools. The developers received a document with issues from the different pilot site, that was specifying the severity of the issue, the tool and the specific task this issue was met and the recommendation from the pilots.

During this phase, some issues were raised and important lessons were learned for the preparation and the realization of the pilots. These lessons will be taken into account when planning the next iteration phases. The evaluation of the auto-configuration provided a lot of valuable feedback, for the next iteration of the design process. The concept was perceived to be very promising and interesting by the participants. The evaluation also revealed that we still have a long way to go with the developers' tools and the way of involving them in the evaluation procedure. Also, there are a lot still to be done with regard to the development of methodologies for evaluation and the design of the measurement instruments.

Acknowledgements. Results presented in this paper have been researched within the Cloud4all project. Cloud4all is an R&D project that receives funding from the European Commission under the Seventh Framework Program (FP7/2007-2013) under grant agreement n° 289016.

References

1. Cloud4all project, CN. 289016, 7th Framework Programme, ICT-2011.5.5 ICT for smart and personalised inclusion (November 2011), http://cloud4all.info/
2. Consolvo, S., Arnstein, L., Franza, B.R.: User Study Techniques in the Design and Evaluation of a Ubicomp Environment. In: Borriello, G., Holmquist, L.E. (eds.) UbiComp 2002. LNCS, vol. 2498, pp. 73–90. Springer, Heidelberg (2002)
3. Belotti, F., Berta, R., DeGloria, A., Margarone, M.: User Testing a Hypermedia Tour Guide. IEEE Pervasive Computing, 33–41 (2002)

4. International Standards Organization. ISO 9241-11: Ergonomic equirements for office work with visual display terminals (VDTs). Part 11: Guidance on usability. Geneva: International Standards Organization (1998)
5. Gould, J.D., Lewis, C.: Designing for usability: key principles and what designers think. Communications of the ACM 28(3), 300–311 (1985)
6. Shackel, B.: Human factors and usability. In: Preece, J., Keller, L. (eds.) Human-Computer Interaction: Selected Readings. Prentice Hall, Hemel Hempstead (1990)
7. Shackel, B.: Usability – context, framework, definition, design and evaluation. In: Shackel, B., Richardson, S. (eds.) Human Factors for Informatics Usability, pp. 21–37. Cambridge University Press, Cambridge (1991)
8. Sharp, H., Rogers, Y., Preece, J.: Interaction design: beyond human-computer interaction. John Wiley, London (2007)
9. Stone, D., Jarrett, C., Woodroffe, M., Minocha, S.: User interface design and evaluation. Morgan Kaufmann, San Francisco (2005)
10. Bevan, N.: Quality in use for all. In: Stephanidis, C. (ed.) User Interfaces for All: Methods, Concepts and Tools, pp. 353–368. Lawrence Erlbaum, Mahwah (2001)
11. Norman, D.A.: The invisible computer. MIT Press, Cambridge (1998)
12. Hassenzahl, M., Tractinksy, N.: User experience: a research agenda. Behaviour and Information Technology 25(2), 91–97 (2006)
13. Hassenzahl, M.: Hedonic, emotional and experiental perspective on product quality. In: Ghaoui, C. (ed.) Encyclopedia of Human Computer Interaction, pp. 266–272. Idea Group (2006)
14. Hassenzahl, M., Burmester, M., Koller, F.: AttrakDiff: Ein Fragebogen zur Messung wahrgenommener hedonischer und pragmatischer Qualität (AttrakDiff: A questionnaire for the measurement of perceived hedonic and pragmatic quality). In: Ziegler, J., Szwillus, G. (eds.) Mensch and Computer 2003: Interaktion in Bewegung, pp. 187–196. B.G. Teubner, Stuttgart (2003)
15. Hassenzahl, M., Law, E.L.-C., Hvannberg, E.T.: User experience: towards a unified view. In: Law, E.L.-C., Hvannberg, E.T., Hassenzahl, M. (eds.) Proceedings of the 2nd COST294-MAUSE International Open Workshop (2006)
16. Rosson, M.B., Carroll, J.M.: Usability Engineering: Scenario-Based Development of Human-Computer Interaction. Morgan Kaufmann, San Francisco (2001b)
17. Rubin, J., Chisnell, D.: Handbook of Usability Testing: Howto Plan, Design, and Conduct Effective Tests. Wiley (2008)
18. GPII, Global Public Infrastructure, http://gpii.net/

Enabling Architecture: How the GPII Supports Inclusive Software Development

Colin Clark[1], Antranig Basman[2], Simon Bates[3], and Kasper Galschiøt Markus[4]

[1] OCAD University, Toronto, Canada
cclark@ocad.ca
[2] Raising the Floor - USA
amb26@raisingthefloor.org
[3] OCAD University, Toronto, Canada
sbates@ocadu.ca
[4] Raising the Floor - International, Geneva, Switzerland
kasper@raisingthefloor.org

Abstract. The Global Public Inclusive Infrastructure is an international effort to build tools, components, services and a sustainable community to support personalized digital inclusion[1]. The GPII is building the critical infrastructure needed by developers to produce the next generation of low-cost assistive technology and highly flexible applications that can adapt to the needs and preferences of individuals across web, desktop, and mobile platforms.

To deliver on these ambitious goals, the GPII architecture team has created an evolving suite of development tools, idioms, and resources to support the creation of an inclusive infrastructure.

Keywords: Accessibility, inclusive design, GPII, development tools, assistive technology, JavaScript, Node.js, Inversion of Control.

1 What Is the GPII Development Platform?

The GPII Development Platform provides reusable frameworks that are employed extensively throughout the GPII ecosystem. These frameworks are designed to reduce the time, cost, and complexity of developing core services that conform to the GPII architecture, as well as ensuring that software is more easily testable, scalable, and capable of accommodating diverse user needs and preferences.

Currently, the GPII Development Platform consists of the following core framework technologies:

1. **Infusion**, a JavaScript application framework built by the Fluid Project to support highly flexible, model-driven, and personalizable applications and authoring environments on the web [7]
2. **Kettle**, a companion framework to Infusion that supports the creation of RESTful, JSON-oriented server-side applications and services[8]

C. Stephanidis and M. Antona (Eds.): UAHCI/HCII 2014, Part IV, LNCS 8516, pp. 368–377, 2014.
© Springer International Publishing Switzerland 2014

3. The **real-time framework**, which provides the core components and lifecycle support for the GPII's "personalization from preferences" functionality[2]
4. The **preferences framework** is built on top of Infusion and the real-time framework and supports the creation of diverse preferences editors and discovery tools that are tailored to users[6]

2 Overview of the Frameworks

2.1 Infusion

Fluid Infusion is a JavaScript library that primarily comprises the Infusion Inversion of Control (IoC) system and the Fluid Renderer. Infusion runs both on the client-side in a web browser as well as on the server and local devices using Node.js[16]. In a web browser, it uses the popular jQuery library[20] as a foundation library. Inversion of Control is a powerful software development technique popularised by Martin Fowler[5] and others, which helps to bridge the worlds of developers, integrators and end users by deferring to a framework the responsibility for wiring together parts of an application. In the case of Infusion, the dependencies between components are specified in a declarative form. Declarative programming as well as the related topic of aspect-oriented programming (AOP) will be discussed in sections 5 and 7.

2.2 Kettle

Kettle, another JavaScript library, lies one level above Infusion in the architectural stack. It is a piece of server-side infrastructure that makes use of Infusion's facilities for declarative programming to help developers express server applications in terms of easily authorable and sharable JSON documents. Kettle is capable of expressing server endpoints using standard web protocols. Kettle currently supports two types of endpoints: traditional RESTful services using HTTP, and WebSockets[3] endpoints that are suitable for realtime, bidirectional communication between client and server. As well as being based on Infusion, Kettle makes use of the popular Node.js server-side JavaScript platform[16] and the Express middleware library[17] for foundational HTTP and WebSockets protocol support.

2.3 The Real-Time Framework

The GPII's real-time framework is itself layered on Kettle and hence also on Infusion. It is responsible for orchestrating the personalization workflow both on local devices (for mobile and desktop operating systems) and in the cloud (for browser-based applications). The real-time framework provides the events and extensible lifecycle points that enable a user to be recognized, their preferences fetched from the cloud, and the appropriate applications and settings to be configured automatically for the user. The real-time framework is composed of several major components including the Preferences Server, Flow Manager, Solutions Registry, Matchmakers, and the Lifecycle Manager. These components are discussed in detail in [18]. When the real-time framework runs locally on a Windows, Linux, or Android device, it interfaces directly with the operating system's applications, access features, and settings storage mechanisms. On the web, it produces a specification that describes the settings required by the user, delegating to the web application itself to actually enact the necessary adaptations.

2.4   The Preferences Framework

The preferences framework is a further JavaScript library that occupies an intermediate position in the technology stack. It is layered on top of Infusion and is capable of interacting with the real-time framework in order to mediate support for editing, transforming, and enacting user preferences and settings. It includes several browser-based user interface components implemented using Infusion, which can be used both to visualize and adjust a user's preference set. It also includes components to store and retrieve a preference set from various sources, including local browser storage and the preferences server component of the real-time framework. It also has the capability to allow a user or an integrator to create their own preference editing interfaces from elements authored by others, rather than requiring the involvement of a developer to write a new application. In order to do this, it makes use of the declarative programming capabilities offered by Infusion's IoC.

3   How the Development Platform Is Used

The Development Platform is currently in active use by a number of teams and projects working to build the Global Public Inclusive Infrastructure and other tools. As mentioned above, Kettle and Infusion are used foundationally across a large number of GPII components, and are used to build the other parts of the Development Platform such as the real-time framework and the preferences framework.

Beyond this, the Development Platform is being used to automatically configure desktop, mobile, and web platforms. The real-time framework can be installed locally on any Windows, Linux, or Android device. Web-based applications can invoke the cloud-based Flow Manager as a web service.

The Cloud4All project is currently developing two applications that enable a user to edit her preferences and device settings. The *Preferences Management Tool* provides a comprehensive web-based user interface for creating, editing, and saving a needs and preferences set to the GPII Preferences Server. The *Personal Control Panel* resides on the user's local device and allows for the adjustment of current settings on-the-fly. For example, the PCP can be used to quickly toggle captions on when the user enters a noisy environment.

The PMT and the PCP use the preferences framework to:

1. render user interface controls that allow the user to change preferences and settings
2. enact in-page previews that show the effect a particular change will have on the system
3. retrieve, transform, and save user preferences to a data source

Further information about the preferences framework and how it can be used by developers of preferences editors is discussed in [21].

Infusion, as the most mature framework in the GPII Development Platform, has also been used for a variety of other applications and projects that preceed the GPII, such as uPortal [22], Fluid Engage [23] and CollectionSpace [24].

The following diagram illustrates the dependency relationships between components of the GPII Development Platform as well as applications that use it. Solid lines represent integral dependencies, while dashed line denote optional or "soft" dependencies that can be swapped out by specifying an alternative configuration. It is worth noting that all dependencies occur downward in a acyclic

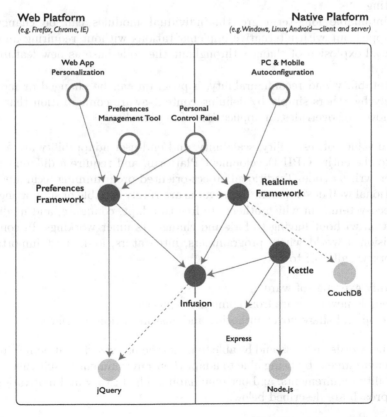

Fig. 1. The components and dependencies of the GPII Development Platform

graph, illustrating the fact that the frameworks of the GPII Development Platform are effectively layered. This ensures that a developer can use a lower-level component without requiring a dependency on higher or more specific layers of the system.

4   Infusion and Architectural Flexibility

The GPII's architectural approach and philosophy is inspired by Infusion, which serves as the technical backbone on which the Development Platform is built. Infusion is an ongoing project of the Fluid community, a key contributor to the GPII effort.

Infusion provides a comprehensive framework and Inversion of Control system that provides developers with a means to weave together many small, self-contained modules into a whole application without requiring hard-coded relationships between each module[4]. This helps to ensure:

1. a high degree of testability; each unit in a program can be tested in isolation, and mock objects can be inserted into a program to support integration testing
2. maintainable long-term growth; individual modules can be changed or swapped out with alternative implementations without requiring an exponential explosion of changes throughout the code base as new features are added
3. adaptability and reconfigurability; a program can be changed or modified freely by others simply by defining context-aware configuration that adds, removes, or overrides an application's functionality

These values of testability, scalability, and end-user adaptability are foundational to the entire GPII Development Platform, and require a different mindset when writing code. Traditional object-oriented programming techniques and conventional web development frameworks are rarely capable of supporting software "ecosystems" in which others are free to adapt, configure, and modify an application without having to fork and change its inner workings. In contrast, we envision a world where programmers, integrators, and, most importantly, end-users are all able to:

1. modify existing software
2. assemble new software from component pieces
3. develop and share novel authoring and customization interfaces

In other words, users should be able to make themselves "feel at home" in their digital environment by being able to adapt their environment to suit their needs, accessibility requirements, and personal habits. The history and motivations for this approach are described below.

5   The GPII Platform in Context of Software Development Trends

Typical programming code is designed for a limited audience. Imperative programming of the '70s and '80s was designed primarily for the compiler. If you wanted to change the behaviour of a program, you needed to find its source code, modify it, and submit it to the compiler again. Object-orientation, a scheme for promoting greater code reuse that became popular in the '80s and '90s, increased this audience marginally; it was possible to *derive* from the originator's implementation without necessarily having access to its source. However, this code still needed to be compiled and then submitted to the user in place of the originator's version.

Later programming developments such as *aspect-oriented programming* (AOP) promised to lengthen the chain of possible creative networks by one more link[12]. With AOP, it was possible to *advise* an existing implementation from the outside in order to change its behaviour, making use of global specifications that match pieces of implementation wherever they may be. Despite this improvement in reusability, these pieces of advice could not themselves easily be advised, creating yet another limitation for extensibility.

We argue that in traditional development environments, users and integrators who want to modify an originator's implementation, but who are more than a certain critical distance from the originator's community, are typically locked out of being able to assemble and distribute modified versions. In this situation, the only recourse is to make a *fork* — to take the original implementation and create a copy that diverges from a snapshot taken of the original at a particular instance in time. The risk of forks in open source software is well-documented[9]. Although tools increasingly exist to reduce the costs of resolving such forks, members of one community are cut off from the benefits of innovation in another. This causes a loss of effort that is proportional to the number of different communities involved. With the GPII, our goal is to enable a "one size fits one" model of accessible development. This entails the creation of many different "versions" or adaptations of an application that can productively coexist and interact. We call this a *community of software creativity*. Such communities require a solution to the problems of large-scale reuse and forking.

6   Supporting Creative Communities

With the GPII Development Platform, we imagine an unbounded sphere of creativity that stretches from the communities of our developers to the communities of our users. A crucial touchstone of our approach is that *any action performed by one creator should be undoable by another*. That is, there should be no limitations in the system that causes the intention of some creators to be privileged above the contributions of others.

To accomplish this technically, the GPII Development Platform attempts to model applications as *documents* encoded as JSON-based *component trees* that can be shared, aggregated, modified, and re-shared without breaking the informational chains which link together diverse communities of interest.

7 Declarative Programming

Above, we described the GPII Development Platform as being declarative in nature. Although there is significant debate about which characteristics are intrinsic to a formally "declarative" system[13], J.W. Lloyd's informal description of the approach is useful as a pragmatic definition. He states that declarative programming entails "stating *what* is to be computed but not necessarily *how* it is to be computed" [14]. The emphasis is on the logical or semantic aspects of computation, rather than on low-level sequencing and control flow. More importantly, Paul Graham identifies the essential characteristic of declarative programming as representing program logic in data structures that can be manipulated by other programs. Discussing Lisp, he says that it "has no syntax. You write programs in the parse trees ... [that] are fully accessible to your programs. You can write programs that manipulate them ...programs that write programs"[19]. This characteristic is essential to Infusion and many other parts of the GPII Development Platform.

Infusion's declarative programming idiom, specifically the JSON-based *component trees* that represent the structure and relationships of a program in a semantically meaningful way, supports the creation of authoring tools and flow-based or model-driven programming environments. Where typical programming code, as described above, is one-directional and opaque to third, fourth, and fifth parties (i.e. the developers, integrators, and end-users who will ultimately customize and adapt their software), the GPII Development Platform attempts to open up the meaning and structure of an application to be editable both by humans and authoring tools.

This declarative approach is applied throughout the GPII Development Platform. For example, Kettle provides a declarative representation of the structure of server-side applications. A developer focuses on configuring her application and routing logic as trees of *server*, *app*, and *data source* components operated by a common framework based on Node.js[16], Express[17], and Infusion. Similarly, the Preferences Framework exposes a higher-level, schema-based representation of user preferences and how they should be bound to web UI controls such as sliders, buttons, or select boxes. This makes it easier for other components of the GPII infrastructure, such as matchmakers, to automatically generate personal control panels that are optimized to the particular user.

8 Third-Party Support Libraries

In addition to the frameworks that comprise the GPII Development Platform, a collection of lower-level third-party libraries is also employed. These help to provide a solid foundation that is aligned with prominent tendencies in open source web development. Aside from saving time and effort while developing the core responsibilities of the GPII, the use of third-party libraries also ensures that the development platform is interoperable with other popular tools available to developers. These prominent third-party libraries include CouchDB, jQuery, Express, and others. A few of these libraries are discussed below.

8.1 CouchDB

CouchDB is a document-oriented database that stores data natively in JSON[10]. Queries (or rather, *Views*) to a CouchDB database are expressed in JavaScript code using a map/reduce approach to enable highly concurrent database indexing[11]. Data is saved and retrieved using a RESTful, HTTP-based API, making CouchDB an effective fit for resource-oriented web applications such as those in the GPII architecture. Notably, storing data as JSON objects avoids common application architecture pitfalls such as the "impedance mismatch" problem common to most object/relational mapping libraries[15]. The Kettle framework provides a built-in *Data Source* for accessing data stored in CouchDB. Data Sources are an abstraction representing an arbitrary source of data that implements the get, set, and delete semantics of HTTP while preserving a highly declarative interface for developers.

8.2 CouchDB

jQuery is a very popular library for managing common front-end web development tasks such as Document Object Model (DOM) manipulation, rendering, and making network requests[20]. jQuery is employed by Infusion to provide a familiar interface for web developers who are developing dynamic HTML-based user interfaces.

9 Results and Next Steps

It is difficult to objectively measure the productivity afforded by a set of development tools without costly and error-prone comparison studies. It is the opinion of the authors that such an approach rarely produces pragmatic information with which our tools can be improved. Instead, it is more effective to listen to the subjective experience of developers who work daily with such frameworks and to measure the success of these tools based on the architectural principles of reusability, extensibility, and the potential for enabling communities of contribution.

Informally, we have observed that the developers of top level GPII components such as the Preferences Management Tool, the Personal Control Panel, and the Real-time Framework's Matchmaker components are able to develop their components in a way that is more effectively isolated from changes occurring in the rest of the system. The PMT and PCP tools, for example, are currently being developed in a distributed manner across two continents and four different time zones. This social complexity is simplified by the system's separation of concerns and layering, where a developer is able to work on their own component or "vertical slice" of an application without being impacted by parallel efforts occurring elsewhere in the codebase.

Another example of the practical benefits we have experienced when using the GPII Development Platfrom is related to a significant recent refactoring of the real-time framework, where Matchmaker implementations were migrated from inside the same runtime as the Flow Manager out into remote, cloud-deployed web services. The Flow Manager's strict decoupling of services from their dependents, provided by Infusion's IoC system, enabled this large-scale refactoring to occur with minimal impact on the Matchmakers themselves. More notably, no changes were required to the portions of the realtime-framework that depend a Matchmaker and its results.

Although the Development Platform has provided a number of observable benefits to developers of the GPII, there have also been significant challenges in adopting the new mindset that accompanies these frameworks. Developers have often found it intially difficult to navigate the unfamiliar landscape of JSON-based configuration, particularly in cases where they are accustomed to writing tightly-coupled code, such when developing user interfaces directly with jQuery. The Development Platform's greater abstraction and emphasis on declarative idioms provides significant production-oriented benefits, but it also represents a learning curve in these situations. This difficulty is compounded by a lack of documentation for many parts of the system, particularly Kettle. To date, we have attempted to address this problem by pairing new developers up with experienced mentors. However, this is not scalable and documentation represents a weak aspect of the system and a major point for future improvement. The GPII community is actively working to improve the comprehensiveness of the Development Platform's documentation, including tutorials, API references, and conceptual background information.

10   Community-Based Sustainability

The GPII Development Platform is open and evolving. It has benefitted from the more than six years of active development invested in frameworks such as Infusion and Kettle, and continues to grow under the stewardship of a federation of open source communities and funded projects such as Fluid, Cloud4All, Prosperity4All, Preferences for Global Access, Floe, and more. The software is available under an "open/open" license, and can be extended, modified, adapted, and commercialized freely.

References

1. GPII: The Global Public Inclusive Infrastructure, http://gpii.net/
2. Clark, C., et al.: A Detailed Tour of the Cloud4All Architecture, http://wiki.gpii.net/index.php/A_Detailed_Tour_of_the_Cloud4all_Architecture

3. The Mozilla Foundation: WebSockets,
   https://developer.mozilla.org/en-US/docs/WebSockets
4. Basman, A., Lewis, C., Clark, C.: To Inclusive Design Through Contextually Extended IoC. In: Videira Lopes, C., Fisher, K. (eds.) Companion to the 26th Annual ACM SIGPLAN Conference on Object-Oriented Programming, Systems, Languages, and Applications, OOPSLA 2011, pp. 237–256 (2011)
5. Fowler, M.: Inversion of Control Containers and the Dependency Injection pattern, http://martinfowler.com/articles/injection.html
6. Clark, C., et al.: Preferences Framework Overview, http://wiki.gpii.net/index.php/Preferences_Framework_Overview
7. Fluid Project: Fluid Infusion combines JavaScript, CSS, HTML and user-centered design, http://fluidproject.org/products/infusion/
8. Fluid Project: Kettle is a framework for building server-side Web applications using JavaScript and Node.js, http://wiki.fluidproject.org/display/fluid/Kettle
9. Viseur, R.: Fork impacts and motivations in free and open source projects. International Journal of Advanced Computer Science and Applications 3(2) (2012)
10. The Apache Software Foundation: Apache CouchDB is a database that uses JSON for documents, JavaScript for MapReduce queries, and regular HTTP for an API, http://couchdb.apache.org/
11. CouchDB Wiki: Introduction to CouchDB Views, https://wiki.apache.org/couchdb/Introduction_to_CouchDB_views
12. Kiczales, G., et al.: Aspect-oriented programming. ECOOP Springer Verlag (1997),
    http://citeseerx.ist.psu.edu/viewdoc/download?doi=10.1.1.115.8660&rep=rep1&type=pdf
13. C2 Wiki: Declarative Programming, http://c2.com/cgi/wiki?DeclarativeProgramming (accessed January 28, 2014)
14. Lloyd, J.: Practical advantages of declarative programming. In: Joint Conference on Declarative Programming, GULP-PRODE 1994 (1994)
15. Neward, T.: The Vietnam of Computer Science, http://blogs.tedneward.com/2006/06/26/The+Vietnam+Of+Computer+Science.aspx
16. Joyent: Node.js is a platform built on Chrome's JavaScript runtime for easily building fast, scalable network applications, http://nodejs.org/
17. Holowaychuk, T.J.: Express is a minimal and flexible node.js web application framework, http://expressjs.com/
18. Clark, C., et al.: A Cloud-Scale Architecture for Inclusion: Cloud4all and GPII. In: Assistive Technology: from Research to Practice, AAATE (2013)
19. Graham, P: Beating the Averages, http://paulgraham.com/avg.html
20. The jQuery Framework, http://jquery.com
21. Clark, C., et al.: How the Preferences Framework Works, http://wiki.gpii.net/index.php/How_the_Preferences_Framework_Works
22. uPortal, http://www.jasig.org/uportal
23. Fluid Engage: Transforming museum content for mobile, web, and in-house experiences, http://fluidengage.org/
24. Goodman, C. et al.: Architecting CollectionSpace: A Web-Based Collections Management and Information System for 21st Century Museum Professionals. In: Trant, J., Bearman, D. (eds.) Museums and the Web 2010: Proceedings. Archives & Museum Informatics, Toronto (2010),
    http://www.archimuse.com/mw2010/papers/goodman/goodman.html

Federating Databases of Assistive Technology Products: Latest Advancements of the European Assistive Technology Information Network

Valerio Gower, Renzo Andrich, and Andrea Agnoletto

CITT, IRCCS Fondazione Don Carlo Gnocchi, Milano, Italy
{vgower,randrich,aagnoletto}@dongnocchi.it

Abstract. Detailed information on the Assistive Technology (AT) Products available on the market is of paramount importance for many different stakeholders: people with disabilities and their family members, AT professionals, manufacturers/suppliers of AT products, researcher and developer, and policy makers. Since 2005 the organizations responsible for the major European AT information systems have joined together to create the European Assistive Technology Information Network (EASTIN). The core of the EASTIN network is the web portal www.eastin.eu that provides, in all the EU official languages, information on AT products and related material. In the last few years the EASTIN association promoted a series of projects aimed at improving the web portal and expanding the network to cover all the EU countries. This paper describes the main results of such projects.

Keywords: Assistive Technology information systems, Database Federation.

1 Introduction

Assistive Technology (AT) is a broad term that can be used to indicate any product, service or technology that can be used by, or aimed at, people with disability to improve functioning in activities that might otherwise be difficult or impossible [1]. The term Assistive, as opposed to Mainstream, refers to products, services or technologies specifically designed in consideration of functional limitations, for instance by providing alternative or augmentative information channels [2]. AT is therefore a term that encompass a wide range of products, including for example mobility devices, products for personal care and daily living activities, products for accessing computers or other information technologies, etc.

The information of what AT products are available on the market is important for many different stakeholders [3]: for **people with disabilities and their families**, in order to get knowledge of what products are available that could help them, and therefore contribute to the *empowerment* process [4]; for **health care and education professionals,** in order to suggest the most appropriate AT solution for their clients, for example during individual AT assessment; for **AT suppliers and manufacturers**, in order to get knowledge of existing competitors in the market; for **researchers and**

C. Stephanidis and M. Antona (Eds.): UAHCI/HCII 2014, Part IV, LNCS 8516, pp. 378–389, 2014.

developers, in order to get knowledge of what are the needs unmet by the existing products; for **policy makers** in order to get knowledge needed to improve the development of AT service delivery systems [2], [6].

The importance of ensuring access to accurate and impartial information on AT products to all the stakeholders needing it, has also been stressed by several studies and research projects [1],[3],[7], and is recognized as a right by article 4 of the UN Convention on the Rights of Persons with Disabilities [8].

Since the early 1980s, several AT information systems have been created in many countries around the world to respond to this need for information. Some among the information systems with the longer history are the Italian SIVA [9], the UK DLF-Data [10], the German Rehadat [11], and the US Abledata [12].

2   The European Assistive Technology Information Network

In 2005 the institutes responsible for the major European AT information systems joined together to create the European Assistive Technology Information Network (EASTIN) [3]. The EASTIN network stems from a project founded by the European Commission (EC) in 2004-2005 within the eTEN programme, and today includes the organisations responsible for the major European AT information systems in Denmark, United Kingdom, The Netherlands, Germany, Italy, France, Belgium and Spain. Associate partners, serving as National Contact Organizations, have also been appointed in 14 European countries. The network is currently operated by the EASTIN Association, a legal entity based in Italy supported by its partners through their annual membership fees.

The core of the EASTIN network is the web-site www.eastin.eu, that provides – in all the EU official languages – information on almost 70.000 AT products and some 20.000 companies (manufacturers, suppliers, and retailers of AT products); it also includes a library containing documents such as fact sheets, case studies, scientific publications, etc.

3   Technical Approach of the EASTIN System

The EASTIN system should not be seen as a database but rather as a search engine that aggregates the contents of several independent national databases (currently eight), each running on a different technological platform. The EASTIN search engine is able to perform AT product searches across all these databases in all EU languages. In order to allow National Contact Organizations that do not have their own national database to upload information on AT products and make them available though the EASTIN website, a Central Database has also been recently added to the system.

Since 2004 the EASTIN partners have worked together to harmonise their databases according to common requirements. The result of this work is the harmonized data structure used to present the product information in the EASTIN website.

The current EASTIN system, developed on Microsoft DOT NET Framework 4.0, is based on a three tier architecture (Presentation, Application, and Data) and the communication between the search engine and the databases of the information providers is ensured by Web Service technology. The user sends a query to the EASTIN system trough the website on his/her browser; the application logic analyzes the query and sends parallel requests to all the distributed databases trough the web service servers; the list of records retrieved from each database is then collected by the application logic and presented to the user on his/her browser Fig. 1.

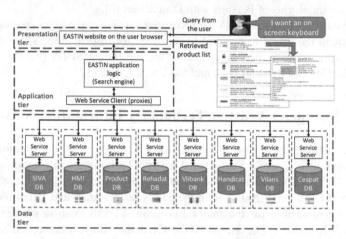

Fig. 1. Functional scheme of the EASTIN system

In the EASTIN portal the AT products, and documents, are classified according to the tasks they are intended for, using the ISO 9999:2011 standard "Assistive Products for Persons with Disability – Classification and terminology" [5].

4   Latest Developments of the EASTIN System

4.1   The Multilingual Query Processing Component

The EASTIN portal has been recently improved through the use of advanced language technologies developed within the EASTIN-CL project, a research project partially funded by the EC under the ICT policy support programme, that ran from March 2010 to June 2012 [13]. The most successful result of the EASTIN-CL project has been the development, and integration into the EASTIN portal, of a multilingual query processing (QP) component for supporting non expert users in retrieving data from the databases.

The QP component developed allows users to forward a free text search request in a "google-like" fashion by entering search terms in their native language. The component analyzes the terms entered and converts the natural language query into a formal query supported by the EASTIN system (i.e. it identifies the appropriate ISO 9999 classification codes). The QP is based on a large multilingual vocabulary (or termlist) that includes over 12000 terms for each supported language (currently English, Italian, Danish, German, Estonian, Latvian and Lithuanian).

The processing of the user query is done in several steps: the user input is split into meaningful single words, decomposed (in case of compound words, quite frequent in German for example), and the canonical forms (lemmata) are found. The lemmata are matched against the termlist. In case no match is found the closest candidate is returned (using a slightly modified Levenshtein distance measure). The QP component is therefore able to manage compound words, inflections (e.g. singular/plural, that are quite important for inflected languages like Italian), and spelling errors (e.g. "mobil" instead of "mobile").

The results retrieved by the QP component are then ordered according to their relevance, on a 1 to 5 scale, computed with a special algorithm that weights the number of words of the query in each "candidate" term found in the termlist, and the number of occurrences of the corresponding ISO 9999 codes.

4.2   The EASTIN Taxonomy for ICT-Based AT Products

The EASTIN association recently promoted the European Thematic Network on Assistive Information and Communication Technologies (ETNA), a project, partially funded by the ICT Policy Support Programme of the EC, aimed at improving the EASTIN portal with special focus on ICT-based AT [14]. The ETNA thematic network worked in conjunction with the ATIS4All Thematic Network   (Assistive Technologies and Inclusive Solutions for All) [15], that was aimed at creating an online community of all the stakeholders involved in the AT field, through a collaborative Portal offering information on AT, inclusive products and services, and cutting-edge technological trends. Both projects run from January 2011 to December 2013.

Within the ETNA project a Taxonomy has been developed for describing the following three categories of resources that constitute the domain of interest of the EASTIN system [16]: 1) Assistive Products, 2) Organizations (including Companies, Service Providers, and Projects), and 3) Information Materials (including Articles, Case Descriptions, Ideas, FAQs, Forums, News, and Regulations).

The Taxonomy identifies, for each of the three categories of resources, a Basic Dataset that represent the minimum set of information needed to: 1) uniquely identify a resource, 2) to understand what kind of resource it is and what it is about, and 3) to make the resource retrievable by the ETNA search engine. The basic dataset for Assistive products is reported in Table 1.

In the EASTIN portal a product record is composed of two parts: the basic information (i.e. the Basic Dataset reported in Table 1) and the technical details that represent the product Detailed Dataset. The Detailed Dataset of a product is composed of an array of Features, selected among the collection of all possible features that constitutes the taxonomy Vocabulary. The taxonomy Vocabulary is based on a two level hierarchy made up of Clusters and Features. Homogeneous Features are grouped together in the same Cluster. For example the Features "Firefox", "Chrome", "Safari", "Internet Explorer" , etc. are all grouped in the Cluster "Browsers", while "Printer", "Visual display", "Tactile display", etc... are grouped in the Cluster "Output devices".

Table 1. Basic Dataset for Assistive Products

Type of information	Item
Record identification	Product Name
	Product Code (database+ID)
Product Typology	Classification code and name
Dates	Insert Date
	Latest update date
Manufacturer information	Name
	Address, Postal code, Town, Country
	Phone, E-mail, Skype
	Website, Social network
Free text description	Description in original language
	Description in English
Images	Product small image url
	Product large image url
Links to further details	User manual
	Video demo
	Brochure
	Other documents
Source of information	Information provider name
	Information provider country
	Link to Full product record
Download/Purchase website	Download/purchase web page

Overall 18 Clusters and 237 Features have been identified so far. In Table 2 all the Clusters included in the current vocabulary are listed.

Table 2. List of Clusters included in the taxonomy

Overall dimensions	Capacity/Range	Energy type
Activation modalities	Operating systems	Visualization
Browsers	Languages	Input devices
Linguistic representations	Functionalities	Output adjustments
Input adjustments	Output devices	Price
Connectivity	License	Subdivisions

For identifying the Clusters and Features a model of ICT based product has been used (see Fig. 2) composed of the following conceptual "elements": Input, Central Unit (for processing and storage), Output, Connectivity (with other products or services),

Environment (in which the product operates), Physical characteristics, and Software characteristics.

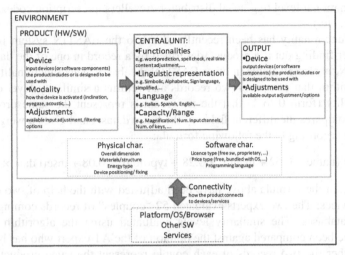

Fig. 2. Model of an ICT based product

A mechanism has been created to put the items of the taxonomy vocabulary in relation with the divisions (i.e. the product categories) identified by the ISO 9999 standard. A matrix has been created to indicate, for each of the item of the taxonomy vocabulary, the "relevance" in relation to the ISO 9999 divisions. Currently a subset of 38 ISO 9999 divisions have been considered (those more strictly related to ICT products). The relevance of a taxonomy item for each of the identified ISO divisions is evaluated by means of a 5-points scale (1 'absolutely irrelevant' to 5 'absolutely relevant'). For instance, for the ISO division "22.36.18 Input Software", the item "Width (Overall dimensions)" is ranked "1" while item "Accelerometer (Input Devices)" is ranked "3" and item "Linux (Operating Systems)" is ranked "5".

This "ranking" of taxonomy items is used in the EASTIN system to present the vocabulary of features ordered by relevance, with respect to the specific product category, in two situations: when a user performs an advanced search, and when an administrator enters a new product to the EASTIN system.

The EASTIN taxonomy is intended to be a dynamically changing vocabulary. New items can in fact be added to the taxonomy (both Clusters and Features) if they are needed. A consensus procedure for deciding on the introduction of new items in the taxonomy has been defined.

4.3   The Similarity Tool

In the EASTIN system multiple records describing the same product may be present in different databases. If a product is available in different countries, say for example

Italy, Denmark and Germany, each national database may have a record describing the product. Each record will include not only information relevant at "international level" (e.g. commercial name, manufacturer, description, etc.) but also information relevant at national level (e.g. local distributors/resellers, prescription codes, tax relief information, etc.).

A new functionality has been recently added to the EASTIN system in order to help the user finding out if a product, described by a record in one of the databases of the EASTIN, is also available in other EASTIN databases. This functionality is based on an algorithm that compares two records and returns a similarity level defined as the probability (form 0 to 1) that the two records represent the same product. The algorithm compares the different fields of the basic dataset and gives a weight to each comparison according to the following formula:

$$\text{similarity} = (\text{name} \times 0.62 + \text{manuf.} \times 0.28 + \text{typology} \times 0.08 + \text{insert date} \times 0.02) \quad (1)$$

The weights in the formula above have been adjusted with the help of two experts of ICT AT devices. The two experts evaluated 52 "couples" of records coming from the EASTIN databases. The similarity levels evaluated using the algorithm for those couples have been compared against the opinion of the AT expert who has been asked to tell whether the two records of each couple represent the same product. Weights were then adjusted to minimize the number of false positives and false negatives.

4.4   The Product Review and Comment Facility

As a result of the joint efforts of the ETNA and ATIS4all projects, a facility has been developed that allows to post reviews and comments on the products available in the EASTIN databases. For capturing the user evaluation of an AT product, a simple questionnaire, based on the QUEST instrument [17] has been used. The user is asked to evaluate the product (on a 1 to 5 scale) along the set of items of the QUEST instrument, and to add any comment he/she wishes. The statistics of the product reviews (Fig. 3) and the details of each review can be accessed from the product detail page.

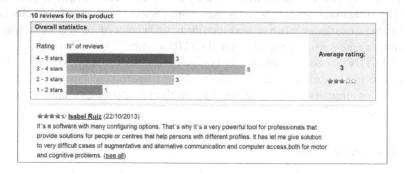

Fig. 3. Product rating facility

5   Federating EASTIN with the GPII Unified Listing

A coalition of academic, industry and non-governmental organizations and individuals have recently come together to promote the creation of a Global Public Inclusive Infrastructure (GPII), i.e. a global infrastructure that can deliver accessibility to every individual, instantly and automatically, where they need it, when they need it, on any device they encounter, and in a way that matches their unique requirements [7]. The CLOUD4all project [18], funded by the EC, aims at advancing the concept of the GPII by augmenting adaptation of individual products and services with automatic personalization of any mainstream product or service a user encounters based on the user's needs and preferences

One of the key component of the GPII is the Unified Listing (UL) of all available solutions to ICT access, including Assistive Technology products, and Accessibility Features and programs built into commercial products [7]. The UL will represent the knowledge base used both by humans (e.g. AT professionals, end-users, etc.) and by machines (e.g. tools for automatic personalization of products and services) to build up the most appropriate AT solution.

The EASTIN network, that represent a unique source of information on the AT products available on the European market and worldwide, will represent one of the main sources of information for the UL [19]. A bidirectional connection between EASTIN network and UL is currently under development and will allow the users of the UL to access information coming from the EASTIN databases, and vice-versa. In the following, the vision is described of how this connection is going to work at the end of the project.

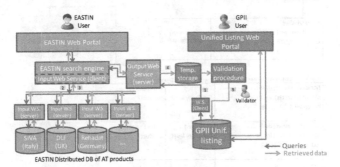

Fig. 4. Scheme of the GPII-EASTIN connection

The connection between the EASTIN search engine and the UL is based on RESTful Web Service technologies. The process of getting the information from the EASTIN databases, in order to store it in the UL, requires the following steps (Fig. 4):

- A Web Service Client sends a query to the EASTIN Web Service Server.
- The EASTIN search engine in turn sends the request to all the information providers that answer the request with the list of products.

- The list is saved to a Temporary Storage.
- Retrieved information is validated and stored in the Unified Listing.

The scope of the EASTIN portal and the GPII Unified Listing are different. The EASTIN information system includes assistive devices for people with disability in general (e.g. assistive devices for personal mobility, assistive devices for personal care, and more) whereas the GPII Unified Listing only includes products for ICT access. On the other side, EASTIN only includes assistive technology products, while the GPII Unified Listing will also include accessibility features in mainstream ICT products and assistive services. Moreover, differently from what happens in the EASTIN portal, where multiple records describing the same product may be retrieved in a search, the aim of the UL is having a single record for each product with multiple layers representing the "original product descriptions". For those reasons, before entering the product records retrieved from EASTIN into the UL database, a Validation Procedure is required, aimed at verifying whether a product is of interest for the UL and cluster "duplicated" records from different databases that deal with a single product into a single record

The validation will initially be a semi-automatic procedure (i.e. it will be performed by a human aided by automatic functions) with automatic processing later for updating the information of products already stored in the UL. A filter, based on the ISO 9999 classification codes, has been implemented to retrieve from EASTIN only products related to ICT and access.

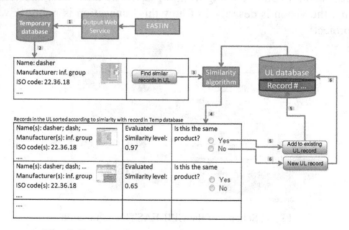

Fig. 5. Functional scheme of the validation procedure

Fig. 5. represents the functional scheme of the validation procedure: a record stored in the Temporary Database is loaded and details are shown; the similarity level of the record loaded with all the other records already stored in the UL database is evaluated (using the similarity algorithm described above). Based on the evaluated similarities the validator decides whether to store the current product into a new UL record or to add it to an existing UL record. In the UL the provenance of the record (database name and ID) is captured and stored to preserve the identity of the source of the record, and to allow for automatic update of UL records when data are updated in the original source database.

A mechanism is also under implementation to propagate modification made in the UL to the other databases that federate with it. When a product record in the UL is modified (e.g. an error is corrected, a new feature is added, a new version becomes available, ...) a feedback notice is provided to the "original sources" (i.e. the DBs where the data have been drawn from) and any other federated databases (Fig. 6).

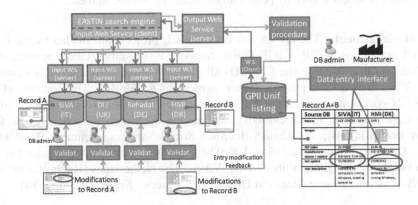

Fig. 6. Bi-directional federation scheme

A bi-directional federation of AT databases can contribute to reduce the effort needed to maintain the data, by sharing it among different information providers, and to improve the quality of data, by keeping all the databases updated on the most recent AT products available. Furthermore, it could provide companies with a more convenient mechanism to update their data across databases, again potentially contributing to reducing the cost and improving the quality of data.

5.1   Licensing and Crediting Sources of Information

For the long-term sustainability of the UL and its sources, it is important to preserve the provenance of the information, by giving appropriate credit to each source, and to establish appropriate license agreements between the UL and its sources. The UL is being designed so to represent an additional entry point to the data included in the federated databases rather than an alternative to those. A possible strategy for that is including information relevant at "transnational level" in the UL web portal while for the information relevant at "national" or "local" level the user will be redirected to the original information sources. In addition UL will also include a mechanism to count the number of visit to each record and communicate it to the original sources of information, so that the information providers can consider this as "indirect visits" to their databases.

6   Conclusions

By disseminating information and knowledge, the EASTIN system can contribute to the empowerment of people with disabilities, to support independence, choice and control in relation to AT, and to inform and develop the work of professionals involved in the disability field. Furthermore, by providing a comprehensive and detailed overview of the European AT market it can help AT manufacturers and suppliers to make their products known by people all over Europe who need them.

Acknowledgements. The ETNA and EASTIN-CL projects are funded by the European Commission's CIP – ICT Policy Support Programme (Grant agreements # 270746 and # 2504327). The CLOUD4All project is funded by European Commission 7th Framework Programme (Grant agreement # 289016). The contents of the EASTIN system are provided by the partners of the EASTIN Association: Fondazione Don Carlo Gnocchi, Italy (Siva DB); Institute der deutschen Wirschaft Koeln, Germany (Rehadat DB); The Danish Board of Social Services, Denmark (Hmi-Basen DB); Disabled Living Foundation, UK (Dlf-Data DB); Flemish Agency for Persons with Disability, Belgium (Vlibank DB); Vilans, The Netherlands (Huplmiddelenwijzer DB); Hacavie, France (Handicat DB); Ceapat Imserso, Spain (Catalogo DB)

References

1. Stack, J., Zarate, L., Pastor, C., Mathiassen, N.-E., Barberà, R., Knops, H., et al.: Analysing and federating the European assistive technology ICT industry. European Commission Information Society and Meida (2009)
2. AAATE. Position Paper: a view on Technology and Disability (2003),
   http://www.portale.siva.it/
   en-GB/databases/libraries/detail/id-135 (retrieved November 7, 2013)
3. Andrich, R.: Towards a global information network: the European Assistive Technology Information Network and the World Alliance of AT Information Providers. In: Gelderblom, G.J., Soede, M., Adriaens, L., Miesenberger, K. (eds.) Everyday Technology for Independence and Care, pp. 190–197. IOS Press, Amsterdam (2011)
4. Eustat Consortium. Assistive technology education for end-users - guidelines for trainers. European Commission, Milano (1999),
   http://portale.siva.it/en-GB/databases/libraries/detail/id-1
   European Commission DG XIII
5. International Organization for Standardization. International standard ISO 9999:2011. Assisitive products for person with disability – Classification and terminology (Fifth ed.). International Organization for Standardization, Geneve (2011)
6. Andrich, R., Mathiassen, N.-E., Hoogerwerf, E.-J., Gelderblom, G.J.: Service delivery systems for assistive technology in Europe: An AAATE/EASTIN position paper. Technology and Disability 25(3), 127–146 (2013)
7. Vanderheiden, G., Treviranus, J.: Creating a global public inclusive infrastructure. In: Stephanidis, C. (ed.) Universal Access in HCI, Part I, HCII 2011. LNCS, vol. 6765, pp. 517–526. Springer, Heidelberg (2011)

8. UN General Assembly. Convention on the Rights of Persons with Disabilities: resolution / adopted by the General Assembly (2007), `http://www.un.org/disabilities/convention/conventionfull.shtml` (retrieved October 04, 2013)
9. Andrich, R., Gower, V., Pigini, L., Caracciolo, A., Agnoletto, A.: Portale SIVA: The Italian National Portal on Assistive Technology. In: Gelderblom, G.J., Soede, M., Adriaens, L., Miesenberger, K. (eds.) Everyday Technology for Independence and Care, pp. 177–184. IOS Press, Amsterdam (2011)
10. DLF Data (n.d.), DLF Data Web Portal: http://www.dlf-data.org.uk/ (retrieved October 04, 2013)
11. Winkelmann, P.: REHADAT: The German Information System on Assistive Devices. In: Gelderblom, G.J., Soede, M., Adriaens, L., Miesenberger, K. (eds.) Everyday Technology for Independence and Care, pp. 163–169. IOS Press, Amsterdam (2011)
12. Lowe, S.: AbleData.com's Leap into the Future. In: Gelderblom, G.J., Soede, M., Adriaens, L., Miesenberger, K. (eds.) Everyday Technology for Independence and Care, pp. 198–204. IOS Press, Amsterdam (2011)
13. Gower, V., Andrich, R., Agnoletto, A., Winkelmann, P., Lyhne, T., Rozis, R., Thurmair, G.: The european assistive technology information portal (EASTIN): Improving usability through language technologies. In: Miesenberger, K., Karshmer, A., Penaz, P., Zagler, W. (eds.) ICCHP 2012, Part I. LNCS, vol. 7382, pp. 215–222. Springer, Heidelberg (2012)
14. Andrich, R., Gower, V., Vincenti, S.: Information Needs Related to ICT-Based Assistive Solutions. In: Miesenberger, K., Karshmer, A., Penaz, P., Zagler, W. (eds.) ICCHP 2012, Part I. LNCS, vol. 7382, pp. 207–214. Springer, Heidelberg (2012)
15. ATIS4all Project (2011), `http://www.atis4all.eu/` (retrieved September 18, 2012)
16. Gower, V., Andrich, R., Lyhne, T.: A Taxonomy for Describing ICT-based Assistive Technologies. In: Encarnação, P., Azevedo, L., Gelderblom, G.J., Newell, A., Mathiassen, N.-E. (eds.) Assistive Technology: From Research to Practice, pp. 254–260. IOS Press, Amsterdam (2013)
17. Demers, L., Weiss-Lambrou, R., Ska, B.: The Quebec User Evaluation of Satisfaction with Assistive Technology (QUEST 2.0): an overview and recent progress. Technology and Disability 14(3), 101–105 (2002)
18. Cloud4all project (n.d.), `http://cloud4all.info/` (retrieved November 11, 2013)
19. Gower, V., Vanderheiden, G., Andrich, R.: Federating Databases of ICT-based Assistive Technology Products. In: Encarnação, P., Azevedo, L., Gelderblom, G.J., Newell, A., Mathiassen, N.-E. (eds.) Assistive Technology: From Research to Practice, pp. 1345–1351. IOS Press, Amsterdam (2013)

The GPII on Desktops in PCs OSs:
Windows and GNOME

Javier Hernández Antúnez[1], Colin Clark[2], and Kasper Galshiot Markus[3]

[1] Emergya, Sevilla, Spain
[2] Inclusive Design Resource Center, OCAD University, Toronto, Canada
[3] Raising the Floor - International, Geneva, Switzerland
jhernandez@emergya.com

Abstract. Since The Global Public Inclusive Infrastructure [1] aims to become an international standard, one of the biggest challenge of the GPII project is to support the many Operating Systems that are running in our Personal Computers. Nowadays, we make an extensive use of personal computers—both laptops and desktops—and their Operating Systems in a lot of circumstances, and as a result of this, we can say that a lot of people could have difficulties when they start using a new computer. Add to this the diversity of different software applications that people use and their many different restrictions of use, and the problem becomes bigger when a person needs some Assistive Technology [2] to use a computer efficiently .As part of the Cloud4all project, the implementation of the GPII on PC OSs is taking place to address these problems. By having a first version of this implementation, the GPII is ready to help the users to solve their problems when using a new PC's OS for the first time.

Keywords: Accessibility, Internet Access, Health, Social inclusion, Cloud.

1 Motivation

1.1 Background

To demonstration how we use personal computers and different operating systems in different contexts, we can describe some real-life scenarios:

- We use our own PCs, either for work or for other personal affairs
- We use others' or shared PCs at work, at home, or at any public place
- We use public "kiosks" [3] that run standard PC OSs such as Windows or Linux for a variety of different purposes

Also, most people with disabilities who need Assistive Technology (AT) to bridge the gap between them and the digital era are using the most popular OSs. These typically include Microsoft Windows, Apple's Mac OS X, or the open-sourced operating system GNU/Linux. Users generally employ a variety of ATs running on their PC OSs.

C. Stephanidis and M. Antona (Eds.): UAHCI/HCII 2014, Part IV, LNCS 8516, pp. 390–400, 2014.

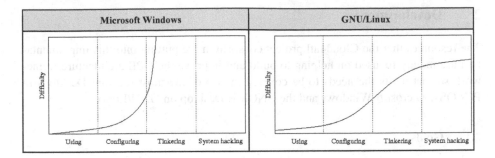

Fig. 1. Learning curves and typical usage of operating systems

If we take a look at the following OS learning curves, we see that there is a progression from beginner to experienced user. It takes some time before a user can properly configure the system to fit his personal needs and preferences. Once a user becomes more familiar with the concept of an OS, what he can do with it, and how he has to use it, the next step in the progression is to be able to configure the system to his needs and preferences. This typically requires more time and it depends on the platform specific built-in capabilities.

1.2   Benefits

Because of the importance of making it easier for users to configure their systems for their personal needs and preferences, the implementation of PC OS autoconfiguration is a key deliverable of the European-funded Cloud4all project. Significant effort has been invested to accomplish this goal and to create a real life demonstration of the benefits of using the cloud-based approach that the GPII project is building right now.

The primary benefit of using the GPII on any PC OS is to take advantage of the Auto-Personalisation capabilities from the users' needs and preferences, which can take into account all the preferences that are coming either from the built-in OS's capabilities, from any third-party application, or from any AT, such as a screen reader for people who are blind, or a screen magnifier for people who are visually impaired. By addressing this implementation, a lot of people will save time and won't have to learn the complex, required platform-specific processes to adapt the system to their needs and preferences.

Another benefit of this implementation is that PC OSs provide more interoperability and flexibility in terms of development, and importantly have significant computing capacity. PC OSs will be the systems where the GPII will run in order to interact with the many different GPII components over the Internet, and taking part in the Cloud infrastructure that will be built around the GPII.

2   Development

The resources that the Cloud4all project consortium are putting into this implementation are mainly focused on helping to build and improve the GPII architecture framework so that it fits the needs to be covered in two of the most relevant Desktops in PCs OSs, Microsoft Windows and the GNOME Desktop on GNU/Linux.

2.1   Goals

From the Cloud4all project perspective, the goals to be achieved in this implementation were explained in detail in the Cloud4all Description of Work document. The main objectives can be summarized as follows:

1. To work with Microsoft, GNU/Linux and GNOME communities, to:
    a. Identify all of the accessibility related features in their respective OS's
    b. Build "auto-personalization from profile" (APfP) capability into:
        i.   the built-in accessibility features in GNU/Linux within the GNOME desktop
        ii. the bundled accessibility software with GNU/Linux within the GNOME desktop
        iii. the built-in accessibility features in Windows
2. To develop translation mechanisms to convert the generic preference profiles into specific settings appropriate for the accessibility related features and software on the OS.
3. To demonstrate the ability of each of these operating systems and accessibility applications:
    a. to automatically load all accessibility related preferences from the OS/application up to the cloud (and other preference storage mechanisms) on user request
    b. to download accessibility related preferences for their OS/ application and apply them either permanently or temporarily (so that original settings return when the user is finished) on user request

2.2   Results

After more than two years of research and development, the Cloud4all project has successfully created the required mechanisms to turn this vision into a reality on PCs. This work included:

*   Finding all the relevant common preferences, provided both by the OS and by third-party applications

- Creating the required mechanisms to interact with all these preferences from many different resources
- Providing cross-platform translation mechanisms for the preferences between the different OSs and third-party software
- Identifying how the environmental context and device's capabilities could affect the people regarding the use of their Personal Computer
- Focusing on covering all the most critical aspects in terms of accessibility

To specifically describe what that this means in terms on this particular implementation of the GPII on Desktops PCs OSs, the efforts of the project could be summarized by the following two points.

- To provide a *technical solution* to:
  - Identify and provide the ability to interact with, and to configure, the most relevant accessibility built-in features from both Microsoft Windows and from one of the most popular desktop environments for the open-sourced GNU/Linux platform, GNOME.
  - Identify and to provide the ability to interact with the most relevant settings in the most popular screen readers that are available on the two focus platforms, NVDA (for Microsoft Windows) and GNOME Orca (for GNU/Linux), and provide the required mechanisms to automatically configure their settings.
- To create the *transformation mechanisms* that will bring the ability to switch from one platform into another. This mechanism will not only be available for these two platforms but for others such as the Android platform or any AT solutions running in the same, or in any other platform.

These two points are explained in detail in the following two points, *Technical solution* and *Transformation mechanisms*.

2.3   Technical Solution

Since the GPII Personalization framework was conceived to cover any need on any platform, it shares the same code base for all platforms. It can even be used by platforms that cannot directly run the GPII by themselves through an online instance of the GPII's Flow Manager [4], which is the component responsible for orchestrating the personalization of any solution on any device.

Having said that, from a technical perspective, the implementation of the GPII on PC OSs is mostly focused in covering the gaps between some of the architectural components of the GPII Personalization framework and the OS itself.

Since the GPII architecture has been already explained in detail in A Cloud-Scale Architecture for Inclusion: Cloud4all and GPII [5], and briefly explained in the following schema,

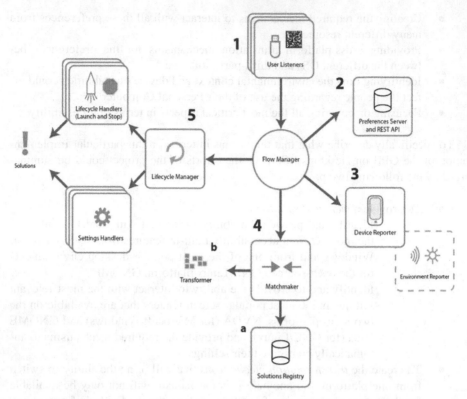

Fig. 2. A *CloudScale Architecture for* Inclusion: Cloud4all and GPII [5]

we would like just to mention those components that are relevant to this specific implementation.

Settings Handlers

In terms of personalization, the GPII's settings handlers are responsible for configuring the settings of an application, access feature, or assistive technology. They are often, but not always, specific to a particular platform, so the GPII provides support for some common standard configuration mechanisms based on well-known formats such as JSON, XML and INI [6].

As an example of a platform specific settings handler, the GNU/Linux implementation makes use of GSettings, the GNOME's configuration system, to make on-the-fly personalizations of the desktop environment, such as:

- Turn on/off some built-in accessibility services and features such as the on-screen keyboard, screen reader, screen magnifier, high-contrast, visual alerts, etc.
- Set specific values to some aspects of these accessibility services such as the magnification factor.

- Change some default behaviours of the user interface that are not specifically accessibility-related such as the preferred applications, background, font-size, windows animations, etc.

This settings handler was created to fill this requirement on GNOME-based PCs. Many other platform-specific settings handlers were written too, including:

- Windows Registry Settings Handler, which deals with Microsoft Windows' registry.
- Windows SystemParametersInfo Settings Handler, which handles Microsoft Windows SPI calls.
- GNOME Orca Settings Handler, which handles GNOME Orca's settings.
- GNU/Linux ALSA, to deal with system's output volumes.
- GNU/Linux Xrandr to deal with the screen's resolution and brightness.

Lifecycle Manager

The GPII has to know about how to orchestrate all these settings handlers in order to automatically configure the system to the user, and this is the responsibility of the lifecycle manager.

In this case, the lifecycle manager usually makes use of well-known cross platform mechanisms, known as *Lifecycle Actions*, to apply a configuration using the settings handlers. They also include some simple platform-specific mechanisms for starting and stopping an application. Since lifecycle actions tend to be simple and can be implemented in a cross-platform compatible way, we haven't had to implement any additional platform-specific component to address this. Instead, we have just to had define, using a declarative JSON specification, how a solution should be treated by the GPII.

Solutions Registry

The solutions registry is where the full information about how to configure a solution is stored, including:

- The application described as a solution
- The settings handler(s) that a solution uses and the way it makes use of it
- The required lifecycle actions to trigger the personalization process
- The available transformations of some settings into the already supported common terms

User Listeners

In order to allow the user to automatically personalize his system through the GPII, a mechanism needs to be provided with every PC OSs implementation called a *User*

Listener. Right now, both Windows and GNU/Linux platforms support the most relevant authentication mechanisms, including:

- USB Drive
- NFC Tag

Since the authentication mechanism is, like the rest of the GPII, an HTTP request, it's very easy to add new user listeners to a platform, such as a fingerprint-based one or by using face recognition.

2.4   Transformation Mechanisms

Nowadays, every   software in the world has a lot of settings that allows to any user to make changes on them to fit their preferences. But this can be a problem, because in most cases, each application defines their own settings without taking into account the settings that other similar software has already defined.

One of the biggest challenges of the GPII and Cloud4all projects is to address these problems, by providing the required mechanisms to easily move any application-specific setting into another, and similar in concept, a different application-specific setting. To explain this we can take some similar settings from two different screen readers, NVDA [7] for Microsoft Windows PCs and GNOME Orca [8] for GNU/Linux PCs.

Table 1.

NVDA	GNOME Orca
speech.espeak.rate	voices.default.rate
speech.espeak.pitch	voices.default.average-pitch
speech.espeak.volume	voices.default.gain
speech.espeak.voice	voices.default.family
keyboard.speakTypedCharacters	enableEchoByCharacter
keyboard.speakTypedWords	enableEchoByWord
speech.symbolLevel	verbalizePunctuationStyle

As you can see in the table, these settings are conceptually the same thing but with different names. Also, another implication is that every setting has different value ranges for its values depending on the application. As an example, if we take both the NVDA's speech.espeak.voice and Orca's voices.default.family, their values aren't structured in the same way:

Table 2.

NVDA's *speech.espeak.voice*	GNOME Orca's *voices.default.family*
en\\en	{"locale": "en", "name": "english"}

By having a *common term* as a general way of defining a preference and its value range, implementers can easily map an application-specific setting into a common term, which can be used to move an application specific preference into another application specific preference.

For this reason, and due to the lack of standardization, the GPII and Cloud4All are putting efforts on creating a Common Terms Registry [9] to provide an unified list of settings to be used during the developments of the GPII personalization framework.

Right now, implementers of the Cloud4all project are making use of this common terms registry within the model transformation mechanisms available in the GPII framework [10] in order to move settings from one platform into another. But this is just part of the solution to the problem.The Cloud4all project is investing a lot of resources on this topic, and they are working on creating the required mechanisms to match the needs and preferences of a user, and move them all from one platform into another. Currently, there are several approaches to *matchmaking* mechanisms, and we have successfully made use of them in this implementation to move the preferences from one platform into another. Right now, we are making use of three matchmakers:

- Flat Matchmaker
- Rule Based Matchmaker
- Statistical Matchmaker

To learn more about these matchmakers, and the general matchmaking mechanisms employed by Cloud4All, we recommend the following references:

- Profile Matching Technical Concept [11]
- Matchmaking on the GPII wiki [12]
- Matchmaking Workflows on the GPII wiki [13]
- Improving Accessibility by Matching User Needs and Preferences [14]

3   Delivering the GPII to the End-Users

A critical goal of the GPII is to deliver this infrastructure to end-users, giving them a way to easily access their needs and preferences on any device, with any platform, and in any place. In case of this particular implementation, both Windows and GNU/Linux repositories can be found at GPII's Github project [15][16] and can be installed and used by any user easily.

These repositories contain all the platform-specific source code that, within the GPII's *universal* repository [17], makes this implementations a reality.

Since users will ultimately either accept or reject to use any software, based on how easy it is to use and how useful it is, it's very important to collect all the valuable feedback that any user of the GPII can provide in any early phase of the developments, and incorporating this feedback into the development process.

For these reasons, and as an early outcome of the implementation of the GPII on PC OSs, which is at the same time the most complex and the most mature one, a first pilot phase with real users has been performed in Germany, Greece and Spain. A second pilot phase is running right now. As part of the Cloud4all project, during these pilots, some focus groups with different disabilities have had the chance to try the GPII and to evaluate the current implementation of the GPII on PC OSs. The results from the pilots have confirmed that this upcoming technology will be very helpful to them in their lives.

3.1   Pilots Scenario

In the pilot tests at the Greek, Spanish and German pilot site, we had 130 beneficiaries: 84 were end users (people with disabilities), 28 were developers and 16 were stakeholders.

While the pilots of Greece and Spain took place in premises of the organizations: CERTH/HIT in Thessaloniki and Technosite in Madrid, in the case of Germany they took place in labs and also in the usual environment (e.g common working places of the participants).

Concerning the duration, all pilots took around 3 months. The methods that have been used per pilot site are described in detailed below. They include basically 3 different approaches:

- For end- users: Usability test / Field test, Mock-up paper or click demo, Observation, Structured interview
- For developers: usability test + Observation + Structured interview
- For stakeholders: Focus group

The participants of the pilots were recruited according to different variables:

user group; gender; age; educational background; and operating system used. In the case of the stakeholders and developers/AT vendors, the recruitment didn't follow socio-demographic criteria but aspects related to their expertise.

Since the auto-configuration on PCs OSs was not the only outcome from the Cloud4all project that has been tested on this pilot iteration, here is a full list of validations that have been done during the pilots:

- Cloud4all concept validation
- Preferences Management tool (PMT) with basic functions validation
- Preferences Management tool (PMT) with extended functions validation

- Auto-configuration scenario validation
- Semantics alignment tool (SAT) validation

The auto-configuration scenario validation, which is related to this implementation (PCs OSs), has been tested by 43 users: 16 in Greece, 18 in Spain and 19 in Germany.

All users that tested the auto-configuration scenario started from platform A and moved to platform B and then configured manually platform B and go back to platform A. So, all users tested both the transformation of the setting from Windows to Linux and vice versa, using one matchmaker when going from A to B and the other when returning from B to A.

3.2   Feedback

The users felt that the system met their needs and preferences when they went from Windows to Linux and from Linux to Windows. In both cases, we did not find significant differences between the performance of the system according to their needs and preferences. However the system met their needs and preferences slightly better when moving from Windows to Linux in Greece. When measuring the difficulties that users faced when they had to perform tasks on each platform, they encountered fewer problems on Windows in comparison to when they had to perform the same task on Linux, especially in Greece. The fact that most of the users are only familiar with the Windows OS in their daily life accounts for these results. We can say the users believe that their needs and preferences are less met when going from Linux to Windows.

The users felt that the system meets their N&Ps when they used both the Rule-based and Statistical MM. It seems that both matchmakers work similarly in terms of their ability to provide the proper auto-configuration to fulfill the user's needs. In the case of users in Spain, there were relevant differences between the statistical and the rule based matchmakers. The Rule-Based Matchmaker worked better than the Statistical regarding the configuration of the preferences of these users. In this case the configuration provided by the Rule-Based MM was rated with almost a 5, while the statistical MM with a bit more than 3. In general, both MMs failed more times with the auto-configuration for low vision users than for blind users.

Also, the users gave some recommendations about the system:

- The auto-configuration should be faster and more refined
- It would be very useful to include some information messages that can guide during the auto-configuration process, such as "loading Cloud4all", "logging out from Cloud4all", etc. Visual and spoken messages.
- Low vision users recommended to include more configuration options

References

1. http://gpii.net
2. http://en.wikipedia.org/wiki/Assistive_technology
3. http://en.wikipedia.org/wiki/Interactive_kiosk

4. http://wiki.gpii.net/index.php/
    A_Detailed_Tour_of_the_Cloud4all_Architecture#Flow_Manager
5. Clark, C., et al.: A Cloud-Scale Architecture for Inclusion: Cloud4all and GPII. Assistive
    Technology: From Research to Practice
6. http://wiki.gpii.net/index.php/A_Detailed_Tour_of_the_Cloud4
    all_Architecture#Settings_Handlers
7. http://www.nvaccess.org/
8. https://wiki.gnome.org/action/show/Projects/Orca#About_Orca
9. http://wiki.gpii.net/index.php/Common_Terms_Registry
10. http://wiki.gpii.net/index.php/
    Architecture_-_Available_transformation_functions
11. http://www.cloud4all.info/pages/news/
    detail.aspx?id=92&tipo=4
12. http://wiki.gpii.net/index.php/Matchmaking
13. http://wiki.gpii.net/index.php/Matchmaking_Workflows
14. Loitsch, C., et al.: Improving Accessibility by Matching User Needs and Preferences.
    Assistive Technology: From Research to Practice
15. https://github.com/GPII/windows
16. https://github.com/GPII/linux
17. https://github.com/GPII/universal

Amara: A Sustainable, Global Solution for Accessibility, Powered by Communities of Volunteers

Dean Jansen[1], Aleli Alcala[1], and Francisco Guzman[2]

[1] Amara.org, USA
{dean,aleli}@pculture.org
[2] Qatar Computing Research Institute, Qatar
fguzman@qf.org.qa

Abstract. In this paper, we present the main features of the Amara project, and its impact on the accessibility landscape with the use of innovative technology. We also show the effectiveness of volunteer communities in addressing large subtitling and translation tasks, that accompany the ever-growing amounts of online video content. Furthermore, we present two different applications for the platform. First, we examine the growing interest of organizations to build their own subtitling communities. Second, we present how the community-generated material can be used to advance the state-of-the-art of research in fields such as Statistical Machine Translation with focus on educational translation. We provide examples on how both tasks can be achieved successfully.

Keywords: Amara, online platform, user engagement, subtitles, translation, crowdsourcing, volunteer communities, lecture translation, statistical machine translation.

1 Introduction

In a globalized world, multilingual subtitles are absolutely essential to the future of web video: they bring more viewers, they make content searchable, and they allow access to content to billions of users who are left out because they are deaf, hard of hearing, or unable to access video because it's in a language different than their own.

Amara is a web service and software toolset for adding captions, subtitles, and translations to virtually any web video. Until now, captioning and translation services have been limited by closed, centralized, and expensive systems; and by tedious user experiences. The Amara system is an open, scalable, flexible, collaborative platform, which allows leveraging the power of crowdsourcing through volunteer engagement. It is the first large-scale, open platform with the potential of making large quantities of videos accessible through high quality captioning and translation.

In this paper, we describe the unique features of the Amara platform, which allow for faster transcription turnaround while maintaining high levels of user engagement.

C. Stephanidis and M. Antona (Eds.): UAHCI/HCII 2014, Part IV, LNCS 8516, pp. 401–411, 2014.
© Springer International Publishing Switzerland 2014

Additionally, we showcase success stories where the platform has allowed volunteer translators to transcribe and translate hundreds of thousands of videos, in communities of varying sizes. Finally, we present a brief summary of cases where the community-generated translations can be used to advance research in the field of automatic translation focused on educational videos.

2   Features of the Amara Platform

To ensure the best user experience, the Amara platform is focused on five important areas: (i) ease of use, (ii) quality control, (iii) compatibility, (iv) ease of integration, and (v) engagement. Below, we explain each of these topics.

1. Ease of use

By separating the transcription step from the alignment step, the Amara interface for subtitle creation is extremely simple and enjoyable. Compared to existing desktop or web subtitling tools, it is easier for a new user to get started.

In addition, by separating subtitle services from video hosting, it lets users add subtitles with simplicity. There is no need to download videos and/or upload them to a new service.

2. Quality controls

The platform puts an emphasis on the production of high-quality subtitles and translations. This is accomplished through transparency, accountability, and a policy of open participation. To that end, Amara quality control works in the same way as Wikipedia's self-regulated community, where members collaboratively solve errors and problems with articles.

3. Compatibility

Amara supports the use of four of the most popular hosting sites (Youtube, Dailymotion, Kaltura, and Vimeo). Additionally, Amara lets users subtitle the vast majority of videos posted online, because it also supports video formats like .mp4 and .webm (the HTML5 standard for plugin-free video playback).

4. Ease of integration

Anyone can add Amara to their website by pasting a single line of JavaScript to their videos. Site owners and their visitors can immediately begin adding subtitles and translations to their videos. Any site using a compatible video host or player can become part of the Amara ecosystem in minutes.

5. Volunteer engagement

Volunteers that caption and subtitle videos are the core element of the Amara project. Therefore, Amara strives to adopt the best current practices and functionalities to

engage and motivate volunteers. Today, hundreds of thousands of volunteers participate on Amara and the numbers continue to grow.

2.1   Key Components

The following components are essential to Amara's success:

- A creation and editing interface that makes it easier to subtitle than any other system for captioning and translating video. This is an essential component needed to
engage and involve millions of volunteers. A snapshot of the interface is shown in
Figure 1.
- A collaborative editing process that facilitates the incremental improvement of
subtitles and captions. This process includes features such as: revision history,
rollbacks, email notifications when changes are made, etc.
- A platform that allows companies and organizations to: (a) collect and organize
video into projects, (b) import / export and manage videos and subtitles through a
powerful API, (c) manage subtitle creation processes involving volunteers, staff,
contractors through flexible workflows, (d) manage the privacy of the content, (e)
build and manage a volunteer team, including an application process and peer review for quality control, (f) synchronize completed subtitles to YouTube videos
- A comprehensive support for more video hosting platforms than any other system,
enabling access to more videos.

Early adopters of the platform include TED Talks, Mozilla, PBS Newshour, and
Udacity. This network of communities is growing exponentially and making tens of
thousands of videos accessible to wider audiences.

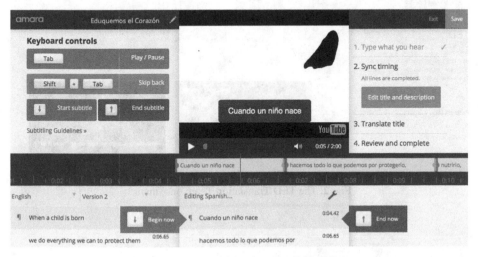

Fig. 1. A snapshot of the Amara subtitle editor

3   Using the Amara Platform: Case Studies

Below, we present different case studies that provide insight into how some organizations are successfully engaging their volunteers, fans, viewers, and students, through the Amara platform, to make their content accessible to more people, in more languages, and around the globe.

3.1   TED Talks

Around 2009, TED Talks[1] started a volunteer translation community using a homegrown system to create translations for their then 1100 TED Talks. During this time, TED built a community of about 7,000 members that focused solely on translating TED's 1100 or so TED Talks.

In 2012, TED migrated to the Amara platform given its ease of use. Additionally, this move was done to address their growing volume of TED, TEDx and TED Ed talks. They needed a subtitle creation tool that: (a) required very little training of their volunteers, (b) was scalable to support large amounts of content, and volunteers.

Since they switched to Amara in May of 2012, TED's volunteer base has grown to nearly 25,000 members. Their video content library is near 29,000 videos and growing steadily: TED Talks has 1600 videos; TEDx Talks, 27,000 videos; and TED Ed around 400 videos; all of which are now being translated by their team of volunteers. The rate at which the team completes subtitles continues to grow, as TED expands their use of the Amara platform.

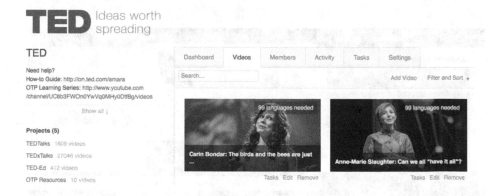

Fig. 2. The TED Translation Team on Amara

---

[1] http://www.amara.org/en/teams/ted/

3.2 Udacity

Udacity[2] is one of the largest Massive Open Online Courses (MOOC), education plat-forms. Udacity began using Amara in late 2012. Their courses focus on advanced math, science, and technology content. When they joined, their greatest concerns given the complexity of their material were: the quality of subtitles, and the volunteer engagement.

Today, Udacity has a strong membership of over 1500 volunteers. Although a smaller team than TED's, this team still manages to translate Udacity's videos into many languages. More importantly, this group of volunteers is passionate about making Udacity's content, education from some of the world's prestigious universities, available to people who do not speak English. Thus, allowing many around the world to benefit from this valuable content.

To ensure a high number of translations, Udacity also uses Amara's "On Demand" service to gain closed captions for all of their courses, making it easier and faster to gain translations from their volunteer community.

3.3 Github

Github[3] is one of the largest open source technology companies in the world. They joined Amara in October 2013 with just a handful of videos, and zero volunteers. Using Amara's standard outreach plan, they quickly grew their community.

To date, they are satisfied with the efforts of their volunteer community, and con-tinue to add videos on a regular basis to keep them engaged.

Interesting Volunteer Behavior Developing across Communities. One of the most exciting things happening with the Github community is the passion of some of their members. So passionate with their participation in fact that they are blogging about it, tweeting and posting on Facebook to invite their friends and family to watch these videos and see the subtitles they created.

This volunteer behavior is a new phenomenon at Amara, and is also happening with TED and Epic Rap Battles volunteers.

This social behavior brings additional benefit to the translation efforts of the volun-teer community. Team member communication gives members the opportunity to share their passion for the organization. At the same time, it also attracts more volunteers and viewers.

---

[2] http://www.amara.org/en/teams/udacity/
[3] http://www.amara.org/en/teams/github/videos/

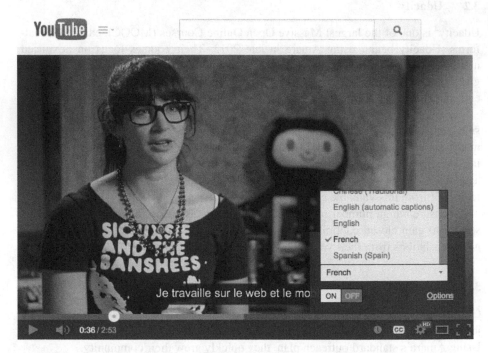

Passion Projects (Docs) • Timoni West (Foursquare)

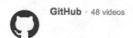 GitHub · 48 videos

Fig. 3. Github's Youtube Videos, translated by community, using Amara

3.4 Maker Studios, Epic Rap Battles Series

Maker Studios is a media company focused primarily on the millennial generation, who are living a mobile, social, and on-demand life. Maker is the number one producer and distributor of online video to this diverse, tech-savvy group of people, attracting over 4.5 billion monthly views, and 340 million+ subscribers.

One of Maker's most popular YouTube channels is Epic Rap Battles (ERB) with about 8 million subscribers. Their viewer demographic for series, are 12 to 14 year-old boys. Therefore, they were cautious about engaging this young ERB community in volunteer subtitling. However, the idea of Amara and building a volunteer community was too compelling. So, Maker decided to do a small, highly controlled test.

Maker's Proof of Concept and Amazing Success Story. Maker chose four videos from their Epic Rap Battle[4] series and put them in an unlisted YouTube channel. They then sent just one tweet sharing this unlisted URL, inviting volunteers to join and help subtitle these four videos. Doing it this way, they figured only a very small subset of their subscribers would actually see the tweet, and an even smaller subset would probably join the effort.

What happened next was amazing: in less than 18 hours, they garnered 210 volunteers who subtitled each of the four videos into over 20 languages per video. Furthermore, after comparing the volunteer translations created in these languages to a set of refereed translations, their reviewers found the volunteer translations to be of higher quality, because they captured humor and tone of the content.

Great takeaway: volunteers who are passionate about the organization and the content have a greater understanding of the content, and are better positioned to create higher quality captions and translations.

After nearly two months, the Epic Rap Battle's community continues to grow both in membership, and the number of subtitles created per video, with no vandalism occurring.

An Epic Social Event and Maker's Upcoming New Amara Communities. Recently, Maker decided to try another experiment. They did a targeted Facebook promotion to different geographical regions around the world. Within hours, their volunteer membership went from around 400 members to over 3,000 members, shutting Amara down for a few minutes in the process. In fact, the Amara platform was not prepared for such levels of traffic jam, but quickly recovered. With this success and the earlier successes shared, Maker is now creating translation communities for three more of their YouTube channels.

Fig. 4. Maker Studios "Epic Rap Battles of History" on Amara

---

[4] http://amara.org/en/teams/erb/videos/

3.5   Summary

In Table 1 below, we present a summary of the engagement statistics for the different case studies introduced previously. Notice how the Amara platform has been successfully used in projects from different sizes. In all four cases, we have observed a widespread adoption by the community of volunteers.

Table 1. Engagement statistics from different organizations using Amara

Org	Videos	Volunteers	Languages (avg)
TED talks	29,000+ videos, 4 times the starting number	25,000 volunteers, 4 times the starting number	40+ languages per TED Talk, 10+ languages per TEDx and TED Ed Talks
Udacity	11,000 videos	1,500+ volunteers	10+ languages
Github	34 videos	450+ volunteers	Between 8 and 9 languages, some with up to 17 languages
Epic Rap	18 videos	3,295 volunteers	40+ languages, some with over 60 languages

These are but a few of the growing number of organizations using the Amara Enterprise platform. As an example, in the next week or so, Scientific American, the United States National Archives, World Vision, and Qatar Computer Research Institute (QCRI) are some of the top organizations launching their volunteer communities on Amara.

In addition, there are ongoing conversations happening with actors from diverse vertical markets, including higher education, film and TV, media companies, online education portals, and major YouTube channels. Amara is experiencing a strong growth not only in interest also in the rate adoption from many different vertical markets.

One market for which there is growing interest is the educational sector. The number of Amara partners, specialized in both higher education and online education, is increasing at a rapid pace. This is a particularly gratifying use of the platform, because it permits volunteers to generate translations for educational videos, allowing such videos to reach wider audiences. Furthermore, these translations are being used to explore how the translations created by volunteers can be used to generate automatic translations for videos that have not been translated by volunteers. This can further help to reduce the language barriers. Below, we briefly summarize such efforts.

4   Using Volunteer Translations for Educational Translation

In this section, we summarize the research presented by [5,6], which use translations generated in the Amara platform to train machine translation systems and improve the state-of-the-art in Lecture Translation in the educational domain.

The automatic translation of educational material has become an active field of research in the wider area of Speech Translation [1,2]. In this area of research, techniques from Speech Recognition and Machine Translation are applied to automatically translate technical lectures from one language (source) to another language (target). To advance the state-of-the-art in this field, researchers have proposed large-scale projects like the EU-funded translectures [3] and evaluation campaigns like the one organized as part of the International Workshop on Spoken Language Translation (IWSLT). However, the main limitation for the success of these is the access to high quality training data.

With the emergence of Massive Online Open Courses (MOOCs), thousands of educational video lectures have already been generated. Organizations like Khan Academy[5], and Udacity[6], etc., continuously increase their offerings of lectures, which range from basic math and science topics, to more advanced topics like machine learning.

However, language barriers limit the access to this content, given that most of the material is in English. This severely limits access to this high-quality educational material for learners who do not understand English.

To overcome these language barriers, volunteers continuously transcribe and translate such lectures into many other languages using the Amara platform. One example is the already mentioned TED Talks[7], for which, so far, more than 25,000 volunteers have generated more than 40,000 translations into a total of 101 languages. However, for many languages the small number of volunteers is insufficient to keep up with the rate in which new content is appearing on these educational platforms.

Statistical machine translation (SMT) can bridge this gap by automatically translating videos for which subtitles are not available. Thus, it has the potential to increase the penetration of educational content, allowing it to reach a wider audience.

To achieve this, an SMT system requires a large quantity of high-quality in-domain training data. Unfortunately, this type of data is very rare and expensive to create by hand. So far, the only openly accessible corpus for the lecture domain has been the TED talks [4], which is also based on volunteering efforts.

To address these issues [5], [6] have proposed to use the transcriptions and translations generated by volunteers in the Amara platform, to create corpora suitable for research in the Machine Translation field. They focus on generating corpora that targets educational content. They observe that the data generated by volunteers can be successfully used for such task. They analyze the output of the machine translation systems, and identify specific challenges that arise when translating highly technical

---

[5] https://www.khanacademy.org
[6] https://www.udacity.com
[7] http://www.ted.com

data, such as mathematical formulae. Furthermore, they observe that the gathered data can also be used to translate other lecture material such as the TED talks, thus showing that the data obtained from the Amara platform can be successfully used for improving lecture translation.

5   Conclusion

Today, video is the fastest growing form of content on the web, with videos being added daily on an exponential scale. Amara's mission of making all video content online accessible, is only possible by providing an open Wikipedia-like solution, where any user, is enabled to participate in addressing this challenge.

Amara is a unique volunteer driven platform that has been tested in real-world scenarios and has helped translate tens of thousands of videos. In the translation communities, volunteers are passionate about the content they translate, and generate high quality translations. Furthermore, contributing volunteers are proud of their achievements, and quickly spread-the-word to their networks, creating a social "contagion" effect. This allows translation communities to grow rapidly. Moreover, the corpora of translations and transcriptions generated by volunteers are being used to improve statistical machine translation systems for educational content.

6   About AMARA

6.1   Amara and PCF

Amara is a project of the Participatory Culture Foundation (PCF), a not for profit 501 (c)(3). Amara's mission is to ensure that all online video content is accessible to everyone regardless of hearing ability or language barriers.

6.2   Amara and Prosperity4All (P4ALL)

The Prosperity4All consortium is comprised of 25 partners from 13 countries who are developing a robust cross-platform spectrum of mainstream and assistive technology-based access solutions required for a sustainable Global Public Inclusive Infrastructure. The Amara platform will be the technology for creating captions and subtitles within this ecosystem.

References

1. Fügen, C., Kolss, M., Bernreuther, D., Paulik, M., Stücker, S., Vogel, S., Waibel, A.: Open domain speech recognition & translation: Lectures and speeches. In: Acoustics, Speech and Signal Processing, ICASSP 2006 (2006)
2. Fügen, C., Waibel, A., Kolss, M.: Simultaneous translation of lectures and speeches. Machine Translation 21(4), 209–252 (2007)

3. Silvestre-Cerdà, J.A., del Agua, M.A., Garcés, G., Gascó, G., Giménez, A., Martínez, A., Pérez, A., Sánchez, I., Serrano, N., Spencer, R., Valor, J.D., Andrés-Ferrer, J., Civera, J., Sanchis, A., Juan, A.: TransLectures. In: Online Proceedings of Advances in Speech and Language Technologies for Iberian Languages, IBERSPEECH 2012, Madrid, Spain (2012)
4. Paul, M., Federico, M., Stüker, S.: Overview of the IWSLT 2010 evaluation campaign. In: Proceedings of the International Workshop on Spoken Language Translation, IWSLT 2010, Paris, France (2010)
5. Guzman, F., Sajjad, H., Abdelali, A., Vogel, S.: The AMARA Corpus: Building Resources for Translating the Web's Educational Content. In: Proceedings of the International Workshop on Spoken Language Translation, IWSLT 2013, Heidelberg, Germany (2013)
6. Abdelali, A., Guzman, F., Sajjad, H., Vogel, S.: The AMARA Corpus: Building parallel language resources for the educational domain. To appear in Proceedings of the Ninth International Conference on Language Resources and Evaluation (LREC 2014), Reykjavik, Iceland (2014)

AT and GPII: Maavis

Steve Lee[1], Gregg C. Vanderheiden[2], and Amrish Chourasia[2]

[1] Open Directive Ltd., USA
steve@opendirective.com
[2] Trace Center, UW Madison, USA
{gv,amrish}@trace.wisc.edu

Abstract. Maavis is a computer framework that provides an extremely simple way to perform common place computer activities like playing media, viewing photos, accessing web information and making video calls. It is ideal for use with a touch screen. A fundamental principal is that it does not appear to be a computer and yet affords access to computer technology that is of benefit and interest to older users, especially those with age related mental health issues. It also has applications for people with learning difficulties or physical disabilities, or even simple kiosk interfaces as it is designed to work best with a touch screen. Integration of Maavis with the GPII has undergone successful validation tests and further development work is ongoing.

Keywords: Accessibility, touch screen, learning disabilities, aging, dementia.

1 Introduction

Individuals with cognitive disabilities such as dementia, often experience diminished independence and social isolation [1]. As we move to a digital world, these individuals find that participation in education, health, employment, school and civic life is becoming increasing challenging due to lack of access to information and communication technologies (ICT).

It has been suggested that assistive technology can reduce social isolation and increase independence [1]. The estimated number of people with dementia worldwide is 27.7 million [2]. As the global population ages the number of people with dementia is also expected to rise. As a result of these demographic shifts, there is a growing interest in technological innovations that can assist individuals with dementia [3].

Maavis is a computer framework that provides greatly simplified access to media, communications, web and programs on a computer. It is primarily designed for people who are either unsure of computers or unable to use them without adaptation. It was designed and developed as part of research into use of technology by people living with dementia.

C. Stephanidis and M. Antona (Eds.): UAHCI/HCII 2014, Part IV, LNCS 8516, pp. 412–420, 2014.
© Springer International Publishing Switzerland 2014

2   Description

The name Maavis was originally an acronym for "Managed Access to Audio, Visual and Information Services". The Maavis project originates from Sheffield University's Advanced Care Technologies Project as a research project investigating technology use by people with dementia living in a care environment. The principal Investigator was Prof. Peter Cudd, of the Rehabilitation and Assistive Technology Research group. A prototype system was used for field testing and this lead to the specification and development of this open source project.

Maavis is tool for creating screens of buttons containing text or images perform simple operations when activated (see Fig. 1). Activation can be with, pointer, keyboard, touch screen or with the built in scanning support for switch users. Speech support is provided using synthetic Text to Speech to read out displayed text.. Screens are arranged in a hierarchy that provides 'activity selection', 'item group selection' and 'item players'. Players are provided for photos, music, information (web pages), video calls and basic AAC. A very simple user login feature is also provided for shared use [4].

Maavis is not designed as an end user ready application but it is expected that a facilitator will provide a configuration in which photos, videos, music will be placed in the correct folders so that they become available through Maavis to the end-user.

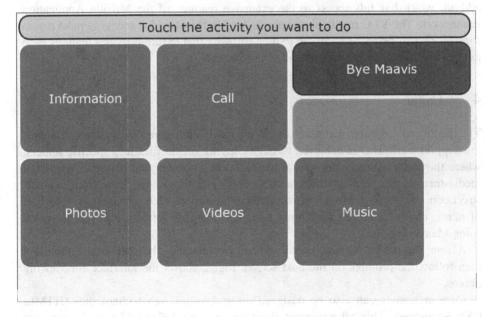

Fig. 1. Maavis interface showing the different options available to a user. The interface is customized for each user.

2.1   Stakeholders

The design of Maavis has kept in mind the people who will be involved and assumed several roles and levels of technical skill [5] :

- End users – no or very little technical interest or experience in IT
- Facilitators – basic IT skills including the ability to get media onto computer copy and rename files
- Technical facilitators – intermediate skills including editing formatted files to update screens and provide web pages.
- Developers
  - Experienced. Ability to create new web pages using XUL (like HTML), JavaScript and CSS
  - Core developers – very experienced – as developers but for platform core, plus possibly Python for Skype integration, C for XPCOM components, Inno setup for installer

3   Design

Maavis builds on other open source technologies, specifically; Mozilla Firefox (PortableApps version), VLC, Outfox and Python. It is implemented as a Firefox add-on, which has full access to the extensive features of the Mozilla Application Framework. The VLC media player plugin for Firefox provides access to most media formats. Outfox provides access to Python software that in turn provides features such as the video conferencing access, and switch access.

4   Usage

The media and programs that users access are easily configured by facilitators including support staff. This is achieved through copying media files into specific folders, where they automatically become available in the choosers and players. Almost all media formats can be played and scalable SVG images such as those from straightstreet.com can be used. More sophisticated configuration, such web items or the order of items, can be achieved by editing basic text files. A settings utility is provided using Maavis buttons.

A user can select the activity to perform by touching the particular button and then follow the prompts on the next screen. Fig. 2 shows the interface for viewing photos.

Custom screens can also be designed using familiar web technologies (HTML, CSS Javascript). This affords great flexibility and predefined Maavis features are accessed using extensions to these standard formats.

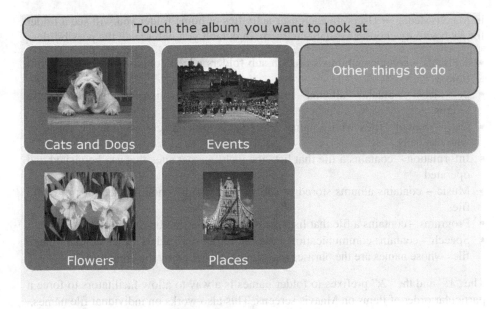

Fig. 2. Maavis interface for viewing photos

4.1 Changing Content That Appears On Screens

In general Maavis screens are arranged into 3 screen levels, providing end users a consistent navigation experience [6]:

- Choosing an activity (Home) – top level screen offering the activity choices
- Activity content chooser (Chooser) – offers selection of the specific 'topic' or content
- Interaction controller (Players) – presents the chosen content and media controls

Each button on the home screen leads to a chooser, the buttons on the choosers perform an action such as making a call or running media players with the selected media set.

Each user has a folder with their name as the folders name. This folder will be referred to as the user activities or home folder. Each activity has a folder located in the latter folder, each with a meaningful name (to the user). These folders will collectively be referred to as chooser folders. The files or folders within these folders that are or identify the content for the activity will be known as content files or content folders as appropriate to the activity.

4.2 Setting up Activities

The content shown in each of the choosers is automatically created from the contents of folders under "MaavisMedia". Samples are provided with Maavis and can be found in MaavisMedia → Users. In each user activities or home folder you will see a folder for each activity/chooser available to them, in default you will see all the possibilities:

- 1;Photos – contains albums stored in sub folders which contain collections of still images
- 2; Videos – contains "albums" stored in sub folders which contain one or more videos
- Call – contains files whose names identify Skype contacts who can be called or who can call1
- Information – contains a file that lists the web/Internet sites that can be visited and operated
- Music – contains albums stored in sub folders which contain collections of audio files
- Programs – contains a file that lists the programs that can be run from Maavis
- Speech – contains communication topics stored in sub folders which contain image files whose names are the phrases that can be generated by the computer

The "1;" and the "2;" prefixes to folder names is a way to allow facilitators to force a particular order of items on Maavis screens. This also works on individual file names.

The names of the folders above have been chosen from the original and obvious use. In fact the type of activity and content is selected by the presence of a file with one of the following filenames _choosmusic, _choosephoto, _choosevideo, _choosecall, _chooseprogram, _choosespeech, _chooseinfo. The name of the folder becomes the name of the button on the Maavis home screen and each folder may contain an image file called Thumbnail which appears on the button. So a facilitator is able to choose any name for the activities, e.g. instead of "Programs" it might be more appropriate to use 'Writing' if the only programs available allow writing.

Any of the above folders/activities can be completely removed as a particular user requires. Similarly the activities can be added if previously removed or duplicated with a new name. For example, if more than one Internet accessing activity is needed, e.g. in a school it may be desirable to separate Art from Science.

4.3 How Folder Names and Contents Are Used

- All folder names within a user activities folder are used as the text on the button on screen.
- An optional image file called Thumbnail that becomes the image on the button for the folder. Most image formats can be used. Note if no Thumbnail file is present Maavis just displays the name of the folder in the button.
- Image, video or audio files in content folders names are used as the text that appears on the button - along with the image itself when that is the type of file
- The player automatically detects Media or content files. Most media formats except Real are supported.

- A content text file _items.ini, which lists the activity, contents and provides access to that content. Each line is of the form "item = value" where value is optional. Item is the name of the item and is shown as the Maavis button text. If an image file of the same name as the item exists it is displayed on the button with the text. The order of the items on the Maavis screen follows the order of the lines in the file. Value depends on the folder the file appears in and may be a skype id, a program filename, a website address or the web address of a media item.

4.4 Videos, Music, Photos

These folders contain subfolders each of which is an album of media content. The audio player and video player play each of the media files in turn in a continuous loop. The audio player allows the user to select individual files to play and uses the media filenames for the button labels. At least for photos instead of multiple media files in the folder there can be a "_items.ini" file with website links that are used instead. Note that if the website address becomes invalid the image is skipped.

Presentation order of media files can be forced using the numeric prefixes as shown in the default user install and mentioned in 'Setting up activities" above.

4.5 Information

This activity uses the _item.ini text file to set up the content. The typical use would require Internet access but web/html pages with a 'local' url would always be accessible.

4.6 Speech

This activity is aimed at people who have difficulty making spoken communication. Setting it up is exactly the same as for Photos, but the difference is how the files in the content folders are used. Instead of all of them being presented one after each other, all appear on screen (or if more than 6 on a sequence of more than one screen) in buttons. When one is chosen the text, i.e. filename, is spoken by the computer.

Presentation order can be forced using the numeric prefixes as shown in the default user install and mentioned in "Setting up activities" above.

5   GPII Integration

The integration of Maavis in the GPII is off to a successful start. As part of the Cloud4all project, a functional prototype with several changeable settings was developed and validated. A webcast of Maavis' integration with the GPII can be found here: https://www.youtube.com/watch?v=F1ATPYSv02Y.

During the technical validation, the following items of Maavis and GPII platform were verified and validated:

- Maavis settings that effect the display theme, automatic speech and switch support
- User Listeners
- Lifecycle Manager
- Lifecycle Handler
- Settings Handler
- Matchmaker
- Preferences server
- Test – Maavis startup/shutdown on insertion/removal of USB key and RFID tag.

Details on the GPII architecture are available on the GPII wiki [7].

Two users were created as part of the testing procedure and professional software testers carried out manual testing. Non-functional requirements crucial for Maavis' functioning such as resource usage, memory usage, response time, number of failures, portability were also evaluated.

The results of the technical validation were excellent. Maavis succeeded to operate using different settings each time, meeting different user's needs and preferences. The user listeners were triggered successfully, while a snapshot of the default settings was successfully taken in order to be restored at the end of each scenario. The Settings Handler managed to find, read and change the settings of the required Maavis configuration file.

The first test cycle did not include all GPII functionalities and but did cover most of Maavis options. Future technical validation tests will include much more functionalities and features in terms of users' needs and preferences.

[Note] for a subsequent second GPII integration validation cycle a new high contrast theme was added, along with a simple internationalisation feature providing easy translations of displayed text.

6   Current Status and Future Work

A HTML5 based prototype of Maavis has been created that that implements key features of the original XUL Maavis in HTML5 and also uses W3C widgets [8]. Creating a new version using HTML5 and Widgets allows Maavis to run on the many platforms that have a Web browser. This includes mobile and tablet devices that are becoming increasingly popular with users since they greatly increase the number of locations and situations in which Maavis can be employed.

In the prototype, key functional areas of Maavis performance were targeted and provided with an HTML5 implementation, which proved they could be made to work. Those functional areas were [8]

- Screens of buttons containing text and images and arranged in grids
- Screens with only buttons that provide navigation and selection
- 'Player' screens containing a viewer (or audio player) plus control button sets, specifically for audio, videos, still image slideshows and information (browser).
- A simple speech screen that speaks words when buttons are pressed

- A text-to-speech processor to read aloud screen titles and other information when requested
- Keyboard access (tab and enter keys to move around and activate screen options)

This prototype demonstrated that a usable HTML5 version of Maavis can indeed be created. However, certain challenges still remain [8].

- Browser Support for HTML5: Perhaps the biggest challenge at present is the variation in browser support for HTML5 and related technologies. In fact, as HTML5 will never be a fully completed specification, but is, rather, a continuous evolution, this may never be completely resolved.
- Security Issue with Cross-domain Access: The browser security concept of same origin policy restricts access to DOM from script on pages in a different domain. When using several widgets, the impact is that code in one widget.
- cannot manipulate another. This means widgets loaded from different sources cannot easily communicate with each other on the client side.
- User Control of Web Page Display: The information viewer raises a difficulty that does not occur in the original Maavis application which shows the Web page in an embedded browser element that is only available in XUL. The control buttons are scripted to control this browser element for pan and zoom. In the HTML pro type the same origin policy means that the control script cannot manipulate the displayed Web page.
- Support for Accessibility Switch Users: The original XUL Maavis provides built-in scanning support to allow control with simple switch devices (briefly a highlight moves between user interface elements until a switch is operated by the user to select or activate that item). Currently browser standards support very limited input devices, namely pointer + click and keyboard, and events (pointer and keyboard), so switches cannot easily be used without extra assistive technology software.
- Keyboard Access Issues: Another observation is when using tab key access to move between elements iframes are tab stops themselves, and so receive focus before subsequent navigation into the contained widget elements.
- Embedded Text-to-speech Support: Synthetic text to speech processing is problematic as that is no standard platform-independent way of accessing speech from a browser in order to create self-voicing HTML applications.

7   Conclusion

Maavis provides individuals with cognitive disabilities a simplified interface to access media, communications, web and programs on a computer. Individuals who are generally not comfortable with computers have also benefitted from Maavis' simplified interface[9]. Maavis has been undergone a successful initial validation and is being integrated in the GPII. A HTML5 prototype of Maavis has been developed to allow it to run on multiple platforms but challenges remain. However, with the availability of newer APIs and tools Maavis will soon have access to new HTML and platform features, thereby providing the opportunity for innovative alternative access to media and communications.

Acknowledgement. Different components of the body of work described in this paper was, and/or is being, funded by the European Union's Regional Development Fund and Seventh Framework Programme (FP7/2007-2013) grant agreement n° 289016 (Cloud4all) and 610510 (Prosperity4All), by the National Institute on Disability and Rehabilitation Research, US Dept of Education under Grants H133E080022 (RERC-IT) and H133E130028 (UIITA-RERC) and contract ED-OSE-12-D-0013 (Preferences for Global Access), by the Flora Hewlett Foundation, the Ontario Ministry of Research and Innovation, and the Canadian Foundation for Innovation. The opinions and results herein are those of the authors and not necessarily those of the funding agencies.

References

1. Todis, B., et al.: Making electronic mail accessible: Perspectives of people with acquired cognitive impairments, caregivers and professionals. Brain Injury 19, 389–401 (2005)
2. Wimo, A., Jonsson, L., Winblad, B.: An estimate of the worldwide prevalence and direct costs of dementia in 2003. Dementia and Geriatric Cognitive Disorders 21, 175–181 (2006)
3. Bharucha, A.J., et al.: Intelligent Assistive Technology Applications to Dementia Care: Current Capabilities, Limitations, and Future Challenges. The American Journal of Geriatric Psychiatry: Official Journal of the American Association for Geriatric Psychiatry 17, 88–104 (2009)
4. Lee, S.: Maavis. n.d. (March 17, 2014), http://maavis.fullmeasure.co.uk
5. Lee, S. User Notes (2010), http://www.assembla.com/wiki/show/bLUCdyxomr3zfBab7jnrAJ/UserNotes (March 16, 2014)
6. Lee, S.: Maavis Facilitator Guide. n.d. (March 17, 2014), http://www.assembla.com/spaces/maavis/wiki/FacilitatorGuide
7. Architecture Overview. n.d. (March 10, 2014), http://wiki.gpii.net/index.php/Architecture_Overview
8. Lee, S.: HTML5 Case Study 3: Re-Implementation of the Maavis Assistive Technology Using HTML5 (2012)
9. Murfitt, N.: Isolated? Not now that I've got MAAVIS: Actress Sylvia Syms logs on to a new service that helps the elderly to stay in touch. Mail Online (2011)

Cloud4all: Scope, Evolution and Challenges

Manuel Ortega-Moral[1,*], Ignacio Peinado[1], and Gregg C. Vanderheiden[2]

[1] Fundosa Technosite, Madrid, Spain
{mortega,ipeinado}@technosite.es
[2] Trace R&D Center & Raising the Floor-International, Geneva, Switzerland
gregg@raisingthefloor.org

Abstract. There are currently important barriers that hinder the access to ICT, especially for the elderly and people with disability. This paper presents the approach adopted by the Cloud4all Consortium to create the technical core of the Global Public Inclusive Infrastructure (GPII). The GPII aims at producing a real impact on achieving global access to ICT. Already in the second half of the project, the current status of developments and main outcomes are presented together with the key components of the architecture. Cloud4all is compared to other approaches to the same problem, defining the scope of the project and unveiling the upcoming new challenges as a result of the research.

Keywords: Cloud4all, Auto-Personalisation from preferences, cloud, accessibility, personalisation, GPII, context-awareness, matchmaking.

1 Introduction

Statistics show the positive correlation between the age and disability prevalence [1]. In 2010, 13% of the population in the United States were over 65, 17% in Europe and about 24% in Japan [2] [3] [4]. The population projection foresees an ageing process of the world population in the next few decades that will cause an increase of disability. Considering that access to ICT is no longer optional and barriers are more important among these population groups, access to ICT becomes a major challenge for a vast percentage of population.

The current situation hinders the access to basic social and economic rights and increases the risk of exclusion from education, health, employment and civic participation [5]. In Europe, the current eAccessibility deployment risks to digitally exclude as many as 110 million Europeans between persons with disabilities and older persons [6]. Additionally, the economic downturn is not reducing the two main barriers for assistive technology (AT) acquisition: cost and lack of information [7]. The problem of cost grows up when the target audience of a given AT is small and mainstream technologies are not available in the market.

---

* Corresponding author.

C. Stephanidis and M. Antona (Eds.): UAHCI/HCII 2014, Part IV, LNCS 8516, pp. 421–430, 2014.

Although the ageing process is an opportunity for AT markets, some studies discussed in 1996 the overwhelming task of discovering which is the most suitable AT product for a user when over 1000 new AT products arrive [8]. Interestingly, that happened before the boom of apps for smartphones, the uprising of browser extensions and wearable computing. Now, the number of devices, markets and platforms is larger and the task of finding the most suitable AT more challenging. Even when users are able to find the appropriate assistive technology, they still need to install it, set it up and learn how to use it [9].

This situation suggests that a new approach could benefit both users and AT developers. Cloud4all is implementing the development of a global infrastructure that could be used from any device, anywhere, to launch and configure the ATs needed reducing the complexity and keeping privacy. This infrastructure will also help users learn about new solutions fitting their needs, hence reducing the gap between supply and demand in the AT market. Next section places Cloud4all inside GPII and other complementary projects. Section 3 explains the approach followed in the project and settles the scope whereas section 4 shows the components of the architecture. Then, in section 5, main outcomes so far are presented, and evaluation procedures and goals are depicted in section 6. Finally, section 7 discusses open issues and future work.

2   Cloud4all and GPII

Cloud4all[1] is a 4-year project from the 7th European Framework partially funded by the EC and led by Technosite, a Spanish company devoted to the accessibility growth. Cloud4all is the technical core of GPII[2], a broader initiative coordinated by Raising the Floor to create a Global Public Inclusive Infrastructure [10] to cope with some of the main problems to access ICT.

GPII stands on three pillar functions [11]:

— Discovery: Providing a way for people to discover useful solutions for them, select those that better fit their needs and store their preferences.
— Personalization: Making it really easy to set-up any device, anywhere.
— Market: Boosting the supply side for the sake of an active and efficient AT market by providing tools, training and help.

There are two FP7 projects contributing to the overall GPII effort and moving this vision towards reality: Cloud4all and Prosperity4all. Whereas Cloud4all is focused on providing simple, instant accessibility for all anywhere and at any device, Prosperity4all centres its efforts on better connecting supply and demand, and providing an affordable method for offering diversity needed.

---

[1] http://cloud4all.info
[2] http://wiki.gpii.net

3   Approach and Scope

Cloud4all steps towards a new way to face accessibility by tailoring any device, any platform, mainstream or minority market solutions, to the user needs and preferences. The goal is to produce an effective impact on access to ICT by moving:

— From individual, hand-operated adaptation of products and services to automatic, instant, simplified activation of any AT product or service.
— From user-group setup of devices, platforms and applications (DPA) to individual customisation, following a one-size-fits-one approach to accessibility and usability.
— From solution-specific activation of accessibility settings to a common easy triggering method, making accessibility easier.
— From isolated non-adaptive DPA configurations to context-aware, adaptive customisations.

Cloud4all researches on effective personalisation to enhance accessibility and leveraging from current solutions rather than creating a new AT. Cloud4all does not create user profiles or user models or defines users as members of categories [12]. The approach is to let users set their needs and preferences defined without aprioristic categorisations. Users will never be requested to name their disabilities but to state how they want to interact with ICT in general terms. Instead of asking users to identify with a cluster of other users labelled as 'low vision', users will only have to state that they prefer bigger font size and higher contrast.

Cloud4all will adapt the accessibility features of different devices, platforms and applications depending on the needs and preferences expressed by the userHowever, this approach is quite different from other research projects on UI personalisation from needs and preferences   [13] [14] [15], that usually rely on a component in charge of generating and adapting interfaces. SUPPLE project defines cost functions to estimate the optimum UIs. First, a feature vector that parameterizes UIs is defined and then optimized considering device features or personal preferences. The INREDIS project created a model of the target device and then represented it according to user needs in a user device (typically PC or smartphone). Although it was inspired by previous works on the Universal Remote Console [16], INREDIS finally implemented an architecture based on an Enterprise Service Bus that iteratively applied XSLT transformations to generate XHTML user interfaces. APSIS4all [17] provides the most similar approach to Cloud4all. A wizard for configuring needs and preferences[3] is alreadyrunning and public digital terminals like ATMs and ticket vending machines (TVMs) use its own interface generators to match user needs. APSIS4all has managed to deploy about 1000 ATMs with this technology in Spain and 24 TVMs in Paderborn. However, the approach followed in this project is focused just on self-service machines using

---

[3] https://cajerofacil.apsis4all.eu/

ad-hoc interface generators. Thus, it can be considered a market deployment of Cloud4all ideas with a technology with the added value both projects are working together to make their technologies compatible. Cloud4all plans to take this concept of personalization from one specific device to any interactive device the user might encounter. Besides, Cloud4all relies on a loosely coupled architecture where components can be running either locally or in the cloud. The architecture launches and manages the settings of available ATs (built-in, installed or cloud-hosted) to configure any DPA according to the user preferences. Instead of being a user interface generator, Cloud4all benefits from the existing solutions and configures them to provide comparable user experiences in any DPA. In brief, Cloud4all is activating adaptions through already existing dedicated software and not creating a new UI generator.

One of the most relevant contributions of Cloud4all are the first steps in developing context-aware systems. Previous work by [18] [19] proposed a commonly used definition and an early use case while [20] [21] categorize content for more complex use cases but still not considering some basic user characteristics like language. The treatment of context in Cloud4all started with environmental variables that may affect the user-device interaction. Some frontiers [22] are defined at thresholds where the interaction mode needs to be switched. For instance, when an excess of light prevents the user from reading a screen, in some cases, the context-aware system may decide to add a screen reader to the interaction. Besides providing the auto-personalization from preferences, Cloud4all will support the personalization of the accessibility features of specific devices or applications depending on the environment where the application is taking place. Similarly, SERENOA project [23] mixes context-awareness with UI generation putting the focus on web applications and UI generation whereas Cloud4all focuses on configuration of available ATs. Both efforts are complementary and improve universal personalisation and accessibility.

4   Components

Cloud4all is developing the technical infrastructure to enable Auto-Personalisation from Preferences (APfP) of any device or platform. In order to gather these preferences, an online tool has been developed. When a user interacts with a device, the preferences are used later to calculate the most suitable ATs and their settings for a user, in a given device, under specific environmental conditions. Finding out the correct settings implies a mechanism for estimating the best possible configuration given other similar configurations for other users or for the user itself in other devices under specific conditions. The matching mechanism is run by the Matchmaker (see Figure 1).

The architecture has evolved from the original designs [24]to include context-awareness. The main components of the Cloud4all architecture are represented in Figure 1 and explained below (see [25] for further details):

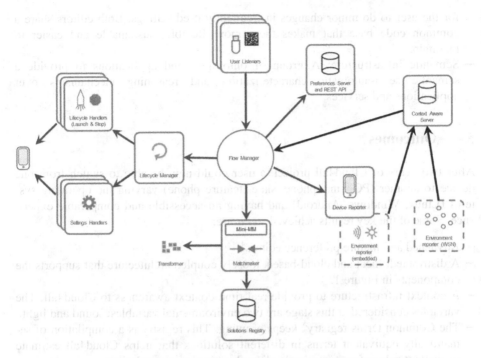

Fig. 1. Cloud4all architecture (Source: Cloud4all [26])

— The Flow Manager is an event-driven asynchronous orchestrator of the whole architecture in charge of managing the workflow of the personalisation process.
— The Matchmakers are in charge of calculating the optimum setting values under certain constraints. There are two implementations: the Rule-Based Matchmaker that relies on an ontology and expert reasoning mechanism, and the Statistical Matchmaker that makes statistical inferences for setting values.
— The Preference server stores and delivers user preferences.
— The Context-aware server centralizes information from sensors about environmental conditions to be used by the Matchmakers.
— User Listener: this component is responsible for reading the user token and starting the process personalization.
— The Lifecycle manager and Settings handlers launch and stop applications with the appropriate configuration and apply changes on-the-fly.
— The Solution registry stores a list of applications, access features and assistive technologies, and replies to queries about the solutions available for a user in a platform.

Other relevant components are:

— Preference editors: 1) a full editor called Preference Management Tool that let users define the value of all possible interaction preferences, and 2) the Personal Control Panel that is a light preference adjuster with an almost always visible GUI

for the user to do minor changes in frequently used settings. Both editors share a common code base that makes them more flexible, sustainable and easier to maintain.
— Semantic infrastructure: A group of ontologies and applications to provide a semantic semi-automatic characterization and reasoning mechanisms over applications and services.

5   Outcomes

After two years of Cloud4all project, a user could now be able to switch from one device to another (PC, smartphone, slate, feature phone) varying the operating systems (Linux, Windows, Android) and having an accessible and comparable experience. Some of the key results achieved so far are:

— Advanced and mature preference editors[4]
— A distributed, local and cloud-based, loosely coupled architecture that supports the components in Figure 1.
— A context infrastructure to provide real time context awareness to Cloud4all. The variables considered at this stage are two environmental variables: sound and light.
— The Common terms registry[5] keeps growing. This registry is a compilation of semantically equivalent terms in different solutions that helps Cloud4all estimate equivalent values for semantically aligned settings across solutions.
— Extensions for Chrome and Firefox. These cross platform web browsers have a combined market share above 50%[6] and represent an efficient way to reach platforms still not compatible with Cloud4all.
— Up to 12 solutions are now compatible with Cloud4all including the aforementioned OS and web browser extensions but also comprising ATs for PCs and smart phones, and feature phones.
— The semantic infrastructure in place let developers register and describe their solutions, and even set relations among the variable settings in their solutions and the existing common terms.

6   Evaluation

The Cloud4all evaluation plan aims to study all factors affecting the user experience and acceptance of the Cloud4all solutions, as well as to provide iterative feedback for developers. The developments carried out can be divided into those with a user interface and those without.

Three iterations are planned. The first iteration has finished successfully, achieving the goal of getting early feedback about the first developments and Lo-Fi prototypes.

---

[4] http://wiki.gpii.net/index.php/User_Preferences_UX
[5] http://wiki.gpii.net/index.php/Common_Terms_Registry
[6] https://blog.shareaholic.com/browser-share-report-10-2013/

The second will take place at Q2-2014. During this iteration, Me-Fi prototypes of the preference editors and the fully integrated APfP architecture deployed with basic functionality will be tested with prospective end users. The last iteration will test the final versions (under the scope of Cloud4all) of the architecture and tools developed.

The first iteration of Cloud4all tests involved 90 users, 30 developers, 15 stake-holders in 3 countries (Spain, Germany and Greece). Three main aspects were evaluated:

— Cloud4all concept: An explanation, a video and some demos helped user under-stand the Cloud4all concept in practice and imagine its future use and how useful (or not) it could be for them and other people.
— Auto-Personalization scenario: Two PCs, one with Windows and one Linux, with similar accessibility solutions, were used to evaluate the user experience of the APfP process. Users were requested to define and adjust their settings in order to perform a common task in one of the platforms, and then move to the other plat-form and do a similar task. The new platform had the configuration calculated by the architecture. These tests were also used to study comparatively the results and accuracy of the two matchmakers.
— The Preference Management Tool and the Semantic Alignment Tool were the two tools available designed within the Project with a GUI. Standard usability studies were performed with each tool's target users: final users for the PMT (usually peo-ple with disability) and developers for the SAT.

On average, users found Cloud4all very useful for their future daily lives, strengthen-ing its ability to make some tasks easier and especially valuable for public devices. Developers and other stakeholders were even more enthusiastic about the Project as they rely on the possibility to open a new AT market. The Auto-Personalization sce-nario turned out to be pretty accurate although 1) the number of devices tested was very limited, and 2) operations on new devices are still a challenge. For instance, shortcuts are completely different for same type of solutions. The tools for managing preferences and align semantically applications are still a work in progress. Usability needs to be improved and new advanced features added.

7   Future Work

Year three of the Project envisions important challenges. First, Cloud4all will have to develop rock solid implementations (reliable and scalable) of some components al-ready developed: the Preference server, user-installable platform modules for Win-dows, Linux and Android, the Common Terms Registry and Unified Listing, and the Matchmakers. The Preference Management Tools and the Semantic Alignment Tool are still in a previous stage, as well as the extension and jetpack for Chrome and Fire-fox, respectively. These plugins for cross-platform web browsers are especially rele-vant as Cloud4all can service this way on still non-compatible platforms. Next year, about 20 applications are expected to be compatible, registered and working with Cloud4all in an ever growing effort to involve a broader community, especially AT developers and mainstream technology providers. A package for developers[7] will be ready to help early adopters make their applications Cloud4all compatible. This will be the first step towards the creation of a more active and efficient AT market although major efforts in this direction are part of Prosperity4all project.

Further research need to be done in the semi-automatic generation of metadata as well as in Context-responsive components. Now, only light and sound variables are considered but the architecture is ready to be responsive to other environmental variables like individual conditions, activity or time. Another important challenge in context management is to decide if some decisions and which ones might avoid user control. Under some circumstances where context conditions prevent users to interact, the context-aware system could add or switch to other interaction mode.

New advanced features relating matchmaking and preference management are planned. Maybe the most important is the ability to suggest new ATs or configurations to a user based on the knowledge gathered about the user interaction.

Next year will also provide some answers to open questions about simultaneously shared devices like TVs. When people with different needs share a device, the optimum settings for each user may not be the optimum for the group. There are also a number of open issues on security. Users are provided with a token to get access to the Cloud4all service, but if the token is lost by the user there is no way to recover it easily without using some contact information. Email is of common use, but other personal details can be traced back from the email address. Additionally, when Cloud4all is used in devices like ATMs, not controlled by the user, settings are downloaded and applied by the device, and can be recorded together with the identification information. The overall problem is to manage privacy levels for different devices, platforms, applications or companies. Users should be able to manage these privacy aspects according to their own interest and preferences should be shared with these solutions up to some point.

Finally, one of the most interesting issues to be covered is the first interaction with a device. How users can know that Cloud4all is running in this device and what key-in methods are available are two problems not solved yet. The project is working in some images and sounds that can be associated to Cloud4all but it also has to do with the creation of a brand.

Acknowledgement. Different components of the body of work described in this paper was, and/or is being, funded by the European Union's Seventh Framework Programme (FP7/2007-2013) grant agreement n° 289016 (Cloud4all) and 610510 (Prosperity4All), by the National Institute on Disability and Rehabilitation Research, US Dept of Education under Grants H133E080022 (RERC-IT) and H133E130028 (UIITA-RERC) and contract ED-OSE-12-D-0013 (Preferences for Global Access), by the Flora Hewlett Foundation, the Ontario Ministry of Research and Innovation, and the Canadian Foundation for Innovation. The opinions and results herein are those of the authors and not necessarily those of the funding agencies.

---

[7] http://blogs.cloud4all.info/developers

References

1. Service, United States Public Health: The Surgeon General's Call to Action to Improve the Health and Wellness of Persons with Disabilities, Public Health Service, Office of the Surgeon General, Rockville, MD (2005)
2. Aging Stats,
   `http://www.agingstats.gov/Main_Site/Data/2012_Documents/Population.aspx`
3. EC Europa,
   `http://ec.europa.eu/economy_finance/articles/structural_reforms/2012-05-15_ageing_report_en.htm`
4. Statistics Bureau, Ministry of Internal affairs and Communications,
   `http://www.stat.go.jp/english/data/nenkan/1431-02.htm`
5. Vicente, M.R., Lopez, A.J.: A multidimensional analysis of the disability digital divide: some evidence of the Internet use. The Information Society, 48–64 (2010)
6. Technosite: SMART 2009-0072: Study on economic assessment for improving eaccessibility services and products, European Commision (2012),
   `http://www.eaccessibilityimpacts.eu/researchResults.aspx`
7. Uslan, M.M.: Barriers to Acquiring Assistive Technology: Cost and Lack of Information. Journal of Visual Impairment and Blindness 9(86), 402–407 (1992)
8. Scherer, M.J., Galvin, J.C.: An Outcomes Perspective of Quality Pathways to Most Appropriate Technology. Evaluating, Selecting and Using Appropriate Assistive Technology, 1–26 (1996)
9. Dawe, M.: Desperately seeking simplicity: how young adults with cognitive disabilities and their families adopt assistive technologies. In: ACM (ed.) Proceedings of the SIGCHI Conference on Human Factors in Computing Systems, pp. 1143–1152 (2006)
10. Vanderheiden, G., Treviranus, J.: Creating a global public inclusive infrastructure. In: Stephanidis, C. (ed.) Universal Access in HCI, Part I, HCII 2011. LNCS, vol. 6765, pp. 517–526. Springer, Heidelberg (2011)
11. Vanderheiden, G.C., Treviranus, J., Chourasia, A.: The global public inclusive infrastructure (GPII). In: ACM (ed.) Proceedings of the 15th International ACM SIGACCESS Conference on Computers and Accessibility, p. 70 (2013)
12. Alvargonzález, Etayo, Gutiérrez, J.A., Madrid: Arquitectura orientada a servicios para proporcionar accesibilidad. In: JSWEB 2010, Valencia (2010)
13. Karim, S., Tjoa, A.M.: Towards the Use of Ontologies for Improving User Interaction for People with Special Needs. In: Miesenberger, K., Klaus, J., Zagler, W.L., Karshmer, A.I. (eds.) ICCHP 2006. LNCS, vol. 4061, pp. 77–84. Springer, Heidelberg (2006)
14. Gajos, K., Weld, D.S., Wobbrock, J.O.: Automatically Generating Personalized User Interfaces with SUPPLE. Artificial Intelligence (174), 910–950 (2010)
15. Casacuberta, J., Sainz, F., Madrid, J.: Evaluation of an Inclusive Smart Home Technology System. In: Bravo, J., Hervás, R., Rodríguez, M. (eds.) IWAAL 2012. LNCS, vol. 7657, pp. 316–319. Springer, Heidelberg (2012)
16. Zimmermann, G., Vanderheiden, G., Gilman, A.: Universal remote console - prototyping for the alternate interface access standard. In: Carbonell, N., Stephanidis, C. (eds.) UI4ALL 2002. LNCS, vol. 2615, pp. 524–531. Springer, Heidelberg (2003)
17. Madrid, R.I., Turrero, M., Ortega-Moral, M.: Applying Human-Centred Design to Create a Collecting Tool of Needs and Preferences for the Personalisation of ATMs. In: Practice, A. (ed.) AAATE 2013, Vilamoura, vol. 33, p. 380 (2013)

18. Dey, A.K.: Understanding and Using Context. Personal and Ubiquitous Computing (5), 4–7 (2001)
19. Dey, A.K., Abowd, G.D., Salber, D.: A Conceptual Framework and a Toolkit for Supporting the Rapid Prototyping of Context-Aware Applications. Journal Human Computer Interaction 16, 97–166 (2001)
20. Zimmermann, G., Lorenz, A., Specht, M.: Applications of a Context-Management System, pp. 556–569 (2005)
21. Zimmermann, A., Lorenz, A., Opperman, R.: An operational definition of context. CONTEXT (2007)
22. Iglesias-Pérez, A., Peinado, I., Chacón, J., Ortega-Moral, M.: Frontiers in context modelling to enhance personalization of assistive technologies. In: Assistive Technology: From Research to Practice, Vilarmoura, vol. 33, p. 380 (2013)
23. Caminero, J., Rodríguez, M.C., Vanderdonckt, J., Paterno, F., Rett, J., Raggett, D., Marín, I.: The SERENOA Project: Multidimensional Context-Aware Adaptation of Service Front-Ends. In: LREC, pp. 2977–2984
24. Vanderheiden, G., Treviranus, J., Usero, J.A., Bekiaris, E., Gemou, M., Chourasia, A.O.: Auto-Personalization: Theory, Practice and Cross-Platform Implementation. In: Publications, S. (ed.) Proceedings of the Human Factors and Ergonomics Society Annual Meeting, vol. 56-I, pp. 926–930 (2012)
25. Cloud4all Consortium: D103.1 Rule sets for the automatic adaptation of the user profile, Madrid (2013), http://cloud4all.info
26. Cloud4all Consortium: D105.1.1 System architecture, Madrid (2013), http://cloud4all.info

Requirements for the Successful Market Adoption of Adaptive User Interfaces for Accessibility

Matthias Peissner[1], Andreas Schuller[1], Daniel Ziegler[1], Christian Knecht[2], and Gottfried Zimmermann[3]

[1] Fraunhofer-Institute for Industrial Engineering, Stuttgart, Germany
{matthias.peissner,andreas.schuller,
daniel.ziegler}@iao.fraunhofer.de
[2] University of Stuttgart, Stuttgart, Germany
christian.knecht@iat.uni-stuttgart.de
[3] Media University Stuttgart, Stuttgart, Germany
gzimmermann@hdm-stuttgart.de

Abstract. The concept of adaptive user interfaces is a promising solution for providing users with a wide range of individual needs with accessible technology. Developers only have to implement one generic solution to offer a multitude of individually optimised concrete user interfaces. Whereas a lot of technical functionalities and characteristics of adaptive user interfaces are already solved, there is still no widespread market adoption of adaptive UI technologies. This paper presents a collection of requirements for adaptive user interface systems that can enable widespread market adoption. Furthermore it identifies strategies and individual answers, how these requirements can be addressed and met in future systems building on the Prosperity4all approach. It gives a comparison of existing research solutions and how they compare with the stated requirements.

Keywords: Adaptive user interface, adaptive systems, accessibility, user characteristics, market adoption, requirements.

1   Introduction

In order to provide accessible technology to end-users, adaptive user interfaces are recognized as one established solution (e.g. [1], [2] and [3]). By recognizing the personal and contextual user needs, the system can dynamically react by providing personalized user interfaces that can overcome usage barriers. Although there is a long term history in the research field of adaptive user interfaces there are no significant approaches established on the mainstream market yet. Our proposition is that there are several essential requirements that adaptive user interface systems must comply before being able to reach significant impact on the software market:

Being able to provide wide ranging user interface adaptations may require a huge knowledge base and complex adaptation algorithms. This can hardly be accomplished in a centralized system. Therefore, we have identified the following prerequisite

C. Stephanidis and M. Antona (Eds.): UAHCI/HCII 2014, Part IV, LNCS 8516, pp. 431–442, 2014.
© Springer International Publishing Switzerland 2014

requirements, which we see as essential to an adaptive user interface system: *Modularity* is necessary to being able to handle the complexity of such a system. In practice, an *extensible* approach is important to allow to focus on a subset of possible adaptive solutions at first and to extend gradually to more elaborated use cases. *Openness* of the implemented approach means that the possibility to integrate external expert knowledge into the adaption system is kept intact. This should also apply after the development has finished.

Ensuring the fulfilment of the previous requirements only represent one necessary prerequisite step toward successful market adoption. Furthermore, we describe three more specific requirements for allowing widespread adoption in software development: *efficiency* in the integration in a general software development processes a *short and easy learning curve* for developers as well as *comprehensible and controllable development processes*. Concluding, an overview and evaluation of existing approaches towards the described requirements is listed and the Prosperity4all concept of reaching these requirements is being described.

2   Prerequisite Requirements

The creation of adaptive user interfaces to lower accessibility barriers for users requires the provision of a broad spectrum of individual solutions. To meet the particular needs of many different users, context variables and target devices, such a system must be able to express and handle user interaction in a great variety of ways. Furthermore, this requires very many adaption rules and complex adaption algorithms. We state the following essential prerequisite requirements that arise from the basics necessities to practically work and handle such an adaptive software system.

2.1   Modularity

Modular approaches are identified by their characteristic to subdivide systems into smaller self-contained elements (modules), by the interchangeable configurability of modules and by clearly specified interfaces between modules. Several modules can be combined in numerous ways, and therefore open the possibility to a large number of possible solutions. Module based solutions with clear interfaces also allow for a facilitated division of work within project teams and for parallel development on different system modules by different project teams or team members.

2.2   Extensibility

When implementing concrete design solutions and corresponding adaption rules, extensibility of all adaption mechanisms should be a key concept. Extensibility means that existing system modules can be scaled within the adaptive system or also added and extended at a later stage. Practically, this can mean to start out the adaptive system behaviour with a subset of user interface elements and to iteratively add more elaborated user interface elements and mechanisms at later project stages. In our previous experience in the MyUI project, this factor of extensibility has shown to be essential and helpful for being able to handle more complex use cases.

2.3   Openness

In order to provide individual design solutions to the needs of particular users, detailed expert knowledge and the knowledge of different user contexts is needed. Even if developers cover all design solutions that work for the known users, they might lack some particular expert knowledge about certain use cases or the characteristics of previously unknown users. Therefore it is essential that the adaption mechanisms in the adaptive system provide a certain amount of openness. This expert knowledge should be easily integrated also at later stages, regardless of an ongoing or closed development process.

3   Basic Requirements for Market Acceptance

In addition to the prerequisite requirements, there are further requirements that are targeted at developers and designers and therefore essential to potential market success and rate of uptake of an adaptive system. To tackle the scepticism towards automatically adaptive user interfaces (as described in [1]) we have identified three key challenges that also resemble our requirements:

— Efficiency in the development process of adaptive user interfaces,
— Short learning curve for developers and
— Comprehensible and controllable development processes for generating resulting user interfaces

These challenges are mainly caused by the approach of model based user interfaces [4] that are generally used for the creation of adaptive user interfaces [5]. This means that an abstract model of a user interface is used as the fundamental structure for generating all possible variants of the adaptive UI. The abstract model describes the commonalities between all variants and is independent of concrete presentation and interaction mechanisms.

The growing requirement of user interfaces running on a multitude of different target devices and platforms has fostered the need for abstract markup languages for automatically generated user interfaces. Some of the most notable recent approaches include TERESA [6] with CONCUR TASK TREES [7], PERSONAL UNIVERSAL CONTROLLER (PUC) [8] for example HUDDLE [9] and UNIFORM [10], additionally UIML (User Interface Markup Language) and CANONICAL ABSTRACT PROTOTYPES (CAP) with newer enhancements CAP3 ([11], [12]).

The work with abstract models is partially difficult to combine with the current practice of the design and development of user interfaces (see [13]). Therefore, the market success of a newly developed adaptive system is also highly dependent on to which extend the previously described requirements are being fulfilled.

3.1   Efficiency in the Development Process of Adaptive User Interfaces

One important precondition for a successful adoption of new software development approaches is their economic viability and efficient implementation. Theoretically, all model based approaches for automatic software generation promise potentially great possible economic savings. Especially for the generation of user interface variants (e.g. different target devices, see [14]), automated processes can relieve the developers of considerable tasks. The user interface is only specified once in an abstract description that resembles the basis for automatic generation different concrete UI variants. Even retrospective changes on the model can be automatically mapped to the different generated variants [15].

To be able to fully benefit from the potential of these automatically generated user interfaces, the following two requirements are of greatest importance:

— *Conciseness and clarity:*
  The adaptive system should keep the manually crafted artefacts (models) in terms of extend and complexity to a minimum (see [16]). Redundancies in the resulting models should be avoided.
— *Reusability:*
  The generation and adaption of the user interface should be based on generic and reusable mechanism and components. Therefore reoccurring components do not have to be created for each application, but reused and referenced in the abstract application model. Precondition is a clear distinction between application logic from the adaption mechanisms of the interface.

3.2   Short Learning Curve for Developers

The creation of a model that describes the user interface independently from the concrete design of the user interface and the used input devices requires a certain ability to abstract on the side of the developer. This abstracted and time consuming working mode of model based creation of UIs doesn't necessarily resemble today's practice, even if some model based systems (like TERESA) employ a graphical editor for the model creation [6]. The graphical visualization of a developed user interfaces is nowadays often an integral part of the development process ([17], [18]). Oftentimes editors with WYSIWYG-functionality are being used. The learning of a new model language is often mentioned as one barrier for employing adaptive systems at all [13].

3.3   Comprehensible and Controllable Development Processes

Developers want to control and understand the automated processes to generate adaptive user interfaces. Myers et al. point out that it can be difficult in some cases to make the connection between the specification of a user interface and the final generated output [13]. One reason for the existing desire to further influence the compiled UI output was that until recently generated user interfaces were not able to satisfy a very high aesthetic level compared to manually designed, non-generated UIs [13].

4   Comparison of Related Work

There have been several research projects in the field of adaptive user interfaces. Not all of them had their particular focus on the support of the interface developers and the market impact, therefore their fulfilment of the aforementioned requirements varies naturally. Table 1 contains the comparison of the related projects in regard to our market requirements; the following sections will briefly describe the most relevant characteristics for each project in this context.

— **DAMASK.** Damask serves as a pattern based modelling approach and tool. Designers can sketch a user interface that can be used for the UI generation on other devices. Accessibility issues are not addressed explicitly. Nevertheless the system's pattern-based approach and practical functions seem to be very beneficial in this context [18].

— **FAME.** Fame, the "Model-based Framework for Adaptive Multimodal Environments", is a model based framework for adaptive multimodal user interfaces. The approach is centered on a behavior matrix, where the developer specifies the system behavior under different conditions. The defined adaptation rules limited to input and output modality. Some interdependencies between adaptable components are not handled which can lead to a potential break of consistence [19].

— **GUIDE.** Guide, "Gentle user interfaces for elderly people", is a European research project. It tries to strengthen the accessibility of interactive TV applications. The user interface adaption is mainly constrained to the augmentation of the original user interface by offering additional input and output modalities. There is no overall abstract application model describing the user interface on a more general level. The augmentation of existing web applications is realized by annotating HTML code ([20], [21] and [22]).

— **MICA.** Mica, the "Mixed-Initiative Customization Assistance" is a system for the intelligent aid for the user to personalize complex user interface. The system is adapting the helping functions that are implemented within a cooperative dialogue with the user (mixed initiative). Nevertheless the user keeps the complete control over the configuration process. Relevant in this context is especially the unique mixed initiative approach in the user dialogue and the focus on controllability of the intelligent system behavior by the user ([23] and [24]).

— **OASIS/ASK-IT.** OASIS "Open architecture for Accessible Services Integration and Standardization") and its predecessor ASK-IT ("Ambient Intelligence System of Agents for Knowledge-based and Integrated Services for Mobility Impaired Users") both have developed and employed a modular, rule based system to adapt the user interface to particular user needs. OASIS developed the so called adaptive widget library which allows for a direct integration in developer tools. However, there is no adaptation of structural aspects of the interaction, i.e. higher abstractions of the interaction flow ([25], [26] and [27]).

— **PUC and HUDDLE.** PUC ("Personal Unified Controller") is a descriptive language that serves for the abstract definition of user interfaces. It can allow for the generation of different UIs for diverse devices and output modalities. HUDDLE builds upon the PUC to offer automatically generated user interfaces for controlling a home cinema system. The approach is relevant, because it is one of the few validated systems employing an abstract user interface description language, and implemented the idea of so called smart templates, that can adapt themselves according to the chosen target device and platform ([8], [28], [9] and [10]).

— **PLASTIC USER INTERFACES.** The basis for plastic user interfaces lays in ubiquituous computing and the easy integration of different user devices. There is a strong focus on providing conceptual and generic descriptions on many different aspects like the user, the social and physical environment and the technical platform. However, the described adaptive mechanisms refer rather to technical device characteristics than of user characteristics ([29], [30], [31], [32], [33], [34], [35], [36], [37], [38], and [39]).

Table 1. Assessment of relevant research projects

Legend:
● Broad coverage, in-depth concepts   ◑ Partial coverage, in-depth concepts
◐ Broad coverage, simple concepts   ○ Low coverage, simple concepts

Requirements	DAMASK	FAME	GUIDE	MICA	OASIS / ASK-IT	PUC / Huddle	Plastic UI	SUPPLE	UUI / AVANTI	MyUI
Modular and extensible adaptation mechanisms (2.1and 2.2)		◐	●	○	◐	◑	●	●	◑	●
Public available adaption mechanisms and open to external contributions (2.3)			◐	○	◐	◑	◑	◑	◑	◐
Efficient Development: reusable components and low effort for the specification with sufficient cardinality (3.1)	◑	○	◑		◑	◑	●	●	○	●
Low thresholds for beginners and low demands for developers` skills (3.2)	●	◑	●		●	●	◐	○	○	●
Generation of the adaptive user interface understandable and manageable from the developers point of view (3.3)					●	◑	◑	○	◑	●

— **SUPPLE.** Supple is one of the most influential adaptive systems for accessibility. Based on a cost function that takes into account used devices, current tasks, user preferences as well as motoric and perceptive limitations. However, performance issues limit the set of characteristics taken to account. Supple also offers the user possibilities to influence the output of the generated user interface ([1], [40], [41], and [42]).

- **UUI/AVANTI.** Avanti is based upon the Unified User Interface (UUI) approach. It offers alterations of the context and user profile both during initialization phase and during runtime. Basis of the adaptions are design patterns that resemble solutions to different user and context profile data. The "Unified User Interface Design Method" describes the process to develop an adaptive application. The model is focused on user characteristics, only motoric disabilities and blindness are mentioned. The different application states are designed to have an easily extensible rule base to mention other user needs ([43], [44], [45], [46], and [47]).
- **MYUI.** MyUI (Mainstreaming Accessibility through Synergistic User Modelling and Adaptability) integrates all aspects of adaptive user interfaces for accessibility in one system [12]. It includes the multimodal design patterns repository, the runtime environment with the adaption engine enabling user interface generation and dynamic adaptations during run-time, the specification of an abstract user interface model and a development tool. MyUI mostly complies with all the described requirements (see Table 1).

5   Prosperity 4 All Approach

Even though MyUI theoretically fulfils most of the requirements for the successful market adoption of adaptive user interfaces for accessibility [48], in practical, it was never used for developing commercial products. Besides having the focus of the patterns and the reference implementation on interactive TV (iTV) the main reason for the absence of market acceptance is probably the missing infrastructure and community.

This is the starting point of Prosperity4All. MyUI and other promising approaches from scientific research will be refined and integrated to a multi-sided-platform, the Global Public Inclusive Infrastructure (GPII). International project participation, the involvement of industry enterprises, cross-platform development techniques and the open source strategy will help adaptive user interface approaches to reach a better market penetration [49]. GPII allows commercial product developers and service providers as well as external technical contributors to easily access and use existing solutions, extend or adapt them in order to fit specific requirements. Additionally crowdsourcing can help making new ideas accessible for diverse end users.

A more concrete plan for integrating and improving the MyUI components is described in the following subsections:

5.1   User and Context Management

The MyUI Context Manager holds a user profile based on variables expressing user capabilities and environmental conditions. The variables are expressed by numeric values an interval common to all of them. Based on collected sensor data the profile variables are updated in a permanent process [12].

The architecture of the GPII as developed by the Cloud4all project uses an ontology of user needs and preferences that are directly linked to user interface and interaction aspects [50]. To enable the integration of MyUI concepts into the GPII architecture a mapping between the stored user preferences and the capabilities based user profile will be established.

Special attention will be directed to MyUI runtime events triggered by sensors and how this information can be used to determine the need for runtime adaptations by refining the users set of preferences.

5.2 Runtime Environment

The MyUI runtime environment will be used to interpret and process information about user needs and environmental factors to generate and adapt accessible user interfaces. Therefor flexible layouts and CSS variations with the newest web technologies will be used similar to those in the "Responsive Design" approach for device specific adaption. If applicable, runtime environments for additional platforms will be implemented. Additionally the MyUI runtime environment will be extended to work with Assistive Technologies (AT) as plugged and configured by AsTeRICS (Assistive Technology Rapid Integration & Construction Set). AsTeRICS allows the creation of flexible solutions for people with disabilities using a large set of sensors and actuators. Possible applications are Computer input, Environmental Control, Toys and Games, Brain/Neural computer interfaces, Android Phone support [51]. In addition the Universal Remote Console (URC) will be integrated which allows users to interact with networked devices and services in their environments in universal and natural ways, utilizing technologies like natural language interaction [52].

5.3 Pattern Repository

The idea and the base of the open and extensible MyUI Pattern Repository will mainly be taken over. Each pattern describes a rule which is interpreted by the adaption engine. They have a defined structure and can be related to other patterns. There will be a machine-readable and a human-readable part in order to allow the contribution from developers and accessibility experts. To preserve platform and technology independence the machine-readable part is written in pseudocode and needs to be transferred to the adaption engine manually. In Prosperity4All the transformation process will be made easier for example by providing generative stubs. Furthermore the repository will be extended with patterns for further applications and devices. The open source character of the project ensures that new patterns will be available to all the interested developers. Additionally quality assurance issues will be addressed in order to guarantee the usefulness of new patterns.

5.4 Development Toolkit

To comply with the in section 3 described basic requirements for market acceptance a development toolkit is an essential component and therefor will also be part of the Prosperity4All approach. It supports industrial user interface developers and designers to quickly create abstract models of adaptive user interfaces which are needed for run-time adaptations. Developers and decision-makers of software enterprises gave positive feedback for the MyUI toolkit in regard to efficiency, learning curve, comprehensibility and controllability [48]. Prosperity4All will also address the mentioned concerns for example regarding more complex projects.

The URC utilizes a User Interface Socket Description to define the abstract interaction possibilities. This approach will be examined for integration of translation possibilities with the MyUI Abstract Application Interaction Model.

6   Conclusions and Outlook

The basic requirements for market acceptance in section 3 as well as the prerequisite requirements in section 2 are described on a rather high level. From a technical point of view to gain acceptance in the real world software market it will be necessary to determine which common software engineering practices have to be supported. Based on the results there may be implications for the structure of the runtime infrastructure and components as well as for the development environment and tools.

A more human-centered perspective brings the developer into focus. It is not sufficient only making developers realize that they have to implement adaptive user interfaces for their software products. Instead it seems necessary to provide an environment where they actually want to do so. One major key may be the user experience of developers working with the components and tools needed.

From the commercial point of view the goal is not to provide special solutions for a distinct market for accessibility solutions but to demonstrate and communicate the potential of adaptive user interfaces for one mainstream market including all users regardless of any kind of temporary or permanent special needs.

Acknowledgments. The research leading to these results has received funding from the European Union's Seventh Framework Program under FP7 Grant #610510 and #248606. The opinions herein are those of the authors and not necessarily those of the funding agency.

References

1. Gajos, K.Z., Weld, D.S., Wobbrock, J.O.: Automatically generating personalized user interfaces with Supple. Artificial Intelligence 174(12-13), 910–950 (2010)
2. Ringbauer, B., Peissner, M., Gemou, M.: From "Design for all" towards "Design for one" – A modular user interface approach. In: Stephanidis, C. (ed.) HCI 2007. LNCS, vol. 4554, pp. 517–526. Springer, Heidelberg (2007)
3. Savidis, A., Stephanidis, C.: Unified user interface design: Designing universally accessible interactions. Int. J. Interacting with Computers 16(2), 243–270 (2004)
4. Szekely, P.: Retrospective and Challenges for Model-Based Interface Development. In: Proceedings DSV-IS 1996. Eurographics, pp. 1–27. Springer, Heidelberg (1996)

5. Cockton, G.: Some critical remarks on abstractions for adaptable dialogue managers. In: Proceedings of the 3rd Conference of the British Computer Society on People and Computers, pp. 325–343. Cambridge University Press, Cambridge (1987)

6. Paterno, F., Santoro, C., Mäntyjärvi, J., Mori, G., Sansone, S.: Authoring pervasive multimodal user interfaces. International Journal of Web Engineering and Technology 4(2), 235–261 (2008)

7. Paterno, F.: Model-Based Design and Evaluation of Interactive Applications. Springer, London (1999)

8. Nichols, J., Myers, B.A.: Creating a lightweight user interface description language: An overview and analysis of the personal universal controller project. ACM Transactions on Computer-Human Interaction 16(4), Article 17, 37 pages (2009)

9. Nichols, J., Myers, B.A., Rothrock, B.: UNIFORM: automatically generating consistent remote control user interfaces. In: Proceedings CHI 2006, pp. 611–620. ACM, New York (2006)

10. Nichols, J., Rothrock, B., Chau, D.H., Myers, B.A.: Huddle: automatically generating interfaces for systems of multiple connected appliances. In: Proceedings UIST 2006, pp. 279–288. ACM, New York (2006)

11. Van den Bergh, J., Luyten, K., Coninx, K.: CAP3: context-sensitive abstract user interface specification. In: Proceedings EICS 2011, pp. 31–40. ACM, New York (2011)

12. Peissner, M., Häbe, D., Janssen, D., Sellner, T.: MyUI: generating accessible user interfaces from multimodal design patterns. In: Proceedings EICS 2012, pp. 81–90. ACM, New York (2012)

13. Lin, J., Landay, J.A.: Employing patterns and layers for early-stage design and prototyping of cross-device user interfaces. In: Proceedings CHI 2008, pp. 1313–1322. ACM, New York (2008)

14. Myers, B., Hudson, S.E., Pausch, R.: Past, present, and future of user interface software tools. ACM Transactions on Computer-Human Interaction - Special Issue on Human-Computer Interaction in the New Millennium, Part 1 7(1), 3–28 (2000)

15. Meskens, J., Vermeulen, J., Luyten, K., Coninx, K.: Gummy for multi-platform user interface designs: shape me, multiply me, fix me, use me. In: Proceedings AVI 2008, pp. 233–240. ACM, New York (2008)

16. Trewin, S., Zimmermann, G., Vanderheiden, G.: Abstract user interface representations: how well do they support universal access? ACM SIGCAPH Computers and the Physically Handicapped (73-74), 77–84 (2002)

17. Newman, M.W., Landay, J.A.: Sitemaps, storyboards, and specifications: a sketch of Web site design practice. In: Proceedings DIS 2000, pp. 263–274. ACM, New York (2000)

18. Lin, J., Landay, J.A.: Employing patterns and layers for early-stage design and prototyping of cross-device user interfaces. In: Proceedings CHI 2008, pp. 1313–1322. ACM, New York (2008)

19. Duarte, C., Carriço, L.: A conceptual framework for developing adaptive multimodal applications. In: Proceedings of the 11th International Conference on Intelligent user Interfaces (IUI 2006), pp. 132–139. ACM, New York (2006)

20. Biswas, P., Langdon, P., Duarte, C., Coelho, J.: Multimodal adaptation through simulation for digital TV interface. In: Proceedings EuroITV 2011, pp. 231–234. ACM, New York (2011)

21. Coelho, J., Duarte, C.: The Contribution of Multimodal Adaptation Techniques to the GUIDE Interface. In: Stephanidis, C. (ed.) Universal Access in HCI, Part I, HCII 2011. LNCS, vol. 6765, pp. 337–346. Springer, Heidelberg (2011)

22. Coelho, J., Duarte, C., Biswas, P., Langdon, P.: Developing accessible TV applications. In: Proceedings ASSETS 2011, pp. 131–138. ACM, New York (2011)
23. Bunt, A., Conati, C., McGrenere, J.: Mixed-Initiative Interface Personalization as a Case Study in Usable AI. AI Magazine 30(4), 58–64 (2009)
24. Bunt, A., Conati, C., McGrenere, J.: Supporting interface customization using a mixedinitiative approach. In: Proceedings IUI 2007, pp. 92–101. ACM, New York (2007)
25. Leonidis, A., Antona, M., Stephanidis, C.: Rapid Prototyping of Adaptable User Interfaces. International Journal of Human-Computer Interaction 28(4), 213–235 (2012)
26. Leuteritz, J.-P., Widlroither, H., Mourouzis, A., Panou, M., Antona, M., Leonidis, A.: Development of Open Platform Based Adaptive HCI Concepts for Elderly Users. In: Stephanidis, C. (ed.) UAHCI 2009, Part II. LNCS, vol. 5615, pp. 684–693. Springer, Heidelberg (2009)
27. Ringbauer, B., Peissner, M., Gemou, M.: From "design for all" towards "design for one"– A modular user interface approach. In: Stephanidis, C. (ed.) Universal Access in HCI, Part I, HCII 2000. LNCS, vol. 4554, pp. 517–526. Springer, Heidelberg (2007)
28. Nichols, J., Chau, D.H., Myers, B.A.: Demonstrating the viability of automatically generated user interfaces. In: Proceedings CHI 2007, pp. 1283–1292. ACM, New York (2007)
29. Frey, A.G., Céret, E., Dupuy-Chessa, S., Calvary, G., Gabillon, Y.: UsiComp: an extensible model-driven composer. In: Proceedings EICS 2012, pp. 263–268. ACM, New York (2012)
30. Calvary, G., Serna, A., Coutaz, J., Scapin, D., Pontico, F., Winckler, M.: Envisioning Advanced User Interfaces for e-Government Applications: a Case Study. In: Practical Studies in E-Government: Best Practices from Around the World, pp. 205–228. Springer, Heidelberg (2011)
31. Ceret, C.: Toward a flexible design method sustaining UIs plasticity. In: Proceedings EICS 2011, pp. 307–310. ACM, New York (2011)
32. Dessart, C.-E., Motti, V.G., Vanderdonckt, J.: Showing user interface adaptivity by animated transitions. In: Proceedings EICS 2011, pp. 95–104. ACM, New York (2011)
33. Demeure, A., Calvary, G., Coninx, K.: COMET(s), A Software Architecture Style and an Interactors Toolkit for Plastic User Interfaces. In: Graham, T.C.N. (ed.) DSV-IS 2008. LNCS, vol. 5136, pp. 225–237. Springer, Heidelberg (2008)
34. Vanderdonckt, J., Coutaz, J., Calvary, G., Stanciulescu, A.: Multimodality for Plastic User Interfaces: Models, Methods, and Principles. In: Multimodal user Interfaces: Signals and Communication Technology. LNEE, pp. 61–84. Springer, Heidelberg (2008)
35. Demeure, A., Calvary, G., Vanderdonckt, J.: The COMETs Inspector: Towards Run Time Plasticity Control Based on a Semantic Network. In: Coninx, K., Luyten, K., Schneider, K.A. (eds.) TAMODIA 2006. LNCS, vol. 4385, pp. 324–338. Springer, Heidelberg (2007)
36. Balme, L., Demeure, A., Barralon, N., Calvary, G.: CAMELEON-RT: A Software Architecture Reference Model for Distributed, Migratable, and Plastic User Interfaces. In: Markopoulos, P., Eggen, B., Aarts, E., Crowley, J.L. (eds.) EUSAI 2004. LNCS, vol. 3295, pp. 291–302. Springer, Heidelberg (2004)
37. Calvary, G., Coutaz, J., Thevenin, D., Limbourg, Q., Bouillon, L., Vanderdonckt, J.: A Unifying Reference Framework for Multi-Target User Interfaces. Interacting with Computers 15(3), 289–308 (2003)
38. Calvary, G., Dâassi, O., Balme, L., Demeure, A.: Towards a new generation of widgets for supporting software plasticity: The "comet". In: Feige, U., Roth, J. (eds.) EHCI-DSVIS 2004. LNCS, vol. 3425, pp. 306–324. Springer, Heidelberg (2005)
39. Coutaz, J.: User interface plasticity: model driven engineering to the limit? In: Proceedings EICS 2010, pp. 1–8. ACM, New York (2010)

40. Gajos, K.Z., Wobbrock, J.O., Weld, D.S.: Improving the Performance of Motor-Impaired Users with Automatically-Generated, Ability-Based Interfaces. In: Proceedings CHI 2008, pp. 1257–1266. ACM, New York (2008)
41. Gajos, K.Z., Weld, D.S.: SUPPLE: Automatically Generating User Interfaces. In: Proceedings IUI 2004, pp. 93–100. ACM, New York (2004)
42. Weld, D., Anderson, C., Domingos, P., Etzioni, O., Lau, T., Gajos, K., Wolfman, S.: Automatically personalizing user interfaces. In: Proceedings IJCAI 2003, pp. 1613–1619. Morgan Kaufmann Publishers Inc., San Francisco (2003)
43. Savidis, A., Antona, M., Stephanidis, C.: A Decision-Making Specification Language for Verifiable User-Interface Adaptation Logic. International Journal of Software Engineering and Knowledge Engineering 15(6), 1063–1094 (2005)
44. Savidis, A., Stephanidis, C.: The Unified User Interface Software Architecture. In: User Interfaces for All – Concepts, Methods and Tools, pp. 389–415. Lawrence Erlbaum Associates Inc., Mahwah (2001)
45. Savidis, A., Stephanidis, C.: Unified user interface design: designing universally accessible interactions. Interacting with Computers 16(2), 243–270 (2004)
46. Kobsa, A., Koenemann, J., Pohl, W.: Personalised hypermedia presentation techniques for improving online customer relationships. The Knowledge Engineering Review 16(2), 111–155 (2001)
47. Stephanidis, C., Paramythis, A., Akoumianakis, D., Sfyrakis, M.: Self-adapting web-based systems: Towards universal accessibility. In: Proceedings of the 4th ERCIM Workshop on 'User Interfaces for All', 17 pages (1998)
48. Peissner, M.: Entwurfsmusterbasierter Ansatz für adaptive Benutzungsschnittstellen zur Überwindung von Nutzungsbarrieren. Dissertation. Universität Stuttgart, Stuttgart (2014)
49. Vanderheiden, G., Treviranus, C., Chourasia, J., The, A.: global public inclusive infrastructure (GPII). In: ASSETS 2013, pp. 1–3 (2013)
50. Madrid, J., Peinado, I., Koutkias, V.: Cloud4all Priority applications and User Profile Ontology (D101.1). Public Deliverable of the Cloud4all Project (2012), http://cloud4all.info/render/binarios.aspx?id=90
51. Ossmann, R., Thaller, D., Nussbaum, G., Pühretmair, F., Veigl, C., Weiß, C., Diaz, U.: AsTeRICS, a Flexible Assistive Technology Construction Set. Procedia Computer Science 14, 1–9 (2012)
52. LaPlant, B., Trewin, S., Zimmermann, G., Vanderheiden, G.: The universal remote console: a universal access bus for pervasive computing. IEEE Pervasive Computing 3(1), 76–80 (2004)

Prosperity4All – Setting the Stage for a Paradigm Shift in eInclusion

Matthias Peissner[1], Gregg C. Vanderheiden[2], Jutta Treviranus[3], and Gianna Tsakou[4]

[1] Fraunhofer Institute for Industrial Engineering IAO, Stuttgart, Germany
matthias.peissner@iao.fraunhofer.de
[2] University of Wisconsin – Madison, Madison, WI, USA
gv@trace.wisc.edu
[3] OCAD University, Toronto, Ontario, Canada
jtreviranus@faculty.ocad.ca
[4] SingularLogic S.A., Nea Ionia, Attica, Greece
gtsakou@singularlogic.eu

Abstract. This paper provides an overview of the recently started Prosperity4All project. Prosperity4all aims at a paradigm shift in eInclusion. It focuses on developing the infrastructure to allow a new ecosystem to grow; one that is based on self-rewarding collaboration, that can reduce redundant development, lower costs, increase market reach and penetration internationally, and create the robust cross-platform spectrum of mainstream and assistive technology based access solutions required. This will be done through a process based on true value propositions for all stakeholders and resulting in a system that can profitably serve markets as small as one, at a personally and societally affordable cost.

Keywords: Accessibility, ecosystem.

1 Introduction

In our global society, access to information and communication technologies and services is increasingly becoming essential for everyone, leaving those who cannot effectively access and use these technologies at risk of exclusion from education, employment, commerce, health information, and almost every other aspect of daily living and civic participation. Those at risk include those who cannot use ICT and services due to disability, low literacy, low digital-literacy or aging related barriers.

In the past those who could not access these technologies could get by, avoiding technology entirely. However, ICT is now becoming so engrained in all aspects of society that this is no longer an option. If we cannot provide access to these groups they soon will be unable to participate in education, employment, commerce, our health system, transportation, or even daily independent living. This need to ensure that everyone is able to access and use ICT however is occurring at the same time we

C. Stephanidis and M. Antona (Eds.): UAHCI/HCII 2014, Part IV, LNCS 8516, pp. 443–452, 2014.

are facing something of a *perfect storm* in accessibility; where a number of factors are all coming together at the same time to create a fatal combination.

1. *Fewer resources*: The new economic realities mean that we will have less resources to address the needs of this much larger population.
2. *Many small groups – together large*: The problem is broader than just disability and includes people facing barriers to ICT from disabilities, literacy, digital literacy, and aging. All of these groups are threatened with an inability to participate as we continually 'technify' everything around them. Although it is many small groups, they are cumulatively large, around 2 billion worldwide (cf. [1, 2, 3])
3. *We never were reaching a reasonable fraction*: We must recognize that, even in the developed countries, we were never reaching more than a small fraction of those who needed special access technologies or features to effectively use ICT. There are no solid data, but assistive technologies (AT) manufacturers estimates of their market penetration, although varying widely, all fall in the very low range of between 3% and 15% of those that need AT being reached, cumulatively.
4. *Focus on the "mainstream" disabilities leaving the tails unaddressed*: Current solutions tend to focus on the larger populations or mainstream disabilities, with fewer or no solutions for individuals at the tails of each disability distribution. With all the types, degrees, and combinations of disability, (digital) literacy, and aging, a large portion of the threatened group falls outside of the mainstream category where all of the current focus lies, and in one of the many 'tails or 'tails of the tails.
5. *Existing solutions focus on biggest few platforms*: A majority of the existing solutions are for one or two major platforms. Yet industry, consumers, and public entities are moving to a wide variety of platforms (operating systems, browsers, mobile technologies, etc.). With the rapid proliferation of platforms developers and vendors are completely unable to address all of these groups, across all of the devices and platforms that these groups are encountering in daily life.
6. *Not just devices, also e-documents, media, and services:* The problem extends beyond devices, and also includes document and media access.
7. *Not just vendors and consumer, also providers:* The rapid proliferation of platforms, devices, and solutions is leaving those who must deliver accessibility (clinicians, educators, libraries, public access points, etc.) confused, perpetually behind, and unable to track or understand what is available, much less which solutions would be best or even effective for their different target groups.

So we find that we not only are not able to provide access to everyone who needs it, but we are actually losing ground. A main problem is that our current eInclusion ecosystem cannot serve but a fraction, focuses on "majority disabilities", cannot address the tails, and is losing ground as technology accelerates and proliferates.

In our recently started EU-funded project Prosperity4All we will create the infrastructure from which a new ecosystem can grow over time that can address these problems. This work began with the FP7 project *Cloud4all,* and is part of an international effort to create a *Global Public Inclusive Infrastructure* (GPII, [4]).

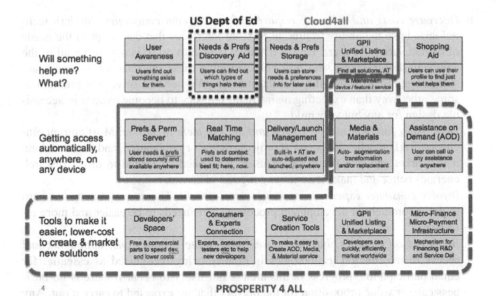

Fig. 1. The Global Public Inclusive Infrastructure (GPII) and its relation to Prosperity4All and Cloud4All

2   The Prosperity4All Vision

We have identified 14 requirements that any such ecosystem must meet. Prosperity4All is built around these requirements, with the requirements becoming the Prosperity4All long-term vision. Prosperity4All is providing the infrastructure and building blocks necessary for reaching the following post-project vision.

1. *Reduce costs*: For developers, vendors, service delivery personnel, public access points, consumers, companies, and governments.
2. *Address the full range of users*: including disabilities, literacy, digital literacy, and aging.
3. Address the tails and the tails of the tails: We can no longer ignore the tails and focus only on the larger groups where it is easier, where there is a larger market, or where there is more return on investment. We need some mechanism to shrink the "unprofitable" so that special measures are affordable to reach them.
4. *Address all technologies*: platforms, OSs, devices, systems, etc. that a person encounters in their lives where they have to use them in 5, 10, and 15 years.
5. *Provide a plan for creating a vibrant and profitable AT market*: Although it would be ideal if all mainstream products could have interfaces that could adapt to the needs of any user, we do not currently know how to do this in any commercially practical fashion, across all disabilities and technologies. We will need AT and will need it for a long time.

6. *Decrease costs and expertise required of mainstream companies*: Modern technologies have the ability to present flexible interfaces that can adapt to the needs of a wide variety of users. However, the expertise to do so is not within all of the company design teams who will be developing these interfaces. Companies are still struggling with usability for the masses. We need to solve this problem in some other way than expecting mainstream industry to become experts in accessible design for any but very mild.

7. *Do a better job of moving research and development to market*: Most current eInclusion R&D reaches life's end at project review or publication, and is not making it to market and into the hands of users who need. We need to direct research energies better and make it easier to get good ideas out.

8. *Involve consumer expertise in product development*: This is easy to say but hard to do in commercial development processes. This needs to be easier and more effective.

9. *Be based on realities, business cases, and value propositions*: although equal access to information technologies is rapidly being recognized as essential for equal participation, progress in this area is not likely to occur if there is no business case or value proposition for the players that are expected to carry it out. Any proposed ecosystem for the creation and delivery of such solutions therefore must be based on economic realities, business cases, and hard value propositions for the implementers.

10. *Recruit and engage more and different players:* We currently do a poor job of enticing and engaging much of the best scientific and technical talent in our society. To address the above challenges we will need to tap the best and brightest, not only in accessibility or inclusion, but the best in other focused scientific and technical areas as well. Any new ecosystem needs to provide a mechanism to allow people to contribute to this area without dedicating themselves to the area, or even having a deep interest in learning much about the area. We also need to be able to figure out how to engage our clinicians and other service delivery personnel who have deep expertise of a different type, that is equally needed and equally thin in our science and technology oriented research core. We involve them as contributors, but we need mechanisms to allow them to become developers and explorers in their own right.

11. *Not forget documents, media, and services*: Information and communication technologies take many forms and all of them must be accessible to individuals with disabilities. Access to an e-book reader but not the books is not sufficient to allow education. Access to the computers in a company but not to the documents, manuals, and communications is not sufficient to allow employment. Access to the website but not to electronic health records is not sufficient for patients. And lack of access to training materials, legal documents, etc. cannot be replaced with access to a home computer or any tablet application. Any ecosystem needs to support and promote access across all aspects of ICT if it is to support inclusion of these groups in all of these environments.

12. *Provide both technology and human accessibility service support*: Any ecosystem must recognize that technology cannot possibly meet all of the accessibility needs

of all of these populations today. Particularly where cognitive or complex aging issues are involved, we do not have assistive technologies, or interface techniques, that can make devices and information automatically usable and understandable to all users. Any ecosystem must therefore, be able to seamlessly integrate human and technology based assistance alternatives.

13. *Work across all domains of life*: any ecosystem must also develop solutions that work across all of the domains that we must operate in as a part of daily life. This includes communication and daily living, work and commerce, education and e-learning, health and safety, mobility and transport, and access everywhere a person goes.

14. *Be applicable, and work internationally*: any ecosystem must be able to create so-lutions that can be applied internationally. The needs are international, and only through international development can development for all users be affordable. And only through international distribution can the economies of scale be brought to the needs of those on all of the tails of all of the distributions. This means that the ecosystem must support solutions that work across languages, cultures, econ-omies and fiscal systems, and legal systems (e.g. copyright, privacy, entitlement etc.)

The Prosperity4All project aims at delivering fully functional key elements – as op-posed to "research prototypes" – of a holistic infrastructure that will entice, engage, and enable stakeholders and individuals to meet the above requirements and create or deliver the required solutions and services. It is self-evident that one project alone, even a large project like Prosperity4All, cannot solve all problems and create all re-quired services within four years. However, we are aiming at laying a sound founda-tion for this and creating a solid base-infrastructure with incremental added value that will enable the full growth into such an ecosystem. As a complete proof-of-concept, Prosperity4All will also deliver numerous real-life implementations of services and applications that are accessible for all, thus proving the feasibility and applicability of the proposed ecosystem infrastructure across technology and user domains.

3   The Prosperity4All Innovative Strategies

Prosperity4All will address these challenges through the following high level innova-tive strategies that are woven throughout the entire project.

3.1   Introduce Holistic Approach to Inclusive Design

Rather than being focused on a particular sector or component or technology, Prosper-ity4All is focused on the creation of an infrastructure as a whole. It does not focus just on supply, or on demand, or on a product or a technology or a technique. Instead it focuses on creating the infrastructure for a system that can bring together the research, development, commercial transfer, service delivery, support, dissemination, and mar-keting etc. aspects, all of which must be in place and work together to address this problem.

3.2   Introduce Technology-Enhanced Crowdsourcing and Gaming Principles in Inclusive Design

We see crowdsourcing and gaming principles not only as powerful new tools, but essential components in any new ecosystem for this area. In the proposed infrastructure they are used in many ways including: to engage new contributors; to enable new ways to collaborate; as a mechanism to draw in new scientists to focus on very specific barriers; and as ways of better tapping the talents of professors and students in our universities as well as our lead clinicians and other service delivery personnel. We intend to incorporate gaming principles not to create game-like interfaces, but within the overall design of the infrastructure and its individual components to encourage participation and collaboration.

3.3   Create a Service-Based Infrastructure for Inclusive Design

We will be introducing and building all of the key infrastructure components for a service-based (versus product-based or device based) ecosystem to augment the current product based system. A marketplace and micropayment infrastructure will be constructed that can support not only the "leasing" of traditional assistive technologies but also selling or leasing of "features" and "enhancement", as well as document and media transformation and Assistance on Demand services of all types. This new service infrastructure has profound implications both for the future of AT and for a diverse new field of 'assistive services' that can both serve and employ less technically oriented users and providers (organizations and individuals).

3.4   Promote a Prosperity-Based Ecosystem for Inclusive Design

The entire infrastructure will be designed to identify and address the issues needed by each of the key players in the development-delivery-support system. A dedicated Sup-Project on Economic Modelling will start by identifying what the needs for each of these players are. These will then be used to shape all of the other activities involved in creating the infrastructure for the ecosystem so that the business case or value proposition for each stakeholder can be met. Where these needs cannot be met by the infrastructure, they will be identified including which other players or forces are needed to provide these components. This approach is in sharp contrast with the usual "social value" or "technology" based approaches of the past.

We see this focus on prosperity/business cases/value propositions as being a critical component to any successful ecosystem. Social justice and human rights might help drive policy and perhaps even service funding, but if policy and service funding do not translate into business cases or value propositions, nothing will happen that actually impacts users in terms of new or better solutions.

3.5   Create a System for Comprehensive Developer Support

A significant part of the project is focused on providing comprehensive support to developers to make it easier and less expensive for them to develop solutions and to enhance the market reach and penetration of their products. This includes support both for assistive technology vendors and for mainstream product companies. It includes provision of background and starter information so that AT and mainstream developers have access to consumer-based needs, as well as information on all existing assistive technologies and access features of other products like there's. It includes both open source and commercial components that they can use to construct solutions (both standard components and special components such as head and body control interfaces, braille translations, web app components, universal remote console sockets etc.). It provides frameworks and tools as well as team support from consumers. It includes a new approach for the mainstream design of web applications that combines the concept of an interface socket or API coupled with an Individual User Interface Generator (IUIG) to allow mainstream vendors to create highly flexible interfaces that can address a wide range of disability, literacy, digital literacy, and aging related barriers without the mainstream vendors having to understand any of these. And it provides tools and components to make it easier to create assistive technology as a service, to tie into the proposed assistive-service infrastructures, and to incorporate the Cloud4all/ GPII auto-personalization from user-preference capability in their products.

3.6   Create Mechanisms That Promote Consumer-Developer Connections

The development of and integration throughout the infrastructure of closer consumer–developer connections is intended to help shift the field from a "push" market (where features are determined by developers and then offered to consumers) towards more of a "Pull" market (where the features that are offered are the result of consumer need and direction). To accomplish this we will be introducing mechanisms throughout the infrastructure to allow consumers to provide a) "feedback" on existing products and features, b) "feed-peer" to allow consumers to communicate the best information on successful solutions to each other as well as strategies for using existing solutions better and in new ways and c) "feedforward" mechanisms to affect the design of future or currently 'in-design' projects. In addition, mechanisms are provided to allow vendors and developers to more closely incorporate consumers in their development process. In the Prosperity4All ecosystem, users will have the chance to identify a desired service and issue donations. Once donations and bids reach critical thresholds, the creation of the service will be possible, even allowing from contest-based decisions on the entity to build the service.

3.7   Develop New Mechanisms to Expand Market Reach and Penetration
(for Vendors and Service Providers)

This includes everything from tools to facilitate localization to other languages, to guidelines for creating products that are acceptable to and support different cultures, to the Unified Listing that will allow them to better reach dispersed user bases and international audiences. The Unified Listing will be expanded from the federated assistive technology database in Cloud4all to one that also includes access features in mainstream ICT, providing enhanced motivation and reach for these products and features as well.

3.8   Develop Targeted Mechanisms to Engage New Players, with New Skills, and to Develop an Expanded Solution Providers Base

In addition to the modularization and other crowdsourcing and gamification efforts discussed above, the infrastructure will build additional specific mechanisms to reach out to specialists who can address specific technical issues such as the use of advanced machine vision to facilitate complex document access, language translation to facilitate internationalization, semantic modelling to facilitate interface transformation etc. We will also be exploring the use of visual/non-visual model-based programming technologies used to push interface development out toward consumers to provide the tools that could be used to explore the introduction of accessibility, and assistive technologies, to early primary education students as a way of both introducing the concepts of accessibility and (through allowing them to create assistive technologies for the example users with disabilities) allow them to discover that they can design, create, and shape technologies to address human/social issues. This might be especially helpful in engaging those individuals who would later be dissuaded from exploring these areas (technology and programming) by social pressures as they grow older.

3.9   Develop New Mechanisms to Target the Tails, and the Tails of the Tails

A key theme throughout the proposal is creating an infrastructure that allows these stakeholders to move beyond the "mainstream disabilities" and to be able to function profitably and successfully in the tails. This goes beyond research and through to delivery, and the ability to provide cost-effective delivery to the tails and the tails of the tails. The proposed infrastructure provides for a robust infrastructure to allow people and organization to develop and deploy a wide range of personal and commercial Assistance on Demand services to address those who cannot be easily addressed through technology. Of particular interest is the proposed user-friendly "do-it-yourself" Assistance on Demand infrastructure tool that will allow an individual to create a personal Assistance on Demand support system for someone in their family. Another important building block to successfully target the tails and the tails of the tails is the Unified Listing and Marketplace. They will make it easier for consumers with orphaned needs to find unique, small market AT. On the other hand, new and small vendors will be supported in reaching thin markets and thus, allowed successful sales to the tails. Finally, the sales of small market AT will be increased by dedicated developer tools and the Unified Listing and Marketplace.

3.10   Integrate an Open Economic Platform into the Ecosystem to Broaden Participation

Another objective is the integration of different infrastructure elements to facilitate a broader participation in the ecosystem by smaller entities and even individuals. This includes a micropayment system to a) allow developers of any size (including individuals) to be able to easily market products or even individual features internationally and have the finances/conversions etc. handled automatically for them, to allow

Assistance on Demand services including micro-Assistance on Demand (for as little as 30 seconds), and b) allow micro-financing (e.g. many users each contribute a small amount to finance future, capability or technology, ala Kickstarter) etc. The infrastructure also includes an Open Marketplace to make it easy for smaller companies that cannot provide their own international marketing to be able to offer their products in a place that can be easily found, that provides international exposure, and that is tied to the new tools being developed to allow users to find solutions that match their particular needs and preferences. The Assistance on Demand infrastructure will also allow anyone, in any country, to set up a service without having to build an infrastructure. It would allow them to provide, and market, any type of Assistance on Demand, in any language, and in a form that is appropriate to local culture and economic scales, by simply providing their service over the Prosperity4All/GPII Assistance on Demand infrastructure.

3.11   Integrate an Innovative Cascading Hybrid Technology and Human Service Delivery Approach into the Ecosystem

There are some groups, (particularly those involving cognitive, digital literacy, or aging related barriers) where what we can do today through technology alone is limited. However where technology could meet part of the needs it is often not employed because it cannot be relied upon – and when it fails it can leave the user stranded and unable to cope. By combining technology and human services in a "try harder" cascading approach it may be possible to have individuals use technology-based solutions that are backed up by human assistance.

4   The Prosperity4All Workplan

In order to realize the project's vision and ambitious objectives, an international consortium of 25 partners has been set up. The 48-months project is broken down into five Sub Projects (SP):

- **SP1 (Economic Model)** focuses on modelling the overall Prosperity4All ecosystem, including its governance scheme, but also the market and business models that will regulate its operation. SP1 aims at ensuring that the project's technical results will have market relevance and a clear potential to be adopted by stakeholders.
- **SP2 (Technological Infrastructure)** is focused on the design, development and integration of the technical infrastructure that will underpin the Prosperity4All ecosystem. This subproject will produce a large number of technologies and infrastructures ranging from perceptive accessible interfaces to technical infrastructures for payment.
- **SP3 (Real-World Applications)** is devoted to testing the applicability and usefulness of the SP2 technology infrastructure and the Prosperity4All ecosystem as a whole through the leveraging and integration of SP2 tools and infrastructures into existing applications, services and platforms.

- **SP4 (Evaluation)** is devoted to assessment, testing and demonstration activities, thus further reinforcing and ensuring a User-Centered-Design of the technology and infrastructure of SP2, as well as the implementations of SP3, but also of the deployment models and market dynamics of the Prosperity4All ecosystem.
- **SP5 (Horizontal Activities)** comprises the management, exploitation, dissemination and sustainability activities of the project

5   Conclusions

The Prosperity4All project aims at providing an infrastructure to facilitate the development of a new ecosystem for eInclusion. One that is based around cross-platform development techniques and that employs modern techniques such as crowdsourcing and gamification to both enable new strategies for the delivery of accessibility services and to enable an entirely new approach to accessibility solution development; an approach that can increase the percentage of research that actually makes it into the hands of users, increases the number of different types of researchers to contribute and enable breakthrough solutions; increase the number and variety of individuals and skills which can be brought to bear on the problem; and broaden the development process out toward users so that users and those living with them, or working with them, can get more directly engaged in the development of effective solutions.

The full development of the ecosystem, populating it with organisations, individuals and stakeholders and the full deployment of solutions are expected to take place after the end of the project, as a result of the EC-funded phase.

Acknowledgements. The research leading to these results has received funding from the European Union's Seventh Framework Program under FP7 Grant # 610510. The opinions herein are those of the authors and not necessarily those of the funding agency.

References

1. World Health Organization. World Report on Disability (2011), http://whqlibdoc.who.int/publications/2011/9789240685215_eng.pdf?ua=1
2. UNESCO Institute for Statistics. Fact Sheets of Literacy (2012), http://www.uis.unesco.org/literacy/Documents/fs20-literacy-day-2012-en-v3.pdf
3. United Nations, Department of Economic and Social Affairs. World Population Prospects: The 2012 Revision (2013), http://esa.un.org/wpp/Documentation/publications.htm
4. Vanderheiden, G.C., Treviranus, J., Chourasia, A.: The global public inclusive infrastructure (GPII). In: Proceedings of the 15th International ACM SIGACCESS Conference on Computers and Accessibility (ASSETS 2013), Article 70, 3 pages. ACM, New York (2013)

Prosperity4All – Designing a Multi-Stakeholder Network for Economic Inclusion

Jutta Treviranus[1], Colin Clark[1], Jess Mitchell[1], and Gregg C. Vanderheiden[2]

[1] Inclusive Design Research Centre, OCAD University, Canada
[2] Raising the Floor Consortium, Switzerland
{jtreviranus,cclark,jmitchell}@ocadu.ca,
gv@trace.wisc.edu

Abstract. People with disabilities are disproportionately affected by systemic global economic problems such as digital exclusion, income disparity, unemployment and poverty. The Prosperity4all project, an international consortium supported in part by the European Union FP7 program, is seeking to address the economic exclusion of consumers and producers at the margins, including people with disabilities. This article discusses the economic or business design models being considered in this emerging initiative. Like the work that the platform supports, the platform itself must be designed for diversity.

Keywords: inclusive design, value chains, user experience, accessibility.

1   The Economic Backdrop

The global economy can be characterized as being in a state of fragmentation and polarization. Much attention has been paid recently to income disparity and the demise of the middle class. Similar patterns can be seen throughout the economic ecosystem affecting more than income but also supply, opportunity, education, employment, access to financial instruments and other essential factors of economic inclusion (1). Fragmentation and polarization lead to redundancies, waste, debt and socially untenable inequalities. While global networks can exacerbate or amplify these vicious cycles, they may also provide a mechanism for addressing these challenges by providing an opportunity to connect, pool, share and repurpose resources thereby reducing redundancy, waste and debt; and also spurring sustainable and resilient innovation.

Like many crisis, people at the margins (most notably people with disabilities) are most profoundly affected. The Prosperity4All project hopes to provide a platform that connects consumers at the margins with producers and suppliers at the margins, thereby addressing the complementary barriers they each face. It is hoped that the platform will support an economically viable means of addressing the diverse "markets of one" that most people with disabilities represent.

C. Stephanidis and M. Antona (Eds.): UAHCI/HCII 2014, Part IV, LNCS 8516, pp. 453–461, 2014.

1.1   Digital Exclusion

Our society is undergoing a disruptive transformation caused by global networks and digital technologies. Accessing online systems is no longer an option for participants in most societies. The social and economic impact of digital exclusion is well articulated in international policies and initiatives on the digital divide [2]. The social and economic costs of digital exclusion are mounting as more and more essential daily activities are mediated digitally (estimated at 55.2 billion a year in the US) [2]. However many of the projections do not take into account the additional technology gap for individuals who cannot use standard ICT systems and resources due to disability, age, language or lack of literacy.

Digital technologies, like most consumer goods, are designed for the average or typical consumer. Specialized accessibility technologies (AT) are intended to bridge the gap between standard technologies and the alternative access requirements of people with disabilities. The small companies that produce these systems have the impossible technical challenge of interoperability with a broad range of rapidly changing technologies. The technical strategies AT developers rely upon will cease to work as software applications inexorably shift to new component-based, distributed paradigms. What assistive technologies exist, are available in only 28% of the world. In most countries they are not sold, maintained or they cost more than 50% of an individual's annual income [3]. While most information and communication technology is going down in price and increasing in functionality, reliability, diversity and availability, most AT is increasing in price and decreasing in functionality, reliability, diversity and availability. The cost of "getting online" for consumers requiring assistive technology is up to ten times the cost when compared to consumers using standard, mainstream systems. Individuals with disabilities are three times more likely to be among the digitally excluded. This means that people with disabilities are not able to be "at the table" when mainstream services are designed, which means they are less likely to be considered in the design. This all leads to barriers of access to education and employment and thereby greater poverty. This makes it even harder to catch up with a quickly changing digitally-mediated world. Against this economic backdrop, the incidence of disability is increasing globally, due to aging and better survival rates from natural and man-made disasters. The incidence of disability increases sharply with aging -- from less than 15% under the age of 25 to more than 64% over the age of 75 [3].

2   Background Work in Personalized Inclusive Design

Within this growing crisis lays both a challenge and an opportunity. Global networks profoundly change the mechanisms of production and delivery. Digital resources are highly mutable. There is a growing awareness of the catalytic and accelerant qualities of global networks and crowdsourcing. Whether it is engaging gamers to catalog the ways a protein can be folded, enlisting citizens to comb through seemingly endless government expense reports, or recruiting global support for political change, global networks have unleashed a new magic that makes the overwhelmingly impossible,

possible, enabling initiatives to realize effects that far exceed available resources or human capacity [5].

This network effect makes it feasible to use networked, collective production to deliver personalized or one-size-fits-one resources and configurations to currently marginalized consumers [4]. For the past 15 years a nascent but growing global consortium has been iteratively refining infrastructure, tools and implementations that enable one-size-fits-one online configurations and resources, on demand, to enable digital inclusion of currently marginalized users. The multiple iterations of this innovative functionality support the consumer in discovering their diverse individual needs and preferences and expressing these in a machine-readable form (using the ISO 24751 or AccessForAll standard). The networked system then reconfigures, augments or replaces resources and interfaces to match these needs and preferences. This functionality has been piloted in education, government online, public access stations, libraries, mobile commerce and other networked contexts. Projects include Web4All (http://web4all.ca), TILE (http://inclusivelearning.ca), FLOE (http://floeproject.org), and Cloud4All (http://cloud4all.info) and most recently Prosperity4All (http://www.raisingthefloor.org/prosperity4all/). With the emergence of cloud technologies the initiatives have moved to the cloud and are coordinated through a global consortium called the Global Public Inclusive Infrastructure (http://gpii.net).

3   Prosperity4All

Prosperity4All (P4A), a multi-partner, multi-sector international initiative, supported in part by the EU FP7 program [6], is the most recent iteration of the GPII initiatives. P4A hopes to address the needs of marginalized suppliers and producers as well as consumers. The project hopes to harness the global network effect to connect consumers at the margins with pooled resources, and if the resources or user experience configurations don't currently exist, with producers and suppliers at the margins who can address those needs. In this way P4A will provide "what you need, when, where and how you need it" to consumers, while also supplying "work where, when and how you can" for currently unemployed or underemployed workers including youth and people with disabilities [4]. P4A is constructing a multi-sided platform that will support the economic viability of addressing marginal consumer needs and thereby provide work for individuals who face barriers to financial independence.

3.1   Aggregating Demand

P4A l and the associated projects coordinated by the GPII are aggregating a growing number of resource gaps or unmet needs from consumers with disabilities and organizations that serve these consumers. Example demands to be filled include captions and descriptions for videos, graphics and audio (for users who are deaf, blind, hard of hearing, or individuals with low literacy levels), file transformations to convert files to screen-reader accessible formats, alternative controls for applications, simplified instructions or demonstrations, applications to provide guidance and better cognitive access, customized casings for mobile devices, tailored grips and handles suitable for manufacture on 3D printers, to name just a few.

This demand is heightened by accessibility legislation in many jurisdictions, including the more than 150 jurisdictions ratifying the UN Convention on the Rights of Persons with Disabilities [7]. These policies or legislative requirements mean that a large number of organizations and businesses must comply with accessibility criteria. This then casts these organizations as consumers of accessible products.

3.2 Supporting Suppliers and Producers

These gaps are being filled in part by crowdsourcing through services such as Amara (http://www.amara.org), however, there remain a growing number of unmet needs. In preliminary trials youth (the group that faces the largest unemployment rates) seem ideally suited to address this gap. As "digital natives" they are more at home in a networked environment developing digital or digitally-mediated resources. The aggregation of demand and other services and resources provided through the multi-sided platform (e.g., training, development tools and resources, accessible building blocks and templates), support the emergence of personalized accessibility or inclusive design as a viable industry for producers and suppliers who face barriers to market entry, as well as youth seeking employment and financial independence.

3.3 Growing a Viable Personalized Accessibility Market Platform

P4A proposes to develop and support the growth and propagation of a globally disbursed demand-driven ecosystem that can sustain "markets of one" as well as mass customization value chains. The platform will connect diverse and distributed consumers at the margins with diverse and distributed producers and suppliers at the margins using supportive cloud infrastructure. The goal is to enable the diversification of demand by enabling each consumer to discover, refine and express their unique individual needs thereby prompting a diversification of supply and triggering greater innovation within the market [8].

As with all multi-stakeholder networks this requires a gardening or organic approach rather than an engineering approach. The project can only create the optimal conditions, plant seeds, monitor and encourage growth and then judiciously prune and graft where necessary. As with most network-dependent market platforms, the majority of the work is done by individuals, organizations and processes external to the project and outside the control of the project. As such there is far greater risk than with traditional applied IT projects, but also the potential for far greater impact and return on investment. As many of the factors that influence this ecosystem will be external and unpredictable, an agile, responsive design approach is needed in developing and "gardening" the network infrastructure and supporting systems.

While "markets of one" have existed in the pre-industrial era (e.g., cottage industry) and at the fringes of current markets (e.g., bespoke or custom services) they have not existed at the scale proposed and there have been no concerted attempts to directly address marginal demands or to engage currently marginalized suppliers or producers.

The hope is to leverage networks, pooling and sharing to make this new industry viable for both the consumers (who frequently live below the poverty line), and producers or suppliers. P4A hopes to create a virtuous cycle that ultimately enables full participation of individuals with disabilities in the economy as both consumers and producers. This participation will help to promote a more inclusive design of market and economic processes that will, in turn, enable more inclusive participation [8].

3.4   Economic Models for Prosperity4All

P4A proposes to create a complex multi-stakeholder network or a multi-sided platform as described by Hagui and Wright [9], but with an unprecedented diversity of products. As such traditional network effect analysis, standard market simulations and economic modeling will not prove helpful without significant adjustments.

P4A will create market models and simulations at both a macro and micro level to determine optimal designs for infrastructure and to determine the impact of market inputs. The full spectrum of ICT design, development and production will be explored from mainstream to specialized, from enterprise to Indie - recognizing that the binary distinctions of mainstream versus assistive technologies are permeable and fuzzy and become ever more so. The intention is also to create a highly permeable and dynamic global market; however to grow or achieve this requires sufficient critical mass or "heat" within a cluster of positive or successful interactions, which may be local. As such, a variety of economic or business analysis tools must be applied, some not yet designed.

The values or principles and design criteria to be achieved in this modeling include, to: a) protect consumer privacy, b) ensure that the services supplied are affordable, c) enable producers and suppliers to create viable businesses, d) encourage innovation, e) support diversification of both supply and demand and discourage a winnowing of demands and products, commensurate with the diversity of users, f) facilitate transparent feedback loops and reviews, and g) support continuous renewal and organic growth of the platform.

3.5   Challenges for the Multi-stakeholder Network

All network platforms face a number of common challenges [10]. These challenges include:

— the "mutual baiting" or "chicken and egg" problem – producers won't come to the platform without consumers and vice versa
— the "ghost town" problem – a platform is initially without activity – neither producers nor consumers are attracted to an inactive platform.
— the double or multiple company problem – it is very difficult to serve both the producers and consumers, or all stakeholders, well at the same time
— the critical mass problem – the value of the network cannot be achieved until there is a critical mass of consumers and producers to achieve an acceptable set of successful interactions

Within the project team the design challenges have been described using a party metaphor. The primary value for partygoers is the people they might meet at a party, or the social interactions they may have. In keeping with the metaphor, to launch a successful "party" you must answer a number of questions: What will attract people to the party? What will keep them at the party until the people they want to meet there get there? What are the conditions that will ensure they have a successful interaction, are satisfied with their experience and will come back? What will prompt them to tell their friends about the party so that more people will come? How do you ensure people's safety and deal with problems, issues or complaints that arise? How do you make sure people behave at the party without being too constraining so that you spoil the fun? These questions will also guide the evaluation of the project.

Potential Stakeholders. The stakeholders or "partygoers" include a highly diverse group of potential participants that would either require inclusively designed services or products; would have services or products to offer, share or refine; would help to finance interactions; would offer training, quality assurance or certification; or, benefit from the aggregated data supported by the platform to shape policy.

Each stakeholder will have diverse motivations or incentives for using the platform. The design team must identify potential successful value chains or interactions that can occur on the platform or at the "party'. As this party is occurring online and all interactions are digitally mediated each of these interactions requires highly usable and accessible user experience designs. To maintain the principle of personalization that P4A is founded upon, these user experiences must transform to match each user's needs and preferences.

Addressing the "Chicken and Egg" Challenge. Two-sided or multi-sided markets require synchronization of producers and consumers coming onto the platform for interactions to happen. Since getting both sides in sufficient numbers simultaneously is difficult to execute, one potential strategy is to design staging processes. To achieve this staging until the requisite critical mass is reached frequently requires a supply proxy or a demand proxy. Candidate supply proxies in P4A include preference discovery interactions in which the standalone value proposition for consumers is the discovery and refinement of individual needs and preferences and an understanding of what works best for them with respect to content and user interface design. Most users find increased self-knowledge or self-awareness highly motivating and valuable. This can be in the form of games, simulations or utilities that enable the adjustment of a variety of settings or configurations. Examples of these configurations could be volume of audio, contrast adjustment and magnification of visual information, structure for text, size and spacing of targets and input fields to enable accurate control, supports such as glossaries or spelling and grammar aids, disambiguation routines that provide word or phrase completion, captions, descriptions, layout options, text translators or simplifiers, to name a few. Consumers could be guided in exploring possible configurations and then testing to see whether they are able to achieve tasks more proficiently with the chosen configuration. The refined configuration then serves as their preference file when requesting resources or services on the platform.

Demand proxies for potential suppliers and producers can include development toolkits, component libraries, training in inclusive design practices or information regarding potential demands. Suppliers and producers may also find the opportunity to create an online profile of their services or competencies as an incentive to "come to the party."

Addressing the "Ghost-town" Challenge. Strategies for attracting producers and consumers to an inactive platform or ghost-town include a variety of incentives, signals of relevant activity, participation by high-profile consumers or producers, access to functionality that has value whether or not the platform is currently active. One strategy being considered is to enable full, highly successful, demand-supply interactions and to grow organically from these successes. This is far more promising than a "waterfall" approach in which all development is completed for the full set of expected users and potential requirements before the process or "party" is launched. One problem that has received a great deal of negative press and is therefore seen as an urgent need is the lack of access to essential government documents by people with print impairments. The candidate interaction cycle might therefore be the conversion of these critical inaccessible PDF documents within a government service to accessible, personally configured HTML5. This would engage consumers with print impairments who require access to important government documents; government agencies that must comply with accessibility regulations and are obligated to provide access to these documents for clients/citizens with print impairments; potential service entrepreneurs such as unemployed youth who can be trained in conducting the conversion to accessible HTML5 and then supplying these converted documents; interaction designers who create interface configurations that meet the needs of the consumers with print impairments; and, quality assurance reviewers. The success of this interaction can then be used to attract other requirements and develop a reputation for successful services. The "story" of this successful value chain would be broadly publicized and high profile users would be recruited to participate in telling the story.

Addressing the "Multiple-Company" Challenge. Partners within P4A have significant experience in articulating and addressing the needs of marginalized consumers and less expertise in addressing the needs of producers whether these producers are marginalized, part of the mainstream, suppliers in specialized markets, volunteers or consumers themselves. The design team will create an engaging process whereby feedback, suggestions and "if only" statements can be garnered from various stakeholders, such that these participants or "party-goers" can be co-designers of the user-experience. A large challenge is to find an incentive for these stakeholders to provide this design input. One strategy is to use an interior design metaphor, enabling the supplier or producer to configure, personalize and decorate their "online office". This would include choosing a set of services and tools. One key to sustaining engagement by all stakeholders is to encourage the sense of ownership and personal investment.

Addressing the Critical Mass Challenge. The critical mass challenge is overcome by constructing a successful demand supply loop. This then sparks further interactions and successful transactions. Like the approach to addressing the "ghost-town" challenge, the team will explore possible ways to "jump start" transaction loops to achieve the critical mass needed to organically address the diversity of demands expected to be addressed by the platform.

3.6   Value Chain Modeling

The design team will use available economic modeling tools to identify potential value chains, recognizing that these will be starter sets and that new possibilities will emerge from the larger community of stakeholders. Possible models include Porter's Cluster model updated to take into account Downes' new forces (Digitalization, Globalization and Deregulation) [11]. These models will help to identify the value proposition for participants in both the demand and supply side. The models will identify potential workflows and inputs required to successfully link specific demands to the appropriate supply, as well as mechanisms of feedback, refinement and resulting correction or adjustment. The team will identify market-ready services and services that are not yet market-ready and the supports needed to enable the maturation of these services. Necessary inputs such as training, incubation, investment, etc. will be identified. The models will also be used to identify factors that result in the greatest impact. Emerging value chains include 3D printing of device casings, handles and grips for people with arthritis, or organizers and labels for people experiencing forgetfulness associated with dementia. Well-established value chains include captioning, translation and description of educational videos.

3.7   Global Solutions Networks

The P4A team will be aided in this by the Global Solution Networks (GSN) effort led by Don Tapscott [12]. This research effort will help to evaluate the success of P4A. P4A fits the criteria for a global solution network as defined by the GSN in that it has diverse stakeholders, extends beyond a single nation state, leverages open networks and has progressive goals. P4A fulfills many of the functions the GSN has identified as potential functions of global solution networks. The GSN is refining evaluation criteria and instruments in concert with P4A.

3.8   Sustaining the Platform

To be successful and achieve the goals of the project, P4A must be sustainable beyond the duration of the project. The P4A design team will explore, develop and evaluate possible sustainability models. Some of the models to be considered include but are not limited to: transaction models, value-added service models, subscription models, advertising models, bartering models and pay-what-you-wish models. P4A will also explore innovative agreements such as cost reduction rewards for cost savings in public service provision and social impact bonds or investments [13].

4   Conclusion

P4A will harness network effects to address an age-old market bias against the outliers or minority needs. It will create the conditions and provide the supports to ensure that addressing outlying needs is economically viable for suppliers and producers and affordable for consumers. By creating a market platform that connects consumers at the margins with suppliers and producers at the margins P4A hope to provide consumers with "what you need, when, where and how you need it" and producers and suppliers with work "when, where and how you can." This will create the conditions for greater prosperity and economic inclusion. The success of the platform depends in large part upon a diverse and responsive set of user experiences that are both usable and accessible.

References

1. Wilkinson, R., Pickett, K.: The Spirit Level: Why More Equal Societies Almost Always Do Better. Allen Lane (2009)
2. Digital Impact Group. The Economic Impact of Digital Exclusion. Econsult Corporation, Philadelphia (2010)
3. United Nations. Factsheet on Persons with Disabilities, http://www.un.org/disabilities/default.asp?id=18 (December 26, 2013) (retrieved)
4. Treviranus, J., Fichten, C.S., Stolarick, K., Kemper, A.: Leveraging Inclusion and Diversity as Canada's Digital Advantage. Social Sciences and Humanities Research Council, Knowledge Synthesis on the Digital Economy (2010)
5. Tapscott, D., Williams, A.D.: Macrowikinomics: New Solutions for a Connected Planet. Penguin Group Inc., USA (2012)
6. http://cordis.europa.eu/fp7/home_en.html
7. http://www.un.org/disabilities/convention/conventionfull.shtml
8. Treviranus, J.: Leveraging the Web as a Platform for Economic Inclusion. Behav. Sci. Law. Wiley Online (2014)
9. Hagiu, A.: Multi-Sided Platforms: From Microfoundations to Design and Expansion Strategies (2006), http://www.hbs.edu/faculty/Publication%20Files/07-094.pdf (February 13, 2013) (retrieved)
10. Choudary, S.P. (2013), http://platformed.info/platform-thinking/
11. Recklies, D.: Beyond Porter _ A Critique of the Critique of Porter (2013), http://www.themanager.org/strategy/BeyondPorter.htm
12. http://gsnetworks.org
13. Pettus, A.: Social Impact Bonds (2013), http://harvardmagazine.com/2013/07/social-impact-bonds

A Novel Infrastructure Facilitating Access to, Charging, Ordering and Funding of Assistive Services

Gianna Tsakou[1], Helen C. Leligou[2], and Nikos Katevas[2]

[1] SingularLogic, Greece
[2] TEI Stereas Elladas, Psahna Evias, 34400 Greece
gtsakou@singularlogic.eu, leligou@gmail.com, katevas@teihal.gr

Abstract. Given that, nowadays, access to ICT is required for almost any kind of education, employment and commerce form, and is increasingly required for travel, it is mandatory to focus on integrating groups of users with any type of disability at a personally and societally affordable cost. In this paper, we outline an ICT-enabled novel infrastructure that significantly facilitates user access to a large set of specialised assistive services and enables small ICT players (e.g. web entrepreneurs) to develop novel services "on user/user group demand" supported by crowd funding. Our vision is to create an infrastructure that can move ideas more quickly from conception to market and consumer availability, that can be more efficient by being better targeted to user needs, that can move users closer to researchers and developers to ensure that the full range of needs are better addressed and that can reduce both the development and operation cost of assistive services. The system we propose consists of the Assistance on Demand (AoD) service infrastructure which aims to be a gateway for accessing on demand diverse types of human and machine-based assistive services. This AoD is accompanied by a flexible payment infrastructure that aims at enabling, for all relevant stakeholders (end users, service providers, etc.), the easy, flexible and reliable handling of multiple bills for different services, while at the same time supporting crowd-funding, as necessary, for user-driven assistive technology (AT) or service development. In this paper, we present the state-of-the-art technologies and approaches that will serve as the basis for the design and development of the AoD and payment infrastructures and then we discuss the requirements that these intertwined systems have to fulfill and draw high-level design directions.

Keywords: Service platform, Assistance on Demand, micro-payments, service description and ranking, non-functional ranking, crowd-funding.

1 Introduction

As information and communication technologies invade our everyday life, they become indispensable for a blooming set of activities including education, employment, commerce, health services, transportation, or even daily independent living. This puts at risk those who cannot use ICT and services due to disability, low literacy, low digital-literacy or aging-related barriers. On the other hand, novel technologies can

C. Stephanidis and M. Antona (Eds.): UAHCI/HCII 2014, Part IV, LNCS 8516, pp. 462–473, 2014.
© Springer International Publishing Switzerland 2014

radically change the scene. For example, the development of digital service market-places have contributed to the decrease of service delivery costs. Similarly, the needs of many small groups can now be catered for in a better way through cloud technologies which allow significant sharing and more intense processing capabilities. The emergence of novel payment models, notably crowd-funding approaches, has contributed towards the creation of new applications and services by web entrepreneurs that fit better the needs of the crowds (individuals/groups) funding them. We argue that by applying the crowd-funding model, it is possible to better serve persons with disabilities, including the unaddressed (up to now) tails (i.e. "non mainstream" disabilities).

Exploiting the latest ICT developments, we design a novel open source Assistance on Demand (AoD) service infrastructure which intends to enable diverse stakeholders to easily set up ICT-supported AoD services catering for individual needs of persons with disabilities, where stakeholders include family members, friends and carers, as well as professionals (individuals and SMEs) offering all kinds of assistive services. This, in turn, enables persons with disabilities to access a wealth of different human- or device- or network-based services. The AoD services that will be built using our AoD infrastructure understands the user's assistance requests, responds to them by filtering the available solutions based on his/her preferences and suggests a possible matching. The AoD infrastructure also caters for different patterns of assistive services: continuous or interruptible, periodic or random and enables the use of different charging models (pay-per-use, pay-per-item, or any other) depending on the type of service and the charging model selected by its provider. The related charges may be of very limited value, they can even be context – dependent and by all means they have to be accountable and justifiable.

The AoD platform creates, in essence, a dynamic ecosystem which brings closer the users, the service providers and application developers, each of which has a set of distinctive requirements that cannot be covered by established e-commerce platforms and one-fits-all solutions. To support the above requirements, it is mandatory to design and implement a charging and payment system, interlinked with the AoD that a) provides smooth and reliable support of fine-grained payments, leveraging on emerging micropayments technologies b) provides reliable and flexible infrastructure that will cater for the charging and payment functionality in order to alleviate the service provider from these burdens and to support the consumer in a seamless way, c) supports the interactivity and the collaborative capabilities among the service providers and the consumers in an enhanced form of crowd-financing focused on accessibility features and d) allows for intelligent and parameterized notification of reaching or exceeding specific amounts.

The "crowd-funding for accessibility support" feature of the payment infrastructure is one of the novel components of the proposed infrastructure because it is expected to contribute to the change of the legacy "service push" approach (from service developers/providers towards consumers) to the "service pull" approach, where users directly define the assistive service requirements and developers undertake the development under a crowd-funding scheme (i.e. a collective effort by consumers who network and pool their money together, usually online, in order to invest in and support efforts initiated by other people or organizations). The proposed system explores the frontier between crowd-funding and group-funding, also providing analytical tools to process useful statistics both for service providers and users and updated information upon request on the progress of the work and appropriate handling of the funds.

The rest of the paper is organized as follows: in sections 2 and 3 we discuss the state-of-the-art related to the design and development of the Assistance on Demand service infrastructure and the payment infrastructure respectively. Then, sections 4 and 5 describe the design of the proposed novel platforms and finally section 6 concludes this article. Both the AoD service infrastructure and the payment infrastructure will be designed and developed in the framework of the Prosperity4All project (FP7-710510) co-funded by the EC [1] that develops a wide set of tools targeting societal groups in the risk of exclusion.

2   State-of-the-Art Technologies for the AoD Platform

To achieve its goals, the proposed Assistance on Demand service infrastructure will capitalize on leading edge Cloud technologies as well as on semantic web service description and web service ranking solutions based on non-functional properties (such as QoS, safety, price).

2.1   Semantic Web Service Description

Web services have evolved through multiple progressive steps since 1990 (when electronic documents in HTML format were first published and linked). XML (eXtensive Markup Language) allowed information produced by any entity to use the same description format and thus enabled structured information collection. The next step was to abstract and describe in a uniform manner the web services to extend their capabilities in the direction of dynamic interoperability, and in particular to address the need for interoperability in the face of heterogeneous standards for representing content communicated between distributed components. There are many situations where systems developed using web services will need to overcome interoperability limitations arising from their inability to agree in advance on the syntax and semantics of interactions and this is the case in Prosperity4All, which targets to bring together and even prioritise diverse service suppliers offering AoD. Users and software agents should be able to discover, invoke, compose, and monitor web resources offering particular services and having particular properties, and should be able to do so with a high degree of automation if desired.

There exists a plethora of service description efforts that can be grouped into different strands with each strand having its own motivation and representation needs for capturing service information. The individual efforts may differ in terms of scope (e.g. capturing IT or business aspects of services or the whole service system), or purpose (e.g. automate a specific task, or offer a reference model), or the ability of the approach to capture business network relationships between services and last but not least in terms of use of standards.

W3 consortium (W3C) has been very active in this area (along with OASIS, OMG and Open Group) and has delivered a set of service description standards. W3C defined Web Service Description Language (WSDL) (already in 2001) which is an XML format for describing network services as a set of endpoints operating on messages containing either document-oriented or procedure-oriented information. WSDL is extensible to allow description of endpoints and their messages regardless of what message formats or network protocols are used to communicate. However, the only bindings described in version 1.1 document describe how to use WSDL in conjunction with SOAP 1.1, HTTP GET/POST, and MIME.

The Semantic Web came to enable greater access to services on the web enabling the dynamic linking and sharing of ontologies contributing to the notions of orchestration, choreography and mediation, since different communities may not always share ontologies directly. Interoperability improves substantially through ontology mappings enabling semantic translation between different representations of concepts based on different ontologies. OWL-S (formerly DAML-S) is an ontology of services that makes these functionalities possible while Web Service Modeling Ontology (WSMO) appeared in 2005 and provides an ontology based framework, which supports the deployment and interoperability of Semantic Web Services.

Semantic Annotations for WSDL and XML Schema (SAWSDL) extended the Web Services Description Language and XML Schema definition language that allows description of additional semantics of WSDL components. The specification defines how semantic annotation is accomplished using references to semantic models, e.g. ontologies. SAWSDL provides mechanisms by which concepts from the semantic models, typically defined outside the WSDL document, can be referenced from within WSDL and XML Schema components using annotations.

The latest W3C work is on the definition of the Unified Service Description Language (USDL) for describing general and generic parts of technical and business services to allow them to become tradable and consumable. USDL builds on the standards for the technical IT description efforts for services such as WSDL, adding business and operational information on top. USDL defines normative UML modules for capturing the "master data" of a service i.e., class models for pricing, legal, functional, participants, interaction and Service Level Agreement aspects. Therefore, both manual and IT services can be described with USDL. Both W3C SAWSDL and W3C SA-REST are designed to be agnostic of any service description schema. Similar holds for W3C SML.

Another interesting and lightweight service model is Minimal Service Model (MSM) [2] which has been adopted by iServe for publishing services and querying them in expressive and extensible manner. iServe intends to be the place on the Web where linked data meets services. The Minimal Service Model, driven by Semantic Web best practices, builds upon existing vocabularies, namely SAWSDL, [3] WSMO-Lite and hRESTS [4]. In a nutshell, MSM is a simple RDFS integration ontology based on the principle of minimal ontological commitment; it captures the maximum common denominator between existing conceptual models for services. Thus, MSM is an integration model at the intersection of existing formalisms (namely, WSMO and OWL-S), able to capture the core semantics of both Web services and

Web APIs in a common model, homogeneously supporting publication, discovery and invocation. Still, MSM is devised so that framework-specific extensions can remain attached, to the benefit of clients able to comprehend and exploit those formalisms.

2.2   Service Selection and Prioritization Based on Non-functional Properties

Service selection and prioritization can turn out to be a very complex and challenging task, especially when more than one services have equivalent/similar functionality and the decision is made upon a variety of different non-functional properties. Non functional properties include information about location, optimal transmission format and protocols, applicable user or system policies (e.g. price), QoS and security policies [5]. The fundamental issues of service selection and prioritization are a) specifying requestor's service requirements, b) evaluation of the service offerings, and c) aggregating the evaluation results into a comparable unit. Of course the requestor's requirements and the service offerings have both functional and complex non-functional aspects, which need to be expressed for evaluation matched against each other.

Before we attempt to match the requestor's requirements to the service offerings, a model to describe the service's non-functional properties. Due to the versatility of non-functional properties (and the fact that new ones might be required at any time) in combination to the fact that the non-functional criteria depend also on the domain, the extensibility and flexibility of the service description scheme are stringent and mandatory requirements. WSDL-S [6] and OWL-S have been proposed to be used to describe the non-functional properties while other researchers decided to build extensions on UDDI repositories to allow expression of non-functional properties [7]. Both are viable approaches, the former might prove more flexible and expandable in the long run, the latter are certainly more immediately applicable as they are based on widely deployed repository technologies. At all cases, in selecting its semantic service description approach, Prosperity4All will have to take into account a variety of non-functional service properties.

To evaluate the service offerings, approaches based on policies [8] have been proposed while others that rely on reports from other users (or even server providers) and previous experiences [9] (reputation based) have also been explored. The policy based approaches rely on policy languages that traditionally only allow expressing a small number of non-functional properties. Given the diversity of AoD services that Prosperity4All aims at enabling, including human and device- based services, it is very likely that different evaluation approaches may need to be supported.

Ranking and selection based on non-functional properties is inherently a multi-criteria decision-making problem due to the presence of multiple parameters that cannot be directly compared to one another. The relative importance of parameters such as price and reliability, thus, varies for different clients and situations. To capture the relevance of the selection criteria, graph and ontologies-based approaches on one hand and context-aware service selection approaches on the other have been proposed [10]. In the latter, the requestor's context is modeled using OWL/RDF which is transformed to be part of the constraint values of the category based and domain specific non-functional service selection criteria. While the initial setup of the weights for the preferences is left to users, the system can modify the values automatically to deal with emergent behaviour (e.g. an emergency status).

To reach a final service selection, the scores related to different non-functional properties need to be combined and compared. While numerical or keyword values have been explored [11], the ontological representation with the help of logical expressions allows semantic ranking to provide more accurate results. The value of a non-functional property of a service may depend on the concrete request data from the client: the service NFP description includes logical expressions that compute concrete NFP values at run-time. For example, given a description of the expected service demand, the NFP expressions can compute the actual price and the expected reliability of the service.

3   State-of-the-Art Technologies for the Payment Infrastructure

While micropayments are not a new idea, the micropayment system together with the proposed AoD will put the user in the driving seat, considering an extensive set of micropayments methods and allowing for dynamic selection depending on the context (and the user preferences – in case they are explicitly expressed). Such methods include the following:

- Electronic check: The electronic check is a digital token that lets a service provider withdraw money from the end user's account at a later date. It is the digital equivalence of a physical bank check while the end user's account can be in a real or virtual bank (main example the Paypal system).
- User – initiated transfers: In this type of payment solution both the user and the service provider have accounts and the end user asks his bank to transfer money to the SP's bank. The banks can be real or virtual.
- Service providers – initiated transfer: This is similar with the previous case with the difference that the user's involvement is not required when making a payment, as long as the SP has the user's account information. The user provides the necessary information. The more typical example in this case is the usage of credit cards. In such a case the account number is replaced by the credit card number (which is typically associated with a bank account).
- Prepaid SP account: In this type of payment solution the user pays money to the SP upfront, who maintains an account on behalf of the user. The account is deducted every time the user makes a purchase or utilizes a service from the SP. This may decrease overhead cost associated with payments.
- Prepaid SP voucher: The SP creates payment codes valid for the specific SP. Instead of using accounts to keep track of how much each user has deposited, the SP sells payment codes to users. The payment codes can then be used at a later date to make purchases.
- Invoicing: The user is invoiced for his purchases at a later date. The specifics of invoicing vary, for example once per month or after a certain debt threshold has been reached.

In addition to the above, the support of crowd-funding is mandatory for the realization of the AoD collaborative vision. Crowd-funding is a collective effort by consumers who network and pool their money together, usually online, in order to invest in and support efforts initiated by other people or organizations. The basic idea of crowd-funding is for an entrepreneur to raise external finance from a large audience, where each individual provides a very small amount, instead of soliciting a small group of sophisticated investors.

4   Assistance on Demand Service Infrastructure Design and Challenges

The target of the presented Assistance on Demand service infrastructure is to enable the rapid deployment of innovative machine/human assistance services on demand by allowing individuals to seek assistance in an organized fashion from a set of predefined sources based on the need, the desired quality of service and other personal preferences.

4.1   AoD Infrastructure Design Considerations

The Prosperity4All AoD infrastructure is designed to offer unique features including the support of:

- Diverse target user groups: This diversity concerns the role they play (service suppliers, service developers, service consumers, consumer relatives and other interested individuals), the targeted application domain (safety, daily leaving, education, entertainment), the socio-economic status/background, other characteristics such as mental, cognitive, emotional, educational, IT-literacy of the individual/group user. To maximize adoption, the AoD infrastructure will support user interfaces that support multimodal interaction and flexible interface configuration with minimal technical knowledge requirements and will provide technical support as a service offered in flexible, possibly collaborative, yet efficient and reliable, way.
- Different types of assistance services including human/machine/crowd-based services: To offer all these services on demand, we need to define a common service description language and employ semantic service annotations to facilitate flexible classification/organization and fast search according to multiple attributes. The AoD infrastructure will enable the creation of "dashboards" of assistance services, customizable (per person or community/group) and supporting a wide set of service selection criteria (e.g. service type, price, developer, presentation, quality and security level) while offering zero/default configuration options for efficiently supporting non professional disabled users.
- (Machine-based) Services created from different developers (companies/ individuals/ organizations/ communities): A mechanism to communicate the service characteristics and infrastructure requirements of each service/application is needed, so as to guarantee proper reservation of resources, given that the proposed AoD

infrastructure aims to offer a dynamic set of services/applications. This mandates the design of a relevant interface between AoD infrastructure and developers' infrastructure. Both Infrastructure-as-a-Service and Platform-as-a-Service paradigms will be pursued to ensure that the AoD infrastructure will be scalable, robust and future proof.

- **Multiple cost models**: To alleviate affordability issues which are even more acute this decade, the AoD will support multiple charging/profitability paradigms. These are expected to lower the usage cost of assistance services. We anticipate that facilitating access to a wealth of assistance services, both paid and free, their utilization will significantly improve and in the end will result in lower cost. To realize this vision, the AoD service infrastructure is responsible for monitoring the access/usage of the offered services and for communicating with the payment infrastructure which is responsible for charging. Different charging models have to be supported (for example, software download or human-offered AoD may follow a one-off payment model, while AoD translation services may follow different charging models depending on expected quality), implying that the AoD Service infrastructure needs to monitor different access/use characteristics per offered service.

- **Quality of Service Differentiation:** Given that usually higher QoS comes at significantly higher price and that the Quality of Service depends on different factors for the variety of supported AoD services, the proposed AoD will enable an intelligent multi-criteria QoS improvement scheme that realizes a "try harder" cascade chain and enables flexible Quality of Service- charge trade-offs. A default quality will be offered at start-up and the user will be asked whether she desires to update the QoS possibly at a slightly higher tariff. Such an approach has to be accompanied by the use of scalable Quality-of-service monitoring tools (machine and human-enabled) to enable flexible and sophisticated billing in cooperation with the payment infrastructure.

- Generic open source infrastructure that meets the current and emerging needs of stakeholders interested in easily setting up AoD services.

The AoD infrastructure will include a "readily available" marketplace for service developers/suppliers. Offering collections of assistance services on demand brings services closer to the users and contributes both to cost reduction for the users and profit creation for the suppliers. This AoD infrastructure will be a meeting point facilitating collaboration among service developers/suppliers, interested users (expert or not, disabled or not, belonging to different mental, societal or other groups), volunteers and persons interested in employment.

4.2 AoD Development Aspects

To cope with all these challenges and offer Assistance on Demand services with unprecedented flexibility, a generic AoD service infrastructure placing emphasis on modularity and specifying the core functionality and interfaces to its subcomponents can be designed. To support different application domain and/or target groups, different instantiation of the generic AoD infrastructure will be possible with more sophisticated implementation of certain modules optimizing different functional and performance aspects. The core of this infrastructure will be based on the semantic annotation of the supported services extending well established vocabularies and annotation techniques to support the wide range of supported services. This will enable fast semantics-based service lookup and composition, service execution and monitoring, and real-time service selection/prioritisation based on customer needs. For the discovery of services, the AoD service infrastructure will interface the developers' infrastructure, while for the support of physical networks of human assistance a different interface will be realized. For the development of the proposed AoD, a semantic service description approach that supports the wide variety of services to be offered and allows for fast service discovery and invocation based on multiple criteria will be designed. For this reason, we will choose widely adopted semantic service description approaches and will extend them to support/describe human-offered Assistance on Demand services and to describe all attributes of interest for the diverse target groups (quality of service, price, input/output interface supported etc.). With respect to service discovery mechanisms, we will adopt state-of-the-art discovery mechanisms (such as Universal Description Discovery and Integration (UDDI) or WS-Discovery) and modify them to support the extended semantic service description approach that will be designed within Prosperity4All.

We will capitalize on existing nonfunctional properties description and ranking approaches and will extend them in order to define generic evaluation and ranking methods that differentiate the property filtering according to coarse criteria such as application domain characteristics. Observing that sophisticated service ranking may introduce significant delay before service starts to be offered, flexible lightweight yet efficient ranking mechanisms will be designed.

5   The Payment Infrastructure Design and Challenges

To complement the functionality of the envisaged AoD platform, the design and development of a payment infrastructure that enables the on-line payment of (multiple) services offered by different suppliers following different charging models on behalf of the end-users and –equally importantly– allowing crowd-sourced financing of R&D, supporting micropayments and bids is necessary. The aim is to alleviate the need for each service supplier to create and maintain her own charging and payment infrastructure. Similarly, for the user the aim is to simplify the process so that, instead of receiving multiple bills from the different suppliers, she will be charged per usage in a way that micro-charges per customer and per service supplier are accumulated in the charging and payment system and billing is made when amounts reach a specified threshold or on a regular basis. The system will operate transparently and accumulate charges on the user's periodic bill without an explicit confirmation for every click (unless otherwise opted by the user), without requiring credential insertion each time it is used. Special focus will be put on usability and simplicity.

In this sensitive AoD region, we consider important to apply the innovative (in this domain and for software-as-a-service cases) concept of charging per use, to allow assistive technologies to be sold as a service (rented) rather than purchased, supporting pay-per-use schemes and dynamic changing tariffs. In typical e-commerce scenarios, charges are calculated according to the types and the quantity of the purchased items/services, either human-, software- or hardware-based. But this is not our case, and one of the main drawbacks of such scheme has been that they psychologically discourage the users from using the service. The flexible support of pay-for-use will offer the possibility to those needing assistance to get it at lower cost by paying for use only instead of paying for purchase. On the other hand, service providers can get higher profits by approaching larger customer groups.

This functionality leads to the following set of design requirements:

- Both machine (software) and human-based services charging should be made through a single infrastructure;
- Multiple charging models from product purchase to product rental on a pay-for-use basis, with highly dynamic tariffs that may change on service/supplier/user/country/time basis.
- Support reliable and fair charging scheme primarily based on the "pay as you go", allowing for the selection of flat charging (if selected by the user).
- Provide detailed logging and accounting information describing the charging and the usage of the services upon requests.
- Allow for intelligent and parameterized notification of reaching or exceeding specific amounts.
- Allow for transfer of charging schemes among users and / or consumers, in the context of the trusted and collaborative community.
- Donation and user bidding schemes for promoting service pulling tilt and crowdsourced R&D financing.
- Personal data privacy and scalability.
- Support of different monetary systems and legislations while flexibility can be further enhanced supporting dynamic price adaptation, either on periodical basis or on demand-response basis (e.g. getting a taxi may be more expensive after a special sport event or physical disaster).

To efficiently support this rich payment system functionality, two discrete subsystems will be defined: the micropayment subsystem and the user bid subsystem, leaving the core charging and payment system of this activity to focus on all other aspects and having the subsystems taking care of a concrete sub set of payment functionality.

For those services, associated with pay-for-use charging models, the micropayment infrastructure will communicate with the AoD infrastructure and the micro charges will be accumulated and classified per user and provider so that payments are done either on regular basis or when the charges reach a predefined threshold to avoid excessive transactions. In the end, customers are charged for all the services they have used and a similar approach for the service providers will be followed.

Micropayment support is considered mandatory for allowing public access points (such as libraries) to make the full range of assistive technologies available to their patrons but only pay for those that the patrons actually use. This will allow many organizations to offer the full range of access solutions to their patrons at reasonable cost.

Central to micropayment functionality is the personal data and privacy management. These issues affect:

- The identification, authentication and authorization mechanisms. There are three mechanisms of authentication, i.e. whether the authentication is based on something the user knows (e.g. username, password), possesses (e.g. token) or is (e.g. biometrics).
- The security of the data: It is important that the service provider convinces the user that the provided information is treated confidentially and the integrity of the data is protected.
- Accountability and logging: The very nature of the micropayment functionality presupposes reliable logging of activities which can guarantee accountability.

With respect to the crowd-funding approach, the large AoD infrastructure customer database will be used to disseminate the initiation of a certain service creation, so that potentially interested users can contribute. Prosperity4All exploits the fact that the AoD platform brings together service suppliers, solution developers and customers to make crowd sourced financing of R&D a reality. Service developers/suppliers will also be notified and will be prompted to declare whether they intend to create the service. In case more than one is interested, they will be asked by the system to prepare an offer, i.e. specify the service one intends to create and possibly set a payment threshold, while volunteering and rewarding will also be supported. A predefined deadline for offers for service creation will be defined to allow for comparing the submitted proposals and trigger the service creation.

6   Conclusions

The proposed Assistance on Demand service and payment infrastructures aims to achieve unprecedented flexibility and high quality experience for any user, to increase the "pull" marketing tilt of the ecosystem and to facilitate successful financing of components, features, and other solutions. This way, market/community/citizen's needs trigger directly the service creation. Leveraging on the current state-of-the-art technologies, the vision of the AoD and micropayment infrastructures will become a reality and will offer a colorful palette of advantages to the most sensitive parts of our society. Our future work will certainly focus on the detailed design, implementation and demonstration of the proposed infrastructures to illustrate the advantages that ICT technologies can bring to our society.

Acknowledgements. This publication is based on work performed in the framework of the Project Prosperity4All (Contract No. 610510), which is co-funded by the European Commission.

References

1. Prosperity4All project
2. Maleshkova, M., Pedrinaci, C., Domingue, J.: Semantic Annotation of Web APIs with SWEET. In: Proceedings of the 6th Workshop on Scripting and Development for the Semantic Web, Colocated with the Extended Semantic Web Conference 2010, Heraklion, Greece (2010)
3. http://www.w3.org/TR/sawsdl/
4. Kopecky, J., Gomadam, K., Vitvar, T.: hRESTS: An HTML Microformat for Describing RESTful Web Services. In: International Conference on Web Intelligence and Intelligent Agent Technology, WI-IAT 2008, December 9-12. IEEE/WIC/ACM, pp. 619–625 (2008)
5. O'Sullivan, J., Edmond, D.: Formal description of non-functional service properties. Technical Report FIT-TR-2005-01, Queensland University of Technology (2005)
6. Oldham, N., Verma, K., Sheth, A., Hakimpour, F.: Semantic ws-agreement partner selection. In: WWW 2006: Proceedings of the 15th International Conference on World Wide Web, New York, NY, USA, pp. 697–706 (2006)
7. Al-Masri, E., Mahmoud, Q.H.: Discovering the best web service. In: WWW 2007: Proceedings of the 16th International Conference on World Wide Web, pp. 1257–1258. ACM (2007)
8. Toma, I., Roman, D., Fensel, D., Sapkota, B., Gomez, J.M.: A multi-criteria service ranking approach based on non-functional properties rules evaluation. In: Krämer, B.J., Lin, K.-J., Narasimhan, P. (eds.) ICSOC 2007. LNCS, vol. 4749, pp. 435–441. Springer, Heidelberg (2007)
9. Wang, Y., Vassileva, J.: Toward trust and reputation based web service selection: A survey. In: Special Issue on New Tendencies on Web Services and Multi-Agent Systems (WS-MAS) (2007)
10. Reiff-Marganiec, S., Yu, H.Q., Tilly, M.: Service selection based on non-functional properties. In: Di Nitto, E., Ripeanu, M. (eds.) ICSOC 2007. LNCS, vol. 4907, pp. 128–138. Springer, Heidelberg (2009)
11. Caverlee, J., Liu, L., Rocco, D.: Discovering and Ranking Web Services with BASIL:A Personalized Approach with Biased Focus. In: ICSOC 2004 Proceedings of the 2nd International Conference on Service Oriented Computing (2004)

Prosperity as a Model for Next-Generation Accessibility

Gregg C. Vanderheiden[1], Jutta Treviranus[2], Colin Clark[2], Matthias Peissner[3],
and Gianna Tsakou[4]

[1] University of Wisconsin, USA & Raising the Floor – International, Geneva, Switzerland
gregg@raisingthefloor.org
[2] OCAD University, Toronto, Ontario, Canada
{jtreviranus,cclark}@ocad.ca
[3] Fraunhofer Institute for Industrial Engineering IAO, Stuttgart, Germany
matthias.peissner@iao.fraunhofer.de
[4] SingularLogic S.A., Nea Ionia, Attica, Greece
gtsakou@singularlogic.eu

Abstract. We propose a multisided platform approach that is user-based but
seeks to provide an infrastructure that supports all stakeholders, making it easier
for vendors to design, market and support access features, products, and services and that makes it easier for consumers to find, secure, and use access
features, products and services, individually or mixed, on any device they encounter. The system is designed to support use by both mainstream and assistive technology developers and to draw new people into the ecosystem in new
roles including developers as resources and users and clinicians as developers.
Central to this latter role is a developer space that provides rich resources in the
form of tools, component, frameworks, service infrastructures, guidelines,
how-to's, mentors, testers, and marketing aids to help both experienced and
new developers enter the market and to broaden the range of people contributing to include both non-disability-related researchers/developers and less
technical consumers and professionals.

Keywords: Accessibility, inclusive design, personalization, GPII, infrastructure.

1   Introduction

The current accessibility ecosystem is based on a competitive push model where
companies compete and consumers choose from what is offered to them that they can
afford. This model has worked well for many consumer goods, especially for the
mass-market and middle-of-the-curve consumers.   However it has not worked well in
the assistive technologies and accessibility area where it is too expensive to market to
the tails' of the distribution tails (those with lower-incidence, severe, and/or mixed
disabilities).   The Prosperity4All project was proposed to attempt to address this
problem and to help develop an ecosystem where more people can be involved in the
development process, and were cooperation on common components is mixed with

C. Stephanidis and M. Antona (Eds.): UAHCI/HCII 2014, Part IV, LNCS 8516, pp. 474–482, 2014.
© Springer International Publishing Switzerland 2014

competition on new capabilities to reduce duplication of effort and create a more diverse and cost effective mix of solutions.

While no project, group or consortium can create an ecosystem, the purpose of the Prosperity4All project is to build key elements of infrastructure that can help the current ecosystem grow in new directions, and develop the capability to profitably benefit all stakeholders while addressing the needs of those not currently addressed by the current ecosystem.

1.1   A User-Based, Multisided Platform/Infrastructure

Prosperity4All (Prosperity for all) is not a promise, but a requirement if any ecosystem is to succeed. If we only attend to the needs of some of the stakeholders then the ecosystem will fail. The Global Public Inclusive Infrastructure (GPII) is an attempt to build a multisided infrastructure that provides support to all stakeholders.   Other projects are working on building the parts of the GPII that would   enable users to find the best solution(s) to match their needs, and to allow them to invoke these solutions anywhere, on any device. The Prosperity4All project focuses on building the portions of the Global Public Inclusive Infrastructure that foster the development of more new, diverse, better, and more affordable solutions so that affordable solutions exist for all users, with all types, degrees and combinations of disability, literacy, digital literacy and aging, in all countries.

To be successful this infrastructure must address the needs of all stakeholders.

- **For users – it must result in a rich set of solutions and services that match their diverse needs.** This includes the ability to use whatever technologies they are confronted with school, work, and their communities, when they vote, when they travel, and they use their health system, when they shop, etc.It also includes the ability to live more independently yet get affordable Assistance on Demand if they need it from family, friends, communities, volunteers, or commercially, if they run into a problem that they cannot handle. It also includes the ability for consumers to be more closely connected to the development processes and people that are generating solutions for them, thus offering a better match between actual needs and abilities, and the realities of their lives.
- **For developers – it must provide the tools and systems they need to more affordably develop, market, and support products that can address the full range of platforms and technologies their customers need to access – in a profitable manner.** This includes better information on the full range of needs for the different market segments, better tools for creating and localizing products that can be sold internationally, ways to reach their users especially dispersed and low incidence users in a much more cost-effective manner, components that can be used to build new products without having to develop them from scratch, especially with regard to emerging technologies such as BCI, advanced eye gaze or gesture (hand and body) recognition, multilingual speech recognition, advanced structure recognition, AI, etc.

- **For mainstream companies - it must provide a way for them to identify the features that they can and should build into their products as well as a means to do so affordably**. If there are accessibility requirements, it needs to help them to address these in a cost-effective way. Where there are no accessibility requirements, it needs to provide them with business cases for the features and tools, information, resources, etc. needed to build them in at low enough cost and with accompanying sales to make the business case. Part of this includes the ability to ensure that those people that can use their access features are aware of the company's products and the access features that the user needs.
- **For clinicians, educators and other professionals – it need to provide a better mechanism to keep track of the rapidly changing array of solutions, the devices and platforms they will work with, which solutions will work with which other solutions without conflict, and which devices, software, or services match the individual needs of each of their different patients/students/clients**. A mechanism is also needed to better connect these professionals with the processes and people generating the solutions so that these professionals can also impact and help direct the development of better solutions for those they are assisting.
- **For schools, libraries, and other public venues that are increasingly relying on ICT, it must provide a realistic and affordable mechanism for them to be able to ensure that their ICT will work with the full range of students/patrons of their facilities**. This includes a way for them to have all of the different types of solutions that would be needed by students/patrons with their individual needs without having to purchase each new solution for each user group that comes out each month. Includes a solution that can allow their IT department to maintain the security they require. It must also provide a mechanism which can be maintained by the individuals at these venues without requiring that they are accessibility experts or even information technology experts.
- **For service providers and NGOs - it needs to provide the information these agencies need to be able to determine which types of solutions would be effective for the different individuals they are supporting, and to provide new models for funding access solutions** when they must change so rapidly in order to keep up with changing technologies in these users environments.
- **For governments - it needs to provide more cost-effective mechanisms for the governments to ensure that the people in their countries can be maximally productive and prosperous in an increasingly digital world even if they face barriers to ICT use due to literacy, digital literacy, disability, or aging**. For countries that do not have the assistive technology or access solutions they need to meet the needs of their people, the ecosystem must provide a way for them to create an effective and economically viable access technology and services infrastructure within their country that can meet the language and cultural needs of their country.

Prosperity4All aims to work collaboratively to make progress toward all of the above facilitating a holistic integrated approach to the design, development, integration, deployment, operation and sustainability of AT technologies and interfaces, regardless of the user's needs/preferences, desired applications and location.

2   Understanding the Structure and Flow of Prosperity4All

The Prosperity4All project is based on meeting user needs. However, the users are not just the end-user or 'consumer' but also include the clinicians, teachers and others who support them, who purchase the access technologies etc. They are all important parts of the ecosystem, and the infrastructure needs to work for all of them. Figures 1 through 5 below present the overall concept of the Prosperity4All infrastructure and its interaction within the ecosystem.

We start with consumers - who need special access technologies in order to use the ICT and MATERIALS they encounter.

- But solutions are not available for
  − users with all types, degrees, and combinations of disability / literacy / digital literacy / aging
  − for all devices they encounter and have to use,
  − and at costs they can afford.
- a problem that is felt both by consumers and by those who are trying to serve them

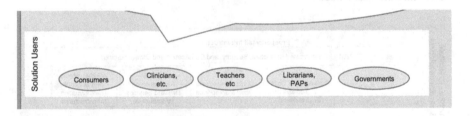

Fig. 1. Consumers, those working with them are the starting point of the ecosystem

We add the Access Solution Developers and Providers.

- Their role is to provide the access solutions the users need.
- But they have trouble reaching more than 3-15% of those they need to serve.
- They have trouble keeping up with all the technologies and platforms being introduced (and updated continually).
- They are not able to create solutions all the technologies in all of the different life domains in which users encounter technology they are required to use.
- The cost to deliver, especially to low incidence groups, is so high that they cannot get their prices down to where many users need them to be.

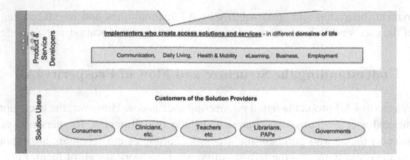

Fig. 2. Access solution developers and providers join the ecosystem in order to provide the access solutions that the users need

This project is about creating an international public infrastructure to facilitate the developers and providers in order to

- Help lower the costs to develop new solutions - and to keep up new technologies
- Help them increase their market reach and penetration - internationally
- Help them (affordably) create solutions for all of the groups who are too small for them to be able to serve today
- Open new types of assistive services they can provide to address unmet needs
- Better connect them to consumers that might use their products if they met or better met the users' needs

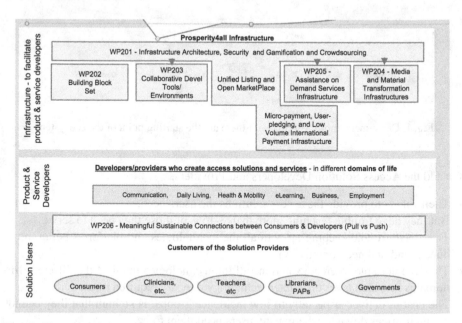

Fig. 3. The core of the Prosperity4All project is the building of the infrastructure to enable developers and providers to develop open, broadly applicable and cost-effective solutions that cover the full range of users and environments/contexts

Such an infrastructure must be constructed to function within the complete ecosystem of developers, vendors, service providers, 3rd party funders, governments and families and support groups.   And to be successful and sustainable

- it must be built on sound business and economic principles;
- civil rights, volunteerism or social responsibility will not keep all the players in place;
- rather the ecosystem must be based on value propositions for each of the stakeholders that are needed for the ecosystem to work.   They must all prosper or they will not be there to play their role.

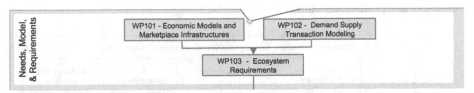

Fig. 4. The Prosperity4All Infrastructure cannot be isolated from the wider ecosystem of developers, vendors, service providers, third-party funders, governments, families and support groups

And of course, any infrastructure, and especially a new one, must be continually evaluated at many levels throughout the development process, and later, operation.

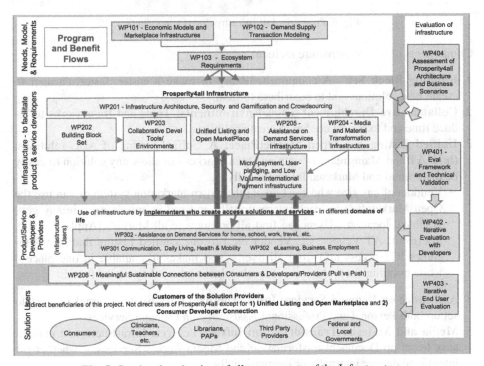

Fig. 5. Continual evaluation of all components of the Infrastructure

3   The Proposed Infrastructure and DeveloperSpace

In the center of the Prosperity4All project is the infrastructure to be constructed and the roles it plays for developers and users alike.   The DeveloperSpace is the name given to the virtual workspace in the cloud that will house the component library, the frameworks, the service infrastructures, payment infrastructures, and other components that stakeholders (incl. "professional" or "amateur" developers) need to create accessible products and services. First we look at the function that the infrastructure/Developerspace will provide. Then we will briefly list some of the characteristics of the DeveloperSpace (DSpace) to facilitate its use by companies, researchers, consumers and professionals alike.

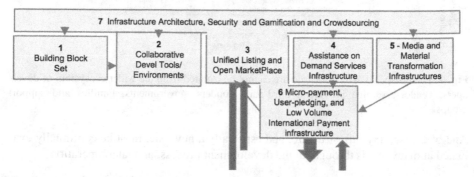

Fig. 6. Prosperity4all Infrastructure Components

Components of the infrastructure include:

1. **Building Block Set:** A component library to make it easier, faster, cheaper to create new solutions and to contribute to field.
2. **Collaborative Development Tools/Environments:** Tools and frameworks to reduce time and expertise needed to create solutions.
3. **Unified Listing and Open MarketPlace:** A Unified Listing of ALL solutions: (both AT and Mainstream) - with an Open Market - to allow any solution to easily be discovered and Marketed Internationally
   − Vendors of any size who can't create their own marketing system or can use the Open Marketplace to reach internationally and sell in any domain, in any geographical location. Users can find all products in all Markets (Apple, Google, Microsoft, AT Vendor, CE Vendor etc.) in one Unified Listing that brings together ICT access info from all over − and makes it available in one place − while pointing out to the various marketplaces where they can be found.

4. **Assistance on Demand Services Infrastructure:** Infrastructure to make it easy to set up both Personal and Professional Assistance on Demand Services.
5. **Media and Material Transformation Infrastructures:** Infrastructure to make it easy to set up Document trasformation and Media Access Services. − whether the intent is to deliver internally or internationally.

6. **Micro-payment, User-pledging, & Low-Volume International Payment Infrastructure:** International fiscal system interwoven into the infrastructure so that anyone, anywhere can make employment from any and all aspects of **development** and **delivery** of **parts, solutions** and/or **services**.
   — Users can pay for product or services in any coin in any amount and vendor or service provider gets it back in their coin.
   — Individuals can function as both users and verdors of services

7. **Infrastructure Architecture, Security and Gamification and Crowdsourcing:** Entire Infrastructure based on Crowd contribution and Gaming Principles (small tasks, challenging, failures quick but investment small, quickly-frequently rewarding, progressive, etc.) to entice and engage new 'players' with new skills

Standardized Modular Infrastructure to make it all work together seamlessly,   and work with Auto-personalization of Cloud4all/GPII to auto-deliver

   — access to ICT access;
   — accessible/transformed Materials;
   — accessible/augmented Media;   and/or
   — Assistance   on Demand;

to meet each user's needs.

4   DeveloperSpace Role and Characteristics

The Developer Space is being designed to connect designers and developers to a larger community of accessibility and usability resources, expertise, and tools. This work will include:

- the establishment of a network of contributors from across a variety of projects and communities, addressing the fragmentation of knowledge that is a typical problem within the accessibility field
- the creation of collaborative forums/tools that will help close the gap between developers and end-users, providing a means for users to influence and participate within the design, development and testing process more actively
- a means for searching, browsing, and contributing (i.e. a set of "libraries" or "shelves") relevant third-party development tools, frameworks, components, and open source applications categorized by type of development need (e.g. JavaScript frameworks, I/O libraries, testing tools, CSS frameworks, etc)
- the creation of a tool to help localize user interfaces into different languages, which can be connected to automated translation tools to allow for crowd-sourced correction. This activity will include a contributed effort from MADA, who have extensive experience with Arabic localization issues.

5   Conclusion

Described is a proposed infrastructure to allow the accessibility ecosystem to either evolve or add a dimension that can better meet the needs of people with low-incidence disabilities, or who have resource limitations that prevent them from being served today. Whether this infrastructure with its tools and services can effect this change, whether it is designed properly, and whether the ecosystem is interested in evolving in this way are open questions. The Prosperity4All project is designed to explore and test these. It is unlikely that the infrastructure will look exactly as described above at the end of this process, and input from all stakeholders is sought throughout the project as are collaborators interested in assisting with or extending any of the components of the infrastructure or ecosystem.

Acknowledgements. Prosperity4All is funded by the European Union's Seventh Framework Programme (FP7/2007-2013) grant agreement 610510, the Ontario Ministry of Research and Innovation, the Canadian Foundation for Innovation and the Consumer Electronics Association Foundation. Work leading up to Prosperity4All was funded by the European Union's Seventh Framework Programme (FP7/2007-2013) grant agreement 289016, by the National Institute on Disability and Rehabilitation Research, US Dept of Education under Grants H133E080022 (RERC-IT) by the Flora Hewlett Foundation, the Adobe Foundation, the Ontario Ministry of Research and Innovation, and the Canadian Foundation for Innovation. The opinions and results herein are those of the authors and not necessarily those of the funding agencies.

Rehabilitation Engineering and Research Center on Universal Interface and Information Technology Access

Gregg C. Vanderheiden[1], Amrish Chourasia[1], Yao Ding[1],
Jim Tobias[2], and Denis Anson[3]

[1] Trace R&D Center, University of Wisconsin – Madison, USA
{gv,amrish,ding}@trace.wisc.edu
[2] Inclusive Technologies, USA
tobias@inclusive.com
[3] Misericorida University, USA
danson@misericordia.edu

Abstract. The incidence of disability is increasing. As we move to a more digital world, people with disabilities, older people, and those with literacy and digital literacy problems face the prospect of losing out due to lack of access to information and communication technology. The rehabilitation engineering research center (RERC) on universal interface and information technology access seeks to promote a new approach to accessibility. This approach involves creating a new infrastructure for the development and delivery of AT and built-in access features. This effort is known as the Global Public Inclusive Infrastructure (GPII). This RERC will move the idea of GPII from laboratory prototypes to real-world implementation. A library GPII system and a cloud-based decision support tool for assistive technology selection are currently under development. The RERC will also support technology transfer and development of standards to promote accessibility.

Keywords: Accessibility, Information and communication technology, Cloud, Library, Decision Support, Technology Transfer.

1 Introduction

As the population in the United States is aging, the number of people with disabilities is also increasing [1]. There are about 56.7 million people with disabilities (18.7% of the civilian non-institutionalized population) in the United States. Disability affects individuals' employment as well as their economic status. Individuals with disabilities are less likely to be employed and more likely to experience persistent poverty than individuals without disabilities [1].

Accessibility impacts not only people with disabilities but also people with literacy and digital literacy problems and people who are older but who don't consider themselves disabled. We live in a society that is increasingly becoming dependent on

C. Stephanidis and M. Antona (Eds.): UAHCI/HCII 2014, Part IV, LNCS 8516, pp. 483–493, 2014.

technology. Today, digital (computer-based) technologies (and their accompanying digital interfaces) are being incorporated into virtually every aspect of life. Ticket agents are being replaced with ticket machines, and many metro train stations no longer have any human attendants at all. If you can't use the machine, you can't buy a ticket or even get through the gate. Jobs increasingly require access to computers or security pads, touch screens or other electronic interfaces. Even janitors must apply for jobs online and sometimes use computer interfaces at their workplaces. Even devices in our homes are going digital.

For those who can use these digital interfaces, this shift provides new capabilities, features, and designs that enhance our lives and our environments - while saving us money. But for those who cannot understand them, or who cannot see or hear or physically operate them or read or understand them, it is scary to live in a time when fewer and fewer things will be operable by them each year. For those who are aging and also have trouble learning new paradigms, it can increase their feelings of helplessness, hastening the time when they are unable to take care of themselves in what becomes an increasingly unfamiliar and inaccessible world.

1.1   Current Approaches for Addressing Accessibility

There are two broad approaches for providing access for these individuals who cannot use the standard interfaces on technology products and systems. One is to use an assistive technology (AT) that provides an alternate interface that the individual can use in place of the standard interface. This is most often done on computers and sometimes on phones.

Today however there is both a proliferation of operating systems on computers and mobile devices (many more than AT vendors can support) and a spread of digital interfaces across different technologies where AT does not exist and/or cannot even be installed or used. Even for computers where AT is most prevalent, we find that there are so many new platforms (operating systems, etc.) that vendors cannot support them all and users find that the AT they are familiar with won't work on all the computers and other devices they encounter and have to use.

Another problem is that solutions don't exist for types, degrees or combinations of disability. Sometimes there just is no AT or no AT for that platform. And even for those devices and those people for whom AT solutions exist, the cost of AT that is good enough to handle modern information technologies, is often out of reach or people never hear of the AT that would help them. According to estimates by accessibility experts and vendors, only between 3% and 15% of those who need special access products or features have them.

The second approach is to have access features built-into (mainstream) products. This has the advantage of zero additional cost for people with disabilities and it is always there when a person encounters the technology. However most products do not yet have access features, and on the relatively small number that do, have features that address the needs of only a small percentage of users – usually those with single or mild disabilities. The features are also often too complicated to invoke, set up, and use. Finally, even when the features exist for a person on a device they need, and it is something they could understand, it is likely that they will never know that it is there or know which device has a feature that would allow them to use it.

Thus we have a rapidly developing crisis where the society is moving digital (in education, employment, travel, health, even household appliances) while it does not have a strategy or systems in place that are capable of providing access for all of those who cannot use the digital interfaces needed to participate in this digital world.

1.2   Our Approach to Address Accessibility

Recognizing this emerging problem a consortium of universities, industry and individuals was built to address this looming issue. The consortium was named the Raising the Floor Consortium – to emphasize the need to ensure that "floor level" AT (AT and other access solutions that was affordable by all) existed and was good enough to provide meaningful access to modern technologies. The problem and the call to form a consortium to address it received widespread recognition by consumers, researchers, mainstream and AT vendors, and the consortium and its supporters grew rapidly. Fairly quickly however it became clear that the goal of the consortium was not attainable with the current accessibility ecosystem. It simply costs too much to develop, distribute and support AT, and reducing the price unilaterally would only serve to run most companies out of business. Similar problems existed with the "built-in" approach. This led to the understanding by the consortium that the only way to address the problem was to create a new infrastructure for the development and delivery of AT and built-in access features. Such an infrastructure would need to address the three central problems blocking widespread, affordable, and usable accessibility:

1. making it much easier for people who need special interface features to be able to find that solutions exist and to find the proper features/aids to allow them to access and use ICT;
2. making it possible for users to invoke the access features they need on any digital technology they encounter and have to use instantly, without requiring users to know how to install, turn on, or configure anything; and
3. making it much easier and less expensive for developers to create, distribute, market, and support new access solutions (AT and built-in features) and to reach the people (internationally) who need their solution(s).

This infrastructure is now known as the Global Public Inclusive Infrastructure (GPII). Major research grants (European Commission grants Cloud4all and Prosperity4all,

U.S. Dept. of Education contract) are working towards building the components of the GPII.

2 Rehabilitation Engineering Research Center (RERC) on Universal Interface and Information Technology Access (UIITA)

The current Universal Interface & Information Technology Access (UIITA) Rehabilitation Engineering Research Center (RERC) at the Trace Center at University of Wisconsin-Madison will use the components built in the other projects and move the GPII from concept, papers and laboratory prototypes to field implementations where we can test the efficacy and viability of the concept with real-world conditions, users and limitations. Fig. 1 illustrates the dependencies between the RERC and the other GPII projects. RERCs conduct programs of advanced research of an engineering or technical nature designed to apply advanced technology, scientific achievement, and psychological and social knowledge to solve rehabilitation problems and remove environmental barriers. RERCs also develop systems for the exchange of technical and engineering information worldwide and improve the distribution of technological devices and equipment to individuals with disabilities [2]

The UIITA-RERC started in October 2013 and is a five-year effort. The RERC will focus its efforts in three areas.

1. Continuing development of the GPII concept – evolving it to address the changing technology landscape and our growing understanding of its role based on discussions with the different accessibility and mainstream stakeholders.
2. Moving the GPII from concept, papers, and laboratory prototypes, through to field implementations. This will include
   (a) The Library-GPII-System (LGS): Development and testing of a package for deploying and applying the GPII in public libraries of all sizes, with a focus on providing libraries with cost-effective ways of serving users with a wider range of abilities – including those with cognitive, memory, and digital-literacy related barriers such as elders and first time users.
   (b) Cloud-Based Decision Support (CBDSS): Development and testing of a decision support tool based on the GPII Unified Listing that can provide users and clinicians with a new capability for tracking and selecting ever-changing solutions for users – including not only comprehensive information on assistive technologies, but also not-previously-available information on the access features that are built into mainstream technologies.
3. Continued work to motivate and facilitate access built directly into mainstream products – through our technology transfer program and our research support of industry standards groups and governmental agencies working on accessibility standards.

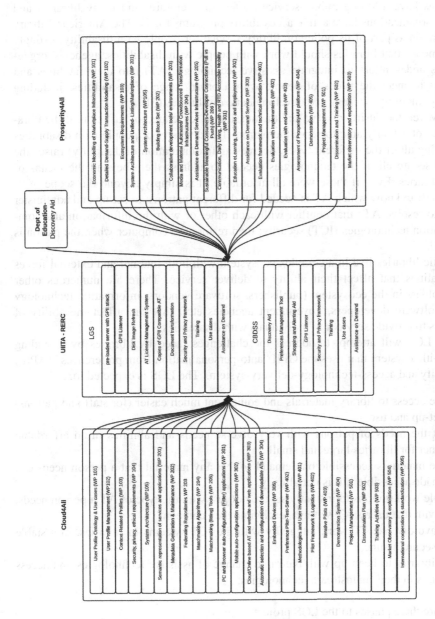

Fig. 1. Dependencies between the GPII projects and the UIITA RERC. (WP = work package, LGS = Library GPII System, CBDSS = Cloud-based decision support system).

3   The Library-GPII-System (LGS)

Libraries have a strong public service professional culture, and many libraries and library organizations have active accessibility programs [3, 4]. The American Library Association as part of its policy on library service for people with disability, strongly recommends that libraries should work with people with disabilities, agencies, organizations and vendors to integrate assistive technology (AT) into their facilities and services to meet the needs of people with a broad range of disabilities, including learning, mobility, sensory and developmental disabilities [3].

However, the desire to serve and the mission to serve are not sufficient if the libraries are not actually able to serve the patron. The diversity of people with disabilities (including all of the different types, degrees and combination of disability) raises the cost to secure all of the technologies needed to address them beyond the means of most libraries. Even if these were all affordable, it is simply beyond the scope of library staff to know which AT is needed for different patrons; to set up and administer them; to resolve ATs that conflict with each other or with the information and communication technologies (ICT) security; then restore the computer when the patron is finished.

Public libraries live in a complex ecosystem with both internal and external forces and realities that affect their ability to deliver service. There are numerous other stakeholders in the ecosystem (publishers, software vendors, information technology staff, software developers, government agencies etc.) that can affect the ability of libraries to provide services to individuals with disabilities.

The LGS will attempt to address the challenges faced by libraries by providing them with a system that uses the GPII "auto-personalization from preferences" (APfP) capability and access-technology-delivery-system. The LGS is expected to:

- make access to library materials and equipment much easier (for staff and patrons) to set-up and use.
- meet the needs of patrons with very diverse needs and abilities in an affordable manner for libraries large and small.
- make materials accessible on demand so that any material that a person needs can be made accessible if it is not already.
- enable workstations to instantly set up, not just with the type of AT a person needs, but with that user's AT settings, each time they come in.
- to have diverse AT work integrally with the ICT systems in libraries, in a stable and secure manner.
- for libraries to keep up with the rapid change of assistive technologies and access features in their mainstream technologies.

There are three phases to the LGS project

1. Needs Analysis – work with stakeholders to define the needs, constraints and specifications for the LGS; the subjects are library patrons, staff, and other library stakeholders specified in the Stakeholder Sample section below.

2. LGS Development and User Testing – results of the stakeholder research on the accessibility needs and issues in libraries and the stakeholder input on the potential use of cloud computing-based accessibility in libraries will be uses to create a prototype cloud-based access solution for libraries.
3. Empirical Field Testing of the LGS in Libraries – Quantitative and qualitative testing of the LGS in diverse libraries (based on size and resources) to determine the LGS's viability and ability to address the issues outlined above.

The Library-GPII-System will be the first real world implementation of the GPII idea. The results from this project will provide us with valuable lessons for other implementations of the GPII in terms of costs, scaling requirements, and perceived benefits. It is expected that the LGS will make it easier for library patrons to use ICT and increase their confidence that they will get the resources and services that they need when they arrive at the library, thereby increasing their use of the library.

If successful the proposed LGS will allow libraries to offer a range of assistive services to their users and either pay a small set cost or pay only for the services that the users actually use. This represents a radical departure from the traditional approach of buying individual software licenses for selected software packages and then only offering those packages to patrons.

We will document the potential impact of the LGS for different library stakeholders (users with disabilities, librarians, library staff, library ICT support, government, publishers, library associations) as a tool to continue the engagement with key stakeholders as GPII approaches implementation. The research findings will help guide development decisions and lead to increased likelihood of adoption and utilization.

More details on the LGS can be found in Vanderheiden et al. [5]

4   Cloud-Based Decision Support (CBDSS)

Most people who need access technologies in order to use ICT often cannot afford a professional evaluation to discover their access technology needs. This problem is particularly serious for elders who often do not qualify for evaluations because they are no longer of employment or school age and hence disqualified from education or vocation based evaluations.

Professionals also have difficulty keeping up with the ever-changing variety of access aids and devices for all the different types, degrees, and combinations of disability that a client might have. This is further complicated by the proliferation of different platforms that each have different solutions that work or don't work on them. Professionals that focus on access AT evaluations are having difficulty, and professionals for whom access AT is only a portion of their practice have no chance of keeping up.

Decision support systems have been widely used in clinical settings [6, 7]. Systematic reviews of studies on clinical decision support systems (CDSS) showed improved practitioner performance, improved patient outcomes, less medication errors, and improved compliance with care standards [6-9].

Despite increasing implementations of CDSS in health care, those for AT selection are few (such as the CAP [10] and Computer Access Selector [11]). To the best of our knowledge, no CDSS for AT selection has been empirically evaluated in clinical settings. Potential needs and constraints of individual consumers and practitioners when using AT decisions support systems are unknown, but the potential, if they can be made to work, is great. Whether computerized decision support for AT selection can be effectively employed in clinical practice, and which factors are important for clear clinical impact needs to be examined.

To address these problems, we proposed a cloud-based decision support to help consumers and practitioners sort through information on all solutions, learn more about them, and select AT (or access solutions built into mainstream products) with less effort and better outcomes.

The project will be carried out in three phases:

- AT Selection Modeling and Needs Analysis: An exploration among consumers and professionals of how decisions are made, and preferred techniques or approaches for supporting the decision-making process.
- Development and Usability testing of a Cloud-Based Decision Support System for ICT access solutions: Creation of a decision support tool (the Tracking/Shopping Aid) based on phase 1 findings, with continual user testing and participation in the design of its interface and functionality.
- Evaluation of the Use of CBDSS in Real-World Settings: Empirically testing the ability of the CBDSS to improve the decision making abilities of individual consumers, and to comparatively test its ability to meet or exceed the selection of aided and un-aided evaluations carried out by professionals who recommend these AT but it is not the bulk of their practice.

If successful, this project will transform the experience of end-users and practitioners in selecting assistive technologies for ICT applications. The proposed system will provide immediate access to all current assistive technology, with information about its features that is updated regularly. The system will select, from the universe of available products, those that are relevant to the needs of a particular client, and assist in making decisions between products of similar function. The system will use information about its users to identify common needs patterns (syndromes). This information can be used by AT developers to create solutions that address multiple related needs, rather than providing a collection of independent accommodations. This information could also be used to suggest to individuals that additional components of their needs pattern could be addressed.

5   Technology Transfer

Although there is much written about the need for products to be more accessible to people with disabilities, and a fair number of papers published and prototypes shown at disability and even mainstream conferences, none of this information or knowledge will directly impact the lives of anybody with a disability until it is built into actual commercial products. When talking about universal design or access to mainstream products, this means that the ideas must be transferred to and implemented by mainstream product manufacturers and available to consumers in the marketplace. However transferring research to commercial implementation is so difficult it is often referred to as the "Valley of Death" [12].

Technology transfer in the area of "universal" or "inclusive" design is particularly difficult. It is a multidimensional effort that needs to occur in many places within an organization in order to be effective. In discussing the development of the BS7000 Part 6 Guide to Managing Inclusive Design, Keates [13] talks about the importance of it being incorporated into the "company ethos" and emphasizes that inclusive design must be a priority at multiple levels within an organization (executive, management, and design) in order to succeed. This is echoed in most every study of technology transfer dealing with universal design or design for all [14-16].

Successful technology transfer has to overcome barriers such as lack of adherence to access regulations; weak business case for universal design (UD); lack of a standard, tested UD process; unrealistic UD guidelines; lack of quantitative measures for comparing solutions or evaluating absolute or sufficient access; poor communication between departments; lack of champions in positions of authority; conflict between UD and push to market and budget; lack of people with disabilities in design or evaluation processes [17]. In addition, successful and consistent practice of universal design is most affected by simple profit, with many of the other factors falling in line if clear profit is perceived [17].

5.1   Project Objective

The objective of this project is to move accessibility advances beyond research so that it is available to users in their everyday lives by:

- Moving the new concept of a Global Public Inclusive Infrastructure (GPII) from research and prototypes to widespread adoption in the field;
- Increasing the building of key accessibility features into mainstream ICT;
- Supporting policy, consumer and consulting groups who foster and support accessibility;
- Facilitating the ability of consumers to discover, select and afford both AT and built-in access features of mainstream technologies.

Specifically we expect to focus on:

- Transfer of the successful aspects of LGS and CBDSS into widespread adoption in the field as part of the broader GPII;
- Coordinating and supporting the work of others who are building the GPII, and creating real-world implementations;
- Continued support of the Access Board, FCC, and other policy makers engaged in development of accessibility guidelines – particularly 508, 255, and M376 (Europe);

- Work with industry on standards around improved APIs and standards to support user definable alternate interfaces for mainstream devices and web services;
- Providing people within companies, and the consultants working with them, with the research, information, tools, and other resources they need to explore, test, sell the concept, implement, and incorporate accessibility features into companies' mainstream products.

6   Conclusion

The RERC is expected to move the GPII from theory and laboratory prototypes and out in the real world. If successful, it will help enable entirely new service and solution delivery options as well as enhance the ability of existing clinical programs to keep up with rapid technology changes in their field. It will also contribute to the innovation and distribution of new and existing technologies that enable individuals with disabilities to access ICT. The RERC is also expected to influence and contribute to accessibility standards and support industry, consumers and the government is achieving their accessibility objectives.

Acknowledgement. Different components of the body of work described in this paper was, and/or is being, funded by the European Union's Seventh Framework Programme (FP7/2007-2013) grant agreement n° 289016 (Cloud4all) and 610510 (Prosperity4All), by the National Institute on Disability and Rehabilitation Research, US Dept of Education under Grants H133E080022 (RERC-IT) and H133E130028 (UIITA-RERC) and contract ED-OSE-12-D-0013 (Preferences for Global Access), by the Flora Hewlett Foundation, the Ontario Ministry of Research and Innovation, and the Canadian Foundation for Innovation. The opinions and results herein are those of the authors and not necessarily those of the funding agencies.

References

1. Brault, M.W. and United States: Bureau of the Census, Americans with disabilities: 2010. In: 2012: US Department of Commerce, Economics and Statistics Administration, US Census Bureau (2010)
2. US Department of Education. Rehabilitation Engineering Research Centers (Program Home Page) (2012), http://www2.ed.gov/programs/rerc/index.html (July 9, 2012)
3. The Association of Specialized and Cooperative Library Agencies (ASCLA). Library Services for People with Disabilities Policy. Library Services for People with Disabilities Policy (2001)
4. The Association of Specialized and Cooperative Library Agencies (ASCLA). Think Accessible Before You Buy, Questions to Ask to Ensure that the Electronic Resources Your Library Plans to Purchase are Accessible. n.d., http://www.ala.org/ascla/sites/ala.org.ascla/files/content/asclaprotools/thinkaccessible/thinkaccessible.pdf

5. Vanderheiden, G., et al.: The Library GPII System. In: 16th International Conference on Human-Computer Interaction, Crete, Greece (2014)
6. Garg, A.X., et al.: Effects of computerized clinical decision support systems on practitioner performance and patient outcomes: a systematic review. JAMA 293(10), 1223–1238 (2005)
7. Hunt, D.L., et al.: Effects of computer-based clinical decision support systems on physician performance and patient outcomes: a systematic review. JAMA 280(15), 1339–1346 (1998)
8. Kaushal, R., Shojania, K.G., Bates, D.W.: Effects of computerized physician order entry and clinical decision support systems on medication safety: a systematic review. Arch. Intern. Med. 163(12), 1409–1416 (2003)
9. Lobach, D.F., Hammond, W.E.: Computerized decision support based on a clinical practice guideline improves compliance with care standards. Am. J. Med. 102(1), 89–98 (1997)
10. Terrell-Lindsay, S.Y., Matthews, B.: Computer/Electronic Accommodations Program (CAP). Work: A Journal of Prevention, Assessment and Rehabilitation 18(2), 205–206 (2002)
11. Stapleton, D., Garrett, R., Seeger, B.: VOCASelect and Computer Access Selector: Software tools to assist in choosing assistive technology. In: International Conference on Assistive Technology for People with Disabilities (RESNA) (1997)
12. Jelinek, M.: Crossing death valley together: Cultural dynamics of industry–university IP. In: Southern Management Association Annual Conference (November 2005)
13. Keates, S.: Developing BS7000 Part 6 – Guide to Managing Inclusive Design. In: Stary, C., Stephanidis, C. (eds.) UI4ALL 2004. LNCS, vol. 3196, pp. 332–339. Springer, Heidelberg (2004)
14. Bauer, S.M., Lane, J.P.: Convergence of assistive devices and mainstream products: Keys to university participation in research, development and commercialization. Technology and Disability 18(2), 67–77 (2006)
15. National Council on Disability, Design for Inclusion: Creating a New Marketplace (2004)
16. Dong, H.: Barriers to Inclusive Design in the UK. In: CHI 2004 Extended Abstracts on Human Factors in Computing Systems. ACM (2004)
17. Vanderheiden, G., Tobias, J.: Universal design of consumer products: current industry practice and perceptions. In: Proceedings of the Human Factors and Ergonomics Society Annual Meeting. SAGE Publications (2000)

The Library GPII System

Gregg C. Vanderheiden[1,2], Amrish Chourasia[1], Jim Tobias[2], and Steve Githens[3]

[1] Trace R&D Center, University of Wisconsin – Madison, USA
{gv,amrish}@trace.wisc.edu
[2] Inclusive Technologies, Matawan, NJ, USA
tobias@inclusive.com
[3] Raising the Floor – USA
swgithen@mtu.edu

Abstract. This paper describes the library GPII system (LGS), the first real-world implementation of the GPII (Global Public Inclusive Infrastructure) system. The GPII aims to utilize cloud computing to create the infrastructure to provide affordable assistive services whenever and wherever a user demands them. The interactions of the different stakeholders in the library ecosystem present various challenges to implement such a system. These stakeholders include the library patrons, library staff, government, publishers, software developers and vendors. The development of the LGS will happen in three phases: needs analysis, development and empirical evaluation. Libraries of various sizes and resources will be involved in the development and evaluation of the LGS. We are currently in the first phase and the results of our stakeholder analysis work to-date are presented.

Keywords: Personalization, GPII, library, assistive technology.

1   Introduction

Public libraries perform several unique functions in society:

- repository of information resources in many forms, including live Q&A on almost any topic to staff of trained information science experts
- community rallying point
- extension of the education system, especially for adult education
- access point for public services (employment, welfare, tax preparation, etc.)
- access to Internet, including digital literacy training
- repository of information resources in many forms, including live Q&A on almost any topic to staff of trained information science experts

Libraries have a strong public service professional culture, and many libraries and library organizations have active accessibility programs [1, 2]. The American Library Association (ALA) as part of its policy on library service for people with disability, strongly recommends that libraries should work with people with disabilities, agencies, organizations and vendors to integrate assistive technology (AT) into their

C. Stephanidis and M. Antona (Eds.): UAHCI/HCII 2014, Part IV, LNCS 8516, pp. 494–505, 2014.
© Springer International Publishing Switzerland 2014

facilities and services to meet the needs of people with a broad range of disabilities, including learning, mobility, sensory and developmental disabilities [1]. It is also recommended that libraries provide training to their staff and employees on available technologies that address disabilities and know how to assist all users with library technology.

However, the desire to serve and the mission to serve are not sufficient if the libraries are not actually able to serve the patron. The diversity of people with disabilities (including all of the different types, degrees and combination of disability) raises the cost to secure all of the technologies needed to address them beyond the means of most libraries. Even if these were all affordable, it is simply beyond the scope of library staff to know which AT is needed for different patrons; to set up and administer them; to resolve ATs that conflict with each other or with the information and communication technologies (ICT) security; then restore the computer when the patron is finished.

The problem is well known and impossible to manage within a normal library budget. In fact many libraries have only one or two assistive technologies, only serving some disabilities. Most leave it to the patrons to adjust the AT to their needs, which is difficult or impossible for many. Many libraries effectively have no AT and leave users to seek library services elsewhere. The problem extends beyond device access to content (books, magazines, etc.) access as well.

As a result librarians find their ability to serve the full spectrum of patrons is blocked; budgetary, technical, and practical constraints leave them with no real options.

Libraries live in a complex ecosystem with both internal and external forces and realties that affect their ability to deliver service. Any solution needs to address these realities. They face staffing and resource constraints and have to deal with other stakeholders such as their local government who may not only decide on their budgets but also provide technology management services to the library, publishers who may or may not provide accessible versions of their materials, software developers and vendors who may or may not address accessibility in their products.

The problem the libraries face is not of awareness or desire to serve, but of the ability to do so within the budget, training and time available and in the library ecosystem. What is needed is a practical integrated solution that addresses these different issues. The solution should:

- make access to library materials and equipment much easier (for staff and patrons) to setup and use.
- meet the needs of patrons with diverse needs and abilities in an affordable manner for libraries large and small.
- make materials accessible on demand so that any material that a person needs can be made accessible if it is not already.
- for workstations to instantly set up, not just with the type of AT a person needs, but with that user's AT settings, each time they come in
- to have diverse AT work integrally with the ICT systems in libraries, in a stable and secure manner.

- for libraries to keep up with the rapid change of assistive technologies and access features in their mainstream technologies.

The Global Public Inclusive Infrastructure (GPII) (www.gpii.net) is an initiative of the Raising the Floor Consortium that aims to utilize cloud computing to create the infrastructure to provide affordable assistive services whenever and wherever a user demands them. The GPII will enable people to learn about and determine what solutions will assist them and store that information in a common, portable, private and secure manner; provide a way to use the stored preferences to invoke and configure needed accessibility and usability features, assistive technologies; and provide tools and infrastructure to developers and vendors to create new solutions for different users in a cost effective and efficient manner. The European Union funded projects, Cloud4all and Prosperity4all are currently underway helping build the GPII.

As part of the Rehabilitation and Engineering Research Center at the Trace Research and Development Center at the University of Wisconsin-Madison, we proposed to develop the first real-world implementation of the GPII. This implementation is referred to as the Library-GPII-System (LGS). The LGS will be developed in collaboration with library staff and other stakeholders in the library ecosystem. Our objectives are to:

1. clearly identify objectives constraints, resources and organization needs for each stakeholder
2. explore the ways that a cloud-based, "auto-personalization from preferences" (APfP) capability and access-technology delivery system like the Global Public Inclusive Infrastructure (GPII) [Reference] might help address these issues and maximize resources
3. develop the LGS, tailored to library needs
4. quantitatively and qualitatively test the LGS in diverse libraries to determine its viability and ability to address the issues listed above.

2   Methods

The LGS development and evaluation is a five-year effort. The study will be carried out in three phases

1. Needs Analysis – work with stakeholders to define the needs, constraints and specifications for the LGS; the subjects are library patrons, staff, and other library stakeholders
2. LGS Development and User Testing - the subjects are the same as Phase 1.
3. Empirical Field Testing of the LGS in Libraries – the subjects here will be libraries, including their staff, patrons, and other stakeholders

In Year 1, we will focus on the stakeholder needs analysis (Phase 1) and use those inputs to create demos and prototypes of the LGS. The prototypes will in turn be used in the stakeholder research to collect further feedback from the different stakeholders and refine the needs analysis. The findings of the stakeholder research will be translated for the development team, which will co-develop the LGS in an iterative design process with three libraries (large, medium and small) in Years 2 and 3 (Phase 2). In Years 4 and 5, we will implement the Library-GPII-System in three test libraries and evaluate its impact (Phase 3).

We will use a qualitative approach for the stakeholder research (Phase 1); participatory research and usability testing in the development of the LGS (Phase 2); and a mixed methods approach to assess the impact of the Library-GPII-System on accessibility practice (Phase 3).

2.1   Population and Sample

Stakeholder Sample. For the needs analysis (Phase 1) we will be recruiting participants from all of the major library stakeholder groups: librarians, library staff, IT staff, administrators, vendors of special library software, AT vendors, mainstream ICT companies, publishers, government bodies, funding agencies etc., and a cross-section of people with disabilities and aging related barriers to library ICT and materials use (including disability advocacy organizations). We will recruit up to 150 participants for the stakeholder analysis.

All samples will be structured samples of convenience since random sampling is not possible. Even if it were possible, random sampling would represent token rather than type (i.e., it would focus where there would be most stakeholders rather than sampling across the spectrum of stakeholders in each category).

Library Sample. We will be testing the LGS in three different libraries: a large public or university library, a medium sized public library, and a smaller rural library.

A convenience sample of 48 participants with disabilities who are patrons at the enrolled libraries will be recruited for the impact assessment. We will recruit participants across the full spectrum of disabilities including individuals with visual, physical, hearing, both hearing and visual, and cognitive, language, and learning disabilities as well as older users and other users with more than one disability. Librarians and library staff at the enrolled libraries will be used for the qualitative impact evaluation of the LGS.

To increase validity of the testing we will use different libraries for the development work than we will for the evaluation of impact of the LGS, to be carried out in Years 4 and 5. The three libraries for the final test will be selected in Year 3.

2.2   Phase 1 – Needs Analysis

The development of the LGS will be carried out as part of the overall GPII development effort. The LGS does not include the development of any AT, but it will provide a means to instantly deliver and configure commercial AT, free AT, and built-in access features in mainstream technologies.

The LGS will be the first real-world implementation of the GPII idea. We will assess its impact on not only on the end users but also the other stakeholders in the library ecosystem along different dimensions (human, organizational, technical, and economic).

We will research and analysis of the needs, constraints, expectations, and motivations of the different stakeholders in the ecosystem; translate the stakeholder requirements into a format that developers can understand and act upon; and encourage continuous dialogue throughout the project regarding each stakeholder's needs/preferences and their current status in the system under development, with refinement and correction as indicated by the stakeholders.

To do this we will use Graham et al.'s [3] Knowledge-to-Action Process Framework (KTA) for facilitating the translation of knowledge for diverse stakeholders. The action cycle begins with a review of existing knowledge, selects and adapts what is most applicable to stakeholder needs, delivers it in context, collects and interprets stakeholder responses, and continues the cycle, monitoring value and effectiveness [4]. Development teams will also be viewed as stakeholders, in that they need to receive the responses of other stakeholders so that the development effort can reflect those needs and increase the likelihood of effective utilization.

Preliminary Research and Analysis. An initial stakeholder analysis report (SAR) for each group will be prepared based on an analysis of trade and academic literature, published interviews, and library-oriented program management reports, and current work. The SARs will address the following questions:

- What are these stakeholders doing now about library accessibility? What are the dominant methods and policies? What is the role of professionals, professional development, and the need for training? How do librarians interact with patrons with disabilities? How do people with disabilities use libraries now?
- What are their motivations, expectations, plans, and outstanding issues? This includes the effect of accessibility laws and regulations on them that inclusive cloud and web computing might help them address. What are the experiences and expectations of people with disabilities? Libraries are concerned about staff training on accessibility when the requests for accessibility are generally low. Can the cloud provide just-in-time training and better technical support?
- What is their role in the market and the ecosystem; where can they influence others to improve accessibility? For example, as libraries migrate to tablets and e-book readers, how can they influence publishers who will store and distribute content via the cloud in a way that will support improvements in accessibility?
- Where does cloud accessibility offer the most value? How can cloud accessibility do at least as good a job for them as other accessibility strategies?
- What would be key barriers to adoption of cloud accessibility in libraries? What is the effect of their current methods of operation on their ability to adopt cloud accessibility? For example, publishers are concerned about the impact of accessibility on intellectual property issues.

Primary Stakeholder Research and Analysis. After our preliminary research based on secondary sources, we will conduct a series of interviews and focus groups. Consider the library staff training issue. We may form a hypothesis that the most acceptable approach would be a mix of general disability/accessibility training and just-in-time training on specific accessibility solutions at the time and place they are being implemented in the library. For the former we might hold a focus group or survey/online poll on whether general accessibility training should be library-specific (such as the popular WebJunction service) or broader; whether the training should be approved by a library organization; whether it should offer continuing education credits; etc. For the latter we would want to know if the just-in-time training should be part of a step-by-step implementation wizard; whether it should involve separate resources for librarians and users, or be an "over-the-shoulder" experience; whether it should be connected to a peer-based service for answering questions and furthering dialogue; etc. Results from this research will be included in revised SARs.

Knowledge Translation between Stakeholder Groups. We will use the knowledge-transfer-action framework to translate knowledge about inclusive-ness of the library ecosystem through: (1) identification of stakeholders' knowledge and information needs, (2) development of effective and accessible materials, and (3) delivery to the specific audiences.

We will initially interview the developers about the kind of input that they need from the other stakeholders (e.g., users with disabilities, library staff) that will help them in the development of the LGS. We will use the input from developers to elicit responses from other stakeholders. The feedback from the other stakeholders in turn will be translated and provided back to the developers to include in the design of the LGS.

2.3   Phase 2 –Development and User Testing of the LGS

The LGS is expected to consist of the following:

- a pre-loaded server that can be connected to the libraries network that contains the full GPII stack – and that interacts with other GPII components elsewhere on the internet, and that also contains;
  - special software that downloads to the workstations to allow them to watch for GPII users to key-in to a workstation and then loads/launches and configures any needed AT or access features built into the mainstream device, OS, or applications
  - (Users can Key-in in any of a wide variety of ways to meet individual user preference including with a NFC keyfob, NFC sticker on their library card or any other handy item, an NFC ring, a printed QR code, a USB, a memorized code typed on the standard keyboard, etc.);
- software that works with the libraries IT system to refresh workstations after each use to restore them to clean and default status;
- a license management system to support different AT sales/licensing approaches;
- copies of all of the free and commercial AT software that is compatible with GPII (This includes software adapted by vendors, software that is made GPII compatible by 3rd parties and software that is works automatically with the GPII generic launch and configure routines, which, if this is successful, will be most all AT);
- a document transformation engine/service;

- other services as identified in the needs analysis (Phase 1 above) or defined in connection with the library and vendor collaborations.

The exact configuration, form, and interface for these functions will be worked out in in this phase by working with the libraries, consumers, and vendors collaborating there.

The development of the LGS will be carried out using state-of-the-art Agile development methods integrated with user-centered design (UCD). Agile software development uses short iterative cycles of development, continuous testing, constant collaboration, and frequent replanning based on current reality (as opposed to a fixed plan developed in the past) [5]. A project is broken down into sub-projects, each of which typically involves planning, development, integration, testing, and delivery [6].

User centered design is a broad term used to describe design processes in which end-users influence the design and development of a product [7]. In UCD the needs, wants, and limitations of the end-users are considered at each stage of the design process. Stakeholder input from R1 will be key here, but will be augmented by the continuous user input from the Agile process as well. Frameworks to incorporate UCD philosophy into agile software development are available [8-10], and there are increasing instances of the integration of agile development and UCD [11, 12]. A survey of 92 practitioners throughout the world, showed that the majority of practitioners (that integrate of agile methods with UCD) perceive that it has added value to their adopted processes and to their teams; has resulted in the improvement of usability and quality of the product developed; and has increased the satisfaction of the end-users of the product developed [11].

Technologies Used. The LGS will be developed using the same state-of-the-art technologies and architecture as the rest of the GPII, which is based on modular design with RESTful APIs [13] and extensive use of node.js [14] and JavaScript. This has given us a robust cross platform architecture which we have been able to deploy across Linux, Windows, and Android platforms to date, and which is easily scalable (used by some of the largest and most used internet sites) and eminently cross platform (supported by all major OSs and all browsers).

Participants and User Testing. Users of all types will be involved throughout the development process. This will include a constructed sample of 20 patrons across the full spectrum of disabilities. A constructed sample will be used to create the best coverage of the spectrum of disabilities including individuals with visual, physical, hearing, both hearing and visual, and cognitive, language, and learning disabilities as well as older users and other users with more than one disability. Participants will be invited to join the design team and to evaluate the LGS user interfaces. They will be given access to the design documents and wikis, and can join design team calls. Other stakeholders including AT developers and vendors, library staff, and library ICT professionals and administrators will also be incorporated into the design process throughout. Ongoing usability testing will be done using standard usability methods and procedures [15]. The results will be used to continually improve designs.

2.4   Phase 3 – Empirical Field Testing of the LGS in Libraries

The goals for the field test and impact evaluation of the LGS are to:

1. Test the study hypotheses that, "compared to existing Library AT practices, the LGS will lead to:
   (a) Increased user satisfaction with library AT service,
   (b) Greater use of AT in libraries,
   (c) Greater use of libraries by a wider range of patrons, and
   (d) Lower unit costs for libraries in providing accessible services.
2. Identify what libraries can do to prepare fellow libraries for GPII implementation
3. Identify ways to improve the design of the GPII library implementations.

Design of Empirical Field Testing. To assess the impact of the LGS, we will use a repeated measures design. Baseline data will be collected before the deployment of the LGS and also after the implementation period.

Preparation for Test. Three libraries in each of the following categories: large public or university libraries, medium public libraries, and smaller public libraries, will be selected on the basis of their existing capabilities to serve users with disabilities (availability of AT, trained staff to help patrons with disabilities). We will work with the IT and other teams at the libraries to support the deployment and integration of the LGS with the IT and other systems in their libraries. The deployment in the development libraries should identify many problems, as expected for an early deployment. Before the deployment of the LGS, we will help the test libraries prepare outreach programs to users with disabilities to inform them about the accessibility services available at the library.

Measures. User satisfaction with the quality of library services is our primary outcome measure. To assess the satisfaction of users with the AT services offered at the libraries, we will use the LibQUAL+ instrument [16]. The LibQUAL+ instrument contains 22 items and an open comments box that measure library users' minimum, perceived, and desired service levels of service quality across three dimensions: Affect of Service, Information Control and Library as Place. The LibQUAL+ scores are rated on a scale of 1 (least favorable) to 9 (most favorable). Since 2000, more than 1,000 libraries have used LibQUAL+ worldwide. LibQUAL+ scores have been found to be reliable [17], valid and primarily measure user satisfaction [18].
We will also collect measures of library operations including:

- Number of users with disabilities served, including number of first time users, percentage of AT users that have returned and number of returns
- Types of disabilities of patrons served
- Diversity of AT offered
- Number of Instances of AT use
- Total cost of AT and AT services, including cost of AT, cost of technical support and training staff in use of AT, unit costs for AT (cost per user hour)

We will also conduct interviews with library staff on how the implementation of the Library-GPII-System has changed the accessibility practice in terms of cost, convenience and effectiveness from their perspective. All measures will be collected at baseline before the outreach program and after the implementation period of two years at all libraries.

Monitoring Plan. For the LGS field evaluation we anticipate the standard operational challenges for a project like this, including subject attrition (planned for up to 33%), staff turnover, changes in interest and activity level from library staff, changes in library ICT resources, and external challenges such as budgetary constraints. We will maintain continuous communication with the libraries both to monitor for any changes in the libraries that could confound the results, and as part of our continual participant input and engagement in the evaluation and development process. Project staff will call the libraries, visit the libraries regularly, interact with library staff on the project wikis and lists, and encourage them to inform us of any unforeseen developments at the libraries.

Data Analysis. Based on the distribution of data, parametric or non-parametric will be used to analyze differences following the implementation of the LGS.

3   Preliminary Results

Data collection is ongoing for Phase 1. We have established relationships with various libraries and communicated with them on the development of the GPII. Previous conversations with librarians have yielded the following findings:

- Lack of control over ICT environment. Library hardware and software is typically limited to that selected by the municipal government or other authority. Control of both the long-term planning and day-to-day operation of library ICT facilities may rest with managers who are not knowledgeable or response to the library's desire to provide more accessible solutions for its patrons.
- Infrequent and unplanned requests for accessibility support. A patron with a given disability may appear at any moment and expect service, or may never appear. The available AT may not match the patron's needs, or library staff may lack the expertise to provide the level of assistance needed for setting up or using the AT. Mismatch can lead to low usage and this makes it hard to justify staff training and equipment provision..
- Training. Even professional librarians and IT staff cannot be expected to become and remain accessibility experts; and many libraries have only one or two professional librarians supplemented by paraprofessionals and volunteers with little or no training in providing accessibility services.
- Assistive Technology (AT). If expensive AT is not used frequently it is viewed as wasted. This only has to happen once for library administrators to be unwilling to repeat such purchases. And users of one type of AT (e.g., screen-reader) may not

be able to use another brand – meaning lower usage of each, or libraries not having one that the person can use.

- E-book readers. 72% of US public libraries offer e-books [19]. These are both an opportunity and a challenge. Their form factor and basic usability settings can make them more accessible to some patrons, but the lack of advanced accessibility features, content usage restrictions, and interfaces (compared to print) can exclude some users [20]. The pace of change in this market and the profusion of competing platforms make accessibility-based decisions more difficult.
- Outreach. Librarians reported that they are unsure of the best way to reach "the disability community," especially in areas where there are special libraries aimed at people with disabilities. Also, once contact is made with disabled patrons there is a good chance that what they need, the library will not have. Couple this with a perception that some patrons insist on solutions they are used to and are not willing to consider alternatives, negotiate, or compromise. This fosters a concern about "inviting trouble" that blocks outreach. The pattern of "drive-by lawsuits" (opportunistic legal actions taken largely to secure court-ordered payment) does not help here.
- Scarcity of information about accessibility. How can libraries inform themselves about accessibility solutions that will work in their environments, especially given how fast technology moves, without needing to dedicate much staff time to the subject? Some librarians indicated that they would prefer to use library-based and vetted information resources rather than vendor sites or generic accessibility resources.
- Installation and setup issues. In addition to the restrictions on libraries' ability to buy and operate hardware and software, libraries must often limit users' abilities to install and operate their own AT or save their set-up (the options and settings they need) for the AT. They may have to reconfigure computers and AT each time they visit or even if they have to leave one computer (to allow another to use it) and then later log-in to another. Staff is usually not available, familiar with the settings on the AT, or able to follow a person around setting up each computer for the patron when they need to use it.

4   Future Work

As part of the needs analysis phase, we will be conducting formal interviews with the different stakeholders in the next few months. We have a shortlist of libraries that we will be approaching to be official partners in the development process. Through these libraries we will collect stakeholder data on entities associated with libraries (staff, IT support, funding agencies, government bodies)

We will also be interviewing other stakeholders (AT vendors, ICT companies, people with disabilities, disability support organizations). We will be attending conferences where these stakeholders convene and also establish one on one communications with individual members of the stakeholder groups. Stakeholder analysis reports are also being developed for various stakeholders.

As part of phase 2, development of the LGS wireframes is currently in progress. As mentioned previously we will be using these in our needs analysis with the stakeholders. Phases 2 (development) and 3 (Evaluation of LGS) will be conducted as scheduled.

The LGS will be including components of the GPII infrastructure that are being developed in the Cloud4all and Prosperity4all projects. The LGS development effort will co-ordinate with these projects to ensure successful completion of the LGS.

5   Conclusions

Libraries face a challenge in providing accessibility services to their patrons. A lack of control on their ICT resources, reduced budgets, cost of AT, unpredictability of AT use, scarcity of information about accessibility issues contribute to the libraries' difficulties in providing service. The LGS has the potential to address these issues. The development of the LGS is ongoing and is happening collaboratively with the other projects building the GPII.

Acknowledgments. The contents of this publication were developed with funding from the National Institute on Disability and Rehabilitation Research, U.S. Department of Education, grant number H133E130028. However, those contents do not necessarily represent the policy of the Department of Education, and you should not assume endorsement by the Federal Government.

References

1. The Association of Specialized and Cooperative Library Agencies (ASCLA). Think Accessible Before You Buy, Questions to Ask to Ensure that the Electronic Resources Your Library Plans to Purchase are Accessible. n.d.,
   http://www.ala.org/ascla/sites/ala.org.ascla/files/content/
   asclaprotools/thinkaccessible/thinkaccessible.pdf
2. The Association of Specialized and Cooperative Library Agencies (ASCLA). Library Services for People with Disabilities Policy, Library Services for People with Disabilities Policy (2001)
3. Graham, I.D., et al.: Lost in knowledge translation: time for a map? Journal of Continuing Education in the Health Professions 26(1), 13–24 (2006)
4. Sudsawad, P.: Knowledge translation: Introduction to models, strategies, and measures, 14 p. Southwest Educational Development Laboratory, National Center for the Dissemination of Disability Research, Austin (2007) (retrieved)
5. Highsmith, J.A.: Agile software development ecosystems, vol. 13. Addison-Wesley Professional (2002)
6. Nerur, S., Mahapatra, R., Mangalaraj, G.: Challenges of migrating to agile methodologies. Communications of the ACM 48(5), 72–78 (2005)
7. Abras, C., Maloney-Krichmar, D., Preece, J.: User-centered design. In: Bainbridge, W. (ed.) Encyclopedia of Human-Computer Interaction, 37th edn., pp. 445–456. Sage Publications, Thousand Oaks (2004)

8. Blomkvist, S.: Towards a model for bridging agile development and user-centered design. In: Human-Centered Software Engineering—Integrating Usability in the Software Development Lifecycle, pp. 219–244. Springer (2005)
9. Chamberlain, S., Sharp, H., Maiden, N.A.M.: Towards a framework for integrating agile development and user-centred design. In: Abrahamsson, P., Marchesi, M., Succi, G. (eds.) XP 2006. LNCS, vol. 4044, pp. 143–153. Springer, Heidelberg (2006)
10. Humayoun, S.R., Dubinsky, Y., Catarci, T.: A three-fold integration framework to incorporate user–centered design into agile software development. In: Kurosu, M. (ed.) HCD 2011. LNCS, vol. 6776, pp. 55–64. Springer, Heidelberg (2011)
11. Hussain, Z., Slany, W., Holzinger, A.: Current state of agile user-centered design: A survey. In: Holzinger, A., Miesenberger, K. (eds.) USAB 2009. LNCS, vol. 5889, pp. 416–427. Springer, Heidelberg (2009)
12. Sy, D., Miller, L.: Optimizing agile user-centred design. In: CHI 2008 Extended Abstracts on Human Factors in Computing Systems. ACM (2008)
13. Representational state transfer, in Wikipedia. n.d.
14. Node.js, in Wikipedia. n.d.
15. Nielsen, J.: Usability engineering. Elsevier (1994)
16. Cook, C., Heath, F.M.: Users' perceptions of library service quality: a LibQUAL+ qualitative study. Library Trends 49(4), 548–584 (2001)
17. Thompson, R.L., Cook, C., Thompson, B.: Reliability and structure of LibQUAL+ scores: measuring perceived library service quality. Portal: Libraries and the Academy 2(1), 3–12 (2002)
18. Thompson, B., Cook, C., Kyrillidou, M.: Concurrent validity of LibQUAL+™ scores: what do LibQUAL+™ scores measure? The Journal of Academic Librarianship 31(6), 517–522 (2005)
19. Library Journal. LJ Survey of Ebook Penetration & Use in U.S. Public Libraries (2010), http://c0003264.cdn2.cloudfiles.rackspacecloud.com/PublicLibraryEbookReport_2.pdf.
20. Junus, S.R.: Chapter 3: E-books and E-readers for Users with Print Disabilities. Library Technology Reports 48(7), 22–28 (2012)

Creating a Global Public Inclusive Infrastructure (GPII)

Gregg C. Vanderheiden[1,*], Jutta Treviranus[2], Manuel Ortega-Moral[3],
Matthias Peissner[4], and Eva de Lera[1]

[1] Raising the Floor – International, Geneva, Switzerland
{Gregg,Eva}@raisingthefloor.org
[2] OCAD University, Toronto, Ontario, Canada
jtreviranus@faculty.ocad.ca
[3] Fundosa Technosite, Madrid, Spain
mortega@technosite.es
[4] Fraunhofer Institute for Industrial Engineering IAO, Stuttgart, Germany
matthias.peissner@iao.fraunhofer.de

Abstract. The current accessibility ecosystem that develops and delivers both assistive technologies and access features in mainstream technologies is not able to keep up, provide the diversity of solutions needed, nor reach more that a small portion of those who need them. To address this a large scale effort was proposed to provide an infrastructure that would allow the ecosystem to evolve into a quite different and purportedly more effective and efficient ecosystem. This paper describes the infrastructure, reports on the progress in securing funding and implementing the various components of the infrastructure. A roadmap for the implementation and a timeline are provided along with a discussion of the major challenges going forward.

Keywords: Accessibility, Digital Literacy, Literacy, Ageing, Cloud Computing, GPII.

1 Why Build a GPII? Why Is It Needed?

There are a number of problems that led to the conclusion that a Global Public Inclusive Infrastructure (GPII) was needed.

The initial problem was identified during standards work on Web Accessibility. One of they key barriers to web access identified by the WCAG working group was the lack of assistive technologies that were affordable by those with limited resources, and that were powerful enough to be able to provide access to modern web content. An attempt to address this gap led to the formation of a consortium called the Raising the Floor Consortium -- whose mission was to identify or create low cost but capable assistive technologies to address the needs of this sector (to 'raise the floor' or base level of access technologies available to all and affordable by all.)

---

* Corresponding author.

C. Stephanidis and M. Antona (Eds.): UAHCI/HCII 2014, Part IV, LNCS 8516, pp. 506–515, 2014.

The consortium quickly realized however that the problem was more complicated and that just trying to create low cost solutions didn't really address many of the problems and, if attempted in isolation, might create others. The consortium also found that people with disabilities were not the only ones facing challenges in using the standard interfaces on mainstream Information and Communication Technologies (ICT), and other products with digital interfaces. There were four interrelated groups who all were experiencing barriers to use of ICT because of their inability to understand and/or use the standard interfaces. These include people who experienced barriers due to disability, literacy, digital literacy, and aging.

The problem in identifying, developing and delivering solutions to these groups was found to be quite severe. AT suppliers and clinicians estimated that only between 3% to 15% of people who need special interfaces were getting them. Although there were sometime hot debates as to which end of this range was more accurate, there was no one who estimated the penetration at higher than 15%.

1.1   Five Key Problems

Five key problems were identified as the reason that such a small percentage of those who needed better interfaces were getting them.

1. Solutions don't exist for all types, degrees and combinations of disability, literacy, digital literacy and effects of aging;

      a.   Many groups are too small to be addressed by AT developers and vendors. They just can't afford the cost to develop for them both because of their small size and the difficult and expensive to solve problems they present.

2. Even when solutions do exist, people cannot find them - or don't even know to search for one;

      b.   Consumer are not aware that solutions exist that would address their problems so may not search. And those that do don't know the terms to use to describe what they need – or where to begin looking for it (other than 'google', which results in a massive redundant listing but no understanding).

3. **Solutions costs too much**   (to develop/market/support, to buy, to deliver);

      c.   The high cost to develop and market, and their limited ability to reach people who need their specific solution, keeps the costs of solutions high; higher than many (most of thosewho need it?) can afford. Even for mainstream companies, the costs to train staff and build in solutions reduces willingness to do so (as does limited uptake/use by consumers who remain unaware of them.

4. Solutions are too complicated;

> d. Those solutions that are built-in to mainstream are too hard to find and set up and adjust. And for shared equipment, too hard to keep setting up and then un-setting for the next user.
>
> e. AT are too hard to install; too complicated to use. They also often do the same things in unnecessarily different ways.

5. Solutions don't work across all of the devices and platforms that users encounter in education, employment, travel, and daily life.

> f. Users encounter different devices they must use – but their solutions are almost all designed for just one platform. What do they do when the encounter all the other device they must use each day in different classes, at work, as they travel, at home, and in the community.

Further it was identified that these problems were interdependent.

- Developers/suppliers can't reduce costs (and thus prices) without reaching a broader audience, and without finding a less expensive way to develop, distribute, market and support the products. (They reported that they tried just reducing prices and it had little or no effect.)
- Low incidence groups cost even more to develop for - and without the ability to reach them companies won't/can't take these on.
- Complexity and cost keep many away that do hear about solutions. But the solutions are not affordable or understandable/ usable for them.
- Solutions that might work are not available on all the platforms/device the people have to use. So they don't address the access problem for these people.
- Developers/vendors can't afford to develop solutions on all of the platforms because of the cost – and low sales volume.
- Many who need things, and could use and pay for what is available, don't know about them – so even these sales are lost.

To address this situation it appears that a fundamentally change in the way Accessibility was approached is required. What was proposed was to create some type of common infrastructure that everyone could use that would:

- a) **simplify finding and using** AT and other access solutions, and
- b) **lower the cost** to develop, market, and support AT so that it can cost less to consumers,
- c) create a common framework and cross-platform components to **reduce duplication of effort and increase compatibility**,
- d) and make it easier to **connect developers/vendors with consumers,** especially for smaller market solutions.
- e) make it easier and lower costs for mainstream companies to build access into their products to meet their own and customer accessibility requirements.

Reexamining the issue from the broader perspective also made it clear that the issues couldn't be addressed with the ecosystem, as it currently existed. But replacing the ecosystem is not an option either. So the focus of the consortium shifted to identifying the key contributing problems, exploring why the current ecosystem couldn't meet them, and determining how to grow or strengthen the ecosystem so that it could.

2   The Global Public Inclusive Infrastructure (GPII)

The GPII is an infrastructure that uses the cloud and the capabilities of the ICT to help evolve the access ecosystem so that it is better able to affordably reach and server all the people facing barriers to digital devices due to disability, literacy, digital literacy and/or aging.

2.1   Goals and Components of the GPII

The GPII cannot and does not attempt to directly address the problem identified in the introduction to this paper. Rather it is an <u>infrastructure</u> that is being designed and built to <u>facilitate</u> the efforts of others in the ecosystem (developers, vendors, clinicians, families, funders, etc.) in meeting these needs and addressing these challenges. That is, the goal of the GPII is <u>not to solve</u> but to <u>facilitate</u> or to <u>make it easier for others to solve</u> the problems identified above and to deliver affordable solutions to those who need them.

The role and goal of the *Raising the Floor Consortium* then is to create this <u>global</u>, <u>publicly available</u>, <u>infrastructure</u> to facilitate <u>inclusion</u>   (the GPII) that can

1. Make it <u>easier</u>…

> …for people to <u>find solutions</u> to their access problems
> …for people to <u>instantly invoke what they need on any device the person encounters</u>.
> …for developers to <u>create new solutions</u>.

2. Make it <u>cost less</u>…

> …to <u>create</u> new solutions.
> …to <u>deliver</u> new and existing solutions.
> …to <u>support</u> new and existing solutions.
>   and in this way – to <u>lower the cost to users</u>.

3. Make solutions <u>work across platforms</u> so that…

> …the solutions a person needs appear on <u>any device they encounter</u>.
> …products work in a fashion that is <u>familiar and understandable to each individual</u>.

> ...solutions appear even on devices a person has never encountered before, instantly, and without the person having to understand how it is done.

4. Make solutions available nationally and internationally

> ...in all of the languages and cultures within, and across, nations.

Figure 1 provides a diagram of the major components of the planned GPII, organized by the three major functions of the GPII.

1. **Making it easy to discover what will help a person** access ICT anything with a digital interfaces in general;
2. **Making it possible to invoke the features or services a person needs anywhere, anytime, on any device they encounter**; and
3. **Making it easer, faster, and less expensive** to develop, distribute, market, and support access solutions (devices and services – including both assistive technologies and features on mainstream products).

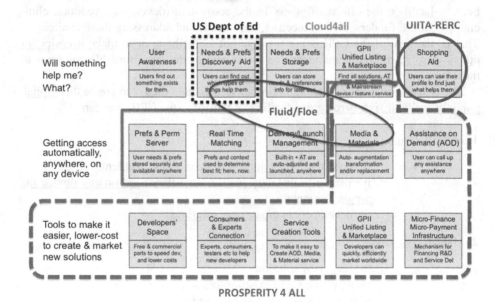

Fig. 1. Major Components of the GPII and the grants providing initial R&D on them

2.2 Vision

The vision of the GPII is to provide an infrastructure that would create a world where everyone, even those with disabilities, or who cannot read, or who cannot deal with technical complexity of any type, and those who are losing sensory abilities or the ability to learn new things due to aging, are able to use any device they encounter.

Any device they approach instantly and automatically changes its digital interface into one that they can use, and that looks and operates in a familiar way.

Any documents sent to them arrive in a form that they can use (print, large print, braille, audio file, accessible ebook, etc) no matter what form it was in when it was sent to them.

Media (movies, audio files, etc) come with captions or video description or text alternatives if they need them in order to use or understand the media.

People with cognitive disabilities for whom technology cannot yet address their needs can call up Assistance on Demand to help them with any interface or documents or media they encounter.

Anyone can set up an "Assistance on Demand" service for anyone who needs it for any reason; visual, hearing, physical or cognitive.   They can set one up out of friends and family members, or set one up with professionals, or both.

Assistive technologies are available as services (pay-as-you-go) so that people are free to try new technologies and switch to them if they are better.   Or people with progressive conditions can easily change their solutions as their conditions change.

Creating new solutions and getting them to market is easy enough that there is a rich set of solutions available including solutions for very small populations.   Consumers and practitioners are also able to become directly involved in the specification and development of new solutions.

Consumer are aware that solutions exist and it is easy for them to find the solutions that best meet their needs.

Solutions are available that are affordable to all who need them in all countries. These solutions are good enough to provide at least full basic access to the technologies they encounter.

3   Who Is Building the GPII

3.1   NPII to GPII and the Establishment of the Raising the Floor Consortium and Raising the Floor – International

Although the initial concept for the GPII began in the United States as a National Public Inclusive Infrastructure (NPII), the concept quickly spread and matured, and within months was rechristened the Global Public Inclusive Infrastructure (GPII). To reflect and facilitate the international nature of efforts, and the strong support and contributions in Europe, the headquarters for the consortium was established as a non-profit organization in Geneva. Switzerland. *Raising the Floor – International* in Geneva now serves as the legal entity and the coordinating point for the *Raising the Floor Consortium* that is building the GPII. The Consortium now includes over 50 companies and organizations from over a dozen different countries. A list of the consortium members can be found at http://raisingthefloor.org.

The GPII is currently under construction with funding from a broad base of funders.

- The National Institute on Disability and Rehabilitation Research, US Dept. of Education under Grants H133E080022 (RERC-IT) and H133E130028 (UIITA-RERC) supported the initial formation of the Raising the Floor Consortium, the coordination of the overall effort, development of the shopping aid, and the first deployment of the GPII in libraries in the US.
- The European Union's Seventh Framework Programme (FP7/2007-2013) grant agreement 289016 (Cloud4all) is funding the development of the core elements for the "auto-personalization from preferences" (APfP) infrastructure including the preference semantic infrastructure, the GPII preference server, the federated repository of information on assistive technologies, the matchmaking architecture, the launch and settings handlers and other run time components and more.
- US Dept. of Education under contract ED-OSE-12-D-0013 (Preferences for Global Access), is funding the development of Needs & Preferences Tools Architecture and the First Discovery Aid.
- The European Union's Seventh Framework Programme (FP7/2007-2013) grant agreement 610510 (Prosperity4All) is funding most of the
- The Flora Hewlett Foundation, the Ontario Ministry of Research and Innovation, the Canadian Foundation for Innovation, has funded much of the foundation research in personalization and the Canadian government the Canadian portion of the Cloud4all work (above).
- The Adobe Foundation, provided the early funding to support the formation of the Raising the Floor Consortium and Raising the Floor – International.
- The Consumer Electronics Association Foundation, IBM, Microsoft and others have provided matching and in-kind contributions to facilitate the GPII work in the Cloud4all and Prosperity4All projects.
- The Raising the Floor Consortium members themselves have also provided matching funding and in-kind funding to support the work.

Figure 1 above shows how some of the major grants relate to the GPII components.

4   GPII Roadmap

The initial research and development of the GPII is being done under support from the Canadian, US, and European governments, and from the foundations, companies, and organizations listed or linked to above. This development work includes implementation and testing of the GPII by companies in their products. Implementations being carried out as part of these R&D activities by AT companies, mainstream companies and research organizations include:

- **3 Operating Systems** – including Windows, Linux, and Android
- **3 Browsers** – including IE, Firefox and Chrome
- **2 Phones** – Smartphones (Android) and Simple Feature Phones (Java)
- **3 Embedded Devices** – Kiosk, Train Ticket Machine, PixelSense

- **2 Home** – DTV, Smart house simulation
- **2 Web Apps** – Online Banking Simulation,   Social Network
- **3 Web/server based AT** – WebAnywhere, SAToGo, Browsealoud
- **4 Installed AT** – NVDA, ReadWrite Gold, SuperNova, Maavis
- **2 Phone AT** – Mobile Accessibility, eCtouch/eCmobile,

(4 of these were not planned or funded but were spontaneous by the companies involved. This will continue in parallel with the funded work)

This development work will be followed by pilot implementations in the field.   The first of these is planned for libraries and just been funded. Other implementations under exploration (but for which funding had not yet been secured) include public access points, educational testing, schools, private homes, travel kiosks, banks (websites and terminals), ecommerce, public service agencies, community centers, and private companies.   A key goal of the pilots is the gathering of metrics on the impact of the GPII in these environments both in terms of increased benefit and decreased cost.

The pilots will then be followed by full rollouts in the different domains where the pilots demonstrate the GPII is ready and beneficial.   These will be done in a staged fashion – with timing based on the ability to support them.

In parallel with the GPII   "auto-personalization from preferences" (APfP) rollouts, the GPII information services will be implemented.   This includes the Unified Listing and Marketplace as well as the DeveloperSpace and its resources. Work on these is funded through 3 grants (each covering different parts) plus matching funding from the Consumer Electronics Association Foundation.

5   Timeline

Initial rollouts in libraries on a development level are expected by next year 2015. This will be followed by full rollouts in test public and university libraries starting the next year.   Rollouts into additional libraries are expected at that year as well.

In parallel with the library rollouts, we will be enabling library patrons to be using the GPII on their personal and home computers as well.   This will be the first general deployment of the GPII in the wild.   This individual deployment will proceed from there based on the success and ability to provide support.

The Unified Listing is expected to be up and in operation internationally by the end of 2014 or the beginning of 2015.   The shopping/Alerting aid is expected to come online for preliminary testing in 2015 with broader deployment in 2016.

The Marketplace is expected to come online in 2016 or early 2017 for initial testing and general use a year later.

6   Challenges

The challenges in this endeavor are significant.   Nothing of this type or scale has ever been attempted. On the plus side, there is almost unanimity that something is needed and the approach on its face seems to be widely accepted as good and powerful approach if it can be pulled off. There is also a very large number of organizations that have gotten behind it and investing themselves in its development and implementation.

On the other side, the infrastructure has a lot of moving parts. Every attempt is being made to both simplify the architectures as much as possible, and to work on an incremental fashion, with basic services implemented first – and more advanced ones added over time. The coordination and planning however are significant challenges.

A second challenge is scaling. Again everything is being designed to be scalable, but until it is deployed and in wide use, it is difficult to anticipate or simulate the loads and unexpected behaviors of the users. Yet when this is done, there will be people depending on it – so failure has significant implications for individuals. The model to be used for the rollout will be important here.

Adoption and incorporation of GPII compatibility in assistive technologies and mainstream products is essential to the GPII's success. Here a chicken and egg situation arises. The GPII works well only if it is deployed widely and works with the access technologies. Until it is deployed however there is little incentive to make access technologies compatible with it. The strategy being used to address this is a combination of selecting domains such as the libraries where there is a demonstrated need and a containable environment. There is also high motivation for access technology vendors to want to have their products work with the system. We are also identifying particular assistive technology applications where the GPII provides unique advantages even for individual vendors. Finally we are developing tools to make it easy to build GPII compatibility into their products. Still this is a definite challenge area.

Funding and sustainability is a fourth challenge. We have had two offers to completely fund the infrastructure by industry. When we explained that they may be less interested because there were two key rules 1) that there could be no data-mining of the needs and preference information on any of the users, and 2) the needs and preference information could not be used to direct advertising (otherwise if we were an insurance company we would like to have our advertising sent to all those who were easily confused) both companies agreed and withdrew their offer. Operating such an infrastructure as a public trust without monetizing it in any way that might be a disadvantage to the users, creates some sustainability challenges. Fortunately, the operation of the "auto-personalization from preferences" (APfP) capability is very light on both server CPU and bandwidth. With continually dropping IT costs, and no human service (other than system maintenance) involved in the infrastructure, the overall cost once up should be nominal. If the service is indeed beneficial, then the cost should be dwarfed by the benefit. To secure funding however this needs to be demonstrated and proven.

7   Conclusion

The Global Public Inclusive Infrastructure (GPII) is a novel and ambitious attempt to take a systematic and holistic approach to addressing a set of severe and growing problems regarding the ability to provide usable interfaces to those who cannot use standard interfaces well or at all. Because we are moving rapidly to a technology based society, incorporating digital interfaces into every aspect of life and into every device around us (including those needed for activities of daily living), the inability to provide usable interfaces to all but a fraction of those who need is as significant challenge and an important priority.

8   Participation

The effort to build the GPII is an open one and any and all are invited to join in. People with every type of skill are needed. The efforts can be followed on http://GPII.net, http://raisingthefloor.org, http://Cloud4all.info and http://Prosperity4All.eu. There are also two dozen papers in these proceedings on different aspects of the GPII work. For those interested in more in-depth information, or who would like to join in, the work of the consortium is conducted in public on the WIKI at http://wiki.gpii.net and the lists at http://lists.gpii.net.

Acknowledgments. This research was funded by the European Union's Seventh Framework Programme (FP7/2007-2013) grant agreement 289016 (Cloud4all) and 610510 (Prosperity4All), by the National Institute on Disability and Rehabilitation Research, US Dept. of Education under Grants H133E080022 (RERC-IT) and H133E130028 (UIITA-RERC) and contract ED-OSE-12-D-0013 (Preferences for Global Access), by the Flora Hewlett Foundation, the Ontario Ministry of Research and Innovation, and the Canadian Foundation for Innovation, by Adobe Foundation, and the Consumer Electronics Association Foundation, with support from IBM, Microsoft, and the participating partners. The opinions and results herein are those of the authors and not necessarily those of the funding agencies.

The GPII Unified Listing

Gregg C. Vanderheiden[1], Valerio Gower[2], and Amrish Chourasia[1]

[1] Trace Center, University of Wisconsin-Madison, USA
{gv,amrish}@trace.wisc.edu
[2] CITT, IRCCS Fondazione Don Carlo Gnocchi, Milano, Italy
vgower@dongnocchi.it

Abstract. Individuals with disabilities are often unable to find assistive technology that meets their needs. While different databases of assistive technologies currently exist, individuals with disabilities are not aware of all of them and unable to take advantage of them. The Global Public Inclusive Infrastructure (GPII) Unified Listing's objectives are 1) to create a single unified listing, that covers not only assistive technologies that relate to accessing ICT but also includes access features built directly in to main-stream ICT as well. 2) to create an open marketplace of accessible and personalizable solutions. The unified listing will be bidirectionally federated with databases such as EASTIN. Development of a method to harmonize and federate the data contained in the different databases is complete and work is underway to create a mechanism to extract information relevant to ICT access from the federated data.

Keywords: Federated databases, EASTIN, accessibility, assistive technologies, access technologies.

1   Introduction

Assistive technologies and access technologies typically cater to small segments of the overall population. There are some products such as Jaws (Freedom Scientific) that are used much more widely than a typical AT product [1] but the typical user base for an AT product is quite small. Additionally, AT developers and vendors often do not have resources to market their products widely. As a result, potential users of AT have a difficult time finding AT that might fit their needs. AT that meets their needs may be available but due to the lack of a resource that allows them to know about it, it is invisible to users who need it. As a solution to this problem, databases of AT have been created. Some of these databases include AbleData, European Assistive Technology Information Network (EASTIN), Open Source Assistive Technology Software (OATS), Open Accessibility Everywhere Group (OAEG) etc.

- Abledata: Abledata's database of assistive technology has over 40,000 products that are available from domestic and international sources to consumers, organizations, professionals, and caregivers within the United States. It is sponsored by the National Institute for Disability and Rehabilitation Research. [2]

C. Stephanidis and M. Antona (Eds.): UAHCI/HCII 2014, Part IV, LNCS 8516, pp. 516–525, 2014.

- EASTIN: The EASTIN website is run by a European network of member organizations running established national information systems in their Country [3]. The EASTIN website aggregates disability product information from its member databases. It contains information on more than 70,000 products and 20,000 AT manufacturers, suppliers and retailers. The databases represented in the EASTIN website include:
  — Portale SIVA (Italy) (http://portale.siva.it/);
  — Rehadat (Germany) (http://www.rehadat.de/)
  — HMI-Basen (Denmark) (http://www.hmi-basen.dk/);
  — DLF Data (UK) (http://www.dlf-data.org.uk/);
  — Handicat (France) (http://www.handicat.com/);
  — Vlibank (Belgium) (http://www.vlibank.be/);
  — Catàlogo de Ayudas Técnicas (Spain) (http://www.catalogo-ceapat.org/)
  — Vilans (Holland) (http://www.vilans.nl/)

The EASTIN database follows the ISO 9999:2011 standard . The ISO 9999 method is considered to be the most widely used method to classify assistive technology devices. The ISO 9999 is a three-level classification system that clusters AT products round "CLASSES" (e.g. mobility, communication, recreation, etc.), then round "SUBCLASSES" (e.g. within class "mobility": powered wheelchairs, cars adaptations, etc.), eventually round "DIVISIONS" (e.g. within subclass "powered wheelchairs": electric motor-driven wheelchair with manual steering, electric motor-driven wheelchair with powered steering, etc.). Each ISO 9999 classification item has a numerical code: for instance, item "electric motor-driven wheelchair with powered steering" has the code 12.23.06, where the first two digits stand for Class 12 "mobility", the following two digits stand for subclass 12.23 "powered wheelchairs" and the last two digits stand for this specific division [4].

- OATS: It is a web based one-stop "shop" for end users, clinicians and open-source developers to meet, exchange notes, promote new ideas, develop new software and download reliable open-source AT software [5]. The OATS website currently hosts more than 150 items of open source assistive technology software.
- OAEG: The key partners of the AEGIS consortium, a European Funded project (AEGIS project, n.d.), together with users' representatives and the active support of the Scientific Advisory Board have developed an Open Accessibility Everywhere Group (OAEG) with the aim to promote the uptake of the AEGIS accessibility open source solutions through a coherent set of incentives and ultimately standardization, and maintain and upgrade the AEGIS Open Accessible Framework and the individual open source software resulting from the project, after the project's lifetime. The OAEG website includes information on accessibility standards, a blog aggregator, and a repository of open source AT software and resources for development [6].

While these databases serves the needs of individuals with disabilities, lack of co-ordination between them means that users still have to search each of these databases individually. In many cases, they might not be aware of the database thus presenting the original problem again, i.e. the lack of information about AT. Co-ordination amongst databases is difficult as each of the databases follows its own conventions and as a result even similar fields in the various databases are different. For example, the "manufacturer name" field EASTIN database is conceptually the same as the field "entity" in the OAEG database.

Mainstream ICT also includes access features that make the products more usable and accessible. Currently, except for the Global Accessibility Reporting Initiative (GARI) database that lists the access features in mainstream phones, tablets and apps [7], there is no other resource that lists access features in mainstream ICT.

AT developers may face restrictions from the established marketplaces for selling their products. Popular marketplaces such as the Apple App Store, Google Play reserve the right to reject an application if it does not conform to their guidelines. Developers also often sell their software directly to avoid paying transaction fees to the marketplaces, or to provide discounts.

To address these challenges, a federated listing of assistive products, called as the Unified Listing was proposed under the Cloud4all project. The Cloud4all is a European Union funded project under the seventh framework program and advances the concept of the Global Public Inclusive Infrastructure (GPII) [8]. The GPII will provide an infrastructure that extends from the content and service providers (authors of Web and ICT content) to the devices used to access these content and services. It builds on existing ICT/Web/Cloud/Accessibility standards and work and will provide additional infrastructure to make it easier to apply and use them to provide anywhere, any device, any content accessibility [9].

The objectives of the Unified Listing are [10]:

- To create a single unified listing, that covers not only assistive technologies that relate to accessing ICT but also includes access features built directly in to mainstream ICT as well.
- To create an open marketplace of accessible and personalizable solutions

2   Targeted Users of the Unified Listing

- Consumers
- Manufacturers
- Vendors
- Clinicians, Teachers, Vocational Counselors, and other Professionals Family, Friends, Caregivers, and others close to consumers
- Funding Agencies
- NGO and other organizations supporting consumers
- Government Funders and Policy makers
- Public

3   Approach

The Unified Listing is a "lossless" "crediting" Federated Database. It contains a full copy of the record fields for the databases it federates with as well as a set of standard common fields. All data is clearly identified with its origin(s) and use data fed back to sources for their crediting and reporting. Maintaining record data for all federating databases also facilitates their matching and use of GPII UL federated data [10].

The unified listing data structure is based on the EASTIN data structure. The EASTIN database aggregates the contents of eight databases on assistive technology products. In order to reflect the contents of all contributing databases, the UL dataset will be the union of the fields of the source databases. However, this may also lead to redundancy as the same fields might be referred to by different names in different databases. To avoid redundancy, similar concepts with different names in different databases will be mapped. For example, the "manufacturer name" field in EASTIN databases is conceptually the same as the field "entity" in the OAEG database).

In the Unified Listing database each record will be represented by a "multi-layer" structure (Table 1) there will be a layer for storing the product description of each of the source databases and a layer for the product description of the GPII Unified Listing as well as each available translation of each database. Specific product settings will also be part of the record. There will also be a "unique product ID" that will allow the Unified Listing to track the same product coming from different databases – and different versions of the same product.

The preliminary dataset for AT products in the Unified Listing is represented in Fig. 1. Each product record is made up of a single GPII product info and N original source product info. If the product is one of the "Cloud4all compatible" applications (i.e. it has been adapted to work with the cloud4all infrastructure), a link to the json file with the specific settings of the product is also included in the dataset.

4   Federation of the Unified Listing with EASTIN

A bidirectional federation between EASTIN network and GPII Unified Listing will be established in such a way that the users of the GPII Unified Listing web portal can access information coming from the EASTIN databases, and users of the EASTIN Web Portal can access information coming from the GPII Unified Listing.

The EASTIN search engine provides a specific set of APIs to receive input data from the EASTIN information providers (online databases) and make them visible in the EASTIN portal. The EASTIN search engine calls a set of Web Services that must be implemented by any information provider that aims to send data to the engine. Both the Web Service functions and the exchanged data format have been standardized by the EASTIN consortium and these standards must be followed by the external information providers. To provide data retrieved by the EASTIN search engine from the EASTIN databases to the GPII Unified Listing, a specific set of Web Services has been be implemented within the Cloud4all project that contains functions

Table 1. Structure of Unified Listing database record

GPII global unique product sync number	5475		
GPII Product Name	Dasher		
GPII Manufacturer Name	Cavendish Labs-Inference group		
GPII Description	Dasher is a special on screen keyboard that….		
…	…		
Information Provider (name-country)	EASTIN-SIVA (IT)	EASTIN-HMI (DK)	AbleData (US)
Product Name	Inference group Dasher	Dasher	Dasher
Product Code (in info prov. DB)	15478	5478	487
Primary ISO code	22.36.18 Input Software	22.36.18 Input Software	-
Manufacturer info	The Inference group	Cavendish laboratory	Inference group
Text description in original language	Dasher è un software gratuito che permette di scrivere…	Auf dem Bildschirm erscheint ein vertikal angeordnetes...	Dasher is a text entry system…
Image			-
…	…	…	…

Specific Settings

Setting name	values
Font size	10- 38 pt
Scanning speed	slow, medium, fast
Voice output	on; off
…	…

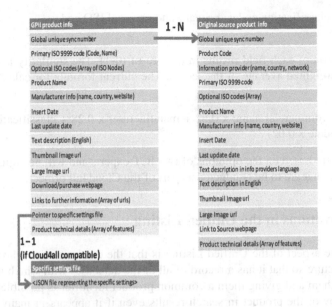

Fig. 1. Preliminary dataset for AT products in the Unified Listing

to extract data using the EASTIN search engine. These Web Services are to be exposed by the EASTIN search engine and will be accessed by a specific application aimed at collecting the data retrieved from EASTIN into the GPII Unified Listing database. (Since the data source is marked when a search is carried out, the fact that the GPII Unified Listing will be part of the EASTIN network will not cause a problem since the data received by GPII Unified Listing from the GPII Unified Listing (Because because it is part of the EASTIN network) can be ignored.)

Details on the federation between the Unifield Listing and EASTIN can be found in the paper "Federating Databases of Assistive Technology Products: Latest Advancements of the European Assistive Technology Information Network" by Gower, Andrich,& Agnoletto to be presented at HCII 2014 Conference [11].

5   Product Similarity

As the Unified Listing will federate information from various sources, it is very likely that the same products could be listed more than once in the listing. In order to prevent this, an algorithm for product similarity is under development [12]. Similarity is a property of a couple of product records A-B. Similarity represents the probability that product described in record A is the same as the one described in record B. The fields to be compared for assessing product similarity are:

- Commerical name
- Manufacturer: name and country

- ISO 9999 classification codes: primary and optional ISO codes
- Insert date

The comparison of each field results in a score of (0-1). The similarity is then calculated as the weighted average of the scores. The current formula for calculating similarity is:

Similarity = (commercial name x 0.62 + manufacturer x 0.28 + classification codes x 0.08 + insert date x 0.02)

The weights are based on the opinions of two ICT experts and will be adjusted further based on tests that are to be conducted as part of the Cloud4all project.

6   Innovations in the Unified Listing

An innovative aspect of the Unified Listing is that the database uses a layered rather than flat structure so that it has a record of all of the databases with which it federates. By aligning them and giving them a common product identifier is possible to provide only one copy of the product in search results even if it appears in many databases. Once it is found an individual can flip through the different descriptions of the product from different databases if they wish. Or look for a description in a language they are most familiar with. The database will allow users to specify preferred languages and the database will automatically display results in the most preferred language that exists for that entry. (It will also auto-translate – but this is of less quality). Because of this 'single record' ability, the user does not need to find the same products repeated many times in search results. Also, because of this feature is possible for differences between databases to be detected and/or corrections to be made to multiple layers of a record. The synchronization with the other databases will then return a corrected record that would match the format for each of the different databases. For the fields are common, a correction need only be made once. Where they differ the change, on the Unified Listing may have to be made to different layers, but this is fairly straightforward for a manufacturer. (Much easier than going to each of the different databases providers and looking up a record in order to correct it.) Federation with the Unified Listing therefore will provide the ability not just access the information in the Unified Listing but also to have corrections that are made in it automatically fed back to each of the databases that federate with it, either directly or with moderation, eliminating the need to reenter data. This approach also solves a major complaint of companies that often will not update any databases because they get requests from so many. The ability to go to one location and correct entries for their products and have it propagate to all of the other databases is of great interest to them.

But perhaps the greatest/largest innovation in the unified database is its coverage of not only assistive technologies but also the access features in mainstream products. As mentioned previously, the only database where this currently exists is the GARI database for mobile phones that was generated in response to government mandate. No similar database exists however for anything outside of the phone accessibility features. The Unified Listing will provide information for the first time on both assistive technologies and on access features in mainstream ICT. It will also draw in the data from GARI and provide a much easier to use interface for consumers – a common complain of GARI. As a result, for the first time, users will be able to conduct a single search and find not only assistive technologies but features that exist in mainstream technologies that they would otherwise not be aware of. It will also help them to determine which of several mainstream devices might be usable directly by them.

To provide information in different languages the database will both store multiple languages for a record where they exist and couple with automatic translation engines from Google to make it easier to serve information in multiple languages. Currently databases are usually available only in one or two languages. In fact the reason that many duplicate databases exist is because they are developed in different languages. The Unified Listing, with its multilayer data records, will allow viewers to store and present different language translations of the data. The translations will be handled using a combination of auto-translation and human correction using crowdsourcing techniques. The auto-translation could also transform the records in to accessible formats.

Important for sustainability, the Unified Listing has also championed a new practice wherein all federated database records that originated from another database are clearly marked as to their origin. The power of a truly federated database is the fact that the efforts to maintain the data can be spread across many database teams who then share the results. However, if the databases are anonymously federated, it can begin to look like all of the databases are redundant. This can cause some or most to lose their funding. Therefore the origin of the data is important to preserve. In addition the unified database will also be introducing another innovation in that it will track the number of times that data from another database was accessed in the Unified Listing. These usage statistics are then fed back to the original source database so that that database can report not only the number of searches done on their database, but also the number of searches done on their data remotely.

7   Open Marketplace

Accompanying the Unified Listing will be an Open Marketplace. Whereas the Unified Listing will be comprehensive, and list all products available from all vendors and marketplaces (e.g. the iOS App Store, Google Play, Microsoft's App store etc.) the Open Marketplace will only contain products that a vendor chooses to sell through the Open Marketplace. The purpose of the Open Marketplace is not to compete with the other marketplaces, or to carry a full range or as many products as possible. Instead the purpose of the Open Marketplace is to provide those individuals or companies who cannot market or market internationally themselves with an easy mechanism for selling their product internationally. This will include the ability to automatically handle the financial transactions needed to purchase products in currencies other than the manufacturer's base currency. Where products are located in any of the app stores, users will be able to find them easily using the Unified Listing, which will then direct them to whichever app store the product resides. If it is in the Open Marketplace and someplace else as well, the user will directed to both. So the Open Marketplace becomes an extension of, or complement to, all of the other markets that are out there. However it is a market where users can upload and sell apps or program or services that cannot be listed elsewhere.

8   Conclusion and Future Work

The Unified Listing is a novel listing that will cover not only assistive technologies that relate to accessing ICT but also include access features built directly in to mainstream ICT as well. It draws upon the standardized data structure of the EASTIN database and will federate multiple databases bidirectionally. The development of the Unified Listing is ongoing. The development effort consists of two phases.

- Development of a method to harmonize and federate the data contained in the different databases, thus creating a single entry point to all available resources. This phase is complete. As part of this activity, the preliminary results of the ETNA and ATIS4AII thematic networks, aimed at creating an online European platform for assistive technology and accessibility devices and services, were studied.
- The next phase involves creating a mechanism to extract information relevant to ICT access from the federated data. This information will be made available to the GPII marketplace so that users who are looking for assistive technology to access mainstream ICT can benefit from it. This phase is currently underway. The success criteria for this phase is a prototype of the single entry point to retrieve the required information and data, and integration of federated data in the GPII marketplace with origin data intact

References

1. WebAIM. Screen Reader User Survey #4 Results (2012),
   http://webaim.org/projects/screenreadersurvey4/ (March 2, 2014)
2. AbleData (2012), http://www.abledata.com/abledata.cfm (March 2, 2014)
3. EASTIN. What is EASTIN (2014),
   http://www.eastin.eu/en-GB/whatIsEastin/index
4. Interational Standards Organization, ISO 9999:2011 Assistive products for persons with disability – Classification and terminology (2011)
5. OATS Consortium, Open Source Assistive Technology Software (2006)
6. AEGIS Consortium. Open Accessibility Everywhere Group (OAEG). n.d. (March 2, 2014), http://www.oaeg.eu/
7. Mobile Manufacturers Forum. Global Accessibility Reporting Initiative. n.d. (March 2, 2014), http://www.mobileaccessibility.info/
8. Cloud4all. n.d. (cited March 10, 2014), http://cloud4all.info/
9. Vanderheiden, G., Treviranus, J.: Creating a global public inclusive infrastructure. In: Stephanidis, C. (ed.) Universal Access in HCI, Part I, HCII 2011. LNCS, vol. 6765, pp. 517–526. Springer, Heidelberg (2011)

10. Unified Listing. n.d. (March 2, 2014),
    http://wiki.gpii.net/index.php/Unified_Listing
11. Gower, V., Andrich, R., Agnoletto, A.: Federating Databases of Assistive Technology Products: Latest Advancements of the European Assistive Technology Information Network. In: 16th International Conference on Human-Computer Interaction, Crete, Greece (2014)
12. Algorithm for Product similarity. n.d. (cited March 2, 2014),
    http://wiki.gpii.net/index.php/Algorithm_for_product_similarity

User Experience in Universal Access

Accessibility Evaluation of an Alternative and Augmentative Communication (AAC) Tool

Sandra Baldassarri[1], Javier Marco[1], Eva Cerezo[1], and Lourdes Moreno[2]

[1] GIGA AffectiveLab, Universidad de Zaragoza, Zaragoza, Spain
{sandra,javi.marco,ecerezo}@unizar.es
[2] Computer Science Department, Universidad Carlos III de Madrid, Spain
lmoreno@inf.uc3m.es

Abstract. People with communication needs use Assistive Technology (AT) to participate in society, be at the family, school among others. There is a variety of different Alternative and Augmentative Communication (AAC) devices due to end-users have different communication needs. AraBoard is an AAC tool developed with the aim to facilitate the functional communication to people with complex communication needs. In this paper, AraBoard tool is presented. In order to ensure the quality of the tool, an accessibility evaluation has been carried out. Following a methodical approach, two main steps have been followed in the evaluation process: (1) Two lists of checkpoints have been developed based on the study and analysis of accessibility standards and related work in the domain of AAC; (2) An evaluation using these resources has been conducted by accessibility experts. The results from the study indicate a high level of accessibility in AraBoard tool, besides some suggestions about new requirements to integrate in the tool have been obtained.

Keywords: Alternative and Augmentative Communication (AAC), accessibility, expert evaluation.

1 Introduction and Background

Many people with communication needs face challenges when trying to communicate with others persons. In order to solve this situation, Alternative and Augmentative Communication (AAC) is a set of strategies and techniques that can be used to support communication for individuals with Complex Communication Needs (CCN) who have little or no functional speech. People who use AAC are a diverse group, as communication disorders can result from physical and/or intellectual disabilities, congenital disability, acquired disability, progressive disorders, and also temporary voice loss [1].

The majority of AAC interventions use unaided techniques (e.g., gesture and sign language) and low-technology devices (e.g., communication-symbol books and letter/word boards). High-technology AACSs are technological aides formed by peripherals, digital ramps and AAC software designed for people with CCNs. They are conceived as support tools for the development of communicational competencies

C. Stephanidis and M. Antona (Eds.): UAHCI/HCII 2014, Part IV, LNCS 8516, pp. 529–540, 2014.
© Springer International Publishing Switzerland 2014

and/or as "communicational prostheses" that help the individual relate to his/her environment.

Recent advancements in technology have expanded the customizability, portability and convenience of AAC devices. The field has witnessed the explosion of mobile technologies (e.g., touch screen smartphones and tablets) with a wide range of apps, including those intended to support communication, extending AAC beyond low-tech systems including new symbol sets, layouts, organizations, selection techniques, and output [2,3,4,5,6,7,8,9]. The advent of digital technologies has resulted in enhanced potential to meet the increased scope of communication needs for a wider range of communication needs [10]. Besides users with cognitive disabilities affecting communication development, these apps can also be used as communication assistants by users with temporal communication difficulties, such us users in a foreign country without knowledge of the local language.

Thanks to mobile technologies, the AAC field is crossing over into the mainstream [11]. The reduced cost and ready availability of AAC apps and mobile technologies has meant that many individuals and their families are becoming active consumers, making their own decisions as they purchase the widely available mobile technologies and apps. But also this "democratization" is expanding to AAC system development, as well [12]. The creation of AAC software applications no longer rests solely in the hands of the traditional assistive technology manufacturers; rather apps are being developed by a wide range of stakeholders, from mainstream programmers to family members requiring AAC tools for their relatives. This model of development differs dramatically from the traditional models of AAC research and development. It supports the rapid development of AAC apps by providing direct links between end consumers and software developers. Unfortunately, this model also has some liabilities. The development of mainstream technologies is largely driven by the needs and preferences of the masses; as a result, these technologies may not meet the needs and skills of individuals with complex communication needs [13], since they are not easily customized, and/or they are not accessible. The limitations are not just restricted to the AAC apps; they also extend to the mobile technologies as well, which use may be difficult or impossible for young children or individuals with motor impairments. Research is urgently needed to tackle these problems to ensure that "democratization" AAC brings benefits for individuals with complex communication needs. We must ensure that communication technology mitigates, and does not exacerbate, disability.

This paper focuses in the study of the accessibility requirements of AraBoard, a shareware application aimed to facilitate the functional communication to people with communication needs. AraBoard allows the creation, edition and use of communication boards especially suited for people with motor disabilities and very basic communication needs.

The structure of the paper is: Section 2 is devoted to present AraBoard tool, formed by two applications: Constructor and Player. Section 3 shows the accessibility evaluation process of AraBoard tool, which includes the development of a checklist and the experts' application of the checklist. In Section 4 conclusions and future work are presented.

2   Alternative and Augmentative Communication (AAC) Tool: AraBoard

AraBoard[1] is a public domain tool developed to facilitate functional communication to people with CCN due to different causes: autism, aphasia, cerebral palsy, etc. The tool has been designed following an Inclusive Design [14] and User Centered Design (UCD) approach [15] in the specific context of users who need AAC technology to communicate. The tool is available for different devices (PC, mobile, tablets) and operating systems (MS-Windows and Android Operating Systems).

AraBoard is formed by two different applications: AraBoard Constructor, for the creation and edition of communication boards and AraBoard Player, for the visualization of the boards previously generated. Each application has a different end user profile. AraBoard Constructor is used by relatives, tutors, educators and therapists; while AraBoard Player is used by the final users (usually children) that have any kind of communicative limitation. Both share the same interface and are used in the same way independently of the device. Moreover, the boards created with the Constructor in one device can be moved, edited and played with the Player in any other device that has AraBoard installed. Each communication board is stored in their own folder in the internal memory of the device, containing the images and audios of each pictogram and an XML file with the board's specification.

In the next sections AraBoard applications are presented as well as the results of a survey completed via web by their users. More detailed information about AraBoard can be found in [16].

2.1   AraBoard Constructor

The AraBoard Constructor application allows tutors and relatives to create and edit communication boards adapted to the particular needs of each user. AraBoard Constructor is characterized by its ease of use in all aspects, since it has a graphical interface designed to make possible anyone to create and edit boards intuitively in a few minutes. Its interface lets to define the number of rows, columns, arrangement of cells, and also to create and configure all elements-visual, auditory, textual, appearance, etc. - that compose the communication board. The possibility to create boards from one to thirty-two cells extends the range of users, from people with severe motor disabilities and very basic communication needs (see Fig. 1.a), offering boards with few cells but with large dimensions, to users with advanced communication needs up to boards with 32 cells (see Fig. 1.b). In order to customize the elements composing the board, the application allows the user to enter resources from the ARASAAC pictograms collection [17] and also personal resources like images, photographs, sounds and voice.

---

[1] http://giga.cps.unizar.es/affectivelab/araboard.html

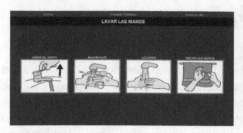

Fig. 1. (a): Simple board for people with severe motor disabilities; (b) Board for people with advanced communication needs

Once the board has been built, the application allows: to export the board in PDF format ready to be printed and used as a communication board in paper, or to save the communication board project, creating a directory in the internal memory of the device for editing or for being used in AraBoard Player.

2.2   AraBoard Player

AraBoard Player is an application that allows users with communication needs to use communication boards previously generated with the Constructor. AraBoard Player shows the board in the full screen, and the user interacts with it by pressing the different cells that compose it. Once a cell has been marked, it plays the audio associated with it (see Fig. 2). In order to be accessible to users with physical disabilities, the audio playback mechanism is designed so that although not stating exactly the desired cell, it always runs the audio associated with the cell closer to the area that has been pressed.

Fig. 2. AraBoard Player

2.3   AraBoard Seen by Its Users

According to the results of a survey carried out to users which have been freely downloaded and used this tool, the users claim to have a high tool's acceptance [16]. During the first year of publication, 295 completed questionnaires have been collected.

Users distinguish as main features that the tool is multiplatform and adaptable to a wide range of users' needs by modifying different parameters like language, number and size of the cells, inclusion or not of audio, selection of colors (background and text), etc. Furthermore, the results reflect that AraBoard Player was mainly used by autistic people. The rest of users presented different types of impairment, which affect their verbal and written expression ability and, the combination of cognitive and motor impairments.

The application is aimed to be used by a higher number and a broad range of final users with communication needs, in an accessible way. In order to ensure this accessibility, a specific accessibility evaluation has been carried out on the AraBoad tool, as it is explained in detail in next section.

3   Accessibility Evaluation of AraBoard Player Tool

An accessibility evaluation done by experts is presented in this section. The evaluation is mainly focused on the AraBoard Player because it is the software which is facing end-users with CCN, although many accessibility requirements are provided by the AraBoard Constructor.

An accessibility evaluation of the AAC tool should be carried out together with its interrelated factors in the AAC environment. For example, communication software is very important, as well as the device the user is employing to access. A variety of AAC device designs and configurations currently exist, because no single device can offer efficient and effective communication to all people with severe communication impairments. The end users of AAC devices are very heterogeneous and with different communication needs access to ICT. Thus, there are a variety of different AAC devices. In this way, AraBoard expands functional communication to a varied range of viable environments due to its compatibility with mobile devices and because of the possibility of directly printing the created communication boards, so that they can be used without any technological device. This feature of AraBoard provides accessibility to the tool. Therefore, the accessibility of the AraBoard Player interface should be evaluated in the different environments in which it is used. In this work, desktop environment is studied.

The evaluation process consists of two steps which are shown below: the generation of a checklist of accessibility requirements and an expert evaluation using the checklist.

3.1   Checklist of Accessibility Requirements for AAC Tools

With the aim of developing a checklist to validate the accessibility in the specific domain of the systems AAC, different works and standards have been distinguished, studied and analyzed to capture the requirements. On the one hand these requirements should help to comply with the characteristics of the AAC tools which should provide support for people with special communication needs; on the other hand, the requirements for access to the software tool must be conformed. In order to obtain these requirements, the following analysis has been made:

1. An analysis of the AAC tool audience was conducted. The data of the user needs were obtained from the results of the end-users survey (see section 2.3).

Resulting of this analysis, needs and users' feedback have been identified. With regard to the suggestions of the users, the level of satisfaction reflected in the results is very high. Their comments show great enthusiasm for the usefulness of the tool. When they were asked about the improvements to incorporate in AraBoard tool, they have coincided on the following improvements:

— Dynamic communication boards that allow linked boards, with the aim of increasing communication needs of users with CCN.
— Functionalities to construct sentences by enabling the accumulation of words and displaying them on screen.
— To provide tutorials, manuals, help guides on characteristics and uses of the tool.
— To allow configuration settings for some features such as speed of response of the auditory messages, ...
— Functionalities for scanning and sweeping through a pushbutton.

2. Following an UCD approach in the specific context of AAC systems, an analysis of related work from the literature and best practices based on formal and experimental studies with real users has been carried out. Works that include characteristics and guidelines for AAC systems [24] [25], and resources of Users Associations [23] [26] among others, have been studied to capture guidelines and requirements that provide the support to the accessibility validation.

Resulting of this analysis, the Checklist (1) shown in Table 1 has been obtained. Each checkpoint of this list should be evaluated by an expert and he/she assigns a value from the following: "No" it is not satisfied, "Yes" if it is satisfied, "Partial" which means it fulfills the checkpoint only in part, and "NA" if it is Not Applied. Not Applied is considered in the case of some accessibility requirements of AAC systems that were decided not to be included in AraBoard because of taking into account the needs of real end-users (following the UCD approach).

Table 1. CHECKLIST (1): Requirements in the specific context of AAC systems

Cod	Requirements for the Player tools	AraBoard Player	Complemented by AraBoard Constructor	Yes, No NA, Par
Theme communication boards and configuration settings				
1	The Player tool has levels (dynamic boards)	No		No
2	Enable to change the boxes size	No	It is possible with the Constructor	Yes
3	Enable to change the boxes layout, position and orientation	No	The Constructor can create templates with different layouts and orientations	Partial
4	Provide a different background colour for each semantic category	No	It is possible with the Construc-tor	Yes

Table 1. (*continued*)

	Content: Pictographic symbols and configuration settings			
5	Allow to introduce external pictures	No	The Constructor allows it	Yes
6	If it allows external pictures, users are informed about which sizes and formats can be used.	No	The Constructor notifies only formats	Partial
7	Allow to include: a picture along with a word|literal?, the pictures are distinguished from the literals?, only a picture?, only a literal?	Partial	The Constructor allows the option of a picture along with a word/literal. Yes, they are distinguishable. However, if the number of rows and columns increases, it becomes more difficult distinguish the text.	Yes
	Output: Messages and configuration settings			
8	Provide flexibility about the number of messages	No	The number of messages is fixed by the Constructor.	Yes
9	Provide speech output digitized speech output or synthetic speech output	Yes	The Constructor allows recording speech and loading audio (digitized speech output)	Yes
10	Provide flexibility in size and edit of messages?	Partial	The Constructor allows change the message associated to symbol.	Partial
11	Allow independence between output messages and hearing scan	NA (lack of the scanning technology)		No
12	Allow volume selection and volume adjustments	NA		NA
	Input: Access and configuration settings			
13	Allow direct access	NA		NA
14	Allow to access with a pointer: Spaciousness to provide enough movement to reach all boxes, Accuracy (boxes with size enough to press comfortably) and strength (it is possible to press the boxes with an average force)	Yes (desktop environments)	It is dependent on the number of rows and columns of the communication board. It is interdependent of the device and platform. It is possible to design boards to ensure spaciousness and accuracy with the Constructor.	Yes
15	Allow to access through eye tracking	NA		NA
16	Allow to access using AT	No, NA	No, It does not. In addition, it does not provide information about it, because this tool is an Assistive tool	No
17	Allow to use assisted scanning technology (and setting configuration)	No		No

3. An analysis of the software accessibility standards and related work about how to develop a user agent (such as a player) have been distinguished and analyzed. These standards have been: the standard ISO 9241-171:2008 - Guidance on software accessibility [21] and standard User Agent Accessibility Guidelines (UAAG) 2.0 [22] of the WAI [18], highlighting the UAAG 2.0 includes comply with the Web Content Accessibility Guidelines (WCAG) 2.0 [20]. With the knowledge gained from this study, a Checklist (2) (see Table 2) has been made. The procedure to assign values to each checkpoint is the same that the one described for the checklist (1).

Table 2. CHECKLIST (2): Requirements based on Software Accessibility Standards

Cod	Requirement ISO 9241 -171	NA/ Yes/ No/Par.	Mapping with other standards
			Suggestion/Comments
8 GENERAL GUIDELINES			
8.1	**Names and labels for user interface elements**	NA	**Guideline 4.1. – UAAG 2.0**
	Provide a name for each user interface element, meaningful names. Make names available to AT		This requirement would be a recommendation if the tool had as an aim to provide support to the AT
8.2	**User preference settings**	NA	**Guideline 2.7 –UAAG 2.0**
	Enable easy individualisation of user preferences. Enable adjustment of sizes and colours of common user interface elements. Enable user control of timed responses		If new features are incorporated in tool as: scan, languages, etc., it is recommended to incorporate user preference settings
8.3	**Special considerations for accessibility adjustments**	NA	**Several guidelines - UAAG 2.0**
	Make controls for accessibility features discoverable and operable. Avoid interference with accessibility features. Inform user of accessibility feature activation		In current version, there are not adjustments because the possible accesses are always available (enabled) and are intuitive to use. But if they are incorporating new features that require configuration settings, it would be recommended to design and integrate mechanisms to keep the simplicity and operability of the interface components
8.4	**General control and operation guidelines**	No	**Guidelines 3.1., 3.2 y 3.4- UAAG 2.0**
	Optimise the number of steps required for any task. Provide "Undo" and/or "Confirm" functionalities. Allow warning or error messages to persist		These requirements should be integrated in future versions.
8.5	**Compatibility with AT**	No	**Guidelines 4.1, 5.1- UAAG 2.0**
	Enable communication between software and AT. Allow AT to change focus and selection. Allow AT to access resources. Accept the installation of keyboard and/or pointing device emulators.		AraBoard tool could be considered a closed system such that the installation of additional technology assistive (it itself is a support product) is not allowed, however: access through Assisted Scan should be provided.
8.6	**Closed systems**	NA	
	Read content on closed systems. Announce changes on closed systems		If it is considered as a closed system, these requirements should be included

Table 9. (*continued*)

	9 INPUTS		
9.1	**Alternative input options**	No	**Guidelines 2.1, 5.1- UAAG 2.0**
	Provide keyboard input from all standard input mechanisms. Provide pointer control of keyboard functions. Provide speech recognition services		The access through screen reader should be provided.
9.2	**Keyboard focus**	Partial	**Guidelines 1.3, 5.1 -UAAG 2.0**
	Provide focus cursor. Provide high visibility focus cursor. Restore state when regaining focus		Access via keyboard is provided only for menu elements. It is not provided for the board boxes (mouse only). The visibility of keyboard focus should be provided
9.3	**Keyboard input**	No	**Guidelines 2.1, 5.1- UAAG 2.0**
	Enable full use via keyboard. Provide adjustment of delay before key acceptance. Provide accelerator keys. Reserve accessibility shortcut key assignments.		Keyboard shortcuts, time setting, allowing configuration settings ... should be provided
9.4	**Pointing devices**	Partial	**Guideline 1.3, 2.12- UAAG 2.0**
	Provide direct control of pointer position from external devices. Provide easily-selectable pointing device targets. Provide adjustment of pointer speed. Provide adjustment of pointer movement direction		Some of these requirements are fulfilled: the mouse-pointing is easy to use but has a strong interdependence of the number of rows / columns, cell/box size and board layout type. Besides, an assistance take the direction to when the user is pointing one box would be recommended.
	10 OUTPUTS		
10.2	**Visual output (displays)**	Partial	**Guideline 1.3-- UAAG 2.0**
	Provide a visual information mode usable by users with low visual acuity. Provide keyboard access to information displayed outside the physical screen		It is recommended to allow to change colours to highlight the focus of the cursor. The access through screen reader should be provided.
10.3	**Text/Fonts**	No	**Guideline 1.4 UAAG 2.0**
	Enable users to set minimum font size. Adjust the scale and layout of user interface elements as font-size changes		It is recommended to allow to change settings such as the font size.
10.4	**Colour**	Yes	**Guideline 5.1 UAAG 2.0 (comply with WCAG 2.0)**
	Provide individualisation of colour schemes. Allow users to individualise colour coding. Provide contrast between foreground and background		The constructor allows it, however, we would recommend that these requirements may be included in the Player
10.6	**Audio output**	Partial	**Guideline 1.5, 1.6, 2.9, 2.11. ..UAAG 2.0**
	Enable control of audio volume. Enable adjustment of audio output. Use specific frequency components for audio warnings and alerts. Synchronise audio equivalents for visual events		The volume control is through the device (PC, Mobile, Tablet ...) but the volume of the AAC should be independent of the device.
	11 ONLINE DOCUMENTATION, HELP AND SUPPORT SERVICES.		
11.1	**Documentation and Help**	Partial	**Guideline 3.3 UAAG 2.0**
	Provide understandable documentation. Provide user documentation in accessible electronic form. Ensure help is available in accessible forms		Although there is documentation, this information and help should be extended and provided for the AAC and not in an external web page.

3.2   Expert Evaluation with the Use of Checklists

Two human experts on accessibility have evaluated AraBoard. Both experts are professionals with the training required and a high degree of Software Accessibility knowledge, besides skills in the use of assistive technologies among others topics, with more than five years of experience in software accessibility evaluations according to standards. The experts have revised manually accessibility issues with the use of the checklists created. The steps followed are:

1. Each expert studied the checklists for the evaluation of the accessibility of the tool.
2. Each expert simulated specific accesses and features.
3. Each expert elaborated a preliminary evaluation report
4. Both reports were compared and a discussion of the results was carried out to confirm the level of conformance the final accessibility.

The results of expert evaluation ({NA, Yes, No, Partial} for each checkpoint) are shown in the fourth column of Table 1: "Checklist (1): Requirements in the specific context of AAC systems", in the third column of Table 2: "Checklist (2): Requirements based on Software Accessibility Standards". Additionally in Table 2 some suggestions are provided. A discussion of the data and conclusions are shown in the next section.

3.3   Discussion of the Data

The AraBoard tool was designed involving users, and this is perceived in the end-users survey (see section 2.3). The purpose of the tool is to provide flexibility in the creation of boards with different layout and sizes, providing external resources as ARASAAC symbols/pictograms, different languages, etc. and all these features integrated into an easy interface. They have a very positive perception of the tool. Users suggested essentially the integration of scan technology.

There are some checkpoints of the checklists which have not been considered (they have been assigned by "Not applied" (NA)) because they are not required by the tool since they come into conflict with user reviews collected in the design phase of the system. Of the remainder, it is noticeable that the evaluation of the AraBoard tools achieves a high level of accessibility, because the most of the checkpoints have achieved rating of "Yes" and others "Partial", except checkpoints related to accessibility requirements such as: provide scan system and configuration settings and provide Documentation and Help.

4   Conclusions and Future Work

In this paper, an overview to the AAC tools has been introduced and the AraBoard tool is described. A user survey was conducted as previous work. To complete this evaluation, an assessment of the accessibility has been carried out and presented in this work. The evaluation process has included two parts: first, the development of checklists applicable to AAC tools based on accessibility standards. These checklists provide evaluation resources for other works in the AAC domain; and second, the evaluation by experts with the use of the checklists.

Taking into account the findings of the results achieved, some suggestions are provided for future releases of the tool. In addition, other requirements proposed by some users have been already included in the new version in process, such as: synthetic speech output, user preference settings and scan.

Acknowledgements. This work has been partly financed by the Spanish Government through the DGICYT contract TIN2011-24660, by the CYTED project 512RT0461, by the Research Network MAVIR (S2009/TIC-1542 and the MULTIMEDICA project (TIN2010-20644-C03-01).

References

1. Waller, A.: Public Policy Issues in Augmentative and Alternative Communication Technologies A Comparison of the U.K. and the U.S., Interactions May-June 2013, pp. 68–75 (2013), doi:10.1145/2451856.2451872
2. Smalltalk, http://www.aphasia.com/products/apps/smalltalk
3. Sc@ut, http://asistic.ugr.es/scaut/index.php
4. Plaphoons, http://www.xtec.cat/~jlagares/f2kesp.htm
5. TalkTable, http://www.gusinc.com/2012/TalkTablet.html
6. TICO, http://www.proyectotico.com/wiki-en/index.php/Home
7. PictoDroid Lite, http://www.accegal.org/pictodroid-lite/
8. Baluh, http://blog.baluh.org/
9. CPA, http://www.comunicadorcpa.com/
10. Light, J., McNaughton, D.: The changing face of augmentative and alternative communication: Past, present, and future Challenges. Augmentative and Alternative Communication 28(4), 197–204 (2012)
11. Rummel-Hudson, R.: A revolution at their fingertips. Perspectives on Augmentative and Alternative Communication 20(1), 19–23 (2011)
12. Menard, L.: A Review of Innovative Communication Apps for Students with Special Needs. In: Proceedings of Society for Information Technology & Teacher Education International Conference, pp. 3292–3298 (2011)
13. Beukelman, D.: AAC for the 21st century: Framing the future. Presentation at the State of the Science Conference for the RERC on Communication Enhancement, Baltimore (2012)
14. Newell, A.F., Gregor, P.: User sensitive inclusive design— in search of a new paradigm. In: Proceedings on the 2000 Conference on Universal Usability (CUU 2000), pp. 39–44. ACM, USA (2000)
15. ISO, ISO 9241-210:2010 Ergonomics of human-system interaction – Part 210: Human-centred design for interactive systems, http://www.iso.org/iso/catalogue_detail.htm?csnumber=52075
16. Baldassarri, S., Marco, J., García-Azpiroz, M., Cerezo, E.: AraBoard: A Multiplatform Alternative and Augmentative Communication Tool. In: 5th International Conference on Software Development and Technologies for Enhancing Accessibility and Fighting Info-exclusion, DSAI 2013 (2013) (in press in Procedia Computer Science - Journal – Elsevier)

17. ARASAAC pictographic symbols from Aragonese Portal of Augmentative and Alternative Communication, Spain, http://www.catedu.es/arasaac/index.php
18. W3C, Web Accessibility Initiative (WAI) (2011), http://www.w3.org/WAI/
19. ISO, ISO/IEC 40500:2012. Information technology: W3C Web Content Accessibility Guidelines (WCAG) 2.0, http://www.iso.org/iso/iso_catalogue/catalogue_tc/catalogue_detail.htm?csnumber=58625
20. W3C, WAI, Web Content Accessibility Guidelines (WCAG) 2.0, W3C Recommendation (December 11, 2008), http://www.w3.org/TR/WCAG20/
21. W3C, User Agent Accessibility Guidelines (UAAG) 2.0, W3C Last Call Working Draft (November 7, 2013), http://www.w3.org/TR/UAAG20/
22. ISO, ISO 9241-171:2008 - Ergonomics of human-system interaction – Part 171: Guidance on software accessibility, http://www.iso.org/iso/iso_catalogue/catalogue_tc/catalogue_detail.htm?csnumber=39080
23. American Speech-Language-Hearing Association (ASHA). Augmentative and Alternative Communication (AAC), http://www.asha.org/public/speech/disorders/AAC/
24. Light & Drager, AAC technologies for young children with complex communication needs: State of the science and future research directions. Augmentative and Alternative Communication 23(3), 204–216 (2007)
25. Owens, J.S.: Accessible Information for People with Complex Communication Needs. Augmentative and Alternative Communication 22(3), 196–208 (2006)
26. Augmentative and Alternative Communication (AAC) Connecting Young Kids (YAACK), http://aac.unl.edu/yaack/index.html

Four Data Visualization Heuristics to Facilitate Reflection in Personal Informatics

Andrea Cuttone, Michael Kai Petersen, and Jakob Eg Larsen

Technical University of Denmark (DTU)
Department of Applied Mathematics and Computer Science
Cognitive Systems Section
Matematiktorvet 303B, 2800 Kgs Lyngby, Denmark
{ancu,mkai,jaeg}@dtu.dk

Abstract. In this paper we discuss how to facilitate the process of reflection in Personal Informatics and Quantified Self systems through interactive data visualizations. Four heuristics for the design and evaluation of such systems have been identified through analysis of self-tracking devices and apps. Dashboard interface paradigms in specific self-tracking devices (Fitbit and Basis) are discussed as representative examples of state of the art in feedback and reflection support. By relating to existing work in other domains, such as event related representation of time series multivariate data in financial analytics, it is discussed how the heuristics could guide designs that would further facilitate reflection in self-tracking personal informatics systems.

Keywords: personal informatics, quantified self, self-tracking, information visualization, feedback, reflection, heuristics.

1 Introduction

In recent years self-tracking and lifelogging have received increased interest with the introduction of a wide variety of low-cost mobile apps, wearable computers, and sensors. These devices allow easy collection of data that can describe various aspects of human behavior. However, making sense of the ever increasing amounts of everyday self-tracking data retrieved across multiple domains create new demands for turning data points and trends into affordances for action. The reflection stage is a fundamental component in modeling and using Personal Informatics (PI) systems [18,8,16] to facilitate an understanding of self-tracking data reflecting daily habitual patterns and to make such data actionable for behavioral change [9]. Different solutions have been suggested to facilitate self-reflection, including the usage of charts [18,20,21,6], avatars [22,12,14], notifications [1], narrative [23] and abstract art [7,10]. Although these solutions may facilitate increased awareness due to the fact that behavioural aspects are being observed, the process of turning observations and insights into actions remains a challenge. Even a recent review of activity trackers in *The New York Times*[1]

---

[1] http://www.nytimes.com/2014/01/30/technology/personaltech/
review-the-fitbit-force-activity-tracker.html Last accessed Jan 29, 2014.

C. Stephanidis and M. Antona (Eds.): UAHCI/HCII 2014, Part IV, LNCS 8516, pp. 541–552, 2014.

emphasized that while self-tracking devices enable the user to collect behavioral data, they fall short of assisting the user in learning how to change habits.

One element of personal informatics is the iterative process with self-reflection questions phrased by a user and feedback provided by a self-tracking system to answer those questions. However, we suggest that state-of-the art systems offer fairly limited flexibility in terms of the types of questions that can be phrased, and the possible feedback that can be provided. In a broader perspective, the self-tracking data obtained might be characterized as quantitative time series data which combines behavioral data with associated discrete events. Similar to how financial analytics like those provided by Bloomberg might combine a vertical flow of business related earning reports or corporate news updates, with distinct time stamped markers, outlined horizontally within the continuous timeline fluctuations of stock values. Thus hierarchically adding layers of relevant information embedded both within the chart and in adjacent panels linked to external events, that may facilitate interpretation or be a direct cause of rising or falling trends visualized in the data [26]. The emphasis of integrating distinct interpretable events in continuous flows of quantitative data within financial analytics reflects a need for these interfaces to provide a foundation for taking concrete action related to aspects of optimizing profits or avoiding a loss. We suggest that these advances within financial analytics software for interpretation of complex data may both provide underlying design patterns for long term comparison of trends in multivariate flows, as well as defining thresholds which could likewise turn quantified self generated data into actionable parameters for optimizing lifestyle in personal informatics systems.

2   Related Work

Several frameworks have been proposed to formalize the reflection process in personal informatics. Li et al. [19] identify six kinds of questions for reflection: *Status* (what is my situation now?), *History* (what was my situation in the past?), *Goals* (what future status should I aim for?), *Discrepancies* (how does my status compare with my goals?), *Context* (what affects my status?), *Factors* (how are different attributes related?). Moreover, two alternating phases are defined: *Maintenance* (known relation between status and behavior) and *Discovery* (not known goals or effect of behavior). Fleck et al. [8] define a multi-layer reflection framework: *Description, Reflective Description, Dialogic Reflection, Transformative Reflection, Critical Reflection*. Each layer builds on top of the previous, and corresponds to a deeper understanding of personal data. Guidelines for facilitating reflection are proposed, including supporting questions and providing multiple perspectives on the data. Rivera et al. [24] apply Boud's reflective learning framework to personal informatics, and identifies two levels of reflection: *Triggering* (active notification or passive feedback) and *Recalling* (aggregating, contextualizing, visualizing).

Several feedback schemes have been suggested including avatar-based feedback that employs a virtual object to represent a judgment on behavior. These solutions exploit participants' empathy with the virtual avatars to persuade them in adopting positive behavioral changes. For example, *Fish'n'Steps* [22] provides feedback about daily step count as a virtual fish, *Ubigreen* [12] using virtual trees and polar bears to provide feedback on green transportation habits, and *UbiFit Garden* [5] represents fitness activity as a virtual garden. *Spark* [7] visualizes physical activity as abstract art through an ambient display, whereas *Lifestyle Stories* [23] provides feedback about mobile sensing personal data in form of stories composed by events of various categories. Many commercial self-tracker systems employ a combination of traditional charts, maps and dashboards (see for example *Nike+*[2], *Fitbit*[3], *Basis*[4], *Jawbone UP*[5], *Mint*[6], *DailyBurn*[7], *Moves*[8]).

3   Reflection as Data Analysis

We suggest to treat reflection as data analysis on personal information. What are the crucial questions or answers that analytics should provide? In Bloomberg financial analytics the ability to couple external events to timeline charts appears crucial for interpreting the causality behind the data. One might in a more general context consider online news media like *The Wall Street Journal* or Twitter feeds an expanded version of this paradigm, providing not only the current market data but also a highly curated selection of background material as well as live updates on events, that would provide the necessary foundation for making informed decisions. Even in admirably simple single sensor quantified self apps like Fitbit, limited to measuring the number of steps taken during the day or week, data might provide valuable insights into user behavior. But it would require that annotations are added automatically with calendar events or smartphone location data, thereby enriching the representation beyond the current ability of manually attaching labels. We see a similar potential for advanced self-tracking devices with multiple sensors like Basis, which likewise translates complex patterns of behaviors into singular goal oriented habits to be fulfilled on a daily basis at regular hours. Coupling calendar events for monitoring heart rate related to specific physical tasks, indicating how this sensor data is correlated to differences in sleep patterns, or influenced by levels of exercise across weeks, might provide additional value.

A user may want to retrieve specific information from his own dataset (current status, progress), or explore it for finding interesting patterns. In order to facilitate this analysis, we propose to use data visualization, that is the representation of data using position, size, shape, color, and text [3]. Visualization facilitates analysis by exploiting the human visual system, which is extremely

---

[2] http://nikeplus.nike.com/plus/
[3] http://www.fitbit.com/
[4] http://www.mybasis.com/
[5] http://jawbone.com/up
[6] http://www.mint.com/
[7] http://dailyburn.com/
[8] http://www.moves-app.com/

good at processing large quantities of information and spotting patterns. Visualization is widely used in Exploratory Data Analysis [28], a statistical technique for exploring datasets, in order to gain insights, obtain a better understanding, spot patterns, trends, correlation, and outliers. In many cases, the data analyst does not know in advance which specific question to ask, so he can explore the data in order to find interesting patterns. This process is highly iterative, as once a question has been posed, its answer often leads to more questions to be asked. Similarly, in PI systems the user may not know which questions to ask, or may not be interested in a specific question but in exploring his own data for curiosity. Indeed, one of the barriers for reflection is not knowing which questions to ask to personal data [18]. We can represent this iterative process as a cycle between questions asked, and feedback provided. We define *question space* the set of all possible questions, and *feedback space* the set of all visualizations. Each feedback type can answer one or more questions, and each question can be answered by one or more type. In data analysis, there are a number of common questions that can be asked: distribution of values (mostly around a central value and gradually less on the sides? Mostly for a value and very rapidly decaying? Multiple peaks?), grouping and outliers (are there values much different than most of the others? Are items clustered into groups?), correlation (what is the relation between x and y? Is there a linear, quadratic, exponential, sinusoidal trend?), geographical (how are values related to locations? Are there locations with similar values?), connectivity (are there items related together? Are there items which are more tightly connected? Are there non-connected items?) We identify the most relevant questions for the goal of self-reflection, and we summarize them into heuristics.

4   Design Heuristics

In this section we introduce four design heuristics that can be applied as a guideline for creating and evaluating interactive visualizations of self-tracking data with the aim to facilitate effective exploration of personal data and make such data actionable for behavior change. Throughout the discussion of the heuristics we relate to existing state of the art self-tracking systems using Fitbit and Basis as examples of personal informatics systems with interactive visualizations. We do not intend to criticize these two systems in particular, but rather consider them as representative and illustrative examples of state of the art in personal self-tracking systems. The scope of the discussion is limited to facilitating the reflection process, while acknowledging that further discussion is needed in terms of providing actionable items as well as other aspects of reflection in personal informatics as mentioned in the Related Work Section.

4.1   Make Data Interpretable at a Glance

Often users want to obtain answers to a question with the minimal effort and time. For this reason, data visualizations optimized for interpretation at a glance are needed, in order to provide a swift overview of personal tracking activities, and to augment and support subjective recollection. Quantified self apps like Fitbit or Basis may aim to simplify visualization of complex patterns by transforming the collected measurements into single activity dashboard dials or progress bars reflecting goal oriented accomplishments. Figure 1 shows the personal dashboard provided by Fitbit, which reduces the collected data to simple indications of (daily) goal fulfillment (percentage) and an overview of daily activity levels. Although it provides an overview of the level of goal fulfillment this division of activities into separate silos makes it a challenge to interpret the data in a larger context. In contrast financial analytics interfaces like those provided by Bloomberg [26] may contain large amounts of data which is nevertheless made interpretable based on established conventions for using dynamically changing font colors to signify up- or downward moving prices, or positive negative outlooks based on earning reports, which when collapsed form independent parallel layers of color coded trend lines that remain surprisingly legible on top of contrasting neutral background screens.

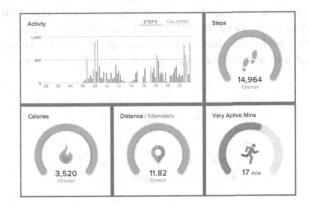

Fig. 1. The Fitbit dashboard show daily goal fulfillment (percentage) and an overview of daily activity

While data visualizations can be very useful they may be complex and difficult to interpret and understand. The complexity of visualizations can range from data-poor, informal infographics for the general audience to complex, rigorous scientific visualization aimed at scholars. Several issues should be considered when designing a visualization, including the technical and domain knowledge of the users, the goals of reflection (exploring data, asking specific questions, testing hypothesis), the time and effort expected from the user (a quick glance or a long interaction?). We suggest to provide a simple visualization as the starting point, and allow advanced users to dynamically increase the level of complexity and details. The usage of explanatory elements, such as text, axes, legends, annotations can greatly facilitate the comprehension. Visualizing data is often compared to storytelling, especially in the fields of journalism and business reporting. Some authors prefer to present the data as raw as possible, with little or no annotations and highlighting, in order to give the reader full freedom in the interpretation of the facts behind the data. Others prefer to editorialize the data to various degrees, by marking samples, comparing with other distributions, providing comments. We argue that a certain editorialization is good for PI system, as it can act as a persuasive force towards positive behavior. For instance a fitness tracker system that encourages the user to be more active by visualizing and forecasting the positive consequences.

4.2   Enable Exploration of Patterns in Time Series Data

There are two fundamental patterns to analyze: global trends (does the variable increase, decrease or remain constant over a period of time?) and periodic patterns (does the variable value change with a repeating pattern, for example hourly, weekly or yearly?).

Although several self-tracking app interfaces emphasize simplified dashboard representations of accumulated data which limits exploration, the recently added Basis sleep monitoring goes far beyond the previous single modality heatmaps by breaking down total sleep duration into the different phases of rapid eye movement (REM) and deep sleep, thereby making it possible to translate these periodic patterns into quantifiable aspects of mind and body refresh, see Figure 2.

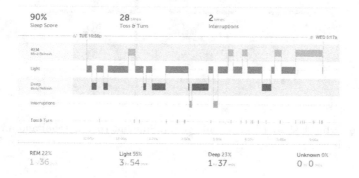

Fig. 2. The Basis sleep visualization interface also break continuous sleep data into discrete sleep phases including rapid eye movement (REM), light, and deep sleep

Time series analysis is a common task for self-trackers, which may be interested in observing changes over time, periodic patterns, rate of change, and time left to reach goals. The most common representation for time series data is *line plots*, which allow to easily see the overall change over time of a variable. Due to the unavoidable noise, it is useful to add *trend lines* such a LOWESS [4] or least squares. This enable the support of forecasting on future status if the current behavior is kept or modified, thus a prediction of future values can be

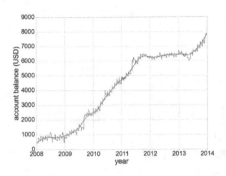
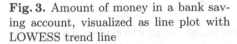

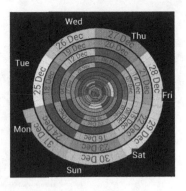

Fig. 3. Amount of money in a bank saving account, visualized as line plot with LOWESS trend line

Fig. 4. Number of steps per day represented as a spiral heatmap, with colors from white (low) to red (large)

visualized [15]. As an example Figure 3 shows the amount over time of money in a bank saving account with a clear trend of increase among the individual month-to-month fluctuations. When the duration of time periods is a factor, *timelines* may be used to represent events in a linear layout to captures the temporal sequence.

Line plots and linear timelines do not however facilitate the exploration of periodic patterns, which are characteristic of human behavior. A familiar metaphor for displaying regular patterns is a calendar. A *calendar heatmap* represents each day as a cell, and the variable value as the color shade of the cells. Cells can be aligned for example by day of the week to allow to spot weekly patterns. Spirals have been recently proposed [17] as another representation to facilitate the exploration of periodic patterns in the quantified-self domain. A *spiral heatmap* represents each time unit as an arc in the spiral, and variable value as the color shade of the arcs. By choosing different periods, periodic patterns at various time scale can emerge. Figure 4 show a step count value over time as calendar as spiral heatmaps, with a color scale ranging from white (small count) to red (large count).

4.3   Enable Discovery of Trends in Multiple Data Streams

Financial analytics may also offer inspiration in terms of comparison of key performance indicators in multivariate data. As an example *The Wall Street Journal* allows for extensive personalization when exploring moving averages for smoothing fluctuating trends in time series data, high and low relative to previous values, weighted blends of values and their variation over time, which may be further customized based on choice of display graphics, adjustable time frames or sensitivity of measures.

The Basis activity details visualization only allows the user limited possibilities of exploring the relations between multiple time series data in an adjustable

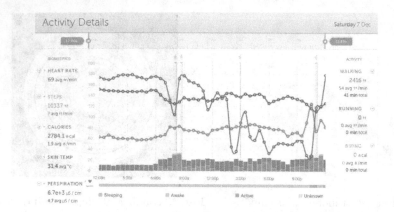

Fig. 5. The Basis Activity Details visualization allows the user to explore the relations between multiple biometric time series data (heart rate, steps, calories, skin temperature, perspiration, and activities) in an adjustable time interval

time interval, as shown in Figure 5. Multivariate analysis is the process of analyzing multiple variables together, in order to find and understand their relation. In the simplest case, two variables x and y are to be compared, and the following relations can exist: direct correlation (y increases as x increases), inverse correlation (y decreases as x increases), or no correlation. For example, fitness trackers may be interested in how the weight loss is affected by exercise and food intake, or productivity trackers may be interested in how coffee intake, sleep patterns, and exercise affect productivity.

The relation between two variable can be visualized as a *scatterplot*, where each variable is represented on one axis. Scatterplots allow to easily spot trends and outliers. If more than two variables are to be compared, a *scatterplot matrix* allows to inspect all possible combinations. A scatterplot matrix is a array of $n \times n$ scatterplots, where the scatterplot S_{ij} displays the relation between variables X_i and X_j. Scatterplot matrices are a very powerful tool, but can also be intimidating for users. A simpler version of multivariate visualization is the *Corrgram* [11] which distinguishes positively and negatively correlation between pairs of variables using color-coding. As a constructed example Figure 6 and 7 show the relation between coffee intake, hours at work, hours of sleep, and steps. The coffee intake appears directly correlated with working hours, and inversely correlated with sleep hours, and no correlation seem to be present with number of steps.

Often users do not need to explore relations of variables between each others, but they are interested in the change of multiple variables over time. A *Streamgraph* [2] can be used when it is important to show the contribution of each variable to a total. Each variable generates a section of different height, and the resulting areas are stacked to form a stream. *Small multiples* [27] allow to display multiple facets of a dataset, often in comparison to time. Each variable is displayed separately in his own subview, and subviews are layed out side-by-side to facilitate

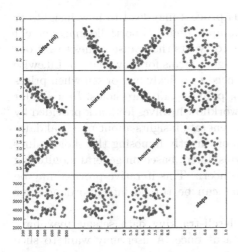

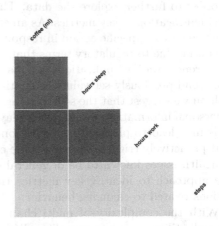

Fig. 6. Scatterplot matrix: all pairs of 4 variables are plotted. The alignment of the data points helps to identify direct, inverse or no correlations.

Fig. 7. Corrgram: the correlation between all pair of 4 variables is represented in a color scale from blue (inverse correlation), grey (no correlation) and red (direct correlation)

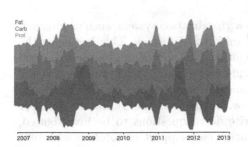

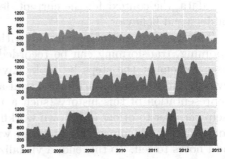

Fig. 8. The composition of dietary intake over time as a streamgraph

Fig. 9. Small multiples: the three variables of dietary intake are shown side-to-side in separate sub-views

comparison. Figures 8 and 9 show the composition of dietary intake over time. The small multiples enable multivariate comparison, and the streamgraph facilitates the understanding of the total caloric intake.

4.4 Turn Key Metrics into Affordances for Action

The emphasis on interaction in data visualization [13] is reflected in a typical analyst workflow including the generation of a data view, exploration of the result, adjustment of parameters or creation of a completely different visualization in order to further explore the data. This process may lead to new insights or the identification of key metrics. As an example, financial portfolio management often requires a specific action in response to events that cause values to get out of bounds due to regulatory terms that trigger alarms for reevaluation. Likewise in currency trading applications one may need to quickly buy or sell when prices transcend previously set values indicating pain or gain thresholds. In a similar fashion we suggest that the self-tracking workflow involves feedback provided by a personal informatics system which may generate insights about personal data. This may lead to phrasing new questions or directly imposing threshold values that proactively trigger responses to be considered, based on general monitoring of health issues known to be of general concern. This iterative process may be one approach to identify key metrics that can be turned into affordances for actions related to changing behavior.

With the complexity of multi channel self-tracking data sets it may have limited utility to try to visualize all data at once. A user may want to slice the data in various ways, such as by time or category. A user may also want to select a specific set of elements that match a given criteria, such as points inside a geographical region, or values between some thresholds. *Filtering* allows to focus on a specific subset of the data. One of the recommended interaction pattern is "Overview first, zoom and filter, then details-on-demand" [25]. *Navigation* may be supported by allowing scroll and zoom views. When focusing on a subset of the data, the context for the current details could hold valuable information to understand behavior.

The long sequence of interactions with a visualization system, such as filtering, zooming, transforming can be recorded in form of *history*. This log helps the user remember the steps he took, navigate in his interaction sequence, undo eventual mistakes and facilitate a trial-and-error exploration. Providing a visual representation of this history (such a timeline or snapshots of the views) can help the user to orient in his own workflow. In the process of reflection, the user may want to document his findings, write down questions to be investigated, add notes to self. To this end, a visualization can support *annotation* with text and sketches.

These interaction techniques can be readily applied in data visualization in personal systems in order to facilitate the reflection process. Imagine a fitness tracking system, where the user is provided with an overview of his activities. He filters the activity log to a specific part of the year. He views his activity both as a timeline of step counter and as a breakdown of his caloric intake and annotated activities.

5   Conclusions

In this paper we have discussed the support of reflection in state of the art personal informatics systems arguing that it is limited in terms of making observations and insights obtained from interactive visualizations of self-tracking data actionable. We have proposed four heuristic principles for the design and evaluation of interactive data visualization feedback that could further facilitate the process of reflection in self-tracking personal informatics systems. Each design heuristic has been discussed on the basis of an analysis of visualization feedback available in state of the art personal informatics systems.

References

1. Bentley, F., Tollmar, K.: The power of mobile notifications to increase wellbeing logging behavior. In: Proc. of the SIGCHI Conf. on Human Factors in Computing Systems, pp. 1095–1098 (2013)
2. Byron, L., Wattenberg, M.: Stacked graphs-geometry & aesthetics. IEEE Transactions on Visualization and Computer Graphics 14(6), 1245–1252 (2008)
3. Card, S.K., Mackinlay, J.D., Schneiderman, B.: Readings in Information Visualization: Using Vision to Think. Morgan Kaufmann (1999)
4. Cleveland, W.S.: Robust locally weighted regression and smoothing scatterplots. Journal of the American Statistical Association 74(368), 829–836 (1979)
5. Consolvo, S., McDonald, D.W., Toscos, T., Chen, M.Y., Froehlich, J., Harrison, B., Landay, J.A.: Activity sensing in the wild: a field trial of ubifit garden. In: Proc. of the SIGCHI Conf. on Human Factors in Computing Systems, pp. 1797–1806 (2008)
6. Cuttone, A., Lehmann, S., Larsen, J.E.: A mobile personal informatics system with interactive visualizations of mobility and social interactions. In: Proc. of the 1st ACM Int. Workshop on Personal Data Meets Distributed Multimedia (2013)
7. Fan, C., Forlizzi, J., Dey, A.A.: A spark of activity: Exploring informative art as visualization for physical activity. In: Proc. of the 2012 ACM Conf. on Ubiquitous Computing, pp. 81–84 (2012)
8. Fleck, R., Fitzpatrick, G.: Reflecting on reflection: framing a design landscape. In: Proc. of the 22nd Conf. of the Computer-Human Interaction SIG of Australia on Computer-Human Interaction, pp. 216–223 (2010)
9. Fogg, B.J.: Persuasive technology: Using computers to change what we think and do. Ubiquity (5) (2002)
10. Frick, L.: Experiments in self tracking, http://www.lauriefrick.com/category/work/ (last accessed December 13, 2013)
11. Friendly, M.: Corrgrams: Exploratory displays for correlation matrices. The American Statistician 56(4), 316–324 (2002)
12. Froehlich, J., Dillahunt, T., Klasnja, P., Mankoff, J., Consolvo, S., Harrison, B., Landay, J.A.: UbiGreen: Investigating a mobile tool for tracking and supporting green transportation habits. In: Proc. of the SIGCHI Conf. on Human Factors in Computing Systems, pp. 1043–1052 (2009)
13. Heer, J., Shneiderman, B.: Interactive dynamics for visual analysis. Queue 10(2), 30 (2012)
14. Hekler, E.B., King, A.C., Banerjee, B., Robinson, T., Alonso, M.: A case study of BSUED: Behavioral Science-informed User Experience Design. In: Proc. of the CHI 2011 Workshop on Personal Informatics (2011)
15. Koeman, L., Rogers, Y.: Enabling Foresight and Reflection: Interactive Simulations to Support Behaviour Change. In: Proc. of the CHI 2013 Personal Informatics in the Wild: Hacking Habits for Health & Happiness (2013)
16. Konrad, A., Whittaker, S., Isaacs, E.: Short and long-term benefits of reflective technologies. In: Proc. of the CHI 2013 Workshop on Personal Informatics (2013)
17. Larsen, J.E., Cuttone, A., Lehmann, S.: QS Spiral: Visualizing Periodic Quantified Self Data. In: Proc. of the CHI 2013 Personal Informatics in the Wild: Hacking Habits for Health & Happiness (2013)

18. Li, I., Dey, A., Forlizzi, J.: A stage-based model of personal informatics systems. In: Proc. of the 28th Int. Conf. on Human Factors in Computing Systems, pp. 557–566 (2010)
19. Li, I., Dey, A., Forlizzi, J.: Understanding my data, myself: supporting self-reflection with ubicomp technologies. In: Proc. of UbiComp 2011, pp. 405–414 (2011)
20. Li, I., Medynskiy, Y., Froehlich, J., Larsen, J.E.: Personal informatics in practice: improving quality of life through data. In: CHI 2012 Extended Abstracts on Human Factors in Computing Systems, CHI EA 2012, pp. 2799–2802 (2012)
21. Li, I., Froehlich, J., Larsen, J.E., Grevet, C., Ramirez, E.: Personal informatics in the wild: hacking habits for health & happiness. In: CHI 2013 Extended Abstracts on Human Factors in Computing Systems, pp. 3179–3182 (2013)
22. Lin, J.J., Mamykina, L., Lindtner, S., Delajoux, G., Strub, H.B.: Fish'n'Steps: Encouraging physical activity with an interactive computer game. In: Dourish, P., Friday, A., et al. (eds.) UbiComp 2006. LNCS, vol. 4206, pp. 261–278. Springer, Heidelberg (2006)
23. Pavel, D., Trossen, D., Holweg, M., Callaghan, V.: Lifestyle stories: correlating user information through a story-inspired paradigm. In: Pervasive Computing Technologies for Healthcare, pp. 412–415 (2013)
24. Rivera-Pelayo, V., Zacharias, V., Müller, L., Braun, S.: A framework for applying quantified self approaches to support reflective learning. In: Mobile Learning (2012)
25. Shneiderman, B.: The eyes have it: A task by data type taxonomy for information visualizations. In: Proc. of IEEE Symposium on Visual Languages, pp. 336–343 (1996)
26. Sorenson, E., Brath, R.: Financial Visualization Case Study: Correlating Financial Timeseries and Discrete Events to Support Investment Decisions. IEEE Information Visualisation (2013)
27. Tufte, E.R., Graves-Morris, P.R.: The Visual Display of Quantitative Information, vol. 2. Graphics Press, Cheshire (1983)
28. Tukey, J.W.: Exploratory data analysis, p. 231. Reading, Ma (1977)

Measuring the Perception of Facial Expressions in American Sign Language Animations with Eye Tracking

Hernisa Kacorri[1], Allen Harper[1], and Matt Huenerfauth[2]

[1] The City University of New York (CUNY)
Doctoral Program in Computer Science, The Graduate Center,
365 Fifth Ave, New York, NY 10016 USA
{hkacorri,aharper}@gc.cuny.edu
[2] The City University of New York (CUNY)
Computer Science Department, CUNY Queens College
Computer Science and Linguistics Programs, CUNY Graduate Center
65-30 Kissena Blvd, Flushing, NY 11367 USA
matt@cs.qc.cuny.edu

Abstract. Our lab has conducted experimental evaluations of ASL animations, which can increase accessibility of information for signers with lower literacy in written languages. Participants watch animations and answer carefully engineered questions about the information content. Because of the labor-intensive nature of our current evaluation approach, we seek techniques for measuring user's reactions to animations via eye-tracking technology. In this paper, we analyze the relationship between various metrics of eye movement behavior of native ASL signers as they watch various types of stimuli: videos of human signers, high-quality animations of ASL, and lower-quality animations of ASL. We found significant relationships between the quality of the stimulus and the proportional fixation time on the upper and lower portions of the signers face, the transitions between these portions of the face and the rest of the signer's body, and the total length of the eye fixation path. Our work provides guidance to researchers who wish to evaluate the quality of sign language animations: to enable more efficient evaluation of animation quality to support the development of technologies to synthesize high-quality ASL animations for deaf users.

Keywords: American Sign Language, accessibility technology for people who are deaf, eye tracking, animation, evaluation, user study.

1   Introduction

Over 500,000 people in the U.S. use American Sign Language (ASL), a separate language from English, with a distinct word order, linguistic structure, and vocabulary [17]. For various educational reasons, deaf and hard-of-hearing students perform, on average, lower than their hearing peers on tests of English reading comprehension [20-21]; these students therefore have difficulty with text on curriculum materials,

C. Stephanidis and M. Antona (Eds.): UAHCI/HCII 2014, Part IV, LNCS 8516, pp. 553–563, 2014.

captioning, or other media. While it is possible to use videos of actual human signers in educational content or websites, animated avatars are more advantageous for several reasons in these contexts. If the information is frequently updated, it may be prohibitively expensive to re-film a human performing ASL, thus leading to out-of-date information. Computer synthesized animations allow for frequent updating, automatic generation or machine translation, animation flexibility, and collaboration of multiple authors to script a message in ASL. Thus, virtual human characters have been favored by sign language synthesis researchers and many educational-system developers. For example, Adamo-Villani et al. [1-2] investigated digital lessons annotated with ASL animation and signing avatars to improve the mathematical abilities of deaf pupils, Vcom3D [3] focused on sign language software tools for early education curriculum, and Karpouzis et al. [15] proposed an educational platform for learning sign language.

Relatively few sign language animation synthesis systems have been developed, due to challenging linguistic aspects of ASL. Signers use facial expressions and head movements to communicate essential information during ASL sentences, and state-of-the-art sign language animations systems do not yet handle facial expressions sufficiently to produce clear and understandable animations. Our lab has recently focused on modeling and synthesizing facial expressions. To evaluate our models, we typically ask native ASL signers to view our animations and then answer comprehension and subjective Likert-scale questions [8–11][16]. The challenge is that signers may not consciously notice a facial expression during an ASL passage [10][14], and some facial expressions affect the meaning of ASL sentences in subtle ways [14], thereby making it difficult to invent stimuli and questions that effectively probe a participant's understanding of the information conveyed specifically by the signer's face.

In this paper, we analyze native ASL signers' perception of ASL animations with and without facial expressions, and videos of a human signer. In a prior study [13], we experimentally evaluated ASL animations with and without facial expressions, using videos of a human signer as an upper baseline. The participants answered subjective and comprehension questions and their eye movements were recorded via an eye-tracker to investigate whether their eye movements can reveal the quality of the animations being evaluated. We found that when viewing videos, signers spend more time looking at the face and less frequently move their gaze between the face and body of the signer, compared to when viewing animations. We also found that the fixation time on the face and the frequency of gaze transitions between the face and the hands was significantly correlated with the subjective scores participants assigned to the animations. Thus, there is potential for eye-tracking to serve as a complementary or alternative method of evaluating ASL animations.

A limitation of this prior study was that we did not observe any significant correlation between these two metrics and participants reporting having noticed a particular facial expression nor their comprehension questions scores. In this paper, we present a second, deeper analysis of the data with more fine-grained Areas of Interest (AOIs) such as the upper face and the lower face of the human or animated signer in the stimuli. This new study also considers a new metric, called Total Trail Distance, which is the aggregated distance between fixations normalized by the stimuli duration.

2   Eye-Tracking and Related Work

The eye tracking literature has been previously surveyed by several authors [6][12][19]. The main benefit of eye tracking for human-computer interaction studies is that it delivers a detailed record of position and timing as subjects gaze at visual stimuli; and it does so in both an unmediated and unobtrusive manner that precludes the use of interruptive methods such as Talk-Aloud protocols [5]. In prior work, eye tracking has been used to record the eye movements of deaf participants who viewed live or video-recorded sign language performances; we are not aware of any prior studies using eye tracking to evaluate sign language animations.

For instance, Cavender et al. [4] explored the feasibility of presenting sign language videos on mobile phones. This study evaluated the understandability of sign language when displayed at different sizes and video-compression rates. Participants were eye-tracked while viewing the videos and then answered evaluation questions. They found that participants' gaze transitioned away from the signer's face during fingerspelling, hand movement near the bottom of the screen, or when the signer pointed to locations outside the video. The participants' total trail distance was shorter for the video stimuli that received the highest subjective scores; and the mouth region of the signer received the highest fixation counts.

Muir and Richardson [18] performed an eye tracking study to explore how native British Sign Language (BSL) signers employ their central (high-resolution) vision and peripheral vision when viewing BSL videos. Their earlier studies had suggested that signers tend to use their central vision on the face of a signer, and they tend to use peripheral vision for hand movements, fingerspelling, and body movements. In [18], native BSL signers watched three videos that varied in how visually challenging they were to view: (1) close-up above-the-waist camera view of the signer with no fingerspelling or body movement, (2) distant above-the-knees view of the signer with use of some fingerspelling, (3) distant above-the-knees view of the signer with use of fingerspelling and body movements. Proportional fixation time was calculated over the following five AOI's: upper face, lower face, hands, fingers, upper body, and lower body. Results indicated that detailed signs and fingerspelling did not accumulate large proportional fixation time, indicating that participants used their peripheral vision to observe these aspects of sign language video. In all three videos, the AOIs on the face region received the most proportional fixation time: 88%, 82%, 60% respectively. In contrast, Video 3 included upper body movement, and participants spent more time looking at the upper body of the signer. Comparing sub-regions of the face, during video 1, participants looked at the upper face 72% and lower face 16%, but during video 2 (more distant view of the signer), they looked at the upper face 47% and lower face 35%. Both these results are of interest to our current study because they indicate that participant's gaze will likely shift under conditions of sign language videos that have lower clarity (i.e., signer is more distant from the camera), in an effort to search for the AOI with the most useful and visible information. This indicates that studying proportional fixation time on the face might be a useful way to analyze eye-tracking data when participants are viewing sign language videos (or animations) of different quality.

Emmorey et al. [7] conducted an eye tracking experiment to explore the differences in eye movement patterns between native and novice ASL signers. It was hypothesized that novice signers would have a smaller visual field from which to extract information from a signer. In turn, this would lead to: less time fixating on the singer's face, more fixations on the lower mouth and upper body, and more transitions away from the face to the hands and lower body. Unlike the previous studies, [7] used live signing performances that presented two stories constructed with differing amounts of fingerspelling and use of locative classifier constructions (signs that convey spatial information, investigated in our prior work [9]). The goal of the study was to induce more transitions in novice signers due to their restricted perceptual span. The results showed that both novice and native signers displayed similar proportional fixation times (89%) on the face. In contrast to this pattern, novice signers spent significantly more time fixating on the signer's mouth than native signers, who spent more time fixating on the signer's eyes. It was also observed that neither novices nor native signers made transitions to the hands during fingerspelling, but did make transitions towards classifier constructions.

3   Prior Work, Eye Tracking Metrics, and Hypotheses

In prior work [13], we conducted a user-study in which native ASL signers watched animations of ASL (of varying levels of quality) while an eye-tracker recorded them. In that prior study, we examined whether there was a relationship between the quality of the stimuli and participants' proportional fixation time on the face of the signer or the number of "transitions" between the face and the hands of the signer. We examined the following hypotheses [13]:

- H1: There is a significant difference in native signers' eye-movement behavior between when they view videos of ASL and when they view animations of ASL.
- H2: There is a significant difference in native signers' eye-movement behavior when they view animations of ASL with some facial expressions and when they view animations of ASL without any facial expressions.
- H3: There is a significant correlation between a native signer's eye movement behavior and the scalar subjective scores (grammatical, understandable, natural) that the signer assigns to an animation or video.
- H4: There is a significant correlation between a native signer's eye movement behavior and the signer reporting having noticed a facial expression in a video or animation.
- H5: There is a significant correlation between a native signer's eye movement behavior and the signer correctly answering comprehension questions about a video or animation.

We found that, when viewing videos, signers spend more time looking at the face and less frequently move their gaze between the face and body of the signer in support of H1. We also found that H3 was supported for animations, there were significant correlations between these two eye-tracking metrics and participants' responses to subjective evaluations of animation-quality. However, the results for H2, H4, and H5 were inconclusive and H3 was only partially supported for videos. A limitation of our earlier study was that we did not distinguish between the upper (above nose) and lower face of the signer in the video. Muir and Richardson [18] had distinguished between these parts of the face, and they found changes in proportional fixation time on the face of signers when the visual difficulty of videos varied. Since many grammatically significant ASL facial expressions consist of essential movements of the eyebrows, in this paper, we separately analyze the upper and lower face.

Since Cavendar et al. [4] had found a relationship between the path length of eye gaze the quality of videos of human signers, in this paper, we also measure the "trail length" of the fixations of the participants eye gaze when watching stimuli. Given that Emmorey et al. [7] found that less skilled signers transitioned their gaze to the hands of the signer more frequently, we predict that there will be longer "trail lengths" of the eye gaze in our lower-quality animations, which are harder to understand.

4   User Study

In [13], participants viewed short stories in ASL of three versions: a high-quality "video" of a native ASL signer, a medium-quality animation with facial expressions based on a "model," and a low-quality animation with no facial expressions. The stories were scripted and performed by native signers, and each story was produced in all three versions. The video size, resolution, and frame-rate for all stimuli were identical. Participants responded to three types of questions after viewing a story: First, they answered Likert-scale subject questions about the grammatical correctness, ease of understanding, and naturalness of movement. Next, they answered on a Likert-scale as to whether they noticed a facial expression during the story. Finally, they answered four comprehension questions about the content of the story. The comprehension questions were designed so that wrong answers would indicate that the participants had misunderstood the facial expression displayed [14].

In [13], only two areas of interest (AOIs) were considered for the analysis of participants' eye gazing behavior: "Face" and "Hands". In this paper, we divided the "Face" AOI to "Upper Face" and "Lower Face" AOI based on the signers' nose-tip height. Fig. 1 illustrates these areas of interest for the animations of the virtual character (with or without facial expressions) and for the videos of the human signer. Note that during a small fraction of time signers may move their hands in front or close to their face thus the two AOIs could overlap. Currently, this is handled by a simplifying assumption that the face should take precedence, and that is why the "Hands" AOI has an irregular shape to accommodate the "Face" AOI. We believe that this limitation in our analysis had a minimal effect on the results obtained, given that the signer's hands do not overlap with the face during the vast majority of signing.

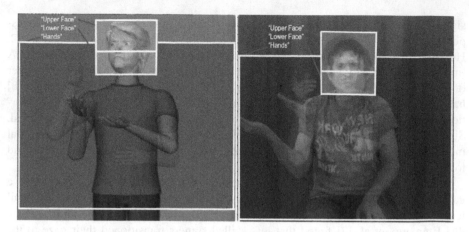

Fig. 1. Screen regions for the upper face, lower face, and hands AOIs

The AOIs were defined identically for all animations (with and without facial expressions). While the area (width x height) of the face AOIs were preserved, the vertical-horizontal ratio was slightly different for human videos: The human would often bend forward slightly, therefore the region of the screen where his head tend to occupy is a little lower compared to the animated character. So, we set the nose-tip line slightly lower for the human signer; to preserve fairness, we kept the area of the "Upper-Face" and "Lower-Face" AOIs as similar as possible between the animated character and human signer (97.6% for the upper and 102.6% for the lower portion).

As described in detail in [13], eleven ASL signers were recruited for the study and were recorded by an eye tracker as they watched the animations and videos. Eye tracking data was excluded from analysis if the eye tracker equipment determined that either of the following conditions had occurred for over 50% of the time of the video or animation: (a) the eye-tracker could not identify the participant's head and pupil location or (b) the participant looked away from the computer screen.

5   Results

This section presents the results of the eye-tracking data analysis from the eleven participants, and the discussion is structured around three types of metrics:

- Transition frequency (i.e., the number of transitions between pairs of AOIs, divided by story duration in seconds) between the upper-face AOI and the hands-body AOI and between lower-face AOI and hands-body AOI.
- Proportional Fixation Time on the upper-face AOI or on the lower-face AOI (i.e., the total time of all fixations on the AOI, divided by story duration).
- Time-Normalized Total Trail Length (i.e., the sum of the distances between all of the participant's fixations, divided by the story duration in seconds).

Transition frequencies are displayed as a box plot in Fig. 2, with the min/max values indicated by whiskers, quartiles by the box edges, and median values by a center line (not visible in Fig. 2(a) because the median value was zero). On the basis of Kruskal-Wallis tests, significant differences are marked with stars ($p < 0.05$). The three groups displayed include "Video" of a human signer, a "Model" animation with facial expressions, and a "Non" animation with no facial expressions. In Fig. 2, there was a significant difference between the transition frequency between upper-face and body-hands, comparing Video and animations (Model + Non), which supports hypothesis H1, but not hypothesis H2.

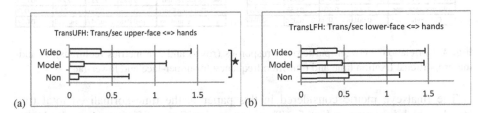

Fig. 2. Transitions per second between: (a) the hands-body AOI and the upper-face AOI ("TransUFH") and (b) the hands-body AOI and the lower-face AOI ("TransLFH")

In order to better understand where participants were looking during the videos or animations, we also calculated the proportion of time their eye fixations were within the upper-face or lower-face AOIs; the results are shown in Fig. 3. In this case, a significant difference was shown between Video and both types of animation (Model and Non) when considering the lower-face AOI in Fig. 3(b). Only the pair Video vs. Non was significantly different when considering the upper-face AOI in Fig. 3(a).

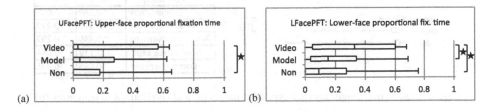

Fig. 3. Proportional fixation time on: (a) the upper-face AOI (labeled as "UFacePFT") and (b) the lower-face AOI (labeled as "LFacePFT")

Since H2 was not supported, Model and Non were grouped together when calculating correlations to investigate Hypotheses H3, H4, and H5. Spearman's Rho was calculated, with significant correlations ($p < 0.05$) marked with stars in Fig. 4. Overall, the metrics using the upper-face AOI were more correlated to participants' responses to questions about the animations; most notably, Fig. 4(a) shows significant correlations between the proportional fixation time on the upper-face AOI ("UFacePFT") and participants' responses to Likert-scale subjective questions in which they were asked to rate the grammaticality, understandability, and naturalness of movement of the animations. This result supports hypothesis H3 for animations, but not for Videos of human signers. No significant correlations were found between the eye metrics and the other types of participants' responses: questions about whether they noticed facial expressions and comprehension questions about the information content of videos or animations. Based on these results, H4 and H5 were not supported.

(a)

Spearman's Rho (* if p < 0.05)	UFacePFT Video	UFacePF T Anim.	TransUFH Video	TransUFH Anim.
Grammatical	0.149	* -0.340	0.166	* -0.305
Understandable	0.056	* -0.346	0.161	-0.145
Natural Movement	0.073	* -0.402	0.191	* -0.213
Notice Face Expr.	0.060	-0.101	0.058	-0.099
Comprehension	-0.001	-0.086	-0.064	-0.090

(b)

Spearman's Rho (* if p < 0.05)	LFacePFT Video	LFacePFT Anim.	TransLFH Video	TransLFH Anim.
Grammatical	0.087	-0.092	0.189	-0.090
Understandable	0.147	-0.156	0.217	-0.660
Natural Movement	0.093	* -0.215	* 0.277	-0.029
Notice Face Expr.	0.023	-0.239	0.198	-0.003
Comprehension	-0.018	-0.047	-0.030	0.027

Fig. 4. Correlations between participants responses (rows) and eye metrics (columns), including proportional fixation time and transition frequency for upper-face and lower-face

The final eye metric considered in this paper is the time-normalized total trail length, which is shown in Fig. 5. There was a significant difference between Video and both types of animation (Model and Non) in Fig. 5(a), further supporting hypothesis H1. The correlations between this metric and the participants' responses are shown in Fig. 5(b). This metric had significant correlations with the greatest number of types of participant responses, as indicated by the stars in Fig. 5(b). While there was still no support for hypotheses H4 or H5, based on the results in Fig. 5(b), hypothesis H3 was supported for both videos of human signers and animations of virtual humans.

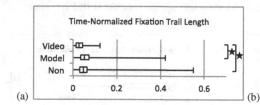

(a)

Spearman's Rho (* if p < 0.05)	TrailLen Video	TrailLen Anim.
Grammatical	* 0.369	0.096
Understandable	* 0.378	* 0.227
Natural Movement	* 0.440	* 0.292
Notice Face Expr.	0.119	0.084
Comprehension	-0.035	-0.035

(b)

Fig. 5. Fixation trail length for each type of stimulus (a) and correlations to responses (b)

6   Discussion and Future Work

This paper has identified how eye-tracking metrics are related to participants' judgments about the quality of ASL animations and videos. We have investigated and characterized differences in participants' eye-movement behavior when watching human videos or virtual-human animations of ASL. The results of our user study are useful for future researchers who wish to measure the quality of ASL videos or animations: eye-tracking metrics that can serve as complimentary or alternative methods of evaluating such stimuli. These metrics can be recorded while participants view stimuli, without asking them to respond to subjective or objective questions, providing flexibility to researchers in designing experimental studies to measure the quality of these stimuli.

In summary, the results presented above indicate that hypotheses H1 and H3 were supported, hypotheses H2, H4, and H5 were not supported; this result is in agreement with our earlier work [13]. There was a significant difference in the eye movement metrics when participants viewed ASL videos (as compared to when they viewed ASL animations), and some eye movement metrics were significantly correlated with participants' subjective judgments of video and animation quality (grammaticality, understandability, and naturalness of movement).

Specifically, the most notable new findings in this paper are:

- If using proportional fixation time to distinguish between ASL videos and animations, the upper-face AOI should be considered; if using transitions/second, the lower-face AOI should be considered. Since our prior work [13] had not analyzed the eye-tracking data in such a fine-grained manner (i.e., the upper-face and lower-face AOIs had been clumped together into a single "face" AOI), this distinction between them in regard to the significance of transitions per second or proportional fixation time was not identified in that earlier work.
- If seeking an eye metric that correlates with participants' subjective judgments about ASL videos or animations, the time-normalized fixation trail length metric (described in this paper) should be utilized. (The only exception would be for predicting participants' grammaticality judgments for ASL animations: the upper-face proportional fixation time was the best correlated.)

Our lab is studying how to design software that can automatically synthesize ASL animations, and in future work, we will continue to investigate the applications of eye-tracking methodologies in evaluation studies of ASL animations. In current work, we are investigating models of ASL facial expression, and we intend to employ eye-tracking metrics in future evaluation studies. Our goal is to produce understandable ASL animations for deaf people with low English literacy – ultimately leading to better accessibility of educational content for deaf students.

Acknowledgments. This material is based upon work supported by the National Science Foundation under award number 0746556 and 1065009. Pengfei Lu, Jonathan Lamberton, and Miriam Morrow assisted with study preparation and conduct.

References

1. Adamo-Villani, N., Doublestein, J., Martin, Z.: Sign language for K-8 mathematics by 3D interactive animation. Journal of Educational Technology Systems 33(3), 241–257 (2005)
2. Adamo-Villani, N., Popescu, V., Lestina, J.: A non-expert-user interface for posing signing avatars. Disability and Rehabilitation: Assistive Technology 8(3), 238–248 (2013)
3. Ardis, S.: ASL Animations supporting literacy development for learners who are deaf. Closing the Gap 24(5), 1–4 (2006)

4. Cavender, A., Rice, E.A., Wilamowska, K.M.: SignWave: Human Perception of Sign Language Video Quality as Constrained by Mobile Phone Technology. Emergency 7(12), 16–20

5. Cooke, L., Cuddihy, E.: Using eye tracking to address limitations in think-aloud protocol. In: Proceedings of the International Professional Communication Conference (IPCC 2005), pp. 653–658. IEEE (2005)

6. Duchowski, A.: A breadth-first survey of eye-tracking applications. Behavior Research Methods, Instruments, & Computers 34(4), 455–470 (2002)

7. Emmorey, K., Thompson, R., Colvin, R.: Eye gaze during comprehension of American Sign Language by native and beginning signers. J. Deaf Stud. Deaf Educ. 14(2), 237–243 (2009)

8. Huenerfauth, M.: Evaluation of a psycholinguistically motivated timing model for animations of American Sign Language. In: Proc. of the 10th International ACM SIGACCESS Conference on Computers and Accessibility, pp. 129–136. ACM (2008)

9. Huenerfauth, M.: Spatial and planning models of ASL classifier predicates for machine translation. In: 10th International Conference on Theoretical and Methodological Issues in Machine Translation, TMI (2004)

10. Huenerfauth, M., Lu, P., Rosenberg, A.: Evaluating importance of facial expression in American Sign Language and pidgin signed English animations. In: Proc. of the 13th International ACM SIGACCESS Conference on Computers and Accessibility, pp. 99–106. ACM (2011)

11. Huenerfauth, M., Zhao, L., Gu, E., Allbeck, J.: Evaluating American Sign Language generation through the participation of native ASL signers. In: Proc. of the 9th International ACM SIGACCESS Conference on Computers and Accessibility, pp. 211–218. ACM (2007)

12. Jacob, R.J.K., Karn, K.S.: Eye Tracking in Human- Computer Interaction and Usability Research: Ready to Deliver the Promises. The Mind's Eye (First Edition). In: Hyönä, J., Radach, R., Deubel, H. (eds.) Amsterdam, pp. 573–605 (2003)

13. Kacorri, H., Harper, A., Huenerfauth, M.: Comparing native signers' perception of American Sign Language animations and videos via eye tracking. In: Proc. of the 15th International ACM SIGACCESS Conference on Computers and Accessibility, p. 9. ACM (2013)

14. Kacorri, H., Lu, P., Huenerfauth, M.: Evaluating facial expressions in American Sign Language animations for accessible online information. In: Stephanidis, C., Antona, M. (eds.) UAHCI 2013, Part I. LNCS, vol. 8009, pp. 510–519. Springer, Heidelberg (2013)

15. Karpouzis, K., Caridakis, G., Fotinea, S.E., Efthimiou, E.: Educational resources and implementation of a Greek sign language synthesis architecture. Computers & Education 49(1), 54–74 (2007)

16. Lu, P., Huenerfauth, M.: Accessible motion-capture glove calibration protocol for recording sign language data from deaf subjects. In: Proc. of the 11th International ACM SIGACCESS Conference on Computers and Accessibility, pp. 83–90. ACM (2009)

17. Mitchell, R., Young, T., Bachleda, B., Karchmer, M.: How many people use ASL in the United States? Why estimates need updating. Sign. Lang. Studies 6(3), 306–335 (2006)

18. Muir, L.J., Richardson, I.E.: Perception of sign language and its application to visual communications for deaf people. J. Deaf Stud. Deaf Educ. 10(4), 390–401 (2005)

19. Rayner, K.: Eye movements in reading and information processing: 20 years of research. Psychol. Bull. 124(3), 372–422 (1998)

20. Traxler, C.: The Stanford achievement test, 9th edition: national norming and performance standards for deaf & hard-of-hearing students. J. Deaf Stud. & Deaf Educ. 5(4), 337–348 (2000)
21. Wagner, M., Marder, C., Blackorby, J., Cameto, R., Newman, L., Levine, P., et al.: The achievements of 100 youth with disabilities during secondary school: A report from 101 the National Longitudinal Transition Study-2 (NLTS2). SRI International, Menlo 102 Park (2003)

Metrics and Evaluation Models for Accessible Television

Dongxiao Li[1] and Peter Olaf Looms[2]

[1] Zhejiang University, College of Media and International Culture, Hangzhou, PR China
80295230@qq.com
[2] Technical University of Denmark, Lyngby, Denmark
polooms@gmail.com

Abstract. The adoption of the UN Convention on the Rights of Persons with Disabilities (UN CRPD) in 2006 has provided a global framework for work on accessibility, including information and communication technologies and audiovisual content. One of the challenges facing the application of the UN CRPD is terminology. The interpretation of concepts such as 'disability' and 'accessibility' builds on national traditions and metrics. A second challenge is implementation diversity: different nations and regions have their own interpretation of how media can be made accessible. A third challenge is the increasing number of platforms on which audiovisual content needs to be distributed, requiring very clear multiplatform architectures to facilitate interworking and assure interoperability. As a consequence, the regular evaluations of progress being made by signatories to the UN CRPD protocol are difficult to compare. Using case studies from three emerging economies (Argentina, Brazil and China) as well as industrialized nations including Canada, Denmark, the United Kingdom and the USA), this paper examines the situation facing television accessibility. Having identified and discussed existing metrics and evaluation models for access service provision, the paper identifies options that could facilitate the evaluation of UN CRPD outcomes and suggests priorities for future research in this area.

Keywords: television, accessibility, access services, metrics.

1 Introduction

How can television be made accessible? For many practitioners in countries with decades of experience, the answer is self-evident: make sure that TV programmes are provided with access services. This paper argues that there is more to accessible TV than access service provision. Some clarification of media accessibility as well as the metrics to assess it will be required. Ideally, some overall evaluation model is needed to facilitate these efforts. What is already in place and what remains to be done in order to make television accessible?

One key instrument to promote television accessibility is the UN Convention on the Rights of Persons with Disabilities, UN CRPD [12]. The convention was adopted in 2006 and came into force two years later. Article 1 contains a broad definition of the scope of the convention: "Persons with disabilities include those who have

C. Stephanidis and M. Antona (Eds.): UAHCI/HCII 2014, Part IV, LNCS 8516, pp. 564–571, 2014.
© Springer International Publishing Switzerland 2014

long-term physical, mental, intellectual or sensory impairments which in interaction with various barriers may hinder their full and effective participation in society on an equal basis with others." Article 2 continues with a clarification of key terms including "communication", "language", "discrimination on the basis of disability", "reasonable accommodation" and "universal design". Article 9, section 1b stipulates that the Convention applies to "Information, communications and other services, including electronic services and emergency services." In the same article, sections 2g and 2h make references to "the design, development, production and distribution of accessible information and communications technologies". Article 30, section b deals with participation in cultural life, recreation, leisure and sport and makes specific reference to the rights of persons to be able to "Enjoy access to television programmes, films, theatre and other cultural activities, in accessible formats".

As regards implementation and monitoring at national level, Article 33 stipulates that nation states "shall designate one or more focal points within government for matters relating to the implementation of the present Convention, and shall give due consideration to the establishment or designation of a coordination mechanism within government to facilitate related action in different sectors and at different levels." Signatories to the Convention and associated Protocol are subject to a regular review of their progress on the implementation of the CRPD, typically at intervals of four years.

The CRPD provides a global framework for media accessibility among governments. For public and private stakeholders, however, clarify what is required to make television accessible – typically the scope of accessible television, targets for access service provision and the means by which compliance can be assessed. Television is both national and international in flavour. While productions such as 'House of Cards' from Netflix have a global following, much of what people view on TV reflects significant differences in taste. The maturity of content providers including broadcasters varies a great deal, too. While broadcasters in some countries have been delivering their content with access services for decades, others have only recently begun to grapple with the issues, often compounded by the transition from analogue to digital distribution. The CRPD will require national legislation, regulation and other kinds of agreement to flesh out the details. The question is what experience has been gained to date and how this can be applied by those embarking on television accessibility?

This paper looks at examples of current practice and suggests areas where the experience gained in one country can be applied elsewhere. The first area to be analysed is metrics for television accessibility.

2   Metrics for Television Accessibility

The term 'metric' is a measure of performance in relation to desired outcomes. Ries (2010) [11] notes that the selection of metrics is crucial if they are to provide a multidimensional assessment of organisational or service performance. In addition he notes that "All metrics should be actionable, accessible, and audible."

National legislation and regulation governing media accessibility does, in some cases, contain metrics and Key Performance Indicators (KPIs) to assess the implementation of a given initiative. A good example of this for access services for individuals who are blind or have serious visual impairments is contained in the Twenty-First Century Communications and Video Accessibility Act, legislation from the US Congress. Section iii, items I to VII of the Act contain both 'supply-side' and 'demand-side' metrics – what programming is available with description and the use of this service by viewers. In essence it is a cost-benefit assessment. Nine years after coming into force, costs to all the key stakeholders in the media industry of providing programming with video description are to be weighed against the use and benefits to 'consumers' of such programming in the top 60 designated geographical areas. This will form the basis of a revision of the Act, new decisions to possibly modify video description and to extend it to further geographical areas. In this sense, the KPIs were an integral part of the accessibility legislation.

3   Supply-Side Metrics

Typical supply side metrics include:

— Applicability: broadcasters, channels and content genres
— Minimum thresholds for each access service
— Scheduling and,
— Quality metrics for each access service.

Each of these 4 metrics will be discussed in more detail.

3.1   Applicability: Broadcasters, Channels and Content Genres

In many territories, the applicability of television accessibility may depend on the distribution network. Terrestrial broadcasting is invariably covered, whereas the demands made of satellite, cable and Internet distribution via broadband or mobile networks may be different.

The television regulator in China, the State Administration of Press, Publication, Radio, Film and Television (SARFT), has accessibility metrics that apply currently to broadcast television but not to broadband distribution.

In the UK, the regulator OFCOM sets targets for both 'domestic broadcasters' based and delivering signals within the UK and to 'non-domestic broadcasters' that deliver signals via satellite from the UK to other European countries. The legal basis for this is the European Union Audiovisual Media Services Directive (AVMS) that contains some broad stipulations covering television accessibility.

The Federation Communication Commission (FCC) has phased in 'network neutrality' provisions when it comes to TV accessibility. The requirements for access services apply not only to network television but also to content delivered on demand, also on the Internet.

In many countries, there are exemptions for broadcasters based on their share of the television market (in the UK, channels with less than 1% market share). In other cases the criterion is urbanization: The FCC in the US exempts broadcasters or networks outside specific urban areas. Campedelli (2014) [4] reports that television access service requirements in Brazil apply "to all free-to-air TV in cities with more than 500,000 inhabitants", an arrangement similar to in the USA.

In some countries, certain categories of TV channel are exempt. In the UK, there exemptions for home shopping channels. Similarly, exemptions may exist for TV genres: most countries have targets for pre-prepared content but have waivers for the provision of audio or video description for live television programmes and some exempt captioning/subtitling for live programmes.

In territories where there is a tradition of providing captions/subtitles, live TV programming is no longer exempt. An example of such changes can be found at KBS in Korea. Han (2013) [7] outlines the timetable for the close captioning of live programming on terrestrial television and national and local level and on satellite TV and explains how the workflows have been adapted so that captioning for live broadcasts can subsequently be enhanced for reuse on other distribution platforms.

Sign language interpretation seems to be the only TV access service where no distinction is made between pre-prepared and live television programming. In Argentina, the president invariably addresses the nation with a sign language interpreter even though captioning of the same direct broadcast is not available. This has something to do with the way in which the two access services are produced.

3.2   Minimum Thresholds for Each Access Service

Access service provision is typically measured as a percentage of the output of a given channel or in terms or the number of hours of programming per day, week or month. In Brazil, Campadelli (2014) reports that "By 2013, television programming shall supply 112 hours weekly of closed captioning per channel."

The introduction of targets for TV access service provision is usually phased in over a number of years. The FCC typically requires compliance within one or two years. OFCOM on the other hand gives broadcasters up to 10 years to reach the final thresholds for access services. The final targets for captioning/subtitles are typically 100% of output, whereas for video / audio description are far lower. In competitive television markets such as the UK, the presence of a public service broadcaster such as the BBC may lead to commercial broadcasters such as Sky exceeding minimum thresholds.

Until recently, compliance with such targets involved self-reporting by the broadcasters in question supplemented with spot-checks by the regulator. Brady (2013) [3] highlights the need for automating the compliance mechanisms not just to ascertain, say, that captioning was present but that it was the right captioning for the content in question. Often such systems are being developed as part of overarching compliance mechanisms being put in place to check advertising play-out.

3.3   Scheduling

Brazil and other countries stipulate not only thresholds for each access service but also when such services shall be offered. The regulator requires broadcasters to deliver captioning primarily from 6 am to 2 am. In the early hours, from 2 am to 6 am, broadcasters can provide the service but the regulator only requires two hours daily during this period.

In some countries such as Ireland and Poland, the targets for captioning/subtitles are stipulated separately for the first airing of a programme and subsequent repeats. The aim of this differentiation is to prevent channels meeting their targets by increasing the number of night-time repeats with access services to improve their overall compliance with access service provision.

Scheduling plays a role for TV content with access services, especially when it comes to the signing communities whose mother tongue is a sign language. As sign language interpretation is 'open' in the sense that it is an integral part of the TV picture, all viewers of a programme with sign language usually have to see it, whether they need sign language or not.

Broadcasters have to juggle the requirements of those needing sign language with complaints or outright resistance from a majority of viewers who do not. For this reason, sign language scheduling strategies include:

- Showing such programmes outside 'prime-time' on major channels;
- Simulcasting programmes with sign language interpretation on a   niche channel; or
- Developing solutions to deliver sign language interpretation as a window overlaid on top of the television picture, allowing the viewer to turn the interpretation on or off.

3.4   Quality Metrics for Each Access Service

Following the successful introduction and scaling-up of an access service such as captioning/subtitles, the consolidation phase often leads to a formal review of how the quality of a given service should be assessed. In the case of Canada, there are quality metrics for closed captioning/subtitling, both for programming in French and English. CRTC (2012) [5] contains the metrics for English programming. These include:

- Lag time for live programming
- Accuracy rate for live programming
- Captions that block other on-screen information
- Correcting errors prior to re-broadcast
- Speed of captions during live programming and children's programming
- Captioning of emergency alerts and
- Monitoring.

In Brazil, the two central documents governing TV accessibility are Portaria MC no 310 de 27 de junho de 2006 [10] and NORMA BRASILEIRA ABNT NBR 15290

[9]. Campadelli (2014) explains that "NBR 15290 contains stipulations for the synchronicity of closed captioning.

The requirements depend on whether the programming is live or pre-recorded. A delay of no more than 4 seconds is permitted for live content whereas pre-recorded content must be "frame-accurate". There are no specifications on how delays should be measured or quantified by regulators, broadcasters and suppliers of closed captioning." NBR 15290 requires verbatim captioning and stipulates a 98% accuracy threshold for live subtitling. No supporting arguments for these decisions are offered.

Other regulators offer more specific quality metrics for access services or include the rationale for their decisions. In the Spanish regulations for closed captioning, the AENOR 15390 [1] document specifies the so-called NER model as the basis for the metrics it has chosen. In the USA, NCRA mentions verbatim captions as a quality metric. Transcriptions using live stenography are recommended but are not mandatory. OFCOM in 2013 has been through a public consultation on quality metrics for subtitles for the deaf and hard of hearing (closed captioning) and the results of this process can be found on the OFCOM website.

Recent studies by the BBC indicate the need to examine the trade-offs between various quality metrics such as the accuracy rate and the lag time for captions/subtitles for live programmes. Armstrong (2013) [2] discusses the link between synchronicity and perceived quality by viewers. The experiments reported take into account differences in viewer preferences. Some viewers turn down the sound completely and rely exclusively on the captioning while others with impaired hearing make an attempt to follow the spoken narrative and use the captions to help in areas where the viewer finds it difficult to follow what is being said.

Synchronicity, or at least a reduction in the delay of the captioning in relation to the content it refers to, has a significant impact on perceived quality. Armstrong reports that "The clearest trend for timing was for people watching with sound where there was a strong and statistically significant increase in the quality score with improved timing (reduced delay). For the range of timings tested, each 1 second reduction in the subtitle delay gave just over 5 points improvement in the quality score." The reduction in the delay is most important for those with some hearing and less important for those who watch with the television sound muted.

There is clearly a need for additional research into the perceived quality of access services so that policy-making and regulation can move from ad hoc decisions to an evidence-based approach around which consensus among key stakeholders can be built.

4   Demand-Side Metrics

While most regulators have targets for access service provision, few have metrics and KPIs for access service use. OFCOM in the UK has KPIs for audio description that came into regular service in 2003. As the targets only call for AD provision for 10% of programming, there was concern that those needing the service would not know of its existence. For this reason, OFCOM conducts regular surveys of AD awareness and use in the UK. This is accompanied by campaigns organized by public service and commercial broadcasters. This allows the television industry to monitor the take-up of Audio Description over time.

Awareness of the existence of television access services among the population at large and the intended audiences is a key first step, a major prerequisite to making television accessible. Arguably, further steps will be needed to assess take-up, use and satisfaction as access services are launched and the provision of accessible TV is consolidated. Davis (1993) [6] provides a good model that could be adapted to monitor the performance of TV access services over time from a user perspective.

The expansion and refinement of an access service such as subtitles can move in unforeseen directions. A case in point is the provision of spoken subtitles on DR1, the main channel of the Danish Broadcasting (DR) in Denmark discussed on Looms (2014) [8]. Adding speech synthesis to Danish subtitles for news items and documentaries in foreign languages has improved the accessibility of these genres for new target audiences including viewers with cognitive impairments and those who are poor readers. In countries with a tradition of using subtitling rather than dubbing for content in foreign languages, spoken subtitles constitute a cost-effective means to make television accessible.

5   Conclusions

This paper has discussed the need to complement conventions and directives governing television accessibility with national legislation, regulation and guidelines so that all the key stakeholders can get a clear, overall picture of performance. There is a wealth of experience when it comes to supply-side metrics. Building consensus and the necessary buy-in from stakeholders can be promoted by the use of evidence-based metrics.

What the discussion of current supply-side metrics indicates is that, as access service provision grows and matures, what constitutes quality from the perspective of all the key players becomes a prerequisite for consolidation and progress. Demand-side metrics are a natural complement. An understanding of service awareness, take-up, use (and enjoyment) can provide an evidence-based foundation on which to optimize television accessibility.

References

1. AENOR (2012). Subtitulado para personas sordas y personas con discapacidad auditiva (Subtitling for deaf and hard-of-hearing people). AENOR Asociación Española de Normalización y Certificación. UNE 153010 Norma española, Madrid, Spain (May 2012)
2. Amstrong, M.: The Development Of A Methodology To Evaluate The Perceived Quality Of Live TV Subtitles. BBC R&D, UK, IBC 2013 (2013)
3. Brady, K.G.: Automated Closed Captioning And Descriptive Video Compliance At Turner Broadcasting. Turner Broadcasting System, Inc., USA, IBC 2013 (2013)

4. Campedelli, G.: Access Services for TV: Quality Metrics and Challenges in the Provision of Live Closed Captioning in Brazil. 浙江传媒学院学报 Issue 3. Journal of Zhejiang Institute of Media & Communications (in press, 2014)
5. CRTC. Broadcasting Regulatory Policy CRTC (2012), -362. Quality standards for English-language closed captioning (2012),
   http://www.crtc.gc.ca/eng/archive/2012/2012-362.htm
6. Davis, F.D.: User acceptance of information technology: system characteristics, user perceptions and behavioral impacts. Int. J. Man. Mach. Stud. 38(3), 475–487 (1993)
7. Han, S., Ha, M., Lee, B., Jung, B.: Capturing Into High Quality Subtitle Files For Multiple Applications. KBS Technical Research Institute, Korea, IBC 2013 (2013)
8. Looms, P.O.: Making TV accessible in the 21st century. In: Liu, Y.-L. (ed.) The Digital Media and New Media Platforms: Policy and Marketing Strategies. Routledge Press (in press, 2014)
9. NORMA BRASILEIRA (2005) ABNT NBR 15290, ABNT NBR 15290. Acessibilidade em comunicação na televisão (Accessibility in TV captions) Section 4.1.9 Sincronia. Secretaria Nacional de Promoção dos Direitos, Brazil,
   http://www.pessoacomdeficiencia.gov.br/app/sites/default/
   files/arquivos/%5Bfield_generico_imagens-filefield-
   description%5D_17.pdf
10. Portaria MC no 310 de 27 de junho de 2006,
    http://www.mc.gov.br/portarias/24680-portaria-n-310-de-
    27-de-junho-de-2006
11. Ries, E.: Entrepreneurs: Beware of Vanity Metrics. HBR Blog Network (2010),
    http://blogs.hbr.org/2010/02/entrepreneurs-beware-of-
    vanity-metrics/
12. United Nations. Convention on the Rights of Persons with Disabilities (2006)

A Comparing Study between People with Reduced Hand Function and Children

Lena Lorentzen[1] and Johan Eklund[2]

[1] Mid Sweden University, 851 70 Sundsvall, Sweden
[2] Unicum – Nordic Design for All Centre,
Fabriksgatan 8, 821 33 Bollnäs, Sweden
lena.lorentzen@miun.se,
johan@statistikkonsult.se

Abstract. This study was conducted in collaboration with Tetra Pak® [1] measuring the hand strength, grip ability, hand size to judge how easy it was to open three packages with a group of 10 people with reduced hand function and 14 children, six years old. The result showed that the hand strength between the group with reduced hand function and the children was quite similar. Also the results from the grip ability test and their judgement of how it was to handle the package was similar. The size of the participants' hands was the only thing that really differed between the groups. This is an interesting input for designers developing products and packages that should be easy to use for children, but may be even more interesting for developing products where there is a need to exclude children or child protective packages.

Keywords: user studies, universal design/design for all/inclusive design, hand function, packaging design, child safety.

1 Introduction

Inclusive design often focuses on how a product is to use for people with different kinds of impairments. Seldom are children involved in user studies to confirm the ease of use for them. Sometimes we are facing a situation where we really want to include or exclude children. Milk and juice packages are examples of products we want children to be able to handle while dangerous products such as packages for pharmaceuticals or detergents can cause the need of exclusion. The traditional way to exclude children to open packages is by a design that requires a lot of strength and good coordination in the hands. The problem is that the target group for pharmaceuticals often consist of sick, weak or elderly people with reduced strength and/or coordination in their hands. Pharmaceutical products that are hard to use can be a great problem for the users. In this study we measured the hand strength, hand function, hand size and assessed how easy it was to open three packages from Tetra Pak with screw caps. The test groups consisted of 10 people with reduced hand function and 14 children, 6-7 years old.

C. Stephanidis and M. Antona (Eds.): UAHCI/HCII 2014, Part IV, LNCS 8516, pp. 572–581, 2014.
© Springer International Publishing Switzerland 2014

1.1   Goal

The goal of this study was to investigate the similarities and differences in the conditions for people with reduced hand function and six years old children to handle every day things and packages.

1.2   The Adult Group

The adult group consisted of ten people with reduced hand function. Eight had rheumatic diagnoses, either osteoarthritis, rheumatoid arthritis or both and one with systemic sclerosis. One suffered from a neurological disease, Multiple Scleroses and one was born with four fingers on each hand where the index fingers have been transferred to thumbs by surgery. The age span in the adult group were between 32-77 with an average age of 61. Two men and eight women participated in the study.

1.3   Child Group

The child group consisted of fourteen children all born the same year with an age between 6-7 years. They were attending the Swedish preschool, in between kindergarten and elementary school. Six boys and eight girls participated in the study.

2   Method

This study compares hand capabilities between two defined groups, six years old children and adults with reduced hand function. Using established test routines considering hand capabilities and sizes comparisons between the groups were made. To estimate the effects in every day life the results were compared to handling consumer packages. The different test methods are presented below. All tests were performed individually with one test person and one test leader.

2.1   Hand Size

The hand size was documented by drawing the outline at the test occasion. Afterwards measurements of the palm width, hand length, thumb, index and middle finger were measured with a ruler.

The way of measuring was according to Anthropometry of infants, children and youths to age 18 for product safety design [2] mesurement 47, 48, 51, 53, 55 in figure 2 and The Digital Human Research Center [3] measurement L1, L3, L4, L5 in figure 2. The methods were chosen since they are correlating and the first is developed for children and the second for adults. Only the key parts of the hand involved in handling the packages in the study were measured.

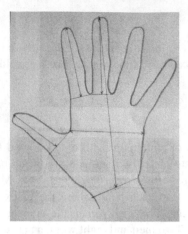

Fig. 1. This figure is an example of an outline of a hand from one of the test persons to show how the hand size was measured in this study

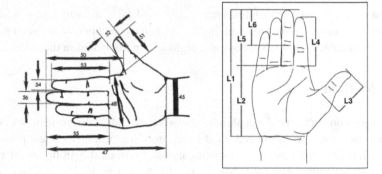

Fig. 2. This figure shows how the hand size was measured by The Highway safety research institute, The University of Michigan (left) and by The Digital Human Research Centre (right)

2.2   Grip Force

Maximum and average value of their grip force was measured for both hands by using a dynamometer called Gripit [4]. The arm was positioned with 90 degrees angel in the elbow and the lower arm resting in a horizontal support with the wrist in a straight position. During ten seconds the test person use all their hand force to grip the handle (black vertical part of fig 3) as hard as they can.

2.3   Hand Function

GAT, Grip Ability Test [6], is a method to measure a person's ability to perform pre-defined actions while clocking the time needed. The test consists of three actions, pouring a glass of water from a one-litre jug, putting a metallic clip on an envelope

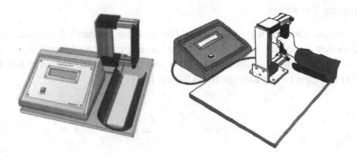

Fig. 3. Grip it is a measuring instrument used for characterising the grip force [5]. It consists of an electronic measuring devise with a display showing the results, a support for the under arm and a handle.

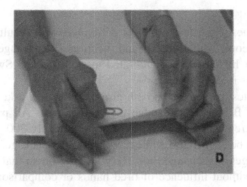

Fig. 4. GAT, Grip Ability Test is way to evaluate the hand function of a person by measuring the time needed to perform three different tasks [9]. This figure is showing on of the tasks - putting a metallic clip to an envelop.

without dragging any of the items to the edge of the table and pulling a gauze tube over the hand until the whole thumb is visible. The method is extracted from the more covering and complicated Sollerman test [7]. In the development of the GAT test they were comparing the results of the different parts of the Sollermantest between people with rheumatism and people without any problems in their hands. The result was analysed to find the variables that was most sensitive to change due to exercise of the hands. Those variables were divided into groups from what kind of grip it involved. A statistic calculation procedure found that the time requirement of the three tasks in GAT were representative for the Sollerman test. The test is sensitive to changes in the hand function and thereby appropriate to use for evaluation of progression from treatment and exercise. The test takes less than five minutes to perform. It is validated and has a high level of reliability [8].

2.4   Judging Packages

Unicum – Nordic Design for All Centre [10] and the Swedish Rheumatism Association [11] has developed a method to measure the experience of handling packages and products. As measuring instruments we use test groups with reduced hand function. The method is a part of the Design for All Test [12]

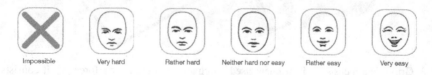

<table>
<tr><td>Impossible</td><td>Very hard</td><td>Rather hard</td><td>Neither hard nor easy</td><td>Rather easy</td><td>Very easy</td></tr>
</table>

Fig. 5. The test person perform every handling step of the package and judge them on a scale from 0= impossible, 1= very hard, 2 rather hard, 3 neither hard nor easy, 4= rather easy and 5= very easy

The average value of the test group is calibrated with results from a reference group of over 100 people with reduced hand function. If a package or product reaches a judgement of 3 or higher from a calibrated test group, The Swedish Rheumatism Association approves it as easy to use.

In this study the test persons from both groups were then asked to open three different packages (A, B and C) and judge their experience. All packages came from Tetra Pak, with a screw cap and a weight of approximately 300 gram. A and B was recently designed to be easy to use while C was an older package. The order that they evaluated the packages was changed for every test person so that every package will be equally judged without influence of tired hands or comparison with the previous package. In all tests, people were observed and captured on movie while performing the task of opening the packages.

Fig. 6. Test of a child (left) and an adult with reduced hand function (right) opening package A Tetra Prisma ® Aseptic 330 DreamCap™ 26

Fig. 7. Test of a child (left) and an adult with reduced hand function (right) opening package B, Tetra Brik® Aseptic 200 Edge with Helicap™ 23

3   Result

The results from the test were analysed and some interesting findings occurred.

3.1   Grip Force

The grip forces between the individuals were more similar in the group of children compared to the adults group. The average values of the groups show that the adults are stronger in their hands than the children. It is still impossible to draw any general conclusions from that fact since the differences are to small and the variety in the adult group too big. We can also see that both the maximum and average grip force of the right hand is overlapping between the two groups.

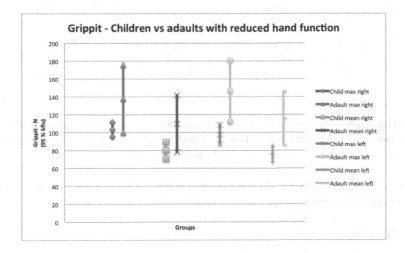

Fig. 8. This figure shows the results from the Grippit tests. Each vertical line represents a 95 % confidence interval for the average strength in the different groups. The longer intervals indicate a larger variation within the group of adults compared to the group of children.

If we compare these groups to the average hand strength of an adult person, that is 370 N for the right hand and 326 N for the left [13], we can se that both this groups has an average value that is less than half. These numbers come from a study with another instrument called Jamar but the concurrent validity between Jamar and Grippit is very high. [14]. These results agree with the study of rheumatic woman made by [4]. In their result they found that women with rheumatic diseases in average had about 30% of the hand force of an healthy woman and that a healthy woman on average has 54% of a healthy mans grip force. They also found that the average value of the grip force in ten seconds were about 70% of the maximum value for the group of rheumatic women. In this study the average value was 80 % of the maximum.

3.2   GAT – Grip Ability Test

The average values from the GAT test shows that the adult group is slightly more successful considering the task to pour a glass of water from a pitcher. In the task where they were supposed to put the clip to the envelope the children managed a little better than the adults. The children were also more successful to pull the gauze tube over the hand. Overall, if we add the time for all tasks, the children had better results on average. But if we look at the varity of the people in each group we can see that the results are overlapping in all results except the gauze tube.

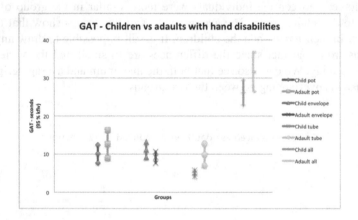

Fig. 9. This figure shows results from the GAT tests. Each vertical line represents a 95 % confidence interval for the average time needed to perform the tests in the different group. The result indicates that both groups has decreased hand function [4].

A GAT score of <20 seconds is considered normal. Higher scores mean decreased hand function. Normative values are not available [4].

3.3   Hand Size

The palm width measurement shows some overlapping but all measured fingers of the participants in the adult group were longer than the children's. The biggest difference between the groups was the length of the hand.

The length of the hand seems to be the strongest difference concerning the hands of adult people with reduced hand function compared to six years old children.

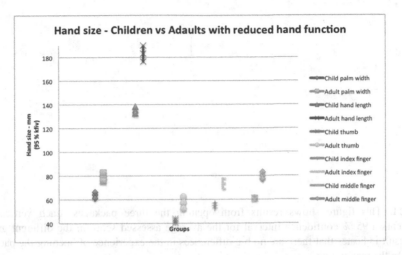

Fig. 10. This figure shows results from the hand size measurements. Each vertical line represents a 95 % confidence interval for the average size of different parts of the hand in the two groups. The results show that children has significantly smaller hands. In average the sizes of the children's hands are about 70% of the adults.

3.4   Judging Packages

The overall experience from the observation study was that the children judged the packages higher than the adult group in relationship to their success in the opening procedure. Despite this difference between the groups we can still see correlating results. The difference in the average values of the judging of the packages was A:0.56, B:0.45 and C:0.33 with an average value of 0.45. A and B were judged higher by the children. C required a lot of force and six children and three adults could not open it at all. Therefor the average value of opening C was lower in the child group.

The two groups were agreeing whether the packages should be approved as easy to open or not. Package A scored 4.36 from the children and 3.8 from the adults. Package B scored 4 from the children and 3.55 from the adults. Both packages scored definitely above 3, the limit to be approved by The Swedish Rheumatism Association [11].

Package C was judged 1.57 on average by the children and 1.9 by the adults which means that they also agreed that this package was too hard to open to be approved.

If we look at the spread of the judgements in the two groups we can see that the intervals overlap, meaning that adults and children were judging the ease of opening these packages as similar.

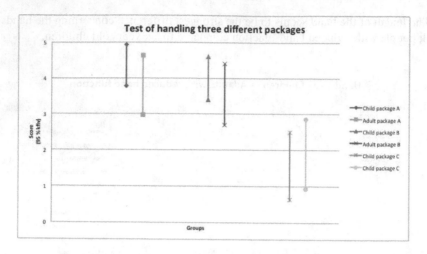

Fig. 11. This figure shows results from opening the three packages. Each vertical line represents a 95 % confidence interval for the average assessed score in the different groups. The result indicates that there are no big differences in the experience of opening the packages between the two groups.

4   Discussion

These findings could have an impact on how to design products and packages depending if we want to include or exclude the children.

In situations where we aim for Design for All solutions, that includes both people with reduced hand function and children we need to consider that their grip force is less than half of an average adult, that both groups are defined by GAT to have reduced hand function and that the hand size of a six year old child is about 75% of an adult. The design should require less than half of an average adults grip force; it should not require complicated coordination skills and should be able to handle with different hand sizes.

If you want to exclude the children the safest way, according to this study, the product or package requires the larger hand size of an adult person.

References

1. Tetra Pak® is the world's leading food processing and packaging solutions company, http://www.tetrapak.com
2. Anthropometry of infants, children and youths to age 18 for product safety design, May 31, 1977 produced for the U.S. consumer product safety commission by The Highway safety research institute, The University of Michigan, Ann Arbor, Michigan 48109, fig 26 "Hand measurement Illustration"
3. Digital human research center, http://www.dh.aist.go.jp/research/centered/anthropometry/L_hand.html.en

 4. Nordenskiöld, U.M., Grimby, G.: Grip Force in Patients with Rheumatoid Arthritis and Fibromyalgia and in Healthy Subjects. A Study with the Grippit Instrument. Scandinavian Journal of Rheumatology 22, 14–19 (1993)
 5. Häger-Ross, C., Rösblad, B.: Norms for grip strength in children aged 4–16 years. Department of Community Medicine and Rehabilitation, Section for Physiotherapy, pp. 4–16. Umeå University, Kolbäcken's Child Rehabilitation Centre, Sweden (2002)
 6. Poole, J.L.: Measures of adult hand function. 61 (2003)
 7. Sollerman, C., Ejeskar, A.: Sollerman hand function test: A standardised method and its use in tetraplegic patients (1995)
 8. Dellhag, B., Bjelle, A.: A Grip Ability Test for use in rheumatology practice (1995)
 9. Brorsson, S.: Biomechanical Studies on Hand Function in Rehabilitation. Halmstad University, School of Business and Engineering, Sweden (2011)
10. Unicum – Nordic Design for All Centre, http://www.unicum.se
11. The Swedish Rheumatism Association, http://www.reumatikerforbundet.org
12. Lorentzen, L., Eklund, J.: Design för alla – En ny metod för att bedöma produkters, tjänsters och miljöers användbarhet (Design for All – A new method to estimate the usability of products, services and environments) (2011)
13. Bohannona, R.W., Peolsson, A., Massy-Westropp, N.: Reference values for adult grip strength measured with a Jamar dynamometer: a descriptive meta-analysis (2006)
14. Svantesson, U., Nordé, M., Svensson, S., Brodina, E.: A comparative study of the Jamar and the Grippit for measuring handgrip strength in clinical practice. Institute of Neuroscience and Physiology/Physiotherapy, Sahlgrenska Academy at University of Gothenburg, Sweden and Department of physiotherapy, Sahlgrenska University Hospital, Gothenburg, Sweden (2009)

T-echo: Promoting Intergenerational Communication through Gamified Social Mentoring

Yuki Nagai, Atsushi Hiyama, Takahiro Miura, and Michitaka Hirose

Graduate School of Information and Science Technology,
The University of Tokyo, Tokyo, Japan
{ynagai,atsushi,miu,hirose}@cyber.t.u-tokyo.ac.jp

Abstract. Intergenerational social mentoring, a mentoring system on social medium between the elderly and the young, will be the one of the platforms for the elderly to make use of their potential. The elderly could have more chances to communicate their knowledge and experience accumulated through their life to the next generations, and the young could try more challenges under the wisdom of crowds. Such systems should 1) have senior-friendly interface, 2) support the rich context-aware communication, and 3) blur some intergenerational gaps. In this paper, we propose "T-echo", a new trial system for intergenerational social mentoring. T-echo is based on the two concepts: "growing gamifictaion" and "calendar-based interface." The field study 15 elderly joined showed that the calendar-notebook interface was friendly for the elderly and have rich contexts for mentoring. Furthermore, growing gamification could be a good mediator between the elderly and the young.

Keywords: social mentoring, growing gamification, intergenerational communication.

1 Introduction

Elderly people are the property of our society. They have much experienced through their lives. The medical development prolong their life, and the number of the elderly who want to work are increasing. However, how to utilize their potential is not known. The elderly's personalities and skills are diverse as the young. They have difficulty to learn a new thing. They want to use their skills but not to be restricted by the organization.

We believe the development information and communication technology (ICT) can be a solution for the problem. We are the members of a research project, "Senior cloud [1]." Senior cloud aims to archive the senior workforce with virtual merging (Fig. 1). In the concept, there are some elderly and young. The elderly might have some skill, knowledge, or experience through their lives including the wisdom for everyday life, while their activeness and cognitive functions decline. The young, on the other hand, are generally active instead of their lack of experience. Then, if we could gather the elderly's experiences and transfer them

C. Stephanidis and M. Antona (Eds.): UAHCI/HCII 2014, Part IV, LNCS 8516, pp. 582–589, 2014.
© Springer International Publishing Switzerland 2014

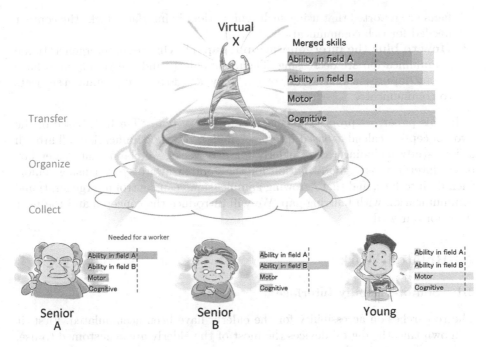

Fig. 1. "Senior cloud": Merging the elderly's rich experience and the young's vigor into a virtual worker

to the young, the virtual workforce will be appeared. To achieve it, we need to collect the elderly's diverse experience and transfer them to young properly.

"Social mentoring" will be the one of the embodiments. Mentoring means that well-experienced people advise the beginners or the young. Mentoring is a good system for both of the elderly and the young. The elderly can communicate with the young and use their skills by transferring their knowledge and experience to the young, which the many elderly desire to. The young, on the other hand, try more challenges under the wisdom of crowds. However, mentoring costs much, and it is difficult to maintain without such as the organisations' effort. It is difficult to get advices from some mentors for the wisdom of crowds. Social mentoring achieves mentoring on social medium. On social mentoring, mentees could meet many candidates for their mentors. It would work with support for communication of medium instead of human costs.

However, we faced some problems for social mentoring.

1. **How to include the elderly on social medium:** The elderly are likely to avoid using new interfaces while the elderly are accustomed to use digital devices these days. Furthermore, they are reluctant to transmit their information because they do not know how and what to do.
2. **How to share the context rich enough for mentoring:** We can simply adopt a senior-friendly interface such as a phone, or email. However, the

facts are reported that using such senior-friendly interfaces lacks the context needed for rich communication [2,3].

3. **How to blur the intergenerational gap** The chances of intergenerational communication are decreasing. Then, the elderly and the young often have wrong impression against each other. They also do have few common subjects to communicate.

In this paper, we propose a social mentoring system, "T-echo", based of the two concepts: "calendar-based interface" and "growing gamification". Through a field study including the 15 elderly for two weeks, we claim that "calendar-based interface" is a good solution for the context-aware system using senior-friendly interface, and that "growing gamification" can control intergenerational communication with blurring gap. We will introduce the concepts and the next steps for our goal.

2   Related Work

2.1   Senior-Friendly Interface

The researches on accessibility for the elderly have been accumulated. First, it is known that the digital devices the most of the elderly are accustomed to use, such as phone or mail, are good means for an approach to include the elderly into social medium. Hiyama et al. [4] used phone calls and e-mails to gather the elderly's skill information. They propose "Question First", a passive interaction model for the elderly who are not accustomed to social communication and do not know how to and what to transmit information. In the model, the system asks some questions to the elderly and all to do for the elderly is simply to answer them. Then, the system can gather some type of answers, such as profile information, their hobbies, and their skills, varying the type of questions. They could collect some skill information just using such simple interfaces, but the participants of their field study sometimes complained that some questions need more contexts of the questioners. Harwood [2] also reported that telephone communication is the most familiar in the intergenerational communication, but Ballagas et al. [3] lacks the context for such communication.

Some studies tried to support richer communication using ICT. Miyazaki et al. [5] used "simple teleda", a social television system, for the elderly. Television is also an digital device the elderly are familiar with. The system provides the conversation topics for the users based on television programs. They argued that such television-based topics could promote their communication.

Touch screen devices, such as smartphones and tablets, are not prevailed in the elderly, but it is important how the elderly can use it for supporting richer context. Kobayashi et al.[6] conducted performance measurements and observational evaluations of 20 elderly participants. Then, they show some guidelines for application design for the elderly.

However, the problems for the elderly to use social mentoring is not just about usability. The elderly has some mental barriers against ICT as Gatto and Tak

[7] pointed out. We should consider how to promote the elderly to transmit their information on social mentoring.

2.2 Context-Awareness

Various appended information has been used as a context. The work progress[8] and location[9] are the examples. Among them, the calendar's context are often focused these days. Previously, within workgroup, various researches have revealed the usefulness of online calendar sharing for collaborative task management. For example, Mosier and Tammaro [10] conducted a research for a group scheduling tool, Meeting Maker, and showed that the system made it easy to schedule meetings and maintain the users calendars. Not only for task management in workgroup, Thayer et al reported that the calendar-based communication can have emotional context among friends using event description. Furthermore, Lovett et al. [11] claimed that calendar events can be the one of the sensors for the users' activities.

From above researches, we believe that calendar-based communication can be a rich context-aware system for mentoring.

2.3 Gamification

Gamification is the use of game mechanics into non-game contexts to motivate or induce the users as the systems expect. For example, Foursquare [12] gives virtual badges to promote the users to "checkin" new places. For the elderly, gamification is also used for rehabilitation [13] and everyday exercise [14].

The gap between the elderly and the young have to be absorbed by medium support. We consider that gamification can be a buffer between intergenerational communication to control it. However, the most of example of the use of gamification is just to motivate or induce the users for some activity.

3 T-echo

T-echo is based on the two concepts: "growing gamification" and "calendar-based interface" (Fig. 2).

3.1 Growing Gamification

Gamification has been mostly used to motivate or induce the users. However, we believe that improved gamification can be used as the buffer of intergeneration gap in mentoring.

We especially focus growing game in various types of games. The users enjoy the characters growing or becoming intimate during taking care of it in growing game. Some growing games have the status for intimacy. When the intimacy status increase, the users are allowed to control from more options, or new behaviour of the character that trust them. Then, the users come to act to the character trust or like the user.

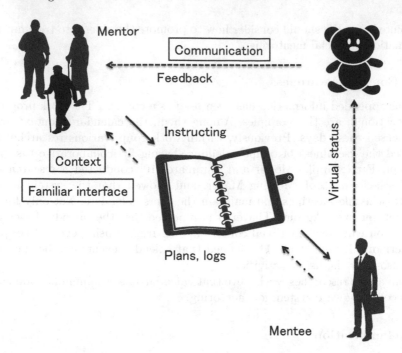

Fig. 2. The concept image for "growing gamification" and "calendar-based interface"

Such game design might be used for social mentoring. A menthe replaces the virtual character. Instructions and growing process are not fictions. The young see the elderly overbearing or stubborn. The intimacy status might be act as the natural protection for the young. For the elderly, on the other hand, the restriction of the actions will decline their motivation. Growing gamification and the intimacy status might make the elderly to act to be thought well by their mentees.

3.2 Calendar-Based Interface

Calendar is very familiar interface for the elderly. Furthermore, the events on the calendar will be the context for mentoring. Then, we propose calendar-based interface (Fig. 3). T-echo's main views have question from mentees, user levels, activities, calendar, and tasks. The views show mentors their mentees what have done and what to do. On calendar, the mentors can praise and criticize (as like communication on Facebook), edit, and talk. For the design of the intimacy status, there are restrictions for mentor actions. Mentors in low intimacy can only evaluate, and middle can edit. Talk is allowed only mentors in high intimacy.

4 Field Study

We conducted a field study including the fifteen elderly for two weeks.

Fig. 3. T-echo's screens: the left is the top view, the right is calendar view

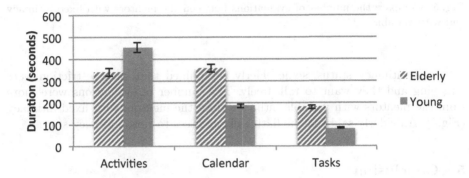

Fig. 4. Mouse over duration. The elderly relied the information on the calendar, while the young people mainly saw activities.

4.1 Participants

The young participants are 17 twenties. The elderly participants are 15, aged from 62 to 82. The young and the elderly do not know each other. The young and the elderly, the 32 users, acted as the mentors for four mentees. The mentees are randomly chosen from the young participants. Intimacy status begin from low in principle. To see the effect of intimacy level, some (almost half) mentorship fixed the status at high.

4.2 Results

We get from the elderly 1954 praises, 98 criticisms, 21 editings, and 299 advices (from the all participants: 5210 praises, 527 criticisms, 104 editings, and 746 advices). From mouse over duration, the elderly viewed mostly the calendar compared with the activities and the tasks (Fig.4). The topics the elderly often commented were about the mentees research (the mentees were university students), life (such as the time of getting up), and the animation on television. Some elderly said they could find the common subjects with the young through their daily life. On the other hand, the topics many advised between the young mentors and the elderly mentors were completely different.

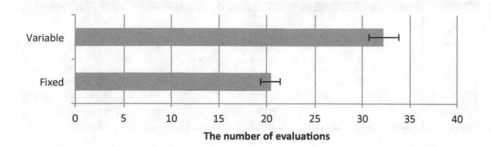

Fig. 5. Compare the number of evaluations between the mentors with fixed intimacy and with variable

About intimacy status, some elderly compained that such restriction were annoying and they want to talk freely. The number of evaluations were more from the mentors with variable intimacy than the mentors with fixed intimacy (Fig.5). An elderly said that he flatter his mentees to raise intimacy status.

5   Conclusion

In this paper, we propose a social mentoring system, "T-echo", based on the two concepts: "calendar-based interface" and "growing gamification." We conducted a field study including the 15 elderly and it shows that calendar-based interface are the familiar and useful context and for elderly. We also showed that intimacy level, the one of the embodiment of growing gamification, can control intergenerational communication for the buffer of gap.

Acknowledgement. This research was partially supported by the Japan Science and Technology Agency, JST, under the Strategic Promotion of Innovative Research and Development Program.

References

1. The University of Tokyo: Senior cloud (2014),
   http://sc.cyber.t.u-tokyo.ac.jp/en/index.html
2. Harwood, J.: Communication media use in the grandparent-grandchild relationship. Journal of Communication 50(4), 56–78 (2000)
3. Ballagas, R., Kaye, J.J., Ames, M., Go, J., Raffle, H.: Family communication: Phone conversations with children. In: Proceedings of the 8th International Conference on Interaction Design and Children, IDC 2009, pp. 321–324. ACM, New York (2009)

4. Hiyama, A., Nagai, Y., Hirose, M., Kobayashi, M., Takagi, H.: Question first: Passive interaction model for gathering experience and knowledge from the elderly. In: 2013 IEEE International Conference on Pervasive Computing and Communications Workshops (PERCOM Workshops), pp. 151–156 (2013)
5. Miyazaki, M., Sano, M., Naemura, M., Sumiyoshi, H., Mitsuya, S., Fujii, A.: A social tv system for the senior community: Stimulating elderly communication using information and communications technology. In: 2013 16th International Conference on Network-Based Information Systems (NBiS), pp. 422–427 (September 2013)
6. Kobayashi, M., Hiyama, A., Miura, T., Asakawa, C., Hirose, M., Ifukube, T.: Elderly user evaluation of mobile touchscreen interactions. In: Campos, P., Graham, N., Jorge, J., Nunes, N., Palanque, P., Winckler, M. (eds.) INTERACT 2011, Part I. LNCS, vol. 6946, pp. 83–99. Springer, Heidelberg (2011)
7. Gatto, S.L., Tak, S.H.: Computer, internet, and e-mail use among older adults: Benefits and barriers. Educational Gerontology 34(9), 800–811 (2008)
8. Persson, J.S., Mathiassen, L., Aaen, I.: Agile distributed software development: enacting control through media and context. Information Systems Journal 22(6), 411–433 (2012)
9. Chon, Y., Cha, H.: Lifemap: A smartphone-based context provider for location-based services. IEEE Pervasive Computing 10(2), 58–67 (2011)
10. Mosier, J., Tammaro, S.: When are group scheduling tools useful? Computer Supported Cooperative Work (CSCW) 6(1), 53–70 (1997)
11. Lovett, T., O'Neill, E., Irwin, J., Pollington, D.: The calendar as a sensor: Analysis and improvement using data fusion with social networks and location. In: Proceedings of the 12th ACM International Conference on Ubiquitous Computing, Ubicomp 2010, pp. 3–12. ACM, New York (2010)
12. Glas, R.: Breaking reality: exploring pervasive cheating in foursquare. Transactions of the Digital Games Research Association 1(1) (2013)
13. Da Gama, A., Chaves, T., Figueiredo, L., Teichrieb, V.: Poster: Improving motor rehabilitation process through a natural interaction based system using kinect sensor. In: 2012 IEEE Symposium on 3D User Interfaces (3DUI), pp. 145–146. IEEE (2012)
14. Lamoth, C.J., Alingh, R., Caljouw, S.R.: Exergaming for elderly: effects of different types of game feedback on performance of a balance task. Studies in Health Technology and Informatics 181, 103–107 (2012)

Answers for Self and Proxy – Using Eye Tracking to Uncover Respondent Burden and Usability Issues in Online Questionnaires*

Erica Olmsted-Hawala, Temika Holland, and Elizabeth Nichols

U.S. Census Bureau, Center for Survey Measurement,
4600 Silver Hill Road, Washington DC, 20233, USA
{Erica.L.Olmsted.Hawala,Temika.Holland,
Elizabeth.May.Nichols}@census.gov

Abstract. In a study of the American Community Survey online instrument, we assessed how people answered questions about themselves and other individuals living in their household using eye-tracking data and other qualitative measures. This paper focuses on the number of fixations (whether participants looked at specific areas of the screen), fixation duration (how long participants looked at the questions and answers), and number of unique visits (whether participants rechecked the question and answer options). Results showed that for age, date of birth and employment duty questions participants had more fixations and unique visit counts, and spent more time on the screen when answering about unrelated members of their household than when answering about themselves. Differing eye movements for proxy reporting suggest that answering some survey questions for other unrelated people poses more burden on respondents than answering about oneself. However, not all questions showed this tendency, so eye tracking alone is not enough to detect burden.

Keywords: eye tracking, usability, questionnaire design, proxy reporting, respondent burden.

1   Introduction/Background

Eye tracking has been used in data collection surveys for a number of purposes to help influence the design of surveys and understand how respondents interact with survey questions. For example, it has been used to identify the usability of branching instructions in paper survey designs - gaze paths (or trails) were used to identify whether respondents read a branching instruction and then followed the instruction to skip a question or move forward to the next appropriate question [1]. Eye tracking has also been used in studying online questionnaires to identify whether participants noticed instructions informing the respondent how to return to the survey if they were

---

* Disclaimer: This report is released to inform interested parties of research and to encourage discussion. Any views expressed on the methodological issues are those of the authors and not necessarily those of the U.S. Census Bureau.

C. Stephanidis and M. Antona (Eds.): UAHCI/HCII 2014, Part IV, LNCS 8516, pp. 590–600, 2014.
International Copyright, 2014, U.S. Department of Commerce, U.S. Government

logged out [2]. Eye tracking helped to visualize what survey designers intuitively understood, that respondents notice the first few response options more than they do the latter response options [3]. However, there are also cautions when using eye tracking with complex survey designs. Researchers recommend using eye tracking in conjunction with other data, such as qualitative results collected from usability testing, when reporting findings because complex surveys may elicit the "blank gaze" where participants recall information while looking at the screen but their attention is not actually on where their eyes are focused [4].

There is plenty of research that investigates how, particularly in household surveys, data quality varies by whether the respondent is answering questions about themselves or other individuals (also known as proxy reporting). Many household surveys rely on proxy reporting because of cost limitations or time constraints. For example, it may not be possible within a certain time limit and budget to have all individuals of a household answer the survey. It is typical then to have one person in the household report for all others in that household. In general, the consensus on whether proxy reporting is reliable is mixed. There are many reasons for this. One primary reason, noted by Moore, in a review of the literature, is due to methodological reasons, such as self-selection bias (e.g. many studies fail to assign respondent to answer as self or proxy a priori [5]. Some researchers have found proxy reports can be accurate depending on the subject of the questions [6; 7]. However, when proxies are asked, questions that are more burdensome or difficult to answer, such as questions about race/ethnicity [8], mental health questions [9], income questions [10], or other questions concerning subsections of the population [11], proxy reporting may be significantly inaccurate. In addition, there are differences in the quality of proxy reporting depending on the relationship of the proxy to the target individual [12]. That is, when the proxy respondent is more closely related to the person they are answering the questions about, the data are more accurate [13].

To date, the evaluation of proxy data has relied on comparing self-reports to proxy reports to examine differences, or on comparing proxy reports to administrative records. We hypothesize that eye-tracking data can be another method to identify difficult questions for proxy respondents. We were specifically interested in evaluating difficult or burdensome questions for people who are unrelated to the respondent. To do so, we compare the eye-tracking behavior for an individual when answering questions about oneself versus answering the same questions about an unrelated person residing in the same household. Based on prior literature that suggests increased eye-fixations and durations can be an indicator of burden (confusion/frustration) [14; 2; 15] we hypothesized that there would be a higher count of eye fixations, an increased duration of eye fixation data and more visit counts (that is going back to the same area of interest multiple times) for the proxy reports of unrelated individuals than for when participants were reporting for themselves.

2   Methods

In the fall of 2013, the U.S. Census Bureau conducted a usability test with eye tracking on the online American Community Survey (ACS). The ACS is an ongoing national survey, administered to nearly 3 million household units per year. The survey generates data to assist in the allocation of more than $450 billion in federal and state funds. The aim of the usability testing was to improve the design of the survey questions and navigation features of the online instrument; thus, minimizing measurement error. Specifically, the testing attempted to investigate whether changes to the instrument would minimize the break-offs and the number of edit messages received at particular screens, especially when answering for unrelated household members [16]. This paper focuses on some of those same screens, including difficult questions for an unrelated individual to answer, such as date of birth, employment information, and wages.

2.1   Participants

Ten participants who lived in unrelated households were recruited from a database managed by the Center for Survey Measurement. These participants resided in the Washington DC metropolitan area and responded to a newspaper advertisement stating they would be interested in participating in research studies at the Census Bureau. Household compositions of participants consisted of a mix of related and unrelated household members. Participants answered detailed questions for all household members, including themselves and all individuals living in the household (related and unrelated). Of the 10 respondents, one had one unrelated person in their household and the others had between two and nine unrelated persons in their household.

Participants were given a $40 honorarium. Participants completed a questionnaire about their computer use and Internet experience. To be eligible for the study, participants had to meet a minimum Internet experience requirement of using the Internet three times a week for at least a year, for more than simply checking their email. If participants met this requirement, and lived in complex households (which we defined

Table 1. Mean (and Range) Participant Demographics

	Participants (range)
N	10
Gender	3 M / 7 F
Age	31 (21-51)
Education	7 < High school & some college 3 > Masters or PhD
Difficulty in learning to use new Websites[a]	1.4 (1-2)
Difficulty in using the Internet[a]	1 (1-1)
Overall experience with computers to use the Internet[b]	1.2 (1-2)
Familiarity with Census Bureau Website[c]	1.7 (1-4)

[a] Scale: 1 (Not difficult at all) – 5 (Extremely difficult)
[b] Scale: 1 (A great deal) – 5 (None)
[c] Scale 1 (Not familiar at all) – 5 (Extremely familiar)

as households having three or more persons with at least one of the three being unrelated to the participant), they were scheduled to participate in a usability test. All participants were considered knowledgeable in navigating the Internet and using a computer, although some were more experienced than others. Participant demographics are presented in Table 1. All participants were unfamiliar with the ACS, and none of the participants reported receiving this survey in the past.

2.2   Procedure

Usability testing was conducted in the Human Factors and Usability laboratory at the U.S. Census Bureau, Suitland, MD. Each participant sat in a room facing a one-way mirror and a wall camera. The room was equipped with a 17" LCD monitor attached with a Tobii X-120 eye tracker.

The test administrator (TA) began the session by reading a brief introduction about the purpose of the study and the uses of data that are collected in the survey. The participant, working one-on-one with the TA, signed a consent form granting permission to be video and audio recorded, completed a short-term memory task, and a brief calibration of their eyes for eye tracking. Once the set up was complete, the participant was left alone in the room. The TA monitored the session from the opposite side of the one-way mirror, communicating with the participant via microphones and speakers. The TA began video and audio recording. After completing a short questionnaire about their Internet search habits and strategies, and a short-term memory exercise, the participant answered the online ACS survey.

During the study, the participant completed the ACS survey in silence. While the participant was answering the ACS survey questions, their eye movements were recorded unobtrusively. At the conclusion of the ACS survey, eye tracking was stopped and the participant completed a satisfaction questionnaire that was loosely based on the Questionnaire for User Interaction Satisfaction [17]. Upon completion of the satisfaction questionnaire, the TA returned to the participant room, asked a set list of debriefing questions, paid the participant, and then escorted the participant from the building.

2.3   Qualitative Usability Feedback

Participants were debriefed at the conclusion of the study, using a list of scripted questions. However, the TA deviated from the script to ask targeted questions based on the participants' responses. This debriefing allowed for an unscripted conversation about the survey questionnaire they had just completed. The verbalized comments from the debriefing were reviewed and transcribed by the authors of this paper.

2.4   Eye Tracking

We recorded the eye tracking data using Tobii Studio [18]. We examined eye movements in predefined areas of interest (AOIs). For each screen analyzed, the AOIs included the question stem, any italic instructional test, and the answer field. We focused on the eye-tracking data related to participants' answers about themselves and other unrelated individuals in their household.

For each AOI, we examined the total number of fixations to assess where participants looked on the screen; total fixation duration to assess how long participants spent on each area of the screen; and the total number of unique visits to the AOIs to assess if participants rechecked the question stem, instructional text or response fields.

Fixation duration and the number of eye-tracking fixations per screen were evaluated to assess the amount of burden experienced by participants when responding to these survey items. We compared the questionnaire screens when a participant answered questions about themselves to the screens when the participant answered questions about unrelated individuals living in the household. The purpose was to identify differences in eye-movement patterns.

3   Results

The analysis plan included a comparison of eye-tracking data of participants who answered questions about themselves and about other unrelated people in their household. This paper reports eye-tracking results on a few of the screens that appeared to have more usability issues and were more difficult for proxy respondents.

A paired t-test was performed to assess differences in fixation duration, fixation counts and visit counts on survey items for the two groups: self-reports and proxy reports for unrelated individuals in the household, which we refer to as proxy reports. Table 2 provides information on the means and standard errors for each AOI in which significant differences were observed.

Table 2. Means and standard errors for AOIs

Screen (AOI)	n	Fixation Duration Mean (SE)		Fixation Counts Mean (SE)		Visit Counts Mean (SE)	
		Self	Proxy	Self	Proxy	Self	Proxy
Date of Birth							
Question Text	7	.74 (.24)**	1.32 (.38)**	3.86	6.71 (1.71)**	2.29	3.71 (.78)*
Italic instructions	3	ns	ns	(.85)**	ns	(.52)*	ns
Response field(s)	8	1.54	2.89 (.93)**	ns	ns	ns	8.25 (1.70)*
Entire Screen	8	(.55)**	8.67	ns	45.25 (10)*	4.75	18.88
		4.48	(1.24)**	23.5		(.84)*	(6.01)*
		(.77)**		(1.81)*		7.25	
						(.56)*	

Table 2. (*continued*)

Employment Duties							
Question Text	5	ns	ns	3.2	9.4 (2.80)^	2.2(.58)**	4.4(.87)**
Italic instructions	5	ns	ns	(1.11)*	ns	ns	ns
Response field	7	ns	ns	ns	ns	ns	ns
Entire Screen	8	5.02 (1.36)*	8.29 (2.39)^	ns 23.5 (4.84)*	35.5 (7.55)^	ns	ns
Employer location							
Question Text							
M		ns	ns	ns	ns	ns	ns
ain	4	ns	ns	ns	ns	4.75	3.00 (.41)**
a	5	ns	ns	ns	ns	(.75)**	ns
b	4	ns	ns	ns	ns	ns	2.25 (.95)*
c	4	.91 (.20)**	.37 (.12)**	5.00	2.25 (.95)**	5.25	1.75 (.48)**
d	4	ns	ns	(1.00)**	ns	(1.60)*	ns
e	2	ns	ns	ns	ns	3.00	ns
f				ns		(.71)**	
Italic Instructions	4	ns	ns		ns	ns	ns
M	5	ns	ns	ns	ns	ns	ns
ain				ns			
a	4	ns	ns	ns	ns	ns	ns
Response field(s)	3	ns	ns	ns	ns	ns	ns
a	4	ns	ns	ns	ns		ns
b	4	ns	ns	ns	ns	ns	ns
c	3	ns	ns	ns	ns	ns	ns
d	3	ns	ns	ns	ns	ns	ns
e	5	ns	ns	ns	ns	ns	ns
f				ns		ns	
Entire Screen						ns ns	
Wages							
Question Text		ns	ns	ns	ns	ns	ns
Italic instructions		ns	ns	ns	ns	ns	ns
Response field(s)		ns	ns	ns	ns	ns	ns
Entire Screen		ns	ns	ns	ns	ns	ns

*p<.10
**p<.05

Date of Birth (DOB). The DOB question had one of the highest number of edit messages of all the screens, in part due to how the edits were designed [16] and the amount of detailed information needed about each individual: including month, day and year of birth and age. Previous research has found that the actual reported age by proxies differs from self-reports; thus, accurate knowledge of these data is a challenge for a proxy [19]. Proxy respondents may know how old someone is but not the date of birth, or they may know a month of a person's birth but not the day, or they may not know a person's age or date of birth and have to decide if they will guess the age based on how old they perceive the housemate to be.

This question, therefore, was ideal to identify if there were different eye-tracking patterns between a self and an unrelated proxy report. When examining eye-tracking patterns for AOI's noted in Figure 1 for the DOB screen, there were significant differences in fixation duration between the self report and the unrelated proxy report for the question text, t(6) = 2.51 p = .05, response field(s) t(7) = 2.30, p =.05, and the entire screen t(7) = 3.42, p = .01. There were also significant differences in fixation counts for the question text, t(6) = 2.55, p = .04 and entire screen, t(7) 1.98, p = .09 and significant differences in visit counts for the question text, t(6) = 2.20, p = .07, response field(s), t(7) = 2.14, p = .07 and entire screen, t(7) = 1.97, p = .09. Overall, there were greater fixation durations and more fixation and visit counts when reporting the age and date of birth of an unrelated household member compared to self-reports of age and date of birth.

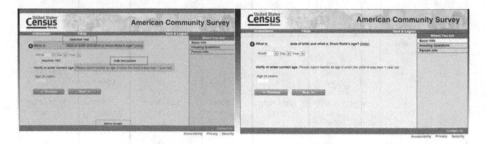

Fig. 1. Screen shot of the date of birth ACS screen, left has AOI's indicated and right is without AOIs. Names have been redacted to protect privacy.

Employment Duties. AOIs for the employment duties screen are outlined in Figure 2. Significant differences in the fixation duration between self report and unrelated proxy report were observed for the entire screen, $t(7) = 1.93$, $p = .09$. There were also significant differences in the fixation counts for the question text, $t(4) = 2.61$, $p = .06$ and the entire screen, $t(7)$ 2.01, $p = .08$. Similarly, these results indicate that proxy reports of unrelated individuals had longer fixation durations, a higher number of fixation counts and visit counts than self-reports.

Fig. 2. Screenshot of the employment duties ACS screen, left has AOI's indicated and right is without AOIs. The duties screen is asking for the most important duties that an individual does at work. Names have been redacted to protect privacy.

Employer Location. AOIs for the screen regarding employer location are noted in Figure 3. There were significant differences in fixation duration for self report and unrelated proxy reports for Question text, (d)-Name of county, $t(3) = -4.91$, $p = .02$. Significant differences in fixation counts were also observed for Question text, (d)-Name of county, $t(3) = -11.00$, $p = .001$. There were significant differences in visit counts for Question text (a)-Address number and street name, $t(3) = -3.66$, $p = .04$, and Question text (c)-Is the work location inside the limits of that city or town, $t(3) = -2.78$,

$p = .07$, Question text (d)-Name of county, $t(3) = -5.00$, $p = .02$. Unlike previous screens, these results show that participants had longer fixations, and more fixation counts and visit counts for self-reports when compared to unrelated proxy reports.

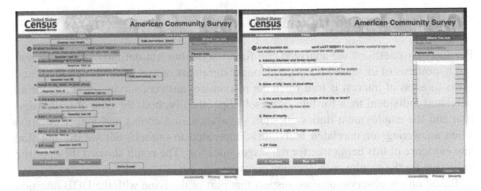

Fig. 3. Screenshot of the employer location ACS screen, left has AOI's indicated and right is without AOIs. This screen is primarily asking the address of where the individual worked last week. Names have been redacted to protect privacy.

Wages. Eye tracking results for the Wages screen revealed that there were no significant differences in fixation duration, fixation visits and visit counts for any of the AOIs outlined in Figure 4 for self-reports and unrelated proxy reports.

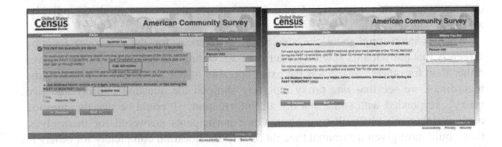

Fig. 4. Screenshot of the Wages ACS screen, left has AOI's indicated and right is without AOIs. Names have been redacted to protect privacy.

4   Assumptions and Limitations

While this study was a convenience sample, done with participants in the DC area, in order to apply the statistical t-test analysis we assume that this was a random sample of the population. Due to time limitations and length restrictions on this paper, we were not able to analyze all the screens from the online ACS. This is something that the authors plan to pursue in future. Also, the sample size of 10 participants is small and not all participants received all screens. However, in usability testing, a sample of

10 participants is often sufficient to identify important usability issues [20, 21]. We plan to increase the sample size by including additional participants in future iterations of this research.

5   Discussion and Conclusion

For the four questions we analyzed, we found some but not definitive evidence that our hypothesis of increased counts and longer durations of eye fixations and increased visits to areas of interest is true when the respondent answers survey questions for an unrelated individual than for him or herself. Specifically, both the date of birth question and the employment duties question show increased counts and longer duration when answering for unrelated individuals compared to oneself, but we did not find any evidence of this being true for the wages question. The result showed the opposite to be true for the employment location question.

Based on our observations, we suspect that part of the issue with the DOB question still surrounds the edit messages. If participants tried to enter in only a part of the age or date of birth information, an error message popped up instructing the respondent to enter as much information as possible. The DOB edit message was activated 9 different times during the study. The increases in eye fixation, duration, and visit counts for proxy reporting suggests that the usability participant needed to spend more time on answering for the unrelated individual by checking and rechecking the question and the answer options before moving onto the next screen.

The longer duration and increased number of fixations for employment duties question suggest that it is more of a burden to answer about other unrelated individuals than about oneself.

What is interesting about the significant differences for the employer location screen is that participants spent a longer time answering the questions for themselves rather than for others, which was the exact opposite of our hypothesis. Observing the recordings, we see that one proxy reporting skipped the question entirely and two proxy's responded with some, but not all, information. It could be that the question itself is inherently difficult to answer. Once participants answered for themselves, they could have given it minimal thought or skip the question completely for others in their household.

Qualitative information gathered during the debriefing indicates that when participants were confronted with questions that they felt they could not answer for the unrelated person living in the household, they guessed, fabricated the data, or said they would have preferred a way to skip the question entirely. This feedback combined with the eye-tracking data, adds insight into the complexities of collecting unrelated proxy information.

While we expected there to be differences in eye tracking behavior on the wages screen, there were none. We speculate that we found no differences because the question is complex and sensitive for everyone. The complexity stems from knowing what income to include, the sensitivity stems from the fact that the usability participants are reporting their income while the test administrator is looking on. Future research could expand the research on this topic.

The results of this analysis suggest that we cannot simply rely on eye fixation and duration data when measuring burden with proxy reports. Results also indicate that other measures, including qualitative data, such as user verbalizations, either during or after the session, needs to be combined with eye-tracking data when targeting questions that have greater burden for respondents. In instances where the respondent doesn't know the unrelated person's information, or for more difficult questions, such as questions related to a proxy's work circumstances, it could make sense to ask the person filling out the form to provide the housemates email and/or phone number so that the survey organization could follow up directly with that individual either through phone or email.

References

1. Redline, C., Lankford, C.: Eye Movement Analysis: A New Tool for Evaluation the design of visually administered instruments (paper and web). In: Proceedings from the American Association for Public Opinion Research Annual Conference, Montreal (2001)
2. Olmsted-Hawala, E., Holland, T., Quach, V.: Usability testing. In: Romano Bergstrom, J., Schall, A. (eds.) Eye Tracking in User Experience Design. Elsevier Press (2014)
3. Galesic, M., Tourangeau, R., Couper, M.P., Conrad, F.G.: New insights on response order effects and other cognitive shortcuts in survey responding. Public Opinion Quarterly 72(5), 892–913 (2008)
4. Jarrett, C., Romano Bergstrom, J.: Forms and Surveys. In: Romano Bergstrom, J., Schall, A. (eds.) Eye Tracking in User Experience Design. Elsevier Press (2014)
5. Moore, J.: Self/Proxy response status and survey response quality. Journal of Official Statistics 4(2), 155–172 (1998)
6. Hays, R., Vickery, B., Hermann, K., Perrine, J., Cramer, K., Meador, K., Spritzer, K., Devinsky, O.: Agreement between self reports and proxy reports of quality of life in epilepsy patients. Quality of Life Research 4(2), 159–168 (1995)
7. Palmer, L., Johnston, S., Rousculp, M., Chu, B., Nichol, K., Mahadevia, J.: Agreement between Internet-Based Self- and Proxy-Reported Health Care Resource Utilization and Administrative Health Care Claims. Value in Health 15(3), 458–465 (2012)
8. Kojetin, B., Mathiowetz, N.: The effects of self and proxy response status on the reporting of race and ethnicity. In: Proceedings from the American Association for Public Opinion Research Annual Conference (1998)
9. Bassett, S.S., Magaziner, J., Hebel, J.: Reliability of proxy response on mental health indices for aged, community-dwelling women. Psychology of Aging 5(1), 127–132 (1990)
10. Tamborini, H., Kim, C.: Are proxy interviews associated with biased earnings reports? Marital status and gender effects of proxy. Social Science Research 42(2), 499–512 (2013)
11. Reynolds, J., Wenger, J.: He said, she said: the gender wage gap according to self and proxy reports in the current population survey. Social Science Research 41(2), 392–411 (2012)
12. Kojetin, B., Mullin, P.: The Quality of Proxy Reports on the Current Population Survey (CPS). In: Proceedings of the Section on Survey Research Methods, American Statistical Association, pp. 1110–1115 (1995)
13. Looker, E.: Accuracy of proxy reports of parental status characteristics. Sociology of Education 62(4) (1989)

14. Ehmke, C., Wilson, S.: Identifying Web usability problems from eye-tracking data. In: Proceedings of HCI (2007)
15. Poole, A., Ball, L.: Eye tracking in human-computer interaction and usability research. In: Ghaoui, C. (ed.) Encyclopedia of human computer interaction, pp. 211–219. Idea Group, Pennsylvania (2005)
16. Horwitz, R., Tancreto, J., Zelenak, M.F., Davis, M.: Using Paradata to Identify Potential Issues and Trends in the American Community Survey Internet Instrument. U.S. Census Bureau: 2013 American Community Survey Research and Evaluation Report Memorandum Series #ACS13-RER-01 (2013),
http://www.census.gov/acs/www/Downloads/library/2013/
2013_Horwitz_02.pdf (accessed January 28, 2014)
17. Chin, J.P., Diehl, V.A., Norman, K.L.: Development of an instrument measuring user satisfaction of the human-computer interface. In: Proceedings of SIGCHI 1988, pp. 213–218 (1988)
18. Tobii Studio version 3.1.3.6615-RC (2012),
http://www.tobii.com/en/eye-tracking-research/global/
19. Bradshaw, B., Akers, D.: Age heaping in the 1960 Census of Population. US Census Bureau memorandum (1962)
20. Nielsen, J.: Why You Only Need to Test With 5 Users. Alertbox,
http://www.useit.com (March 19, 2000)
21. Faulkner, L.: Beyond the five-user assumption: Benefits of increased sample sizes in usability testing. Behavior Research Methods, Instruments, & Computers 35(3), 379–383 (2003)
22. Goldberg, J., Kotval, X.: Computer interface evaluation using eye movements: Methods and constructs. International Journal of Industrial Ergonomics 24(6), 631–645 (1999)

Experiences from a Long Run
with a Virtual Personal Trainer

Paolo Pilloni, Lucio Davide Spano, Fabrizio Mulas,
Gianni Fenu, and Salvatore Carta

Dipartimento di Matematica e Informatica, University of Cagliari
via Ospedale 72, 09124 Cagliari, Italy
{paolo.pilloni,davide.spano,fabrizio.mulas,fenu,salvatore}@unica.it

Abstract. In this paper, we report on our two-years experience with the commercial application *Everywhere Run!*, a mobile app that allows people to self monitor their running sessions and stay motivated in pursuing a wellbeing life-style. We consider a time interval of two-years, taking as breakpoint the first release of the application that improved the Virtual Personal Trainer presentation. The quantitative data we report comes from a remote logging of the app usage, while the qualitative data comes from the application reviews on the Google Play Store.

Keywords: self-monitoring, wellbeing monitoring, virtual trainer, running, Design for Quality of Life Technologies.

1 Introduction

The pervasive adoption of mobile technologies improved different aspects of our everyday life, providing different ways for supporting different tasks on the go, tracking or logging data that can help us in maintaining or changing our habits.

In the last years, such kind of technologies have been progressively adopted to support people in their daily physical routines. Many research studies provide solid evidence that peoples motivations may benefit from the guidance provided by mobile persuasive systems.

In this paper, we describe our experience with *Everywhere Run!*, a mobile application that allows self-monitoring during running sessions. *Everywhere Run!* differs from other similar apps by means of a Virtual Personal Trainer, able to guide users during a workout as if a real trainer was there with them. The virtual coach analyses the live input provided by the device's sensors, such as the covered distance and the elapsed time, in order to provide users with a broad set of performance metrics. The system provides a real time guidance and support during a workout by comparing a planned pace (i.e., the time to cover a certain distance) with the actual pace kept by the user.

In particular, we discuss the improvement we registered when radically re-designed the UI for presenting more effectively the monitored training parameters and their comparison with the planned values. We analyze the effect of the aforementioned redesign from both a quantitative and qualitative point of view, through a long run experience in the market.

C. Stephanidis and M. Antona (Eds.): UAHCI/HCII 2014, Part IV, LNCS 8516, pp. 601–612, 2014.
© Springer International Publishing Switzerland 2014

2   Related Work

This section, with no claim of being exhaustive, puts forward some research studies and some technological systems relevant to the field of mobile persuasive technologies designed to promote an active lifestyle.

Berkovsky et al. [1] present a new game design to motivate people in changing their sedentary playing habits. They suggest to stimulate users' motivations by means of virtual rewards users can gain only after performing some physical activity for real during a game. For this purpose, they recommend to modify some native components of traditional video games in addition to the interaction model between players and the game environment. For example, they proposed to introduce virtual rewards to motivate physical activity, to provide an external activity monitor to users in order to calculate the proper virtual reward, and to play the game by means of a modified game controller specifically designed to favour the active gaming experience. Their proposals have been implemented and evaluated through an empirical test on 180 participants in an exergame called Neverball. Obtained results revealed that the proposed design stimulated users to be more active by augmenting the total amount of active gaming.

Hoysniemi in [2] presents the results of a study conducted on users of a dance-based exergame called Dance Dance Revolution. She sets up an online survey to investigate, among others, users' playing styles, motivational, social, and perceived effects of active gaming. The responses of more than 500 users allowed the author to conclude that playing the game have had a positive outcome on users' motivations, physical health, and social life.

In [3], authors propose an exergame called Jogging over a Distance to conduct a series of experiments investigating how social and exertion interactions can affect users while training at a distance. The application exploits a wireless heart rate monitor that allows users to measure their heart rate in real time and also to input a desired heart rate intensity in order for them to specify a physical effort (in terms of that intensity) best suited for their physical skills. By means of a remote server the system elaborates the heart rate data collected in order to modify the 2D position of the audio sent to the jogging partner according to their current performance. If the two runners maintain the heart rate at the level they had previously specified, they can hear the audio of the partner as if they were jogging side-by-side. The results obtained from a qualitative study put emphasis on the importance of social interactions for exertion activities in addition to provide some guidance for researchers that aim at taking advantage of social factors to favor an active gaming experience.

In [4], authors present a mobile system called UbiFit Garden designed to push sedentary people to an active lifestyle. The software consists of three main components: a *fitness device* that automatically records and transmits the data of the physical activity performed both to the *glanceable display* and to the *interactive application*. The application stores all the information of the users' activities and provides a journal where users can consult and edit the data of their activities. The display is placed on the background of the device's screen and it shows a stylized representation of user's physical activities and attained goals in order to stimulate her motivation. The current level of physical activity is represented through the metaphor of a garden that becomes gradually more and more luxuriant as the user performs physical activities throughout the week. Results from a three-week field trial, revealed that users were positively surprised by the novelties the application introduced and their responses helped authors to derive some guidelines for the design and the evaluation of this kind of systems.

Chittaro et al. [5] propose a location-based exergame based on the famous Snake mobile game in which the snake is guided by users' movements. Authors set out to encourage users to walk more frequently, to introduce new evaluation metrics for this kind of persuasive systems, and finally, to demonstrate the effectiveness of the proposed solution by means of standard questionnaires mainly used in the medical field. Obtained results point out how users' behaviour and lifestyle can be positively influenced by the enjoyment resulting from the game.

In addition to the academic research studies and prototypes listed above, there exist several other commercial applications specifically designed for mobile devices.

One of the most famous application is Nike+ [6]. Some of its main strengths are: the advanced vocal cues and music management system, the availability of several features to favour social interactions with social networks, the support of a web community where users can create their training plans and socialize with other people, in addition to the possibility to enrich the training experience through ad-hoc devices. Along with Nike+, there exist several other commercial examples of such a kind of applications. Among the most popular ones: Adidas miCoach, Endomondo, MapMyFitness, RunKeeper, and Runtastic (see Section "Bibliography" for the references). All the applications share roughly the same core features: position tracking, statistical reports of users' activities, and support for social interactions through social networks and ad-hoc communities.

The experiences reported throughout this work are based on statistics from real users that chose our application freely for their training. With respect to the state-of-the-art proposals, our case study is the first example of mobile persuasive software born as an academic project and soon became a product with some characteristics similar to the most popular commercial products. Differently from the academic studies listed above[1], our application is allowing us to carry out a series of long-term experimentations, thus limiting the biasing factors typical of the most part of research studies on this field.

3   Experiences from a Long Run

In this section, we set out the main changes in design that have been made during the two years period under consideration. For the purposes of this work, we provide a comparison of the old and the new design of some of the most important screens and features of the application as a key to integrate and facilitate understanding of the data, the statistics, and all the remarks presented

---

[1] Please note that there are no publicly available statistics or results of experimentations for commercial products.

in Section 4. The new version of the application interface was introduced in February 2013.

Let us start with the workout creation screen for the old and the new design, respectively (see Figure 1 and Figure 2). The menu gives users the possibility to create relatively complex workout plans like the one, called "Monday", we show in the two figures: the training consists of several "sessions", called "traits", defined in terms of a distance and a pace/speed to keep. For example, the "trait 1" (see Figure 1 or Figure 2) is a training session of 2 km that the user should run at a pace of 5 minutes per kilometer (please note that runners generally express speed as the time to run one kilometer or mile). "Trait 1" is followed by "trait 2" where the user plans to run 10 km at a slightly higher pace than before. The new screen allows users to design a training plan with the same flexibility and complexity as before, albeit it is completely different in terms of usability. In particular, we decided to introduce a bar in the topmost part of the screen to make available to users both global application settings and some screen specific options in order to favour a more comfortable and effective use before, during, and after a training session (please note that these considerations hold for all the new design screens). In addition, we removed the set of buttons on the bottom part of the interface, in order to better support the primary task in the training creation, through a direct selection of the existing traits and automatically saving the edited values.

Fig. 1. Workout creation UI (old design)   **Fig. 2.** Workout creation UI (new design)

As previously pointed up, the most important feature of the application is its ability to act like a real trainer. In short, this functionality sets out to support and motivate the runner during the whole workout in order for her to adhere to the goals set by means of the workout creation screen (see Figure 1 or Figure 2). Figure 3 and Figure 4 show the ongoing workout screen and how the virtual personal trainer feature works.

Figure 3 shows the virtual trainer represented by the orange stick man in the left center of the screen. The virtual trainer acts like a pacemaker (a pacemaker is a runner that leads the race to keep the pace for other participants) so that the

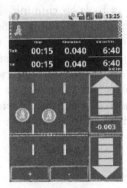

Fig. 3. Virtual personal trainer UI (old design)

Fig. 4. Virtual personal trainer UI (new design)

user (the green stick man in the center of the screen) has just to keep the pace of the trainer focusing solely on the run. In both designs, the horizontal bar in the topmost part of the screen provides a global overview of the whole workout (please note that the length of the workout has already been established during the workout creation) with the actual position of the runner with respect to the virtual trainer. Just below that bar there is a dashboard that reports current speed values, distances, and times regarding both the current trait and the whole training session. The two buttons in the bottommost part of the screen (only for the old design) allow to zoom in/out the part of the whole workout showed in the central part of the screen.

In the old design, the two big arrows in the right side of the screen suggested to the user if she has to slow down or to speed up. In between the two arrows is reported the current distance gap of the runner to the trainer. Moreover, the arrows will be alternatively filled proportionally to signal the need of slowing down or speeding up. All that can be observed in Figure 3. It depicts a runner just 3 meters behind the virtual coach, thus none of the arrows is filled signalling that the user is running with the planned pace.

At this point we discuss some other differences between the two designs: in addition to the aforementioned bar in the topmost of the screen, we concentrated to redesign the screen area that depicts the user and the virtual coach during a workout (i.e., the "personal trainer" area in the lower half of Figure 4). We decided, inspired also by some advices and comments from real users, to simplify some of the components originally present in the early design. First, in addition to a general graphic improvement, we changed the orientation of the "personal trainer" area from vertical to horizontal to be consistent with the whole workout perspective. In addition, we removed the zoom in/out buttons and one of the two arrows, and finally, we moved the distance gap indicator near the icon representing the user, on its left.

In this way, we simplified the overall appearance of the screen for an immediate readability, which is crucial for this kind of application: while running, the user should be able to read and understand the monitored parameters without spending too much time, since her primary task is to keep running. The new layout is more effective in providing such kind of information, since it facilitates the recognition of specific UI elements which are hidden as soon as they are not needed any more (e.g. the arrow for increasing the speed). The first version instead relayed on short term memory for finding differences between two states of the same element. This change allows users to receive immediately a coarse grained information at a first look, and to focus more on the UI only when more precise information is needed, enhancing the efficiency of the self-monitoring task.

4   Application Usage

From the first releases of the application, we monitored the size and the composition of our user set. By now, we counted about 54000 trainings performed by our 12500 users. As we detail better in the following sections, most of the users (76.5%) are returning ones, which means that once they tried the application once, they continued using the application for further training sessions. Such numbers highlight an overall success of the application in satisfying our target users needs.

In our analysis, we report three different metrics we gathered using Google Analytics [7], which has been designed for collecting statistics about the usage of a website. We associated the end of a training with the visit to a particular URL. In this way, we were able to collect the following metrics:

1. *Number of trainings*, which is the total number of trainings registered in a given time unit (e.g. day, week or month). It corresponds to the definition of *Visit* in [7], which is a group of interactions that take place in the application (or a website in general) within a given time frame. Since a visit may consist of different accesses to the application, it finishes either after 30 minutes of inactivity or at midnight. Provided that we record through Google Analytics only one interaction per training, the term visit can be interchanged with training in our case.

2. *Returning user trainings*, which is the number of trainings created by users that have registered at least another training before the current one [7].

3. *New user trainings*, which is the number of trainings created by first-time users [7]

In the following sections we discuss the data about these metrics in detail.

4.1   Number of Trainings

Figure 5 shows the total number of trainings, starting from the 1st of October 2011 and ending to the 30th of November 2013. The data is reported considering a week as time unit, so each point on the graph represents the number of trainings recorded during the considered week (e.g. the one starting at the 11th of August 2012).

The plot shows an increasing trend for the number of trainings, starting from the first launch of the application: we fitted the data with a linear model and

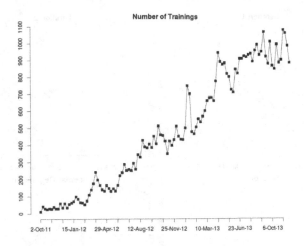

Fig. 5. The number of trainings created with *Everywhere Run!* from the 2nd October 2011 to the 30th November 2013

we obtained $a = 9.99$ as slope and $b = -99.37$ and intercept ($R^2_{adj} = 0.94$, $F_{(1,112)} = 2035$, $p < 2 \cdot 10^{-16}$), which means an increase of about 10 trainings per week.

In addition, we are interested here in establishing whether such trend can be considered as a constant during the whole application life-cycle, or if it possible to identify different phases during the examined interval. In order to identify possible slope changes, we exploited the algorithm described in [8,9], which is able to fit the relationship between the response and the explanatory variable (respectively the number of trainings and the week in our case) through a piecewise linear model, estimating the position of the breakpoints.

We started considering the whole time interval (from week 1 to week 114), and we proceeded iteratively excluding the interval higher or lower than the week selected as breakpoint. Figure 6 shows the result of the three iterations:

1. At the first iteration, the algorithm found a breakpoint at week 36. It corresponds to the 2nd of June, 2012.
2. At the second iteration, we considered the interval between week 36 and week 114. This time the algorithm found a breakpoint at week 98, corresponding to the 10th of August, 2013.
3. The last iteration considered the interval between week 37 and week 98. The algorithm found a breakpoint at week 70, corresponding to the 26th of January 2013. After this iteration, the algorithm was not able to find more breakpoints.

We defined a piecewise linear regression model for the data, starting from the breakpoints, the slopes and the intercepts identified for each segment by the algorithm. The resulting model is depicted in figure 6, bottom-right part ($R^2_{adj} = 0.97$, $F_{(7,106)} = 447$, $p < 2.2 \cdot 10^{-16}$).

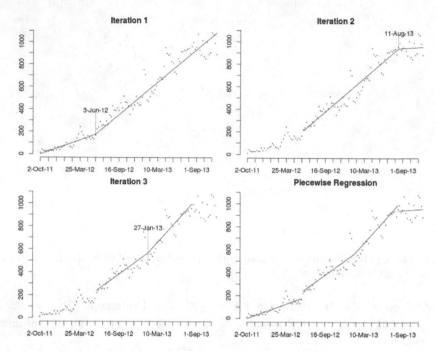

Fig. 6. Breakpoints and piecewise linear regression model of the total number of trainings from the 1st October 2011 to the 30th November 2013

While the straight-line model prediction of the values can be considered already good, the piecewise linear regression is more precise. We compared the two linear models with an ANOVA analysis and they resulted significantly different ($p < 4.3 \cdot 10^{-9}$). In addition, the piecewise regression provides some interesting insights for discussing the history of the application, especially if we compare the breakpoint positions with the dates of the application versions published on the Google Play Store.

The first segment shows the increment of trainings recorded in the months after the first application release, which can be quantified roughly in 5 more trainings for each week.

The first breakpoint (about the 3rd of June 2012) corresponds with the launch of the 2.0 version of the application, which happened in the 30th of May 2012. The version introduced the monitoring features, with the first UI version (see section 3). The update caused a steep increment of the training count, since the increase rate changed from 5 to 10 trainings per week. This means that the new features were able to better satisfy the users' needs, and the changes were considered useful for our audience.

The second breakpoint sets an additional increment of the slope, which is about 15 in the third segment. The breakpoint date is the 27th of January 2013, which is close to the release of the version 2.1 of the application (the beginning of February 2013). In that version, as already discussed in section 3, the self-monitoring features included in the application have been organised in a clearer and more effective way.

Finally, the last segment of the piecewise regression shows that at the beginning of August the increasing effect of the improvement finished, but we were able to maintain almost constant (with a slightly increasing trend) the number of trainings recorded.

4.2   Returning User Trainings

The number of trainings registered by returning users follows the same trend discussed for the total number of trainings, which is shown in the left part of figure 7. We recall that a user is defined as returning if she registered at least another training through the application in the past [7].

Following the same methodology we used in section 4.1, we found the same number of breakpoints:

1. Week 35, corresponding to the 27th of May 2012
2. Week 102, corresponding to the 1st of September 2013
3. Week 68, corresponding to the 13th of January 2013.

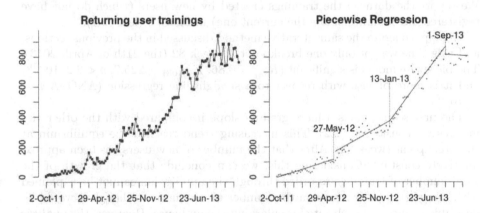

Fig. 7. The number of trainings created by returning users (left) and its piecewise linear regression (right)

Figure 7, right part shows the corresponding piecewise regression model ($R^2_{adj} = 0.96$, $F_{(7,106)} = 432.6$, $p < 2.2 \cdot 10^{-16}$). Provided that the breakpoints are located more or less in the same weeks, we can associate the changes of slope in the model to the same events we identified for the total number of trainings. Again, the ANOVA analysis found a significant difference between the simple straight-line regression and the proposed piecewise model ($p < 2.2 \cdot 10^{-16}$).

As a consequence, the trainings created by the returning users follow the same trend of the total number of trainings. This fact, together with the trend identified for the trainings created by new users discussed in section 4.3, allows us to conclude that our application has been able to satisfy the new users that tried *Everywhere Run!*, transforming most of them in returning ones.

This is confirmed also by a more deep insight on the composition of our user base. If we consider the time span between June 2012 (corresponding to the first breakpoint) and August 2013 (corresponding to the third breakpoint), we have that in the first period, one third of our 4300 users (30%) tried the application only once, while the other two thirds (70%) were returning ones. Our system registered a total of 7800 hours of running, with an average of 30 minutes per workout. Each user had 0.41 trainings per month (calculated excluding the one-time users).

After introducing the improvements discussed in this paper, we registered a consistent increment of the application usage. We doubled the number of users (7900) and, in addition, we increased the number of returning users reaching the 80% and the average training rate to 0.56 per month. The total running time increased from 7800 to 21700 hours (almost tripled), with the average value passed from 30 to 36 minutes per workout.

4.3   New User Trainings

We report the data on the trainings created by new users (which do not have registered any training before the current one) in figure 8 (left part).

We applied again the same iterative method discussed in the previous sections, and this time we got only one breakpoint at week 82 (the 21th of April, 2013). The piecewise model is significant ($R^2_{adj} = 0.86$, $F_{(3,108)} = 225.7$, $p < 2.2 \cdot 10^{-16}$) and it is more precise with respect to a straight-line regression (ANOVA $p < 2 \cdot 10^{-7}$).

The first segment has a more gradual slope if compared with the other two metrics we considered (2.2). This increasing trend reached the equilibrium at the breakpoint (week 82). After that the number of new users has been approximatively constant. Considering this, we can conclude that the growth of the total number of trainings recorded through the application cannot be explained with any particular increase on the number of new users, although it would be desirable to increase such rate for enlarging the audience. However, the analysis in section 4.2 shows that people usually create other trainings after the first one, therefore the application is able to convince people in using *Everywhere Run!* for further trainings after the first try.

4.4   Users' Feedback

We analysed the user reviews in the Google Play Store, in order to assess how our users feel and think about the app, and to see whether the difference between the two designs was reflected also in the ratings. In the first version of the UI, we had an average rate of 3.6, increased to 4.5 with the new version (5.0 is the maximum rate). Comparing such quantitative feedback with the qualitative comments of the app reviews, we collected the evidence that the key factor for

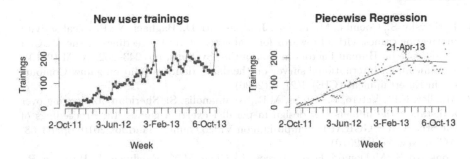

Fig. 8. The number of trainings created by new users from the 2nd October 2011 to the 30th November 2013

such improvements is the ability to guide step-by-step the user in their workouts in realtime, providing a precise position tracking together with different professional-level metrics (particularly important for high-end runners), which are shown to the users for a comparison with previous sessions.

5 Conclusion and Future Work

In this paper we discussed our experience with *Everywhere Run!*, a mobile application for self-monitoring during running sessions. The application provides a virtual trainer which allows the user to monitor her performance while running and to motivate her for reaching a planned result.

The analysis of the data, collected through Google Analytics in two years, shows an increase of trainings in correspondence to the introduction of the self-monitoring features, together with an additional increase when the UI has been enhanced. The trainings from returning users followed the same trend, showing that the application is able to fulfil our target user's needs.

For further improvements of the application, we plan to add the support for tracking the altitude and the calories burned. In addition, we are starting some experiments for using other external sensors, such as the heart-rate belts, for monitoring the runner's physical state.

Acknowledgments. This work is partially funded by Regione Sardegna under project SocialGlue, through PIA - Pacchetti Integrati di Agevolazione "Industria Artigianato e Servizi" (annualità 2010).

We also gratefully acknowledge Sardinia Regional Government for the financial support (P.O.R. Sardegna F.S.E. Operational Programme of the Autonomous Region of Sardinia, European Social Fund 2007-2013 - Axis IV Human Resources, Objective 1.3, Line of Activity 1.3.1 Avviso di chiamata per il finanziamento di Assegni di Ricerca.

References

1. Berkovsky, S., Coombe, M., Freyne, J., Bhandari, D., Baghaei, N.: Physical activity motivating games: virtual rewards for real activity. In: Proceedings of the SIGCHI Conference on Human Factors in Computing Systems, pp. 243–252. ACM (2010)
2. Hoysniemi, J.: International survey on the dance dance revolution game. Computers in Entertainment (CIE) 4(2), 8 (2006)
3. Mueller, F.F., Vetere, F., Gibbs, M.R., Agamanolis, S., Sheridan, J.: Jogging over a distance: the influence of design in parallel exertion games. In: Proceedings of the 5th ACM SIGGRAPH Symposium on Video Games, Sandbox 2010, pp. 63–68. ACM, New York (2010)
4. Consolvo, S., McDonald, D.W., Toscos, T., Chen, M.Y., Froehlich, J., Harrison, B., Klasnja, P., LaMarca, A., LeGrand, L., Libby, R., Smith, I., Landay, J.A.: Activity sensing in the wild: a field trial of ubifit garden. In: Proceedings of the SIGCHI Conference on Human Factors in Computing Systems, CHI 2008, pp. 1797–1806. ACM, New York (2008)
5. Chittaro, L., Sioni, R.: Turning the classic snake mobile game into a location-based exergame that encourages walking. In: Bang, M., Ragnemalm, E.L. (eds.) PERSUASIVE 2012. LNCS, vol. 7284, pp. 43–54. Springer, Heidelberg (2012)
6. Nike: Nike+ gps, nikerunning.nike.com (accessed January 29, 2014)
7. Google: Google Analytics, http://www.google.com/analytics/ (accessed January 13, 2013)
8. Muggeo, V.M.: Estimating regression models with unknown break-points. Statistics in Medicine 22, 3055–3071 (2003)
9. Muggeo, V.M.: segmented: an r package to fit regression models with broken-line relationships. R News 8(1), 20–25 (2008)
10. Runtastic: Runtastic, http://www.runtastic.com (accessed January 29, 2014)
11. Endomondo: Endomondo, http://www.endomondo.com (accessed January 29, 2014)
12. RunKeeper: Runkeeper, http://runkeeper.com (accessed January 29, 2014)
13. MapMyFitness: Mapmyfitness, http://www.mapmyfitness.com (accessed January 29, 2014)
14. miCoach: micoach, http://www.adidas.com/fi/micoach (accessed January 29, 2014)

Self-monitoring and Technology:
Challenges and Open Issues in Personal Informatics

Amon Rapp and Federica Cena

Università di Torino – Dipartimento di Informatica
C.so Svizzera, 185 10149 Torino, Italy
amon.rapp@gmail.com, cena@di.unito.it

Abstract. Personal Informatics (PI), also known as Quantified Self (QS), is a school of thought which aims to use technology for acquiring and collecting data on different aspects of the daily lives of people. These data can be internal states (such as mood or glucose level in the blood) or indicators of performance (such as the kilometers run). Some research was conducted in order to discover the problems related to the usage of PI tools, although none investigated how common users use these tools for tracking their behavior. The goal of this paper is to provide some insights about challenges and open issues regarding the usage of PI tools from the point of view of a common user. To this aim, we provide a theoretical background of personal informatics and a brief review on the previous studies that have investigated the usage pattern of PI tools.

Keywords: Personal Informatics, Quantified Self, Behavior Change, Self-tracking, Gamification.

1 Introduction

Personal Informatics (PI), also known as Quantified Self (QS), is a school of thought which aims to use technology for acquiring and collecting data on different aspects of the daily lives of people. These data can be internal states (such as mood or glucose level in the blood) or indicators of performance (such as the kilometers run). The purpose of collecting these data is self-monitoring, performed in order to gain self-knowledge or some kind of change or improvement (behavioral, psychological, therapeutic, etc.). PI tools are systems that help users to collect their data, enabling self-monitoring activities, their aggregation through some forms of reasoning, and feeding them back through computerized visualizations. PI tools can be apps running on users' mobile devices (such as Moves for automatic tracking of steps or eDreams for manual collection of dreams) or they can be ad hoc smart devices (such as Jawbone UP).

Some research was conducted in order to discover the problems related to the usage of PI tools [1], [2], although none investigated how common users use these tools for tracking their behavior. To this date, research has been carried out through surveys or interviews with people who already have a strong interest in collecting

C. Stephanidis and M. Antona (Eds.): UAHCI/HCII 2014, Part IV, LNCS 8516, pp. 613–622, 2014.

personal information, such as users of blogs and forums dedicated to personal informatics and information visualization, or users with prior experience in using PI tools [1], [2], [3]. The goal of this paper is providing some insights about challenges and open issues regarding the usage of PI tools from the point of view of a common user. To this aim, we provide a theoretical background of personal informatics and a brief review on the previous studies that have investigated the usage pattern of PI tools.

2   Theoretical Background

Personal Informatics systems have been defined as "those that help people collect personally relevant information for the purpose of self-reflection and gaining self-knowledge" [1].

For collecting personal data, PI tools rely on *self-monitoring*, the activity of observing and recording one's own behavior (i.e., actions, thoughts and emotions). Self-monitoring is a well-known technique in cognitive and behavioral psychology, much older than the possibilities offered by current PI technologies. Originally conceived as a clinical assessment method for collecting data on behaviors that only the patient could observe and record (e.g. eating, smoking), self-monitoring has become a standalone intervention technique, because of its reactive effects. Reactivity refers to the phenomenon in which the process of recording behavior causes the behavior to change [4]: self-monitoring often changes behavior, and this change is typically in the desired direction.

In *cognitive psychology,* self-monitoring is often interpreted as the first stage in multistage models of self-regulation as it signals a disengagement from automaticity or a transition from mindlessness to mindfulness [5]. Bandura [6], for example, states that self-monitoring is a subfunction of the self regulative mechanism that motivates and regulates human behavior: people can discover the factors that influence their behaviors, thoughts and emotional states, gaining self-knowledge through personal experimentation. The Transtheoretical Model of Behavior Change states that people apply different *processes of change*, i.e., different self-change strategies, for moving and progressing through different stages of behavior change [7]. Self-monitoring could be used as means of intervention in some of these stages, as a technique for favoring the consciousness raising and developing realistic changes, e.g. for individuating potential triggers of undesirable behavior patterns and planning strategies tailored to the individual [8].

In *behavioral psychology,* self-monitoring is usually directed at specific target behaviors (such as the number of smoked cigarettes). Some behavior theorists suggest that self-monitoring is effective in changing the behavior since it evokes self-evaluative statements that could either reinforce the desired behavior or punish the undesired one [9]. Kanfer [10] proposed a three-stage model for explaining reactive effects of self-monitoring: in the first stage, the self-monitor observes and records the target behavior; in the second stage, the self-monitor compares the occurrence of the behavior to a standard performance; in the third stage, the self-monitor rewards or punishes herself for having matched or having failed to meet her self-standard.

Malott [11] suggested that self-monitoring improves performance because of guilt-control: seeing undesirable behavior produces guilt feelings that can be avoided by improving the performance. However, beside how exactly self-monitoring works, the reactive effects on the behavior are sometimes temporary and modest and thus may require other techniques for maintaining the behavior change. For this reason, self-monitoring is often part of a self-management procedure in which contingencies of reinforcement and punishment are included [9].

Personal Informatics technologies enhanced the self-monitoring process in different directions. First, they make the data tracking easier for users, allowing to record the data potentially everywhere at every time, even in automatic manner. Second, they allow collected data to be organized and then given back to users in an aggregated visualization. Fogg states that self-monitoring is one of the strategies for informing the design of persuasive technologies [12]. Eco-feedback technologies, that may be seen as an extension of research in persuasive technology [13], are based on the hypothesis that "most people lack awareness and understanding about how their everyday behavior, such as driving to work or showering, affect the environment; technology may bridge this "environmental literacy gap" by automatically sensing these activities and feeding related information back through computerized means" [13]. Most of PI tools rely principally on cognitive models, since giving behavior information back to the user for causing insightful reflections is their main objective. Thus, with their newfound understanding of themselves, people may tailor their behavior to match their goals [1].

This approach, however, has some problematic points since it relies on the assumption that individuals are rational actors that seek to optimize their activity based on what they know [14]. Nevertheless, it is known that even if a person knows well how a specific behavior, despite its short-term benefits, is harmful for her wellbeing in the long term, she may irrationally choose to persevere in that behavior, ignoring the future consequences [15]. During their everyday lives, individuals often do not act according to rational choices, rather according to irrational methods, such as heuristics and rules of thumb [16]. Irrational behavior persists even when the individuals have been properly informed [17].

However, regardless of the principles of behavior involved, the act of self-monitoring is often an effective procedure for changing one's behavior [9].

Self-monitoring itself shows some practical issues. Korotitisch & Nelson Gray [18] identify eight variables affecting accuracy of the data collected: awareness of accuracy checks (self-monitors are more accurate when they are aware of accuracy checks); topography of the target behavior (if the target behavior is well defined); training in self-tracking (if the individual is trained in the use of self-monitoring); compliance (compliance can be enhanced if, for example, verbal commitments or contracts are made); accuracy-contingent reinforcement (accuracy is improved if reinforcement is provided contingent on the accuracy of self-monitored data); nature of the recording device; concurrent response requirements (the accuracy decreases when self-monitors are required to engage concurrently in other responses); valence of the target behavior (the accuracy may be lower for negatively valenced behavior than positively valenced behavior). Moreover, they identify other eight variables affecting reactivity of self-monitoring: target behavior valence (positively valenced behavior increases in frequency); motivation for change (increased reactivity in persons desiring to change the behavior being monitored); topography of the target behavior (greater reactivity occurs for nonverbal behavior); schedule or recording (greater reactivity happens if each occurrence of target behavior is recorded); concurrent response requirements (reactivity decreases when multiple behaviors are monitored concurrently); timing of recording (reactivity is improved if the recording occurred before rather than after the behavior); goal-setting feedback and reinforcement (providing feedback and reinforcement contingent on behavior change improves reactivity); nature of the self-recording device (the obtrusiveness of self-recording device can influence reactivity). Other practical issues related to training, maintaining data quality and compliance are showed in [19]. For example authors highlight that systematic training improves performance, recommending multi-component training that provides self-observers with definitions of what they should observe, feedback on accuracy, models of correct performance, and so on [19].

3   Previous Studies on Personal Informatics

There are a number of research works in Personal Informatics. Some authors investigate the role of self-monitoring through technological means, such as Maitland & Chambers [23] who investigate the role of self-monitoring in health behavior change within the context of cardiac rehabilitation programs. Other authors design and develop systems that allow users to collect and visualize personal information for therapeutic and rehabilitation purposes or for promoting behavior change towards healthier and more sustainable habits. For example, we can cite UbiGreen [20], a mobile application that provides personal awareness about green transportation behavior through iconic feedback; Mobile Mood Diary [21], a mobile and online symptom tracking tool for adolescents with mental problems; and Lullaby [22] a system for tracking sleep that combines temperature, light, motion sensors, audio, photos and an off-the-shelf sleep sensor for helping people to understand their sleep behavior.

Currently, there are also many commercial applications and devices for self-tracking behavior data (see [24] for an overview). For example, among the most popular, Moves (movement), Nike+ (sport activities), MoodPanda (mood), MyfitnessPal (calories and food), Jawbone (sleep, physical activity, mood and food) track users' behavior and give information back to users, allowing visual exploration of the data gathered and showing patterns and trends. These applications are at the disposal of all individuals interested in self-monitoring, but the modalities of their usage by common users are not yet well investigated. In fact, researchers focus mainly on users with a previous experience with Personal Informatics tool. For example, Li et al. [1] carry out a survey with users with an intrinsic interest in Personal Informatics, i.e., participants to blogs and forums dedicated to personal informatics and information visualization. Based on their findings, they suggest a stage-based model for Personal Informatics usage. The *Preparation stage* occurs before users start collecting personal information: in this stage users have to choose the right tool for satisfying their needs, and they can have problem to find the most suited one among the available ones. In the *Collection stage*, users collect information about their thoughts, behaviors, interactions with people and the environment; some problems arise in collecting information (e.g. users fail to track their behaviors). The *Integration stage* is the moment when the information gathered is combined and transformed for the user to reflect on: users can encounter problems when data come from multiple inputs and are visualized in multiple outputs. The *Reflection stage* is when people reflect on their personal information: problems here occur because of difficulties in exploring and understanding information. Finally, in the *Action stage* people decide to change their behavior based on the understanding of their data. Li et al. [2] further investigate the usage of self-monitoring tools in another study, focusing on the Reflection stage. In this stage, people's information needs can change, from the *Discovery phase*, when users do not know theirs goal or the factors that influence their behavior, to *Maintenance phase*, when they already know their goals and the factors that influence their behavior.

Results of their work show that the current commercial tools do not have sufficient understanding of users' needs. They suggest to i) alert and assist the users when they don not meet their goal; ii) reduce the burden of data collection; iii) support different kinds of collection tools, integrating them in a system and presenting data together; iv) reduce the upfront cost of data collection v) support transition between Discovery and Maintenance phases.

As seen above, these two studies recruited i) participants from a blog dedicated to Personal Informatics (http://quantifiedself.com), a blog about general information visualization (http://flowingdata.com) and forums at two Personal Informatics web sites (http://slifelabs.com, http://moodjam.org), ii) participants currently using a Personal Informatics tool (they had to have used it for a month or more). Thus, these users are familiar with Personal Informatics. As the authors themselves note about the first research, there is the suspect that these participants encountered only a subset of problems that common users may experience: this limitation suggests to study users with little or no prior experience with Personal Informatics systems to find specific issues that they may encounter [1].

Following this suggestion, we decided to emphasize some open issues that common users could encounter with PI tools and the challenges that this kind of applications have to face in the next future. These remarks are conceived as a starting point for a further study in which we aim at investigating the pattern of usage of PI tools by common users.

4   Challenges and Open Issues from a Common User Perspective

We define "common users" as users that are not intrinsically interested in tracking their behavior and do not have prior experience with PI tools. Intrinsic interest for using PI applications could be related to: belonging to a community dedicated to self-tracking or believing that technology could lead to knowing thyself (as the members of the Quantified Self community), being affected by a chronic disease that requires a continuous self-monitoring (e.g., diabetes), or having a strong motivation for changing a specific behavior (e.g., going on a diet). On the other hand, common users can be seen as people with no familiarity with self-monitoring activities and tools, not belonging to a community of shared interests in self-experimentation, and not having strong motivation for changing their behavior. For such common users, an occasion for trying one of these applications could emerge from the suggestions of friends or significant others, the exposure to commercial ads, news or reviews, a casual glimpse to an application or device that attracts their attention.

The main differences that distinguish common users from intrinsically interested users (that we will call PI users from now on) are the lack of initially strong motivation for self-monitoring and the absence of prior experience with PI tools. Less motivation and less familiarity with self-monitoring activities and PI tools open new issues with respect to those already highlighted [1]. These issues are related to the process of tracking, managing and visualizing of self-monitored data.

First, regarding the *data tracking*, common users may not be so compliant in tracking their own activities. This issue is also present in clinical settings, where the therapist compels the patient to track her own behavior, and among PI users, as Li et al. [1] highlighted. Patients and PI users often fail to self-monitor themselves due to lack of motivation, time or forgetfulness. However, we may expect that common users would be even less compliant in tracking their own behavior. Since they are not compelled or intrinsically motivated for tracking each occurrence of the target behavior, we could imagine that self-report activity would be accomplished with less continuity, perseverance and accuracy.

Second, regarding the data *management,* common users may not be so interested in deeply investigating the data gathered by PI tools. One of the characteristics of PI users is their interest in self-experimentation, i.e., their willingness to discover patterns and correlation among data. At the same time, patients under psychological assessments, people affected by a chronic disease or individuals strongly motivated for changing an unhealthy behavior have a strong interest in searching for and knowing better the factors that may influence their condition. This interest could overcome the burden of choosing the right tool for tracking a specific behavior, exploring data with different tools and correlating information that could not be visualized together. Many PI users, in fact, as reported by Li et al. [1], use different strategies for managing their data, for example using paper graphs. For common users the situation is different. They most likely start from using a single tool or device without knowing what kind of information will be useful to them. The effort in exploring data for finding correlations between variables that may affect their behavior would probably be weak. The engagement in managing different sources of information would decrease rapidly if not supported and incentivized by the tool itself. However, forcing users to interact daily with the data gathered for enhancing their involvement, as suggested by Li et al. [2] for PI users, may not be the optimal solution for common users, since reports and alerts could be easily ignored by them, representing a source of noise.

Finally, regarding data *visualization*, common users are usually not very familiar with visualization of quantitative data that PI tools provide for them. In clinical settings, interpretation of the data gathered through self-monitoring is usually provided by the therapist/physician: she evaluates the patient's logs, discusses with her the data that represent potential triggers of undesirable behavior and plans strategies of intervention tailored to patient's behavioral patterns. PI users, instead, are used to interpret the data on their own, determine by themselves if their current actions are in line with their goals. However, also PI users can find some difficulties in retrieving, understanding and interpreting the data when they are not supported by the tool they are using [1]. This is especially true for common users. For them, a meaningful representation of their data, able to provide useful information, is essential for engaging them in the usage of the tool and for compensating the self-monitoring burden. Moreover, common users could be moved by unrealistic expectations and become easily disappointed by ambiguous representations, excessive complexity and unintuitive interaction modalities.

All these issues that we expect to encounter in common users should be investigated in an additional user study. However, we can highlight some challenges that PI tools will have to face in the next years for overcoming some of such problems.

Personal Informatics has to find new ways for reducing the burden of self-monitoring. One possibility is to completely automate the collection of data, improving sensor technologies and algorithms for inferring new information from the existing data. We could expect that in the upcoming years wearable technologies and ubiquitous computing could face this challenge providing new devices that could silently and invisibly track users' behavior. Problems of using this automatic tracking concerns confidence of data reliability and privacy issues. Furthermore, not all the data are suited to be automatically detected, such as mood and emotional states.

Another way for reducing these barriers is to make self-monitoring more fun and enjoyable. From this perspective, the world of games could suggest some strategies of improvement. *Gamification*, as the use of game elements in non game context [25], highlights how the addition of simple mechanisms derived from videogames can stimulate participation, improve motivation and make cumbersome activities more enjoyable. However, gamification, as it is currently conceived, shows many problems when it is applied to PI, since it is mostly based on design techniques that provide extrinsic rewards and stimulate competition among users, using points, badges and leaderboards. PI tools, instead, are mainly conceived as personal instruments, especially when the self-monitored data relates to sensible information (such as wellness, health, weight, dreams etc). Thus, the mechanical implementation of leaderboards and badges (that are often added without considering the context of their application) is not always appropriate in this context. Moreover, points and external rewards could reduce intrinsic motivation in users [26] and their effects could vanish in short time frame, after an initial hype.

Personal Informatics tools should promote a long-term usage. PI tools require a long-term compliance from their users in order to work well, since their benefits increase over time. For a long lasting engagement it is essential that users perceive the self-monitoring as meaningful *per se*, for the benefits that it provides, and not only as means for obtaining prizes, points and extrinsic rewards. Thus, it is necessary to go beyond the current gamification practices, considering more complex game elements and adapting them to the PI context, stimulating the self-monitoring and transforming it in a "playful" [27] and "gameful" [28] activity. Identification of kinds of game elements which are suitable for the PI context is the challenge that should be considered.

Personal Informatics tools should provide meaningful data visualizations. The data presentation should immediately engage users, giving sense to the self-monitoring activity. In addition, as we have seen above, the data gathered from different sources and related to different behavior should be integrated in an intuitive way that could reduce the cognitive load on the users. In the last years, many researches have focused on the role that storytelling can play in data visualization, since visualizing data has analogies with the ability to tell engaging stories [29]. However, very few applications tried to implement narrative elements within the flow of data visualization (e.g., [30], [31]). In PI tools, visualizing human behavior data means putting the individual at the center: thus, the character, the point of view from which a narration takes form, acquires a great importance. Considering this point, we can look once again at the video game world for taking inspiration, for finding novel modalities for displaying behavioral data. As a matter of fact, video games succeed where hypertexts failed, creating an engaging narrative form that requires active user interaction, deeply involving the players and, at the same time, leaving them the power to determine the story. Video games give the players the possibility to reflect and identify themselves in an alter ego, the avatar, that acts at their place in the game world. Reflecting in an image that user can recognize, at the same time, as herself and as something else (as usually happens when a player identifies with her avatar and simultaneously feels a sense of empathy that leads her to nurture the character) could be more effective than a simple presentation of behavioral data, because of the emotional link that could be established between the user and her avatar. How to adapt this peculiarity of video games in the PI field, taking into account the difference between a game and an application used for recording personal behavior, is another challenge that should be considered.

5   Conclusion and Future Works

Personal Informatics commercial tools seem nowadays more interested in collecting data and transforming them in beautiful representations and visualizations than improving people's daily activities [32]. They open new problems and issues: how are they used by common people? How much are users accurate and compliant in using these applications? Could they be effective in changing user's behavior? What kind of meanings are provided through the display of user's behavior information?

As future work, we aim at answering these questions with a user study in order to discover how PI tools allow common people to self-track their behaviors, how they are perceived by individuals, which are the difficulties and the problems encountered during the self-monitoring process, whether the provided information is useful for the users, whether the information visualization is effective for the user purposes or it is necessary to move beyond and think about other design features that could leverage the act of self-monitoring.

References

1. Li, I., Dey, A.K., Forlizzi, J.: A Stage-Based Model of Personal Informatics Systems. In: SIGCHI Conference on Human Factors in Computing Systems, pp. 557–566. ACM, New York (2010)
2. Li, I., Dey, A.K., Forlizzi, J.: Understanding My Data, Myself: Supporting Self-Reflection with Ubicomp Technologies. In: The 13th International Conference on Ubiquitous Computing, pp. 405–414. ACM, NY (2011)
3. Khovanskaya, V., Baumer, E.P.S., Cosley, D., Voida, S., Gay, G.K.: "Everybody Knows What You're Doing": A Critical Design Approach to Personal Informatics. In: SIGCHI Conference on Human Factors in Computing Systems, pp. 3403–3412. ACM, New York (2013)
4. Miltenberger, R.G.: Behavior modification: Principles and procedures, 4th edn. Wadsworth, Belmont (2007)
5. Karoly, P.: Mechanisms of self-regulation: A systems view. Annual Review of Psychology 44, 23–52 (1993)
6. Bandura, A.: Social Cognitive Theory of Self-Regulation. Organizational Behavior and Human Decision Processes 50, 248–287 (1991)
7. Prochaska, J.O., Velicer, W.F.: The Transtheoretical Model of Health Behavior Change. American Journal of Health Promotion 12(1), 38–48 (1997)
8. Rosal, M.C., Ebbeling, C.B., Lofgren, I., Ockene, J.K., Ockene, I.S., Hébert, J.R.: Facilitating dietary change: the patient-centered counseling model. Journal of the American Dietetic Association 101(3), 332–341 (2001)
9. Cooper, J.O., Heron, T.E., Heward, W.L.: Applied behavior analysis, 2nd edn. Prentice Hall, New York (2007)
10. Kanfer, F.H.: The many faces of self-control, or behavior modification changes its focus. In: Stuart, R.B. (ed.) Behavioral Self-management: Strategies, Techniques, and Outcomes, pp. 1–48. Brunner/Mazel, New York (1977)
11. Malott, R.W.: Notes from a radical behaviorist. Author, Kalamazoo (1981)
12. Fogg, B.J.: Persuasive Technology. Using Computers to Change What We Think and Do. Morgan Kaufmann, San Francisco (2003)
13. Froehlich, J., Findlater, L., Landay, J.: The design of eco-feedback technology. In: SIGCHI Conference on Human Factors in Computing Systems, pp. 1999–2008. ACM, New York (2010)
14. Brynjarsdóttir, H., Håkansson, M., Pierce, J., Baumer, E., Di Salvo, C., Sengers, P.: Sustainably unpersuaded: how persuasion narrows our vision of sustainability. In: SIGCHI Conference on Human Factors in Computing Systems, pp. 947–956. ACM, New York (2012)
15. Nakajima, T., Lehdonvirta, V., Tokunaga, E., Kimura, H.: Reflecting Human Behavior to Motivate Desirable Lifestyle. In: Conference of Designing Interactive Systems, pp. 405–414 (2008)
16. Tversky, A., Kahneman, D.: Judgment under uncertainty: heuristics and biases. Science 185, 1124–1131 (1974)
17. Brown, L.R.: Eco-Economy: Building an Economy for the Earth. Earthscan, London (2001)
18. Korotitisch, W.J., Nelson-Gray, R.O.: An overview of self-monitoring research in assessment and treatment. Psychological Assessment 11, 415–425 (1999)
19. Foster, S.L., Laverty-Finch, C., Gizzo, D.P., Osantowski, J.: Practical issues in self-observation. Psychological Assessment 11, 426–438 (1999)

20. Froehlich, J., Dillahunt, T., Klasnja, P., Mankoff, J., Consolvo, S., Harrison, B., Landay, J.: UbiGreen: Investigating a Mobile Tool for Tracking and Supporting Green Transportation Habits. In: Proceedings of the SIGCHI Conference on Human Factors in Computing Systems, pp. 1043–1052. ACM, New York (2009)
21. Matthews, M., Doherty, G.: In the mood: engaging teenagers in psychotherapy using mobile phones. In: The SIGCHI Conference on Human Factors in Computing Systems, pp. 2947–2956. ACM, New York (2011)
22. Kay, M., Choe, E.K., Shepherd, J., Greenstein, B., Watson, N., Consolvo, S., Kientz, J.A.: Lullaby: a capture & access system for understanding the sleep environment. In: The 2012 ACM Conference on Ubiquitous Computing, pp. 226–234. ACM, New York (2012)
23. Maitland, J., Chalmers, M.: Self-monitoring, self-awareness, and self-determination in cardiac rehabilitation. In: SIGCHI Conference on Human Factors in Computing Systems, pp. 1213–1222. ACM, New York (2010)
24. Marcengo, A., Rapp, A.: Visualization of Human Behavior Data: The Quantified Self. In: Huang, L.H., Huang, W. (eds.) Inovative Approaches of Data Visualization and Visual Analytics, pp. 236–265. IGI Global, Hershey (2013)
25. Deterding, S., Dixon, D., Khaled, R., Nacke, L.: From game design elements to gamefulness: Defining "Gamification". In: 15th International Academic MindTrek Conference: Envisioning Future Media Environments, pp. 9–15. ACM, New York (2011c)
26. Deci, E.L., Koestner, R., Ryan, R.M.: A meta-analytic review of experiments examining the effects of extrinsic rewards on intrinsic motivation. Psychological Bulletin 125(6), 627–668 (1999)
27. Ferrara, J.: Playful Design. Creating Game Experiences in Everyday Interfaces. Rosenfeld Media, New York (2012b)
28. McGonigal, J.: Reality is Broken: Why Games Make Us Better and How They Can Change the World. Penguin, New York (2011)
29. Gershon, N.D., Page, W.: What storytelling can do for information visualization. Communications of the ACM 44(8), 31–37 (2001)
30. Eccles, R., Kapler, T., Harper, R., Wright, W.: Stories in geotime. In: IEEE Symposium on Visual Analytics Science and Technology, pp. 19–26 (2007)
31. Heer, J., Mackinlay, J., Stolte, C., Agrawala, M.: Graphical histories for visualization: Supporting analysis, communication, and evaluation. IEEE Transactions on Visualization and Computer Graphics 14(6), 1189–1196 (2008)
32. Rapp, A.: Beyond Gamification. Enhancing user engagement through meaningful game elements. In: 8th International Conference on the Foundations of Digital Games, pp. 485–487 (2013)

A User Test with Accessible Video Player Looking for User Experience

Johana Maria Rosas Villena, Rudinei Goularte, and Renata Pontin de Mattos Fortes

Mathematics and Computer Science Institute,
University of São Paulo P.O. Box 668 - Zip Code: 13560-970 São Carlos, SP, Brazil
{johana,rudinei,renata}@icmc.usp.br

Abstract. There is a huge availability of videos that have been produced in a very fast and wide way, along with the popularity of Internet. The video authors should carefully consider the scenario since many users have different needs. It is important to keep in mind the user experience because involves a person's behaviors, attitudes, and emotions about using a particular system, for example, the video player. In addition, usability and accessibility of video players need to be considered. The object of this study is to examine users' needs, expectations and requirements for accessible videos. We developed an accessible video player to evaluate with users. We present the results in the form of guidelines, which highlight the characteristics of users; the characteristics that the video need to satisfy the users' needs and the context in which users commonly watch the videos.

Keywords: user experience, video accessibility, user test.

1 Introduction

The popularity of the Internet has boosted many possibilities of media dissemination. Along with the technological advances on the Internet, there is a huge availability of videos that have been produced in a very fast and wide way. The video authors should carefully consider the scenario, since many users have different needs. Thus, it is very important to keep in mind the user experience because it involves a person's behaviors, attitudes, and emotions about using a particular system, for example, the video player. In addition, usability and accessibility of video players need to be perused.

ISO 9241-210:2010 specifies that usability, when interpreted from the perspective of the users' personal goals, can include the kind of perceptual and emotional aspects typically associated with user experience [4]. It also affirms that usability criteria can be used to assess aspects of user experience. Nevertheless, the standard does not go further in clarifying the relation between user experience and usability.

The accessibility requirements must be considered in order to produce and reproduce videos, so that any user can access their contents regardless of the limitations imposed by either deficiency or some temporary restriction. The current video players present barriers for many people, especially to the elderly, for example, the videos do not have subtitles nor change the font size on video subtitle.

C. Stephanidis and M. Antona (Eds.): UAHCI/HCII 2014, Part IV, LNCS 8516, pp. 623–633, 2014.
© Springer International Publishing Switzerland 2014

The object of this study was to examine users' needs, expectations and requirements for accessible videos. We conducted studies with twenty five users, the participants were between 23 and 82 years old. We have applied triangulation methodology of the survey, user test and observation to identify the requirements, problems and users' needs. Thus, we also developed an accessible video player to test with these users.

The results are presented in a list of guidelines, which highlight the characteristics of users, the characteristics that the videos need to satisfy the users' needs and the context in which the videos will be used. Both academia and industry can benefit from knowledge of these requirements when designing the further studies and development work concerning the user experience of watching videos in an accessible video player.

The paper is organized as follows: Section 2 describes the concepts of user experience, usability and accessibility; the accessible video player is presented in Section 3; Section 4 addresses the user requirements; finally, Section 5 concludes the paper and suggests some future works.

2   Usability, Accessibility and User Experience

ISO 9241-11:1998 explains that usability extent to which a system, product or service can be used by specified users to achieve specified goals with effectiveness, efficiency and satisfaction in a specified context of use [2].

ISO 9241-171 defines accessibility as: the usability of a product, service, environment or facility by people with the widest range of capabilities [4].

There are many definitions of User Experience (UX) that explore different perspectives. The ISO 9241-210 defines UX as person's perceptions and responses that result from the use or anticipated use of a product, system or service [3]. Hassenzahl, Law and Hvannberg explained that UX goes beyond usability [5]:

- Usability focuses on performance of and satisfaction with users' tasks and their achievement in defined contexts of use; UX balance these aspects with beauty, challenge, stimulation and self-expression.
- Usability has emphasized objective measures of its components, such as percentage of tasks achieved for effectiveness and task completion times and error rates for efficiency; UX is more concerned with users' subjective reactions, their perceptions of the system themselves and their interaction with them.
- Usability has often focused on the removal of barriers or problems in systems as the methodology for improving them; UX is more concerned with the positive aspects of system use, and how to maximize them, whether those positive aspects be joy, happiness, or engagement.

Petrie [6] categorized the methods for usability, accessibility and UX evaluation in: automated checking of conformance to guidelines and standards, evaluations conducted by experts, evaluations using models and simulations, evaluation with users or potential users, and evaluation of data collected during the use of a system.

There are guidelines on accessibility: IBM Human Ability and Accessibility Centre, ISO standards (10779, 9241-20, 9241-171), WAI guidelines (WCAG, UAAG, ATAG), Section 508 of the Rehabilitation Act of the United States Federal government[6], automatic tools (AIS Toolbar, Opera, WAVE, etc.), guidelines in important companies (Firefox, Microsoft, Joomla, Eclipse, Adove Flash, etc), etc.

There are guidelines on usability: Heuristic evaluation proposed by Nielsen, expert walkthrough evaluation, parts 12-17 of the ISO 9242 standard [6], golden principles of good interface design by Shneiderman, automatic tools (LIFT, WebSAT, etc.), evaluations with users, etc.

3   Accessible Video Player

We have developed an accessible media player, Facilitas Player, using HTML5, JavaScript, jQuery, jQuery UI and CSS to provide functionalities to make videos accessible. The current controls include basic controls as play/pause, stop, volume controller and full screen and new controls as caption, search, list with search result, links, speed up, speed down, rewind 10 seconds, forward 10 seconds, configuration, help, and light on/off. Some functionalities of accessibility include highlight and keyboard access. The link for the Facilitas Player is http://5.135.182.74:8080/.

Some of the accessibility features of Facilitas player are in conformance with the UAAG: G1.1: Alternative content, G1.3: Highlighting, G1.4: Text configuration, G1.5: Volume configuration, G1.8: Orientation in Viewports, G2.1: Keyboard access, G2.4: Search, G2.7: Preference settings, G3.3: Help and G2.8: Toolbar configuration.

Link control enables the developer to add links to the video. Each link is linked to a specific time in the video. Links provide a short description of the video content and a long description when the link is selected, facilitating the search into the video.

Fig. 1. Facilitas Search Control and Link Control

For instance, in Fig. 1, the video has six links. If we select the "Tip: dark chocolate" link, the video skips to the third link time and a long description appears.

The search control enables the search for a word or phrase that appears in the sub-title text. The player will show all results and when a result is selected, it skips to that point on the video. For instance, in Fig. 1, we searched for the word "butter", return-ing a set of two entries. When a result is chosen, the player reproduces the selected part of the video.

A light functionality is represented as a lamp icon on the video (Fig. 1) and is used to distinguish the video from the rest of the page. Another functionality of Facilitas Player is the configuration, which enables text configuration to change style, color and size in real time, as shown in the bar at the right side of Fig. 2.

Fig. 2. Facilitas Caption background Color

A control to move the Facilitas toolbar still in development, the toolbar will be docked at the top or bottom of Facilitas Player. A control to change the caption back-ground color was developed (Fig. 2). A Help Control show the keyboard shortcuts of Facilitas Player. Finally, each control have a description to facilitate the navigation.

4   User Requirements

We have applied triangulation methodology on the basis of a survey, evaluation with users and observation to identify the requirements, problems and users' needs. Our aim was to target both explicit and implicit requirements when choosing the three different methods. All of these studies took a place concurrently during the year 2013.

4.1   Survey

Surveys are commonly used as a method to identify requirements. The questionnaire in the earliest phase of product development is exploratory, surveys can help to identify current practices, needs of and attitudes to the new system ideas and does not aim to confirm any particular theory [7]. For this research, the survey allow to collect data to identify the user profile, problems and users' needs. The data-collection was carried out using a questionnaire in Portuguese for 24 Brazilian people and 1 Peruvian. Besides the questionnaire, a Term of Agreement was elaborated to clarify the objectives of the research, the risks, benefits and their freedom to participants to quit their participation at any time. The user requirement questionnaire contained 18 questions related to user profile, problems and users' needs. It is important to mention that we have invited the participant users during the user center design we had adopted while developing the Facilitas player.

The data gathered by the answers to the questionnaire were collected in two places, the local Educational Institute to attend to Informatics courses for elderly and the university. The questionnaire represents overall view of users' requirements of video players. It should be observed that this research was aimed at the elicitation of user needs. We meet with each participant individually to collect the data. The total number of respondents was 25 and a description of the user profile is given in Table 1. None participant were between 41 - 50 years old.

Table 1. Description of user profile

	Age 23-30	Age 31-40	Age 51-60	Age 61-70	Age 71-82
Age	28%	8%	20%	32%	12%
Gender					
• Female	43%	50%	80%	43%	100%
• Male	57%	50%	20%	57%	-
Marital Status					
• Single	71.4%	-	-	-	-
• Married	14.3%	100%	80%	87.5%	33.3%
• Cohabiting	14.3%	-	-	-	33.3%
• Divorced	-	-	20%	12.5%	-
• Widow	-	-	-	-	33.3%
Occupation					
• Pensioner	-	-	20%	75%	33.3%
• Student	71.4%	50%	-	-	-
• Unemployee	-	-	40%	12.5%	66.6%
• Seller	-	50%	20%	-	-
• Entrepreneur	-	-	20%	12.5%	-
• Employee	14.3%	-	-	-	-
• Teacher	14.3%	-	-	-	-

About digital awareness, the participants presented the characteristics as shown in Table 2. We can see that the majority of people with some kind of impairments are the elders. It is worth to notice that older participants present less time of use the computers.

Table 2. Digital awareness and impairments

	Age 23-30	Age 31-40	Age 51-60	Age 61-70	Age 71-82
Use of the computer					
• <2 years	-	-	25%	25%	100%
• 2 and 4 years	-	50%	25%	12.5%	-
• 4 and 6 years	-	-	25%	-	-
• > 6 years	100%	50%	25%	62.5%	-
Visual Impairment					
• Big difficulty	14.2%	-	-	12.5%	33.3%
• Some difficulty	14.2%	-	100%	87.5%	66.6%
• None	71.4%	100%	-	-	-
Hearing Impairment					
• Big difficulty	-	-	-	12.5%	-
• Some difficulty	14.3%	-	40%	12.5%	100%
• None	85.7%	100%	60%	75%	-
Motor Impairment					
• Some difficulty	-	-	-	-	33.3%
• None	100%	100%	100%	100%	66.6%
Cognitive Impairment					
• Some difficulty	-	-	-	50%	100%
• None	100%	100%	100%	50%	-

The participants reported that the most common Video Players on the web they watch were: YouTube (30%), followed by News (28%), None (10%), and others (32%). The most used controls of Video Player were play/pause (29%), followed by stop (13%), language (11%), change the caption size or color (7%), full screen (7%), and others (33%).

The common problems the participants faced were when they wanted to watch a video in another language (20%), to set the volume to higher (20%), unavailable caption (15%), caption size (13%), quality (10%), fast caption (8%), codecs (8%) others (6%).

The main motivations for watching a video are to be entertained (42%), to obtain information (26%), to learn new things (23%) and the rest of the participants did not watch videos on Internet, they only watch TV.

The most common video content for entertainment was about music, followed by movies, foreign television series, sports, soup opera and anime. The most common video content for obtain information was news, followed by documentaries, education and capture images. Regarding to interest in learning new things, the participants reported that the most common video content was cooking videos, followed by learn languages, how to do videos and tutorials.

4.2   User Test

We used two applications of Morae software[1], i.e. Recorder and Manager, to facilitate the research process and data analysis. Recorder enabled the capture of audio, video, user input and on-screen activity. Manager application enabled the analysis of the video records.

We performed an experiment to identify the more important functionalities of videos and those the participants chose to complete some tasks. The participants were provided with five videos using Google Chrome browser. We have asked them to choose two of them. They completed a series of tasks in which they had to answer three questions for each video. The first two tasks were questions about the video content. For each question about the video content, they had to show the scene where the answer could be found. They used some controls to find the scene: search, link, speed up, speed down and time bar. The third task referred to subtitle configuration and they used the settings panel to configure the color, size and font.

We used five videos with subtitles in Portuguese for the testing. Two of them have audio in English and three in Portuguese. For each video, we created between 2 and 7 links (5 on average). The videos lasted 4 to 10 minutes (6 on average).

As we had mentioned before, we used user center design to developed the Facilitas player. The process was divided in two parts. First with 10 users, where the participants completed some tasks, some problems were identified and solved; the process was explained in [9]. The second part was a user test with 15 older people, where was reported issues related to their personal difficulties during the user test are [8].

Considering all 25 users, the main characteristics that the video need to satisfy the users' needs are:

- The language: 40% of the participants explained that foreign language difficult the video understanding. Another problem of the foreign videos is that the participants (12%) can not read all subtitles because the personage speak is fast. One participant has problem with the language of the video, he/she started watching the video with English speak and Portuguese subtitles, but after 3 minutes, we notice his/her difficulty and we needed to change the video. Also 96% of the participants watched the video with subtitles, whereas that some videos are in the native language.
- Volume: 28% of the participants said that the low volume is another difficulty that frequently appear when they watch a video.
- Subtitle configuration: 28% of the participants explained that, in the common players on the web, the   size and the color of the subtitle can not configured.
- Subtitle: 20% of the participants reported that videos have unavailable subtitle.
- Quality: 12% reported that the video quality is an issue when they watch videos.
- Other reported problems were the codecs, the contrast of captions, small screen, lack of keyboard navigation and shortcuts, going back (rewinding) to some part of video to hear it again and fear to make mistakes and close everything.

---

[1] Morae Software - http://www.techsmith.com/morae.html

We list the context in which the videos would be used and the controls that can be used for that content. The participants are labeled with a letter followed by a number (P1 = Participant 1).

- Learning: P1 and P3 watch videos to learn languages, so P3 has focused on search control because she thinks that it is a tool to review the meaning of the word she did not understand during her study. P3 said that for studying languages it would be interesting to hear the word pronunciation, for this reason, she used speed down control. 28% of the participants said that controls to rewind 10 seconds and to forward 10 seconds are useful for learning. P3 said that she would like to use annotations. P15 said that she would like to use search control when she is cocking and need to find some information in the video, also she liked the links of the video, because it should be easy follow the videos gradually. P20 watches videos to learning online courses and he said that links would be interesting to jump to some chapter. P23 would like to use the links on videos to learn about how to do videos (i.e. details of fix or maintain a car).
- Biography: Participants want to create videos, which were strongly related to their personal life, such as family meetings, trips, past experiences or important dates. P1 wants to create a video with his biography, he wants to talk, record short films, show photos and include subtitle. P1 is retired and wants to show his life to his grandchildren. P14 wants to create familiar videos; she would like to use the links to show some important parts of the video.
- Teaching: P4 suggested a new control to mark some parts of video to show them again to other people, since he is a speaker. He said that the links are important when he asks something to the public, after that, he wants to show the answer using the link. P5 wants to capture images of video, since she likes to paint pictures, she could use the marks to found the image. P25 said that the links are useful because she always makes annotations of the time of the video to show their students, instead, she would like to create the links.
- Entertainment: P7 and P13 used to watch soup opera. P8 had hearing impairment and she likes to watch ballet videos, but the volume not enough. P13 used to watch movies and horse raising, he would like to use links to return to some important part of the movie or speed down control to saw with detail the champions of the raising. P13 said that change background color of the subtitle is interesting and it should be related to the type of the video, for example, for beach scene on a sunny day, the background should be white.

In Fig. 3 we can show an example of how the specific controls can help to reach the objective. We identify, that there are two types of user needs, when the user want to produce a video and to reproduce a video. To reproduce a video there are some special controls, for example, the most requested ones, by the participants for learning a new language, were the search, speed down, rewind, forward, links and annotations. To produce a video, for example, for teaching, the participants said that marks and links are essential.

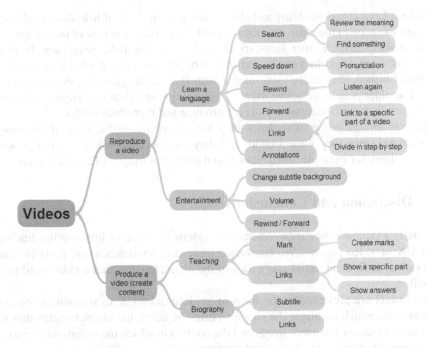

Fig. 3. Context in which the videos would be used and the controls for that context

4.3   Observation

Observation is way of gathering data by watching behavior, events, or noting physical characteristics in their natural setting. Observations can be overt (everyone knows they are being observed) or covert (no one knows they are being observed and the observer is concealed). The benefit of covert observation is that people are more likely to behave naturally if they do not know they are being observed. However, the observer will need to conduct overt observations because of ethical problems related to concealing his/her observation [1]. For our experiment, the observations method was the overt one.

There are three groups of older people that we observed during two months, they regularly frequent the local Educational Institute to attend to Informatics courses for elderly. The summary of this course includes themes as email, Facebook, Skype, download programs, excel tips, videos, etc. When they learned how to watch the videos, they used YouTube. There were some problems identified: older people forgot how to access to YouTube, the steps to find or search a video and the use of headset to listen the video, also they felt fear to make mistakes, had difficulty to click into the button, to make double click and to move the mouse, etc.

Some of the participants expressed they not only go to the Institute to study but also to make friends, most of them are pensioner and they like to participate in groups of elderly people. Most of them have some kind of disability (visual, hearing, cognitive or motor), but not all accept this disability. One female participant declared that she did not have visual disability and she did not use any kind of help device (glasses) but when she goes to the class, she always needs to increase the font of the webpage.

The participants are also familiarized with spending time with their Institute friends, they organized barbecues, and they took photos and recorded videos. When the class finished, they share these media with their colleagues and shared in Facebook. The older people are active users of technology, and then it is important to contribute with them with accessible tools for produce and reproduce media.

There is another group of students, they have computer skills, most of them used the computer since they were a child, and they were excited when new things were shown to them, for example, links, search, and subtitle settings of Facilitas Player.

5   Discussion and Conclusions

This study examined user requirements for videos in order to improve the findings about UX of video players. We conducted three user studies, survey, users test and observation, to form an initial user's idea of the characteristics that a video need to be accessible.

The results are presented in the form of guidelines of UX to summarize the user requirements, which highlight the characteristics of users; the characteristics that the video need to satisfy the users' needs and the context in which the videos will be used. Researchers, designers, developers and content producers can use them.

The guidelines about the characteristics of the video depending on the user's perspective are:

- The video need to satisfy entertainment, information and learning needs.
- Provide different languages, volume configuration, available subtitle, subtitle configuration and quality configuration can improve the User Experience.

The guidelines about the characteristics that the video need to satisfy the users' needs are:

- The language of the video is the main characteristic: it is important that the video be in the tongue language because can difficult the understanding.
- Configuration of the volume: allow increase the volume is important for all type of users not only when the user present hearing disability.
- Subtitle configuration: the configuration of color, size, font and background of subtitle make a positive impact in the user experience.
- Subtitle: when a video have a subtitle, the users prefer watch with the subtitle, regardless of the language of the video.
- Quality is an important characteristic that need to be considered.

The guidelines about the context in which the videos will be used are:

- To learn new things: include languages, how to do videos as carpentry, make up or cooking, tutorials or online courses.

- To make a biography: produce a video with basic characteristics to show for a specific public.
- To teach: prepare some parts of the videos to show to a specific public.
- To entertainment: watch different types of videos, for example, music, films, soup opera, sports, foreign television series or anime.

There are some limitations of the current results and the need for further work. Increasing the quantity of the participants, we can collect more requirements for videos. In addition, we can specify better the user needs for a user objective in some context.

We identify, that there are two types of user needs, when the user want to produce and reproduce the video. In this paper we focus in reproduce part, it is necessary research about the production part.

Acknowledgments. The authors would like to acknowledge to the program *Estudantes-Convênio de Pós-Graduação – PEC-PG,* of *CAPES/CNPq – Brazil* for the financial support provided to this project.

References

1. Evaluation Eta, Data Collection Methods for Program Evaluation: Observation. Evaluation Briefs (16) (2008)
2. International Standards Organization, Ergonomic requirements for office work with visual display terminals (VDTs) - Part 11: Guidance on usability, ISO 9241-11:1998. Ed.1 (1998)
3. International Standards Organization, Ergonomics of human-system interaction. Part 171: Guidance on software accessibility, ISO 9241-171 (2008)
4. International Standards Organization, Ergonomics of human system interaction - Part 210: Human-centered design process for interactive systems, ISO 9241-210:2010, Ed. 1 (2010)
5. Hassenzahl, M., Law, E.L.C., Hvannberg, E.T.: User experience: towards a unified view. In: Proceedings of the 2nd COST 294-MAUSE International Open Workshop (2006)
6. Petrie, H., Bevan, N.: The evaluation of accessibility, usability and user experience. In: Stepanidis, C. (ed.) The Universal Access Handbook. CRC Press (2009)
7. Jumisko-Pyykkö, S., Weitzel, M., Strohmeier, D.: Designing for user experience: what to expect from mobile 3d tv and video? In: Proceedings of the 1st International Conference on Designing Interactive User Experiences for TV and Video (UXTV 2008), pp. 183–192. ACM, New York (2008)
8. Rosas-Villena, J.M., Ramos, B.C., Fortes, R.P.M., Goularte, R.: An accessible video player for older people: issues from a user test. In: Procedia Computer Science of the 5th International Conference on Software Development and Technologies for Enhancing Accessibility and Fighting Info-exclusion - DSAI, Vigo, Spain (2013)
9. Rosas-Villena, J.M., Ramos, B.C., Fortes, R.P.M., Goularte, R.: Web Videos – concerns about accessibility based on User Centered Design. In: Procedia Computer Science of the 5th International Conference on Software Development and Technologies for Enhancing Accessibility and Fighting Info-exclusion, DSAI, Vigo, Spain (2013)

Can Animated Agents Help Us Create Better Conversational Moods? An Experiment on the Nature of Optimal Conversations

Masahide Yuasa

Department of Applied Computer Sciences, Shonan Institute of Technology,
1-1-25 Tsujido-Nishikaigan, Fujisawa, Kanagawa 251-8511, Japan
yuasa@sc.shonan-it.ac.jp

Abstract. We describe a method using animated agents to investigate how humans recognize conversational moods. Conversational moods are usually generated by conversation participants through verbal cues as well as nonverbal cues, such as facial expressions, eye movements, and nods. Identifying specific rules of conversational moods would enable us to construct conversational robots and agents that are not only able to converse naturally, but pleasantly and excitedly. Additionally, these robots and agents would be able to assist us with proper action to generate improved conversational moods in different situations. We propose methods for developing agents that can help improve the quality of our conversations and facilitate greater enjoyment of life.

Keywords: animated agent, turn taking, nonverbal behavior, conversation.

1 Introduction

Humans share moods and emotions under various settings in everyday life, including both joy and sorrow. For example, we enjoy talking and eating together and sometimes we have confrontational discussions. Shared emotions are important for humans as they contribute to the development of better relationships.

Emotional moods are produced by physical behaviors during interactions. Humans exchange behavioral cues, including gaze direction, facial expression, head orientation, and turn-taking patterns. These behavioral cues help us to comprehend the emotion of a conversation and the mood changes accordingly.

However, it is difficult to establish rules that guide conversational moods due to several critical issues. For instance, which verbal and nonverbal cues facilitate conversational moods? How do we comprehend our present mood, and infer subsequent ones? Although several researchers have investigated mechanisms of multi-party conversations and the relationships between verbal/nonverbal information and conversational moods, significant contributors to these moods have yet to be determined. Heuristic aspects of salient conversational components and automatic processing are key factors in nonverbal exchanges. These factors are difficult to explain by nature

C. Stephanidis and M. Antona (Eds.): UAHCI/HCII 2014, Part IV, LNCS 8516, pp. 634–640, 2014.
© Springer International Publishing Switzerland 2014

because they are experienced involuntarily and implicitly. Thus, we need an effective method for investigating shared conversational moods.

To investigate accurately the mechanisms underlying conversational moods, we proposed an approach using animated agents. We developed a conversation evaluation system that generated conversational moods by controlling the turn-taking patterns and facial expressions of animated agents. This allowed us to model human behaviors during conversation via bottom-up processing. Further, by testing participants' impressions on agent behaviors using a stepwise model, we were able to ascertain the psychosocial mechanisms of conversational moods.

2   Conversational Mood Simulation System

We developed a conversational mood simulation system using animated agents [4]. In this study, we focused on three parameters based on previous research: facial expression, time lag, and turn taking. As Bartel indicated, facial expressions are major cues for producing conversational moods [1]. Moreover, the time lag between utterances affects communication moods, such as familiarity, politeness, and preference [8]. In addition, we considered turn-taking patterns.

Fig. 1. Animated agents and the TVML control panel

We assumed that turn taking significantly influences mood [3], [5]. Specifically, "a lot of turn taking" might produce excited or energetic moods (e.g., an amusing conversation), and "little turn taking" might imply sorrow moods (e.g., at funerals). We developed a conversational mood simulation system using animated agents. We used TV Program Making Language (TVML) [7], which is a toolset that controls virtual characters. We selected three characters from the TVML set as conversational agents that can produce various facial expressions, gaze directions, and mouth movements.

In this system, we could choose the turn-taking patterns and facial expressions, and control the timing of turn taking using the slide bars on the control panel for generating various moods (Fig 1). For an unbiased evaluation, the agents said random words from the word set with no meaning (e.g., ARABAHIKA or UKUJARAH).

3   Experimental Procedure

Previous research [4], [5] has demonstrated that the next speaker was selected in the following turn-taking patterns. Case 1: the person being looked at by the previous speaker would be the next speaker, and Case 2: the person not being looked at by the previous speaker would be the next speaker, even though the previous speaker had looked at another listener.

We prepared video stimuli for the experiment. Regarding turn taking, the following two conditions were evaluated (also see Fig. 2).

- T1: One of the hearers must speak (Case 1: 100%)
- T2: Overlap of utterance may occur 75% of the time (One of the hearers behaves in Case 1, and the other hearer behaves in Case 2.)

T1 indicates that the person who is being looked at by the speaker starts to speak without exception. T2 is a pattern where, most of the time, two hearers—the one who is being looked at by the speaker as well as the one who is not being looked at—begin speaking simultaneously. Watanabe and colleagues demonstrated that the time lags between the utterances of participants at turn taking convey negative impressions of robots [8]; thus, we considered several time lags as parameters for conversational moods.

We conducted the experiments using 16 video clips, which included two turn-taking conditions (T1 and T2), two facial expressions (HAPPY vs. ANGRY), and four time lag conditions (0.0 s, 0.5 s, 1.0 s, and 2.5 s). In each condition, all three agents behaved under the same parameters: turn-taking patterns, facial expressions, and time lags. The duration of each video was approximately 2 min.

In the experiment, volunteers filled out a questionnaire after they were shown the stimuli. Based on previous research using evaluation of impressions (e.g., [2]), we introduced a semantic differential method using pairs of adjectives. The subjects rated moods using the following pairs of adjectives on a scale ranging from -2 to 2 after watching each clip: cooperative-uncooperative, friendly-hostile, good terms-bad terms, closely-distantly, harsh-gentle, elated-depressed, hot-cool, tense-relaxed.

T1   T2

Fig. 2. Turn-taking conditions. T1: One of the hearers must speak, T2: Overlap may occur at 75%.

HAPPY   ANGRY

Fig. 3. Turn-taking conditions: Happy and angry

4   Experimental Results

A total of 19 computer science student volunteers participated in the experiment. Factor analysis was used to determine the data structure by using pairs of adjectives. The dimensions were assessed in terms of valence (unpleasant-pleasant) and arousal (high-low activation). Additionally, we conducted a 2 x 4 within subjects ANOVA using the factorial scores for valence and arousal: T1 vs. T2 and four time lags for each facial expression. Fig. 4 shows HAPPY and ANGRY for valence. Fig. 5 shows HAPPY and ANGRY for arousal.

For HAPPY in valence, there was a marginally significant interaction effect between the turn taking and time lags, $F(3, 54) = 2.50$, $p < .10$. Multiple comparisons using the LSD method showed that, at the T1 level, 0.5 s and 1.0 s scores were significantly greater than 2.5 s (MSe = 0.5505, $p < .05$). For ANGRY, there was a significant main effect for turn taking, $F(1, 18) = 7.20$, $p < .05$. (T1 > T2), and there was no significant interaction effect for arousal.

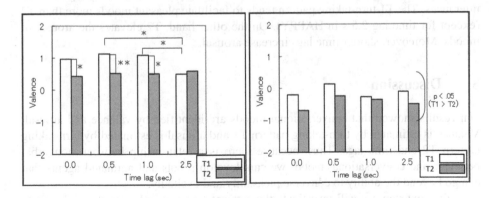

Fig. 4. Valence scores for HAPPY (left) and ANGRY (right)

For HAPPY in arousal, there were significant main effects for turn taking, $F(1, 18)$ = 15.15, $p < .01$. (T2 > T1), and time lags, $F(3, 54) = 12.39$, $p < .01$. According to multiple comparisons using the LSD method, the score for 0.0 s was significantly greater than the others and the score for 0.5 s was significantly greater than that for 2.5 s (MSe = 0.5063, $p < .05$). Furthermore, there was no significant interaction effect for arousal. In the case of ANGRY, there was no significant interaction effect of arousal. There was a significant main effect for turn taking, $F(3, 54) = 16.41$, $p < .01$. (T2 > T1), and time lags, $F(3, 54) = 16.41$, $p < .01$. Multiple comparisons using the LSD method indicated that the score of 0.0 s was significantly greater than the others and the scores for 0.5 s and 1.0 s were significantly greater than that for 2.5 s (MSe = 0.5063, $p < .05$).

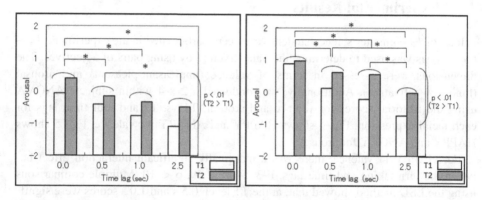

Fig. 5. Arousal scores for HAPPY (left) and ANGRY (right)

Conversational moods consisted of valence and arousal. Further, moods were significantly influenced by facial expressions, turn-taking patterns, and time lag between utterances. The T1 turn-taking pattern tends to facilitate pleasant moods more than T2 (except for time lag 2.5 s in HAPPY). On the other hand, T2 elevates the arousal of moods. Moreover, shorter time lags increase arousal.

5   Discussion

Our results showed that conversational moods are identified by valance and arousal. Valance is estimated by turn-taking pattern T1 and arousal is estimated by turn-taking pattern T2 and time lags. Thus, because there is a relationship between nonverbal behavior and conversational mood, we can develop robots and animated agents that can go beyond the ability to converse pleasantly and excitedly.

In the next step, we will investigate the patterns (valence and arousal) conducive to positive human conversation. By using the experimental results and ideal speaking patterns, we can develop robots and agents that can express their moods using turn taking, facial expressions, and time lags. Regarding the comprehension of turn taking, we developed an agent system that can use cameras and gaze equipment to interact with a user. Further, we will develop a robot system that can detect user actions (Fig 6). Our agent system detects head orientation (right/left) and head height (high/middle/low) using cameras situated around two displays in front of the participant. The system estimates whether the participant gazes at the right or the left display.

Based on these findings of the three-agent system, and the two-agent and robot system involving a user, we will be able to develop conversational agents and robots to comprehend and express users' moods, and thus enrich communications with humans. Agents and robots are a universally known interface for humans. Not only are they easy-to-use and friendly, but they also facilitate enjoyment and delight. Moreover, if they can comprehend our mood and create better moods, they may enhance not only our communication style, but also our future lifestyle.

Fig. 6. Conversational agents and robots

In addition, we focused not only on the parameters in this experiment, but also facial expressions that expressed utterance attitude [6]. As a preliminary test, we developed facial expressions that expressed the desire to start speaking and positive attitude, and another that expressed a neutral attitude to show disinterest in the conversation (Fig. 7). We hypothesized that subtle differences in such behaviors would affect comprehension of conversational moods.

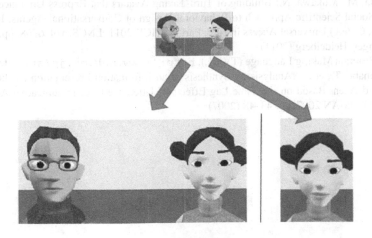

Fig. 7. Utterance attitude (left) and neutral attitude (right)

In our preliminary test, a user noted that the expressions of the desire to speak generated better moods than an interested but neutral attitude. This suggests that showing a positive attitude in conversations can create better moods. In the future, we aim to conduct additional tests to investigate the relationship between attitude and mood in conversations.

6   Conclusions

We believe that the findings of this study will be instrumental in designing agents that behave in a way that influences conversational moods in humans. Such conversational robots and agents would be able to assist in improving human interactions and communication by helping people cultivate better conversational moods in various situations, which would enrich relationships and even increase enjoyment of life.

References

1. Bartel, C.A., Saavedra, R.: The Collective Construction of Work Group Moods. Admin. Sci. Q 45(2), 197–231 (2000)
2. Fukayama, A., Ohno, T., Mukawa, N., Sawaki, M., Hagita, N.: Messages Embedded in Gaze of Interface Agents–Impression Management with Agent's Gaze. In: Proc. CHI 2002, pp. 41–49 (2002)
3. Matsusaka, Y., Fujie, S., Kobayashi, T.: Modeling of Conversational Strategy for the Robot Participating in the Group Conversation. In: Proc. Eurospeech 2001, pp. 2173–2176 (2001)
4. Yuasa, M., Tokunaga, H., Mukawa, N.: Autonomous Turn-Taking Agent System based on Behavior Model. In: Jacko, J.A. (ed.) Human-Computer Interaction, HCII 2009, Part III. LNCS, vol. 5612, pp. 368–373. Springer, Heidelberg (2009)
5. Yuasa, M., Mukawa, N., Kimura, K., Tokunaga, H., Terai, H.: An Utterance Attitude Model in Human-Agent Communication: From Good Turn-taking to Better Human-Agent Understanding. In: Proc. CHI Extended Abstracts 2010, pp. 3919–3924 (2010)
6. Yuasa, M., Mukawa, N.: Building of Turn-Taking Avatars that Express Utterance Attitudes - A Social Scientific Approach to Behavioral Design of Conversational Agents. In: Stephanidis, C. (ed.) Universal Access in HCI, Part IV, HCII 2011. LNCS, vol. 6768, pp. 101–107. Springer, Heidelberg (2011)
7. TV Program Making Language (TVML), http://www.nhk.or.jp/strl/tvml/
8. Watanabe, T., et al.: Analysis by Synthesis of an Information Presentation Method of Embodied Agent Based on the Time Lag Effects of Utterance to Communicative Actions. In: Proc. ROMAN 2007, pp. 43–48 (2007)

Author Index